CHARLES GRANDISON FINNEY, 1792–1875

Charles Grandison Finney in 1860. Courtesy Oberlin College Archives.

CHARLES GRANDISON FINNEY

1792-1875

Revivalist and Reformer

KEITH J. HARDMAN

BAKER BOOK HOUSE
Grand Rapids, Michigan 49516

Paperback edition 1990 by
Baker Book House Company
ISBN: 0-8010-4348-4

This book was published with the assistance of a grant from the
John Ben Snow Foundation.

An earlier version of chapter 9, "The Free Church Movement," appeared in
New York History LXVII/4 (October 1986).

The paper used in this publication meets the minimum requirements of American
National Standard for Information Sciences—Permanence of Paper for Printed Library
Materials, ANSI Z39.48-1984. ∞ ™

Library of Congress Cataloging-in-Publication Data

Hardman, Keith.
    Charles Grandison Finney, 1792-1875.

    Bibliography: p.
    Includes index.
    1. Finney, Charles Grandison, 1792-1875.
2. Evangelists—United States—Biography. 3. Revivals—
United States—History—19th century.   4. United
States—Church history—19th century. I. Title.
BV3785.F485H37 1987   285'.8'092'4 [B]   86-23119
ISBN 0-8156-2397-6 (alk. paper)

TO

MY MOTHER AND FATHER

KEITH J. HARDMAN, who received his Ph.D. from the University of Pennsylvania, is the author of *The Spiritual Awakeners: American Revivalists from Solomon Stoddard to D. L. Moody, Ingredients of the Christian Faith,* and numerous articles. He is Professor of Philosophy and Religion at Ursinus College in Collegeville, Pennsylvania.

CONTENTS

PREFACE

In recounting the history of the United States, historians have been slow to credit the nation's spiritual awakenings with any great influence over the minds of its citizens. As Timothy L. Smith has written:

> Church historians of a later day, anxious to make plain the origins of modern religious outlooks, wrote the history of the great popular sects in such a way as to becloud the memory of evangelism's power. . . . The myth persists that revivalism is but a half-breed child of the Protestant faith, born on the crude frontier, where Christianity was taken captive by the wilderness.[1]

The key figure in American religion for the second quarter of the nineteenth century was the revivalist Charles G. Finney (1792–1875). It is impossible to have a full-orbed understanding of the middle period of American history without some inclusion of his role in it. And yet some accounts of American religious history barely mention Finney, if at all. He has suffered the same neglect as have a number of other distinguished spiritual leaders of the age. His only substantial biography (other than some good but unpublished doctoral dissertations) was published in 1891.

This volume aspires to establish Finney's proper place in history. During the antebellum period, he was a catalyst and often a prime mover in achieving the enormous shift that occurred in Protestant church practices and theology. Finney became the national focal point for this massive redirection in emphasis and activities. He and his writings were so well known, and he traveled so extensively and had so much firsthand acquaintance with the religious situation throughout the land, that wherever he journeyed, the controversy over this shift was highlighted. Perry Miller has written,

> Not only could he slay his thousands in the frenzy of a revival, but in 1835 could articulate his *Lectures on Revivals of Religion,* indisputably the most powerful theoretical statement of the significance of the titanic enterprise. Overnight it sold 12,000 copies in America, soon was translated into Welsh, French, German. No religious leader in America since Edwards had commanded such attention; no one was to do it again until Dwight Moody. Hence Finney's book stands . . . as the key exposition of the movement, and so a major work in the history of the mind in America. Its study is imperative if one wishes to pursue the mental adventure of the country.[2]

Finney's long lifetime extended over a period during which the nation was rapidly changing. In his early, formative years, the nation's secular and religious situations included the following:

1. the extraordinary length of the Second Great Awakening, from 1795 to 1835, and the general interest in revivals during that time;

2. the shift away from Calvinist election and predestination, and the inertia that was perceived to be induced by "hyper-Calvinism," to an Arminian view;

3. an upward mobility allowed to common people, in which they assumed more power in civil life, and in the nation's churches as well;

4. the liberalizing tendencies of "the New Divinity" and all the devices used by the Protestant denominations (beginning with more "means" and "measures") to cause a greater number of conversions, and hasten church growth;

5. the search for social panaceas, which created innumerable reform movements and frequent experimentation in perfectionistic and communitarian schemes.

A consideration of these developments in themselves serves somewhat to set the background for Finney's life, and to explain his appeal and success, granting the predilections of the times. But they take us only so far.

In the eighteenth and early nineteenth centuries, why was much of America so prone to revivalistic influence? Numerous factors may have contributed to this. Among them we may mention that some of the American colonies, New England especially, had been settled by people committed to the doctrines of regeneration and a distinct separation between the church of "visible saints" and the world at large. The gathered churches that they formed were in New England a potent influence in colonial life. The reception of new members into the church was achieved in some cases through the Half-Way Covenant (which permitted children of church members to become members themselves, with restricted privileges, before they could give evidence of being "savingly converted") and in others through awakenings in the churches. From early New England days, Calvinists were trained to look for "outpourings of God's Spirit," and to expect that at such times numbers of people would come under conviction, seeking forgiveness and conversion, and thus swelling the church's ranks. Many of the towns there experienced periodic awakenings until at least the 1830s. As part of their spiritual training, New Englanders were taught to decry periods of declension and aridity, and the overall declines in membership were finally answered by the Great Awakening of the 1740s. This seemed to many to be God's verifying his determination to alternate declension with renewal in the churches.

In the decades following the Great Awakening, the frontier of America began to move westward rapidly, luring multitudes with the promise of free land and riches. At least one scholar, influenced by Frederick Jackson Turner, has used the interpretive key of the frontier to explain the dominance of revivalism in nineteenth-century America. The frontier at this period was surely unusual; the settlers were largely uneducated and crude, society was raw and untamed, and it was necessary for the clergy to use persuasive methods to win converts. All of this meant that revivals in the West would be boisterous and devoid of theological subtlety, and the emphasis would be on rapid conversion rather than on pastoral ministry. There the concept of itinerancy was modified by the circuit rider, and great camp meetings proved to be the solution to reaching the pioneer with the gospel. The entire appearance of revivalism changed.

However, as the Second Great Awakening entered its later period, the focal center of revivalism shifted to the East and its cities, allowing a different kind of mass evangelism from that of the camp meetings. But this simply underscored the fact that the entire nation was susceptible to revivalism in its varied forms. The clergy's function was regarded as essentially evangelical. When the country was faced with the challenge of a new form of mass evangelism in the 1820s and 1830s, with a new theological base, there were no institutions of adequate authority to outlaw it. Congregationalists slowed the entry of Methodism into New England, and Old School Presbyterians did their best to fight the new ideas, all to little avail. But pragmatism won the day. It was statistics—numbers of converts—that counted, not status quo. And revivalism provided converts in quantity. The structure of churchly authority was too loose, and its power too frail, for the new practices to be restrained for any length of time. And Charles G. Finney, preeminently, was at the center of this controversy.

Many questions surround a study of Charles Finney. He has often been regarded as the initiator of modern mass evangelism. He supposedly developed innovative methods to bring about more conversions, a new style of preaching to audiences, and from these the entire attitude toward evangelism was transformed. Stemming from Charles G. Finney, some have held, are all the techniques and attitudes of modern large-scale evangelism: Dwight L. Moody, J. Wilbur Chapman, Billy Sunday, and Billy Graham carried the attitudes forward virtually unchanged, and modified the techniques only as later times demanded.

Such an interpretation must be severely revised. For one, although Finney did use some "new measures," he by no means initiated mass evangelism. It could be argued that his illustrious predecessor, George Whitefield, reached as great and, at times, greater audiences, and his impact, though much compressed in time, equalled or surpassed Finney's, as Whitefield spread the 1740s Awakening throughout the American colonies. Secondly, as to revivalistic theory, the shift toward the promotion of revivals by human instrumentality had been occurring long before Finney—as early as Solomon Stoddard, as we shall see. Thirdly, the crucial role of America's Baptists, and especially the Methodists, in altering the approach toward awakenings, must be considered. Even the credit for changing the revival expectations of the nation's Presbyterians and Congregationalists does not belong singly to Finney, but must be shared with Nathaniel William Taylor, Lyman Beecher, and others. As regards these Calvinists, their attitudes toward awakenings changed not so much from new trends, but from the recognition that Methodist and Baptist evangelism was producing great numbers of converts in the first third of the nineteenth century, far

outstripping the numerical gains of the Congregationalists and P
byterians.

Such overarching interpretations aside, when we begin to examine Finney's life, because it was so lengthy and filled with controversy and influence in many areas, we are confronted with numbers
of problems. Some of these are:

What were the effects of his formative years on Finney? The influences of a legal training, and his own demand for individual responsibility, made Finney impatient with the doctrine of original sin
and inability. What additional effects did his frontier upbringing have
on his later life?

How could a man of so little education rise to such eminence
in the antebellum Protestant world? Was it the force of Finney's character, and his determination that his way alone was correct, and nothing should stand in his way, that bowled over the obstacles?

Wherein lay the phenomenal power of this man over his multitudes of followers? Was it an intellectual power, or psychological
force, or what? Why was he so effective among middle-class Americans? Was it his lawyerlike ways in the pulpit? And why did he remain influential for so many years, long after his methods were no
longer new?

If Finney has been falsely credited with some achievements, what
was he truly responsible for? We shall examine his use of a new style
of freer, largely extemporaneous preaching; the concept of citywide,
cooperative evangelism; and the wedding of evangelism and reform —
his genuine contributions.

To what degree did Finney's theology and moral impulse moti-
vate the developing antislavery movement, especially as seen in Theodore Weld and those abolitionists converted in the national revival
of 1831?

Definitive answers to problems of such magnitude may need
longer treatments than I am able to give in these pages. The problems
are complex, and Charles Finney was a complex individual. Two massive difficulties are involved in producing a critical biography of Finney: the superabundant nature of the primary source materials, and,
paradoxically, the meager amount of documents from Finney, so that
— apart from his reflections many years later in his *Memoirs*, and his
lectures and sermons — in essence we have very few sources from the
man himself. It is apparent that Finney read back into his *Memoirs*
his elderly reactions and positions, and we shall see how unreliable
his *Memoirs* are at times, granting their charm. What is the quintes-

sential Finney? What were his original motives? At some of this we can only speculate, relying on other materials for guidance.

Among the myriad of details, the broader themes of that time—changes in the nation's culture, antislavery, temperance, the millennial thrust, and the democratization of Protestantism, to name a few—must be traced. In all of these, Charles G. Finney had a major influence, and he deserves to be seen as the chief "prophet" of the nation's religion then, who captured the spirit of the age, gave it voice, and shaped and reshaped its spiritual institutions in ways that have endured.

ACKNOWLEDGMENTS

As the size and character of this volume will undoubtedly suggest to readers, it owes its very existence to the help of a number of good people who have encouraged and aided me over the years. My deepest thanks are for my wife, Jean, who bore with me, critiqued the manuscript, and lent support in a hundred ways. I must also make amends to my children, Carolyn, Keith, and Colleen, who recall so many times when the research for this book denied them their father's time and energies, but who have been, withal, most understanding and the diversion that I needed when the going was difficult.

Among scholars, my greatest debt is owed to Richard A. G. Dupuis. I value highly the friendship of this gentleman, who has studied Charles Finney for years. A British psychotherapist, he has amassed a large collection of materials on Finney and has always been happy to place it at my disposal. He has made many excellent suggestions and corrected innumerable errors of fact and interpretation in my work, doing all this with graciousness and ease.

I owe another great debt to William G. McLoughlin, the foremost scholar of revivalism. Throughout this project, Professor McLoughlin has encouraged me, thoroughly critiqued the manuscript, and given me invaluable advice. While Richard Dupuis and William McLoughlin are in no way accountable for the faults that remain, their great enthusiasm for the topic has supported my work, and I wish to express my gratitude for their encouragement at every turn.

Other colleagues, including Earle E. Cairns and David K. McMillan, have read portions of the manuscript and made many helpful suggestions. I thank them for all the ways in which they have saved me from error and exonerate them completely from the flaws that still remain.

I have had an interest in the life of Charles Grandison Finney from my days in seminary, one that was deepened during my graduate work by two excellent teachers, Robert T. Handy of Union Theological Seminary, and Don Yoder of the University of Pennsylvania, who continue to provide friendship and inspiration. During periods of research on other books my interest matured, especially in recognition of the lack of a critical biography of Finney. The renewal of scholarly attention to America's evangelical religious heritage in the last decade heightened my awareness that there was a real need to organize and interpret the overwhelming amount of original source material on everything connected with Finney and his revivals, his associates, Oberlin College, abolitionism, the Benevolent Empire, and the theological movements of antebellum America, especially in the light of recent research. I am well aware of the difficulties in doing this, for there are manifest problems in writing on Charles G. Finney. Some of these stem from the abundance of materials, the changes that occurred to him over his long and very busy life, and his own complex and occasionally eccentric personality.

The staffs of many archives have been of great help. No biography of Finney could be completed without the full cooperation of the archivists at Oberlin College, especially William E. Bigglestone, Anne Pearson, and Edsel Little. During my numerous visits and calls for assistance, they have been unfailingly cheerful in providing whatever I needed. I have also spent many hours at the Presbyterian Historical Society in Philadelphia. Here again the entire staff, including Norotha Robinson, William B. Miller, and Gerald W. Gillette, have been of great assistance.

Such a project needed a large amount of time, and I am grateful for the sabbatical leave granted me by the administration of Ursinus College. The staff of the Ursinus library, especially Joan Rhodes, Margaret B. Staiger, Judith E. Fryer, and Marty Mann, have also been of invaluable assistance on many occasions. My thanks are also extended to the librarians of Princeton University, the Library of Congress, the Congregational Library in Boston, Harvard University, and many other archives where I have spent much time.

The staff of the Syracuse University Press deserves much gratitude for making a huge pile of manuscript into a book, and doing it so competently.

Audubon, Pennsylvania   K. J. H.
September 1986

Finney's Revivals in America

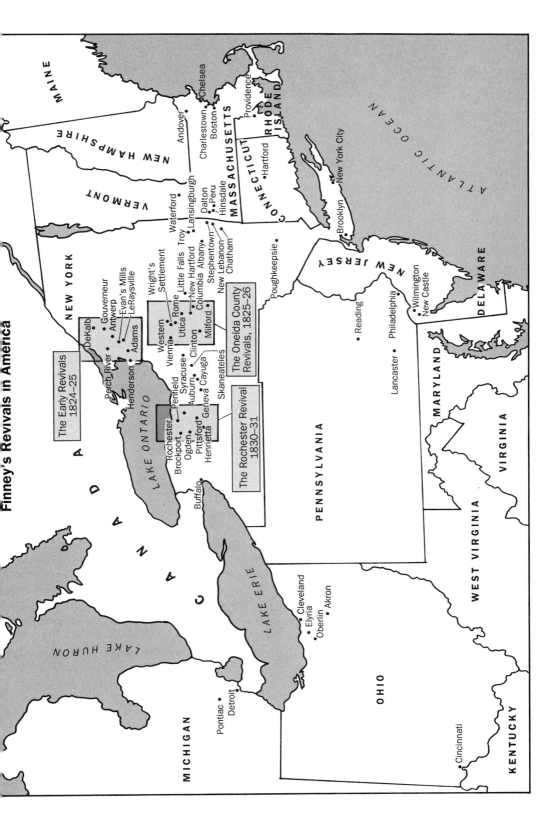

I

INTRODUCTION

In his book *Revivals, Awakenings, and Reform* William G. Mc-Loughlin uses an anthropological approach in examining the prejudices and misconceptions of awakenings that imagine them to be "brief outbursts of mass emotionalism" or "periods of social neurosis." Against such views McLoughlin argues:

> Awakenings begin in periods of cultural distortion and grave personal stress, when we lose faith in the legitimacy of our norms, the viability of our institutions, and the authority of our leaders in church and state. . . . They are times of revitalization. They are therapeutic and cathartic, not pathological. They restore our natural verve and our self-confidence, helping us to maintain faith in ourselves, our ideals, and our "covenant with God" even while they compel us to reinterpret that covenant in the light of new experience. . . . In short, great awakenings are periods when the culture system has had to be revitalized in order to overcome jarring disjunctions between norms and experience, old beliefs and new realities, dying patterns and emerging patterns of behavior.[1]

The last nineteen centuries are studded with awakenings, or periodic restorations of Christians after times of indifference and decline. Kenneth S. Latourette, the church historian, has demonstrated that the progress of Christianity, both as a religion and as a social influence, has been by marked stages of advancement followed by marked periods of decline, followed again by periods of advance.[2] Latourette has compared this pattern to the incoming sea as it moves toward high tide; there is constant movement, even withdrawal and wavering, but the advance is greater than the retreat. Major advances over the centuries—the spread of the early church, the Franciscan movement, the Reformation, the Puritan movement in England, the great awakenings in America and Britain, the Evangelical Revival of the eighteenth and nineteenth centuries, the worldwide missionary movement of the nineteenth century, the Welsh revival of 1904–1905, and so on —all are examples of the periodic nature of such activity.

For the life of Charles Grandison Finney, the proper background is provided by the years after the Great Awakening of the 1740s, when other matters agitated the colonies and there was a general decline in religious interest. The French and Indian War, which lasted from 1754 to 1763, had major effects on all Americans especially in the areas of morals and religion, as deism first began to invade the country. The Revolutionary War period continued this influence, bringing a drop in membership to the churches. Deism and skepticism became popular among the educated of the East coast. On the rapidly expanding frontier of Ohio, Kentucky, Tennessee, Virginia, and the Carolinas after the Revolution, the rigorous life was demoralizing, and at first the churches made slight penetration. Some predicted a rapid decline for the Christian faith. Many churches along the Eastern seaboard received few new members and were at the same time losing multitudes to the allurements of the opening frontier. By 1800, nearly one million people had deserted the East for a new life and, it was hoped, riches, in the Allegheny and Ohio River valleys. That number increased greatly in the next decades as new states were formed from the enormous increase in United States territory after 1803, the year of the Louisiana Purchase.

Members of the churches were greatly troubled by the rise of deism and what they considered infidelity—the Americanization of the Enlightenment as expressed in the ideas of Tom Paine, Ethan Allen, Elihu Palmer, and Thomas Jefferson. Some of those who agreed with deism and other ideas gathered into the Democratic-Republican political party being formed under Jefferson's leadership. He was an avowed deist who had openly declared his doubts of Christian doctrine as early as 1781. This was confirmed in him during his years in France from 1783 to 1789, when he had been strongly influenced by the *philosophes*. When Jefferson became president in 1801, this was viewed by many as a distressing event, ominous for the future of religion in America. As might be expected, new ideas from Europe were particularly welcomed by students in the colleges. Whatever exaggerations were made elsewhere about the drift from Christian ideas, it is certain that the colleges were in difficulty. At Maine's Bowdoin College, there was but one professed Christian in the student body in the 1790s, and things were almost as bad at Presbyterian Princeton. Bishop Meade of Virginia declared that the College of William and Mary was "the hot-bed of French politics and religion."[3] Of those who were swept into the vortex of French infidelity, the president of Yale, Timothy Dwight, reflected:

> Youths particularly, who had been liberally educated, and who with strong passions and feeble principles were votaries of sensuality and ambition, delighted with the prospect of unrestrained gratification and panting to be enrolled with men of fashion and splendour, became enamored of these new doctrines.[4]

In actuality, however, awakenings had hardly ceased since the 1740s. Numerically they were small by comparison with the Great Awakening, but they did continue despite the depressed conditions. There were some small awakenings in New England in 1763 and 1764, and the Methodists, under the dynamic Bishop Francis Asbury, began to see revivals throughout the states in 1787. The first of the series began in Brunswick County, Virginia, an area known as a center of Methodist piety, and there were some emotional excesses (shouting, swooning, and weeping), but the ministers denounced any wilder behavior.[5] In the same year Hampden-Sydney, a small Presbyterian college in Virginia founded during the Revolutionary War, became the center "of the great inter-denominational Awakening which marked the final triumph of evangelical Christianity in Virginia, and . . . left Hampden-Sydney throbbing with a new zeal for its mission."[6] In Connecticut local revivals broke out for three decades: Norfolk in 1767, Killingly in 1776, Lebanon in 1781, New Britain in 1784, Lyme and East Haddam in 1792, New Hartford and Farmington in 1795, and Milford in 1796. Edward Dorr Griffin, a perceptive observer of these events, wrote that the period of general awakenings dated from 1792 and that he "saw a continued succession of heavenly sprinklings at New Salem, Farmington, Middlebury, and New Hartford . . . until, in 1799, I could stand at my door in New Hartford, Litchfield County, and number fifty or sixty contiguous congregations laid down in one field of divine wonders, and as many more in different parts of New England."[7]

But it was the West—that surging, chaotic frontier that was moving sinuously onward—that disturbed the settled East most deeply. The Eastern seaboard might have its depressed periods religiously, but it still retained its churches, and they could be revitalized at any time. The West, however, was fundamentally different; it had never been won to Christian ideas, and it had no churches. There, lawlessness seemed to be the order of the day. Morals were low, the Christian faith was mocked and shunned, deism and atheism were rife, and the vast spaces and extremely low density of population stretched the resources of circuit riders and missionaries to the breaking point. The early settlers of Kentucky named some of their towns after prominent French infidels, as LaRue, Bourbon, Rousseau, Altamont, and other names indicate. It seemed beyond contradiction that several hundred thousand people on the frontier were "hair-hung and breeze-shaken over the pit of hell."

Suddenly, the tidings changed. The Presbyterian General Assembly of 1800 declared, "The success of the missionary labours is greatly on the increase. God is shaking the valley of dry bones on the frontiers, a spiritual resurrection is taking place there."[8] From different points of western Pennsylvania, Kentucky, and Tennessee came specific reports of spiritual interest. As E. H. Gillett has remarked, "Thus, the century which was just closing, and which had threatened to close with dark and dismal prospects, was destined to leave behind it a brighter record. A new era had dawned upon the Church—an era of revivals."[9]

The history of the Second Great Awakening in the West properly begins with James McGready (1758?–1817). Of Scottish-Irish parentage, he was a fiery Presbyterian preacher who had observed the 1787–89 revivals in Virginia and was much impressed by the dignified evangelistic preaching of John Blair Smith, president of Hampden-Sydney College. But McGready knew that what might be acceptable in settled communities would have to be greatly modified on the frontier. Those in the wilderness worked, lived, and died hard, and most of them were illiterate. They would not be patient with the finer points of theology. With this in mind, McGready went to become pastor of three small churches in Logan County, Kentucky, in 1796. The response to his powerful exhortations came quickly, and by the summer of 1798 many were "struck with an awful sense of their lost estate."

It was not until June 1800, however, that unusual events began to occur. That month several hundred members of McGready's congregations came to Red River for a communion service. Three Presbyterian pastors (McGready, John Rankin, and William Hodge) were joined by two brothers, the Presbyterian William McGee and the Methodist John McGee. The first three days of the meetings were reverent and solemn as the ministers spoke, and all remained in order. On the final day John McGee began to exhort the throng that "there was a greater than I preaching" and that they should "submit to him." Immediately the congregation joyously and frantically began to cry and shout.[10]

Astonished, the pastors agreed that the Lord was moving, and they scheduled another sacramental service for late July 1800 at Gasper River. Unprecedented crowds assembled at the appointed time, many from distances as great as one hundred miles. Although the term "camp meeting" was not used until late 1802, and large outdoor services had had a long history, this was the first true camp meeting in which the continual meeting was combined with the planned practice of camping out. Wagons with provisions were brought in, the underbrush around the area cleared, and tents erected everywhere. Continuous preaching began, and the ministers were kept busy counseling the penitents. On Sunday, after three long, tense days, the emotions of the crowd were at breaking point. That evening, with the rough pulpit lighted by flaming torches, William McGee delivered a throbbing exposition of a doubting Peter sinking beneath the waves. McGready recalled:

> The power of God seemed to shake the whole assembly. Towards the close of the sermon, the cries of the distressed arose almost as loud as his voice. After the congregation was dismissed the solemnity increased, till the greater part of the multitude seemed engaged in the most solemn manner. No person seemed to wish to go home—hunger and sleep seemed to affect nobody—eternal things were the vast concern. Here awakening and converting work was to be found in every part of the multitude; and even some things strangely and wonderfully new to me.[11]

The perspective of time would show that the Gasper River camp meeting was the turning point in the Second Awakening in the West; after that, in meeting after meeting, large crowds came and similar revivals began, until the awakening spread to Tennessee as well. However, its full force was yet to be experienced.[12] Barton W. Stone (1772–1844), a Presbyterian clergyman from Bourbon County, Kentucky, was pastor of the Cane Ridge church, and in the spring of 1801 he traveled across the state to see for himself the sensational events. He declared that "the scene was new to me and passing strange. It baffled description." Impressed, he returned to his congregation and laid plans for a protracted meeting to be held at Cane Ridge in August 1801.

In June and July the word was spread and preparations made. Baptist and Methodist preachers were invited, for this was to be ecumenical in every way. But when August came, no one had anticipated or prepared adequately for the numbers who responded. Estimates ranged from ten to twenty-five thousand, coming from as far as Tennessee and Ohio. Even ten thousand was a staggering number at a time when Lexington, the largest town in Kentucky, had at most eighteen hundred inhabitants.

Stone, astounded at the hosts pouring in, declared that "the roads were crowded with wagons, carriages, horses, and footmen moving to the solemn camp." The arrangements for the cleared grounds for tents and wagons, the cooking areas, and the seating on logs in several separate congregations with different pulpits, all proved hopelessly inadequate, but somehow the unanticipated throngs were provided for. The work began, and despite the difficulties Stone rejoiced that "all appeared cordially united in it. They were of one mind and soul: the salvation of sinners was the one object. We all engaged in singing the same songs, all united in prayer, all preached the same things."[13]

John Finley was one of the participants, and he wrote to his uncle on September 20, 1801:

> The Governor of our state was with us and encouraging the work. . . . Great numbers were on the ground from Friday until the Thursday following, night and day without intermission engaged in some religious act of worship. . . . At Cynthiana, Paris, Flat Creek, Point Pleasant, Walnut Hill and Georgetown, great congregations are in all these places.[14]

Since the fanaticisms of James Davenport in 1741 and 1742, wild antics and frenzies had been generally condemned, especially by the Congregationalists and the Presbyterians. Excesses, or "enthusiasms," were viewed with great distaste and suspicion by most evangelists, and the years since Davenport had brought awakenings admirable by the absence of excesses, with some minor exceptions in the rural South. In 1746, after he had had time to think through all the aspects of the Great Awakening, Jonathan Edwards had written in *A Treatise Concerning Religious Affections:*

> Great effects on the body certainly are no sure evidences that affections are spiritual. . . . And if great affections about things *purely natural* may have these effects, I know not by what rule we should determine, that high affections about *religious things*, which arise in like manner from nature, cannot have the like effect.[15]

In the aftermath of the 1740s, prorevivalist New Lights had soberly pondered these words and agreed that the likes of Davenport and his ilk could not be tolerated again, at any cost.

The hard-bitten character of the pioneer, however, demanded a far more exuberantly emotional religion than many back in the settled East would have liked. It was natural that frontier dwellers would demand this; that they would cry aloud in wrestling with their guilt, and that they would laugh and jump and shout with joy when they had purged their souls. Two factors combined to bring about unchecked emotionalism at times. The bleak hardness of pioneer life was one, with its absence of restraint and sparsity of social contact. Second was the fact that in the camp meetings the traditionally slow cycle of conviction, despair, repentance, and release was inevitably compressed into a few days, and pent-up feelings when finally released could be explosive.

Such reactions rarely brought about the disastrous results they would have produced in more civilized areas. Indeed, to the unlettered on the frontier, the index to a preacher's baptism with the Holy Ghost was to be manifested in his lungpower, his ability to array hell and its horrors before the wicked so that they would quake and tremble, and his dual capacity to portray first a wrathful God judging and condemning to fire, and then a loving and merciful God receiving the penitent and forgiving all sins. Theological subtleties were of no value on the frontier, and the minister who lacked both capabilities and could show only love and a gentle spirit did not impress many as a true man of God.

The Second Great Awakening in the West spread with impressive speed, and brought about many conversions. Portions of western

Jonathan Edwards (1703–1758). Without question, Edwards remains the most brilliant theologian America has produced. The influence of Edwards was so great after his passing that all leaders in the Reformed tradition, including Lyman Beecher, Asahel Nettleton, and Charles Finney, claimed to follow him faithfully, whether they did or not. Oil by Joseph Badger, courtesy of Yale University Art Gallery. Bequest of Eugene Phelps Edwards, 1938.

Pennsylvania, the Ohio territory, Maryland, Tennessee, Georgia, and the Carolinas were influenced in a short time. The Methodists especially favored camp meetings, although usually the combined efforts of neighboring pastors of other evangelical denominations were required to provide the personnel necessary for all the preaching and

Timothy Dwight (1752–1817). Grandson of Jonathan Edwards. Dwight's concern over the inroads of secular thinking in America helped to bring about the Second Great Awakening. As the president of Yale College, he became the leader of those forces seeking to revitalize the church, and ultimately the nation, through spiritual awakenings. Oil by Deane Keller, after John Trumbull. Courtesy of Yale University Art Gallery.

counseling that went on. Bishop Francis Asbury regarded camp meetings with great favor, and he confided to his journal, "I pray to God that there may be a score of camp-meetings a week. . . . I rejoice to hear that there will be perhaps four or five hundred camp-meetings this year."[16]

The vast congregations of Cane Ridge and Gasper River were seldom repeated, but in 1811 there were more than four hundred of them, and by 1820 almost a thousand had been held.[17] In their wake, the denominations hastened to consolidate the gains into established churches. Gradually the moral tone of the frontier was raised, and the sins that McGready, Stone, and other revivalists scourged—atheism, murder, drunkenness, adultery, and many more—became things of the past.

Church members of the Eastern seaboard could put aside their despondency of the previous decade for other reasons. Awakening was renewing the East as well, in the churches and on the college campuses. Those seeking revival in the East found their leader and theologian in Timothy Dwight (1752–1817), a grandson of Jonathan Edwards and, after 1795, the president of Yale College. Yale, like most colleges at that time, had its troubles. It was not a large and thriving institution; with only 110 students it had come through the unenlightened presidency of Ezra Stiles, an older man of declining vigor who had clung to the methods of the mid-eighteenth century. There was a vast amount to be done when Dwight assumed the presidency. Discipline was notoriously slack. "Intemperance, profanity, gambling, and licentiousness were common," Lyman Beecher reported; "most of the class before me were infidels, and called each other Voltaire, Rousseau, D'Alembert, etc., etc."[18]

President Dwight, at forty-three, possessed boundless energy, much experience, and an openness to innovation. And, although he was distressed by the lack of seriousness on the part of the students, he had the wisdom not to show it and thus alienate them. By example he would demonstrate the intrinsic worth and integrity of the Christian position. The academic direction changed perceptibly in a short time. One student reported home, "We now see the advantage of having an able director at the head of affairs, one whose commands are energetic, respected, and obeyed."[19] Although Dwight's instruction and administration impressed the students, above all they came to admire his character, his "sound understanding," "open, candid and free behavior," his "handsome and graceful person," and "engaging manner."[20]

By 1800 Yale had achieved greater prestige than ever before, but Dwight's ultimate designs were far beyond making the academic machinery hum briskly. Having won the students' respect and loyalty, Dwight advanced to new strategic positions. Lyman Beecher, looking back on his days at Yale, recalled:

[the students at first] thought the Faculty were afraid of free discussion. But when they handed Dr. Dwight a list of subjects for class disputation, to their surprise he selected this: "Is the Bible the word of God?" and told them to do their best.

He heard all they had to say, answered them, and there was an end. He preached incessantly for six months on the subject, and all infidelity skulked and hid its head. . . .

He was universally revered and loved. I never knew but one student undertake to frustrate his wishes.[21]

The battle lines were drawn; to Dwight there were but two alternatives, Christianity or infidelity. He then began a sledgehammer attack on paganism that lasted for seven years. In his chapel messages he carefully explained the dangers to public morals of all departures from revealed truth. A series of sermons that lasted for four years was delivered, then repeated for the new students. Thus Dwight presented an entire system of divinity in which the philosophy of skepticism was answered and overthrown.

Changes in the mood of the college became perceptible shortly after Dwight assumed the presidency. In 1796 some students organized to improve moral conditions. In 1802 two seniors were distressed with conviction of sin. Shortly they professed faith, and joined the college church. This made a large impact, and in the ten days preceding vacation fifty young men declared themselves "serious inquirers." Conviction multiplied, and religion seemed to be the only topic of conversation. "The convictions of many were pungent and overwhelming; and 'the peace in believing' which succeeded, was not less strongly marked," Professor C. A. Goodrich declared.[22] During the revival that followed, no stated college activities were set aside, nor was preaching more frequent than usual. Dwight disapproved of any emotional displays, and order prevailed everywhere.

Many feared that when the students left on vacation the awakening would end. The opposite occurred. The young men carried the spirit to other schools, and when they returned to New Haven, more than half of the senior class considered itself converted. Eventually one-third of the class entered the ministry. In time the awakening of 1802 faded, but a new revival came in 1808, then another in 1813, and a fourth in 1815.

Following Yale's lead, awakenings began to occur elsewhere. Middlebury College had a succession of revivals in 1805–1806, 1809, 1811, and 1814.[23] In Vermont from 1801 to 1810 there were almost continual awakenings, and they brought in the Baptists as well as the Congregationalists. Western Massachusetts and Rhode Island underwent revivals at the same time. In Connecticut the peaks came in 1807–1808, 1812, 1815–16, 1820–21, and 1825–26.[24] Charles C. Cole, Jr., says that "Indeed, there was no complete interruption of revivals in the state during the first four decades of the century."[25]

Inevitably, the intellectual and psychological ramifications of awakenings were enormous. In each awakening positions were taken, and people were driven into different camps. Beginning with the Great Awakening of the 1740s, parties emerged that were perpetuated into the nineteenth century. Initially, the Great Awakening divided the clergy into two basic camps of Old and New Sides, but after a few years of cooling and reflection, three distinct groups appeared in New England.

"The Arminians," as they were inaccurately termed, inclined toward liberalism and grew in number slowly from 1740 through 1800. For greater precision they might be called "rationalistic Arminians" to distinguish them from the "evangelical Arminians" who accepted John Wesley's theology. Following Wesley's continual stress on the abject human need for divine grace, the evangelical Arminians took a pessimistic view of human nature. The pivotal issue upon which Wesley's theology was based (and all Reformed theologies, whether "Arminian" or not) was the sovereignty of God and the depravity of human nature. Wesley's theology departed from Calvinism in major areas, such as its reinterpretation of the strict Calvinistic understanding of atonement, grace, and the sanctifying work of the Holy Spirit. Rationalistic Arminianism, on the other hand, took an optimistic view of human nature, and its departure from the basic spirit of Calvinism was apparent. Its adherents in New England believed that humans are born with the capacity both for sin and for righteousness, and they can respond to one as well as to the other; that life is a discipline by which, with God's aid, the bondage to sin may be gradually broken.[26]

The Arminians were mainly products of the "broad and catholic" approach furthered at Harvard since John Leverett's presidency, and they frequently were called to the pastorates of churches of eastern Massachusetts. Ebenezer Gay of the Hingham church, Charles Chauncy of the First Church of Boston, and Jonathan Mayhew of the West Church were among the most important and influential of this party. Some, like Chauncy and Mayhew, were accused of Arianism, although neither of them accepted that designation openly. But when the disruptive events of the Unitarian controversy upset the settled order in Massachusetts between 1805 and 1820, most of this party placed themselves in the Unitarian camp, as did the churches they pastored.[27]

Perhaps the largest party at the beginning was that of the Moderates, or Old Calvinists. Sidney E. Mead has said of them:

> Recent studies, as, for example, the work of Perry Miller, indicate that the Calvinism of the New England Puritans was already greatly modified by their "Covenant theology." In this view it also appears that the pre-Revolutionary Old Calvinists, not the Edwardeans or Consistent Calvinists, were the direct theological descendants of the Puritans. It seems, then, that the line can be drawn from Puritanism to Old Calvinism, each the system of the dominant party in its era. It is possible, in brief, that Edwardeanism or Consistent Calvinism was never *the* New England theology.[28]

In the Great Awakening those who would form this party were heartily in favor of revival. However, when the excesses of Davenport, Gilbert Tennent, and others drew reproach upon it, the Moderates felt betrayed and withdrew some of their support. Such respected Boston pastors as Thomas Foxcroft (Charles Chauncy's senior colleague at the First Church), Joshua Gee of the Second Church, and Joseph Sewall of Old South Church, were early proponents of Old Calvinism. Later, this party was represented by such able men as Joseph Willard, president of Harvard (1781–1804), Thomas Clap, president of Yale (1740–66), David Tappan, professor of divinity at Harvard (1792–1803), and Ezra Stiles, president of Yale (1778–95). All the Old Calvinists regarded themselves as orthodox in every way, and indeed they were, taking into account that those who were at Harvard were of a somewhat more liberal tendency than those at Yale.

The third group were variously called New Divinity men, Edwardeans, or Consistent Calvinists. Looking back to Edwards as their mentor, they attempted to "improve" upon his ideas and rework his great theological system. Almost without exception they were graduates of Yale, pastored churches in Connecticut or the Connecticut River Valley, and were knit not only by a fealty to Edwards but also by kinship, marriage, and student-teacher affiliation. Estimates of their contributions have varied widely. Admirers of Edwards are quick to dissociate him from "Edwardeanism" and to point out that the genuine but restrained mysticism that kept his metaphysical expositions from becoming sterile was entirely lacking in his followers, and their heavy-handed treatment of the same themes is ponderous indeed.[29] Joseph Haroutunian has declared:

> The profound tragedy of Edwards' theology was transformed into a farce by his would-be disciples, who used his language and ignored his piety. . . . The logic of Calvinistic piety was being transformed into a vast, complicated, and colorless theological structure, bewildering to its friends and ridiculous to its enemies.[30]

The oldest of the Edwardeans was Joseph Bellamy (1719–90), who graduated from Yale in 1735 and studied with Edwards for a time before assuming a half-century of ministry at Bethlehem, Connecticut. In 1750 Edwards wrote a laudatory preface to Bellamy's *True Religion Delineated*, but in Bellamy's later writings he departed from Edwards' thinking in major areas. The first of these departures, and possibly the most basic, was the exoneration of God as the cause of sin through a stress on the divine *permission* of sin as the necessary means of achieving the greatest good in this best of all possible worlds. Secondly, Bellamy softened Edwards' stress on the unity of mankind with Adam, which then allowed him to remove the idea of original sin in all of Adam's progeny. For Bellamy, as with Nathaniel William Taylor and Charles G. Finney, people were sinful simply because they sinned, and there was no one who did not indulge in sin.

Bellamy wished to dissociate the guilt of his contemporaries from the consequences of Adam's disobedience, recognizing that it is unfair for anyone to be punished for what Adam had done, but this did not mean that humankind was any the less guilty. Hence Bellamy stands as a major source of the influence flowing copiously from Yale Divinity School under the driving insistence of Nathaniel William Taylor's teaching after 1822. Taylor insisted that people become sinful only by their own breaches of God's law, and that "sin is in the sinning." In Taylor's well-known phrase, mankind always had "power to the contrary," to do good instead of evil because of the freedom of the human will, even though in actuality sin was inevitable. In time, Charles Finney would thoroughly agree with Taylor's position.

Slightly younger than Bellamy and the originator of the harsher school of Edwardeans, Samuel Hopkins (1721–1803) has had his name erroneously made synonymous with the entire New Divinity. At many points his theology paralleled Bellamy's, and he went even further in his disavowal of *original*, as distinguished from *actual*, sin. Among the well-known ideas that made up "Hopkinsianism," none gained more repute than the teachings that sin and self-love are identical, and his expansion of the theme of Edwards that true virtue is "disinterested benevolence," so that, in Hopkins' view, a Christian should be willing to be damned if that would be conducive to the glory of God. Again, he prepared the way for Taylor and Finney by going further in asserting the freedom of human will than any American Calvinist before him. He declared that it is self-evident that the will is free, because of the conscious choices we make. In that it is free, it is therefore accountable, especially for its lapses into sin and rebellion. The fact that there are many circumstances beyond our control does not alter the fact of free will.

Doubtless aware that this insistence on freedom of choice would be an appalling abridgement of Puritan doctrine to the Old Calvinists, Hopkins defended himself by declaring that he still held to the divine decrees, and that he could entirely harmonize human free will with predestination. This he attempted by stating that "regeneration" is a totally imperceptible work of the Holy Spirit, in which a human being is entirely passive. As Sydney Ahlstrom explains:

> "Conversion" was then made to rest wholly upon the active exercise of the human will, which leads to growth in positive holiness. In this dualistic view, regeneration lays a foundation "in the mind for holy exercises, for hungering and thirsting after righteousness"; while conversion consists in the volitional "exercises of the regenerate, in which they turn from sin to God, or embrace the Gospel." Against this background one can easily understand how Hopkins could work so large a moral and reformatory effect in the church, and yet be a champion of both revivalism and intellectualism.[31]

Once original sin had been set aside as the active agent in human depravity, and the responsibility for sinning placed squarely upon each individual, along with the understanding that one's will was indeed free and capable of being active in the choice of conversion, the stage was set for Taylor and Finney, and they could easily build upon these Hopkinsian foundations.

Two other important New Divinity men remain to be mentioned. Jonathan Edwards, Jr. (1745–1801) had little of his father's theological originality, and he did not contribute greatly to the development of the New Divinity. But he was instrumental in furthering the teachings of his father, Bellamy, and Hopkins, and he eventually became the president of Union College in Schenectady, New York. Nathanael Emmons (1745–1840) spent fifty-four years in a rural pastorate in Franklin, Massachusetts, which allowed him to spend abundant time in writing and preparing over eighty young men for the ministry. He admitted that his concepts were basically derived from Samuel Hopkins, yet as he taught and published, his system took on its own color and tone and received the designation of "Emmonsism." He opposed the old Puritan doctrine that God had entered into a covenant with Adam. Rather, God established a "law of paradise" and decreed that if the first parents broke this law, they would fall into sin. Old Calvinists might grumble at this interpretation, but they were horrified when Emmons went on to state that God had placed within Adam's mind an inclination toward evil, for in their view this would make the Lord directly liable for the coming of sin.

Whatever judgments one may make regarding the New Divinity, there can be no doubt that the Edwardeans were far and away the most prolific and creative of these three parties, and that they executed their task against massive difficulties. By the midpoint of the eighteenth century, Americans were increasingly preoccupied with secular matters; doctrinal issues and disputes did not have the same claims to preeminence as in the previous decades. Problems of war, Indians, trade, difficulties with England, and nation-building absorbed more and more of the colonists' energies and attention. "Never have theologians struggled against greater odds," Sydney Ahlstrom has said of the Edwardeans. "For the churches their works served as a highly effective sheet anchor during the period's political storms, enabling the New England religious tradition to move ahead again under the fair winds of the new century."[32]

The New Divinity preachers not only tried to further Edwards' ideas but also to fan the fires of spiritual zeal into new revivals. In the latter attempt they had little success for many years, due in part to their censorious and astringent practices. They persisted nonetheless in attempts at cultivating religious concern, and their churches were the first to be rewarded by the Second Great Awakening after 1800.

By then a distinct change was coming over the New England expectations of awakening, and it was not confined to the New Divinity men. Timothy Dwight and others shared in the new approach to revivals. It has often been stated that the history of evangelism in

America is, in one method of interpretation, a history of the development of "measures" for bringing about conversions. One soon sees why the terms "revival," "revivalism," and "evangelism," if placed on a continuum, are often confused. Until the Great Awakening of the 1740s few "measures" or "means" were thought to be of any efficacy. The theology of revivals held both in the Old World and in eastern Massachusetts was that awakenings would come only at God's pleasure. The prevailing Calvinist concept of election had a massive dampening effect: people must simply wait, perhaps all their lives, and if they were of the elect, in God's own time salvation would surely come. Individual initiative was therefore discouraged. Pastors would preach on God's methods, but stop short of inviting a congregation to accept regeneration. Solomon Stoddard (1643–1729), the grandfather of Jonathan Edwards, was the first in New England to attack this teaching of futility, and to suggest "measures." He thus strikingly introduced what was to become the paramount question in the theology of revivals, namely, to what extent can clergy and laity be partners with the Almighty in the bringing of awakenings? Stoddard's entire approach assumed that pastors and people could indeed assist in bringing down spiritual fire, and his methodology was the first to delineate the steps necessary to cooperate with God in this.[33]

Stoddard would have made a large contribution had he done no more than assail the despair many felt in their assumption that they were not of the elect. He taught that election cannot be known for sure in this life, and therefore all should respond to the gospel as if they were elect. Although this new, pragmatic, and optimistic approach to evangelism had only limited geographical influence, with no effect on most of New England to the Great Awakening, it was, inevitably, the wave of the future. Among their other modifications of Puritan doctrine the Edwardeans picked up this democratic approach, and added to it free will and the canceling of original sin. It takes little insight to see that these were enormous shifts of emphasis.

Stoddard's great-great-grandson, Timothy Dwight, exemplified the new determination as he set himself to "preach down a revival" at Yale. Although by birth and training an heir of the Edwardeans, Dwight had rejected some of their ideas to accept the Old Calvinist position on original sin and the use of "means," or measures. Edwardeans were generally opposed to the use of means, mainly on the ground that this fostered pride by giving individuals too much power in their own salvation, even though paradoxically they were the ones who had opted for free will. The Old Calvinists, following Stoddard,

urged those seeking salvation to do all they could. Sidney E. Mead
has pointed out:

> As a practical man with his heart set upon results, [Dwight] re-
> jected firmly the idea of the utter sinfulness of all "unregenerate
> doings" and argued like an Old Calvinist that, as a matter of fact,
> "wherever the Gospel has been preached, and read, mankind have
> actually been made disciples of Christ," whereas in those coun-
> tries where it has not been preached, "disciples have not been
> made." Since then "it is the soul, which is thus taught, alarmed,
> and allured, upon which descends the efficacious grace of the Holy
> Spirit," therefore "the Means of Grace ought to be used by sinners,
> and by Christians, for the purpose of promoting the salvation of
> Sinners." As for ministers, and Dwight was especially interested
> in getting ministers to act, they "ought to advise, and exhort, sin-
> ners to use the means of Grace."[34]

It was not that Dwight believed the prayers of a person under
conviction of sin had any moral goodness; that could not come until
the Holy Spirit imputed the righteousness of Christ to the soul in
regeneration. But, said Dwight, the sinner's prayers for deliverance
and the experience of being under conviction of sin had definite purposes. Unless sinners knew their guilt and danger, and recognized their
complete dependence upon God's grace, they could not appreciate the
love of God in saving them. Indeed, it was to everyone's interest to
use the means of grace, Dwight taught, for they were the usual methods by which God regenerated the lost soul. The Lord would not have
provided them if they were forbidden.

All of this dramatically changed the old Puritan idea of a prolonged period of conviction to one in which conversion could come
within a relatively brief period. "Whosoever will may come," the text
most dear to the heart of the evangelist, took on new meaning and
gave him a new urgency. Dwight and all his friends who longed for
awakening were utterly convinced that revival was the work of the
Holy Spirit, but there was increased feeling that God *invited* human
beings, by their praying and preaching for awakening, to cooperate.
The significance of this was that evangelism came a great distance
within the space of only sixty years. Even Edwards, the master psy-
chologist and dialectician of the soul, was genuinely surprised when
the revivals began in 1734 and 1740 as the result of vivid preaching.

Sidney Mead has remarked that, "To Edwards the revival was a by-product of his shared experience; to [Dwight, Beecher, and Taylor] revivals were the calculated means to an end."[35]

Any lingering unpredictability in awakenings was swept away in 1835 by Charles Finney, when he stated at the outset of his *Lectures on Revivals of Religion*, "A revival is not a miracle, nor dependent on a miracle, in any sense. It is a purely philosophical result of the right use of the constituted means."[36] The continuum was now complete; it had swung from the Puritans' astonishment at the mysterious workings of God and the awesomeness of it all, to the post-Enlightenment, sanitized and respectable cause-and-effect relationship of an efficiency principle, with no dangling metaphysical ends. Finney's virtual abandonment of the older understanding made more epistemological sense, but many were shocked and wondered if something had not been lost in the translation. Finney surely was referring to *evangelism*, but did he really mean *awakenings*? When he referred to "means," he meant specific evangelistic techniques that he had found to be successful in persuading people. New methods of persuasion had been discovered since the days of Stoddard, and old methods had been refined, and Finney meant by "means" what Stoddard had meant by "preparations" and "converting ordinances," for bringing people to the state of conversion. But Stoddard (as well as Edwards, the New Divinity men, Old Calvinists, and Dwight) never identified the conversion of individuals with a general awakening, as Finney did continually. They knew that there had been awakenings, such as the Franciscan revival and the Reformation, where evangelism and conversions played almost no part, and that therefore the two concepts were complementary and mutually contributory, but not identical.

The New Testament refers to individual conversion (but certainly not to awakenings) in such places as Matthew 13. In his *Lectures on Revivals* Finney took this passage and showed his merger of the two concepts:

> What are the laws of nature according to which it is supposed that grain yields a crop? They are nothing but the constituted manner of the operations of God. In the Bible, the Word of God is compared to grain, and preaching is compared to sowing the seed, and the results to the springing up and growth of the crop. A revival is as naturally a result of the use of the appropriate means as a crop is of the use of the appropriate means.[37]

One of the decisive events that prepared the way for Charles Finney's successes was the growing cooperation between the Congregationalists and the Presbyterians and the adoption of the Plan of Union in 1801. During the revivals of 1798–1801 in central and western New York, missionaries of the two denominations frequently met, and leaders began to explore the possibilities of a combined effort in the West. In 1800 Jonathan Edwards, Jr., then president of Union College in Schenectady, proposed the plan whereby Presbyterians and Congregationalists in any community could form themselves into one congregation and have a pastor from either denomination. If the majority of members were Presbyterian, the church could be organized as such and affiliate with a local presbytery. If Congregationalist status was preferred, they could join with a Congregational association. In case of difficulties between a pastor and the congregation, the problem could be referred to the association or presbytery of which the pastor was a member, or to a suitable council.[38]

This "presbygational" arrangement first operated in New York, and eventually spread into Ohio, Indiana, Illinois, Missouri, Tennessee, and Kentucky. Although it was intended to be completely fair to both groups, in time it worked in favor of the Presbyterians. In many of the areas mentioned above, early Congregational churches were almost uniformly received into local presbyteries. But in doctrinal matters, the reverse frequently occurred: exponents of the New England theology, especially the Edwardeans, many of whom had participated in the Second Awakening, began to have a strong influence on Presbyterians. In time Old School Presbyterians realized that the doctrine of which they heartily disapproved was rapidly infiltrating their denomination. By an ironic twist of fate, the Presbyterians' welcoming of Congregationalist missionaries into their fold greatly furthered the influence of the New Haven Theology of Nathaniel William Taylor, and this in turn was a vast stimulus to the New School Presbyterians, helping to bring about the schism in this denomination in 1837.

This laudable desire to foster interdenominational cooperation also gave rise to the American Home Missionary Society (AHMS). By the 1820s there were numerous local missionary groups throughout New York, many of which were affiliated with the statewide Domestic Missionary Society. In 1826 the local groups banded together with the smaller societies of other states to form the American Home Missionary Society. One year later, the AHMS was supporting 169 evangelists, and of this grand total 120 were laboring in the state of New York. New Englanders were naturally concerned about the multitudes who had migrated from their area into New York and the other new regions, and leaders of New England were heavily represented among the officers of the AHMS. Its first president was the former Federalist patroon Stephen Van Rensselaer; other officers were Leonard Woods, David Porter, Nathaniel Taylor, and Archibald Alexander. Among its directors were the New Englanders Justin Edwards, Joel Hawes, Heman Humphrey, Bennet Tyler, and Nathaniel Beman.

All of these developments demonstrate conclusively that, for some time, the "mix" was right for the emergence of a new type of evangelism among American Calvinists, possibly similar to what the Methodists had been practicing for years. The supporting ideology was already present; it had been developing ever since Solomon Stoddard gave revivals a new twist, and it was virtually completed when Nathaniel Taylor shocked the clergy by denying original sin. Now, a practitioner was needed to implement the design, a fearless and bold man, one who was utterly confident of the rightness of his cause, one who brooked no opposition, even from those who were high-placed and powerful, a man of driving determination and ambition.

Charles Grandison Finney fitted those particulars exactly.

2

GROWTH AND SEARCHING

After the Revolutionary War, New England Yankees and Pennsylvanians began to look on the frontier west of the Adirondack and Catskill Mountains of New York State as a choice area for settlement.[1] Most of New England and parts of Pennsylvania were settled, and many in the younger generation felt the compelling attraction of a beckoning frontier. New York was that. Well watered, with a variety of fine lakes and rivers, undulating hills and fertile valleys, in 1790 it was very sparsely populated except for Manhattan and the Hudson River valley. It stood fifth in population among the states, being exceeded by Virginia, Massachusetts, Pennsylvania, and North Carolina.

Timothy Dwight, Yale's dynamic president, reflected on this vast exodus from New England when he pondered, some years later, his own tour of New York.

On Tuesday, September 19, 1799, I set out in company with Mr. W. S. H., of Charlestown, S.C., on a journey to the western parts of the state of New York. . . . The state of New York contains about forty-five thousand square miles, about five thousand less than England. Almost all of it is capable of cultivation. . . . As the soil is rich, the climate favorable, and the inhabitants sufficiently intelligent and industrious to avail themselves of their advantages, the state is capable of sustaining a population as great in proportion as that of England, or from seven to nine millions of inhabitants. . . .

No country can be more advantageously situated for commerce. . . . The Hudson in proportion to its size is inferior to no
river in the world in commercial faculties. The great lakes on the
East, North, and West yield a navigation nowhere equaled by waters of the same kind.

The rapidity with which the population of New York has
increased is without a parallel. In the year 1790, they amounted
to 340,120; in 1800, to 484,065; and in 1810, [to] 959,220.

A great part of the population thus rapidly accumulated has
been derived from New England. From three fifths to two thirds
of the inhabitants have originated from that country. The proportion is continually increasing. New York is, therefore, to be ultimately regarded as a colony from New England.[2]

In at least one way, the area of New York west of the Adirondack
and Catskill Mountains differed from other newly opened frontiers
in other periods of the nation's history. Much more than anywhere
else, settlers in central New York were inclined to a wide variety of
causes, crusades, enthusiasms, and eccentricities to such an extent
that the region has been called a "psychic highway."[3] Some of these
movements were respectable and needed for the amelioration of societal ills, but others were bizarre. Where there were individuals who
initiated these movements, they tended to have their beginnings in
New England and to have moved into New York to take advantage
of the rapidly increasing population and the upheavals of the area.
An entire gamut of experiments promoting the perfection of humanity and the bringing of millennial bliss, unorthodox religious beliefs,
new cults, and new political parties caused the area even then to be
called a "burnt" or "burned-over district."

Although these agitations came to full fruit between 1825 and
1850, the symptoms are to be detected from the first settlements. The
term "religious ultraism" was used to describe the propensities of the
Burned-over District as early as 1835, when W. B. Sprague published
a sermon in Albany bearing that title and defining what was meant
by "ultraism" at that time.[4] Whitney R. Cross, in his study entitled
The Burned-over District, says that "the stage of religious emotionalism immediately preceding heterodoxy was that which contemporaries
called ultraism."[5]

A fuller sociological analysis of these phenomena must bring
into account the excitement and opportunities for prosperity that were
created by the impetus to construct an inland waterway across New
York State, and the hordes of people this brought to the region. Ca-

nals as a means of inland communication had intrigued Americans since prerevolutionary days, but little actual work was completed until DeWitt Clinton opened his famed Erie Canal in 1825. This canal connected Buffalo with Albany, and thence (via the Hudson River) to New York City. With the success of this venture, the nation succumbed to canal fever, and canals of varying length and·financial return were attempted in Massachusetts, Connecticut, Pennsylvania, New Jersey, Maryland, Ohio, Indiana, Illinois, Virginia, and elsewhere.

While the Erie Canal was being dug, and for years afterward, the demand for laborers and practitioners of every enterprise brought hundreds of thousands of migrants into the area, many of them bound for the western regions of Ohio, Indiana, and Michigan, but many others settling along the path of the canal. In New York, as well as throughout the nation, inaccessible markets plagued all economic producers before 1825, but especially the farmer, the country's chief entrepreneur. To make matters worse, the nation was steadily expanding, bringing even greater distances between producers and consumers. But in New York, with the opening of the Erie Canal, the state was traversed by a convenient waterway that assured farmers and producers a route to markets for their crops and products. Cities and large towns grew rapidly along the canal, as packing houses, distilleries, and flour mills prepared the meat and grain of the region for shipment to the outside world. Within a few years there was a new wealthy class, composed of successful bankers, jobbers, commission merchants, and proprietors of the many types of factories and mills opening in the thriving new communities. And for every member of this class, there were dozens at the bottom of the social ladder, factory workers and common laborers, who were eager to work hard if it might bring eventual success and upward mobility.

For the Burned-over District, all of this meant upheaval and rapid socio-economic change to a people who had known settled habits, quiet isolation, and unquestioned values. Of the many enthusiasms that agitated the region, among the first was Mormonism. Joseph Smith (1805–44) had been born in Vermont, where each of several economic ventures left his family poorer than the one before. In 1816 they came to the vicinity of Palmyra, New York,[6] where Joseph reported that he was greatly disturbed by the religious controversies rampant in the region. "In the midst of this war of words and tumult of opinions, I often said to myself, what is to be done? Who of all these parties be right? Or are they all wrong together?" He claimed he was then led to discover long-buried golden plates nearby, and in 1830 Smith's translation of the *Book of Mormon* was published. In time Smith was aided by a clerical assistant, Oliver Cowdery, who had also come from Vermont, where he had embraced some "extraordinary doctrines, apparently involving millennial expectations and direct revelation as well as some mysterious treasure hunting."[7] While one writer has observed that the "Latter-Day Saints might never have existed except for the extraordinary mental agitation about religious matters which pervaded western New York in this period,"[8] it is interesting to note that for both Smith and Cowdery, Vermont seems to have provided the seedbed for their ideas.

Another of the movements exciting the Burned-over District was anti-Masonry, which provided a great agitation beginning in 1826, as multitudes charged that the Freemasons, who included many important people, were plotting to take over the government of the nation. Shortly after that came the great clamor over the Millerites. William Miller (1782–1849), who had served as the sheriff of Poultney, Vermont, migrated to Low Hampton, New York, and took up farming while maintaining a fascination with calculating the date of Christ's return to earth. In 1828 he felt a "call" to proclaim that Christ would return to earth "about 1843." Interest in his teachings mounted; adherents bearing his message were sent on speaking tours; tracts, catechisms, children's books, and much else were published; camp meetings were held. In January 1843, Miller proclaimed that Christ would return to earth between March 21, 1843 and March 21, 1844. Although there was no general abandonment of business, no preparation of ascension robes, and no gathering in cemeteries and on hilltops by the Millerites, as has often been reported, multitudes were led to expect the second coming. When nothing happened, Miller recalculated the date at October 22, 1844, and again many who trusted were infuriated at being deceived. So widespread was the clamor after the second disappointment that churches generally were mocked, including those that had condemned the excitement from the beginning. At the peak of the Millerite fever, one scholar has estimated, there were probably more than fifty thousand devoted adherents and perhaps as many as a million who were peripherally involved.[9]

But this was not the end. In one memorable year, 1848, two more fads and extravagances shook New York. Spiritualism (or spiritism) burst upon the state when the Fox sisters, Leah, Margaret, and Katie, of Hydesville, some twenty miles from Rochester, imitated spirit "rappings," which some neighbors took seriously.[10] The way had to some extent been prepared by Emanuel Swedenborg (1688–1772), who claimed to have received communications from the spirit world that gave him knowledge of all things, and by the spread of Mesmerism, which promised to open the secrets of the next life through its hypnotic trances. Spiritualism soon made important converts, such as Horace Greeley, editor of the *New York Tribune,* and claimed at its height in the mid-1850s sixty-seven periodicals, thirty-eight thousand mediums for "personating, writing, painting, etc.," and two million believers, "in and out of the church." New York alone had four hundred twenty thousand adherents, according to the statistics of the movement, and Ohio two hundred thousand.

The second movement that convulsed New York in 1848 was the perfectionist Oneida Community of John Humphrey Noyes, who was born in Brattleboro, Vermont, in 1811. Noyes gathered a small band of perfectionists at Putney, Vermont, in the early 1840s, and instituted a communism of property. When he extended his idea of "spiritual union" to renounce conventional marriage in 1846, in favor of what he called "complex marriage," outraged citizens threatened violence, and the community was moved to Oneida, New York, in 1848. Because his followers were equally yoked in their faith, Noyes reasoned, the practice of primitive Christian communism was acceptable, and this included the marriage relationship. Also, some isolation from the sinful world was necessary to bring about perfectionism; "salvation from sin, though possible under the conditions of ordinary society, must have for its full objective development a reconstructed society."[11] Horrified disbelievers labeled his "complex marriage" merely free love, but the community persevered for years.

Such an environment of enthusiastic religion, bizarre fads, crusades and eccentricities was already in the making when Sylvester Finney, his wife Rebecca, and their numerous children followed the flood of Yankees into New York State in 1794. Sylvester traced his lineage back to early New England stock. Sometime before 1635 a John Finney, Sr., and his wife, known as "Mother Finney," came from England to Falmouth, Massachusetts, with their daughter and two sons. One of the sons, John, Jr., was married three times, fathered many children, and lived at various periods in Swansea, Bristol, and Barnstable, Massachusetts.[12] At Barnstable in December 1665, his ninth child, Joshua, was born, and he in turn sired a large family.[13] A son, Josiah, was born to Joshua Finney on July 26, 1701, and in time he became one of the earliest settlers of Warren, Connecticut, in Litchfield County. The town records indicate that it was he who purchased the ground upon which the first church was built and then gave it to the Congregational society.[14]

On February 24, 1727/28 a son was born to Josiah Finney, whom he named after himself.[15] The fact that there was a Josiah Senior and a Josiah Junior has caused a bit of confusion to some genealogists, but it seems conclusive that Josiah Junior married Sarah Curtis, the sister of Major Eleazer Curtis, an officer in the Revolutionary War.[16] A second son, Sylvester, was born to them in Kent, Connecticut, on March 15, 1759. As a young man Sylvester also served in the Revolution, and on April 29, 1779, he married Rebecca Rice (born August 9, 1759) of Kent, a member of a large family prominent in the early records of Norwich and New London, Connecticut.[17]

Little is known of Sylvester and Rebecca Finney. Several letters of his are extant, and they show that he was not illiterate, but certainly he had enjoyed few educational advantages. His spelling is appalling. He was a typical frontier farmer, and like most of them, he was occasionally (if not often) in financial straits.[18] Rebecca Rice Finney was apparently a quiet and unassuming woman, who became an invalid by 1818. After her death on August 19, 1836, at their farm in Henderson, New York, Sylvester moved to be with his son Charles at Oberlin, Ohio. There he lived to be eighty-three, dying on June 26, 1842.

Along with most couples of the time, Sylvester and Rebecca Finney reared a large family. Their seventh child, born at Warren, Litchfield County, Connecticut, on August 29, 1792, was named Charles Grandison.[19] They called their son after the hero of a popular novel by Samuel Richardson (1689–1761), an English author who had written several works of fiction widely popular in America.

Of Charles' brothers and sisters, little is known. He had three sisters, Sarah (b. 1780), Deliah (b. 1781), and Chloe (b. 1785), and five brothers, Zenas (b. 1783), Sylvester (b. 1787, d. 1798), Harry (b. 1790), George (b. 1795), and a second Sylvester (b. 1802, d. 1803). Other than Charles, the only one to achieve any prominence was George. After working as a blacksmith for some years, George entered the ministry and, although he had a very limited education, was quite successful as a clergyman.[20] From the scant evidence, Zenas and Harry were farmers in Jefferson County.[21] Thus, with the exception of Charles Finney, the family was not outstanding, and left few records by which we can trace their activities.

Information on the early life of Finney is neither plentiful nor as reliable as the historian would like to have it. It appears that when Charles was two years old his parents no longer could resist the tide of western immigration, and the lure of good, cheap land in New York. Moving into the frontier wilderness of Oneida County, the Finney family settled first in Brothertown for a short period. There are no official records of Finney's youth, but family memories held that they soon moved nearby to Hanover, near the town of Kirkland, seven miles to the north.[22] Here they remained for the next fourteen years, during which this area was rapidly settled and domesticated.

The New England tradition insisted that even on a primitive frontier there should be schools, opened at least for the several months each year when college students home on vacation could be employed as teachers. Finney's daughter, Julia Finney-Monroe, and his grandson, William C. Cochran, believed that he attended the backwoods schools of Oneida County until he was fourteen, and that in 1806 he was enrolled at the Hamilton Oneida Academy at Clinton, several miles from his home, although Finney does not mention this in his *Memoirs*.[23] Some doubt must remain that Finney ever attended the academy, as there are no known records indicating that he did. But records at that time were often poorly kept and incomplete. Let us assume for the moment that Cochran was correct, for if Finney did attend it explains several things, such as his training in music and his friendship over the years with Thomas Hastings.

The curriculum at Hamilton Oneida Academy was quite respectable for that day, offering "English Grammar, Reading, Writing, Arithmetic, Bookkeeping, Dead Languages, French, Logic, Rhetoric, Composition, Moral Philosophy, and Natural Philosophy."[24] Hamilton Oneida Academy may have brought several important influences to bear on the impressionable lad. At the academy was the famous missionary to the Indians, Samuel Kirkland. Another teacher was Seth Norton, later a professor at Hamilton College after the academy was incorporated in 1812. L. Nelson Nichols held that it was Norton who detected musical talent in Finney and urged him to appreciate music and to take up the playing of the violin and the bass viol. In addition young Charles fell in with Thomas Hastings, it is held, a student who led the choir of the Congregational church,[25] and under his influence the love of music was further stimulated. It was a love that was to last throughout Finney's life.

Still, Finney considered himself very ignorant of religion. "My parents were neither of them professors of religion," he recalled in later life; "I seldom heard a sermon, unless it was an occasional one from some traveling minister."[26] Although Finney could remember not a single thing that these itinerants had said, he well recalled the grammatical errors they made and the merriment of the townsfolk afterward, when the preacher had departed, as they joked at his strange ideas and "the absurdities which had been advanced."

When Charles reached sixteen, in 1808, it appeared that at last the community would be privileged to have the services of a settled, educated clergyman. A meeting house was erected and a pastor selected. At that point, Finney's family moved to Henderson, a town in a remote area of Jefferson County on the shore of Lake Ontario. Charles Finney gave only sketchy information about his early life in the *Memoirs*, and additional sources are unreliable. One item is certain, however: he became a good athlete during these years. At Hamilton Oneida Academy he engaged in sports such as riding, wrestling, hunting, and running, and later when he lived by Lake Ontario he took advantage of it, becoming proficient in sailing, swimming, and rowing.[27]

Young Charles must have displayed some proficiency in the rudiments of education, for the townspeople adjudged him qualified to teach in the district school at Henderson from his sixteenth to his twentieth year. His students grew to love him, and one of them remembered:

> There was nothing which anyone else knew, that Mr. Finney didn't know, and there was nothing which anyone else could do that Mr. Finney could not do—and do a great deal better. He was the idol of his pupils. He joined in their sports before and after school, and although at first there were older and larger boys than he in the school, he could beat them at everything. He would lie down on the ground and let as many as could pile on top of him and try to hold him down. He would say, 'Are you ready?' Then he would make a quick turn, rise up and shake them all off, just as a lion might shake off a lot of puppies. In school, all was different. He was very dignified and kept perfect order. Should any boy attempt to create a disturbance, one flash of Mr. Finney's eye would quell the sinner at once. Oh, I tell you, they all loved and worshipped him, and all felt that some day he would be a great man.[28]

In 1812 war with England brought concern to the Americans along Lake Ontario. Persistent rumors of an impending invasion from Canada caused the militia to be called. In Sacket's Harbor, a few miles north of Henderson, a fort was built. This was the day of rampant republicanism, where in the military the soldiers elected their officers and enlistment was taken quite lightly. Finney, stirred by the danger as much as the other young men of the area, went to Sacket's Harbor to inquire about serving in the maritime branch of the militia. Apparently the furor calmed and the militia was disbanded after a time, for Charles returned home, irritated with the low morality and roughness he had encountered.[29]

In the latter part of 1812 he returned to Warren, Connecticut, to live with one of his uncles for a period. It was his desire to attend the academy located there and possibly to prepare for entrance into Yale College. For the first time in his life he came under the influence of regular religious services as he attended, Sunday by Sunday, the Congregational church in Warren that had been organized at his grandfather's home in 1756.[30] The aged pastor, Peter Starr, had come to the church in 1771; he was "an excellent man and greatly beloved and venerated by his people." Finney's curiosity led him to seize this opportunity to hear the Christian faith presented. Having developed some abilities in speaking and leading himself, he naturally expected to find theology preached with a certain amount of vigor and dynamic. It was not to be. To observe Starr's methods, Finney sat in the balcony where he could look down on the pastor's performance and note his techniques. To his chagrin, he found that the pastor "read his sermons in a manner that left no impression whatever on my mind. He had a monotonous, humdrum way of reading what he had probably written many years before."[31]

Finney noted critically that Starr used manuscript notes each week that fitted neatly into a small Bible, and that the preacher placed his fingers at the different pages of scripture to be quoted at appropriate points in the rendition of the sermon. This made it necessary to hold the Bible in both hands, and precluded the possibility of any animating gestures that might have helped the homily along. Starr liberated his fingers one by one, until the fingers of both hands were read out of their places. When he was down to his last finger, the congregation could also expect to be set free presently.

Finney was profoundly disappointed after listening to months of such preaching. It was not only he who thought the sermons were dry. The rest of the congregation as well, while they revered Starr, were at a loss to detect any practical application to their lives. "It seemed to be always a matter of curiosity to know what he was aiming at," Finney lamented. Although Starr's homiletical abilities suffered greatly from his declining years, and his methods were already woefully antiquated, it is important to note that Starr was one of only two preachers (the other was George W. Gale) to whose sermons Finney was exposed for any length of time before his conversion. Thus, when Finney in 1822 condemned before the presbytery the regulation style of preaching then in vogue, he was in large measure reacting to the poor performances of Peter Starr.

During the time that Finney spent in Warren, he made several other decisions that were to be fateful. For one, he took his uncle's advice and joined the local Masonic lodge, believing that it would be to his future advantage in finding fraternal help everywhere. He spent some time in the lodge rising through the membership levels, and finally he was raised to "the sublime degree of Master Mason."[32] Secondly, at the Warren academy he asked his teacher, a graduate of Yale College, about the feasibility of his attending that institution. Taking into consideration Finney's abilities and the fact that he was past twenty years of age, the teacher replied that it would be a waste of time, because he could accomplish Yale's entire four-year curriculum in two years if he applied himself. "He presented such considerations as prevailed with me," Finney recalled, "and as it resulted, I failed to pursue my school education any farther at that time. However, afterward I acquired some knowledge of Latin, Greek, and Hebrew."[33]

Finney accepted the judgment eagerly. Whatever may have been his teacher's motives, for one to rise to the prominent positions Finney would eventually occupy, it was certainly an unfortunate judgment. Perhaps his teacher assumed that Finney would immediately go through the Yale curriculum on his own, but that was not to be, and to the end of his days he felt the gaps and inadequacies in his education. But such regrets are the Finney of seventy-five years reminiscing in his *Memoirs;* the young man in his early twenties possessed enormous self-assurance, and in a few years he would be defying a presbytery of learned clergymen when it requested as a routine matter that he attend a seminary for systematic study before ordination. The elderly Finney may have had his regrets over an incomplete education, but still he could not bring himself to admit he had been wrong.

About 1814 Finney left Connecticut and traveled to New Jersey, teaching in public schools there for several years. He intended to travel farther south and continue a career as school teacher, but in 1818 his mother's poor health induced him to return to the family homestead in Henderson, Jefferson County, New York. During his absence of six years, few changes had occurred. It was still a primitive area in most respects. While the region around Oneida County, containing the city of Utica, was rapidly becoming settled, the movement was generally westward, to Syracuse and the Finger Lakes region, and the population increase in Jefferson County to the north was much less. In the two decades from 1800 to 1820, the population of Connecticut had increased by only ten percent, whereas that of New York had doubled.[34] It was a raw frontier life in Henderson, and there were few cultural amenities. But religiously, the situation had improved somewhat since 1812. At that time there was practically no settled ministry in this region, and in 1816 a clergyman who passed through reported, "To the north as far as the St. Lawrence and east to Champlain, there are probably not six gospel ministers."[35] However, the denominations were responding to the challenge, and local congregations were being organized.

In 1816 religiously inclined residents of Sacket's Harbor, a few miles to the north of Henderson, had called Samuel F. Snowden to be their pastor. A man of excellent qualities, Snowden was able to organize a Presbyterian church by February 1817. And in Adams, to the east of Henderson, a Congregational church, soon to become Presbyterian, was organized under the ministry of Edward W. Rossiter at about the same time. In addition, a revival had swept through the region in 1815.[36] Finney returned, therefore, to an area where the Christian faith had made strong inroads. In addition, where in 1812 his family had had no religious connections, by 1818 one of his brothers had given himself to God in his absence, as Finney later described:

> I well recollect, when far from home, and while an impenitent sinner, I received a letter from my youngest brother, informing me that he was converted to God. He, if he was converted, was, as I supposed, the first and only member of the family who then had a hope of salvation. I was at the time, and both before and after, one of the most careless sinners, and yet on receiving this intelligence, I actually wept for joy and gratitude, that one of so prayerless a family was likely to be saved.[37]

In Finney's consideration of a lifetime career, teaching may have paled; certainly the profession was insecure enough and poorly paid. Back in Henderson, Finney gave the impression that he was somewhat unsettled, looking to put down roots but not altogether clear

as to what other callings might be open to him. Certainly he was reacting to the restlessness of the area, for even in remote Jefferson
County the tenseness of expectancy that pervaded central New York
was in the air. The common man was becoming a greater factor in
politics, and canal fever was beginning to grip the populace as realization came that the contemplated Erie Canal could bring a great economic boom for miles around.

Finney had reason to take stock; he was twenty-six, and his future seemed cloudy. He possessed many admirable characteristics,
however, and had much in his favor. One writer, perhaps reading too
much of the later Finney back into him at this point, described him
as a "splendid pagan—a young man rejoicing in his strength, proudly
conscious of his physical and intellectual superiority to all around
him."[38] A more balanced view was given by George W. Gale:

> He was a young man of strong impulses, great vivacity of spirit,
> bold and fearless, which qualities are strongly imprinted on his
> physiognomy, independent and self-reliant, but full of kind and
> tender feeling and strong attachment to his friends. He [had] light
> complexion and light hair, large and prominent light blue eyes.
> . . . His first appearance was not prepossessing, and his manners
> plain and bordering strongly upon the rough and blunt, but his
> warm heart, sincere and unchanging attachments, and affection-
> ate manner, made him many friends. His was a guileless, honest,
> frank heart. He is said to have been a very wicked man before his
> conversion; that was the common report. He might sometimes
> when excited have used rough, or even profane, language, but he
> was not, that I know, addicted to any low vices.[39]

Handsome in a virile way, Finney was soon to learn as a young
law clerk how to capitalize upon his striking features, so valuable and
persuasive in a courtroom—or behind a pulpit. No description of Finney from this period failed to mention his prominent forehead and
those remarkable, hypnotic eyes, which many remembered for years
as his most conspicuous characteristic, for it seemed that he could
pierce through a person with his stern glance. His grandson, William C.
Cochran, described Finney's eyes as "large and blue, at times mild as
an April sky, and at others, cold and penetrating as polished steel."[40]
In addition to those unforgettable eyes, observers were always impressed with his rich and strong voice, which was a perfect accom-
paniment to the piercing gaze. In later years, when Finney had learned

how to use his appearance and voice for maximum effect upon audiences, he was able to modulate his vocal power to be immensely persuasive, as well as to be explosive—perhaps melodramatic by the standards of today—with his verbal pyrotechnics. But that was still future.

In Henderson, Finney devoted himself to the social life. He became well known throughout the county for his dancing, playing of the bass viol, and his athletic prowess, and he was regarded by the opposite sex as a most eligible bachelor. It was widely acknowledged that Charles Finney was dynamic, magnetic, and arresting.

Perhaps it was these qualities that led friends to suggest a legal career to him. Certainly Finney was fitted for the law: he had an orderly, logical mind, and his physical characteristics and abilities could impress judges and juries. It seemed a sensible choice and might lead in due time to a further career in politics, where again he would be an impressive figure. The law was certainly to be preferred above the shaky profession of schoolteacher, positionally and financially. Because law schools were still embryonic, it was the common custom to study under a local lawyer of repute. Finney chose the law office of Wright and Wardwell in the nearby town of Adams.

For three years all went well. It seemed that Charles G. Finney had found his place in life. He became an apprentice to Benjamin Wright, one of the partners, who had opened this law firm some years earlier and was soon elected surrogate of the county, or "side judge," holding this office for many years.[41] Under Wright's instruction, Finney read a great deal of Blackstone during this time.

A good source for this period of Finney's life is the *Autobiography of Rev. George W. Gale*, who was to play such an important role in the immediate future. Gale gave this appraisal of Finney as a student of law:

> When I was preaching at Adams, before my settlement, he was in the office of Wright and Wardwell, a student at law, where he continued till his conversion in the fall of 1821. He was expecting at the time of his conversion, to be licensed soon in the Supreme Court. He could have been licensed some two or three years before, according to the usages, or laws, of the State, in the Court of Common Pleas, but he did not choose to do so. He had all the business he wanted, and that was enough to support him, in Justice's Courts. He proposed having all the time he could for study. He was a good student and had attained a knowledge of the law, it is said, which many practitioners had not attained in that sec-

tion of the country, and when meeting them, as his opponents in Justice's Courts was more than a match for them.[42]

Benjamin Wright in time became more than a tutor; he became a friend of Finney, one for whom the younger man had a deep regard. Wright appears in the sources available to us as mild-mannered and affable, although his student speaks occasionally of Wright's "pride," which prevented him from making a ready acceptance of Christian faith. Despite this, when Finney made such a profession Wright did not deter him in any sense or ridicule him and was eventually converted himself.[43]

The law, then, was to be Charles Finney's life work—or so he thought. But as events would have it, a strange combination of factors continued to display Christianity to him as an attractive option. At the same time, he regarded himself "as ignorant of religion as a heathen"[44] and declared that he was one of the most careless of sinners. George Gale's appraisal of Finney is similar, but he was reacting at that time to Finney's self-protective sarcasm of the faith. Thus Gale's verdict that "the common report" of Finney was that he was "a very wicked man before his conversion" may need to be discounted somewhat in view of Gale's annoyance. One historian has suggested that Finney's morals were no worse than those of the average young man of that time and region.[45]

In later life, Finney endlessly referred to his conversion as a miracle of God's grace. However, the historian would also wish to bring in the psychological context that was working so powerfully on him in those years. In a sense, although it was hardly inevitable that Finney would turn from his irreligion to God, the forces operating on him were so strong that for him to resist them successfully may seem to us unlikely. Mentally and spiritually, Finney was undergoing a conditioning that provided a powerful impetus toward religion, and he already possessed all the requisite propensities.

The first factor that operated on him was biblical authority. "In studying elementary law, I found the old authors frequently quoting the Scriptures," he said. Especially quoted were parts of the Mosaic code. Finney had read the Bible only perfunctorily until that time, if at all. "This excited my curiosity so much that I went and purchased a Bible, the first I had ever owned. . . . This soon led to my taking a new interest in the Bible, and I read and meditated on it much more than I had ever done before in my life. However, much of it I did not understand."[46] Nevertheless, it is apparent that his mind absorbed a great deal and it simmered there for some time, and in addition there was a profound correlation made by him between Blackstone's legal commentaries and the Bible, which was to affect the rest of his life.

In Blackstone's discussions of crime and guilt, the concept of free will played a crucial role. Inasmuch as a legal tradition came into existence through the exercise of free will, Blackstone argued that only those violations of the law that were committed voluntarily, with a will that was free, could be justifiably punished. As he wrote:

> All the several pleas and excuses, which protect the committer of a forbidden act from the punishment which is otherwise annexed thereto, may be reduced to this single consideration, the want or defect of will. An involuntary act, as it has no claim to merit, so neither can it induce any guilt: the concurrence of the will, when it has its choice either to do or to avoid the fact in question, being the only thing that renders human action either praiseworthy or culpable.[47]

This contribution of Blackstone to Charles Finney's presuppositions and categories is basic for an understanding of him in later years as a preacher and theologian. Foundational to Finney's approach both to evangelism and to theology is the unquestioned assumption that, forensically and religiously, human beings are responsible to higher law. Because Blackstone was inculcated in him before a study (however tentative) of Calvin and the Westminster Standards, it would later enrage him to learn that the reformers taught that the human will was in bondage, encumbered with inherited guilt and not free to obey or disobey the Creator. Such a teaching, to Finney, vitiated human responsibility for acts of good or evil. One has but to read any sermon of his taken at random to observe this conviction at work. Above all else, however, his own experience of conversion bore out in fact what Finney learned from the legal tomes of Blackstone concerning the "God-given faculty of the will." Although the full development of Jacksonian democracy was not to be realized until the election of 1828, Finney's demand for individual freedom meshed perfectly with the developing mood in America, found in the rationale of Thomas Jefferson, of greater trust in average people and their responsibility and involvement in government.[48]

Another factor that operated on Finney was church attendance. He recorded no particulars as to how he was first drawn to the Presbyterian church at Adams, although it may have been his musical ability. His talents enabled him to take the position of choir director, and he found an immediate liking for the energetic young pastor, George W. Gale. Gale was three years Finney's senior, a graduate of Union College and Princeton Theological Seminary. In personality and in the friendship he extended toward his choir director Gale was an altogether different type of divine from the aged Peter Starr of Connecticut. But Finney discovered, to his surprise, that in the pulpit George Gale and Peter Starr were somewhat similar. For one, they both preached Calvinism, which stressed the sovereignty of God, election, and the impossibility of bringing about one's own salvation. At first that was merely a curiosity to the young law clerk; later, his questions about some doctrines of Calvinism and the arguments between him and Gale served as catalysts leading to his own conversion. But the thing that immediately rankled Finney was that Gale, although a far more lively preacher than Starr, still had been trained in the regulation style that was somewhat formal and did not address the congregation directly, avoiding the use of "you." As a law student, Finney had already mastered the use of vigorous, direct address to juries and witnesses on the stand. In comparison with such plain speech, Gale's preaching seemed mild and ineffective. An indelible impression had been made on Finney by his legal studies, and his patterns of thought and style of speaking were fixed for life during his three years of apprenticeship under Benjamin Wright.

In addition to reading the Bible and attending church, Finney was increasingly discussing religion with Gale and others, and devoting more time to spiritual matters than he realized. Then, at some time during his legal training, he began to court Lydia Andrews of Whitestown, Oneida County, who had a sister living in Adams and frequently came to visit her. Lydia, a very devout young lady, began to pray for Finney's conversion, and doubtless this was another factor that swayed him.[49]

Eventually, Pastor Gale, recognizing Finney's talents and potential, singled him out for special attention. With Finney's position as choir director there were many opportunities for Gale to initiate conversations and cultivate friendship. The pastor never allowed this fine young law clerk, who was scoffing at religion but clearly uneasy in his mind about it, to move far from its influence. Gale got into the habit, Finney wrote naively, "of dropping in at our office frequently, and seemed anxious to know what impression his sermons had made on my mind. . . . I now think that I sometimes criticized his sermons unmercifully."[50] Finney mistook Gale's objectives in forging friendship as a desire to have stimulating discussions, but he never suspected that this was merely good pastoral work.

At that point, in the summer of 1821, George Gale left the town of Adams for a time to visit a sick relative. No ordained clergyman being available to supply the pulpit, Gale asked Jedediah Burchard to conduct the Sunday services and read prepared sermons to the congregation. Burchard, a man of thirty-one, had suffered bankruptcy in the panic of 1819, and was converted soon afterward.[51] When Gale returned to Adams, he was delighted to find that the sporadic awakenings that had begun in 1815 were continuing. B. B. Warfield has written:

> The revival of 1815 already mentioned as sweeping over this region, had been followed by others without intermission. Sixty-five converts were added to the little church at Adams in 1819, at the opening of Gale's ministry there. Seventy were added to the church at Sackett's Harbor in 1820. In 1821 the whole region was stirred to its depths; from eight hundred to a thousand converts were reported from Jefferson County—no fewer than seventy or eighty from Finney's home hamlet, Henderson. In Adams itself one of the churches received forty-four new members and the other sixty or seventy.[52]

As for Burchard, Gale encouraged him to enter the clergy and took personal charge of his theological training. Gale persuaded the Black River Congregational Association to license him, and after a while Burchard was ordained by the Presbytery of Watertown and remained active in promoting revivals in St. Lawrence and Jefferson counties.[53]

According to Charles Finney's account of this period, he was going through much soul-searching and consternation. He avoided Gale and others as much as possible.[54] Then, reversing himself, he attended his first inquiry meeting and "trembled so that my very seat shook under me. At that time I had never received such instruction as I needed; for if I had, I should have been converted at once."[55]

Now this was hardly fair to Gale, especially in light of the abundant criticism that Finney himself admitted he had made of Gale's work and every aspect of the church, and of Gale's discussions and friendship with him. The pastor's recollection of Finney's attendance at this inquiry meeting (the same one, it would appear) was somewhat different. Gale recalled:

He looked at me, with an air of solemnity I shall never forget. . . .
"I am willing now to be a Christian. . . . Do you think there is any
hope in my case?" I told him he might be converted, but if he were
it would be something very similar to God's exercising miraculous power. . . . It was not teaching that he needed. It was com-
pliance with what he knew already.[56]

The resolution of Finney's spiritual struggle came quickly. He
determined, "on a Sabbath evening in the autumn of 1821,"[57] to settle
the issue. In the next two days he became increasingly agitated, and
on Wednesday morning he set out for the law office of Wright and
Wardwell feeling greatly weighted down. An impulse made him halt,
and he determined to spend no more time in indecision. About half
a mile north of the town was a large wooded tract, and he began walking in that direction, resolving to "give my heart to God, or I never
will come down from there." Finding a remote spot where he hoped
to escape the notice of anyone passing by, Finney knelt. And suddenly
it became clear; until then he had believed scripture intellectually,
but he had not realized that faith was a voluntary trust, not an intellectual state. It was to place oneself under the mercy of a supremely
forgiving heavenly Father. From the deep depression that held him
shortly before, making him wonder if he had committed the unpar-
donable sin, he found himself in a totally different state, full of joy.

Elated at this breakthrough, Finney gave himself to prayer amid
the tangle of trees. Hours passed, although he had no consciousness
of the passage of time. "I prayed," he recalled, "till my mind became
so full that, before I was aware of it, I was on my feet and tripping
up the ascent toward the road." His mind now was "most wonderfully
quiet and peaceful." Almost involuntarily he said, with great emphasis, "If I am ever converted, I will preach the gospel."

Charles Finney's complex personality is well illustrated by this
sequence of events. For much of his life, a fixed determination, rigidity of purpose, and absolute conviction of the rightness of his way
seem to dominate his character. Yet here is Finney in a very different
key, pliable, admitting his need, uncertain, joyful—hardly the stern,
implacable man so familiar to multitudes over his lifetime. Scholars
have been aware of this ambivalence in Finney's thought between
pietism, as well illustrated in his conversion, and a determined pragmatism that ruled his plans and methods.[58]

Walking back to the town, Finney found that his entire outlook
was changed. It was the tenth of October, "a very pleasant day," and

Concerning his conversion, Charles Finney wrote in his *Memoirs*, "North of the village [of Adams], and over a hill, lay a grove of woods. . . . I turned and bent my course . . . into the woods, I should think, a quarter of a mile. . . . I crept into this place and knelt down for prayer." From an old wood engraving in the author's possession.

he had gone into the woods immediately after an early breakfast. Now it was past noon, and "the most profound spiritual tranquility had taken possession of me." He went to the law office, which he found empty, took out his bass viol, and began to play and sing some of the hymns he knew. That caused him to weep, and it seemed "as if my heart was all liquid." Eventually Benjamin Wright entered, and they spent the rest of the day moving books and furniture to another office.

When Wright left, the emotional impact of Finney's decision hit him again. Christ appeared to him, "face to face," and Finney believed this was a physical manifestation, not a vision. As he sat by the fire he received "a mighty baptism of the Holy Ghost," an altogether unexpected phenomenon, and he soon cried out, "I shall die if these waves continue to pass over me. Lord, I cannot bear any more." A member of the choir entered and was astonished to see him weeping. Asking if Finney was in pain, the man received the answer, "No, but so happy that I cannot live."

The next morning Finney told Squire Wright what had happened. The lawyer was amazed, but made no reply, and soon left the office. Finney recounted:

> I thought no more of it then, but afterward found that the remark I made pierced him like a sword; and he did not recover from it till he was converted.
>
> Soon after Mr. Wright had left the office, Deacon Barney came into the office and said to me, "Mr. Finney, do you recollect that my cause is to be tried at ten o'clock this morning? I suppose you are ready?" I had been retained to attend this suit as his attorney. I replied to him, "Deacon Barney, I have a retainer from the Lord Jesus Christ to plead his cause, and I cannot plead yours." He looked at me with astonishment, and said, "What do you mean?" I told him, in a few words, that I had enlisted in the cause of Christ. . . . He dropped his head, and without making any reply, went out. A few moments later, in passing the window, I observed that Deacon Barney was standing in the road, seemingly lost in deep meditation. He went away, as I afterward learned, and immediately settled his suit.[59]

This new attorney for Jesus had prepared himself for whatever might come next.

3

A RETAINER FROM THE LORD

Charles Finney took his conversion with the utmost seriousness. From the first a determination and urgency dominated his mind. He took every opportunity to tell everyone he met, friends and strangers alike, of his turnabout in sentiments. News of Finney's conversion naturally excited curiosity, many of the townspeople reacting with disbelief because his previous scorn of the church was very well known. Some said that he was trying to play a practical joke not only on the church but on the entire populace.[1] Yet Finney persevered. He stopped at a shoemaker's shop in town and heard the son of one of the church elders espousing Universalism, which was a frequent opponent of the Congregational and Presbyterian churches at that time. According to Finney, he "was enabled to blow his argument to the wind" in a few moments, and soon thereafter the young man was converted.[2]

That evening, a prayer meeting was held in the schoolhouse as was the custom, and Finney eagerly attended. The Reverend George Gale was there as well. The house was filled to capacity, but no one seemed ready to begin the meeting. Without waiting to be called on, Finney rose and proceeded to tell the crowd what had happened to him in the last few days. His evident sincerity convinced the audience that this was no joke, and many were greatly impressed. No sooner had he concluded than Gale arose and, crestfallen, began to speak in a very humble manner. He confessed that he believed Finney was truly converted after hearing this account, but that when he had earlier heard it he would not accept it. This was wrong, he said, and all along he had been in error in discouraging others from praying for Finney, because he had thought that the choir director was beyond the reach of the gospel. Dejectedly, he stated that he had little faith, and begged forgiveness.[3]

Finney then turned to devoting his energies to influence the young people of the town whose minds he had previously prejudiced against Christianity. He was surprised at the response, and took this for God's blessing on the work. In a short while all but one of them professed to have followed Finney in believing. Then his concern turned to his parents, neither of whom had previously made any profession of religion. He went to their home in Henderson, and his father met him at the gate. After greeting him, Finney said that he had never heard a prayer in his father's house. The old man lowered his head and burst into tears, saying, "I know it, Charles; come in and pray yourself."[4] Again Finney was gratified when both his father and mother accepted the Christian faith.

According to what Finney said in his *Memoirs*, even before he had turned from his irreligion he was in disagreement with George Gale's Calvinism. In listening to his sermons from week to week, Finney claimed he had the same reaction that struck him when he sat under the ministry of the Reverend Peter Starr in the Congregational Church of Warren, Connecticut. Although he readily granted the absolute sincerity of these two men, and admired their good characters, he could not agree with the Westminster Standards Calvinism that they preached.

To what extent these statements in the *Memoirs* may be taken at face value is open to question. The thesis has been advanced that even at the time of his early revivals he possessed a novel and distinctive theology,[5] but proof for this is lacking and the idea rests entirely upon his own claims. Whitney R. Cross has stated:

> In fact, not only was his doctrine at this time by no means distinctive or original, but it is fair to question whether he had at the beginning anything whatsoever which deserves the title of a theology. Adequate examination of the subject must refuse to take him at his own evaluation or to read back into his early ministry notions developed in the course of a lifetime.[6]

Although Finney had no positive theology to offer for some time, it may be that he entertained some doubts about Calvinism, and that long before he developed any theological sophistication of his own, he felt that some of what Gale taught was problematic and contradictory. It would have taken little theological acumen to balk at Calvinism's destruction of human pride, Finney's claims notwithstanding. When Calvinism made God sovereign and humans puny, Finney simply reacted with the unordered Pelagianism of the man in the street who wants to consider himself in control.

This is not to say that Finney rejected all that George Gale preached. Finney certainly agreed, not only at the beginning but throughout his days, that he and all mankind were at enmity with God, as the scriptures taught, and deep in sin and in need of divine forgiveness. But from this point on, Finney claimed that he differed from Gale. The pastor was expounding nothing novel, of course, but in company with multitudes of others of that day he was simply repeating the high and undiluted Reformed creed first set forth in John Calvin's *Institutes of the Christian Religion*, further refined in the Westminster Confession of Faith completed in 1646, and taught at his alma mater, Princeton Theological Seminary. According to this widely held interpretation, human beings were sinners by nature, having moral depravity and their wills inclined inexorably toward evil. Humans were capable of committing sin, but were not free, because of the old Adamic nature, to do right and follow the laws of God. For this sinful nature, as well as their own transgressions, all mankind was condemned to eternal damnation. Gale went on to teach that Christ died only for the elect, exact justice having been satisfied by his death on the cross, whereby their debt to God's righteousness was paid and the penalty required by the divine law was discharged in full. Regeneration, whereby a person was converted, was a physical change wrought by the Holy Spirit independently of human agency, acting directly upon the substance of the soul. In this process sinners were passive. Nothing they could do, nothing anyone else could do for them, would help in their salvation. In due time, strict Calvinism taught, those who were of the elect, God would convert; but those who were of the nonelect would remain without hope and without God in the world. If he preached on repentance, Gale would be sure to inform his hearers that they could not repent of their own power, but only when God's time came and he worked repentance in them. And if he preached on saving faith, Gale would tell his congregation that they could not believe until their natures were changed by the Holy Spirit.

Even before his conversion, Finney—the law student demanding human accountability—felt that Gale's Calvinism overly demeaned human motivation and action, and he may have told the pastor that in their discussions. And although Finney was consciously unaware of it, he was voicing the concerns of many Americans at that period who were abandoning Calvinism and predestination, or at least rejecting the very elements that were most repellent to the unconverted, the ideas that they were mired in sin and unable to exert moral choice. To Finney this was irrational and utterly unfair, and thus unknowingly he concurred with the mood of the New Divinity in New England, represented by Timothy Dwight, Lyman Beecher, and Nathaniel William Taylor, which was attempting to dissociate itself from the older ideas. As one who had studied law and traveled around the states somewhat, Finney was quite aware of the broader mood of expansive individualism that gripped the population then, and of the search of the American people for national unity and identity, and all of these had major implications for his theology.

At the heart of Finney's difficulty was the crucial idea of human nature, the question of how much power of choice and action was left to the unsaved. It was not only the problem of a free or unfree will, but also whether sin was inherited from Adam's fall, and if original sin had so vitiated human power to obey God that there was no possibility of obedience before salvation. The idea of a fallen will, necessitated and unable to freely choose, was especially repugnant to the mind of the young attorney. He was convinced, from the influence of the courtroom, that ability was commensurate with responsibility, that people were not sinners from birth but from choice, that they were endowed by nature with all the powers of moral agency and what was required of them was not to alter these powers but to use them in the service of their Creator. Therefore, he began to think, regeneration was not a physical change, a change in the substance of the soul, but merely a change in the overall preferences of the mind, brought about by the moral influence of the Holy Spirit in persuading people through interior motives, to embrace the truths of the gospel. Because it was in their power to do so, therefore it was their duty to repent, believe, and obey the gospel. It had been so in Finney's own conversion, for as long as he felt inhibited by Gale's preaching and the idea that he was powerless to choose for God, nothing had happened; but suddenly he had realized it need not be so, that he did have the power to choose. "Gospel salvation seemed to me to be an offer of something to be accepted; and that it was full and complete; and that all that was necessary on my part, was to get my own consent to give up my sins, and accept Christ."[7] *My own consent!* And as soon as he realized this, he was enabled to go to the woods north of Adams, pour out his heart before God, and accept the gospel. To Finney, it was all so simple and logical.

Whenever it was that these ideas matured, Finney prided himself that his own intellect had brought him to question Calvinism, and that few others had discovered the same ideas previously. It was hardly so. These were similar to the arguments that had been advanced by Pelagius, attacked by Augustine, and condemned at the Third General Council in Ephesus in the year 431—the tendency of thinking that has come to be called Pelagianism.[8] And somewhat parallel notions of free will had been advanced by Erasmus and attacked by Luther in 1524 and 1525. Entirely ignorant of the long history of this dialectic, Charles Finney had become convinced from his own study of the Bible (influenced, certainly, by his legal training) that the broken relationship with God could be healed if mankind would simply turn in repentance to Christ. Finney's innate self-assurance asserted itself and convinced him that it was a matter of admitting that they were sinners, and of accepting what Christ had done, that brought people salvation. What held them back was not that they were not of the elect, but their own obstinacy and lack of determination.

Unfortunately, there are only two contemporary sources of information for the next two years of Charles Finney's life, his *Memoirs* and George Gale's *Autobiography*, which give much material. They are in general agreement on factual matters, but Gale's work is brief and Finney's, written decades later, is often unreliable and filled with anecdotes, which, if interesting, are hardly satisfying in terms of historical detail, and leave much unsaid. But several definite facts emerge. For one, in a short while the friendship forged between the two men grew somewhat stronger, and Finney changed his boarding house to move into the manse of Gale and his wife.[9] Secondly, Finney turned away from the study of law almost immediately after his conversion, which had major implications because it cut off the source of his income and left him dependent on some funds he had put aside previously. He declared:

> I had been very fond of my profession. But as I have said, when I was converted all was dark in that direction, and I had, no more, any pleasure in attending to law business. I had many very pressing invitations to conduct lawsuits, but I uniformly refused. . . .

The business itself of conducting other people's controversies, appeared odious and offensive to me.[10]

A third development came about with the decision that Charles Finney would enter the ministry. That this was a momentous decision hardly needs to be said, for it meant that this man of twenty-nine years, who had already been a schoolmaster and then a law student, would enter the third profession of his lifetime. But as to the source of this decision, we must remain in some doubt, for Gale and Finney give opposing statements. "He [Gale] had it fixed in his mind that I should be a minister," Finney claims, "and he took pains to inform me that if I did not become a minister, the Lord would not bless my labors."[11] Gale's recollection is entirely different:

> After a few months, as I had anticipated, although I said nothing to him, he came to me and wanted to know what I would think or advise in regard to his leaving the law and studying for the ministry. I said, "I will say to you, as an old minister of my acquaintance said to a young lawyer who came to him with a similar question. It may be best but I would not advise you to turn too short a corner, take time to consider." I told him he might resume his study of Latin and commence the Greek language, and review the studies of moral philosophy and rhetoric, to which he had given some attention. This would do him no harm, but good, whatever conclusions he might come to after he had had time to try his feelings and duly consider the subject. He took this course, and I became his teacher.[12]

It may have suited Finney's conceit in old age to have believed that Gale was eager to claim him as a protégé for the clergy, but the facts seem to be otherwise, and Gale's version is to be preferred. His *Autobiography* makes it abundantly clear throughout that the pastor was not so overwhelmed and impressed with Finney's abilities as the latter would have us think. Gale, arguing with his boarder constantly over theological questions, was justifiably irritated over the positions his "pupil" took, and he must have felt that seldom has a pupil been more obstinate, or more convinced that he was destined for greatness. On the other hand, Finney asked Gale at the time of his conversion if he "did not feel the house tremble while we knelt,"[13] but Gale had not noticed any such thing. On another occasion Finney approached Gale and suddenly "the glory of God shone upon and round

about me, in a manner most marvellous. . . . I think I knew something then, by actual experience, of that light that prostrated Paul on
his way to Damascus."[14] But Gale saw no light, and must have been
disturbed by these mystical tendencies in Finney, with which his rock-
ribbed Calvinism would have little sympathy.

Whatever reservations George Gale entertained about Finney, he
overcame them when he sponsored his friend before the local presbytery, that Finney might begin preparing formally for the ministry.
The Presbyterian system encompassed three stages for such candidates for the cloth: being "taken under care" of the presbytery, which
meant that future studies might be directed and in time examined
for sufficient mastery; licensure, which would allow the candidate
limited preaching opportunities, but not the administration of the sacraments; and last, the actual ordination to become a "presbyter," or
teaching elder. Ordination, which allowed the administration of the
sacraments, was done under one of two justifications: the receipt of
a "call" to be pastor of a particular congregation, or as an evangelist,
with no fixed congregation and a wide-ranging ministry whose latitude would be determined by the presbytery.

In the midst of his activities, Finney was taken under the care
of the Presbytery of St. Lawrence at a meeting held at Adams, June 25,
1823. George Gale, filling the role of a faithful pastor, was naturally
hoping that Finney would be accepted into a theological seminary
where he would receive professional training. By this point, with several seminaries established throughout the East, the older custom of
young men studying under the supervision of experienced pastors was
quickly disappearing.[15] Finney claimed in 1868 that the presbytery offered to see that his expenses would be paid if he went to Princeton
Theological Seminary,[16] but Gale, whose memory played fewer tricks
on him, recorded in 1853 that he "had written to Andover, to Princeton, and to Auburn, to see if they would admit him as a student and
aid him from their funds while in the pursuit of his studies, but getting no encouragement I advised him to this course, and to study what
should be prescribed, and as long as the Presbytery thought proper."[17]
Gale's account went on to state that the presbytery moved ahead in
a routine fashion to take him under its care, and appointed Gale and
George Boardman, pastor of the Presbyterian church at Watertown,
New York, to supervise his studies. Apparently there was little out
of the ordinary in what transpired at the meeting of the presbytery,
except that the candidate's application for admission and financial
aid had been rejected by three seminaries. But this is hardly Finney's
recollection, which differs at many points:

In the Spring of this year, 1822, I put myself under the care of the Presbytery as a candidate for the Gospel ministry. Some of the ministers urged me to go to Princeton to study theology, but I declined. When they asked me why I would not go to Princeton, I told them that my pecuniary circumstances forbade it. This was true; but they said they would see that my expenses were paid. Still I refused to go; and when urged to give them my reasons, I plainly told them that I would not put myself under such an influence as they had been under; that I was confident they had been wrongly educated, and they were not ministers that met my ideal of what a minister of Christ should be. I told them this reluctantly, but I could not honestly withhold it. They appointed my pastor to superintend my studies. He offered me the use of his library, and said he would give what attention I needed to my theological studies. But my studies, so far as he was concerned as my teacher, were little else than controversy.[18]

It is to be seriously doubted that dignified, competent clergymen of many years' experience would meekly accept the tongue-lashing of a rather arrogant, newly converted law clerk who patently knew nothing of theology and whose application for scholarship aid had just been rejected by three seminaries! In all likelihood Finney merely *thought* what he claimed he said, as he chafed under the embarrassment of his rejections and the governance of any authority. And what was the impact of these rejections by seminaries and churches on Finney's character and career? No data remain to tell us, but it is a safe conjecture that they went far to solidify his pietistic insistence that he could learn all he (or any *true* man of God) needed from a solitary study of the Bible, and that all human institutions and organizations, including church and clergy, inhibited his work for God. Pietism as well as anti-intellectualism are at work here. One thing is certain; Finney during his Oberlin years may have overcome his aversion to institutional loyalty, but all his life he remained nondenominational, and the seeds of this were surely planted at this time.

For some reason, George Boardman had little to do with Finney's instruction, and the entire burden fell upon Gale's shoulders. The wrangling between them continued. Finney said at one point, with uncharacteristic humility, "I was however but a child in theology,"[19] and then proceeded to portray their disputes as a contest between equals: "We went over the whole field of debate between the old and new school divines, upon the subject of atonement." He certainly learned more from Gale than he ever chose to admit, but at the same time evidently he was unwilling to follow any systematic plan of study or instruction. He claimed that he spent much of his time in prayer consulting his Bible, deriving all his doctrine from an intense scrutiny of that source alone, without any human admixture. "Indeed I read my Bible on my knees a great deal during those days of conflict, beseeching the Lord to teach me his own mind on those points."[20] In Gale's recollections he hardly mentioned the controversy between them, whereas Finney endlessly dwelt upon it. But Gale does unhorse the notion that Finney was theologically precocious or totally opposed to Calvinism:

> His peculiar views, adopted since he has been at Oberlin, were no part of his theology at that time, and for a number of years afterward. . . . Of the doctrine of Election Mr. Finney in his preaching said very little. His reason for it was that he was dealing with the impenitent chiefly, and he thought it was adapted to converted, or the mature Christian, rather than to the impenitent. This I always thought in some degree a wrong judgment. . . . Had Mr. Finney taken a different view of it, and dwelt upon it more, his faith would have been more firmly anchored, and he would have been saved from the position in which he has found himself, and some of his converts, and some young ministers, who regarded him as a model, would have done more good. *When he was licensed and first labored as a missionary, he was very firm and faithful in bringing out this doctrine.*[21]

Fortunately, Finney had learned some of the classical languages while a student at the academy in Warren, Connecticut, and after a bit of brushing up, this served him in good stead for the language examinations of the presbytery. "I read several books of Virgil & Cicero's orations in Latin," he wrote, "& my Greek testament so far as to pass the usual examination before Presbytery, & so much Hebrew as to be able to satisfy myself of the meaning of a text when I felt in doubt upon the subject."[22] In all likelihood Gale assisted here, as well as guiding Finney through a review of rhetoric and ethics in addition to the theology over which they argued. The studies continued for some time, although gradually they were eclipsed by evangelistic efforts until early in 1824.[23] Finney's initial labors as a winner of souls commenced, then, under George Gale's guidance. "During the summer" of 1823, Gale recorded, "I labored hard, with such assistance as Mr. Finney could give, to arouse the church and bring the impenitent to Christ, but it was uphill work and the fruits not abundant. A few were converted."[24] But Finney's zeal was not dampened by these early discouraging experiences, as events would demonstrate.

A few months after Finney was taken under care of the presbytery, George Gale became ill and was unable to preach in the church at Adams. At that juncture a Universalist minister came to town and began to interest the residents in his doctrines that all would be saved. Gale, alarmed and too ill to respond, asked Finney to answer the Universalist publicly if possible, lest some be led astray. Finney eagerly accepted the suggestion. He presented two discussions in answer to the intruder, in which he claimed in his *Memoirs* that he was forced to set aside the stance that the atonement literally paid the debt for sinners. Instead, he took the position in these two lectures that "Christ, in his atonement, merely did that which was necessary as a condition of the forgiveness of sin; and not that which cancelled sin, in the sense of literally paying the indebtedness of sinners."[25] The Universalist, vanquished, immediately left town.

Finney may have routed his opponent, but it is highly suspect that he was able to do it with the theological profundity he claimed. In all likelihood the debate hinged on no subtleties from either side, but was more in the nature of a verbal give-and-take that the country folk could appreciate. The account of the debate was written long after the event, and Finney interjected his later theological position into it, as he did with all of these incidents.

Normally the procedure of presbytery was to allow a year between the time when a candidate for the ministry was taken under its care, and the next step, his licensing. But Finney was somewhat older than the usual candidate for the ministry, and in his case this was moved up.[26] George Gale explained the circumstances that brought about the advancing of this step, and his own departure from the church at Adams:

> He [Finney] was licensed six months sooner than he wished, or expected to be, that he might supply the pulpit made vacant by my sickness and dismission. . . . Finding myself without any prospect of being able to labor longer as the pastor of the church I requested Presbytery, that held its winter session there, to dissolve the connection, in which the congregation united from the same necessity. But I felt that they ought to have a pastor. At this meeting I suggested the propriety of licensing Mr. Finney, that he might, for a time or until they could obtain a pastor, supply the pulpit, and this was done.[27]

The Presbytery of St. Lawrence met at Adams on December 30, 1823, to consider the propriety of licensing Finney to fill this specific need, only six months after he had been taken under its care. He recorded in his *Memoirs* that the clergymen dealt gently with him, and avoided asking doctrinal questions that would highlight the differences in their views. He was, after all, not their ordinary candidate, but an older man than they would normally take under care, and one who came from another profession. Gale, doubtless, had privately informed his colleagues of Finney's diligent service and success in evangelistic endeavors, and of his disputatious nature. Although the gentlemen of the presbytery confined their questions to matters regarding his development and progress, as the examination proceeded one of them haplessly asked Finney if he subscribed to the Westminster Confession of Faith—the bulwark of Presbyterian Calvinism. Incredibly, Finney claimed that he had not read it! "I had not examined it. . . . This had made no part of my study. I replied that I received it for substance of doctrine, so far as I understood it."[28]

Finney had claimed for the previous twenty pages of his *Memoirs* that the controversies with George Gale had centered around his "old school library" containing books that advanced the Reformed viewpoint. "I had the use of his library, and searched it thoroughly on all the questions of theology, which came up for examination; and the more I examined the books, the more was I dissatisfied."[29] It is utterly inconceivable, if there were indeed such discussions with Gale, how the Westminster Confession would not often have come up, and it is difficult to understand under any conditions why a Princeton graduate like Gale would omit any study of it in preparing a candidate for the Presbyterian ministry.[30]

Another aspect of his examination was the presentation of two trial sermons on texts assigned by the presbytery. Inasmuch as Finney was primarily an extemporaneous speaker, he was not especially at home with written sermons, but apparently his performance was satisfactory, for the presbytery voted unanimously to license him. Immediately he was pressed into service, on the next Sunday, to fill in for the ailing George Gale. As Finney came from the pulpit after the service, he recalled that Gale came up to him and said, "Mr. Finney, I shall be very much ashamed to have it known, wherever you go, that you studied theology with me."[31] As usual, Gale's recollection of the period differed: "Mr. Finney supplied [the pulpit] for a number of weeks, but 'a prophet is not without honor, save in his own country.' Some were not pleased."[32]

Charles Finney was not acceptable to the people of the Adams

Presbyterian church to be considered for the pastorate, but George Gale again came to his aid. Through his influence he procured for the younger man a commission to be "a missionary to labor in the Northern parts of the County of Jefferson and such other destitute places in that vicinity as his discretion shall dictate"[33] for the Female Missionary Society of the Western District of the State of New York. The commission was for a period of three months, beginning on March 17, 1824, and Finney said he "intended to go into the new settlements and preach in schoolhouses, and barns, and groves, as best I could."

He went to the northern part of Jefferson County and began his labors in the village of Evans Mills or Le Ray. Here there was no church building, and two small and dispirited congregations, the Baptists and the Congregationalists, worshiped in a large schoolhouse. Finney was able to hold services on alternate Sundays there, and on any evening. But it proved to be slow going. Crowds came to hear him, but no more substantial results were forthcoming, and opposition built up. A local resident kept a tavern where all the opposers of Finney's work gathered, and there was a general fear of him throughout the village. The consternation of the churchgoers may be imagined when suddenly this tavern keeper appeared at one of Finney's meetings. Naturally it was assumed that he had come to make a disturbance, but Finney noted that he "sat and writhed upon his seat, and was very uneasy." In the course of the meeting he arose, made a heartbroken confession, and begged forgiveness for all the harm he had done over the years to the populace of Evans Mills.

It was at this time that Finney became acquainted with the Reverend Daniel Nash (1774–1831), one of the first and most resolute members of Finney's "Holy Band," with whom he was to be associated for several years. George Gale's estimate of "Father Nash," as he was called, is balanced and insightful:

> Mr. Nash had been for many years pastor of a church in the Black River country, as it was called. A plain, good man, but not much of a preacher. After hearing Mr. Finney he experienced a sort of new conversion, and he went about a good deal with him, attending prayer meetings. Mr. Finney did not permit him to preach much when with him, and he did not wish to do so. He thought his gift was prayer. He had great fluency and fervor, prayed very loud, often even in what ought to be called secret prayer. He kept lists of names of persons for whom he prayed, and at times had great distress for souls, which he called spiritual travail. At a prayer

meeting which I attended in Rome at the early stage of the revival, he cried out while an individual was praying, it being a private prayer meeting of ministers and deacons, in which prayer was offered for some prominent individuals. . . . He often had impressions with regard to the conversion of individuals, felt assured that they would be converted. This he called the prayer of faith. Great confidence was had by many in the prayers of Father Nash, as he was called. He died in Oneida Co. a few years after this. Mr. Finney thought highly of him, but did not think it best afterwards to have him with him.[34]

The first time Charles Finney saw Nash was at the time of his licensure at presbytery, December 30, 1823, and at that time Finney was puzzled by him because Nash was in the pulpit "looking all over the house, as if he were talking to the people." In a minute Finney realized that in actuality Nash was praying, despite his eyes being open. Shortly thereafter his eyes became inflamed, and he was forced to spend several weeks in a darkened room. When he was able to venture into the light again, it was only with a double black veil over his face.

When Daniel Nash appeared at Le Ray, or Evans Mills, the young missionary welcomed the older, much experienced man. Needing a close confidant and co-worker, Finney formed a friendship with Nash that lasted for several years, until he left the frontier phase of his work and moved to urban areas where Nash might feel uncomfortable. Nash was wise in the folkways of the backcountry, but he was not a rustic bumpkin. He had read widely, knew the works of Jonathan Edwards and quoted from Alexander Pope, and later wrote a popular series of articles for the *New York Evangelist*.[35] He shouted at times because of his deafness, and this irritated many, as Gale has inferred, but he was in actuality a humble and faithful man. Whitney Cross has said of Nash, "No other letters written to Finney during the New York campaigns compare with his in vigorous crisp simplicity of style and in the evidence they reveal of constant agonizing self-humiliation in the service of his God and fellow men."[36]

In the news-starved rural areas, tidings traveled rapidly, and it was not long before what Finney was doing in upper Jefferson County was well known. Excitements of one type or another, religious or secular, had agitated the area for some years, and Charles Finney soon became aware that he was up against a resistance to religion that grew out of previous religious excitements.[37] Many were fearful of revivals because of earlier experience:

I found that region of country what, in the western phrase, would be called, "a burnt district." There had been, a few years previously, a wild excitement passing through that region, which they called a revival of religion, but which turned out to be spurious. . . . It was reported as having been a very extravagant excitement; and resulted in a reaction so extensive and profound, as to leave the impression on many minds that religion was a mere delusion. . . . Taking what they had seen as a specimen of a revival of religion, they felt justified in opposing any thing looking toward the promoting of a revival.[38]

The situation was difficult because there was, as has been noted, a predilection on the part of the settlers to excitements, bizarre fads, and eccentricities that could hardly be stifled at any rate. So, to Finney and others, the alternatives seemed to be either suffering wild erraticisms, or attempting to direct the propensities of a rough, emotional frontier people into useful orthodox channels. There is no doubt that Charles Finney was concerned with results, not dignity, at this early stage of his ministry, but even then he exercised enough good sense to recognize that there were many things he could not allow in his meetings. He reported that he used "simply preaching, prayer and conference meetings, much private prayer, much personal conversation, and meetings for the instruction of earnest inquirers."[39] In order to contain emotional outbursts, he would call on certain ones to pray, then he would speak for a short period, and then call on another one to pray. By these means he hoped to keep emotionalism within bounds, knowing at the same time that pioneering people demanded enthusiastic preachers and direct, provocative preaching. In Charles Finney, they got both.

But the frontier of New York State was not the frontier of Kentucky and Tennessee, where emotionalism and fanaticisms had run riot since the Cane Ridge camp meeting of August 1801, and the protracted meetings had drawn incredible throngs of as many as 25,000. The Kentucky camp meetings had become synonymous with wild gyrations of many sorts, and in all fairness nothing in the Burned-over District of New York, even at its most eccentric, began to compare with the Cane Ridge tradition. With the release of tidal waves of feeling in the early Kentucky camp meetings, beginning approximately in June 1800 at Red River, convulsive physical "exercises" became somewhat common. Hysterical laughter, occasional trances, the "barking" exercise, and the infamous "jerks" were witnessed in many places of Kentucky. By the second decade of the century these extreme manifestations of fanatic behavior had tapered off, and at later camp meetings shouting, crying, and falling down were the only physical reactions to rousing preaching.

These reactions did not produce the disastrous results they would have engendered in more settled communities such as the Burned-over District. Professor John Boles states:

> These grossly exaggerated revival exercises, which have been cited widely to discredit the revival, were probably restricted to a comparative few. Only among some of the splinter groups that developed in Kentucky did they become ultimately respectable. . . . Except at the very start, they were never a significant factor in the camp meetings.[40]

Professor Bernard Weisberger agrees: "Many stories of unusual transports of holy joy and anguish were undoubtedly stretched. Some came from supporters. . . . Others were planted by opponents, who were trying to underscore the element of caricature in the meetings."[41]

In New York State, even in the farming hamlets along the Ontario frontier, nothing comparable to what occurred in Kentucky and Tennessee was experienced. In his first few years as an evangelist Charles Finney would be accused of allowing or promoting excesses, but to keep the matter in perspective it is important to understand the extent of emotionalism he allowed, and what he would not tolerate. Surely the New England background and traditions of Finney and the people of New York played a large part in inhibiting unbridled emotionalism there, both negatively and positively, as opposed to the much more heterogeneous culture of Kentucky in the early nineteenth century.

Finney, the convert of only two years, was learning rapidly the requirements that would fit him to be the preeminent evangelist of his time. As a man in his early thirties, he brought with him a goodly amount of psychological baggage: driving forcefulness, at times verging on ruthlessness, high hopes for personal success, a pietistic approach to religion, a backwoods conviction that he was engaged in personal combat with a real Devil, and a modest stock of apprehensions and anxieties — offset by his ambition. These interior dynamics of the man are everywhere apparent. Would they adequately fortify him for the days ahead, and for his entire career?

4

THE HALCYON DAYS

Another in the list of excitements that agitated the Burned-over District from 1825 to 1850 was anti-Masonry.[1] Sporadic actions against the Masons had flared up previous to this period, and clergymen of the various denominations found themselves on both sides of the issue. Perhaps because he had heard propaganda against the Masons seeming to indicate that membership in the group would be detrimental to his calling, Charles Finney resigned from the lodge shortly before his ordination. On May 7, 1824, he received a discharge from the local chapter.[2] Not long after this, the sensational events surrounding William Morgan erupted in the western portion of the state, and began the largest movement against the Masons that had been seen to that time.

In 1823 William Morgan became a Mason in Rochester. Later he moved to Batavia and applied for membership in that chapter, but was refused. Infuriated, Morgan wrote a long exposé of the secrets of the society, *Illustrations of Masonry,* and persuaded a local printer to publish it. Word of what he had written got out, and a series of strange happenings then befell him. First he was arrested on a debt claim, so that his home could be searched for the manuscript. On September 8, 1826, groups of strangers appeared in Batavia, with rumors that they came from Canandaigua, Buffalo, and other towns. There was an attempt to burn down the printer's shop, but the fire was extinguished. Then Morgan was charged with a crime in Canandaigua, and taken there to be held in jail while awaiting trial. On the evening of September 12, 1826, he was kidnapped from the jail cell. Rumors swirled, some saying that he had been released in Canada, and others that he had been drowned in the Niagara River, but no evidence surfaced to prove he had been murdered. The ensuing events—defeated investigations by the state legislature, panicky rumors of gigantic conspiracies, village committees organizing politically against the accused fraternity—took on the form of a great, statewide crusade that in turn became merely another eccentricity of western New York.

As the reverberations from this rumbled across the state, Charles Finney may have congratulated himself on resigning from the Masons earlier. But more important matters engaged his attention. Only a few months after he had been licensed by the St. Lawrence Presbytery, Finney was already an evangelist of notable achievements. The area to the north of Watertown was aflame with religious interest, and no one questioned that most of the credit was his. Conversions were multiplying, and the previously dead churches there were receiving new members. On the other hand, some of the clergy were disturbed by the tales they had heard of Finney's rough, extemporaneous style of speaking, which they opposed as undignified. In all likelihood Finney suspected that opposition would increase, and the longer it continued the more difficult it would be for him to join the ranks of the clergy. He therefore inquired of the influential moderator of the presbytery, the Reverend Adams W. Platt, pastor of the Presbyterian church in Rutland, N. Y., as to the possibility of being ordained at its next meeting, and received this reply:

Rutland, New York, June 22, 1824

Brother Finney,
I hasten to communicate to you the result of my inquiries respecting the possibility of there being any opposition to your being ordained at our next meeting. I spoke to Mr. Dutton about it, on my way home from you. He seemed pleased with the idea, and thought it a matter of considerable importance that you should be ordained either then or soon after.
I visited Mr. Boardman yesterday. Mr. Boardman will make no opposition, but fell in with the idea cheerfully.... I think you may calculate upon its being done, without any opposition, if the matter is brought forward in a proper manner.

> I find there is a little more feeling amongst my people than usual. Some of the dead Christians are beginning to awaken. . . .
>
> Adams W. Platt[3]

Accordingly, on July 1, 1824, the Presbytery of St. Lawrence convened at Evans Mills for the purpose of conducting routine business and considering the propriety of ordaining Charles Finney. It was the custom of the Presbyterian Church to have candidates either submit written sermons or preach before an assembly, for they had previously examined Finney in theology and other matters. But he declared in the *Memoirs*, "I had not the remotest thought of what was in the minds of the brethren of the presbytery. . . . I saw in a moment that it was the design . . . to put me on trial, that they might see if I could do as they had heard I did—get up and preach on the spur of the moment, without any previous preparation."[4]

In light of the above letter from Adams Platt, revealing that Finney was seeking ordination and that it would likely come about, such a statement that he "had not the remotest thought" is somewhat ludicrous. If he was to be ordained that day, as this was the last opportunity for him to be examined for his preaching abilities, and he had not been asked to submit a written sermon, why would he not assume that he would deliver it verbally? At any rate, he arose to preach when asked, but disdained the "high, small pulpit up against the wall," which would have cramped his rough-hewn style, and chose instead to walk up and down the aisle. He chose a text he had often preached on previously, "Without holiness no man shall see the Lord." Apparently, although Finney's account is confused,[5] some of the ministers were not favorably impressed by his performance. He claimed that he was criticized for speaking too much like a lawyer, and in a colloquial manner, using "you" to shock the audience, and that his entire approach to homiletics brought down the dignity of the pulpit. Because Finney did not claim that these were criticisms leveled that day, it is more likely that he was giving a compendium of judgments he received over the years. From all the evidence, however, it appears to be certain that in these early years Charles Finney had a crude and denunciatory style that may have rattled the rustics, but would have offended or insulted anyone of sensitivity or education.

Although they may have had their reservations, and Finney was full of complaints about procedures that were completely routine, the men of the St. Lawrence Presbytery moved to ordain him that evening. Because he had no call to a particular church, he was ordained as an evangelist. In the ordination service Adams W. Platt presided, George S. Boardman delivered the charge to Finney, Samuel Snowden offered the consecrating prayer, J. Clinton preached the sermon, and E. Bliss and W. B. Stowe led the devotions at the opening and closing of the service.[6]

After his ordination, Finney returned to his work for the Female Missionary Society in upper Jefferson County. In the area there were some Methodists, and the rumor spread that Finney was afraid to teach the Reformed doctrine of election and predestination (which Methodists rejected), because if he did his converts would not join the church. Undaunted, Finney did exactly that—but with his own version. In his view, he said, election was a doctrine not only of the Bible but also of reason; "that it opposes no obstacle in the way of the salvation of the non-elect," and what was more, it was "not inconsistent with free agency"! Even though by foreknowledge God knew from eternity who would be of the elect, having chosen them, the duty of responding to the gospel fell upon both elect and nonelect alike. Hearing this, the Methodists were convinced, and agreed that they could accept election, if that was what it meant.[7]

The work in Jefferson County was proceeding so well that the Presbytery of St. Lawrence took notice of the general revival there under the labors of several men. The presbytery report, however, did not name any individuals, but said:

> A minister was sent in May to Le Ray by the Female Missionary Society of the Western District. He was stoutly withstood at first, but the Lord wrought with him and through him, and soon began to prevail. Party spirit was then aroused for another encounter; but, wherever it appeared, prayer laid it. . . . At least eighty forsook all and followed Christ.

The historian of New York Presbyterianism, P. H. Fowler, took this to refer to Charles Finney, and he concluded, "Thus early in his career, that remarkable man [Finney] was as fully disclosed and his remarkable modes of procedure as fully mapped out, and his remarkable success as fully achieved as at its culmination, and the same conflicting sentiments and surprises agitate us."[8]

In the fall of 1824, the eighth report of the Female Missionary Society contained Finney's own account of his activities in Jefferson County. Surprisingly, whereas the reports of the other missionaries are a quarter to a half page each, the Society allowed Finney's to run to two and a half pages, possibly indicating their approval of his work. His account is a striking combination of legal objectivity and earnest dedication, as shown in these excerpts:

> The work has commenced among the first class of society, in point of talent and influence; and our earnest prayer to the blessed Head of the church is, that the foundations of Satan's empire in that place may be rased. . . . My method of preaching to them has been simple and familiar, but as plain and pointed as I was able. I have endeavored to convince them that the religion of such of them as had not been born again, was insufficient, and altogether an abomination to God. . . . I have spent in the execution of your commission, 12 Sabbaths, preached 77 discourses, attended 36 prayer meetings, and 13 conference meetings, and made 469 family visits. I have collected no monies, nor made any application for any as yet, believing that the interests of religion would suffer by it.[9]

By October of 1824, compelling interests were drawing him away, if only temporarily, from the field where he had given devoted service. One of these was the annual meeting of the Synod of Albany at the First Presbyterian Church of Utica early in October.[10] Meetings of the Synod drew together representative numbers of Presbyterian clergymen from throughout the state, and according to the roll, the Rev. Charles G. Finney was in attendance.[11]

But of far greater moment was his marriage to Lydia Root Andrews on October 5 in Whitesboro, Oneida County. Finney had been engaged to her since his days as a law clerk in Adams. Lydia, born on March 8, 1804, was twelve years younger than her husband, and had been converted at the age of eleven under the ministry of the Rev. John Frost of Whitesboro, or Whitestown.[12] Before the Finney family had moved to Henderson in 1808, they lived in Kirkland, a few miles from Whitesboro, for fourteen years. The two families had become close friends at that time and continued their friendship after the Finneys moved to Jefferson County. In addition, Lydia's sister coincidentally lived in Adams, and when Finney joined the firm of Wright and

Wardwell in that town, it was there in 1820 that the eye of Lydia Andrews was drawn to this dashing young man.[13] Lydia attended Pastor Gale's services when visiting her sister, saw Finney become the choir director of that church, realized he was not converted, and began to pray for him.[14] It is apparent that he returned her interest, and in time they decided to wed. Until she died twenty-three years later, this sincere lady was a cherished wife, constant aid, and unfailing support to Finney, and the mother of their six children.

The newlyweds spent a short honeymoon in the vicinity of Utica, and then he returned alone to Evans Mills, intending to find a home for them in that town. He left Lydia at her parents' home in Whitesboro with their goods, expecting to return for her within a week with a wagon. But when he arrived in Jefferson County he found religious interest still high. He had previously preached in Perch River, perhaps seven miles west of Evans Mills, and he heard that the work was growing. A messenger implored him to return and preach again. Finney obliged, and his original intention to stay for one or two days stretched out to a full week. Then word came that the revival was spreading in the direction of Brownville, six miles to the south of Perch River and west of Watertown. In late October, with the harvests largely gathered in and the onset of the indolent winter season, country folk could turn their thoughts away from their heavy labors to things of the spirit.

At Brownville, there was a settled pastor who gave a "pressing invitation" to Finney to remain there and fan the sparks of revival into flames. The evangelist could not ignore such persuasion, and he wrote to his recent bride that "such were the circumstances that I must defer coming for [you] until God seemed to open the way." He threw himself into the work mightily, leaving Lydia Finney to ponder alone the responsibilities of marriage to a messenger of God's grace, and soon the entire winter had passed. This long separation from his new wife might be taken for callous indifference, but G. Frederick Wright comments on this, accurately:

> It would be doing the keenest injustice to Finney to attribute this long separation from his wife, so soon after their marriage, to any indifference of feeling. It is to be taken purely as an index of the strength of his devotion to the ministerial work to which he felt himself called. For, throughout his life, he was passionately devoted to his family, and was never separated from them except

upon occasion of necessity, and then with much self-sacrifice and solicitude.[15]

Early in the spring of 1825, before the ice began to break up, he set out with his horse and sleigh to get Lydia in Whitestown. The roads were icy, and the horse was smooth shod, so he stopped at Le Rayville, a small village about three miles south of Evans Mills, to have the horse reshod. Learning he was in their town, the people flocked to him and he was persistently requested to preach. As soon as he consented and held several services, a revival began and he felt compelled to continue there. With Lydia waiting for him in Whitestown, Finney was at a loss to know what to do until he found a man who was willing to take the horse and cutter, and go south for the evangelist's patient wife.

As the work progressed in Evans Mills, Brownville, Perch River, Le Rayville and the surrounding communities, Lydia joined him and they set up housekeeping. It was then that "God revealed to me, all at once, in a most unexpected manner, the fact that he was going to pour out his Spirit at Gouverneur, and that I must go there and preach."[16] Gouverneur was thirty-five miles northeast of Evans Mills, in St. Lawrence County, and if Finney was to extend his labors in that direction, it would be the first time he worked outside Jefferson County. Confronted with this challenge, Finney quickly wrapped up his work in Le Rayville, left Lydia at Evans Mills, and traveled to this new field. The spring rains were very heavy, and it took him two days to reach Gouverneur. When he arrived he found "Father" Nash already at work, with crowded meetings and great interest among the populace.[17]

Finney later portrayed his sermons at that time as somewhat intellectual, emphasizing that his debates with opponents were indeed contests of wits. In his *Memoirs* Finney suggested frequently that logic and appeal to the intellect were indispensable parts of his evangelistic technique at this stage of his career. This is very doubtful. By 1868, when the *Memoirs* were written, Finney had polished his style by forty years of contact with sophisticated congregations in major eastern cities, who would tolerate none of the backwoods ranting and bluster of itinerant preachers. To ascertain the real tenor of his work, a most valuable insight into the methodologies and personality of Charles G. Finney during the revival at Gouverneur is given by the letter sent to him at that time, on May 13, 1825, by C. C. Sears of

Hamilton College, in Clinton, New York. Sears corresponded with Finney on an occasional basis, and the letter is of consequence because it shows that what he was doing in northern New York was becoming well known at some distance, and also that Finney was cultivating important friends wherever he could find them:

> Dear Brother Finney,
> . . . Brother Maynard showed me a l[etter] from you, with which I can not but find some little fault. I know not how you derived your impressions but I have no hesitation in saying that you have either been misinformed, or that you have changed your maxims since I knew you. If there are any Christians among us, I believe Brother Maynard is one. You charge him at least by implication with "a cold heart" "endless theories" "baptizing ungodly and carnal policies into the sacred name of prudence." I am inclined to think that your ear has been foully polluted by some designing person or that you wrote without much consideration, and intended merely for counsel what you expressed in the language of very severe reproof. I confidently presume that . . . you did not mean that everything in a revival was right, and that no degree of rant and passion could be wrong. . . . [I] shall also take the liberty of expressing a very serious doubt of the genuineness of that revival which is conducted upon the principle that no degree of animal feeling is too great, and that every excitement however raised, is to be cultivated and cherished. . . . I have written as a friend to a friend. . . .
>
> C. C. Sears[18]

Whether Sears is repeating a direct quote from Finney, that "no degree of animal feeling is too great, and that every excitement however raised, is to be cultivated and cherished," or paraphrasing other preachers, cannot be determined, but the letter without doubt accuses him of censoriousness and the promotion of emotionalism.

From Gouverneur Finney went to De Kalb, another twenty miles to the north, to begin evangelistic work there. He came with the approval and cooperation of the local Presbyterian pastor, but he found that the town had been riven by a feud between the Methodists and the Presbyterians several years before. The Methodists had been engaged in evangelistic meetings, and during the services some minor excesses had occurred, especially fainting, which the Methodists called "falling under the power of God." The Presbyterians disapproved of the fainting, and there had been hard feelings between the two congregations ever since.

When Finney heard of this, naturally he sided with the Methodists, doubtless thinking ahead to the predictable results of his own evangelism. "The Presbyterians had been decidedly in error," he pronounced. As his meetings began, with both Methodists and Presbyterians in attendance, it was not long before a man fell from his seat to the floor. Some of the congregation gathered around to take care of him. Finney assumed that it was another case of "falling under the power of God" by one of the Methodist brethren, and he feared that this would revive all the old feelings. To his delight he found that it was one of the leaders of the Presbyterians who had fallen. Further, as the meetings went on, it was the Presbyterians who continued to fall, and none of the Methodists did so! He was gratified that this led to "great cordiality and good feeling among them."

Father Nash also worked alongside Finney at De Kalb in the conversion of souls, devoting himself as usual to much prayer. The entire countryside was stirred by the impact of the meetings, and many came from Ogdensburg, twenty miles to the north, to see for themselves. One wealthy businessman from Ogdensburg, John Fine, befriended Finney and offered to employ him as a missionary to work throughout St. Lawrence County. When the evangelist declined, Fine gave him sixty dollars as a gift and Finney was able to purchase a buggy, the first he had owned, having previously used only his horse.

Toward the close of the labors in Gouverneur and De Kalb a concern came upon Finney, in his private devotions, regarding the future. He had a strange premonition that changes were coming, and that great difficulties would have to be overcome. It drove him to more intense prayer, and some of his concerns alarmed him lest his health break down. This was not an imagined fear, because he had not been well only two years before, in the fall and winter of 1823. "When I left Adams my health had run down a great deal," he related. "I had coughed blood; and at the time I was licensed, my friends thought that I could live but a short time."[19] But the outdoor life of a rural evangelist had effected the cure, and in six months in the environs of Evans Mills his health was entirely restored. Now, he worried, would he be equal to the new tasks that seemed to be crowding upon him? Altogether he had worked as a missionary for approximately eighteen months in Jefferson and St. Lawrence counties, and might remain there, or be sent elsewhere, for all he knew.

Whatever was the nature of these premonitions, this period of his life was brought to a close, and the greatest episode of Finney's life inaugurated, by an unforeseen occurrence. It was to catapult Finney from the position of a backwoods missionary to that of a nationally known figure, and it ushered in eight years of probably the most spectacular evangelistic activity the country has ever witnessed. It came about because Finney wished to combine a visit with his wife to her family at Whitesboro, with attendance at a meeting in the vicinity of Utica. After spending some time at this meeting, Finney and his wife were returning from Utica on the way home to Jefferson County when, to their surprise, they met George Gale at Westernville, a few miles north of Rome.[20] Gale recalled:

Toward the latter part of September I proposed to my wife to go down to Rome and visit our acquaintances there, particularly the family of the pastor, Rev. Mr. Gillet. On our way down I saw a gentleman and lady coming in a buggy from the other direction, and as they came a little nearer I said to my wife, "That is Charles Finney and his wife. They are coming to see us." I said, "I don't know but the Lord is sending him to help us. He is just the man to labor in this field." We were soon hold of each other's hands, and our wives were no less glad to see their husbands respectively and each other. Mrs. Finney had been with her sister a good deal, at Adams, before her marriage, and was a most amiable, intelligent, and pious woman. As soon as we arrived home I spoke to Mr. Finney, as we stood upon the steps before entering, and said, "You have been sent here I hope to help us. Can you not remain? This is a needy place. I hope you will remain with us." He replied, "I do not know. I have been down to Whitesboro to visit my wife's parents, and I have a commission to labor as a missionary, from the 'Ladies Society' at Utica. I was on my way back to the County of [St.] Lawrence, where I have been preaching the last year, and where the Lord has been pouring out the Spirit, and where they are desirous to have me return, but my commission is general; I would take no other. I heard at Rome that you were here, and I turned out of my course to see you. I cannot say what I ought to do. We will pray about it."

After dinner we went down to the meeting house and had a season of prayer. The result was he concluded to remain, a few Sabbaths at least, but as God would have it he stayed nearly three months, he and his wife and child occupying my study and bedroom. The evidence of God's Spirit being present soon appeared, and the work continued to spread and increased in power while he remained, and altho, as he said, it was one of the hardest fields he had seen, some forty or fifty were cherishing a hope. I visited with him and aided him what I could.[21]

As George Gale mentioned above, and as Finney reiterated in his *Memoirs*, what probably assisted the decision to do evangelistic work at Western was the prayer meeting held on the afternoon of his arrival. The church at Western had no settled pastor, and George Gale's health, although somewhat improved, was still too poor to allow him to preach consistently. The two arrived at the schoolhouse near the church and found perhaps a dozen people present, "but they were the leading members of the church." Gale introduced Finney, and the three elders present asked him to lead the meeting, but he declined, wishing rather to hear what they had to say. After some opening devotions, one of the elders began a long prayer, which consisted for the most part in lamenting the fact that they had been praying for years, and God had not answered their requests. The other two elders prayed also, and said basically the same thing. As they were about to adjourn, one of them asked Finney if he would like to make some concluding remarks.

Finney arose and dissected their prayers, saying that they were only mocking God by putting all the blame on him. At first the elders became angry, but the first elder suddenly burst into tears, exclaiming "Brother Finney, it is all true!" Then followed a general repentance, with all the members weeping and asking God's forgiveness. "This scene continued," Finney recalled, "for an hour; and a more thorough breaking down and confession I have seldom witnessed."[22] He was unable to resist such conviction, and began to feel that here might be a fertile field in which to labor.

While he had as yet no inkling that pastors in Oneida County would seek him out to conduct meetings, its churches were certainly superior in every way to those up north. Their memberships were larger, their pastors often more prominent, their constituencies more urban and better educated, and the region was along the newly completed Erie Canal, where there was challenging potentiality for growth and a better publicized sphere of activity. Indeed, revivals were already in progress in this section of the state; the village of Manlius, east of Syracuse, reported that about twenty converts had been added to the Rev. Mr. Cushman's congregation,[23] and there were similar reports elsewhere. These factors were decisive for Finney. Committing himself to this new field, he began the "Oneida County revivals," which culminated in April 1827. The next year and a half made Charles G.

Finney a figure of national repute, and severed his ties to the cross-roads hamlet forever.

That Sunday, he preached at the Western church in three separate services, and during the next weeks he spoke in the schoolhouses and in other locations almost every night. Immediately he began to come into contact with some important people. One of the elders, Judge Brayton, was the father of nine children, all of whom were converted eventually through the influence of Finney's work.[24] Perhaps the most important convert was the widow of William Floyd, a signer of the Declaration of Independence. Floyd had served in the Continental Congress from 1774 to 1777 and 1778 to 1783, and later was elected as a New York state senator, where he strongly advocated a practical and conservative financial policy. During his earlier years he adhered to Christian principles, but in 1795 he was on board a sloop bound for Long Island when he came across a copy of Thomas Paine's newly published *The Age of Reason*. Knowing the reputation of this book, at first he was repulsed by it, but later, out of curiosity, he perused it and in time became an atheist, as did his wife. He then placed his wealth at the service of anti-Christian causes until his death at an advanced age in 1821. George Gale, settling nearby in 1824, learned of the man's activities and declared, "The influence of General Floyd had been very injurious to the people."[25] Therefore, when Floyd's wife was converted, it made a powerful impact upon many in the surrounding countryside.

"Convictions and conversions" soon became general throughout the area, and in many instances whole households were converted.[26] Despite the earlier condition of the people, described by the clergy as being sunk in "universalism, unitarianism, deism, and a great ignorance of divine things," conversions totaled 140 by the time Finney had preached through the months of November and December 1825.[27]

The fact that Finney was now in a far better publicized sphere of activity than his previous work in Jefferson and St. Lawrence Counties ensured notoriety for him and also a greatly increased number of invitations to conduct evangelistic campaigns elsewhere. The correspondence that came to Finney, carefully preserved for this period of his life, records a surprising quantity of calls to preach over a wide area for one so relatively new to the ministry and evangelism. Previous to his work at Western the invitations had been few and local. It is very apparent from the evidence of the collected correspondence that the revival at Western, and the succeeding months, brought rapid fame to Finney throughout the eastern part of the United States. Invitations during the first half of 1826, from Cleveland, Ohio, and New York City are preserved, in addition to many at closer range, showing that his name was already becoming well known, and that as far as many were concerned, a new star was blazing brightly in its orbit in the religious firmament of America.

If Charles Finney was dazzled by this attention suddenly lavished upon him, from all evidence he did his best to conceal it. New-found adherents and advisers flocked to his side, and he soon discovered that fame would bring not only friends but also bitter critics and enemies, attacks and ridicule. If he had time to stop and take stock in the increasingly frenzied world into which he was entering, he must have marveled that it had all taken place so quickly. Here was a young man, but four years a Christian, and ordained to the clergy for only eighteen months, with no traditions of refinement behind him, and no experiences of preaching except as a frontier missionary, suddenly being called to speak in important places by people of consequence who obviously were willing to give him opportunities, even if they did not as yet completely follow his leading. Many others with his relative youth and inexperience would have picked up pointers, modified their methods to suit the new demands, and learned all that was required of them as quickly as possible. Finney did accommodate, obviously, to a degree. But the stern, unbending aspects of his nature, which were to be so manifest in later years, were already coming to the fore. They would have to take Finney as he was, rough-cut and self-educated. His preaching was paralyzing in its intensity and its ability to rivet an audience and bring it under quick conviction. Of course, those attributes were what many of his supporters desired. Finney brought excitement and a new dynamic onto the religious scene, and, many argued, that was exactly what was needed to combat ennui and other difficulties.

The revival at Western generated so much excitement that people from the communities of Rome, Elmer's Hill, and Wright's Settlement flocked to see for themselves. Among them was the Reverend Moses Gillet, pastor of the Congregational church at Rome, and a member of the Oneida Presbytery.[28] George Gale knew him well, giving this account of him and also indicating his own changed attitude toward Finney's theology and methods:

> Late in December of 1825, after Mr. Finney had been at Western nearly three months, he met Rev. Mr. Gillet of Rome, and after

much solicitation agreed on an exchange with him. It was in the height of the revival at Western. . . . He said if I had been with him he should not probably have consented, but he could not alone resist Mr. Gillet. He was a very good man but a very different one from Mr. Finney. Moderate in his delivery and much tied to his notes. . . . Prayer was offered that God would help Brother Gillet. He came and prayer seemed to be answered. . . . Mr. Gillet returned home, but Mr. Finney did not come back. We expected him on Monday, and still more on Tuesday, but he did not come. On Wednesday morning as we heard nothing I told my wife I would go down to Rome and see what was the matter. I arrived at Mr. Gillet's a little before dinner, when he and Mr. Gillet had just come in from visiting. Both expressed a great deal of satisfaction that I had come. Said Finney, "You never saw such a state of things. In some of the families we have visited today some of the young ladies are unable to sit up, and young men and old ones can attend to no business."[29]

Captivated as always by a new challenge, Finney plunged into the work at Rome soon after the beginning of 1826, and the town of Western was left behind. This is not to say that he abandoned Western, for we have numerous letters from places such as this attesting to his continued concern after his departure. But for the most part his expressed interest was that other preachers could take up where he left off, and that God would continue the work.

Where Western was a rather unimportant village a few miles from the main thoroughfares, Rome was a town of much greater consequence and promise. For decades it had been in competition with Utica, its neighbor. Before 1800 Rome was larger than Utica, and seemed to have a brighter future. As the tides of immigration began, and land values along important roads soared, many towns along this east-west route either prospered or suffered according to the land policies adopted by their leaders. In 1820 Rome had a population of 3,569, whereas Utica was still behind it with 2,972. With the coming of the canal Rome began to drop back, for the route went a half mile to the south of its boundaries, and then passed directly through Utica. Because of this and intelligent land policies, Utica grew at a very rapid pace and by 1830 it boasted 8,323 citizens, with Rome lagging along at 4,360.[30] During this decade when the canal caused such growth and enthusiasm, Rome also slipped behind its neighbor in commercial, political, cultural, and religious dominance of the area.

And yet, to Charles Finney, the town of Rome was a major departure from the crossroads hamlets he had labored in for the past year and a half. For one thing, the canal fever and the prosperity it brought were vivid contrasts to the rural slumber of the northern backwoods. In addition, he had been invited to preach at an important church by its pastor, who was a man of stature in the community. Finney's preaching at the Congregational church in Rome soon gripped the entire area. According to Moses Gillet, "religion was the principal subject of conversation in our streets, stores, and even taverns."[31] Finney came to feel in a short time that the people of this area were quite ready for an awakening, and succeeding events proved him correct. A spirit of expectancy prevailed, and when Gillet called for a meeting of inquiry, to allow questions and counseling but no preaching, he asked Finney to be present. But Gillet had no awareness of the spiritual temperature.

The meeting was held in the home of one of the deacons, and to Gillet's shock the large sitting room was "crowded to its utmost capacity." Unprepared for such a turnout, he was doubly perplexed to find that some of his most stalwart members were among the seekers! "I soon saw that the feeling was so deep," Finney stated, "that there was danger of an outburst of feeling, that would be almost uncontrollable."[32] Gillet became increasingly agitated, never having confronted such massive concern on the part of so many, and Finney had to calm him repeatedly. Calming the inquirers as well, Finney spoke softly, explaining the central tenets of salvation to them. Then he knelt and led in prayer, and after several minutes he concluded and sent them home, requesting them to remain quiet on their way.

This became the pattern for the next four weeks in Rome, from approximately the turn of the new year to the first of February 1826. Prayer meetings, or meetings to counsel with inquirers, were held in the morning or afternoon, and Finney would preach in the evening in the Congregational church.[33] It was a gruelling schedule for Finney and also for Gillet, but the thoroughness of their attention not only to the townspeople but also to the surrounding area soon began to manifest itself. To vary the schedule somewhat, Finney did not always preach his usual type of sermon lasting as long as two hours, but, as Gillet says, "sometimes there was preaching, and sometimes only prayers with short addresses."[34] Finney quickly became convinced that, unlike the town of Western where initially it was rough going against the opposition, the town of Rome was prepared for a revival, and the population expectant. In his *Memoirs*, the chapter on the Rome revival glows with his recollections of people who were as sensitive and prepared as any he was to meet, who needed little to stimulate them toward religion.

As the work progressed, it gathered momentum. Both Finney and Gillet were pleased that so many cooperated in furthering the awakening. Secular business was largely suspended:

> Merchants' and mechanics' shops were many of them closed in the evening, that all might attend meeting. . . . Many who had regularly attended public worship for twenty years, and lived through revivals unmoved, were now made to tremble and bow to the cross. Four lawyers, four physicians, all the merchants who were not professors before, and men of the first respectability in the place, are hopeful converts.[35]

After several weeks, Moses Gillet was gratified to note that there was much to be grateful for; there was a marked reformation in morals that was "too apparent to be denied." Throughout the town, convictions were "more sudden and more pungent" than he had witnessed in previous revivals. The Sabbath was now strictly observed. Drunkenness and profanity seemed to be things of the past. Quarreling and fighting stopped, and the church was blessed with peace and harmony, opposers apparently being nonexistent. The new converts were eager and earnest, and a delight to all. Word of all this, obviously, traveled fast, and Finney was not one to hide his light under a bushel. There is some evidence that he may have begun to speak in surrounding communities, although it was not until later that he did this as a regular practice in the endeavor to spread the revival as far as possible. Visitors came with regularity to see for themselves. "Ministers came in from surrounding towns," Finney recalled, "and expressed great astonishment at what they saw and heard, as well they might."[36] He might well bask in the untroubled sun; difficulties would come soon enough.

From the evidence, it does appear that the Rome revival was conducted without excesses or fanaticism, under the nervous eye of Moses Gillet. Finney was careful to point this out with pride in several places: "It is difficult to conceive so deep and universal a state of religious feeling, with no instance of disorder, or tumult, or fanaticism, or anything that was objectionable, as was witnessed at Rome."[37] His techniques, under the new demands of the prosperous area along the Erie Canal, were being formulated, and they did not yet include some of the "new measures" that caused so much objection in years to come.

The means that were used to promote evangelism were "much prayer, secret and social, public preaching, personal conversation, and visitation from house to house."[38] In that list he neglected to mention one practice that he began in Rome, speaking of it elsewhere: "Every evening, at the close of my sermon, I requested all who had been converted that day, to come forward and report themselves in front of the pulpit, that we might have a little conversation with them."[39] From this evangelistic invitation the anxious bench or seat would develop in time. By all accounts, he had not regularly issued an invitation to new converts to respond in a tangible fashion on previous occasions, although in the midst of his work at Evans Mills Finney had asked converts to rise, and on a single occasion at Rutland he had asked those who wished to give their hearts to God to take the front seat.[40]

By late January, spectacular results were everywhere apparent. The effects of the revival became obvious in Verona, New Hartford, Clinton, and other towns.[41] The Reverend Ira Manly, who supplied the Presbyterian church in Boonville, New York, described the spread of the revival to that town:

> About this time, also, I received an account of the revival in Rome, from two of our young men, who had been there on a visit, and had become hopeful subjects of grace. Their warmth and zeal were a blessing to me. The next evening, in meeting, I gave an account of the revival in Rome. It was attended with a divine impulse. From that time our meetings increased, till they were full to overflowing. Presbyterians, Baptists and Methodists, rushed together, and seemed to participate of the same spirit. We endeavoured to avoid exciting any party feeling. . . . Ministers from abroad preached with much engagedness. Conversions became frequent. . . . Sixty-seven have been added to the Presbyterian church. . . . The whole number of converts is probably towards one hundred.[42]

That was as nothing when compared with Rome. There, every church benefited, including the Methodists, the Episcopalians, and the Baptists. But it was to be expected that the Congregational church, which had done most in backing Finney's labors, would reap the greatest benefit. On March 12, 1826, Pastor Gillet admitted into membership upon profession of faith 167 persons as the "fruits of the great revival." Altogether, the church received 284 new members by the fall, and Gillet estimated the total number of converts in Rome and adjacent areas to be five hundred.[43] This is indeed an astonishing number when it is considered that the town could claim little more than four thousand in its entire citizenry.

Among the converts was a prominent merchant who came to one of the morning prayer meetings. Entering after the meeting had begun, he came to the front and took a seat near where Finney was speaking to the assembly. "He had sat but a few moments, when he fell from his seat as if he had been shot," Finney recalled. "I stepped to the pew door, and saw that it was altogether an agony of mind," and not some physical attack that had beset the merchant.[44] Nearby in a pew sat a physician who was a skeptic. Coming to the fallen merchant, the physician examined him, "said nothing, but turned away, and leaned his head against a post that supported the gallery, and manifested great agitation." The physician later told Finney that he recognized by his examination that there was nothing physically wrong with the merchant, but that he had gone into a fainting spell caused by his extreme conviction. What delighted Finney was that this so struck the doctor that his complacency and skepticism were completely shattered, and both the merchant and the physician were soon converted.

Among the tide of the redeemed was Moses Gillet's own wife. This was his second marriage, and his wife was a sister of the founder of foreign missions in America, Samuel J. Mills, Jr. (1783–1818), who had been instrumental in bringing into existence the American Board of Commissioners for Foreign Missions in 1810. But Mrs. Gillet was given to finery and fashionable dress, and she had come to believe that this would keep her out of the kingdom of God. Finney thought little of it. She "wore about her head and upon her person some trifling ornaments; nothing, however, that I should have thought of as being any stumbling-block in her way, at all."[45] But it was an obsession with her that this prevented her salvation, and she approached Finney so often concerning it that he "tried to avoid her," which was difficult because he was staying with the Gillets! After weeks of this, Finney decided that kid-glove tactics with his hostess were not helping, and rougher treatment was called for. When she next implored him to pray for her, he turned away rudely, saying (as he had rehearsed to do) that it was no use, for she was depending upon his prayers, and would not simply have faith in Christ. This worked the desired cure, for in a few minutes "she came rushing across the hall into the parlor, with her face all in a glow, exclaiming, 'O Mr. Finney! I have found the Saviour!'" She overcame her fondness for dress, and thereafter found that her way was strewn with no more difficulties.

Charles Finney placed little blame, as he had in previous locations, upon the inhabitants of Rome for their attitude toward the work he had undertaken, and their spirit of prayer. Indeed, he was impressed that prayer was spontaneous throughout the town, and seemed to bring about a deep awesomeness among the populace, "as if God pervaded the whole atmosphere." Moses Gillet, reporting a few months later on the events during the revival, was similarly impressed, saying, "Indeed, *the great instrument in this glorious work has been prayer.*"[46] And, after Finney left, conversions continued and the spirit of awakening remained for many months, largely due to the well-organized and well-attended prayer meetings that drew hundreds.[47]

Finney's innate self-confidence and resourcefulness was immensely buoyed by the events in Rome and environs. He had proved that his abilities were superior to those of the ordinary backwoods exhorter, and that he possessed the precise formula for revivalistic work in more urbane areas. His hopes and motivations kindled by success, his stature as an evangelist had grown in his own eyes and in those of his many colleagues. He was ready for greater conquests.

5

GATHERING STORM CLOUDS

T he tidings of awakening in Rome, N.Y., traveled in all directions, but nowhere with more effect than ten miles to the east, to the bustling town of Utica. In 1826 this canal port of approximately five thousand was the commercial, financial, and transportation center of central New York state. Many people commuted between the two towns, and those in Utica who tended to ridicule the revival were often silenced by those who had seen for themselves its undeniably impressive results. During the month of January 1826, first curiosity, then fascination, held the residents of Utica as they gazed in wonderment toward Rome.

Then, at the end of January, a prominent elder in the First Presbyterian Church of Utica died, and Charles Finney was invited to attend the funeral. It was conducted by the Rev. Samuel C. Aikin, pastor of the church, who knew well of the evangelist's labors in the neighboring town.[1] George Gale was helpful in bringing Finney and Aikin together, and left this account:

> Mr. Finney after remaining three or four weeks at Rome, went, on invitation to preach at Utica. I was there, and Brother Aiken, who was pastor of the church (First Presbyterian) and some others made a great many inquiries about Mr. Finney. He had heard a good many things said, and some that were unfavorable. I told him that Mr. Finney had some peculiarities, some things that were

not practicable that I would alter, but many things said had little or no foundation, that he was a good man and God was with him. "Tell him," said he, "I want him to come. A great door is open for him." He soon after prevailed upon him to go, and a great good work was wrought. He was afraid that his refined and literary people would be disgusted with his plain Saxon, and unpolished manners, if not offended and driven away by his direct and powerful application of offensive truth. But they were pleased as well as impressed by his business and offhand way of presenting the truth, which had more the air of the forum, or the stump, than the pulpit, or rather which resembled the class of orators who address a jury rather than a popular audience. And yet this does not express it fully. He often made strong appeals to the feelings, but not usually until he had endeavored to satisfy the reason of the truth he would enforce. . . . He possessed a masterly power in unmasking men and systems of false religion. A professor in college, who heard him in several instances expose the absurdity of the Universalist's system, said that his reasoning came the nearest to a mathematical demonstration of anything he had heard. . . . In his course of argument, or of illustration, he always selected his arguments or figures such as any man would appreciate or understand. . . . If judged by strict rules of rhetoric it might sometimes be a subject of criticism, but after a few sentences all criticism would be forgotten by an intense interest in the subject. I have sometimes sat in a sort of tremor, with hot and cold flashes running through my system. Nobody who heard him could help feeling delighted, interested, or enraged, according to his character or prejudices. He seldom made his audience weep. He said he had remarked that weepers seldom receive any lasting good. Men would often go to hear him full of malice, or with a proud defiance, who would return deeply convicted, and sometimes converted.[2]

Finney was now hammering out the techniques that he would use for the remainder of his long ministry, and opposition was beginning to build, so it is only elementary fairness to him to point out that an evangelist is always in a very controversial position. By the very nature of his position, an evangelist arouses strong emotions and reactions pro or con. The most irenic of people have found it to be so, despite their attempts to remain affable. If an evangelist bends over backward to avoid hurt feelings in his audience, then he softens the message and becomes largely ineffectual. But if he allows the challenge of evangelism to come through undiluted, hearers are immediately divided and a controversial situation ensues. Thus the dissension that was beginning to build around Finney was only partly of his own making; the remainder went with the very function of evangelism.

The revival in Utica was more prolonged than that in Rome, due partly to Finney's preaching in the surrounding towns at the same time, and partly to the cooperative nature of Finney's work in this town. Much more than at Rome or Western, it was a united endeavor, involving not only the churches in other towns but also the Methodists and Baptists of Utica, as well as the Welch Congregational church and the two Presbyterian churches.[3] Finney himself was vague on the point, but it seems from other sources that a cadre of preachers assisted, conducting services concurrently with his. These other meetings, held throughout Utica and the vicinity, may have been started as a result of Finney's work, but they were conducted independently.[4] Nonetheless, it was Finney's preaching that galvanized the area, and the others remained backwaters, sustaining but not threatening his centrality. Almost all the members of the Oneida Presbytery supported him, with the exception of one or two, and this in itself was a notable accomplishment. Daniel Nash labored mightily at his side the entire time, and Nathaniel Smith, a man recently ordained by the presbytery, did much preaching especially at the First Presbyterian Church.[5]

Rolling on a successful tide of clerical and lay support, Charles Finney preached in and around Utica from approximately February 1 to May 20, 1826. It may have been that the revival began at a propitious time, inasmuch as the canal was closed for the winter and some of the citizens had more time on their hands, but as spring came these factors could hardly be credited for its success. Putting aside his initial caution, Samuel Aikin became ecstatic over the results of Finney's work: the churches of Utica were "thronged, and the stillness of the sepulchre reigned"; indeed, there had been some noise, but not from anyone affected by the revival! "It has been on the other side — among the enemies of the revival, as it was in the days of the Apostle." Aikin was delighted that his sizeable congregation maintained its staunch support; "Never was so large a church more happily united than we have been . . . and it is so still."[6]

As in Rome, the converts mounted. By the end of the year, Aikin estimated the number to be five hundred in Utica, and three thousand for the entire county of Oneida. Over one hundred had united with his church.[7] Opposition developed, especially from the local newspaper, the *Sentinel and Gazette*, but it hardly hindered the awakening. The Oneida Presbytery met from September 6 to 8 to behold with joy the fruits of the gospel. According to Finney, during the session an aged clergyman arose to address his peers. He was a Scotsman, recently arrived in America, and had never previously witnessed a revival. What he had seen in Utica irritated him greatly, for "he found the public mind all absorbed on the subject of religion." As he began to speak to the assembled presbyters, he made "a violent speech against the revival," which "greatly shocked and grieved the Christian people who were present." After denouncing for some time what Finney was doing, the old minister ceased, and the dumfounded leaders of the presbytery adjourned the meeting. The pastors and the laypeople present left the church shaking their heads in anguish, and Finney reported that there was much prayer sent to God that evening, "that he would counteract any evil influence that might result from that speech."[8] According to the *Memoirs,* the old Scottish clergyman was found dead in his bed the next morning. But other evidence has shown that the man, a Rev. Southworth, did not die until nine days later.[9]

Among the strong supporters of Finney's work were two members of the presbytery, Noah Coe,[10] pastor of the church at New Hartford, just south of Utica, and John Frost, pastor of the church at Whitesboro, where Lydia Andrews Finney had grown up, to the west of Utica. Finney preached occasionally in both places, as often as his schedule would permit, and saw to it that both friends were supplied with help in their work and preaching whenever they needed it by Henry Hotchkiss, James Eells, Daniel Nash, and others who were joining his "Holy Band" at this time.[11] Both towns responded with awakenings, but the one at Whitesboro was especially powerful. Frost had come to the church immediately after his ordination in 1813, and had brought about remarkable growth in membership. Revivals were held in 1819 and 1821, and 111 new members united with his church. After that, revivals had come with less frequency, but Finney's work in Rome during January 1826 excited deep interest, and soon numerous prayer circles were formed. By March the work was more powerful than anything Frost had witnessed previously.[12] He was pleased that he did not have to goad his congregants into concern, but that throughout the summer members gathered at five o'clock in the morning, at the ringing of the village bell, for prayer meetings. By fall, the results were extremely gratifying: 116 had united with the Presbyterians, about one hundred with the Methodists, seventy-eight with the Baptists, and a few with the Episcopalians. "The whole number who have indulged hope, is not far from three hundred," he reported jubilantly.[13]

By the time of the Utica revival, Charles Finney's "measures" or methods were beginning to change from the style he had used in Jefferson and St. Lawrence counties. The first stage in his evolution had been that of the Lake Ontario frontier, where, as was customary with revivalists in the backwoods, Finney had not seen a great need for education, but had opted for dramatic showmanship and violent portrayals of a hell yawning for unbelievers, and had used his legal training to impress his listeners with plain, straightforward language that jettisoned the dignity of the pulpit in the cause of quick results. Even in the early days of his career there were those (the long-suffering George Gale is of course the best example) who pled with Finney, probably sensing his potential for better things, to rise above the level of the ignorant ranter when the intellectual level of the backwoods enticed him to descend to that. Although he never became merely another firebrand of the Cane Ridge variety, there is no question that in the first stage of his development Finney's language was coarse, vituperous, and extremely inflammatory.

The second stage in Finney's evolution began with the work at Western and Rome, and especially Utica, when he realized that the paroxysms of excitement that passed for conversion in Jefferson County would not satisfy a better educated audience, and that he would have to tone down his sensationalistic techniques somewhat. But, given Finney's native intransigence, this realization and willingness came slowly to him. He did not, after all, have any model of a more stately evangelist on which to pattern himself. The dignified Old School style of Asahel Nettleton—long before Finney met him—had been criticized by enough people that he could not be taken as a pattern fitted to Finney's needs. Nettleton, the best known of the itinerant evangelists conducting campaigns in New York and New England, was far removed from the ranting frontier exhorter, but his emotionally restrained style was considered out of date by many. A strict Hopkinsian, Nettleton stressed total dependence on God's sovereign grace, and this meant that any gimmicks or techniques that could be interpreted as "getting up a revival" were unacceptable to him.[14] Clearly, Charles Finney was cut out of an entirely different cloth.

There is some evidence that members of the Oneida Presbytery tried to exercise a moderating influence on Finney during the year 1826. Undoubtedly some of them were shocked by Finney's defamatory ways in the pulpit. While statements from Asahel Nettleton must be taken with caution, there is probably considerable accuracy in his statement regarding Finney's favorite terms for sinners:

The phrases "blistered," "skinned," "broken down," and "crushed" were coined and are current only among the friends of the new measures. . . . And yet when the above was read in the Oneida Presbytery the language sounded so harsh when used by others, that one of these very men remarked that "the man who wrote it was instigated by the devil."[15]

Whether Moses Gillet, Noah Coe, Samuel Brace, or other members of the presbytery attempted to influence Finney during his time with them, cannot be known with certainty. But in one pastor, Samuel C. Aikin, Finney met his match. Dignified and commanding, and approximately Finney's own age, Aikin was a graduate of Middlebury College and Andover Seminary, and knew far more theology than did Finney. The First Presbyterian Church of Utica, which he pastored, was large and important, conferring prominence and authority on its minister. He was well liked by his parishioners and by the entire community, and had an earnest and engaging manner of preaching.[16] Finney knew that before this congregation of well-educated and respected people some of his uncouth ways would not be tolerated, and a perceptible change came about at this time, although it was only the beginning of a metamorphosis for him. Aikin described some of what happened in a letter to Lyman Beecher dated April 20, 1827:

When I first became acquainted with him, I think he used too frequently the word "devil," and harsh expressions; but he is greatly reformed, and I apprehend that reading those very quotations which you make from Edwards on Revivals was the means of his reformation. Until he came to my house (at Utica) he had never read the book, and here it was frequently in his hands during the revival; also other volumes of that great writer; and he often spoke of them with rapture. Indeed, next to the Bible, no book was read so much in my family as Edwards on Revivals and on the Affections.[17]

Staying in Samuel Aikin's home for several months,[18] Finney became close friends with the pastor, and the fact that he readily took Aikin's suggestion to read Jonathan Edwards' *Thoughts on the Revival of Religion in New England* and *Treatise Concerning Religious Affections* shows the influence the dignified clergyman had on the revivalist. Almost immediately, Finney's preaching showed its effect. He began to cite Edwards, and he became somewhat more restrained in his use of inflammatory language. There was much improvement still to make, but it was a beginning.

By the time of the Utica revival, Finney's "new measures" were already a source of great discussion whenever religion was spoken of. Although opponents such as Asahel Nettleton would later list as many as twenty-nine practices they considered objectionable, only five or six caused widespread controversy: public praying by women in mixed audiences; protracted series of meetings (i.e., daily services); colloquial language used by the preacher; the anxious seat or bench; the practice of praying for people by name; and immediate church membership for converts.[19] Nettleton would add to this list in 1828 the invasion of towns by itinerants without invitations from local pastors; attacks upon clergymen who opposed revivals, and attempts to "break them down" or "skin" them; too great familiarity with the Almighty in prayer, "This talking to God as a man talks to his neighbor . . . telling the Lord a long story about A. or B. and apparently with no other intent than to produce a kind of stage effect," and so on.[20] But very few, if any, of the new measures originated with Finney; many of them had been used previously by the Methodists. The inquiry or anxious meeting had a long history in New England, and, while he was careful to come only upon invitation, Asahel Nettleton was himself an itinerant, which was something of a violation of the New England tradition. In all fairness to Finney, it must be noted that he was not an innovator for the sake of innovation; if a measure was found effective in promoting conversions, he used it, but not slavishly. What John Frost said in a letter to Finney was correct: "Say what is true, that you have introduced no new measures but have followed such as you found in the church when you entered it."[21]

Charles Finney's aggressive side has frequently been noted, but even in the earlier period of his ministry another, more tactful side can be seen. On one occasion a man acknowledged to Finney his belief in God, but admitted that he did not worship or obey the deity as he should. In a kindly but firm fashion Finney replied:

> Then why should I give you further instruction and further light, if you will not do your duty and obey the light you already have? When you will make up your mind to live up to your convictions, to obey God according to the best light you have; when you will make up your mind to repent of your neglect thus far, and to please God just as well as you know how, the rest of your life, I will try to show you that the Bible is from God. Until then it is of no use to do any such thing.

Seeing that Finney said this without rancor and was merely try-ing to live up to his pastoral responsibility, the man admitted the reasonableness of this position, went on his way, changed his habits, and soon became a generous and useful member of his church. He kept in contact with Finney, who continually encouraged him, and in time the man became a trustee of Oberlin College and a firm sup-porter of the revivalist's ministry.

It would seem that Samuel Aikin sensed criticisms were to come, and he defended the practices used in Utica, feeling as he did that Finney was not to be castigated for them. They were, he said, substan-tially the same as those used in the Great Awakening of the 1740s by Edwards and Whitefield. The doctrines preached were completely biblical, and it would be difficult for any orthodox person to find fault on that count. Although Aikin did not want to draw undue attention to them, there were, he stated, two unpopular practices that had been used extensively—females praying in public, and the demand for sin-ners to respond immediately to the invitation to accept Christ. Aikin declared:

> Nor have we failed to urge sinners to repent and submit to Jesus Christ, and that *immediately,* as the only condition of forgive-ness, warning them at the same time, that so long as they refused to comply, all their tears, and prayers, and efforts, are not only in vain, but sinful. . . .
>
> We have also had various small circles for prayer, as well as stated and public prayer-meetings; and in the former, *females,* in some cases, though more seldom than we could wish, have taken a part.[22]

The idea of immediate response was of course Finney's, but there is convincing evidence that the practice of women praying in public was borrowed by Theodore Weld from the practices of groups such as the Methodists and Free Baptists. It was still generally frowned upon by those of the Reformed tradition. While Finney was not re-sponsible for the practice, he offered no resistance to it, and from this time on increasingly became a patron of women's public speaking and praying.

Finney admitted he needed polishing, and could learn from Ed-wards, but on the matter of immediate response to the gospel he would brook no interference. It was one of the greatest reasons for his suc-cess. As Samuel Aikin explained:

Formerly it had been supposed necessary that a sinner should remain under conviction a long time . . . and they evidently had
the impression that the longer they were under conviction, the
greater was the evidence that they were truly converted. We taught
the opposite of this. . . .

Such sudden conversions were alarming to many good people; and of course they predicted that the converts would fall away,
and prove not to be soundly converted. But the event proved, that
among those sudden conversions, were some of the most influential Christians that ever have been known in that region of the
country.[23]

Something else during the Utica revival worthy of mention was
the use of Thomas Hastings as leader of the choir during the meetings.
Hastings had been a classmate of Finney's at Hamilton Oneida Academy, and was currently a music teacher, and editor and publisher of
the pro-revival *Western Recorder* in Utica.[24] Hastings would be
associated with Finney at the Chatham Street Chapel and the Broadway Tabernacle in New York City from 1832 to 1837. But it must not
be assumed that Hastings was allowed to do anything innovative with
music during the meetings, such as lead the congregational singing
or sing solos himself, as Ira Sankey with D. L. Moody in the 1870s.
Whatever innovations Finney might bring in elsewhere, music was
not among them, and he maintained basically a very conservative approach toward the use of music in prayer meetings and worship
services.[25]

The Utica revival was also notable for the acquisition of Charles
Finney's most famous convert, Theodore Dwight Weld. Born on November 23, 1803, at Hampton, Connecticut, Weld was the son of the
Rev. Ludovicus Weld, a Congregational clergyman. When Theodore
was still a youth the family moved to western New York, the father
taking the Congregational pulpit at Pompey. At the age of seventeen
Theodore entered an academy to prepare for college, but intense study
affected his eyes and he left school for two years to become an itinerant lecturer, traveling through the South and East. Then, his sight
restored, he began to take some courses at Hamilton College at Clinton, New York, in 1825.

In nearby Utica lived Weld's aunt and uncle, and in their home
he met Captain Charles Stuart, forty-two years of age, principal of the
Utica Academy, much beloved by all, but possessed of many eccentricities. Weld formed a very close friendship with Stuart, and the lat-

ter directed his great talents toward a reformer's career. His uncle in Utica, Erastus Clark, was a founder and trustee of Hamilton College, and offered to finance Weld's education. Despite his peripheral status at Hamilton, Weld soon became one of the most influential students at the school. Shortly thereafter the Oneida County revivals began, and the students went to hear Finney preach. Many of them were converted, and others were stirred by what they saw, but Weld heard of Finney's flamboyant style and immediately denounced him. Then Weld heard that his cousin Sophia had attended the awakening in Utica, and was frightened by Finney. This enraged him. "My father," he said, "was a real minister of the Gospel, grave and courteous, and an honor to the profession. This man is not a minister, and I will never acknowledge him as such."[26]

His uncle Erastus having died, Weld visited his aunt in Utica, but declared to the students at Hamilton that the revival was fanaticism or enthusiasm, and he would have nothing to do with it. When his aunt asked him to attend a service, Weld said that he would go to the church in the morning, when Mr. Aikin usually preached, but that he would not go to hear Finney, who preached in the afternoon and again in the evening. She immediately sent word to Aikin, who suggested to Finney that he preach in the morning, and this was agreed to. As Finney recalled it, "She took pains to have him so seated in the slip [pew] that he could not well get out, without herself, and one or two other members of the family, stepping out before him."[27] Samuel Aikin took the introductory part of the service, and Weld suspected nothing, although he saw Finney sitting next to Aikin on the platform. As Weld recalled:

> But by-and-by Mr. Finney rose, with those great staring eyes of his (never was a man whose soul looked out through his face as his did), and took for his text, "One sinner destroyeth much good." I stooped down and took hold of my hat; but just as I rose, Aunt Clark put her mouth close to my ear and whispered, "Theodore, *you'll break my heart* if you go!" I gave it up, and resigned myself to my fate; and then, for an hour, he just held me up on his toasting-fork before that audience.
>
> You see, they all knew; they had heard about me. And finally he wound up, "And yes! you'll go to college, and use your influence against the Lord's work," and described all the different methods of destroying good.
>
> I went home, and on the way aunt said, "Why, Mr. Finney

never preached in the forenoon before, but *always* in the afternoon." So I suspected nothing.

On the next day, while Theodore Weld was in a store in the city, Finney, alerted by friends, came into the place. Weld was trapped, and he called upon "all the vocabulary of abuse the language afforded" to vilify Finney. The evangelist meekly accepted this, "only he would every now and then just take my feeling and show it to me." Finney's unwillingness to return Weld's venom and spite made him the more furious, and he left, humiliated. "I was so ashamed I could not live," he admitted. "Finally, I made up my mind I'd go and ask his pardon." When he came to Samuel Aikin's home where Finney was staying, the latter exclaimed on seeing Weld, "Ah! Is it not enough? Have you followed a minister of the Lord Jesus to his own door to abuse him?"

"Mr. Finney, I have come for a very different purpose. I—"

Finney grasped what had happened immediately, if he had not already suspected that it would. He threw his arms around Weld's neck and dragged him into the parlor and down on their knees, both men "sobbing and praying, and sobbing and praying. That put an end to my studying," Weld declared. "I was with him in his meetings, speaking and laboring, all that summer."[28]

Finney's description of these events in his *Memoirs* adds extended details, claiming that the young man's conversion took a longer period of time, but essentially there is general agreement, except for this, between the two accounts. At any rate, Finney knew a valuable adherent when he encountered one, and as he had used his persuasive power to swing Weld to a prorevival stance, once the new convert was available, Finney utilized him to the fullest. Weld assisted in the meetings at Auburn in July and August, and in the meetings at Troy through the fall. A natural leader, Weld was not hesitant in expressing himself, and it was he who first encouraged women to speak publicly during prayer meetings. This was a violation of Paul's injunction in 1 Corinthians 14:34–35, and Finney was excoriated for this daring breach of biblical custom, although he was innocent. In reality when he first heard women praying and speaking in public at Utica, he assumed it was a local practice. Until later he had no idea that Theodore Weld had initiated it.[29]

Finney's increasing urbanity was shown in the calmer, more confident way he treated others by that time. When he met a tailor by the name of Godly, he inquired as to the man's name, and when told he replied, "Well, are you a Christian, Mr. Godly?" "No, sir." "Well, then," Finney said with a sigh of sadness, "it might just as well be Un-Godly." And on another occasion he returned from a fire at a grist mill that attracted a multitude, and to one person he said, "Good evening, we've had quite a fire, haven't we? Are you a Christian?" From such accounts, where Finney does not resort to the browbeating he earlier used, we begin to see the character of the mature man emerging, with a dignity that remains for the rest of his life. It is less brash, more lawyerlike, and matter of fact.

Evangelistic services were held throughout the area from approximately the first of February to the end of May, while invitations begged him to come to other cities. Hiram H. Kellogg, a Presbyterian clergyman, urgently asked him to come to nearby Clinton, the seat of Hamilton College.[30] His request, dated May 20, 1826, refers to "Dr. N.," and the context makes it clear that this is Asahel S. Norton, pastor of the church at Clinton:

Dear Brother Finney,
. . . I want a general meeting of inquiry, but I fear to have one and have it come under Dr. N's direction, for I rather that anxious sinners should see no one than to converse with him. He appears desirous of doing his duty, but he is not plain-telling sinners to repent and *that immediately*. His feelings are *too tender*. Now can you not come? Does not duty call this way? Look at the college which commences in about two weeks, and at the various schools there are here—at the state of feeling in our church among the wicked. . . .

In haste yours, H. H. Kellogg

P.S. I wish you would not mention what I have written especially what I have said respecting Dr. N. I do not speak of it even here and would not to you only that you may see my true situation and that of this people.[31]

Certainly Theodore Weld seconded this invitation, and the thought of many young students, plus the state of Kellogg's work, was an irresistible lure to Finney, who saw young college men as having great potential for the ministry. Throughout his lifetime, Finney's attitude toward them was always solicitous, for he felt that if he could make them prorevival preachers at the beginning of their ministries, they would henceforth be of inestimable blessing to the church.

Finney set up camp in Clinton about the first of June and

preached for approximately three weeks. Apparently, however, the situation misfired in some way, for he mentioned nothing of Clinton in the *Memoirs,* and the opposition from Norton and Hamilton College President Henry Davis may have been formidable. The full truth may never be known, but Davis and the Universalist editor A. B. Grosh were quick to spread disparaging accounts that, while Finney and his wife were eating breakfast at their boarding-house, an unidentified youth removed their belongings from their room and loaded them onto a carriage. He then called the Finneys to the door and invited them to depart from Clinton immediately. The story claims that they did so, although Finney was scheduled to preach that evening. Whatever the truth of that, it is certain that no revival occurred in Clinton. On June 24 Orin Gridley wrote to Finney from Clinton, stating that Asahel Norton was unaware that the evangelist had departed; "Indeed," Gridley wrote, "I think he [Norton] most sincerely desires your return, and I am certain his *people* do: I write by his special request."[32]

Whatever the specific opposition was in Clinton, it was to be only the beginning. From there Finney moved eighty miles to the west to the town of Auburn, leaving Oneida County behind. And at this time he had a premonition of what awaited him:

> The Lord showed me as in a vision what was before me. . . . I never spent a waking hour in thinking of it; when to all outward appearance, it seemed as if all the churches of the land, except where I had labored, would unite to shut me out of their pulpits. This was indeed the avowed determination, as I understood, of the men that led the opposition. They were so deceived that they thought there was no effectual way but to unite, and, as they expressed it, "put him down."[33]

Dr. Dirck C. Lansing, pastor of the First Presbyterian Church of Auburn, had journeyed to Utica to observe Finney's work there, and it was he who had issued the invitation to Auburn.[34] The fears that occasionally came to Finney that he would be fought by powerful people came true increasingly, and at Auburn it was to be some members of the theological seminary located there, and especially one of its faculty, Professor James Richards (1767–1843). He had studied for a year at Yale, and served as a Congregational and Presbyterian minister in Massachusetts and New Jersey for thirty years. In 1805 he had been elected moderator of the Presbyterian General Assembly, and in 1823 a professorship at Auburn Seminary was offered him. He and others of the faculty were in sympathy with the promotion of revivals, for this school had been founded specifically to promote New School views. But some there were critical of Finney's methods and suspicious of his theology. Yet, surprisingly, Richards took an active part in the awakening, at the same time making it known, to Finney's intense annoyance, that he did not approve of some of its aspects. "One of his published discourses is a criticism of Mr. Finney's theory of faith in prayer," said Henry Fowler, "and ably presents the orthodox view."[35] It may be that some of Finney's anger derived from his own lack of training in a theological seminary, and his unwillingness to stand scrutiny from professors and students of a seminary.

The work at Auburn lasted approximately two months, from June 24 to August 28, 1826, and seems to have been filled with more than the usual number of unexpected occurrences. In one service a man stood in the congregation clutching some silver dollars in each hand and shouted back at Finney, "These are my gods!" A writer reported that, under the evangelist's withering gaze, the man was converted in short time.[36] All told, in spite of the numerous problems encountered, about five hundred people were converted in the Auburn revival, according to one estimate.[37]

With the center of New York State aflame with revivals, it was no longer possible for city sophisticates in the East to think of Finney's work as that of a backwoods ranter. By the mid-point of 1826 he had made some influential friends, among them Judge Jonas Platt of the New York State Supreme Court. Judge Platt and his son Zephaniah had felt the magnetic power of Finney's preaching during the Utica revival, and had then moved to New York City. On June 19, 1826, Zephaniah Platt wrote to Finney from Albany:

> Reverend and Dear Sir,
>   I have just arrived here from N. York to see my wife and family, and to take them home with me. I have made several attempts lately to visit Jamaica and to see the great and good man Mr. Nettleton who has been and is still labouring there. . . . Dr. [Gardiner] Spring too is arising as a man from sleep; he preaches Repentance and Submission to Christ, and is faithful in warning sinners against the Hell for the wicked. . . . There is to be a meeting of the Albany Presbytery here on Thursday of this week. . . . Mr. Nettleton also has been invited to attend, and probably may be expected. Now I propose that (if you can think it your duty) you attend this meeting, and proceed from there to New York and Jamaica. If I know anything of the human heart I am ready to say

that some of our N.Y. churches are in readiness for *your preaching*.
Dr. Spring will gladly invite you to his pulpit and so will Ludlow;
and even their congregations are prepared to hear *the truth*. . . .
I dare also assure you that you will be sustained and supported
by many Christians.

Z. Platt[38]

In New York City, the Platts, father and son, belonged to the well-
known Brick Presbyterian Church where Gardiner Spring was pastor.
But Zephaniah Platt may have been mistaken in assuming that Spring
would allow Finney to preach in the church, for in July of 1827 Lyman
Beecher would invite Spring to join him against Finney at the New
Lebanon Convention, and Spring, as a conservative Hopkinsian, probably would have gone but something prevented his attendance. At any
rate, Finney chose not to attend the meeting of the Presbytery of Albany, and thus effectively postponed his first confrontation with Asahel Nettleton.

Shortly thereafter Finney took another action that may have been
motivated by his sense of impending clash. The minutes of the Presbytery of Oneida meeting at Whitesboro on September 8, 1826, record
that "The Reverend Charles G. Finney presented a letter of dismission from the Presbytery of St. Lawrence, with a request to unite with
this Presbytery, and his request was granted."[39] Strategically this was
an intelligent move, for the Presbytery of St. Lawrence was a rural
association with little power or influence, whereas the Oneida Presbytery was filled with Finney's associates and co-revivalists, and had
far more importance in the denomination. The wonder is that Finney
had not transferred his membership previously. This move to close
ranks with sympathetic pastors who agreed with the new measures
came none too soon. Opposition from a number of fronts—Old School
Calvinists, Universalists, Unitarians, deists, and atheists—was beginning to build, and Finney would in time need all the support he could
find, from members of his "Holy Band" and from every other possible
source.[40]

At this period, by far the most vitriolic attack on the new measures revivalism was a 103-page book published by Ephraim Perkins,
who identified himself as a "plain farmer" from Trenton, New York,
and a deacon of the Unitarian church. The title, given in full to illustrate its approach, was *A "Bunker Hill" Contest, A.D. 1826. Between the "Holy Alliance" For the Establishment of Hierarchy and*

Ecclesiastical Domination Over the Human Mind, On the One Side, And the Asserters of Free Inquiry, Bible Religion, Christian Freedom and Civil Liberty on the Other. The Rev. Charles Finney, "Home Missionary" and High Priest of the Expeditions of the Alliance in the Interior of New York, Headquarters, County of Oneida. Throughout this work, Perkins portrayed Finney's methods as wild and fanatic in the extreme, and concluded, "To represent you as a sincere deluded enthusiast or misguided fanatic, would be to misrepresent you."[41] It is full of stories reported as fact even when they were completely unsubstantiated and on the face of them quite improbable, and which most unbiased people would have dismissed as concocted exaggerations or rumors. Perkins, perhaps urged on by others, apparently nursed such a hatred of Finney that he was willing to malign him by the invention of any lie that might serve his purpose. Unfortunately, this rancorous pamphlet has been accepted uncritically by some undiscerning historians as an accurate portrayal of Charles Finney's early ministry. When it is carefully considered against the known facts, its distortions immediately emerge. Everything considered, it is safe to conclude that Perkins' booklet should be accepted only with great caution and qualification.

Because the charges in the booklet were so slanderous, and its style sufficiently polished, there have been those from its first appearance who have stated that either Perkins was only a front for the Unitarian clergymen who were the actual authors, or that he did not even exist, and the Rev. Henry Ware, Jr., an itinerant Unitarian preacher, was the writer. Ware was thought to be the author because he had written to a friend about the Utica revival, "it is proposed to write a history of the thing and publish it."[42] But sufficient evidence has surfaced to prove that Perkins existed, although it is possible that Henry Ware did influence him. He was a prominent member of the Oneida Agricultural Association, whose records show him to have been a horse breeder. Extant church records also testify to his existence, as does correspondence from him.[43]

Among Perkins' many unsubstantiated charges, he alleged that the Presbyterians, along with other denominations, were in the process of using concerted action to bring in surreptitiously a national church, by whose strength "all the opposition of infidelity would be borne down and overpowered." The inquiry meetings held during the revivals were described as follows: "They are generally, if not always, held in the night. The room is darkened, so that persons can only see to walk and discover each other; and the reign of universal silence is interrupted only by now and then a dolorous groan from different parts of the room." It was claimed that the leaders walk about softly, whispering to each individual some questions such as "Do you love God?" An occult element was suggested in the statement that "Mr. Finney would go round, and, by putting his eyes on each individual for a few seconds, tell the exact state of their mind."[44]

Full of such palpable exaggerations, A Bunker Hill Contest would have been rejected by most serious inquirers. However, the Oneida Presbytery thought it best not only to answer the opposers, but also to substantiate all the good the revivals had done. So, at the meeting of September 8, 1826 (the same day in which Finney transferred his membership), the presbytery appointed a committee consisting of Noah Coe, John Frost, and Moses Gillet to collect a large amount of data from pastors in whose churches revivals had occurred, including those where Finney had not preached. The three went at the task avidly, and secured testimonials from nine clergymen representing as many towns. The accounts varied in length, those from Lee, Camden, Boonville, and Trenton taking about a page to list the outstanding events and benefits the revivals had brought to them; those from Western, Rome, Whitestown, New Hartford, and Utica were much longer. The report was entitled A Narrative of the Revival of Religion in the County of Oneida, Particularly in the Bounds of the Presbytery of Oneida in the Year 1826, and appeared as a bulky booklet consisting of sixty-seven closely printed octavo pages.

The Narrative consisted of three parts, first the accounts of revivals, then "Remarks on the Character of this Revival of Religion," and finally "Means which Appear to have been Blessed in Promoting this Revival." The committee was anxious to answer some of the charges of A Bunker Hill Contest, and asked, "Why did not these authors, after describing the darkness of the rooms at these meetings, say that Mr. Finney professed to have powers of vision that he could see the faces of the converts in the dark, as well as 'tell the exact state of their mind'? This would have increased the wonder."[45]

Regarding Ephraim Perkins, whose name appeared as the writer, the authors of the Narrative charged that the book was too polished for a mere farmer to have written. Perkins, they claimed, was only a puppet acting on the stage, and the Unitarian ministers of the area had probably combined their writing skills to produce the booklet.[46] Instead of A Bunker Hill Contest, a better and more accurate title might be:

*THE TRENTON SHAM FIGHT, A.D. 1826, Between Unitarians,
Writers of Anonymous Letters, and Opposers of Bible, Tract, and
Missionary Societies and Revivals of Religion; in Support of "The
Prince of the Power of the Air," On the One Side; And Bugbears,
Sprites, Fairies, Ghosts, and Hobgoblins, of Their Own Conjura-
tion, on the the Other. MR. EPHRAIM PERKINS, Deacon of the
Unitarian Church, and Commander in Chief of the Allied Forces
in the Interior of New York: Headquarters, Oldenbarnevelt, Near
Trenton Falls.*[47]

The *Bunker Hill* pamphlet made many serious charges that Coe,
Frost, and Gillet were eager to refute. One was that Finney and the
students of Auburn Seminary had paraded around the streets of Trenton to stir up local interest and annoy the Unitarians there. The *Narrative* replied that not a single "itinerant from Auburn Theological
Seminary" was in Trenton, and Finney had gone to the town during
his meetings in Utica only once.[48] Another charge was that, immediately before the Finney meetings, many handbills had appeared in
Utica depicting the day of judgment; they were offensive and in poor
taste. The *Narrative* replied that the Unitarians were showing incredible ignorance here; Finney had had nothing to do with the handbills,
for a Methodist had distributed them after a new theater had opened
in Utica, and they were to combat its bad influence, and never mentioned the Finney meetings! The text in the handbills was taken from
the writings of John Wesley, and the same handbills had appeared in
London, Baltimore, and other cities, and had been published in the
Baptist Register and *Zion's Herald.*[49] The *Narrative* stated that the
opposers of revivals must be desperate indeed in their search for incriminating material against Finney, if they must stoop to such per-
versions of truth as their technique. In a long section Finney himself
was discussed; he possessed, said the *Narrative*, "a discriminating and
self-balanced mind," a "good share of courage and decision," and "is
as well-calculated to be extensively useful" in awakening the churches
through evangelism as any man alive.

The Unitarians and the Universalists could be counted upon to
be enemies, but another antagonist appeared during the Oneida
County revivals from a much closer quarter. No critic of Finney appeared more vexatious than William R. Weeks, pastor of the Congregational church at Paris Hill, south of Utica. Finney was not alone
in his irritation; even the mild-mannered and moderate George Gale,
now thoroughly won over to Finney's ways, wrote that Weeks "has

doubtless been as instrumental as any other man in exciting unfavorable impressions against the work of God here."[50]

Weeks had been born in Connecticut in 1783. Before his conversion he had worked at a number of trades, and then he turned to study theology under the direction of a cousin in the ministry. In addition he took one year of study at Andover Seminary, and was ordained in 1812 by the Presbytery of Albany. A difficult person to deal with, he held two pastorates within a year's time, and then spent a year without a charge. Finally in 1815 he received a call to a church in Litchfield, Connecticut, where he did his best to cultivate the friendship of Lyman Beecher, already an important figure in Congregationalism. For some reason the local Congregational association there refused to install him in the pulpit to which he had been called. The historian P. H. Fowler states that the reason was because Weeks differed somewhat in theology.[51] This is difficult to accept, however, because Weeks was a Hopkinsian, although he had some leanings toward the teachings of Nathaniel Emmons,[52] and both theologies were common in that region.

In 1818, having had little success in Connecticut, Weeks moved to Oneida County and attempted to begin anew, seeking a call to a church there. The congregation at Paris Hill was divided into two factions: those who favored the Presbyterian form of government, and those who preferred the Congregational. The latter group issued a call to Weeks to be pastor in 1820, which he accepted eagerly. Under the "Presbygational" Plan of Union, Congregational clergymen such as Weeks and Moses Gillet usually attended the meetings of the local presbytery, and these two were counted as members on the roll of Oneida Presbytery at this time. For some reason (one can hardly help wondering if his irascible nature was not at the bottom of it all) history repeated itself, and he remained at Paris Hill for twelve years without ever being installed by the presbytery. The likelihood (from subsequent events) was that he defied the authority of presbytery and the power of the Plan of Union arrangements, claiming Congregational autonomy, and in light of the already split congregation, Oneida Presbytery simply declined to act and hoped that in time he would come around.

It was not to be, however, for in 1825 Weeks was one of the leaders in organizing the Oneida Congregational Association, comprising a few clergymen who were dissatisfied with the Plan of Union. With some Presbyterians in his congregation, he was bound to attend some of the meetings of presbytery, and as Charles Finney went through the area in 1826, Weeks heard most of the members of Oneida Presbytery praise the evangelist. Almost predictably, Weeks reacted negatively to Finney, and attempted to turn his colleagues against him. The hundreds of Finney converts streaming into the churches effectively stalled that attempt, and this grated exceedingly on Weeks. Unable to influence the Oneida Presbytery against Finney, he denounced this organization and made the Congregational Association, which had only the feeblest existence and was completely dominated by Weeks, into an anti-Finney body claiming to represent those pastors who opposed the new measures.[53]

As a Hopkinsian Weeks had few associates, for this school was not popular in western New York, despite Finney's claim that "this view of Mr. Weeks, was embraced, to a considerable extent, by ministers and professors of religion in that region."[54] The historian Fowler says that Finney's "broad inferences from narrow premises are illustrated in his charging on 'ministers and professors of religion in that region' a concurrence 'to a considerable extent' in the Hopkinsianism of the Rev. Dr. Wm. R. Weeks, whereas that divine stood almost entirely alone, with little or no countenance from his surrounding brethren."[55] But Hopkinsianism was, or had been, the stance of Asahel Nettleton,[56] and in casting about for support against the avalanche of new measures, Weeks quite naturally turned to the one who until recently had been the most famous revivalist, and also a fellow Hopkinsian. It is altogether likely that Weeks, more than anyone else, alerted Nettleton first about the threat of Finney, and kept the New Englander posted on what to him were the latest outrages.

On May 11, 1827, the *Pastoral Letter of the Oneida Association on the Subject of Revivals* appeared, and Weeks was generally credited with its authorship.[57] In the *Letter*, Finney and his associates were charged with "calling men hard names"; "reporting great, powerful revivals which afterwards came to little or nothing"; "ostentation and noise"; "not guarding against false conversions"; "injudicious treatment of young converts, such as turning them into exhorters and teachers"; "giving heed to impressions, feelings, and supposed revelations"; "allowing anybody and everybody to speak and pray in promiscuous meetings of whatever age, sex, or qualification"; using means of exciting fears, such as saying to a sinner, "If you don't repent today, you will be in hell tomorrow"; "you are a reprobate, you are going straight to hell"; familiar use of the words "devil," "hell," "cursed," and "damned" in a tone and manner like profane swearing; the calling of elderly persons by youths "old hypocrites," "old apostates"; imprecations in prayer; interference, by ministers and others, with congregations to which they did not belong; female prayer and exhortations in public, and so on.[58]

Now, these allegations were measured, not the sort of wild stories that were printed in the papers of the Universalists. Therefore they seemed to merit a certain amount of credence. Undeniably, such offenses *had* occurred in the past, such as in the Great Awakening of the 1740s, whether Charles Finney had actually been guilty of any of them. Guilt by association was at work, and Weeks was very clever in never specifying whether Finney or one of his subordinates, or anyone at all, had committed the breach recently; they were general charges, without documentation or evidence.

Weeks continued by alleging that the Finneyites used the principle that the end justifies the means, a pagan principle that had no place in Christian practice.[59] In regard to females, or ones not qualified, speaking or praying in "promiscuous" meetings, he stated that human nature would see to it that the modest and the meek would be hesitant, whereas those who suffered from egotism would thrust themselves forward, and upset the intended purpose.[60] In addition, said Weeks, the new measures raised false hopes in many hearts. When some heard of the conversion of others, they would attend the meetings hoping to duplicate the experience of another person:

> They ask to be prayed for, themselves, with raised expectations that the same prayers will be successful in their own case. The prayers are made in their presence, and they are exhorted to submit before they rise from their knees. . . . The expectation that now they shall be converted, removes their distress. Their countenances indicate that their burden is gone. They are inquired of, perhaps, if they do not feel better, and they answer in the affirmative. Joyful congratulations succeed, and thanks are returned to God that another soul is brought into the kingdom.[61]

The *Pastoral Letter* stung, far more than anything that opposers had previously published, and it led Herman Norton to write that it was the "most wicked thing that I have seen in print."[62] A year later, the pot was still boiling sufficiently that the Oneida Presbytery appointed John Frost, Samuel Aikin, and George W. Gale on February 8, 1828, to inquire of William Weeks "whether he has any evidence that any member of this Presbytery used any of the exceptionable expressions quoted" by him. By then the New Lebanon Conference was history, and Asahel Nettleton and his confidant William Weeks had suffered wrenching setbacks to their cause. When approached by the committee from Oneida Presbytery, Weeks defiantly challenged their authority, knowing that he had nothing further to lose, and the committee reported back to presbytery that "he had refused to give them any information" on the subject.[63]

Weeks, as well as other antagonists, held Charles Finney responsible for the behavior manifested at all times by all of his "Holy Band." In one sense, this is patently absurd, for no one person could possibly control even those closest to him to such an extent that he could be truly held accountable for their actions. Yet, in another sense, this very thing is done frequently, as when parents are held responsible for the behavior of an errant child even if they are absent when certain activities occur. If Charles Finney had only the most circumspect of assistants, this might have been an acceptable policy. But that was not the case. The eccentric ways of Daniel Nash have already been noted, and when all of Finney's associates have been studied, it soon becomes apparent that none of them were so enamored of him to yield to his every wish. Many were individualists and went their own ways. Yet, Weeks and others held him responsible for what they did, even when he himself was entirely innocent of a particular practice.

Charles Finney's preaching has been presented sufficiently for a word of assessment to be given. Not only during this early period, but throughout his life, the aspects of Finney that struck others most were his fierce countenance, and his powerful "denunciatory" style of preaching, which savagely tore at public composure and lethargy in the attempt to awaken his audiences to a revival. Indeed, in Finney this took on the nature of a formula: if one were not in the heat of revival fever, then the only alternative was religious "stupidity," or lassitude and ennui. To him, there was no such thing as a deep, quiet spiritual life as in Blaise Pascal, John Bunyan, or John Woolman. No other alternative existed. More than almost anyone before him, this oversimplification of the life of the spirit demanded constant, frenzied activity for God, so characteristic of Finney's own life, and so in harmony with the activism of the period of Jacksonian democracy in America.

Such an activistic approach contradicts Solomon Stoddard's theory that the spiritual life has peaks and valleys, because human nature is incapable of continual spiritual awakening. But Stoddard believed in the unpredictability of divine working, whereby the law of alternation operated everywhere, in natural things as well as in spiritual, and where a resurgence of God's power might be expected at some point after decline set in. Finney, of course, did his best to remove the unpredictability in God's working, and operated on what John Calvin's followers would have called Pelagian principles. Finney, the "pragmatist's pragmatist," would of course be displeased with unpredictabilities.

Finney often stated that among the enemies he was fighting was that of the supposed impotence in conversion bred into people by Calvinistic preaching on election. To some extent that may be true, but in removing God's unpredictability and restoring human choice, Finney's theology still remained quite negative. He may have broadened the possibility of salvation, but his portrayal of God was still as a wrathful deity. God's love for humans, and our response in love, played a very small part in Finney's appeal to audiences, as a broad reading of his sermons and lectures will demonstrate. Indeed, one can read in his writings for dozens of pages, and the prominent biblical term "love" will never appear.

But that is not all. Lyman Beecher and others were correct in calling Finney's preaching "denunciatory," for the scourging he gave would surely not be tolerated by any audience today! When one reads through all of Finney's sermons, and his lectures on systematic theology and revivals, it seems that he was not merely trying to awaken his hearers to spiritual jeopardy, for he went far beyond that. He was not satisfied until he had "blistered," harrowed and castigated a congregation beyond measure. The basic point is, Finney never seemed to understand, all his life, that unbelievers can be won to faith as much (and perhaps far more) by the preaching of God's *love*, as by threats of damnation and the presentation of God as wrathful and threatening. Dwight L. Moody also preached a judgmental God, until 1868, when his growing friendship with the Englishman Henry Moorhouse made him reexamine his preaching and completely change its emphases. Moorhouse preached seven evenings in Moody's Chicago church on the theme of the love of God, based on John 3:16. Moody was astounded. Before that, Moody had appealed to his hearers to repent and flee the wrath to come, out of fear of judgment. He saw the vast difference in Moorhouse's stress, and began to teach that sinners should be drawn to God by love, for God wants sons and daughters, not slaves.[64]

The importance of Lydia Andrews Finney in her husband's ministry deserves brief consideration at this point. An extended treatment of her role has been developed by Leonard I. Sweet.[65] The role of the clergyman's wife in eighteenth-century America was generally that of the helpmeet, who gave herself to undergirding her husband in whatever quiet and self-effacing ways he asked and predictably received little public appreciation. Sweet has found that by the 1820s changes began to affect the minister's wife, and it was Charles and Lydia Finney who expanded the possibilities for her role. These allowed her public leadership and personal growth while encouraging the perception that she was not merely his support but a real adjunct to his ministry, operating even in areas of the church's work where he rarely intruded. Thus Leonard Sweet characterizes Lydia's role as "the assistant model." Where Finney's understanding of theology and the activism of each Christian meshed so well with the developing mood in Jacksonian America, so the part played by women in the nation was broadening significantly at this time, and Lydia Finney was among the first to exemplify the changes. "Not until Lydia Finney did the change in the minister's wife's legacy to the world become clearly apparent," Sweet has written. "It would become not merely a life, but a career."[66]

In the newly heightened status of evangelist's wife that she created, Finney's wife found her opportunities chiefly in two areas: visitation, and the organization of female prayer meetings. The extant correspondence to Lydia Finney contains letters from a significant number of women, who wrote concerning prayer groups, ministries of visitation, their spiritual lives, their churches and pastors, their families, the state of their towns before and after a revival conducted by Finney, and much more. Several observations may be drawn from this correspondence. First, a large number of women came to respect and rely upon Mrs. Finney's advice and support. This is clear evidence that she possessed sufficient leadership and personal attraction to cultivate and maintain such trust for an extended period, and she apparently enjoyed being in a position of trust and leadership. Again, there is no indication that her husband discouraged or envied this, but rather he had the good sense to recognize what a valuable contribution it could make to his total ministry.

Finney had found that campaigns of evangelistic visitation before and during a revival were a significant help in encouraging prospective converts to attend his meetings, but he was not the first to use this device. As with many of his practices, Methodists had pioneered the use of visitations; in 1810, the wife of a judge in western New York had called on many homes with a circuit rider, and from this came forty new members for their church.[67] But it was Lydia Finney who discovered here the vital part she might play as a revival unfolded, and play it she did in one location after another for a period of several years, organizing church women into teams of two or three for wholesale, house-to-house visitations over a large area. Each duo or trio could make perhaps ten to twenty brief calls in an afternoon or evening throughout a district, and when those calls were multiplied by the number of teams, the result could be significant. In the early nineteenth century, in the desire of females for a more liberated lifestyle, here was a needed activity that they were abundantly capable of performing, had the time to do, and which had the desirable effect of taking them from their homes to further the revival and bring in converts.

The second activity Lydia Finney took up was to organize women's prayer meetings. This was in perfect concert with her husband's emphasis, for he became convinced immediately after his conversion of the centrality of prayer for the success of any spiritual undertaking. No revival could ever be brought about, even with the most devoted preaching, house-to-house visitation, and other organizational backing, without massive intercession. In his 1835 work, *Lectures on Revivals of Religion,* Finney devoted almost a quarter of the book to the subject of prayer, meetings for intercession, and the "prayer of faith," and he fully intended to impress upon his readers the crucial nature of the subject.

In practice, Finney made prayer meetings an integral part of his revival technique. Leonard Sweet has stated the matter with precision:

> For a proper understanding of why the words "praying women" were Finney's basic recipe for revivalism, we must first divest ourselves of the unfortunate association of "prayer" with words like "private," "personal," and "passive." Finney believed that prayer, like love, was in its truest form not an attitude but an activity, and, as Sandra Sizer has shown, a predominantly social activity at that. . . . Weekly female prayer meetings were more than social parentheses or pious pep-rallies. When animated by the hope of revival, they became directed gatherings, pulsating centers of creative energy and zeal.[68]

Finney's determination to have his work in any area supported by a large ministry of lay intercession meshed nicely with the potential of women for such a task. Of course, as we have seen in the Utica revival, there was still some prejudice against females speaking or praying in what was called "promiscuous," or mixed, assemblies (although there is some evidence that among Methodist and Baptist groups the practice had been carried on for some years).[69] Knowing well the sentiments based on St. Paul's injunction, Lydia had to be cautious with her meetings. At first such gatherings were restricted to women; no one could object to that. Gradually, under one expedient or another, men were included—at first men who thought St. Paul's warning was misapplied or anachronistic, and later others who could be convinced of this—until finally a custom was established and accepted.

As Leonard Sweet has pointed out, "Where Lydia fits into the debate over public prayer by women is difficult to determine. . . . There is no direct evidence that she spoke publicly."[70] And her sensitive and humble nature was not readily prodded into aggressive roles. It is likely that she was content to encourage competent women, whenever she found them, to take active parts. It can safely be assumed, however, that Mrs. Finney's great trust in her husband's ministry would have moved her to do all that she could, overcoming her own reticence, to further that.

Letter after letter to Lydia Finney in the period 1826–31, attests to the importance women had learned to assign to their ministry of prayer, largely through her insistence. In 1827 Christian women in Troy had organized prayer groups and covenanted with each other on four promises: "that we will attend unless necessarily detained; . . . that we will commence at the hour though but two should be present; that all shall lead in prayer each in turn; that we will live together as dear sisters in the Lord."[71] Other statements show that in many parts of New York State church women were promising to uphold various worthy endeavors and each other in intercession at stated times, and that they considered it a sacred trust to be involved in such a ministry, to be continued by oneself when forced to be separated from the other women.

A good deal more was at stake in these liberating acts, and there were few who were so naive as not to realize it. Women speaking publicly in groups and out visiting in strange surroundings gained a new self-confidence, and to their surprise found themselves at the heart of the conversion process. When they gathered for prayer, they were physically separating themselves from their unconverted spouses, children, and townspeople, and theologically they were assuming the role of the chief intercessory agents of salvation. Never before had they dared to take to themselves, in the male-dominated society of that day, the assumption that here, at least, they were equals. Charles and Lydia Finney taught them that they were indeed.

6

CIVIL WAR IN ZION

Charles Finney's startling successes in the Oneida County revivals began to bring appeals from a clergyman in Troy, on the Hudson River, as early as June 9, 1826. The Reverend Nathaniel S. S. Beman, a stranger to Finney, and the pastor of the prestigious First Presbyterian Church in that city, explained in his letter that Finney's preaching was much needed there.[1] Then on June 17 Finney received a message from a layman, probably Truman Hastings, seconding Beman's invitation. If Finney replied, it must have been in the negative. Again on August 3 Beman wrote with the same request, and Finney tentatively accepted.

Nathaniel Beman was, by the summer of 1826, facing a trial before his presbytery on the charge of un-Christian conduct, and it may be that his determination to bring Finney to his pulpit was a maneuver to distract attention from the trial. If it was, it did not work, for Finney's coming only made the situation worse, causing new charges to be added to the original ones. Unquestionably the Old School clergymen of the Presbytery of Albany were only too happy to see Beman brought to trial, for his advocacy of New School views was increasingly irritating to them. By 1826 his influence was becoming felt throughout his denomination. In the previous year he had published four sermons upon the atonement espousing those views, and he was seen, correctly, by Old School adherents as a definite threat.[2] But the charges against him did not deal so much with his theological views. G. F. Wright has explained:

> Charges were preferred against him by certain disaffected members of his church, and the Presbytery was assembled to investigate both them and the revival methods which Dr. Beman had come to endorse and advocate. No charge of heresy or immorality was brought against him, but the specifications related mostly to infelicities of conduct connected with and growing out of the urgency used in trying to persuade men to consider their lost condition and accept the gospel. Dr. Beman's domestic life also was not the most happy, his wife being a notorious vixen; and among the charges against him was that, when his original call to Troy was pending, he did not unfold to his future parish the uncomfortable side of his wife's character.[3]

Inasmuch as ecclesiastical trials were relatively rare in the Presbyterian fold (though from this time they would increase in number), Charles Finney surely had heard of Nathaniel Beman's predicament. Their two presbyteries were neighbors, and anything of such notoriety as a trial made the rounds of gossip. So Finney could not have walked into this situation unaware. But a larger question than why Finney would involve himself in a potentially nasty circumstance is, why would he travel east to begin with, where the new measures and New School theology were being roundly criticized (as in the charges against Beman), and where there were many supporters of Asahel Nettleton and his methods? In the Oneida Presbytery Finney was among friends, and he had the entire western part of New York, from Utica to Buffalo, where the new measures would be readily accepted. He also must have been aware of this. It seems, then, that Finney went to Troy in the belief that he could patch up differences with the Old School supporters, or, failing this, that Finney was perfectly willing for a showdown that he knew might come. What he did *not* know, as his correspondence makes quite clear, was that when Nettleton would find out that Finney was preaching in Troy, the New Englander would deliberately come to that region to see for himself if the many rumors he had been hearing were true.

The evangelistic meetings began in Beman's church about the first of October, 1826. After Finney had preached for approximately one month, with things seeming to go well, he left to attend to his previous commitments, intending to return to Troy as soon as pos-

George W. Gale (1789–1861). The son of Josiah and Rachel Gale of
Dutchess County, New York, Gale graduated from Union College
in 1814 and studied at Princeton Seminary. He was ordained by
the St. Lawrence Presbytery on October 29, 1819, and became minister of the Adams Presbyterian Church, the only pastorate he ever
held. A distinguished educator, he directed the Oneida Institute
at Whitesboro from 1827 until 1834, and in 1837 founded Knox College and Galesburg, Illinois. From a daguerreotype, courtesy of
Knox College.

sible. Naturally, Nathaniel Beman wished the meetings to continue,
so he invited Horatio Foote to substitute for Charles Finney until the
latter's return. The faction in the congregation who were preferring
the charges against Beman, annoyed with everything he did including
the invitation to Finney, became even more antagonized by Foote's

Nathaniel S. S. Beman (1785–1871), pastor of the First Presbyterian Church of Troy, New York, was already embroiled in a trial before his presbytery when he begged Charles Finney to come preach from his pulpit. The two were close friends until Finney espoused perfectionism. From a steel engraving, courtesy of the Presbyterian Historical Society.

preaching. Whereas Finney was beginning to learn the value of diplomacy, Foote would have none of it, and "he bore down upon them with the most searching discourses," Finney reported.[4]

For decades there has been disagreement among historians concerning this dissident group, some claiming that soon they left to form the Second Presbyterian Church of Troy, and others believing that the Second Church was not the result of a split, but came about simply as a result of normal growth in the First Church starting a daughter congregation. The first position holds that this group, already antagonized by actions of Beman, became irreconcilably provoked during the evangelistic meetings of Finney and Foote, and thus the break and the founding of Second Church were outgrowths of this.[5] The second position holds that the rapid expansion of the city, and the proliferation of members through Finney's evangelism, made the beginning of the Second Church inevitable, and that plans for it had been underway for more than a year before Finney set foot in Troy.[6]

During the months that followed, this opposition to Finney and Beman remained very active, providing constant troubles for the two of them. One man, Joseph Brockway, wrote a lengthy pamphlet detailing his objections to the methods used. "I venerate his talents," Brockway wrote of Nathaniel Beman, "but, through what I have considered a wrong direction of his talents, he has given me more pain by his preaching, than any man I ever heard, Mr. Finney excepted."[7] In addition, he said, both Beman and Finney praised the Methodists far too often. Brockway wrote:

> He [Beman] had before said, in one of his lectures, that the only reason why the Methodists were so much blessed, and why they had grown up, as it were, in a day, to so great a people, was because they preached the simple truth of God. Mr. Finney, too, bears testimony to the same point, and says that there has been more of the spirit of religion among them, and they have done more good than all other denominations put together. I say then, let them go to the Methodists.[8]

Shortly after Brockway's booklet appeared, another protest from the dissident group was issued by a "number of the late church and congregation." This was even more scathing in its denunciation of Finney than Brockway's book had been, stating:

> While things were in this state . . . Mr. Beman [introduced] into his pulpit the notorious Charles G. Finney. This man had acquired a high reputation as an active and successful promoter of revivals; and a message had been transmitted to him that Troy would

be, at the present juncture, a suitable theatre for his labours. The character of the man must be too well known to require any illustration from us; and, as we shall be compelled to make some allusions to him, we shall treat him with but little more ceremony than an acknowledged outlaw. If no other objections could be urged against him, it was not proper to obtrude upon an unwilling auditory a man who was not qualified, either by his talents or acquirements, to instruct or please an enlightened community. But his shocking blasphemies, his novel and repulsive sentiments, and his theatrical and frantic gesticulations, struck horror into those who entertained any reverence either for religion or decency.[9]

Charges against Finney in this booklet were many and, for that age, serious. The main assertion was that the evangelist's language was coarse, violent, and entirely inappropriate. On one occasion, it charged, Finney and Beman called at the home of a Mrs. Mosier, and immediately Finney began to browbeat her mercilessly, asking, "Do you love God?" The lady responded, "I think I do." Then Finney shook his fist in her face, saying, "You lie! . . . You ought to go to hell, and you must repent." The lady responded that she could not repent. Finney, irate, said that she could be converted immediately, and when the lady still insisted that she could not, he declared, "You ought to be damned."[10]

The picture of Charles Finney that is conveyed by many such accounts, friendly and antagonistic, is of a forceful and resolute person who has all the unbridled zeal of the recent convert. Clearly, the interior dynamics of the man were complex, and his youthful zealotry would in time be smoothed off by increasing urbanity. Samuel Aikin claimed that Finney became more dignified and cerebral after reading Jonathan Edwards during the Utica revival the previous spring, but here we find him, during the Troy campaign, reverting to the antics of an earlier day, if this account is accurate. The answer may lie in the company with which he was associating; Aikin demanded sane and dignified behavior from Finney, and he got it, whereas Beman himself set the tone of questionable actions and language.

In a situation where a church was dividing, friends were important. As always, Finney appealed to the attorneys in his audiences, and a solid friend was made in John P. Cushman, a lawyer in Troy who became a frequent correspondent. When Finney left Troy to preach in Utica on November 6, 1826, Cushman, a close friend of Nathaniel Beman, wrote to the evangelist some surprising news: "We learn this evening that Mr. Nettleton is in Albany, and preached for Mr. Weed yesterday. He may remain but a few days and not so long as that. . . . He wishes to see *you*, but how strong this desire is, I cannot know until I see him."[11] Nettleton across the river from Troy, in Albany! It could mean, of course, only one thing—that although he might attempt to conceal his true purpose by doing a bit of preaching, in actuality he had come to the area to find out more about the "new measures" and its chief exponent.[12]

By any standard, Asahel Nettleton was an unusual person.[13] He was born on April 21, 1783, in North Killingworth, Connecticut, the son of a farmer. Nettleton's childhood was not exposed to religious influences, and he was thinking of opening a dancing school when he was converted in 1801. He graduated from Yale College in 1809 and began to take postgraduate studies there when he was requested to take an interim preaching assignment in eastern Connecticut. During that stint his abilities as an evangelist became evident, and, as this area had been very susceptible to excesses in the Great Awakening, Nettleton used only the most cautious techniques, as he did for the rest of his ministry. He was ordained as an evangelist by the Consociation of Litchfield County in 1817, never took a settled pastorate, and never married.[14]

Nettleton began his evangelistic career by adopting methods reminiscent of the strongly intellectual approach practiced by Jonathan Edwards, and he immediately achieved great success. Conservative in practice, retiring in demeanor, and determined to bring about awakening by involving the local pastor in every aspect, he found himself to be something of a sensation, and in great demand, throughout New England and New York. Lyman Beecher described his preaching:

> The power of his preaching included many things. It was highly intellectual as opposed to declamation, or oratorical, pathetic appeals to imagination or the emotions. It was discriminatingly doctrinal, giving a clear and strong exhibition of doctrines denominated Calvinistic, explained, defined, proved, and applied, and objections stated and answered. . . . But, with all this intellectualization and discriminating argument, there was in some of his sermons unsurpassed power of description, which made the subject a matter of present reality. . . .
>
> But all these would have been comparatively feeble but for the ubiquity and power of his personal attention where exigen-

cies called for it, and the little circles which he met daily, when many were interested, to instruct and guide. . . . To these were added a meeting of inquiry for all who were willing to attend and receive exhortation and personal instruction.[15]

Nettleton had worked out a careful methodology for the creation of the proper sensitivity to spiritual matters in a congregation where he might be working, involving his powerful but sober sermons, a systematic approach to home visitation, personal conferences, and a great deal of follow-up instruction designed to prevent new converts from relapsing. But this seemed, for all its success, to be an obsolete approach, and his tenacious insistence on preaching the doctrine of original sin put him increasingly out of touch with Nathaniel Taylor, Lyman Beecher, and of course Charles Finney. His health broke in 1822, and from that point on he was forced to restrict his efforts. Nonetheless, Lyman Beecher defended him for years, pretending to a unity in theological viewpoint that was not there, in order to present a solid front to the Unitarians and other threats to the traditional New England way. A year after Nettleton went to Albany, on December 18, 1827, Beecher was still busy defending Nettleton:

> Now, that such a man as he, should be traduced, and exposed to all manner of evil falsely, in order to save from deserved reprehension such a man as Finney, (who, whatever talents or piety he may possess, is as far removed from the talent, wisdom and judgment, and experience of Nettleton, as any corporal in the French army was removed from the talent and generalship of Bonaparte,) is what neither my reason, nor my conscience, nor my heart will endure.[16]

The real parting of the ways between Nettleton and Beecher came in 1829, when the former, increasingly alarmed at the theology of Nathaniel Taylor emanating from Yale Divinity School, sided with Bennet Tyler (1783–1858) in his attack on Taylor's address *Concio ad Clerum*. Because Taylor and Beecher were close friends, and the "Tyler-Taylor Controversy" soon became a dominating topic throughout New England, the facade of unity could be maintained no longer. More and more, Beecher drew away from Nettleton after 1829, and when Charles Beecher edited his father's *Autobiography* in 1864 the picture drawn of Nettleton is not very favorable:

He himself [Nettleton] was old and broken, Mr. Finney young and robust. The one was reverential, timid, secretive; the other bold, striking, demonstrative. The style of the one was subdued, that of the other full of éclat. The atmosphere most congenial to Mr. Nettleton was one of hushed, mysterious stillness. . . . Mr. Finney is described by an admirer as "frank, open, giving his opinion without solicitation in a strong style, somewhat dictatorial. He keeps nothing to himself. In this respect he is perfectly at antipodes with Mr. Nettleton. . . ."

It is not probable that any course of measures Mr. Finney could have adopted would have failed to jar more or less painfully on Mr. Nettleton's susceptibilities. Both were originals, both had their eccentricities, but their eccentricities were of opposite kinds. . . . If we might presume to illustrate the difference of the two men in their styles of labor by comparison, we should say that the latter set snares for sinners, the former rode them down in a cavalry charge. The one, being crafty, took them with guile; the other, being violent, took them by force. Yielding to this powerful antagonism . . . it is not strange Mr. Nettleton should come to regard him as sustaining to himself the relation of a [James] Davenport to a Whitefield.[17]

There is much of value in the above comparison, and it is accurate in portraying Nettleton, after his health failed in 1822, as less than vigorous. But Charles Beecher's statement that Nettleton in 1827 or thereabouts was "old and broken" is not literally true. He was only *forty-four*. Many historians, forgetting to check dates, have perpetuated Charles Beecher's picture of a superannuated, crotchety patriarch tottering around and casting maledictions at younger generations. Frail health forced restrictions on him, and certainly his evangelistic practices were becoming antiquated, but old he was not.[18]

When Charles Finney received John Cushman's letter of November 6, 1826, he reacted predictably. "I had had the greatest desire to see him," Finney said, "so much so that I had frequently dreamed of visiting him, and obtaining information from him in regard to the best means of promoting a revival. I felt like sitting at his feet, almost as I would at the feet of an apostle."[19]

Finney concluded his preaching at Utica and returned to the area of Troy and Albany immediately. Calling on Nettleton of an afternoon, Finney found him to be somewhat complaisant and predictably aloof, but apparently in agreement with Finney on doctrinal matters. "I observed that he avoided the subject of promoting revivals," Finney recalled. "When I told him that I intended to remain in Albany, and hear him preach in the evening, he manifested uneasiness, and remarked that I must not be seen with him."[20]

In writing his *Memoirs* in 1868, Finney checked the biography of Nettleton written by Bennet Tyler and found an assertion that at this meeting the New Englander was "hoping that by a free consultation, their views might be brought to harmonize. . . . But in this he was painfully disappointed."[21] This angered Finney, "for certainly he never attempted to do it. As I have said, at that time he could have moulded me at discretion; but he said not a word to me about my manner of conducting revivals, nor did he ever write a word to me upon the subject. He kept me at arm's length."[22]

Tyler's *Memoir of the Life and Character of Rev. Asahel Nettleton, D.D.* put an entirely different cast upon the meeting between the two men, claiming that there were indeed two meetings:

> In the winter of 1826–7, at the earnest request of some of his brethren, he visited Albany, while Mr. Finney was preaching at Troy. He had two interviews with Mr. Finney, hoping . . . that they might co-operate in promoting the interests of Christ's kingdom. But in this he was painfully disappointed. He found that Mr. F. was utterly unwilling to abandon certain measures which he had "ever regarded as exceedingly calamitous to the cause of revivals," and which, of course, he could not sanction. He perceived also that there could be no hope of convincing Mr. F. of his errors, so long as he was upheld and encouraged by ministers of high respectability.[23]

Samuel Aikin also stated that there were two meetings, saying "Mr. Finney had two short interviews with Mr. Nettleton in Albany previous to my receiving his letter in January."[24] Attempting to justify his failure to persuade Finney regarding the new measures, Nettleton explained to Beecher, "You may thing it strange that I did not receive him and run the risk of molding him. But I could not do it without sanctioning all that he had done. . . . Besides, if I should not succeed, it would ruin us both, and if I should have succeeded, the disorganizers would say I had spoiled him."[25]

Seeing the power that Charles Finney was amassing, Asahel Nettleton turned to a writing campaign to frustrate him. First he wrote to Lyman Beecher in Boston on January 2, 1827, pleading with Beecher to intercede directly with Finney, and ending with the expressive appeal, "Dr. Beecher must write to these men. Somebody must speak, and *who*, WHO, I ask, shall do it, if not some one from New England?"[26] Then on January 13, 1827, Nettleton revised and expanded this letter and sent it to Samuel C. Aikin in Utica, and twenty other Presbyterian pastors in New York, fully intending that it should fall into Finney's hands. Aikin gave it to Finney when he visited his wife's parents in nearby Whitesboro. Nettleton began the missive by stating that "there is doubtless a work of grace in Troy. Many sinners have hopefully been born into the kingdom." But that was as much as Nettleton would concede. What good had been done, he went on, was at "an awful expense," considering the schism in Beman's church, and "the names of God used with such irreverence." What is worse, Nettleton stated, "the spirit of denunciation" in the New York revivals has alienated many, and some who have visited there from other areas have returned "soured and denouncing ministers." Nettleton saw this as a great rent in the body ecclesiastic, and he termed it, very accurately, "a civil war in Zion—a domestic broil in the household of faith."[27]

"The evil is running in all directions," Nettleton intoned, and he diagnosed its symptoms as anger, wrath, malice, envy, and evil-speaking, all of these attributable to the intense desire of "the friends of Finney" not so much to convert souls to Christ, as to convert clergy and laity to their peculiarities.[28] And if Christian leaders could not be made to agree with Finney immediately, then it was the practice to "get ministers to agree with him only by 'crushing' or 'breaking them down.'" Pastors subjected to these pressures, and even some of Finney's strongest supporters, expressed great doubts as to his methods, saying, "I have been fairly skinned by the denunciations of these men, and have ceased to oppose them, to get rid of the noise. But I warn you not to introduce this spirit into your church and society." Much of the problem was with the inexperience of Finney and his helpers; they had not had the benefit of years to observe the effects of what they had done. "I heartily pity brother Finney," Nettleton stated, "for I believe him to be a good man, and wishing to do good. But nobody dares tell him that a train of causes is set in operation" that could be nothing but disastrous.[29]

Positively, Nettleton wished to suggest, as the alternative to "disorganization and disorder," the proper method of conducting evangelistic campaigns. To avoid all of Finney's difficulties, settled pastors should "occupy nearly the whole field of operation. They have, and ought to have, the entire management of their own congregations.

. . . No itinerant has any business to interfere or dictate." But the young exhorters now crowding the field "are continually violating the rules of ministerial order, and Christian propriety, in these respects. Impatient to see the temple rise," their clumsy and inexperienced hands are in actuality doing violence to the very thing they claim to be building.[30]

Nettleton could not help but referring, with understandable concern, to the excesses of the Great Awakening, and their "likeness to the present." Gilbert Tennent, James Davenport, John Cross, and a host of others drew opprobrium upon what had been, before their fanatical intrusion, a calm and orderly awakening, and the very same activities were occurring at that time. "The young itinerants, in their zeal to extend the work, began to denounce all those settled ministers who would not go all lengths with them." Sides were immediately taken by the congregations, for the pastors, or for the itinerants, and as soon as this had happened, the Spirit of God retired and the movement foundered over discord and rancor. And all of this would be repeated if Finney did not learn from history, Nettleton inferred.[31]

Thus Nettleton's letter of January 13, 1827, to Samuel Aikin. Having read it as it was intended he should, Charles Finney was predictably infuriated. Perhaps if Nettleton had given him the courtesy of true counsel and concern in their conferences, he might have reacted less strongly. But Nettleton's pretense of friendliness at their Albany meetings, and his evasive way of writing letters to others to accomplish his objectives, rankled Finney. Should he take the trouble to answer Nettleton directly? He decided against it, and maintained the policy he kept all along, of not replying in print to the scurrilous pamphlets that were a stock in trade of that age. Instead he used against Nettleton a mightier weapon, which he wielded with precision—the sermon (which would, of course, appear in print).

On the following Sunday, from Aikin's important Utica pulpit and with his permission, Finney preached one of his most resounding messages, from Amos 3:3, "Can Two Walk Together Except They be Agreed?" Casting aside almost every one of Nettleton's bothersome allegations, Finney went to what he discerned as the heart of the matter: sincerity, which must be manifested in affections, or emotions. The sermon, which was immediately published, began:

> For two to be agreed, implies something more than to be agreed
> in *theory,* or understanding. . . . We have reason to believe that holy
> angels and devils apprehend and embrace *intellectually* the same

truths, and yet how very differently they are affected by them. ... The difference in the effect consists [in] the heart or affections ... truths to which the experience of every man will testify ... founded upon principles incorporated within the very nature of man.[32]

Believing that the essence of the disagreement between him and Nettleton lay in their different approaches to sincerity, Finney went on to explain his reasons for withstanding "cold ministers." To him, a person who is spiritually awakened must be "grieved and distressed" by "heartless, unmeaning" preaching that does not appeal to the perilous state of the unsaved. And any true preacher of God's grace would have "great heaviness and continual sorrow" of heart for "unfeeling" sermons. Yet on the other hand, persons differing on doctrinal points or belonging to separate denominations "will often walk together in great harmony and affection, because they *feel deeply* and feel *alike*. ... They walk together while in heart they are agreed."[33]

Finney proceeded to describe the effect of increased "feeling" in an awakening, placing the fault for controversy on those who resisted "spiritual affections," or religious emotions:

Again—We see why young converts love to associate with *each other;* and with those older saints who have most religious *feeling;* these walk together because *they feel alike.*

Again—We see why lukewarm professors and impenitent sinners have *the same* difficulties with *means* in revivals of religion. We often hear them complain of the *manner* of preaching and praying. . . . It is the fire and spirit that disturbs their frosty hearts.

Again—We see why ministers and Christians visiting revivals, often, at first, raise objections to the means used, and cavil, and sometimes take sides with the wicked. The fact is . . . the praying, preaching, and conversation, are above their present temperature. . . . Now, while their *hearts remain wrong,* they will, of course, cavil, and the nearer right any thinking is, the more spiritual and holy, so much the more it *must* displease them, while their affections grovel.

Again—We see why lukewarm Christians and sinners are not disturbed by dull preaching or praying. It does not take hold of their feelings at all, and therefore does not distress or offend them.

Again—We learn why churches are sometimes convulsed by revivals. . . . For as those who are awake become more engaged, more spiritual and active, the others, if they *will not awake*, will be jealous and offended, and feeling rebuked by the engagedness of others, will cavil, and find themselves the more displeased, as those that are more spiritual rise above them.[34]

Finney insisted that "wrong feeling in wrong hearts" is the expected effect of awakenings that automatically divide all people, including church congregations, into two groups, those who receive the Holy Spirit's grace, and those who reject it. "Whenever the Holy Spirit comes," Finney pointed out, "the opposite spirit is disturbed of course."[35] He claimed that his exhortations had one overriding objective: to show the sinner "that he hates God and His truth." In the process, he thought it only "natural" that as his preaching increased in "spirit" (in other words, as it became more imbued with religious power) opposition would increase:

> Hence it appears, that *other things being equal*, those means, and that preaching, both as *matter* and *manner*, which call forth most of the native enmity of the heart, and that are most directly over against wrong hearts, are nearest right.[36]

To anyone familiar with the writings of Jonathan Edwards, it is apparent that Charles Finney was invoking the authority of that work which he had recently perused in Samuel Aikin's home, *A Treatise Concerning Religious Affections*, and which had given him new conviction and confidence. No higher authority except scripture itself would have more telling effect to silence Nettleton, who of course professed to be a faithful Edwardean. How fascinating to note that in his letter to Aikin, printed and reprinted, Nettleton also appealed to the spirit of Edwards—to defend his own position!

Who, then, was interpreting Jonathan Edwards correctly?

In actuality, both men were somewhat faithful to Edwards' intentions in *Religious Affections*. But Edwards was more subtle than either Finney or Nettleton. In a distinction that Jonathan Dickinson, first president of Princeton, had first made in *The Witness of the Spirit* in 1740, it was carefully specified that those moved by God's Spirit, and not by mere enthusiasm, will have the Spirit's graces in abundance. There will be a readiness to follow Christian things, to adhere to the Bible, be full of joy, to mortify lusts, and be truly humble and zealous for the glory of God. But those who are deluded, pretending to have this extraordinary witness of the Spirit, are not humble and gracious, mortifying the lusts of the flesh, but are rather proud and conceited, thinking themselves possessed of some special qualities that have made them worthy recipients of God's immediate revelation, which is in reality only enthusiasm. This was a clear and easily applicable distinction, which, if followed widely, would have rescued both the First Great Awakening and the Second from much disillusionment, putting lay people on their guard, warning them not to confuse an enthusiast's rhapsodic allegiance to fancies of subjective origin without a shred of objective evidence, with true possessors of divine grace whose lives were permanently changed.[37]

Jonathan Dickinson's *Witness of the Spirit* went through three printings, in 1740 and twice in 1743, and it is almost certain that Edwards knew the work, because the themes and conclusions are so similar. In 1746 Edwards had put out his own *Religious Affections* [read "emotions"], saying:

> The Author of our nature has not only given us affections, but has made them very much the spring of actions. As the affections not only necessarily belong to the human nature, but are a very great part of it; so . . . holy affections not only necessarily belong to true religion, but are a very great part of such religion. And as true religion is practical, and God hath so constituted the human nature, that the affections are very much the spring of men's actions, this also shews, that true religion must consist very much in the affections.[38]

Here Charles Finney found his arguments against Nettleton, in the first tenth of Edwards' work, and embodied them in "Can Two Walk Together. . . ." To Finney, Nettleton was far from the spirit of Edwards, for he knew nothing of this central truth of religion, with his fear and prohibition of any emotion whatsoever among the congregations in his revivals. For Charles Finney, Nettleton epitomized the warning of Jonathan Edwards:

> We may hence learn how great their error is, who are for discarding all religious affections, as having nothing solid or substantial in them. There seems to be too much of a disposition this way prevailing at this time. Because many who, in the late extraordinary season, appeared to have great religious affections . . . and run into many errors . . . hence religious affections in general are

grown out of credit with great numbers, as though true religion did not at all consist in them. Thus we easily and naturally run from one extreme to another. . . . But of late, instead of esteeming and admiring all religious affections, without distinction, it is much more prevalent to reject and discard all without distinction. Herein appears the subtilty of Satan. . . .

This manner of slighting all religious affections, is the way exceedingly to harden the hearts of men, to encourage them in their stupidity and senselessness, to keep them in a state of spiritual death as long as they live, and bring them at last to death eternal. . . . And let it be considered, that they who have but little religious affection, have certainly but little religion.[39]

So Finney drew his arguments from the *first* part of Edwards' book. But Asahel Nettleton took his position from the remainder of it, for the great theologian of New England had not stopped with a wholesale acceptance of all emotions, as Finney suggested. Rather, Edwards had gone on to a careful delineation of dispositions and attributes that all could have, as against those that only the Holy Spirit would implant, following Jonathan Dickinson's leading. Said Edwards:

On the other hand, it must be observed, that a natural [unregenerate] man may have religious apprehensions and affections, which may be, in many respects, very new and surprising to him; and yet what he experiences, be nothing like the exercises of a new nature. . . .

Gracious affections arise from those operations and influences which are spiritual, and that the inward principle from whence they flow, is something divine, a communication of God, a participation of the divine nature, Christ living in the heart, the Holy Spirit dwelling there, in union with the faculties of the soul, as an internal vital principle, exerting his own proper nature in the exercise of those faculties. . . . Indeed the power of godliness is exerted in the first place within the soul; in the sensible, lively exercise of gracious affections there. Yet the principle *evidence* of this power is in those exercises of holy affections that are practical; conquering the will, the lusts, and corruptions of men, and carrying them on in the way of holiness, through all temptation, difficulty, and opposition.[40]

Edwards was holding to the old Puritan concept that one's regenerate state is best demonstrated by one's "fruits," or, in other words, by the Christian striving throughout life, so that by good works, salvation might become evident or certain. Therefore, Edwards was saying, both those who paraded only "feelings" as the badge of their regeneration, and those who "content themselves without clear and sure evidences of their sanctification and adoption," were equally devoid of salvation.

Thus Jonathan Edwards on the place of emotion in religion—a carefully balanced, precise set of definitions that were meant, as far as is possible with such entities, to be empirically applied, and would serve as a greatly needed curb on those who thought that emotions run amuck proved their religious authenticity. Edwards had done his best to arrive at a mean between the age-old extremes represented by Finney and Nettleton, to set forth the arguments against cold formality in religion, and yet to point out as powerfully as possible that many emotions are deceitful and misleading, and that quiet and peaceable good works were the real proof of one's salvation by faith.

It must be judged that on the whole, Nettleton was by far the better interpreter of Jonathan Edwards. If Charles Finney claimed to derive his arguments from Edwards' *Religious Affections*, the question can be legitimately asked, Had Finney read beyond the first thirty pages? Inasmuch as it is only in that initial part that Edwards defended the emotions, and then went on for another two hundred fifty pages to state the cautions that Finney never mentioned in "Can Two Walk Together" or anywhere else, it seems beyond doubt that Finney skimmed the book, took from it what he agreed with, cast the remainder aside—and then claimed to be following Edwards!

On the other hand, Asahel Nettleton was violating no specific injunction of Edwards. Although his conservative and cautious techniques in evangelism played down the emotions, he did not deny them. In a sense, by encouraging in his meetings a hushed, mysterious stillness, Nettleton was shifting attention from the demonstrative, outward manifestations and "feelings," which could be easily mimicked, to the very things that Edwards put far above them, the "special and peculiar influences of the Spirit." Nettleton was very discriminating, and this was exactly what Edwards had encouraged. A remove of many years had made Edwards the ultimate authority in these matters, and it has often been assumed, because of his "Sinners in the Hands of an Angry God," that he brought as much dramatic showmanship and denunciation into the pulpit as Charles Finney did. Not so. Eyewitnesses to Edwards' homiletics testified to his holding up one small scrap of notes after another, delivered without vehemence. "'Mr. Edwards in preaching,' remembered one of the townsfolk, 'used no gestures, but looked straight forward'; Gideon Clark said 'he looked on the bell rope until he looked it off.'"[41] Thus, if Charles Finney had traveled back in time to witness Edwards preach, there is the distinct possibility that for his average performance Edwards would have been labeled by Finney as another "cold minister."

Perceiving the epistemological difficulties in Finney's sermon, Nettleton determined to answer it upon Edwardean ground. Using his tactic of writing letters, he shot off to Gardiner Spring, pastor of the Brick Presbyterian Church in New York City, the following rebuttal to Finney, which was soon published in the *New York Observer* and then in pamphlet form:

> The sermon in question entirely overlooks the nature of true religion. It says not one word by which we can distinguish between true and false zeal, true and false religion. If the tone of feeling can only be raised to a certain pitch, then all is well. The self-righteous, the hypocrite, and all who are inflated with pride, will certainly be flattered and pleased with such an exhibition; especially if they are very self-righteous and very proud. False affections often rise far higher than those that are genuine; and this very preacher, in seasons of revival, has had occasion to observe and correct.[42]

Nettleton continued in a similar vein for several pages, adducing the same arguments that Edwards had previously used. The letter was warmly supported by Lyman Beecher, Heman Humphrey, president of Amherst College, and other prominent New Englanders. James Richards, professor of divinity at Auburn Theological Seminary, who had opposed Finney previously, wrote to Nettleton, "Your review of Finney's sermon has gone to the very core of the business, and will surely be effective in dissipating much of the illusion which is connected with these mournful innovations."[43]

Shortly after this, in January 1827, the trial of Nathaniel Beman before the Presbytery of Albany began. Joseph Brockway and the other dissidents urged the rightness of their views before Beman's peers, but because part of their complaint was against Beman's wife, and the rest of the charges were so broad and all-encompassing, the presbytery came to the conclusion that, although there may have been some substance to the charges, there was also fault on the part of the plaintiffs, who seemed to be malcontents. Therefore the presbytery exonerated Beman,

and the plaintiffs immediately announced their intention of appeal-
ing to the next higher court, the Synod of Albany, which would meet
in October 1827.

Having preached "Can Two Walk Together Except They be
Agreed?" from Samuel Aikin's pulpit in Utica, Finney proceeded to
give the same message in several other towns, and returned to Beman's
pulpit in Troy to deliver it on March 4, 1827.[44] His correspondence indicates that he conducted the revival in Nathaniel Beman's church
until approximately April 20, 1827, in an on-again, off-again fashion
with several breaks where he preached in other cities and left the
preaching in Troy to members of the "Holy Band." Horatio Foote's aggressive preaching has already been noted, and, after another absence,
Finney returned to find that Augustus Littlejohn had created more
mischief in Troy. According to the vitriolic Ephraim Perkins, whose
word must be taken with great caution:

> After the evening was spent, there having been no fainting, fall-
> ing, or crying aloud for mercy . . . Littlejohn said, "Can't we roll
> the wheels a little harder?" These were his very words. He then
> raised his voice to the highest pitch, threw himself forward from
> his knees to the floor, and pounded, torturing himself in extreme
> agony, sometimes groaning and sighing—ostentatiously for poor
> sinners. "You don't pray here tonight—you don't agonize—you don't
> groan—you han't got into the harness—you must wrestle harder
> with Jacob's God!"[45]

Could it have been that, after hearing of such antics from Foote
and Littlejohn, Finney pondered again the solemn and weighty warnings of Jonathan Edwards, and the angry charges of Asahel Nettleton?

A graver problem than Littlejohn's idiocies appeared in late
January 1827 when Lyman Beecher himself entered the literary fray.
Beecher (1775–1863), "father of more brains than any man in America,"
was a pupil of President Timothy Dwight of Yale, and became Dwight's
lieutenant in the effort to bring revivals to New England, and to maintain an established, tax-supported church system throughout the region. When Dwight died, Beecher inherited the leadership of the campaign, and immediately broadened it to include an amazing number
of enterprises. A founder of the American Education Society and the
American Bible and Tract societies, he endlessly promoted home and
foreign missions, almost single-handedly began the temperance movement in New England, and was a major figure in the crusades against

Sabbath-breaking, deism, dueling, theater-going, profanity, and other causes of the day. Incredibly energetic, Beecher had a penchant for leadership, publicity, and popular oratory which he used for over forty years, from the early years of the nineteenth century until well into the 1840s, to keep himself on center stage in American life as the most prominent pastor in the nation, and the one to whom many turned for expressions of ecclesiastical opinion whenever relevant issues arose. A superb organizer, Beecher managed to keep in contact with a multitude of important people, and to use them for his purposes whenever occasion demanded.

For years Beecher had been fighting the radically liberal Unitarianism that had quietly been growing within the New England churches, and he early learned, from his mentor Dwight, that the best offense against this threat lay in revivals that would bring into trinitarian churches far more new members than the Unitarians could match. In 1826 he left his church in Litchfield, Connecticut, and moved into the heartland of Unitarianism, Boston, becoming pastor of the Hanover Street Congregational church. There he hoped to continue the career as revivalist that he had pursued at Litchfield, embodying in himself the concept that most distinguishes the evangelical resurgence of the next half-century, what Sydney Ahlstrom has called "the intimate association of evangelism in its broadest sense with moral reform and social benevolence."[46]

Theologically, Beecher had been drifting for some time from Hopkinsianism. He formed a very close friendship with the Yale theologian Nathaniel W. Taylor, which lasted for many years, and he and the Yale divines created the New Haven Theology, or New Divinity, which attempted to increase the effectiveness of orthodoxy's appeal by modifying its methodology and some of the harsher aspects of Calvinism, especially original sin and the impotence of the human will. Beecher was the first to get into trouble on this score; in 1823 he published a sermon entitled "The Faith Once Delivered to the Saints," in which he stated that "men are free agents, in the possession of such faculties, and placed in such circumstances as render it practicable for them to do whatever God requires." He was at once assailed by many Old Calvinists and Edwardeans for what was taken to be a departure from the doctrine of predestination. But Beecher, always the adroit sophist, sidestepped the charge and declared that he could reconcile his views with Calvin and the Bible, and that he was at all points orthodox, even if he did not always agree with Hopkinsianism or other stances.

Asahel Nettleton (1783–1844), about 1825. Several years prior to this Nettleton had contracted typhus fever, and he never fully regained his health. When he heard that Charles Finney was superseding him as an evangelist, and in addition using questionable "new measures," his anger knew no bounds. Attributed to Samuel Lovett Waldo and William Jewett. Courtesy of the Connecticut Historical Society. Gift of Adelbert H. Stevens.

Asahel Nettleton supported Beecher in these attacks against the 1823 sermon, writing to him at that time, "I believe it to be a matter of fact that you and I are *really* a different kind of Calvinists" from the Edwardeans and Old Calvinists, and "that we do preach moral obligation and dependence different from many of our old divines—that in some things the Calvinism of Connecticut or New England has undergone an important change."[47] As an evangelist, Nettleton had naturally been tempted to assert to his congregations some measure of free will, to overcome the paralysis induced by strict predestination, and to assist people in making the decisions he so much sought.

Beecher's obsession with unity was in the interest of a master plan he held dear, that of "the great evangelical assimilation which is forming in the United States." In his mind it had begun with the Plan of Union, bringing together the Congregationalists and the Presbyterians. Although he affirmed the legitimacy of denominationalism, Beecher hoped that all evangelical Protestants could join together in some way, perhaps in interdenominational voluntary associations.[48] To this exalted end he felt that other benevolent causes and programs were subservient, and that it was a goal worthy of the expenditure of his total energies. This gradual combining of the Christian forces in the nation might take some years, but it seemed to his mind that tendencies were moving toward it, and that he might serve as the grand architect of union by the dextrous manipulation of factors and agents. Compromise was, therefore, essential, and it took all of Beecher's great skill to bring leaders of diverse groups together in New England against the common foe, Unitarianism, which was the first step in the master plan.

In attempting to find common ground on which Old Calvinists, Arminians, Edwardeans, Hopkinsians, Taylorites, and all others could somehow agree and join together in furthering revivals, Beecher had managed in New England to piece together a shaky alliance whose only real common tie was a dislike of Unitarianism. Often some of these parties expressed disagreement with the New Divinity that Beecher supported, but a combination of his pacifying efforts and the assumption of co-leadership by Nettleton, recognized leader of the conservative New England revival tradition, served to keep all members within the alliance. There were frequent rumblings of discontent, but overall the parties showed a willingness to overlook differences, at least for the duration of the danger, at the same time that they warned they would withdraw from the coalition if the new practices went too far.[49]

In his grand strategy for orderly and productive revivals, Beecher believed that one frenzied episode of the James Davenport or Cane Ridge type would throw the cause of evangelical assimilation back to a bygone time. And such a threat, in his estimation, had recently materialized: Charles Finney and his followers. Beecher knew of Finney and his methods only by hearsay, mostly from Asahel Nettleton, and at this point he was still persuaded by all he heard. So, in January 1827 Beecher wrote to Nathaniel Beman, charging:

> We are on the confines of universal misrule and moral desolation, and no time is to be lost in forestalling and holding public sentiment correctly, before the mass shall be put in motion by fierce winds before which nothing can stand, and behind which, when they have swept over the land nothing will remain.[50]

As with Nettleton's letter to Samuel Aikin, so Beecher's to Beman was of course intended for Finney to see. Were such harbingers of chaos as Finney and the new measures revivalists who followed him to succeed, said Beecher, "it would be the greatest calamity that could befall this young empire." Working from this hypothesis, Beecher declared that Finney's brand of revivalism was most dangerous, because it was not based on decorum, as in New England, but tended toward uncontrolled emotionalism, as well as being opposed to well-educated clergymen. A master of stinging rhetoric, Beecher flung the charge that Finney's revivals would lead to "barbarism," reminiscent of the collapse of the Roman empire. According to Beecher, Finney's techniques attacked three pillars of society—"popular taste," learning, and an educated ministry. When these three are debased or destroyed, he declared, it would be similar to the time when the Teutons swept down on the Romans and violated every civilized custom and decency that existed. In the same way, denunciatory revivals "would stop all our improvements, and throw us back in civilization, science, and religion, at least a whole century." Then, gathering his oratorical powers for one mighty thrust, Beecher strained all credulity by declaring, "it would constitute an era of calamity never to be forgotten, and be referred to by future historians as the dark age of our republic."[51] Giving almost a visible shudder, Beecher cast a horrified glance at Kentucky and the Cane Ridge fanaticisms:

> There are parts of our nation to which I might refer you, which were burnt over by such revivals some 20 years ago, where the

abiding evils may still be seen in the state of society which has followed. And there too, with all their extravagances of falling, and groaning, and laughing, and jumping, and dancing, were regarded by many, by some very good men, as a new dispensation of the Spirit,—a new mode of conducting revivals with power; and those who rode on the foremost waves, thought themselves to be reformers.[52]

Another area of Beecher's concern was that of women praying in public. This practice had become, in the communicating of it, so exaggerated by the time it reached Beecher's ears in Boston that it was not simply a violation of St. Paul, but an outrage against public decency and a scourge to morality. Indeed, Beecher practically omitted the biblical aspects of the issue, and concentrated instead on a psychological theorizing, which must bring at least a smile today: there is generally "in female character, a softness and delicacy of feelings which shrinks from the notoriety of public performance." This guards female virtue, and is "invaluable in its soothing, civilizing influence on man." A greater evil could not befall womanhood, or the very nation, than "to disrobe the female mind of those ornaments of sensibility, and clothe it with the rough texture of masculine fiber."[53] But when ladies are allowed to speak and pray publicly, Beecher insisted, their femininity is ruthlessly violated, and they will in time inevitably become coarse.

Then, changing his tone entirely, Beecher showed his remarkable ability to straddle a fence and be conciliatory. It was not Finney's theology that was so objectionable, he stated; rather, it was the new measures that threatened the order of the churches, because they were the wrong measures. Having excoriated Charles Finney in the earlier part of the letter to Beman, Beecher now turned about completely and held out an olive branch:

> I would not, brethren, on any account, deter you from the propagation of revivals; and I believe if Brother F. will take counsel, he may be an invaluable blessing. The thing which I have wished to accomplish is, to enable you so to perceive the defects and dangers of your mode of conducting revivals, as that you shall be induced to part with its unseemly warts and excrescences, without diminishing at all the energy and warmth of the healthful pulsation of their hearts, or abating the moral courage or humble boldness with which you pray and preach, or the directness and power with which you address the consciences of men.[54]

The campaign of letters continued. Beecher, feeling that with his power and leverage he could still swing Finney around to his ways and thus gain an ally, wrote later to the *New York Observer* saying he had no doubt that there might be some good coming from the new measures. Beecher did not want to limit Finney's usefulness to the kingdom of God, but he did feel that Finney must abandon his peculiarities if he wished to be received by his fellow evangelists.[55]

Then, shortly after the letter to Nathaniel Beman, Lyman Beecher apparently felt that still more explanation was needed, and he sent off another letter, this time to John Frost. Referring to his letter to Nathaniel Beman, he wrote, "My object in that letter, was to justify them against . . . the haters of revivals of religion, and to suggest emendations . . . yet without checking the ardor, and boldness, and moral momentum with which I did not doubt Brother Finney was moving on." Nonetheless, Beecher's support was not without its conditions, as he made clear; "*This, however, makes it necessary that Brother Finney should come upon ground on which we can sustain him, for we can not justify his faults for the sake of his excellencies.*"[56]

Beecher sent a copy of this letter to Nathaniel Beman to Nettleton, with this note:

> There must be immediately an extensive correspondence and concert formed. Ministers must come together and consult, and churches must be instructed and prepared to resist evil. The mask must be taken off from Satan coming among the Sons of God, and transforming himself into an angel of light. . . . Should all these measures fail, then we *must* publish, your letter to Aiken must be published and mine to Beman if it is thought best. . . . Brother Finney and Beman [must be] kept within their orbit.[57]

Nettleton, who had collaborated with Lyman Beecher for years, knew that like any politician, Beecher was most adept at working both sides of the fence. Here Beecher was at it again: in his letter to Beman he offered, if Finney met the conditions, to "sustain him," yet in his note to Nettleton he suggested no conciliation, for Finney was "Satan," and "we *must* publish"! Nettleton, confused, was appalled at Beecher's willingness to compromise with Finney, and his vacillation between threats and acceptance. Piqued by Beecher's politics and ambiguities, and emboldened by Beecher's own suggestion of publishing, Nettleton furnished an extract of the letter to the moderator of the Troy Presbytery, which was about to try Beman. The moderator, in turn, passed it on to a friend, and then Nettleton found, to his shock, that it was presented to the public by Dolphus Skinner in his *Utica Evangelical Magazine,* a Universalist publication!

When Beecher heard of this, his fury knew no bounds. His letter to Beman appearing in—of all things—a Universalist paper was "as if a man should throw a firebrand on a train of powder which another was attempting to guard against ignition."[58] He heard nothing suppliant from Finney or Beman, but he received angry complaints from "every direction." Moses Gillet of Rome wrote, with no trace of respect for Beecher, "Had it come from an obscure minister, I should have set him down as an enemy of revivals. . . . What I lament is that it strengthens the hands of opposers;—published in the first number of a Universalist paper at Utica!"[59]. Beecher responded by howling, at the same time, his wrath and his own innocence in the matter. The letter's publication was "an outrageous violation of authorized confidence for which neither Brother Nettleton nor myself are accountable."[60] Nettleton whimpered to Beecher, as if he were completely without blame, "I regret the surreptitious publication of that letter of yours to me."[61] Yet surely, with such a crude method of circulating ideas and wishes as letters handed about from person to person, something of the sort was to be expected, and should have surprised no one.

But worse was to come for the beleaguered Beecher. Imagine his mental state when, in May of 1827, he found that a Unitarian paper, *The Christian Examiner and Theological Review* of Boston, expressed some agreement with him. One of Beecher's admonitions it could adopt, the paper said, although he had expressed the matter too strongly, and it "betrays something too much like a panic, viz., 'We are on the confines of universal misrule and moral desolation.'"[62]

Lyman Beecher's discomfort was heightened because the reconciliation with Charles Finney that he had hoped to accomplish seemed as far away as ever. He, as the most famous Congregational clergyman of the day, was clearly miffed that neither Finney nor Beman had bothered to answer his letters, privately or, if it must be, in print. "I did expect, that Brother Beman or Brother Finney would have written to me, and that the correspondence would have softened down into mutual explanation," he complained.[63] A bit later, his annoyance turning to anger, Beecher was on the verge of charging that the new measures men were not even gentlemen: "I am certain, for I have tried it for more than one whole year thoroughly, as my correspondence will show, if called for, that no kindness and magnanimity on our part will be appreciated."[64]

By April, events began to move more quickly. For one, during the winter a revival had started in the town of New Lebanon, a few miles west of the Massachusetts border on the Albany-Pittsfield turnpike. The Congregational pastor, Silas Churchill, has secured the assistance of Father Nash, and the two wrote to Charles Finney on March 8, 1827, asking for his presence there, informing him that eighty converts had already come into the church. In Troy, thirty miles distant, things had been going well. With Nathaniel Beman's trial before the presbytery decided in his favor in January, he turned his full attention to Charles Finney's preaching and the revival in his church, which was gradually concluding. On April 6 Silas Churchill wrote another letter to Finney, more urgent than the first, and the evangelist transferred his labors to the Presbygational church in New Lebanon about the third week of April, remaining there until the end of May.

By this point many were weary of the constant exchange and publication of letters between the two factions, and hoped that a breakthrough was near. Some signs pointed to that, and no one anticipated the crippling blow to the cause of accommodation that would come on May 11, when William Weeks dispatched his *Pastoral Letter of the Oneida Association on the Subject of Revivals.* After all the speculation and rumors that had been circulating for months, the close relationship between Weeks and Asahel Nettleton was well known. Thus it was immediately felt that Weeks, who had been supplying Nettleton with his "information" about the new measures and Finney, was backed by Nettleton in putting out the vitriolic *Pastoral Letter.* George Gale was especially exasperated; "One man is chiefly at the bottom of all the trouble that has been made," he wrote to Finney: "the hand of Brother Nettleton is in this thing, and the same is true of the explosion made in Troy."[65] Nathaniel Beman felt that this *Pastoral Letter* was the last salvo that could be tolerated in the literary battle. He begged Finney to lend his support to a coordinated counterattack, a barrage of pamphlets, letters, and books directed against Nettleton and Weeks, especially capitalizing on the widening rift between Beecher and Nettleton. "If Dr. Beecher does not ultimately forsake him, I shall be much disappointed," Beman declared.[66]

Another tack—the possibility of a meeting between Beecher and Finney—was at this time being explored. Two merchants of Utica, Milton Brayton and James Whipple, friends of Finney, had journeyed to Boston, listened to Beecher speak, and later conferred with him, writing on May 18 that he preached with an ardor not unlike Finney's. No definite plans for a meeting were made, but they reported back to Finney that Beecher was certainly open to such an interview.[67] Then, in the first week of June, an attempt was made by the new measures faction to bring about a meeting of Nettleton with Finney, and they gained the backing of two of Nettleton's chief supporters, Edward Griffin and David Porter. Nettleton himself then hesitantly agreed. Joel F. Benedict, a pastor from Norwich, New York, and one who anxiously wished the controversy to cease, went to Nettleton, and began to make preparations for a gathering of the major figures. All seemed hopeful for some type of settlement of the acrimonious debate, when suddenly Asahel Nettleton declared his unwillingness to participate. Joel Benedict wrote to Finney on July 5, 1827:

> I was much pleased to learn that you were willing to meet any number of your brethren & have a full disclosure of all the circumstances of the case. . . . You have doubtless heard that Dr. Porter and Mr. Nettleton were decidedly opposed to calling a meeting of ministers as was proposed. To me their conduct is most mysterious; as but a few days before they manifested their most cordial approbation of such a meeting and were agreed on the men, time and place.[68]

Disgusted with Asahel Nettleton's tactics, Nathaniel Beman determined that the New Englander might continue in this obdurate way for some time unless something was done. Beman was feeling triumphant; the appeal of his trial before the Synod of Albany had been found in his favor, and, flushed with victory, he traveled to Boston and met with Lyman Beecher, explaining all the circumstances. Characteristically eager for compromise, Beecher agreed that a meeting must be held immediately, despite Nettleton's opposition. This obviously put Nettleton in a very bad position, for the meeting would be held with or without him, and if he refused to attend, he would appear to be a defiant obstructionist and would lose most of his clerical support.

Beecher and Beman set the time for the assembly as Wednesday, July 18, 1827, at ten in the morning, and agreed that a mutually convenient place for the delegates was the town of New Lebanon, where Finney had been preaching.[69] Each agreed to invite up to a dozen participants to take part in the discussions. Ecstatic, Beman immediately wrote to Charles Finney, "My dear Brother, . . . You have heard from

Brothers Lansing and Frost what I have been doing in the Nettletonian war, and I trust you will attend the contemplated meeting. . . . You must come."[70]

Until this time, Finney had enjoyed almost unparalleled success, and his path had been strewn with few obstacles. Now he was confronted by two of the most powerful figures in American religion, and they seemed intent on smashing him down as a pretentious interloper. Finney was forced to contemplate the possible end of his career!

7

NEW LEBANON AND ITS AFTERMATH

In his *Memoirs*, Charles Finney put a serene and tranquil design upon his own approach to the New Lebanon Convention. Writing forty years later, he could look back with equanimity, as if condescending to attend. In reality, as still a relatively young man and a neophyte to revivalism, confronted by the giants of the day, he must have approached the meetings with some apprehension. Finney's interior dynamics—resolute determination and utter self-confidence—were put to their severest tests in that village.

By mid-morning on Wednesday, July 18, 1827, the town of New Lebanon was hot. Dignified clergymen had been alighting from carriages for some time, gathering in small circles to confer, or making their way inside Dr. Betts' residence. It was apparent to the perceptive onlooker that there were actually two groups of ministers coming here, for each clergyman was quite cordial with some who seemed to be good acquaintances, and took a different, more reserved attitude toward others to whom he was introduced. Finally, when the clock on the church steeple chimed ten, those remaining outside, chatting in little knots, nodded and proceeded inside the home.

In the large parlor, a plain-looking, enormously energetic little man, Dr. Lyman Beecher, clapped his hands to get attention and asked if each one would be seated so that the meeting could get underway. He then introduced the members of the convention from the East, New England, whom he had brought with him: Heman Humphrey, president of Amherst College, subsequently chosen as moderator; Asahel Nettleton, evangelist from Connecticut; Justin Edwards, of Andover, Massachusetts; Caleb J. Tenney, of Wethersfield, Connecticut; and Joel Hawes, of Hartford. Then Beecher indicated that he had also invited, as members of his party, Henry Weed, of Albany, New York; Asahel Norton, of Clinton, New York; and William R. Weeks, of Paris Hill, New York.

That formality over, Beecher then turned to a taller, younger, and strikingly handsome man, Charles Finney, and asked if he would introduce the rest of the men. Finney smiled as Beecher seated himself, and followed the same procedure with the men from the West: Nathaniel S. S. Beman, of Troy; Moses Gillet, of Rome; Dirck Lansing, of Auburn; John Frost, of Whitesboro; Henry Smith, of Camden, New York; and the host pastor, Silas Churchill. Then Finney said that he was expecting two others who should arrive at any time, George W. Gale of Western; and Samuel C. Aikin, of Utica.[1]

In their remarks and demeanor, both Beecher and Finney attempted to project an air of dignified reserve, confidence, and, at the same time, cordiality. Despite their best attempt, however, there was tension in the atmosphere, and frequent furtive glances among the men, which indicated the uncertainty under which they labored concerning the direction in which the meetings might go. Fortunately the large room still preserved the coolness from the previous night, but during the afternoon session heat would build up, making the sessions stuffy and uncomfortable, and adding to the tension.

Was Finney on trial? Technically, no. This conference of important leaders had been called to decide only issues in which he was involved. In addition, the randomly selected clergymen had no specific authority, and the informal meetings had been given no delegated powers by duly constituted denominational agencies. So, at best this was a representative forum for the airing of grievances, very much on the "town meeting" model of New England.

G. F. Wright says, "This was not in any sense an ecclesiastical court . . . [Finney] was not in any sense on trial. It was the measures which he and his coadjutors were employing which were on trial."[2] Nonetheless, it can hardly be denied that the man would rise or fall with the measures; if they were to be condemned by ranking clergy, Finney's career might suffer irreparable harm, and it would inexorably work to his discredit. After all, if this informal assembly found against the new measures, that could well signal Finney's many enemies that the time was ripe, and sufficient support could be found, to proceed to formal church court proceedings. Much was on the line, and everyone knew it.

Most of Wednesday, July 18, was taken up with preliminaries. Devotions were conducted, and Heman Humphrey was nominated for moderator, and elected. The proceedings were interrupted by the midday "dinner," and when business began again George W. Gale arrived, was introduced, and the meeting proceeded. It was agreed that they would adjourn each day before seven P.M., and then go to the supper that was prepared and waiting for them.[3]

It was mid-afternoon before the specific matters under consideration could be discussed. Two resolutions were introduced by the New Englanders, the first a formality stating the need for each of the members to spend time in prayer both publicly and privately during the coming week (which was passed immediately), and the second an attempt to frame the purpose of the convention. It stated that the object was "to see in what respects there is an agreement between brethren from different sections of the country, in regard to principles and measures in conducting and promoting revivals of religion."[4] This encompassed a number of concerns, and so the members for the first time put aside the introductory matters that had occupied them, and turned to the reason for which they had come. An hour, then two, went by, and Dr. Humphrey announced that the discussion would have to be suspended until the next morning, because it was approaching seven o'clock.

On Thursday morning Samuel C. Aikin arrived and was introduced around. The meeting was called to order, and the suspended discussion began again. When the question was called for, the resolution was passed by a vote of fourteen yeas, one nay, and two abstentions. John Frost then put forth a declining resolution, seconded by Samuel Aikin, in which he stated that he "understood the object of the meeting to be, to correct misapprehensions, and restore peace among brethren."

Dr. Humphrey then recognized Justin Edwards, who proposed a series of formal resolutions that might be issued to the churches and reading public at the conclusion of the meetings. They dealt with general concerns of evangelism and revivals, on which all these members of the Congregational-Presbyterian union were in agreement. There was unanimous assent to the resolutions. They included the following:

That revivals of true religion are the work of God's Spirit, by which, in a comparatively short period of time, many persons are convinced of sin, and brought to the exercise of repentance towards God, and faith in our Lord Jesus Christ. . . .

There may be some variety in the mode of conducting revivals, according to local customs, and there may be relative imperfections attending them, which do not destroy the purity of the work, and its permanent and general good influence upon the church and the world; and, in such cases, good men, while they lament these imperfections, may rejoice in the revival as the work of God.

There may be so much human infirmity, and indiscretion, and wickedness of man, in conducting a revival of religion, as to render the general evils which flow from this infirmity, indiscretion, and wickedness of man, greater than the local and temporary advantages of the revival: that is, this infirmity, indiscretion, and wickedness of man, may be the means of preventing the conversion of more souls than may have been converted during the revival.

In view of these considerations, we regard it eminently important, that there should be a general understanding among ministers and churches, in respect to those things which are of a dangerous tendency, and not to be countenanced.[5]

In light of the unanimous assent to each of these resolutions, it may be thought that the participants were not in such disagreement as had been thought. But a careful examination of the resolutions shows them to be of a rather general nature, and not specifically calculated to be a censure of Finney (with one or two possible exceptions), so that all the convention members could begin by agreeing on broad principles.

That done, Heman Humphrey recognized Justin Edwards, who proceeded to be more specific about "things which are of a dangerous tendency." He introduced the motion, "In social meetings, of men and women, for religious worship, females are not to pray."[6] Suddenly, amiability and broad agreement vanished. Animated debate flashed back and forth, with Humphrey at times having difficulty keeping order. In New England, for women to speak in public and openly pray aloud while men were present was thought, by both sexes, to be a horrid violation of social decorum. Lyman Beecher and Nathaniel Beman carried the weight of debate, and Thursday afternoon passed by rapidly. The dispute was heated when the time came for adjournment, and nothing had as yet been settled on this extremely controversial point.

The Friday session took up where debate ceased on Thursday, and continued all morning. Nathaniel Beman asked, and received, permission to present arguments from scripture allowing women to speak and pray publicly. Finney recalled that Beman examined the eleventh chapter of First Corinthians, and attempted to prove that the praying or prophesying of a woman was not what was condemned, but rather doing so "with her head unveiled" (verse 5), which was a violation of Oriental tradition. Beman, according to Finney, showed that "the apostle did not reprove the practice of their praying, but simply admonished them to wear their veils when they did so." To the New Englanders, whose women always wore hats and bonnets to church, the uncovering of the female head was certainly not the problem, but unable to prove Beman wrong they grudgingly had to admit that the Christian women of Corinth were not praying and prophesying privately, but in mixed groups. "It was manifestly too conclusive to admit of any refutation," Finney remembered with pleasure.[7]

But the New Englanders were not going to abandon their traditions easily, and as things moved into the afternoon session, Samuel Aikin and Charles Finney proposed that certain "matters of fact" be brought before the members. They asked for documentation of the New Englanders' claim that women had been praying in mixed or "promiscuous" assemblies. At this point Lyman Beecher bristled, and protested that to divulge such information was a violation of authorized confidences. According to Finney's *Memoirs*, Beecher said brusquely, "We have not come here to be catechised; and our spiritual dignity forbids us to answer any such questions."[8] Finney, keeping his temper, thought that this was strange, that "when such things had been affirmed as facts, which were no facts at all; and when such a storm of opposition had been raised throughout the length and breadth of the land; and we had come together to consider the whole question, that we were not allowed to know the source from which their information had been obtained."[9]

Irritated by the request for documentation, which apparently did not exist, Lyman Beecher retorted that the new measures supporters should not be accepted as legitimate witnesses to their own activities, because of personal involvement. Rather, he argued, their testimony should be excluded because they were the objects of inquiry at this conference. Finney knew, from his legal background, that this was the flimsiest of pretexts, and he rose to point out that in any court of law there was abundant expectation that defendants would be allowed to testify on their own behalf. Moderator Humphrey, agreeing with the obvious, took the position that they were the principal parties in the inquiry, and that they would have to be heard; he therefore overruled Beecher's motion.

It should be noted that, in regard to their request for documentation, the westerners were on solid ground. They believed, based on his *Pastoral Letter*, that William Weeks was the one who had supplied Nettleton with all the charges, and if the New Englanders would admit who was the source of their information, the entire issue could be quickly resolved. Yet he sat throughout the entire convention in their midst, saying hardly a word.

Samuel Aikin, to move matters along, withdrew his motion concerning "matters of fact," and the vote was called for on the issue of "females are not to pray." The members split evenly, on an east-west basis: Beecher, Humphrey, Nettleton, Tenney, Norton, Weeks, Hawes, Weed, and Edwards voting affirmatively, and the rest declining to vote. The new measures advocates then took the initiative and Frost moved the question, "Is it right for a woman in any case to pray in the presence of a man?" After Edwards had withdrawn his earlier motion, unresolved, Dirck Lansing offered a substitute motion to Frost's, stating, "There may be circumstances in which it is proper for a female to pray in the presence of men." When the vote was taken, Finney, Frost, Gale, Aikin, Gillet, Lansing, Beman, and Churchill voted in favor of this rather vague proposition, and Henry Smith changed over, declining to vote along with the nine on Beecher's side. Thus this attempt to clarify the women's issue failed also, manifesting the stubborn resistance of the easterners to accept innovation and social change. The role of women in public worship, which was a central issue in the "civil war in Zion," remained unresolved by the New Lebanon Convention.

On Saturday, the fourth day of the meetings, Justin Edwards introduced the motion, "The calling of persons by name in prayer ought to be carefully avoided." This was discussed and a compromise motion was agreed to, reading, "The calling of persons by name in prayer may take place in small social circles; but in all cases, ought to be practiced with great caution and tenderness." On this note the delegates adjourned until Monday morning.[10]

When Heman Humphrey brought the delegates to order on Monday, it was noticed by everyone that Asahel Nettleton was absent. The previous week, as the debates had continued, Nettleton was seen to be increasingly irritated and impatient. Although he had said little, it was plain to all that the meetings were not going the way he thought they should, with Finney and his men being roundly denounced and threatened with expulsion from the normal activities of the churches. Charles Finney wrote concerning Nettleton's absence:

> As the facts came out in regard to the revivals, Mr. Nettleton became so very nervous that he was unable to attend several of our sessions. He plainly saw that he was losing ground, and that nothing could be ascertained that could justify the course that he was taking. This must have been very visible also to Dr. Beecher.[11]

With Asahel Nettleton's frail health, it is understandable that the proceedings put him under a great strain, but on the other hand with his absence the easterners lost a crucial vote, and they needed every one of their members present if they hoped to carry the coming motions.

Debate resumed upon the issue of public prayer and continued through to the afternoon. Dirck Lansing then introduced the motion, "Audible groaning in prayer is, in all ordinary cases, to be discouraged; and violent and boisterous tones, in the same exercise, are improper." It passed handily, with fourteen assents and three (Weeks, Norton, and Hawes) abstentions. But by the careful wording of the motion, "In all ordinary cases," the suggestion was deliberately left that there could be extraordinary ones in which groaning was allowable. This permitted the possibility of the "agonizing prayer" so important to Finney's new measures.

Unwilling to allow the initiative to pass to the westerners, Justin Edwards then brought the focus of attention around to the alleged "denunciatory" tactics of the new measures preachers. His next motion submitted was, "Speaking against ministers of the Lord Jesus Christ, in regular standing, as cold, stupid, or dead, as unconverted or enemies to revivals, is improper." Another crucial issue was joined, and anxiety again could be felt. Nathaniel Beman was not willing to allow all the reproach to be on the westerners, however, and he rose and asked to amend the motion by adding "or as heretics or enthusiasts, or disorganizers, as deranged or mad." Again Justin Edwards rose, recognizing that this addition would probably frustrate the voting, and amended his own wording by proposing that all "epithets" be dropped. In this form the motion passed.

Tension remained, however, for the New Englanders were determined to bring what they considered Finney's aberrations out into the open. Edwards next moved to condemn the "hasty admission of converts" to church membership, which was obviously a slap at the new measures. Before this motion could be carried, Dirck Lansing relieved Beman of the full weight of speaking by moving a counter-resolution aimed at the methods of Nettleton and Beecher. Lansing's motion denounced "the writing of letters . . . complaining of measures supposed to have been employed in revivals, being calculated to impair the confidence of the members . . . in their ministers, and to encourage the wicked to oppose." This provoked a storm of discussion until 7 P.M., when Heman Humphrey gratefully declared it was time to adjourn, which they did without a vote on the motion.

When the members came together on Tuesday morning, Justin Edwards took the initiative from Lansing by immediately speaking of the threat to the "institution of a settled ministry" made by itinerant evangelists who create "an excitement of popular feeling . . which is calculated, or at least liable, to . . . fill the churches with confusion and disorder."[12] Edwards moved to condemn "harsh language" in preaching, and this motion was passed by a vote of twelve yeas to five nays.

Whether ultimately they would win, the New Englanders seemed to be getting the upper hand in remaining on the offensive, keeping the new measures men on the defensive. Seizing this initiative, Justin Edwards then presented a list of eight resolutions dealing with the most prevalent complaints of the easterners against the new measures. The westerners were overwhelmed at this sizeable list, feeling it was a barrage of accusations being thrown at them in an attempt to ram through the motions before each charge could be adequately answered. But the moderator allowed the reading of the entire list, and there was nothing the new measures spokesmen could do for the moment. It condemned "all irreverent familiarity with God," "uneducated and ardent young men" making "invidious comparisons between them and settled pastors," stating "things which are not true . . . for the purpose of awakening sinners," "unkindness and disrespect to superiors in age or station," conniving "at acknowledged errors," and justifying a measure "without regard to its scriptural character, or its future and permanent consequences." In addition it urged that "great care should be taken to discriminate between holy and unholy affections [emotions], and that revivalists should adopt no measures that they are "unwilling to have published to the world."[13]

When the list had been read, the chief complaint of the new measures side was that these evils had never occurred under their ministries, although very possibly some of them may have been committed elsewhere. At any rate, if they voted in favor of these propositions it would suggest that they did exist. The easterners said this was not so; that to vote in favor would bolster their position and let the public know where they stood. Eventually the new measures men acquiesced, half-heartedly, and then the motion was passed by a unanimous vote. At that Joel Hawes of Hartford, eager for concord and convinced of the innocence of the westerners regarding these points, said to all, "Well, I profess I am satisfied."

Lyman Beecher, unwilling to let up on the pressure that had been placed on the westerners, and fearful that some of his forces might defect, turned on Hawes and said, "Stop, Brother Hawes, don't be in a hurry and decide too quickly." Then, turning to Finney and his friends, Beecher scolded:

> Gentlemen . . . you need not think to catch old birds with chaff; it may be true that you don't go personally into ministers' parishes; but, in the noise and excitement, one and another of the people in the towns want you to come and preach, and you are mighty reserved, and say, "Ah no, we can not come unless ministers invite us," and so you send them back like hounds to compel them to call you.[14]

With that, Heman Humphrey closed the morning session with prayer. During the dinner hour, it was apparent to each side that there was work to do. Beecher, laboring without Nettleton to assist him, had to rally his forces, and the new measures pastors were presented the opportunity in the afternoon meeting of responding, taking the initiative in the consideration of subjects for discussion and action. As the two groups conferred, dinner became of secondary consideration.

When they had reconvened, Nathaniel Beman once again became the spokesman for Finney's men, and naturally the subject shifted to the tactics of the opposition. Beman first moved a resolution stating that "great caution should be exercised in listening to unfavorable reports." Secondly, Beman stared directly at Lyman Beecher as he read, "Attempts to remedy evils which exist in revivals of religion, may . . . do more injury and ruin more souls than those evils which some attempts are intended to correct." Thirdly, "the best conducted revivals are liable to be stigmatized and opposed by lukewarm professors, and the enemies of evangelical truth." In these carefully worded statements, Beman had taken the language of Justin Edwards' earlier motions and reversed the meaning, thus attacking the assumptions and activities of Nettleton and Beecher. Doubtless Finney and his friends smiled smugly at this turnabout.

Beman had done his work well, and it was immediately apparent to the New Englanders that the tables had been turned. Conferring quickly, as each of the three resolutions was read and seconded and the vote called for, Beecher's allies refused to vote, saying "As the previous does not appear to us to be, in the course of Divine Providence, called for, we therefore decline to act."[15] So, as with some of Edwards' motions, although it was impossible because of the split to pass them, Beman's points had been forcefully made on the easterners.

Beman then yielded the floor to Dirck Lansing, who drove the new measures position further home in a motion directly aimed at Lyman Beecher and Asahel Nettleton's devices:

> The writing of letters to individuals in the congregations of acknowledged ministers, or circulating letters which have been written by others, complaining of measures which may have been employed in revivals of religion; or . . . conferring with opposers . . . thus strengthening the hands of the wicked, and weakening the hands of settled pastors, are breaches of Christian charity, and ought to be carefully avoided.

When the vote was taken, the easterners declined, and advanced a dissenting resolution that defended the "duty of ministers of the gospel freely to communicate, by letter or otherwise . . . [to] give notice of approaching danger."

With limited time remaining, Lyman Beecher realized that the reciprocal condemnations were largely resulting in a draw. Surely, by no stretch of interpretation could it be portrayed that the easterners had won, as yet, a clear-cut victory over the new measures. Asahel Nettleton's absence due to his "nervousness" was not helping the cause, for it meant not only a crucial vote lost but also the loss of his leadership. On Wednesday, therefore, Beecher and the other New Englanders prevailed upon Nettleton to return to the floor of the conference for the last day of meetings, Thursday.

Finney recalled that Nettleton entered the meeting room on Thursday "manifestly very much agitated,"[16] and with Moderator Humphrey's permission he produced "a historical letter" that detailed the various evils of the new measures. As he read it, Finney, who possessed a copy, noted that "I was seldom mentioned in it, by name. Yet the things complained of were so presented, that there was no mistaking the design."[17] It was "as long as a sermon," and although no evidence exists to demonstrate it, this letter was probably the same as the one first composed by Nettleton to plead for Beecher's aid against Beman and Finney and then lengthened and sent to Samuel Aikin on January 13, 1827.

When Nettleton was done reading, Charles Finney arose and said that he was glad this letter had been read before them, for he had a copy and would have read it himself had Nettleton not done it. He then stated that not one of the charges was true. Then he turned to his friends and said of them, "They know whether I am chargeable with any of these things, in any of their congregations." He demanded that if there was an eyewitness to his performance of any of these charges, that it be so stated immediately. Each of the new measures men affirmed that the charges in the letter were untrue, to their knowledge.

Finney then asked Nettleton for the source of his information, and of course the New Englander refused to give it, probably thinking of the precedent set by Beecher early in the meetings. Weeks, who was sitting at the front of the room recording the minutes of the convention, kept silent (although certainly Finney and the others stared at him) and would not admit to supplying Nettleton with data or writing the *Pastoral Letter*. Apparently Beecher and Nettleton expected Weeks to be man enough to speak up, but because neither he nor Nettleton had ever personally witnessed the things they criticized, Weeks refused to admit that what he charged was based on secondhand and distorted information. "No one there pretended to justify a single sentence in Mr. Nettleton's historical letter," Finney stated. "This of course was astounding to Mr. Nettleton and Dr. Beecher. If any of their supposed facts had been received from Mr. Weeks, no doubt they expected him to speak out, and justify what he had written. But he said nothing."[18]

Soon after this, the convention was ready to be adjourned for want of any further proceedings. According to Finney's *Memoirs*, he proposed that the members should pass another resolution against "lukewarmness in religion, and condemning it as strongly as any of the practices mentioned in the resolutions."[19] Taking this as a rebuke, Lyman Beecher snapped that there was no danger of lukewarmness, and Heman Humphrey, weary of all the infighting over the last week, declared that the convention was indeed adjourned. In his *Autobiography* Lyman Beecher claimed he said, probably toward the end of the convention when he realized how little he had accomplished:

> Finney, I know your plan, and you know I do; you mean to come into Connecticut and carry a streak of fire to Boston. But if you attempt it, as the Lord liveth, I'll meet you at the State line, and call out all the artillerymen, and fight every inch of the way to Boston, and then I'll fight you there.[20]

In *his* memoirs, Finney said he recalled no such remark, "but, as Dr. Beecher does, let it illustrate the spirit of his opposition."[21] In all likelihood the statement was never made, at least audibly. Bernard Weisberger has humorously commented, "But if the remark was actually made, [Finney] should have treasured it, for no one else ever heard Lyman Beecher admit that he would retreat *before* a battle started!"[22]

And so, the famous New Lebanon Convention concluded. What had actually happened, beneath all the acrimony and division, and what was accomplished, if anything? One thing is sure: Lyman Beecher's omnipresent self-confidence was rattled, and he was aware that he may have blundered badly. As G. F. Wright has said:

> The full effects of the convention upon Beecher's mind were not seen at once, but on his way home he dropped a casual remark in the presence of the landlord of the hotel where he stopped for dinner . . . which revealed as clearly as words can do the most important result of the conference. "We crossed the mountains," said he, "expecting to meet a company of boys, but we found them to be full-grown men."[23]

Interpretations of the convention have varied, and a final analysis is difficult. Some faulty conclusions are easily dismissed, such as that the conference resulted in a condemnation of Finney's methods.[24] Although the new measures were relentlessly attacked, Finney, Beman, and Lansing succeeded in separating many of the wilder charges against them from the facts of what had been occurring, and, with the exception of Nettleton, it seems that all the easterners, including William Weeks, went home convinced that in the future they must stop listening to stray gossip and unfounded, secondhand distortions. Nettleton, history shows, went on choosing to believe what he wanted to believe of Finney.

One cannot make the case that Finney was the clear loser at the convention, because some of the practices of Beecher, Nettleton, and Weeks also came under withering fire, especially the direct and explicit rebuke they received for the writing of letters with unverified charges. In addition, Finney succeeded in fending off many of the allegations against him by the simple expedient of having his compatriots deny that they had ever happened. When the trusted, dignified western pastors declared this, the impact was obvious: much of the argument against the new measures took on the complexion of willful exaggeration and distortion, in which little confidence could be placed. The balloon was badly punctured, and it sagged ignominiously for all to see. What was especially dispelled was the idea that Finney and all his followers were fanatics and violent disturbers of the settled order. The New Englanders were persuaded that that was not so, but still many regional prejudices, misunderstandings, and cultural tensions remained, along with a rejection of the new measures. The many frictions between East and West, between old, entrenched views and the newer, less stately institutions of New York, were not eased by the New Lebanon Convention.

As to Lyman Beecher, he left New York being forced to recognize that younger men, led by Finney, with newer ways were threatening and in places supplanting those represented by Nettleton and himself. It was beginning to become disturbingly clear to Beecher that Finney's network of influence had in an astoundingly short period extended over a great area, possibly eclipsing his own! The young upstart, whom Beecher had tried to discredit, not only survived the attack but had emerged, for some baffling reason, with even more influence than previously. More frustrating yet was the fact that the carefully chosen members of Beecher's personal coalition had failed to uphold him and Nettleton, and had shown at times entirely too much propensity to be lenient and tolerant.

As to Asahel Nettleton, he was the real loser at New Lebanon. He had come to the conference expecting that the power of Lyman Beecher would vanquish Finney forever, and to his horror he found that Beecher's influence was not what it claimed to be, and that the eastern coalition all too readily treated Finney as an equal, rather than a scoundrel! Being unable to accept defeat or recognize that he had been sadly misled on almost all counts, he left the conference to continue demanding support from Beecher, and receiving less and less of it.

As to Charles Finney, by any estimation he must be counted the real victor at New Lebanon. Coming to the conference with everything to lose and little to gain, he emerged with more than he dared hope for. At age thirty-five, his already growing reputation soared after the convention, and he had to be accounted, by friend and foe alike, as one of the leaders of the Presbyterian-Congregational campaign for awakening America. This was the opening to his being eventually recognized as the head of the latter phase of the Second Great Awakening, and the real inheritor of the mantle of Jonathan Edwards and Timothy Dwight. He had withstood the two greatest contemporary evangelists, and gained at least a draw.[25]

Although in some ways the results were inconclusive, the new measures men were quite aware of the extent of their success. Charles Finney was pleased beyond measure, for George Gale wrote to him on July 28, only two days after the end of the meetings, to "impress upon his mind" that "we shall be in danger of boasting of what we have done and *not* done—how we have foiled our enemies and opposers instead of ascribing the honour to God. . . . You ought therefore to have power over your tongue." Gale went on to caution Finney that Nettleton would be watching everything done in the future, perhaps redoubling his efforts to collect incriminating evidence against the new measures. Regarding Finney's method in conducting evangelistic meetings, Gale urged, "Look at, examine it and be not afraid to use the pruning knife wherever faults are found."[26]

Estimates of the convention were rendered almost as soon as it was concluded. The Unitarians were delighted that there had been no reconciliation between Finney and Beecher, and they printed the proceedings of the convention in full in the *Christian Examiner and Theological Review* of Boston, adding only the brief comment, "There can be but one deep feeling of regret and even shame among all enlightened Christians at the disgrace, which such proceedings as we have here recorded, are adapted to bring to religion."[27]

Other interpretations came from friendly camps. The *Western Recorder*, organ of the new measures people, seized upon what their opponents were trying to make of the convention in portraying it as a complete failure. But their mistake is apparent, the *Recorder* declared; "The enemies of religion . . . may see abundant cause for mortification in the degree of unanimity which prevailed on all points of radical importance."[28]

When the New Englanders had reached their homes, Nettleton refused to allow the dust to settle. Growing increasingly infuriated,

possibly at the realization that his own absence from many of the
meetings had helped in the frustration, he kept up a salvo of letters
to Lyman Beecher. Nettleton insisted that because the convention had
been ineffective, it was imperative that they intensify their efforts to
bring Finney down and reclaim their leadership over the revival coalition. He wrote to Beecher on October 29, 1827:

> We think to forestall public opinion by silent measures, but this
> is giving them all the advantage they want. We can correspond
> with our friends who are already firm and need no correction, but
> this does not touch the evil. It is the irregulars themselves, and
> the *ignobile vulgus,* and the whole host of insurgents, that need
> to know our opinion and our determination to make a firm and
> decided stand against these measures. A few letters like that of
> Dr. Porter would soon turn to flight the armies of the aliens. It
> is not mere argument, but names, that will turn the current against
> the ragamuffins.[29]

On December 29, 1827 he wrote to Beecher,

> I never was attacked on so many *awkward* points. Silence is con-
> strued into sullenness, unwillingness to be corrected, envy, etc.;
> and so many good people are made to believe.[30]

Why Nettleton supposed that he was being silent is difficult to
conceive. In reality he was causing as much commotion as ever, be-
rating Finney publicly in New York City[31] and everywhere else that
he traveled, so much so that Samuel C. Aikin wrote to Charles Finney on December 18, 1827, claiming that he saw "in Bro. Nettleton a
fever that could only be allayed by drowning."[32]

Beecher's reaction to this drumbeat of demands was increasing
annoyance. He looked back on the New Lebanon meetings with frustration, realizing too late that his task there had been impossibly difficult. As William G. McLoughlin has said, "Short of taking Finney
into his confidence, Beecher could not have hoped to achieve anything
at New Lebanon."[33] Always pragmatic, Beecher vowed to himself that
he would be a fool to attempt any more confrontations with Charles
Finney, and he had come to the realization that there was little more
that he (or Nettleton) could really do. It would seem that he grasped
the fact increasingly that, theologically, Finney was not at odds with

him. In addition, perhaps some of the new measures could be reconciled with his own methodologies, at least the measures that promised quick results and did not tend toward fanaticisms.

Beecher had been well aware, even before New Lebanon, that the real bone of contention between them was the relationship of revivals to the social order. Through revivals, moral reform, home missions, and a host of other controls, Beecher and the New England Congregationalists hoped to bring about and keep an orderly, regulated social structure. For Beecher, the "regular ministry" was the backbone of this structure, and occasional decorous, well-organized revivals would serve to breathe new zeal and life into the churches so that deists, Unitarians, and all other threats to the social order would be kept down. The settled pastor regulated society by molding converts into obedient subjects of the Almighty's moral government, which was intertwined, in the mentality of the New England theocrats, with the Puritan heritage of their land. When the Congregational churches had been disestablished in New England, these ideas of social control had been wedded to "voluntarism," and all latter-day Puritans such as Beecher had made radical adjustments in their thinking to accommodate the new demands. Still, it seemed to work. The Deity had ordained a specific social order, to which mankind had been invited in covenantal participation. This order, which Beecher identified with the status quo of New England, was repeatedly threatened by democrats, pagans, and disturbers of peace. The latest threat was the new measures revivalism of New York, which had all too many demographic links with New England.

To Beecher, Charles Finney represented the frenzied upward scramble of the lower classes and Jacksonian democrats, the very forces that promised to overturn the New England settled order. In Beecher's view, Finney did not call his converts to propriety and preservation of the old, but rather to enthusiasm and unpredictability, and he posed the menace of detaching religion from the institutional framework, for he believed the churches to be lukewarm and impotent.

However, Beecher realized, Charles Finney was still young, and youth must have its fling. He was a recent Christian, and when he matured a bit more, there was the possibility that he could be influenced toward a more institutional approach. So Lyman Beecher counseled himself to be patient, and ignore Nettleton's complaints as much as possible.

Through the winter and spring of 1828 Beecher moved steadily in the direction of conciliation with Finney, believing that nothing was to be gained by opposition. Charles Finney began preaching in

Philadelphia in mid-January 1828, and was still there when the Presbyterian General Assembly met in annual conclave at that city in late May. Lyman Beecher attended as well, and took that as an auspicious opportunity to draw the revival ranks together in a truce. He explained to the interested parties that, to retain public confidence and stifle Unitarian and Universalist exploitation, internal squabbling would have to cease, and he was willing to make the overtures. The following statement was drawn up:

> The subscribers, having had opportunity for free conversation on certain subjects pertaining to revivals of religion, concerning which we have differed, are of the opinion that the general interests of religion would not be promoted by any further publications on those subjects, or personal discussions, and we do hereby engage to cease from all publications, correspondences, conversations, and conduct designed and calculated to keep those subjects before the public mind, and that, so far as our influence may avail, we will exert it to induce our friends on either side to do the same.[34]

In his old age Finney, in writing his *Memoirs*, and still trying to put the best construction on the entire controversy to make it appear that he was aloof from it, wrote, "I was not a party to the agreement entered into at Philadelphia."[35] But G. F. Wright says, "his signature is unquestionably upon it."[36] The document, dated May 27, 1828, bears the signatures of Finney, Lyman Beecher, Dirck Lansing, S. C. Aikin, John Frost, Noah Coe, Nathaniel S. S. Beman, Joel Parker, A. D. Eddy, Sylvester Holmes, Ebenezer Cheever, and E. W. Gilbert.

Lyman Beecher's later affiliation with Charles Finney remains to be examined, but their supposed convergence on all matters was expressed—even exaggerated—in a letter Finney received from Beecher written August 2, 1831. Finney must have been startled to read from his former adversary, that Beecher had no prejudices about "past difference of opinion about measures," for "with very little difference, and that now on points of discretion unessential, you and I are, as much, perhaps even more, *one* than almost any two men whom God has pleased to render conspicuous in his church."[37]

Beyond doubt, Charles Finney had every reason to be immensely pleased with his progress. He had aspired to the seats of the mighty, and increasingly they were forced to accept him as an equal. His motivations and hopes were vindicated. He took this as the evident blessing of God upon his ministry.

8

INTO THE LIONS' DEN

When Charles Finney left the towns and small cities of the New York State "Burned-over District" for the major metropolises of the eastern seaboard, there was, as might be imagined, at first only partial acceptance. But gradually he won more and more adherents to the new measures and to his theological position. This introduces problems of historical and theological interpretation into our discussion. In the years after 1827, why was Finney so successful, in the face of the opposition of Beecher, Nettleton, the Old School Presbyterians, and others? More importantly, what great watershed in American culture was being established, and why did it occur then?

Put as sharply as possible, to attempt to answer the questions that arise over Finney's methodologies and vast influence, we can no longer follow the environmental interpretation that has served until this point. This has seemed to offer an adequate explanation for Finney's New York successes: regional factors made the Burned-over District different from the rest of the country, and therefore that district was so susceptible to many new religious ideas and movements. But an environmental interpretation will carry us only so far; it will not tell us why Finney became such an important figure elsewhere — in the more pragmatic, "practical" East, in New England, and among Midwestern clergymen and churchgoers. The Burned-over District had provided the breeding ground for the new measures, and Finney's theological views were derived thence and from several other sources, but the spread of these views and practices nationwide calls for a broader interpretation.

In the light of what Finney did between 1828 and that point in 1836 when he left the Presbyterian Church and assumed his duties as professor of theology at Oberlin Collegiate Institute, it becomes possible to see his intentions and determination as he came to the East. At New Lebanon, having bested Beecher and Nettleton, two of the most important divines in the nation, he became emboldened to take on the entire leadership of American Calvinists, both Presbyterian and Congregational. How could one individual, however self-assured, be so audacious?

Several possible answers suggest themselves, and go far toward explaining Finney's great success. None may be adequate singly to explain what happened. There is first his determination to democratize American Protestantism, and the relationship between this force embodied in his career and the democratizing influence of President Andrew Jackson's political thought, who was elected to the nation's highest office in 1828. Just as Jackson railed against privilege, monopoly, and property qualification for voting, Finney railed against the social conservatism of the Presbygational church structure. Increasingly, Finney came to regard the Old School theology as disastrous to the cause of evangelism at a time when multitudes needed to be reached and brought into the churches, and the Old School hierarchy of the Presbyterians as a top-heavy bureaucracy with entrenched power. His calling, as he came to view it, was to overthrow its stifling theology of election, and do what he could to redistribute its power in a more democratic fashion, among the laity itself. So, Jacksonian democracy and Finney's desires complemented each other. Speaking of all the revivalists of the age, Perry Miller has well said:

> But as compared with Finney, they all seem pallid. This is not necessarily because he possessed (in the phrase of the time) more "animal spirits" than they (Lyman Beecher was a man of tremendous physical vigor), but because all the others, whether in Connecticut or Kentucky, were linked with the eighteenth century, striving to enact anew the Great Awakening of 1740. Finney's preeminence lies in his embracing the Revival out of no academic theological training, but fully imbued with the spirit of the nineteenth century. . . . The story of his whirlwind deeds across northern New York, in New York City and Philadelphia, and even in Boston, has often been told, but it is still difficult for us to con-

ceive how revolutionary he loomed. . . . Not Thomas Jefferson,
or Madison, or Monroe led America out of the eighteenth century. Lyman Beecher was a spiritual grandson of Edwards, as Timothy Dwight was in the flesh; neither of them ever faintly glimpsed
the possibility that the battle would not still be fought in inherited terms. So, Beecher attacked Finney's "methods," and made a
great show of bringing him to reason. Actually, Beecher did nothing of the sort. The famous New Lebanon Conference . . . was, like
many later diplomatic arrangements, one in which the rebel
seemed submissive, only to continue upon his original course,
never again to be challenged. Nettleton withdrew to the seminary
in East Windsor, and poor Beecher, magnificent though he was,
in so far as he was related to the Revival, for the rest of his life
remained a tail to the Finney kite.[1]

A second reason for Finney's immense success lies in the expectations of Americans themselves, including the millennial thrust of
the times with which he resonated so perfectly. This factor must be
stressed, but in our cynical, secular time it is difficult for us to appreciate anything so antithetical to our own mind-set. Most Protestants then were postmillennialists, which meant that they had been
taught to dream that, theologically, their efforts for the kingdom of
heaven were helping to bring in the thousand years of the golden age
foretold by Isaiah and other Old Testament prophets (Isa. 2, 4, 65, etc.)
and Revelation. It was an exciting hope. All American Christians were
invited to contribute, by their labors and funds, to the many-orbed
activities of the "Benevolent Empire" in which Finney became so central. It was not hoped in some vague fashion, but expressly believed,
that with massive efforts toward eradicating slavery, war, alcoholism,
and a myriad of other human ills, the gospel would reign in human
hearts and overshadow the world. "If the church will do all her duty,"
Finney thundered with incredible confidence, "the millennium may
come in this country in three years."[2] Then Christ would return to
this beneficent scene at the end of the millennium.

Charles Finney's later perfectionism also fitted perfectly into this
pattern.[3] By the year 1831, although he had not yet adopted perfectionist views, he had already entered into his career as a reformer, which
he kept to the end of his days. All the causes that he advanced, and
all the words that he ever wrote, assumed this postmillennial scenario.
On the national scene, it would mean that Finney in several aspects
assumed the role of a prophet — a leader who captured the spirit of
his age, gave it voice, shaped and reshaped its religious thought and

institutions, and stepped boldly into the future. Thus he fitted so well into the regimens of the time: the patterns of expansive individualism on the one hand, and the search for national unity and identity on the other.[4]

Still another reason for Finney's successes and the general acceptance of his views was that clergymen themselves were ready to accept new methodologies, and were passively waiting for a leader. In studying the situation as Finney came into Philadelphia, that bastion of Old School Presbyterian orthodoxy, there would seem to be no other rationale that adequately explains what happened. *Why* did that city's Old School pastors allow New School doctrines? Three possible reasons seem to advance themselves. One is that some of these clergymen were themselves in a transitional phase, and were not sufficiently imbued with Old Schoolism to prevent them from being at least curious about the newer ideas, if not actually willing to experiment with them. Another is the reason Finney advanced for the openness of Eliphalet Gilbert, Finney's host in Wilmington, Delaware: "Mr. Gilbert was very old-school in his theological views, but a good and earnest man. His love of souls overruled all difficulty on nice questions of theological difference."[5] In other words, evangelism to Gilbert was more important than theological position, and if Finney's demand for immediate response to the gospel produced more converts, then pragmatic considerations would prevail and the older view would be laid aside. Still, these two reasons do not altogether explain why, in months to come, some devoted Old School adherents would be willing to allow a man into their pulpits whose views they disliked. A third answer, on the psychological level, may be that, for some of these pastors, their invitations to Finney were implicit admissions of the hindrances to evangelism that Old School views presented.

These, plus other facets that may be glimpsed in Finney's career, are the reasons for his preeminence. They are also major issues of historical interpretation of this period of America's past. As Finney came into national prominence, these are some of the broader themes that should be enunciated in describing his thought and work.

After the New Lebanon Convention, Charles Finney's star went into its ascendency in a new and more spectacular way. The abundant correspondence he kept from this period (over seventy personal letters from August through December 1827) demonstrates this in the form of messages from important people, requests for his advice, and invitations from the large cities of the eastern seaboard. His own self-confidence, never small, received a great boost from his remarkable

Theodore Dwight Weld (1803–1895). In 1832 H. B. Stanton wrote to him, "You are ardent, fear no danger, have great personal courage, can shake hands with toil, and call peril by his Christian name. You possess a very vigorous physical constitution." In none of this was Stanton exaggerating. Weld was a sincere, wholesouled man whose unselfish service for others makes him almost larger than life. From an old engraving.

success in standing up to "the great gun at Boston" and emerging from the bout almost unscathed, and some thought he was the hands-down winner. Even before the confrontation with Beecher and Nettleton, Finney had received invitations to preach in their home territory of New England, in Vermont and New Hampshire, and on April 20, 1827,

Gardiner Spring (1785–1873) was pastor of the Brick Presbyterian Church in New York City from the time of his ordination in 1810 to his death, and one of the most prominent clergymen in the nation. He helped to organize numerous voluntary societies. Originally opposed to Charles Finney, in time he warmed somewhat toward the evangelist. Courtesy of the Presbyterian Historical Society.

he had been urged to come to the Old School Presbyterian stronghold of Philadelphia. The Rev. James Patterson, one of the prominent pastors of the city, wrote on that date, "It is my prayerful desire that you would visit this great and wicked city . . . tho' there are many here still who look aghast at revivals, yet latterly don't talk so freely against them. To oppose them openly would be unpopular."[6]

Confident that the future was his, Finney bided his time and waited to choose only the best opportunities. All his friends urged him not only to be humble, but also to remain in the West, for the East had snares aplenty. George W. Gale wrote to him on September 8, 1827:

> Some considerations speak favorably of your going east, others seem to forbid it. One against it which would weigh much is You would have to sustain the weight of the contest with Unitarians and instead of receiving aid from those who ought to aid you you would probably find them throwing obstacles in your way. Let Doct. Beecher & co who have buckled on the harness to fight Unitarians fight it out. The Presbyterian Ch. furnishes an ample field, and is the field where you have been born and nurtured. You will have to fight here but it will be a different warfare. . . . Many in New York and in Philadelphia, as well as others south will be your warm friends and supporters. . . . Your sermon and our Narrative have been republished there and well received by many.[7]

Gale was certainly correct regarding the Unitarians; there was plenty of time for that sort of thing later, and if Beecher wished to lock horns with them, that was his choice. But other cities held many allurements for Finney, and the promise of audiences far larger than he had ever addressed in the small towns and cities of the West.

After Finney concluded his work at Little Falls, New York, in July 1827, he accepted an invitation to preach at Stephentown, a few miles to the north of New Lebanon, and he worked intermittently there until November 30. Finney's work at Stephentown was interrupted on October 4, 1827, by the annual meeting of the Synod of Albany, which convened at the Second Presbyterian Church of Utica. There, among the many items of business, the dissidents from Nathaniel Beman's church in Troy appealed their defeat at the Presbytery of Albany in January 1827 to the next higher church court, the Synod. Charles Finney attended the meetings of Synod, not only from general interest in the business of the church, but also because of real concern for the man who had defended him so well at New Lebanon. There were wider issues here than merely the squabble in Beman's church, and Finney knew this. Some of the charges by Joseph Brockway and his fellows dealt with the new measures as used by Beman in the First Presbyterian Church of Troy, and this involved Finney, although he was not named in the complaint. Nonetheless, had the Synod found against Beman, all the Old School party throughout the denomination who felt they had been frustrated at New Lebanon would have taken heart, and the New School would suffer a decisive setback in the defeat of Beman, one of their leading representatives. Possibly, had Beman suffered defeat, the Old School would have then mustered its forces to move against the new measures and New School ideas, wherever they were found.

However, this did not happen. After a week of other business, on October 11, 1827, the Synod heard testimony from "a delegation from a legal majority of the congregation of the First Presbyterian Church in Troy." As with the Presbytery of Albany, the delegates to the Synod found that the plaintiff's petition had difficulties connected with it, and action on the matter was "indefinitely postponed." Frustrated, but unwilling to admit defeat, Brockway's group immediately gave notice of their intent to appeal to the highest judicatory in the church, the General Assembly, which would next meet in Philadelphia in May 1828.[8] Immensely relieved, but still not free of this nasty matter, Beman and Finney rejoiced.

When Charles Finney had been preaching at New Lebanon, he was heard by the Rev. Eliphalet W. Gilbert, pastor of the Second Presbyterian Church in Wilmington, Delaware. Gilbert was very impressed by Finney's preaching, and invited the evangelist to labor at his church. Here was exactly the opportunity Finney was seeking—to leave the confines of small towns and cities in New York, and emerge into the centers of influence and prestige on the eastern seaboard. Wilmington was not a major city then, but it was in close proximity to Philadelphia and Baltimore, and it would be the first time Finney had ministered outside of New York State. Eager for the challenge, Finney was becoming aware that a group of prominent businessmen in New York City wished to meet him and some of his associates to discuss the possibilities of his coming there. So, he concluded his activities in Stephentown and went to New York City, arriving there about the first of December 1827, to participate in a productive meeting with the Platts and others. After this he left for the state of Delaware, arriving in Wilmington about December 10, and began preaching in Gilbert's church almost immediately.

The theological situation there was entirely different from that in New York. Many of the New Yorkers had migrated from New England, where Hopkinsianism was the most widely accepted form of

Calvinism.[9] In addition to Samuel Hopkins' ideas coming strongly into New York, there was also the New Haven theology of Nathaniel William Taylor and Lyman Beecher, with its insistences that free agency be recognized. However, among Presbyterians in Pennsylvania, Delaware, and New Jersey, the Old School theology emanating from Princeton Seminary held Hopkinsianism in considerable suspicion because of its virtual denial of original sin and the fact that most of its adherents had abandoned the doctrine of a limited atonement for the position of a general atonement. Charles Finney may have claimed to denounce Hopkinsian ideas,[10] but in actuality his views contained more of Hopkins' theology than he ever acknowledged.[11] All of this meant that there was a far more relaxed theological atmosphere in New York than in Pennsylvania, New Jersey, and Delaware, and Finney knew full well that in traveling south he would encounter less latitude, and possibly more resistance.

It was so. For the first time he found himself deep in Old School territory, and in the pulpit of a man who had preached views of predestination and human inability to his congregation for years. To us, this may be reminiscent of George Gale's early perplexity over what to do with the rebellious Finney, when Gale still taught Old School doctrines, except that he would not allow Finney to preach in the Adams pulpit. Gilbert's pulpit in Wilmington was the first in a series of such situations that continued for several years.

Charles Finney's account of his onslaught on the paralysis in Wilmington is vivid. As the first of his attacks on Old School ideas on the eastern seaboard, Finney presented this as something of a classic textbook case that could stand as his method for all forthcoming assaults on error. It reads, in part:

> I soon found that [Gilbert's] teaching had placed the church in a position that rendered it impossible to promote a revival among them, till their views could be corrected. They seemed to be afraid to make any effort, lest they should take the work out of the hands of God. They had the oldest of the old-school views of doctrine. . . .
>
> The next Sabbath, I took for my text: "Make to yourselves a new heart and a new spirit; for why will ye die?". . . I preached about two hours. . . .
>
> As I came down the pulpit stairs, I observed two ladies. . . . The first we reached, who was near the pulpit stairs, took hold of Mr. Gilbert as he was following behind me, and said to him, "Mr. Gilbert, what do you think of that?" She spoke in a loud whisper. He replied in the same manner, "It is worth five hundred

dollars." . . . She replied, "Then you have never preached the Gospel." "Well," said he, "I am sorry to say I never have. . . ."

Mr. Gilbert's views became greatly changed; and also his
style of preaching, and manner of presenting the Gospel.[12]

After several weeks of launching this devastating attack on the
Presbyterians of Wilmington, Charles Finney received another letter,
from the Rev. James Patterson of Philadelphia. This Presbyterian pastor invited Finney to preach in his church, and mentioned the fact
that Asahel Nettleton had just left Philadelphia.[13] His church was the
First Presbyterian of the Northern Liberties, located perhaps six blocks
north of Market Street at Sixth and Buttonwood Streets, on the northern boundaries of the burgeoning city.

Even the redoubtable Charles Finney stood a bit in awe of Philadelphia, the very stronghold of Presbyterian orthodoxy. At the time
there were approximately sixteen Presbyterian churches in the city,
all hale and hearty like Patterson's, and as many clergymen, mostly
Old School. Finney must have mulled over the invitation to come to
the Northern Liberties. Was he ready yet to enter into battle in the
heartland of Calvinism?

Nothing daunted, in he went. After all, he was being invited in.
But so as to have recourse if he were invited out, he did not sever his
ties with Eliphalet Gilbert's church in Wilmington immediately. Instead, he began by preaching at Philadelphia twice a week: "I went
up on the steamboat and preached in the evening, and returned the
next day and preached at Wilmington; thus alternating my evening
services between Wilmington and Philadelphia. The distance was
about forty miles."[14]

In the year 1828, Philadelphia was a rapidly growing city,
cosmopolitan, and stately. Although it was no longer the capital of
the United States, it was still larger than any other city including New
York proper, and boasted of being the cultural center of America, and
the metropolis of science, commerce, finance, literature, and art. That
was no idle boast, for it solidly backed up every claim, and many of
the most important leaders of various fields in the country chose it
as their home. Philadelphia was the greatest manufacturing city in
the nation, producing carriages of every sort, soap, glass, shot, carpets,
paint, and a myriad of other products. Its population in 1820, including the Northern Liberties, Penn Township, and the southern districts
of Southwark, Passyunk, and Moyamensing, was 114,410.[15] This was
a deceptively small figure, for there were many outlying districts not

counted, and on its consolidation in 1860 the population had grown
to 565,500. Its great rival was New York City, which was already over-
taking it in several ways. Economically, New York had the inestimable advantage of being an all-weather shipping port whose rivers did
not freeze over (as occasionally the Schuylkill and the Delaware would
do), and it had already overtaken Philadelphia in volume of imports
and exports. In addition, the opening of the Erie Canal in 1825 was
an enormous advantage to New York in giving access to the country's
interior, and in that day when canals (and not yet railroads) were seen
as the method of transportation for goods, Philadelphia was desperately scrambling to open canals of its own.

Still, Philadelphia was by common consent a fine city, in many
ways superior to New York. In George Washington's day High (later
Market) Street was the fashionable part of the city, but by 1828 the
twice-weekly markets and hundreds of Conestoga teamsters had
spoiled this area for the residents of high society, and they had moved
to the neighborhood of Third and Spruce Streets, well to the south.
But many substantial Quaker families had settled to the north of High
Street, on Arch Street, or in the Northern Liberties. For the most part
this burgeoning new area of the Northern Liberties was identified with
market vendors, drovers, and butchers. The black and poor white areas
were farther to the south, beyond Cedar or South Street.

Possibly, of its many distinctions, the two for which the city was
most famous were its fine houses, and the checkerboard or grid pattern of its grand design, laid out by William Penn in 1682. Visitors from
a distance, especially those from the twisted, narrow, and crowded
thoroughfares of Europe, never failed to be impressed by the broad and
regular avenues of Penn's design. In 1817 a Frenchman, Montule, had
pronounced Philadelphia "the most beautiful and the largest city in
the United States."[16]

With its tolerance and welcome extended to all groups, the City
of Brotherly Love had been religiously heterogeneous. There were four
Roman Catholic churches in 1828, but Catholics did not become a
significant force in civic life until the Irish immigration of the 1840s.
And the Jewish community was miniscule, with less than five hundred members and only one synagogue. William Penn's broad policy
of religious toleration had brought to Pennsylvania, and to the city,
a vast mixture of different groups, and Philadelphia was probably as
religious a place as any in America, including Puritan Boston.

Among all the Protestant churches, it was the Presbyterians who
held the most power in the city. By 1828 there were at least sixteen

Presbyterian congregations throughout the area.[17] Almost every one of them was in a thriving condition, and a large number of the more affluent and educated citizens had gravitated toward this denomination for decades. There were good reasons for this. Throughout the nation, Presbyterians were among the largest of the denominations. They had wealth, capable leadership, learning, and numerical strength in the most vital areas of the country.

One reason for their strength had been their solid support of the Revolutionary War. So energetic had been their furtherance of the colonial cause that the war was frequently labeled "a Presbyterian rebellion." In 1777 an agent of Lord Dartmouth stated, "When the war is over, there must be a great reform established, ecclesiastical as well as civil; for, though it has not been much considered at home, Presbyterianism is really at the bottom of this whole conspiracy, has supplied it with vigor, and will never rest, till something is decided upon it."[18] The denomination emerged from the war years in a strong position, with a national organization capable of propagating churches in newly settled areas, and a well-educated ministry eager for the work ahead. Pennsylvania, along with New Jersey and New York, had gradually become the center of Presbyterian power for several reasons, not the least because of the heavy Scotch-Irish influx into the region. These immigrants, coming from Scotland and the north of Ireland between the years 1706 and 1750 in great numbers, were mostly Presbyterian. The city of Philadelphia, which retained some of them, seemed the natural center of the church, and national General Assemblies had met annually in the city since 1789.

The Presbyterians of Philadelphia had not been lax in taking advantage of their prestige. Seizing the opportunities, they had established new churches in a steady progression as the population shifted and moved in other directions. First Church, "mother church" of the denomination, had always occupied a prominent place in the city's affairs from its founding in 1698. Until 1821 its edifice had stood on Market Street between Second and Third, but with demographic shifts the congregation moved in that year to Seventh and Locust Streets and built there a fine new sanctuary on Washington Square. The Second Presbyterian had grown out of the "New Building," or Tabernacle, erected for the preaching of George Whitefield during the Great Awakening, and after this Gilbert Tennent had gathered his New Side congregation there. By 1746 both Tennent's Presbyterian congregation and Zinzendorf's Moravians were using the building, but for all practical purposes it had become the Second Presbyterian Church, immersed in revival concerns from its beginnings.[19] The remainder of the sixteen churches had been founded in fairly rapid succession until 1828.

For the most part, Philadelphia's Presbyterian churches were the bastion of Old School orthodoxy, in general alignment with the moderate theologians at Princeton. Over the years some moderating had been occurring in a quiet way. The most prominent pastors were Dr. James P. Wilson, of the First Church, and Dr. Thomas H. Skinner, of the Fifth Church. Widely respected throughout the denomination, these two were leaders of the moderate wing of the church, which dominated it from the time of the Plan of Union in 1801 until shortly after Charles Finney's visit to Philadelphia. Nominally Old School, Skinner and Wilson were sympathetic to revivals and open to some innovations, if they did not violate their demands for decency and order. Holding strictly to original sin and the Westminster Confession, they nonetheless accepted a general atonement and the possibility of immediate conversion. Indeed, Dr. Skinner had conducted powerful evangelistic campaigns himself at Fifth Church over the years, and revivals had followed.[20] The prorevival sympathies of his congregation at Fifth Church were amply demonstrated after his departure, when they tried to secure the pastoral services of Lyman Beecher, and on April 15, 1828, presented a call for Beecher before the Presbytery of Philadelphia.[21] Beecher, liking his conspicuous and exposed position in the Boston Hanover Street Church battling the Unitarians for all the country to see, knew full well that if he moved to Philadelphia the fanfare would diminish and he would be just one among many distinguished pastors. He mulled over the possibilities of conducting revivals in Penn's city for a brief time, and then rejected the offer.

In 1777 the Second Church, at Third and Arch Streets, recognized that some of its members were moving north to a newly laid out area called the Northern Liberties, beyond the current city limits. The church wisely planned to begin missionary endeavors there, with an eye to planting a new church in due time. It was not until 1813 that sufficient population had entered the area to do so, and in that year the First Presbyterian Church of the Northern Liberties was organized. On January 11, 1814, the congregation received the Rev. James Patterson as its first pastor. Born in 1779 and a graduate of Jefferson College and Princeton Seminary, Patterson was a moderate in theology, generally of the same persuasion as Wilson and Skinner.[22] Tall, with piercing eyes, dark hair, and the visage of a prophet, James Patterson impressed Charles Finney in 1828. "He would preach," Finney recalled, "with the tears rolling down his cheeks, and with an earnestness and pathos that were very striking. It was impossible to hear him preach without being impressed with a sense of his intense earnestness and his great honesty."[23] Finney and Patterson became close friends, and the evangelist called him "one of the truest and holiest men that I have ever labored with," "remarkably teachable," and "a lovely Christian man, and a faithful minister of Jesus Christ."

When Patterson had begun as pastor in the Northern Liberties, things looked anything but promising. The wealthy still lived at the core of the city, and this area had at the start poorer and less educated residents. Fifty-two made up Patterson's initial congregation, "¾ of them women, $\%_{10}$ of them poor, all untrained, undisciplined."[24] In describing the region, Patterson said, "Ignorance and vice, its most invariable concomitant, abounded; the sanctuary and institutions of religion were neglected by very many of its inhabitants."[25] But Patterson was undeterred; energetically he promoted the church through a variety of means: home visitation, prayer meetings, a thriving Sunday school, and especially, an annual emphasis on evangelism. In time he became loved and revered universally. Because of his genuine interest in all, old and young alike, his kindness, and his year-in, year-out evangelism, he was able to take into membership over eighteen hundred persons before his death in 1837.[26] In addition, Patterson was responsible for sixty young men entering the ministry, truly a remarkable number. He was especially concerned with young men coming from poor families who showed aptitude for the clergy, and he often raised money for their education.

With this tradition of evangelism at the church, it was to be expected that Patterson would invite Charles Finney to conduct a crusade, and Finney began preaching there about January 17, 1828. From the start, all went well. The people responded eagerly. For Patterson, Finney had only praise and good wishes. James Patterson proved to be the best of hosts, much like Eliphalet Gilbert in Wilmington. He accepted everything Finney did without question.[27] There was, however, one bone of contention. In all his evangelistic preaching, Patterson had taught his congregation that they could not expect instantaneous conversion. At this early point in Finney's visit, Patterson had not yet understood Finney's demand that people choose for Christ immediately, because "every moment they remained impenitent, without submission, repentance, and faith, they were increasing their condemnation."[28] But when Finney had realigned Patterson's theology on this point, all went well after that.

With the revival underway, much of Philadelphia became curi-

ous as to what was occurring in the Northern Liberties. Fearing that
his brother presbyters would rage when they learned Old School ideas
were being challenged, Patterson said, "Brother Finney, if the Presbyterian ministers in this city find out your views, and what you are
preaching to the people, they will hunt you out of the city as they
would a wolf."[29] Finney knew that his host could not protect him
against an inquiry by the Philadelphia Presbytery, if that should even-
tuate, and so he prepared for the worst. But nothing of the kind happened. Instead, to their astonishment, Finney began to receive invitations from several of the other pastors to speak in their churches. Most
amazing of all, he was requested to preach in the prestigious First
Church by its very influential pastor, Dr. Wilson! After fulfilling that
assignment, he received an invitation from Mr. Livingston, pastor of
the Dutch Reformed Church, and he preached there also.

The news flew, and Finney's friends were jubilant. David L.
Dodge, a wealthy dry-goods merchant in New York City who was trying to get Finney there, wrote to him on February 25, 1828:

> Dear Brother Finney,
> . . . modern Cities are dangerous places to souls, not so much from
> the example of the world, . . . not from opposition, but flattery. . . .
> You need double the grace my dear Brother in Phila. or N. York. . . .
>   If the Lord appears in power at Phila. opposition will soon
> spring up and if possible without sacrificing truth and plainness
> do try to keep under the wings of some of [the] good ministers
> that they may share the responsibility with you. Dr. Wilson hav-
> ing taken you into his pulpit it has almost petrified opposition
> here. He has more weight here than perhaps any minister in the
> Presbyterian Church. By the way, he is a wise man, tho probably
> not much acquainted with powerful revivals, yet it may be well
> to keep if practicable in his good will and often advise with him.
> Thousands will be on the look out, besides special spies.[30]

Zephaniah Platt, son of Judge Jonas Platt, who had recently
moved to New York City from Utica, expressed even more astonishment than David Dodge when he wrote to Finney on March 10, 1828:

> Dear Brother Finney:
> . . . When I first heard of your preaching in Dr. Wilson's and Mr.
> Livingston's churches, i could hardly credit my senses; for I had sup-
> posed that the orthodox Dr. Wilson was far more inaccesible. . . .
>   Our N.Y. churches are generally in a cold, stupid, state; but

I am happy to tell you that there is a very general change of sentiment here in regard to yourself and the Western revivals. . . .
    But since you left us, I have made a point of introducing
the subject on every admissable occasion, and I have often been
surprised to find myself warmly and zealously supported by men
who not long since would have voted you a room in the Lunatic
Asylum.[31]

But Charles Finney could not sail along on such waves of euphoria
forever. After preaching for Mr. Livingston in the Dutch Reformed
Church, opposition asserted itself, and Finney thought it best not to
extend himself too far. Better to cease preaching in the center-city
churches for a while, he thought, rather than attempt to storm their
bulwarks so early. So he gave up preaching in the important congregations and retired to James Patterson's church in the Northern Liberties in early March. But then, this upset some who wished Finney to
be extremely aggressive, for they feared he was losing his nerve. Eliphalet Gilbert, pastor of the Wilmington Second Church, was watching
Finney's actions closely and wrote a scorching tirade on March 14,
1828:

Dear Brother,
    . . . I heard the other day, that you had left Mr. Livingston's also!
Is it so? I hope not. If you have done so I fear you have *shut yourself out of the city altogether.* I don't understand your motives
in this matter. Are you so *fearful* of opposition? . . . Satan will
never let go such a *stronghold* without a mighty resistance. It is
his metropolis—his headquarters—the citadel of his power so [far
as the] Pres. chh is concerned. . . . What did you mean by retiring
as soon as the great guns began to load?[32]

Finney fumed. Although the Old School adherents of Philadelphia were cordial to him, and were inviting him to preach from their
pulpits, still the city was not capitulating to his onslaught. He found
churchgoers much more cosmopolitan and refined than any he had
previously encountered, and, except for the poorer classes in Patterson's Northern Liberties church, they did not go into paroxysms of
joy or fright over his pulpit pyrotechnics; they merely sat and politely
listened. This was a new experience for Finney; these city sophisticates of the East coast were certainly quite different from the enthusiasts of Oneida County. He reported in his *Memoirs,* "The revival

spread, and took a powerful hold."[33] But he was in Philadelphia for a full year, and in several sections. To what does he here refer? And that was the memory of his elderly years; in 1828 he was not so sanguine about the situation, as his very critical and frustrated letter of March 27 to Theodore Weld reveals:

Philadelphia

My Dear Weld.

    I seize upon the present moment as it rushes past, to write you a single line. The good work of God is deepening and spreading in this AntiRevival city, much to the joy of the friends of revivals, and I have no doubt to the no small annoyance of many who would be thought to be the *greatest* friends of the Redeemer's Kingdom. . . . The fact is, that here we are all hereticks, Alias Hopkintians who dont sit quietly down in a corner of the Triangle and wait God's time. . . .

    The churches here are in a dreadful state. This city inste[a]d of being the "radiating point," the "mainspring and rallying point [of Christian] enterprise of the presbyterian church," is almost solid darkness; [she reeks o]f corruption and in her putrid embrace, she holds all the [country, north] and south, locked up in loathsome horrid death. The work goes on [in sev]eral of the congregations.

    N.B. I am in a land where many would entangle me in my talk. Be careful what you do with my letters. Love to all Friends. Yours affectionately

C. G. Finney[34]

Finney's caution to Weld to protect this letter from prying eyes was well taken, for if the clergymen of Philadelphia had heard of his low opinion of their churches—indeed, his *contempt* for them expressed above—certainly they would not have given him the reception they did. In truth, from what we know of the way he was treated on all hands, the sentiments expressed in the second paragraph of this letter, especially when written so surreptitiously to Weld, reveal a very ungrateful side of his nature, which surfaced occasionally.

In a short while Charles Finney recovered from Eliphalet Gilbert's rebuke, and his failure to capture the Philadelphia churches immediately. Then it was that he received Theodore Weld's April 22 answer to his letter, and Weld's probing of Finney's increasing urbanity must have further distressed him:

... I thought I saw when at Stephentown—and I have more clearly discerned it in your letters this winter—(unless I strongly mistake) that *revivals* have become with you matters of such every day commonness as scarcely to throw over you the least tinge of solemnity. I fear they are fast becoming with you a sort of trade, to be worked at so many hours every day and then laid aside. Dear brother, do you not find yourself running into *formality*. . . . The machinery all moves on, every wheel and spring and chord in its place; but isn't the *main spring* waxing weaker?[35]

Here was a charge that he received from others also, and must have irritated him greatly.

Then, beginning on May 15, 1828, the General Assembly met in the First Church. Some scholars have asserted that Charles Finney was invited to preach before the assembled delegates, but a search of the extensive minutes fails to turn up even a passing mention of his name. He was doubtless a visitor from time to time, however, for it was here that Lyman Beecher signed the agreement with Finney and his friends in which both sides promised to cease publishing attacks upon each other. But a more pressing matter was the appeal of the dissident group from Nathaniel Beman's church in Troy to the General Assembly.[36] This nagging case was discussed at three different points on the docket, and, without possibility of any further appeal, was finally resolved in Beman's favor on May 27. Beman, Finney, and all the new measures advocates were ecstatic at the victory.

Despite Finney's feeling that Philadelphia was an "antirevival city," which he confided to only a few, there were many who wished that opposition might be overcome by having him preach continuously in some central location. This would bring a stop to his having to alternate between several churches, and would present a seemingly united front of churchly support for his endeavors, which would be more difficult to criticize. Accordingly, some friends sought to secure permission for him to preach in the city's largest auditorium, which was the German Reformed Church at Fourth and Race Streets, when the fall came.

It was at this point that Lydia and Charles Finney underwent the experience of parenthood for the first time. In some of his letters in the spring of 1828, he referred to Lydia's "frail health," but he does not specify whether this was a matter connected with her pregnancy. At any rate, on June 8 Lydia gave birth to a daughter, Helen Clarissa, the first of the six Finney children.[37] In order for his wife and the baby to escape the heat of summer in the city, Finney began planning to close his meetings for a time. When this was announced, the residents of the Northern Liberties were appropriately grateful for all that had been accomplished. Impressive numbers of converts had been won and were joining the church. On July 14, James Patterson and the session of the church sent this testimonial to Finney: "Resolved that we consider him a truly evangelical Preacher, sound in the faith, mighty in word and doctrine, and sincerely devoted to the cause of his Lord. . . ."[38]

Finney was exhausted after seven gruelling months of preaching, and Lydia was eager to show the baby to her parents in Whitesboro, and so the three left the sweltering city in mid-July and traveled to New York City. There Finney met again the New England Congregationalists who had befriended him on his previous visit early in December 1827. They arranged for Finney to preach in the Brick Presbyterian Church on Sunday, July 20.[39] Finney, his wife, and their month-old child then continued on to Whitesboro, and on his return trip to Philadelphia in mid-August he stopped again in New York, this time for an extended conference with the New Englanders. Because his preaching in the Brick Church had gone so well, they arranged for Finney to preach in Samuel H. Cox's church on Sunday, August 17. Hopes were brightening that Finney might be invited officially by the clergy of New York City for an extended campaign there, and after his conference he continued on to Philadelphia, heartened by the rest he had gotten, the situation in New York, and the challenge of the continuing work in the home city of Presbyterianism.

The German Reformed Church, which had been selected for the union meetings, was large and rather centrally located in the city. At the beginning of August 1828 a letter was sent by a number of signers, including George Troutman and Caspar Schaeffer, to the consistory of the church. It read, in part:

> Gentlemen, We the undersigned members of the Presbyterian Church, and others, desirous to have a more favorable opportunity of enjoying the benefits of the lectures and sermons of the Rev. Mr. Finney, a Presbyterian minister in good and regular standing, and feeling animated with the conviction that he would be more extensively useful, should he labour in a central part of our city, respectfully solicit you to pass a resolution, to invite him to your church.[40]

In accepting the invitation to speak in this church, Charles Finney inadvertently became part of a long-standing squabble, which diminished for the period of his meetings, but flared up again after his departure and continued to involve him later. The pastor, Samuel Helffenstein, D.D., was at the center of the difficulty. He had been installed there on January 14, 1799, and was confronted by the fact that the German language was fast passing out of use among younger members. Helffenstein was himself bilingual, and he conducted the services in German until 1804, when he yielded to the demands and began doing some of the preaching in English. This was the "first of many serious troubles,"[41] which continued unabated for years as the older and more powerful members demanded he use German exclusively. A defiant and irascible man, Helffenstein tried to domineer the congregation, and an attempt was made in 1817 to oust him, which failed. One of the congregation's complaints was the pastor's "interference with elections," as he tried to manipulate the voting to ensure that his favorites would be elected to offices.

The meetings at the new location of Fourth and Race Streets went well, drawing large crowds from all the churches month after month. But Samuel Helffenstein was less and less pleased as Finney's dynamic and vibrant preaching to capacity crowds made the congregation increasingly displeased with his own anemic and stilted performances. With the arrival of the new year and the coming of the snows of winter, Finney and his supporters decided to end the Philadelphia campaign by January 5, 1829. On that date Charles Finney wrote a letter of thanks to the pastor, elders, trustees, and deacons of the German Reformed Church for their cooperation, and the use of the sanctuary, and on the same date the corporation of this church resolved to thank him "for the zeal, fidelity, and truth with which he has assisted the Pastor of this church. . . . Resolved that we entertain the highest opinion of the talents and piety of Mr. Finney and believe that his labours in this church have been the cause of doing much good for the cause of Christianity."[42] One needs little skill in reading between lines to see that the corporation was more dissatisfied with Helffenstein than before, but on the other hand, few pastors would profit from being compared with the dashing itinerant Finney!

In addition, the congregation had realized another thing during Finney's glorious months in their pulpit—their pastor had little taste for Finney's type of evangelism. He had supported Finney and the meetings only halfheartedly, they believed. Caspar Schaeffer was among those who had invited Finney to the church, and he wrote to Finney after his departure, on May 7, 1829, describing the situation succinctly:

> . . . I was informed that Mr. Helffenstein's people are becoming very much dissatisfied with him. . . . Their object is to get clear of Mr. Helffenstein, introduce a popular preacher, and alter their charter. So unpopular has the old gentleman become that no one of the name would be agreeable, consequently *Jacob* [his son], as their *pastor*, would be out of the question. . . . If Papa Helffenstein can be peaceably and quietly disposed of . . . I think there is a reasonable prospect that this church may yet be made the centre of revival operation. . . . Mr. Beman has been confidentially proposed as pastor.[43]

This contrasts sharply with Finney's disclaimer in his *Memoirs* that "there was no jar or schism among them, that I ever knew of; and I never heard of any disastrous influence resulting from that revival."[44]

Whatever Finney's elderly memories may have been of his year in Philadelphia, the evidence is clear. For the most part he was treated well, even by Old School adherents, despite his secretly raging against them. He continued the revival tradition at James Patterson's church in the Northern Liberties, and made many converts. In the city as a whole there were conversions but no widespread awakening. The Presbyterian General Assembly met in the city for two entire weeks during his revival preaching, but did not see fit to take special notice of it. And at least one church was split by Finney's preaching, although the troubles at the German Reformed Church predated his coming by many years, and in all fairness he can hardly be blamed for what happened there.

Although conservative Philadelphia may not have been over-enamored of Charles Finney, above and beyond the statistics or lack of success of his campaign in that city an advance of a different kind should be noted, and this in the area of methodology. One treatment of Finney's ministry has declared that he was not a "mass evangelist" in the "sense of conducting city-wide crusades as was true of D. L. Moody later. He was a 'local church revivalist.'"[45] But this statement is not accurate for either the Philadelphia or Rochester revivals, or for his evangelistic activities in Boston, Providence, Reading, and for much of his work on his two visits to the British Isles, where in each case he tried to "go citywide" among a number of cooperating churches and clergymen. In this he was harkening back to the precedent set by George Whitefield in the Great Awakening.

Finney's four months of preaching at the German Reformed Church in Philadelphia was a truly cooperative effort among a number of churches to reach the entire populace, in the largest auditorium of the city. The same was true of the Rochester revival of 1830–1831, where all the denominations of the city united in the work, and it became truly ecumenical. The point is that, from 1828 on, Charles Finney was always willing to cooperate with as many churches and clergymen as would join in united work in a city; he was a "local church revivalist" only when conditions prohibited that and only one church, or a few, were open to him.

Even if Philadelphia did not capitulate to his revivalism, Finney's hopes were being met in some areas, and there had been accomplishments: he had succeeded in uniting the New School adherents in the heart of Presbyterianism, and even some of the most important moderate leaders had given him encouragement. But if anything, the year in Philadelphia was as much a moral victory for Finney as he could expect. He had held his positions in Old School territory, and came through unscathed. Now, there was one remaining conquest — New York City. Would it go as well there?

9

THE FREE CHURCH MOVEMENT

In the latter part of his Philadelphia campaign, Charles Finney received an invitation to preach in the town of Reading, Pennsylvania. Fifty miles to the northwest of Philadelphia, up the Schuylkill River, Reading was deep in that region where multitudes of Germans had settled. In the town there were naturally several German-speaking congregations, Lutheran and Reformed, and in addition there was a Presbyterian church belonging to the Philadelphia Presbytery, under the pastorate of the Reverend John F. Grier, D.D.[1]

Dr. Grier and his elders had invited Finney, and he arrived in Reading on January 9, 1829, in the dead of winter.[2] It is somewhat to be wondered at that he accepted the invitation, for it might be guessed that there would be difficulties there. Surely Finney knew, from having preached in the German Reformed Church in Philadelphia, that Reading was heavily settled by Germans and that he could not possibly reach a large proportion of the inhabitants because of the language barrier. He had invitations to preach in other cities, but perhaps none of them seemed propitious at that time. So, for whatever reasons, he began to labor there, and was soon irritated beyond measure at the condition of religion in the area. He wrote to Theodore Weld, on March 30, 1829:

My D[ea]r Weld,
. . . This is a most horribly wicked place. Those who know, say it exceeds New Orleans. Nothing like a revival here, ever before.

The mass of the people are Germans. They are nearly all members of the church. But Oh, such churches. Why Weld, they dont pretend to select pious men for Elders. You would be astonished at such ministers and professed christians. . . .

I am exceeding glad to hear you speak of Burchard as you do. I love that man. Do give my love to him. I am strongly inclined at times to recommend him to this people as a Pastor, as his talent would fall in peculiarly with the taste of this people. They need a pastor immediately and it is greatly desirable if possible, to obtain one who can speak German, this makes me hessitate about recommending any man from the north, although they must have [a] revival man, and I know not where they can get one here.[3]

Against such adversity, Finney, indomitable as always, plunged ahead. Apparently he exercised what for him was unusual restraint in tolerating Grier's shortcomings, and in everything Grier "made no objection to this, as he had left everything to [Finney's] judgment." One cannot help wondering if Grier and his elders regretted the invitation to Finney, knowing now that they had a tiger by the tail! There is probably no greater instance in Finney's career where a pastor and people were so utterly divergent from the standards of spiritual life and churchly activity that Finney had come to know and expect, considering the size of this congregation, than that of Reading.

Finney preached for several weeks, having accommodated himself to lowered expectations, and then felt the time was ripe for an inquiry meeting. Grier made no objection, but Finney thought he doubted that "many, if any, would attend such a meeting." On a cold, snowy Monday evening Finney himself was beginning to have some doubts that many would come, and "behold! the lecture-room, a large one—I think nearly as large as the body of the church above, was full." Grier was dumbfounded. He stated that he could hardly assist in the counseling, for he knew nothing of evangelism. Finney then proceeded to address the people, and to instruct them in the steps to assurance of salvation. After covering the doctrine of justification by faith in a simple fashion adapted to their understanding, Finney then stated that he wished to converse with each one for a moment, and he would circulate among them. He did this for some time, and then returned to the desk and explained that they could each one make an immediate decision for Christ. Then he invited all of them to kneel while he prayed for them, and besought God to accept each one in faith.[4]

Midway through Finney's stay, the *Western Recorder* reported on his work:

Reading, situated about fifty miles from Philadelphia, and containing about 10,000 inhabitants, has never before witnessed a revival. Religion and morals in the place had degenerated to a degree almost beyond parallel. But the work, we learn, has assumed a promising aspect. Many are awakened, some among the higher ranks, and an usual proportion of the number are men.[5]

By the early part of May 1829 Finney determined that he had done all he could for the town of Reading, and he prepared to conclude his activities. He had received an invitation from the town of Lancaster, approximately thirty miles to the southwest of Reading, and he probably began his preaching there on Sunday, May 10. The Presbyterian church in Lancaster had no pastor, and Finney had been invited by the leading elder of the church to minister there. He found, to his distress, a situation very similar to what had existed at Reading, with the faith of church members at a low ebb, and a great ignorance of evangelistic methods. Again there were no prayer meetings, and the elders of the church were unaccustomed to taking part in any such activities. Finney established standards of activity for the leaders, and began meetings for prayer and inquiry. He stated, "I remained at Lancaster but a very short time. . . . I left at so early a period as not to be able to give anything like a detailed account of the work there."[6] But he later declared that he remained in the town until June 15, which indicates a residence of perhaps five weeks.

After a year and a half of steady evangelism, Charles Finney was tired. He, with his wife Lydia and their year-old child, took the opportunity of release from further assignments to return to their beloved Whitesboro, and renew their acquaintances with the friends of Oneida County who never ceased to write to them and pray in their behalf. In letters he occasionally mentions problems with his health, and a severe inflammation of the eye, which left it very weak for months. Attempting to recover his strength, Finney made several short trips, the function of which was to confer with trusted friends and renew contacts after so long a time away from home. He preached in Utica for Dirck Lansing, and in Rome for Moses Gillet, and then made an extended trip to Albany and Troy to have meetings with Nathaniel Beman and Edward N. Kirk in July.[7] Beman had kept him abreast of the situation in New York, and he found that his friends in the Albany Presbytery were still very much under fire for their use of the new measures.

But above and beyond all of these reasons to take some time off

from preaching, Charles Finney needed to rest and recover his vitality for one overriding purpose: to be ready for New York City. The
invitations had been coming for some time, and things seemed to be
ripe. His numerous friends there had been pleading for his presence,
and undeniably, the attraction of the city to Finney was almost overwhelming. It is quite apparent to one who attempts to probe the mind
and the motives of Charles Finney, through his writings and his actions, that New York City exerted an irresistible pull on him. All of
his close friends in Oneida County sensed this, and they spoke of it
in numerous letters. It is as if, with Philadelphia behind him (whether
that campaign was a "triumph" or not), there was now one other major conquest to make for God, and he could not rest until he had in-
vaded Satan's last outpost. Although Finney had come far from being
a countryman, he was still a bit wide-eyed at the wickedness of the
cities, and his slashing denunciations must be balanced against his
eagerness to preach to the great audiences that could be gathered in
them.

It was not that Charles Finney had developed this interest in New
York entirely by himself; his interest had been whetted for some time
by the urgings of a group of remarkable businessmen there who had
large plans not only for that place but for the entire country. At the
center of this group was the wealthy silk merchant Arthur Tappan
(1786–1865), an orthodox Calvinist from Massachusetts who throughout his lifetime generously supported a host of evangelical causes and
in so doing inspired other businessmen to similar stewardship. Arthur Tappan had begun his New York business in 1826, and was joined
by his younger brother Lewis (1788–1873) in the rapidly growing firm
in 1827.[8] With their Puritan background, the Tappan brothers were convinced that well-to-do Christians were absolutely obligated to give of
their wealth to the kingdom of God. This conviction led them into
ever-widening areas of causes, and into close contact with the burgeoning "Benevolent Empire" of societies for the amelioration of societal
ills, which desperately needed the financial backing of men such as
the Tappans.[9] The brothers were beginning to bring together a group
called the "Association of Gentlemen," men generally from rural Connecticut and strict Congregationalists, in the banking and mercan-
tile trades, to support these worthy causes. Besides the Tappans their
number included David Low Dodge, Anson G. Phelps, Moses Allen,
Peletiah Perit, Silas Holmes, Zachariah Lewis, Knowles Taylor, Elea-
zar Lord, and Judge Jonas Platt and his son Zephaniah, the latter two
friends of Finney, recently moved to New York from Utica.[10]

David Low Dodge (1774–1852), born in Brooklyn, Connecticut, became a wealthy drygoods merchant in New York and in 1815 founded the New York Peace Society. In December 1827 he and other Yankee businessmen met with Charles Finney to persuade him to hold extended revivals in New York. Courtesy of the Presbyterian Historical Society.

In New York City the Presbyterians had gotten a firmer hold than the Congregationalists, and the leading pastor there was Dr. Gardiner Spring, of the Brick Presbyterian Church. Anson Phelps and the Platts belonged to this church, and most of the other "Gentlemen" on coming to New York had joined Presbyterian churches, their Congrega-

Arthur Tappan (1786–1865), born in Northampton, Massachusetts, came to New York City and established a silk-jobbing firm in 1826. Two years later his brother Lewis joined him. He was the unfailingly generous benefactor of Auburn and Lane theological seminaries, Oberlin and Kenyon colleges, and a host of other social reform movements. From an engraving by J. Andrews, in [Lewis Tappan], *The Life of Arthur Tappan.*

tionalism feeling comfortable enough there. But these prominent men, used to authority not only in business but also in the self-sufficient Congregational worship, soon grew restive under the stricter ecclesiastical polity of their new church, with its rigid hierarchy of judicatories and far greater authority given to the clergy than in New

England. Writing to Lyman Beecher in Boston on February 16, 1828, Lewis Tappan complained that the Presbyterian clerical establishment "keep in obscurity many persons who might be highly useful."[11] There was an increasing flow of Yankees from New England into New York City, young men for the most part looking for advancement and promise in the aggressive business world of the metropolis. Many of them were Congregationalists, and the New Englanders realized that here were the makings of a rival Congregational system, if someone were to organize it.

Within a month of his arrival in New York, Lewis Tappan decided to do exactly this. With Arthur to give financial aid, Lewis proposed a chain of Congregational churches throughout the city, each of which could continue to spawn other churches led by laymen, without the oversight or interference of a presbytery. Tappan's plan came quickly to the ears of Gardiner Spring, and he realized what a threat this presented to his denomination. Spring acted immediately to squelch the idea, and Tappan raged to his diary, "The Dutch & other interests here have paralized even N[ew] England men, and they feel the benumbing influence of timidity, & a compromising spirit, and a fear of man."[12] Hearing of the angry clash among men whom he needed as allies, Lyman Beecher begged Tappan to compromise with Spring. Tappan gave in for the moment, and Gardiner Spring moved ahead to divert the thrust of the idea. As a result, only one "Pilgrim" church was begun, and the members of the Association of Gentlemen were confirmed in their conviction that entrenched interests would continue to frustrate their benevolent efforts.

Coincidentally, at almost this exact time the New Lebanon Convention was being drawn together. Needing influential pastors on his side, Lyman Beecher invited Gardiner Spring to join him against the new measures pastors. Spring was of the same persuasion as Dr. James P. Wilson and Dr. Thomas H. Skinner of Philadelphia, all leaders of the moderate wing of the church which dominated it from the time of the Plan of Union in 1801 until the 1830s. When the schism came in the Presbyterian Church between the Old School and the New in 1837, Spring would side with the Old School. In 1827, he was already suspicious of the new measures, and his attitude is summed up in his statement, "Revivals are always spurious when they are got up by man's device and not *brought down* by the Spirit of God."[13] Certainly Gardiner Spring would have been happy to interrogate Charles Finney at New Lebanon, but he told Beecher that he would have to forego the pleasure because he had other pressing engagements and could not attend.

After the frustration of the New Lebanon Convention, Asahel Nettleton was wise enough to realize that although he could not bring Charles Finney down in fair combat, he could still rally pastors against the new measures. One of the cities to which he went on his errand of alarm was New York, and there Dr. Spring was one of the clergymen to whom he complained. While in the city he also conducted evangelistic meetings, which failed to produce any converts. To many of the New York pastors this was a more damaging blow against Nettleton than his continual harangue against the new measures.

In the midst of this situation, with their plan for "Pilgrim" churches brought down by Gardiner Spring, it was not difficult to convince the Association of Gentlemen that they should have a meeting with Charles Finney. Judge Jonas Platt and his son Zephaniah declared that Finney was the very man to provide the energetic leadership needed to go around the timid Presbyterianism that claimed to provide direction for the city's Calvinists. Accordingly, the Platts arranged a meeting during the first week of December 1827, and Finney, having preached at Stephentown until the last of November, then went to Troy and took a packet boat down the Hudson. When he arrived in New York, he was immediately taken under the care of the Platts. There, for several days, Finney met with the Yankee merchants, including David L. Dodge and his son William E. Dodge, Anson Phelps, and possibly with the Rev. Samuel H. Cox, pastor of the Laight Street Presbyterian church, which the Dodges attended.

The ostensible purpose of the meetings was to allow Finney to answer Nettleton's charges, and to give his version of the revivals that had been conducted in the last several years. Although it was unannounced, surely there was the additional hope on the part of the Platts that as the New Englanders listened to Finney they would not only be persuaded by his honesty but also come under the influence of his personal charm. Much prayer was offered as part of the meetings, and because there was no adversarial relationship as at New Lebanon, apparently the conference was successful in allaying fears about the new measures. At the conclusion, Finney parted from them and went on his way to Wilmington, to begin preaching at Eliphalet Gilbert's church in a few days. Almost immediately, enthusiastic letters followed him to Wilmington from the New Englanders. David L. Dodge wrote to Finney on December 18:

Dr. S[pring] voluntarily stated that he was uncommitted either way, but regretted Mr. N[ettleton]'s publication, said it was al-

together uncalled for. . . . I believe at least four ministers in our
Presbytery would give you not only the right hand of fellowship
but open their pulpits to you if they could be satisfied, you would
not introduce some things that [have] been such an occasion of
handle to opposers. . . . [Nettleton] has met with decided disap-
probation here from quarters he highly respects and has entirely
failed in enlisting some individuals in his favour.[14]

Two days later Zephaniah Platt wrote to Finney with the latest news:

Since you left us, Messrs Phelps and Dodge have had an interview with Dr. Spring, and the subject matter of the Western Revivals was fully and frankly discussed. The Dr. expressed the
kindest feelings towards yourself. . . . Upon the whole Mr. Phelps
is satisfied that your visit among us has resulted in good, and
that many an old prejudice has been softened, if not eradicated.[15]

Anson Phelps was especially pleased with Finney's demeanor
at the meetings and wrote to him on January 7, 1828, "We shall expect
to see you In our Stupid, Poluted, and Perishing City."[16] However, on
January 17, 1828, Finney began his work in Philadelphia, and this was
as important and auspicious a field as New York; he therefore postponed any thoughts of immediate service there for the time being.
Letters continued to flow between the two cities, the New Englanders delighted at his success to the south but fearful that if Finney did
not take advantage of the opportunity in their city soon, it would be
lost. Mindful of this, when he took a vacation at Philadelphia in mid-
July, on his way home to Whitesboro he stopped at the metropolis.
Gardiner Spring invited Finney to preach in the Brick Presbyterian
pulpit on Sunday, July 20, and Anson Phelps exulted to his private
diary:

Last Sabbath Doct. Spring Invited Brother Finey to Preach for Him
which was Verry Gratifying to Me and Many of His Friends Who
Espoused his Cause. . . . His Sermon was Excellent and I Believe
gave Great Satisfaction to Doct. Spring and A Numerous Congregation all of whom Now are anxious To Hear Him again and I
Cannot but Hope the Lord will Open a Door for Him.[17]

Departing from New York, Finney continued on to Whitesboro.
On his return, at the request of Phelps and his friends, he brought

Beman, Aikin, and Lansing for the extended conference that made William E. Dodge write, years later, "I shall never forget those days. Such prayers I never heard before. These men had all come from the influence of the recent wonderful revivals, and were all filled with the Spirit."[18] Then Finney preached at Samuel Cox's church on August 17.

As far as Finney knew, Cox, who was vacationing, had agreed to the invitation, and so he gladly complied. At Cox's Laight Street church the congregation was satisfied that Finney's preaching was not "fanatical," but when Samuel Cox returned he was quite angry, and word circulated quickly that he resented Finney's preaching from his pulpit. By this time Finney was back in Philadelphia beginning his work at the German Reformed church at Fourth and Race Streets, and when the rumor of Cox's anger reached him, knowing the damage this could do to a future campaign in New York, Finney wrote to Arthur Tappan. Tappan replied on September 25, 1828:

> Your letter rec[d] this morning is the first intimation I have had that Mr. Cox has expressed any dissatisfaction at your having preached for us during his absence. I can scarcely believe it true, but will make inquiry and write you again.
>
> Whatever Mr. Cox's sentiments may be upon the subject, I can assure you I have heard but one sentiment from his people and that is entire approbation and satisfaction. As it regards the report that "you intruded yourself upon us" I can say from my own knowledge, having been particularly instrumental in obtaining your assistance, that it is so far from being founded on fact that directly the reverse is the truth.[19]

From the available evidence, it appears that the laymen of New York City were quite pleased by Charles Finney's preaching, and the entire opposition came from Samuel Cox and a few other clergymen who were still excessively influenced by Asahel Nettleton and Lyman Beecher, and fearful of alienating the New England clergy. But Anson Phelps, David Dodge, the Tappans, and the other New Englanders had an impressive agenda of projects, and bringing Finney into New York on a permanent basis was only one of them. So, until the clerical opposition softened somewhat, that project would have to be tabled.

By the summer of 1829, when Charles Finney was concluding his evangelism in Lancaster, once again the New Englanders had decided that his preaching in New York was essential to their program. Even if Gardiner Spring and the Presbyterian hierarchy had supported them, they understood that revival, and numerous conversions, was not something that Spring could promise. On the other hand, the possibilities of Finney's sweeping in with his aggressive, time-tested program that was almost sure to produce results in the form of many converts, was an allurement difficult to resist. All other projects, even in the planning stage, would benefit enormously from an influx of new members who were pliable and eager for service. However, the New Englanders were shrewd enough to realize that they should not pin all their hope on Charles Finney, but with his loosely-organized cadre of fellow evangelists there was a ready pool of personnel from which they could draw capable and experienced men. Nathaniel Beman was named frequently as a likely candidate for a city church, and it may be that, with his long-standing troubles in Troy, he encouraged invitations to his relocating.

Increasingly irritated at the reluctance of the New York clergy to invite Finney, the New Englanders finally decided to cease waiting for the timid ministers, and on their own to invite Finney for a prolonged stay. As a leading member of Gardiner Spring's church, Anson G. Phelps must have been especially annoyed with his pastor, and he took the lead on this occasion. Phelps (1781–1853) had moved to New York City from Connecticut before the War of 1812. A poor orphan, by determination he had risen to become New York's leading importer of metals. His daughter Melissa married William E. Dodge, son of David L. Dodge, and William left his father's dry-goods store to join his father-in-law in the firm of Phelps, Dodge and Co., laying the foundation of the great Dodge fortune.[20] As Anson Phelps had led the way in the first meeting in December 1827, so once again he took a courageous stand. He wrote to Nathaniel Beman and others, urging them to persuade Finney to come immediately and preach in the metropolis.

Beman, who was very much concerned with the plan for "Pilgrim" churches, wrote to Finney on October 15, 1829:

> The call from N. York for revival preaching has become *loud* and *commanding;* and if those dear friends of ours are not speedily supplied they will give up and never think of making another similar effort. Do come out and see me. . . . The thing has lingered so long that they are almost in despair. . . . if N.Y. is not supplied *immediately,* the whole cause is *carried headlong!*[21]

At the very time Beman wrote to Finney, Anson Phelps was taking no chances that his pleas fell on deaf ears, and he traveled to the

Albany-Troy area to converse personally with the new measures pastors and urge them to persuade Charles Finney to come to the city. Samuel C. Aikin wrote to Finney on October 12:

> I saw in Albany Mr. Anson G. Phelps of New York. He told me that the two parties belonging to the Bowery Church have separated; that he and his friends are agoing to build. . . . He says Mr. Beman will probably be their pastor, but cannot go for several months. He wished me to say to you that he and his friends who have withdrawn from the Bowery, want you to come on without delay and occupy their pulpit, which is now wide open for you and will be at your entire disposal.[22]

Finney must have pondered the pros and cons of the situation for a time. On the one hand he was coming to the metropolis without clerical support, and if he dared invade the city without it, that might well solidify the opposition against him so that he would never be able to gain it. On the other hand, over a year had passed since he had preached in Samuel Cox's and Gardiner Spring's pulpits, and in that time they did not seem to have warmed to him. In addition, although he lacked ministerial endorsement, he was coming under the auspices of some of the most prominent and wealthy businessmen of the city, who had now provided money of their own for a church. This certainly demonstrated amazing determination, and to turn them down would be tantamount to cruelty. Furthermore, this might be the last chance he would have, and if he rejected it the New Englanders would in all likelihood wash their hands of him. Convinced that he should not disappoint them, Finney promised to come to New York City.

Overjoyed, Anson Phelps found a vacant church building on Vandewater Street, which he leased for three months. It was dedicated as the Union Presbyterian Church, with Charles G. Finney as its temporary pastor.[23] The news traveled that the renowned evangelist was now occupying a pulpit of his own, and many came, if only from curiosity, to behold the new measures at work. Certainly some attended because the rumor circulated that here was a man that the established clergy did not want the public to hear!

From Troy Nathaniel Beman dashed off another in his long series of admonitions to Finney (even Father Nash did not dare to speak this way to the fiery-eyed evangelist) on October 23, 1829, saying, "You never were situated, in all your life, as you are *now*. You have no Lansing, or Aikin, or Frost, or Gillet, or Beman to stand by you, and assist you; but all are lookers on, and will make their own *inference*."[24] Three days later Moses Gillet added his own advice:

> I have heard you remark, that Mr. Nettleton became proud and lost a spirit of prayer, in consequence of being patronized and flattered by great Doctors. . . . You may be surrounded by men of wealth and distinction, whose attention and flattery may not be the most favorable to prayer, and a humble dependence on God.[25]

From the beginning, the Congregationalism of the New England merchants, with which Finney was in full concurrence, asserted itself. They may have joined Spring's and Cox's churches, but their hearts were obviously elsewhere. Arthur Tappan wrote to Elias Cornelius, "I have all the feelings of an eastern man, and but little of the Presbyterian except the name."[26] The Union Church was the first of several *free* Presbyterian churches founded in New York, Rochester, Boston, and other cities by Finney and his followers. Carrying out the egalitarian nature of the enterprise, the merchants were eager to reach the abundant poor of the city who had often come from the countryside and needed to be protected from the malignity now surrounding them. To attract them, the usual custom of that day in supporting churches through the renting of pews was set aside, and all seats were free. Transients and the poor were welcomed at every service. The Union Church was enlisted in the ranks of the Presbytery, but it became clear from the start that it would take an irritatingly "congregational," independent attitude toward sectarianism. And, embodying the principles of the Benevolent Empire, the stated worship services and the pulpit preaching, however crucial they might have been, were just the beginning of a program of organized reformism and philanthropic endeavor calculated to reach the whole person.

Finney's own interests in social reform had been developing for several years, and they found a marvelous resonance in the devoted stewardship of the Association of Gentlemen. It was well and good to wish for reform in the abstract, that society might be lifted and its wounds healed, but when one found sincere men dedicated to using their wealth in concrete, specific ways, that was something else, and Finney immediately saw the possibilities and the value of joining forces with them. Finney's recognition of the need for Christian social action would continue to develop until the time of the Rochester revival, when a determined attack on the liquor interests of that grain-processing city would not only be extremely successful, but would seem a logical corollary to the entire endeavor of redeeming it. But alcoholism, the rationale went, was only one cancer that gnawed at society. What of the other maladies? Here, in New York City, were a phalanx of men who were already renowned throughout the nation for their generosity to reform causes, and they were explicitly inviting Finney to join their number. The implications were enormous.

When this impetus toward social reform began to take hold in the new and impressionable converts of Finney's revivals, under his careful tutelage, it became a thing of immense power. Gilbert Barnes, in *The Antislavery Impulse,* found that revivalism, and especially Finney's own preaching, provided the roots for the abolition movement. Theodore Weld is the best example of a reformist convert, but Weld was only one of many young converts whose idealism is difficult to conceive in our cynical modern period. Evangelism and the conversion of the individual remained the first priority with Finney, and without that nothing further could be done. Having that accomplished, urgent concerns could then be addressed, such as the ubiquitous poor of New York City, and the conditions that trapped many women in that day. Finney was appalled at women's plight in the city, and began to preach for female emancipation, in concert with the moral reform movement that was gathering strength. Carroll Smith Rosenberg has fully documented Finney's close ties to moral reform, and shown that it was his disciples who first manifested concern. After some initial activity under Finney's encouragement, the New York Female Moral Reform Society was organized in his church, the Chatham Street Chapel, on May 12, 1834, and its founders, officers, and supporters came from among his followers. Historians of women, including Barbara Berg, Nancy F. Cott, Mary P. Ryan, Keith Melder, Paul Boyer, and Carroll Smith Rosenberg, have described the movement's goals: distributing food and clothing to the destitute, seeking jobs for the unemployed, eliminating the double standard, eradicating prostitution, and in general highlighting women's rights and equality. In 1839 Calvin Colton, looking back on all this, remarked acutely on Finney's shift of emphasis:

[It had remade Calvinism into] a very practical affair, and adapted it well to American tastes and habits. It encourages mankind to *work* as well as to *believe.* Let loose from the chains of predestination, and in accordance with this new light, the scheme has been set on foot in America, of converting the world *at once* . . . a very natural excess of such emancipation of the mind, and of the overflowings of benevolence.[27]

With the poor encouraged to attend, and the wealth of the Gentlemen supporting the endeavor, congregations at the Union Presbyterian Church began to increase under Finney's vibrant preaching. Here, however, the situation was quite different from that in Philadelphia, where he had had the backing of the clergy, and the unchurched poor were not the special target of his evangelism. However, the Gentlemen were encouraged enough that when the lease ran out in three months on the Vandewater Street church, Anson Phelps once again stepped forward and purchased outright an abandoned Universalist church uptown on Prince Street near Broadway, which was about to be sold under foreclosure of mortgage. Now in a building of their own, Finney and the Gentlemen were delighted that the work could go forward on a more permanent basis. The poor were not the most substantial persons upon which to build the work, but with the assured financial backing of several wealthy men, it seemed that the future was auspicious. On May 29, 1830, the infant *New York Evangelist* stated,

> From the fruits of this revival, 103 persons have joined this church by profession, and 42 by letter. Many . . . have united with other churches. Probably more than 200 have been hopefully renewed by the power of the Holy Ghost. . . . The work is still progressing.[28]

The Association of Gentlemen recognized that their benevolent work needed a spokesman to combat the sneering references of other newspapers, which would grow far worse in the next few years. They had nurtured a hope for some time that a newspaper could be founded that would serve to advertise their program. Early in 1827 Arthur Tappan began the New York *Journal of Commerce* as a paper that would refuse undesirable advertising from theaters, breweries, and so on. Tappan had several ideas to put the paper on a firm base. Distributed free of charge at first, it soon proved a fierce competitor in scooping rival papers by the expedient of sending a small boat out to sea to meet incoming ships, thus getting the latest news from overseas, and for this Tappan received the undying enmity of other publishers. But he chose the wrong man as editor, and religious and commercial news did not coexist profitably in the same journal. Then Arthur Tappan gave full control of the paper to his brother Lewis, who ran it for several months and wisely sold it to David Hale, in whose hands it rapidly grew into a leading political and financial paper.[29]

Having sold the *Journal of Commerce,* the Gentlemen hoped that their next experiment in journalism would be more successful. After the December 1827 conference at Anson Phelps' home, David Dodge wrote to Charles Finney: "I do not think the time is very distant when we shall have a strictly religious periodical in the City—one of a decided and independent character. It is greatly needed."[30] In April 1830 the Gentlemen tried again, organizing the *New York Evangelist.* Its financing largely came from Zephaniah Platt. N. C. Saxton was chosen as editor. Saxton was an able man, but the going was uphill and there were many competitors. He wrote Finney on September 27, 1830: "Unless we can receive 2000 more subscribers between this and the first of April next we will be in trouble."[31] They were not forthcoming, and in 1831 the Tappans appointed the Rev. Joshua Leavitt, an energetic Connecticut Yankee Congregationalist, as editor.

A practicing attorney before graduating from Yale College and Seminary, Leavitt (1794–1873) had come to New York in 1828 as secretary of The Seaman's Friend Society. In 1830 he published a hymn book, *The Christian Lyre #1,* sending an examination copy to Finney and writing, "It will contain, as far as I can procure them, the favorite tunes and hymns of various denominations. . . . If you approve the work, allow me to request of you the favor to aid its circulation."[32] Finney was pleased with the book for several reasons, not the least of which was that he might use it to replace Asahel Nettleton's *Village Hymns* in his services! With their common legal background, the two soon became close friends, and Finney eagerly supported the choice of Leavitt as editor of the *Evangelist.* Almost immediately the circulation of the paper began to increase as Leavitt brought in innovative ideas, and the Gentlemen hoped in time it would supplant the *New York Observer,* an Old School paper that upheld Nettleton and condemned Finney and the new measures. Most of their hopes were realized in the next few years as the *Evangelist* ably advocated the free church movement, and served as the literary voice of Finney's evangelism and the benevolence work of the Association of Gentlemen.

For months on end Charles Finney labored away in the church on Prince Street, functioning more as a settled pastor than he had ever done previously. As always, his friends fussed over him and worried about him. Would the city, with its millionaires, corrupt him? Was he becoming formal? Was it not true that spiritual unction and true power came only in the country, and, fight it as one may, faded in the cities? Was not Finney growing tired of staying in one place, and did he not long to preach to his enthusiastic and emotional friends in the "Burned-over District," rather than to the jaded and work-worn faces in Gotham? Of many such letters, George Gale's of January 21, 1830, expressed this as well as any:

> I am still of the belief that cities are poor places to promote Re-
> vivals, at least such as we have in the country. The business, the
> hustle, the dissipation, the etiquette and a countless number and
> variety of things seem to stand in the way of good. . . .
>   I have heard the question asked will not brother Finney catch
> the same fever or language to that effect. Will he not have his mind
> turned off at least from the business of converting souls to Christ
> to the business of converting men to some peculiarity of senti-
> ment to some theory or speculation?[33]

Succumbing to the constant suggestions, apparently Charles Finney did begin to feel a bit boxed in. At that point he had not definitely decided to leave New York, but there was the possibility that he might take another church begun with Tappan or Phelps money, and thus build up an entirely new congregation before moving on to still another field of labor. The evidence for this is slight, but apparently Finney explained this to the leaders at the Prince Street church, and recommended Dirck Lansing as his successor. An invitation to be pastor of the church was extended to Lansing, for he replied to Finney on May 25, 1830, from Utica: "I have come to the conclusion that I must not listen to an invitation from abroad, at least for the present. The ch[urch] of Prince St. must, therefore, turn their attention to some other man."[34]

Whatever Finney's place in its future, the free church movement in New York seemed to have a propitious start. In May the Gentlemen invited the Rev. Joel Parker (1799–1873) of the Third Presbyterian Church in Rochester, New York, to attend a meeting. Although the Prince Street church was performing a very adequate ministry to one area of the city, there were still areas too far from there to be touched by Charles Finney's preaching. At the meeting with Parker, Lewis Tappan volunteered to find a suitable place for worship on the lower East Side, which teemed with the poor. Parker, a revivalist preacher, was eager for such a ministry in tandem with Finney, and at the meeting pledges of financial support were secured from the Gentlemen. Parker was accepted as pastor of the proposed church.[35] On June 26, 1830, the *New York Evangelist* reported:

A Hall has been hired in Thames Street, near Broadway, being the room formerly occupied by the Rev. Dr. Romeyn's church as a lecture room. It is conveniently fitted up and will contain about 400 persons. Several families belonging to other churches have formed an association to worship in this place. An invitation has been given to the Rev. Joel Parker, of Rochester, N.Y., to become minister; he has accepted the call . . . and will commence his ministry in this city the next Lord's day.[36]

The new outpost was named the First Free Presbyterian Church, and the Dutch Reformed of New York cooperated in its founding. The specific intention of this move was to absorb the surplus of converts from the evangelism Finney had been conducting at Prince Street. Joel Parker, who had had extensive experience with the American Home Missionary Society (AHMS) work in western New York, led in applying for membership with this group, because the church conceived of itself as a "free mission" to the poor. However, the AHMS feared a conflict of interest with the two existing presbyteries of New York, and prudently refused the application. Next Parker appealed to the First Presbytery of New York for membership, which also refused, and objected to the name "free church" as unauthorized by itself. In addition the First Presbytery stated that no new church was needed in the lower part of the city. So, for the time, Parker's church was indeed "free," in that it lacked any denominational affiliation.

By the summer of 1830, Charles Finney was anxious to leave the city and spend some time in Whitesboro. A second child had been born to Lydia on March 28, their first son, named Charles Beman, after Nathaniel Beman. Finney redoubled his urging of the leaders of the Prince Street congregation to look for another pastor, and toward the end of August the congregation extended a unanimous call to his very dear friend Herman Norton.[37] Delighted with the leaders' acquiescence, Lydia and Charles Finney and their two children quickly left the summer heat of the city and made for their rural retreat. At Whitesboro, he considered a number of pressing invitations before him. Should he return to New York? James Patterson was continually urging him to return to Philadelphia, where the situation for the acceptance of new measures looked more promising than ever. Patterson had written to Finney on March 26, 1830, regarding the changing circumstances at the important First Church: "Dr. Wilson's people have called Rev. Mr. [Albert] Barnes of Morristown, N.J. Dr. Green, Dr. Ely, and Mr. Potts, it is said, don't like that he should come into this Presbytery because of his New Divinity. He is a revival man. . . . I think he will be an acquisition to the cause of revivals in this city."[38] And there were other invitations, equally compelling, requesting his preaching in cities and towns across the nation.

While Charles Finney pondered his prospects, the free church movement in New York went ahead without him. On September 13, 1830, a Dr. Brown advised Finney that Joel Parker "has a crowded house," and that efforts were continuing to affiliate with some organization. Overtures had also been made by the Gentlemen to the Second Presbytery of New York, and these had met with rebuff. But, although the free churches were small and new, the Association of Gentlemen itself had a great deal of influence because of the combined wealth of its members, and they determined upon a new tactic. This was to appeal to the Synod of New York for the establishment of still a third presbytery in the city. The General Assembly had approved the principle of "elective affinity," whereby several presbyteries might coexist in the same geographical area, and newly formed churches could choose which they wished to join.

The Synod granted their request, accepted eleven churches into this arrangement, and set the date of January 4, 1831, for the erection of the Third Presbytery.[39] Its stated objective, as approved by the Synod, was conversion of the lower social classes. With such a liberal structure granted by the Synod, churches within this arrangement were free to initiate what for many would be radical stands, such as the amalgamation of new measures revivalism and Benevolent Empire causes, "immediate conversion" and "immediate reform," and the Presbyterian hierarchy would be powerless to hinder them. Demonstrating that such an arrangement was desired by many in New York is the fact that its "free missions" claimed a total membership of 3,863 by May 1832.[40]

Surely, as Charles Cole has demonstrated, the free church movement was a valid attempt to apply the social teachings of Christianity —love, fellowship, and the grace of God—to a festering society where the poor were trapped in immobility.[41] With the pew tax arrangement, and the sale of pews in most churches of the day, the poor were effectively excluded from all but a peripheral place among the congregations. This had the inevitable effect of allowing wealthy families not only to restrict the poor to balconies and undesirable areas of the sanctuaries, but also to allow the wealthy to dominate the affairs of the churches. Thus, a class system was perpetuated in the church, and the social teachings of Christianity were frustrated and overturned. The free church movement was designed to attack these evils by transforming the church into a classless institution that disregarded social, economic, and racial distinctions. It is perhaps especially surprising that such a system was largely designed by some of the wealthy upper class of New York City. At Prince Street, and in his later New York pastorates, Finney used the free church movement as an important democratizing force in breaking down the social conservatism of Presbyterianism.

Herman Norton came as pastor of the Prince Street church in September, and set to work with a will. As Charles Finney's closest friend, he labored to perpetuate the gains made by Finney during the previous year, but he found it hard going. Perhaps part of the problem was that people had been mesmerized by Finney's preaching power, and were somewhat disappointed with Norton's lesser abilities. His letter of November 1830 to Finney illuminates many of the problems encountered at the time:

> ... I found this church in a very scattered state. The feeling which existed when you left was entirely dissipated. Every one had gone his own way. Everybody had been preaching here. A mighty effort was necessary to rally the church. ... I do not know that these men of business ever will wake up this side of eternity. The members of this church you know have come from all parts. Although called the Union Church no general bond of union has yet been formed among them. ...
>
> A third Presbytery is to be formed [in] this City in January by order of the Synod. I expect to belong to it. It will take in the uptown churches.[42]

The free church movement in New York was off to an auspicious beginning, but its best days were still ahead. It would have to do without Charles Finney for a time, for other interests were drawing him away. He could not know it, but his greatest revival, and one of the best years of his life, were immediately ahead.

10

REVIVAL AT ROCHESTER

Among the many invitations Charles Finney received in 1830 were letters from Josiah Bissell, an elder of the Third Presbyterian Church of Rochester and the owner of the famous Pioneer Stage Line, known throughout the East because he would not allow its coaches to move on Sunday. Bissell had sentiments similar to those of the Association of Gentlemen in New York, being involved in many societies. Very generous to Christian causes, he had financed the construction of both the Second and Third Presbyterian churches of Rochester, and to the latter had promised "a half of his bisquit as long as he had one."[1] In addition, he personally financed the militant *Rochester Observer*, and headed the Monroe County Bible Society. Bissell had written to Charles Finney on September 15, 1829, in an attempt to persuade him of the necessity of holding a campaign in the city on the Erie Canal:

> Your ideas of the importance of N York are correct—this is the Waterloo of the world—Here a mighty contest is commenced & must be carried on. Here God is displaying His wonders and will display them more and more untill the great interest of Zion shall triumph. Your glance at the *Canal* too, is an important one and there are many whose hearts are stirred within them on this subject. Dr. Phelps, minister from Pittsfield, says on one of his passages on the Canal this summer the Captain told him the line

which he was in, had already dismissed nine women from their boats in a stage of pregnancy, and that a [boy] driver might as well be sent to state prison as to the Canal.[2]

Bissell's pastor, the Rev. Joel Parker, also urged Finney's coming, and when he was called to be pastor of the First Free Presbyterian Church in New York City in May 1830, he advised the Rochester congregation to invite Finney to preach after he left.

But Finney, through his friends, had also heard that the Christians of Rochester were quarreling in ways severe enough to constitute impediments to the success of any widespread evangelism there. Hearing this, Finney had drawn up short. The strife had taken place in several denominations, but among the Presbyterians, upon whom Finney would largely lean for support, most of the difficulties revolved around one individual, interestingly—Josiah Bissell. His Pioneer Stage Line, and the attempt to stop the nationwide delivery of mails on Sunday, in which he was deeply involved, had already made him in the eyes of many, even church members, the symbol of repression and coercive methods. Even more recently Bissell had been involved in a nasty wrangle with two Presbyterian clergymen of the city. It started when Bissell saw the Rev. William James of the Second Church on a weekday riding in one of the seven-day coaches. Outraged, he intruded into the affairs of Second Church and told James that his people wished him to leave. Possibly Bissell had taken a dislike to James, for one paper said of his generous but imperious ways that the pastor did not "*draw well in Mr. Bissell's harness.*"[3] Because Bissell had financed the construction of their building, the congregation was startled and obediently "requested the dismission of Mr. James," alleging that "pecuniary embarassments demanded it." Bissell wished for Asa Mahan, pastor of the church in Pittsford, to come to the Second Church.[4]

All this demagoguery was carefully watched by the pastor of the First Church, Joseph Penney. Not a man to knuckle down to wealth, Penney was provoked by Bissell's ways, and saw James' dismissal as simply a maneuver on Bissell's part to get his own man into Second Church. Penney was threatening to take the entire matter before the Rochester Presbytery and expose Bissell's chicanery. Since this would bring a powerful and generous man into a position of widespread notoriety and possible rebuke, tempers were ready to flare on all sides, and the Presbyterians of Rochester were hardly in any spirit to welcome Finney and a revival.

At Whitesboro, Finney pondered this problem and the others he

knew to exist in Rochester, and resolved to lay the entire matter before his friends in nearby Utica. He, Lydia, and the children went there,
trunks packed and ready to go where God seemed to be guiding, "and
in the evening quite a number of the leading brethren, in whose prayers and wisdom I had a great deal of confidence, at my request met
for consultation and prayer, in regard to my next field of labor."[5] After
explaining the situation at Rochester, he "laid all the facts before
them" regarding his invitations to other cities. "Rochester seemed to
be the least inviting of them all."

It was decided. "They were unanimous in the opinion that
Rochester was too uninviting a field of labor, to be put at all in competition with New York, or Philadelphia, and some other fields to
which I was then invited. . . . At the time, this was my own impression and conviction." Thanking his well-intentioned friends, he retired for the night, composed in his mind that in the morning his route
was clear, to go east. But then the matter returned to him, and he
rehearsed the reasons that seemed to render Rochester a poor choice.
An almost mystical feeling came over him, as it occasionally did in
his life when he claimed to feel the direct presence of God guiding
his actions. It seemed that all the reasons he advanced against Rochester, in another light were the very reasons he should go there. "Something" spoke to him saying, "Certainly you are needed at Rochester
all the more because of these difficulties. . . . If all was right, you would
not be needed."[6] Finney felt ashamed, and lacking in faith. He could
not deter the impression, and the pull toward Rochester was irresistible. Accordingly, early the next morning he and his family boarded
the first packet boat headed west.

Although he had traveled the Erie Canal many times in the past,
Finney still enjoyed the leisurely and stately ride aboard the canal boat,
towed by the rope attached to the horses on the tow path. His little
son Charles, barely five months old, would have no interest in the
passing sights, but daughter Helen, now two, would show a lively
curiosity as her father pointed out an approaching eastbound boat,
passengers on its deck as on this, and as the boats passed each other
a quick exchange of greetings and bits of news. Then, west of Jordan
and Weedsport, the canal entered the broad plain which forms the
southern shore of Lake Ontario. Here the soil was rich, and in that
early September the lush green crops, and the endless fields of golden
wheat tossing gently in the breeze, were magnificent sights. Finney
knew that almost all of this wheat would be sent to the mills of
Rochester, and the flour made from it would go to faraway places. In

the distance were well-kept and prosperous farmhouses and barns, and every few miles a bustling village would appear, its shops and mills on the very brink of the canal, and deriving much of its livelihood from it.

East of the Genesee River, the captain announced that Rochester would soon be in view. Lydia and Charles Finney gathered their belongings, and almost immediately the fields of wheat stopped, a few last stands of old trees passed by, and the houses that made up the outskirts of the nation's newest city surrounded the canal. In a minute, impressive new buildings were to be seen, obviously busy with prosperous commerce. Then the moment approached that would bring forth exclamations of surprise and delight from first-timers on the boats, as the canal passed high over the river on the famous stone aqueduct.

Even before the opening of the canal, Rochester was important by virtue of its location and natural advantages. Rochesterville was founded in 1812 by Nathaniel Rochester, William Fitzhugh, and Charles Carroll, and it was seen immediately that it offered a perfect site for mills at its falls. As an atlas of the 1830s described:

> The fall in the stream between the city and the lake [Ontario] is 271 feet, 268 of which are within the city bounds, affording cascades of exceeding beauty. The power they afford is estimated to be equal to 38,400 horses, giving motion to 21 large flouring mills, 11 valuable sawmills, 1 cotton, and 3 woollen factories, 9 large machine shops, and numerous other hydraulic works.[7]

When laborers digging the canal reached Rochester in 1821, it was then a busy village of fifteen hundred, and from then on its growth was almost meteoric. The through route to New York City was completed in 1823. Almost immediately the fertile Genesee Valley became one of the world's most important grain-producing areas, and this place on the Erie Canal was turned into the nation's first inland boom town. The motivation for it was everywhere apparent: before the construction of the canal the cost of transportation for the flour milled here had eaten up much of the profit. But with the opening of the canal to New York City, transportation costs tumbled and easy access to world markets was made possible for the first time. Seizing the opportunity, farmers felled the remaining stands of trees, plowed under their corn, and planted wheat in every possible place. An index of the town's growth is to be found in its production of barrels of flour. In 1818, an average year before the canal began operating, 26,000 barrels of flour were produced. In 1828 the figure stood at 200,000, and by 1840 reached over 500,000.[8]

Such sudden wealth drew not only hordes of laborers seeking employment and riches, but also its share of upheaval and trouble. In his thorough study of the background of the Rochester revival, Paul E. Johnson had termed these transients, many on their way farther west, "a bottom-heavy and unstable urban population," culturally closer to the small town than to larger east-coast cities.[9] In 1830, amazingly, three-fourths of the population was under thirty years of age. In addition to the land boom and the possibilities of quick riches, other factors had conspired to make the Rochester boom-town years less than tranquil. For one, the anti-Masonic frenzy had not only centered on Rochester (the events surrounding the disappearance of William Morgan had occurred in the area) but it also attacked the town's elite as nowhere else. A large number of local wealthy and powerful men were Masons, and deep jealousies between Masons and non-Masons had festered for years before the Morgan incident. After that, in retaliation, anti-Masons not only mounted a protest movement against entrenched power, but even transformed themselves into a political party in 1828. This reached into the very core of religious life in Rochester, for the rector of St. Luke's Episcopal Church, the Rev. Francis Cuming, was closely tied by marriage to many of the most powerful people in town, and he was elected in 1826 the Grand Commander of the Masons. After Morgan's disappearance it was Cuming who was indicted on the charge of providing the carriage in which the abductors had fled.[10] Happily for Finney's revival in 1831, the furor over that had died down after Cuming had resigned from his pulpit in 1829 and left the area.

After that, the city of Rochester reeled over the excitement of the temperance crusade. Fortunately, this did not split the churches as the anti-Masonic movement did. Rather, the middle class here and in much of America united as on few other issues, as they began to realize that they had largely lost control of the lower-class, blue-collar workers due to the ravages of Demon Rum. It was Lyman Beecher, grand strategist of almost every reform cause, who in 1828 had sensitized the conscience of the American middle class with his published *Six Sermons on the Nature, Occasions, Signs, Evils, and Remedy of Intemperance*.[11] Already alarmed over its unruly and frequently drunken young workers, Rochester rallied to the Beecher banner with alacrity, realizing that here might be a method of social control that was desperately needed. Paul Johnson has found that, whereas the temperance question did not exist in 1825, "three years later it was a middle-class obsession."[12] It was also an important adjunct to revivalism, and would play an ongoing role in the coming revival.

Playing right into the hands of the temperance movement was the fate of Sam Patch in 1829. Sam had previously leapt over both the Niagara and Genesee Falls with no resultant damage, and he decided to try the Genesee Falls again. When he did not appear at the bottom of the falls, a search for his body was begun, which lasted four months.[13] Then rumors began to spread. He had been drunk, and was coaxed to it by some instigators! These evil persons, the rumors continued, knew that Sam needed all his faculties when performing his famous leaps, but that had not deterred their foul deed. The temperance forces in Rochester made the most of the rumors, taking marvelous advantage of the national publicity. Rochester was once again famous — or infamous — in the eyes of the nation.

At about the same time came the furor over Sabbatarianism, which split the churches of Rochester as had the anti-Masonic fever. In 1828, many who had grown up in quiet New England towns where from sundown Saturday little was done but attend church, and who wished to see the New England Sabbath replicated in New York, began to pressure transportation companies to stop doing business on Sundays. Sabbatarians demanded that good church members patronize only boat and stage lines that ceased operations on the Lord's day.

It was then that Josiah Bissell, with contributions from wealthy citizens and important donors to worthy causes like Lewis Tappan, started his Pioneer Coach Line. Attempting to attract all decent people, the Pioneer line observed the Sabbath, its stage drivers were nondrinkers, and at stops hot coffee, instead of the customary liquor, was served to passengers. This was met with objections: if Sunday travel stopped, mail delivery would be hindered. Then, Bissell went to Washington to secure contracts from the post office for his stage line. He was flatly rejected. Infuriated, he joined with Lyman Beecher and Lewis Tappan to organize a nationwide movement to stop Sunday deliveries of mail. As Paul Johnson has commented, "Overnight, Rochester was at the center of a national crusade to maintain Sunday as sacred time."[14] It would dissipate almost as quickly as it came, however. Many church members did not agree with the arrogant Bissell, fearing that if the canal boat crews were idled on Sundays, and marooned in Rochester and elsewhere, they would become drunken menaces, carousing and rioting. Because of massive opposition, within a year Bissell's six-day line had ceased operation and had become a laughingstock of the country, and the name of Rochester a byword.

All of this, within a period of only three or four years, would have been enough agitation to suit any middle- or large-sized city. But that it happened to an upstart of a town of merely ten thousand souls is startling. And so much of the hostility dealt directly or indirectly with the churches of Rochester. It was no wonder Finney and his friends had qualms about them. Yet, it was there he went.

Arriving at his destination about September 9, Finney prepared to fill the pulpit of the Third Church. A cousin, who was an elder in the First Church, introduced Finney to his pastor, Joseph Penney, and an invitation was extended to Finney to preach in the First Church as well. Then, Penney and Josiah Bissell realized the importance of unity, and their quarrel was resolved and "all the distractions and collisions that had existed there were adjusted," and peace prevailed.

The first union meeting was held on September 10, and from then until March 6, 1831, Charles Finney preached ninety-eight sermons and attended numberless "anxious meetings."[15] In so many previous campaigns time had been required to overcome the "stupidity" of people and awaken their consciences, but it seemed that here the populace was ready and eager for Finney's challenges. Alternating between the churches, Finney faced crowds from the beginning. People came in from surrounding towns in a wide radius. To assist in the spread of the revival spirit, Finney accepted occasional calls to preach in such places as Ogden, Brockport, Penfield, and Clarkson.[16] The press was generally favorable from the start, and Finney was fortunate that the town had the specifically revivalist paper, the *Rochester Observer*, which threw its entire weight behind his work.

After years in the wealthy, worldly, and starched metropolises of Philadelphia and New York City, Finney was again among people who understood him thoroughly, and whose New England roots were still strong. Finney simply appealed to Yankee consciences that had been carefully honed in earlier years, but had been dulled during the canal boom years of the 1820s. He did not revert to his earlier haranguing pulpit style. With the abundant material from the Rochester revival we are able to appraise Finney at this time, and it is apparent that a subtle change had occurred from the influences of the great cities. A final phase in his oratorical development had come about; his mannerisms and terminology were more studied, and the last remnants of countrified speech and rustic bombast and crudities had been carefully refined out. His friends from Oneida County might have termed it "formalism," but it was inevitable after close contact with the magnates of finance, industry, and theology, and it was the Finney who was to remain. He had whetted his logic to a fine point, and he played upon his background and reputation as a student of law, so that this was perhaps the prevailing impression that came across to multitudes of auditors. And, although Finney always stressed that he was an extemporaneous speaker (to separate himself from the stuffy tied-to-notes pulpit pedantry of the past), ironically this was no longer strictly true, for years of repeating a stock of sermons over and over in various places had removed some of his earlier freshness and élan, while allowing him to polish each one of that stock to a brilliant lustre. Still, he portrayed God as vengeful, and rarely mentioned God's love, other than as an impersonal "disinterested benevolence."

Feeling a marvelous resonance with the community, Charles Finney was at his superb pinnacle during those months in Rochester. One scholar has commented:

> No more impressive revival has occurred in American history. . . .
> But the exceptional feature was the phenomenal dignity of this awakening. No agonizing souls fell in the aisles, no raptured ones shouted hallelujahs. . . . Lawyers, real-estate magnates, millers, manufacturers, and commercial tycoons led the parade of the regenerated.[17]

Not only was Finney dignified and superbly logical, but he now possessed complete self-confidence to experiment with, and introduce innovations into, his technique. Although "anxious meetings" had been standard until then with him, the opportunity afforded in them to come to an immediate decision was not carried over to the large worship services. For some time he had felt this to be a lack, and so at Rochester he brought in what was to become a staple of mass evangelism, the opportunity to respond immediately to the evangelist's invitation by some overt physical activity such as walking forward. Finney's comments on this decision are so important they deserve to be quoted:

> I had never, I believe, except in rare instances, until I went to Rochester, used as a means of promoting revivals, what has since been called "the anxious seat." I had sometimes asked persons in

the congregation to stand up; but this I had not frequently done. However, in studying upon the subject, I had often felt the necessity of some measure that would bring sinners to a stand. From my own experience and observation I had found, that with the higher classes especially, the greatest obstacle to be overcome was their fear of being known as anxious inquirers. They were too proud to take any position that would reveal them to others as anxious for their souls. . . .

At Rochester, if I recollect right, I first introduced this measure. This was years after the cry had been raised of "new measures." A few days after the conversion of Mrs. M———, I made a call, I think for the first time, upon all that class of persons whose convictions were so ripe that they were willing to renounce their sins and give themselves to God, to come forward to certain seats which I requested to be vacated, and offer themselves up to God, while we made them subjects of prayer. A much larger number came forward than I expected, and among them was another prominent lady. . . . This increased the interest among that class of people; and it was soon seen that the Lord was aiming at the conversion of the highest classes of society. My meetings soon became thronged with that class. The lawyers, physicians, merchants, and indeed all the most intelligent people, became more and more interested, and more and more easily influenced.[18]

The campaign had scarcely begun, on October 1, 1830, when a frightening experience occurred. The old First Church building was being used that evening, with every seat taken and hundreds standing in the aisles. Dr. Penney was leading the first prayer, with Finney kneeling behind him, when a sound like a gunshot and the cracking of glass startled the congregation. Finney reported that "Dr. Penney leaped from the pulpit almost over me. . . . The original alarm was created by a timber from the roof, falling end downwards, and breaking through the ceiling, above the lamp in front of the organ."[19] Panic followed, with the congregation of almost two thousand people stampeding through the doors, and some leaping out the windows. Finney tried to restore calm, calling loudly for order, but two women rushed up to the pulpit and, one on each side, bodily carried him out of doors. He reported that "As I did not know that there was any danger, the scene looked so ludicrous to me, that I could scarcely refrain from laughing." Finney was not aware that others had been concerned with the state of the building for some time, for the rear wall of the church stood on the brink of the canal and, due to the ground being very wet, the walls had been settling. Many were frightened that the roof would collapse or the walls buckle. In their stampede to get out, people trampled one another. One elderly woman opened a large window that overlooked the canal, and many leaped out into the water below. Eventually it was found that some were hurt, but no one was killed, and the inside of the church was littered with the bonnets, shawls, hats, and gloves that the congregation had abandoned in its flight.[20] The clergy of the St. Paul's Episcopal Church offered the use of that building, but it was decided to keep the remainder of the meetings in the Second and Third churches. Finney was concerned lest the work suffer from this event; however, it seemed to stimulate public interest rather than deter it.

Finney was busy from morning till night. He preached several times during each week, and three times on Sunday, in addition to conducting innumerable meetings for prayer and inquiry at other times in various churches throughout the city. His pace was so demanding that Theodore Weld wrote cautioning him to tend carefully to the condition of his lungs and throat, and adding:

> The influence which the revival at R[ochester] and vicinity has had to do away prejudice against you is beyond calculation. Dont be in haste to leave that region I beseech. . . . Why not go to Buffalo and to the intermediate towns between there and Rochester? Once get that region thoroughly soaked and all hell cant wring it dry you know.[21]

An especially perceptive observer of the revival was the journalist Henry Brewster Stanton, who recalled Finney's demeanor:

> In October, 1830, Charles G. Finney, the famous evangelist, came to Rochester to supply the pulpit of the Third Presbyterian Church. I had been absent a few days and on my return was asked to hear him. It was in the afternoon. A tall, grave-looking man, dressed in an unclerical suit of gray, ascended the pulpit. Light hair covered his forehead; his eyes were of a sparkling blue, and his pose and movement dignified. I listened. It did not sound like preaching, but like a lawyer arguing a case before a court and jury. This was not singular, perhaps, for the speaker had been a lawyer before he became a clergyman. The discourse was a chain of logic, bright-

ened by the felicity of illustration and enforced by urgent appeals from a voice of great compass and melody. Mr. Finney was then in the fulness of his powers. He had won distinction elsewhere, but was little known in Rochester. He preached there six months, usually speaking three times on the Sabbath, and three or four times during the week. His style was particularly attractive for lawyers. He illustrated his points frequently and happily by reference to legal principle. It began with the judges, the lawyers, the physicians, the bankers, and the merchants, and worked its way down to the bottom of society, till nearly everybody had joined one or the other of the churches controlled by the different denominations. I have heard many celebrated pulpit orators in various parts of the world. Taken all in all, I never heard the superior of Charles G. Finney.[22]

Some of the articles carried in the local papers were critical, but for the most part the journalistic tone was positive. This was inevitable, for in all objectivity there was little to criticize or condemn, look as hard as one might. Finney had the constant backing of the evangelical *Observer*, and after a few weeks it reported:

On the Sabbath no place of worship is large enough to contain the multitude that assembles. . . . Such a revival, perhaps, was never experienced where less disorder was witnessed, or less open opposition manifested. . . . Indeed Christians of different denominations are seen mingling together in the Sanctuary on the Sabbath and bowing at the same altar in the weekly prayer meeting.[23]

In its eagerness to follow Charles Finney's ministry, the *New York Evangelist* stated:

Mr. Finney is preaching to overflowing houses. Multitudes assemble who cannot get within reach of the preacher's voice. Conversions are daily occurring. . . . So large a proportion of men of wealth, talents, and influence have rarely, if ever been known to be the subjects of revival in that vicinity.[24]

These were the regular descriptions of the revival's progress in October and November. Then in December the *Observer* related that the awakening was going on "with unabated interest and power," although, it added, Finney was showing some signs of a physical break-down from his crushing labors.[25]

The uniform support that he received from much of the citizenry encouraged Finney, for the first time in his ministry, to extend the revival emphasis into an area of social reform in which he was vitally interested. In addition, he had been determined to involve Theodore Weld in some aspect of his ongoing work, convinced as he was that Weld would be an invaluable asset. Finney had begun to solicit his help as early as 1828, when Weld was only twenty-four, writing on March 27 of that year to him from his Philadelphia campaign, "O how much I want your help and that of 20 others who understand revivals."[26] One problem was evident, however: although Weld was unusually mature for his age, intelligent, and extremely personable, his education was still deficient, and he had enrolled at the manual labor school George W. Gale had just founded, Oneida Institute, in the fall of 1827 to study for the ministry. So his lack of ordination seemed to prevent Finney from using Weld in a full-fledged capacity to preach the gospel, despite his mesmerizing powers as a speaker. Where, then, to use him?

In Rochester the obvious solution appeared. In this grain-processing city where distilleries were busy, temperance advocates had been vocal since 1828. Paul E. Johnson, in studying the background to the revival, has declared that "by 1830 the temperance crusade was, on its own terms, a success: society's leading men were encouraging abstinance."[27] But there was much left to do. Grogshops were common, distilleries still bought grain from the farms and mills, and grocers and merchants generally offered ardent spirits in their stores. The lower-class workingmen, with the most tenuous connection to Rochester's churches (if any at all) were frequently drunk, even at work, and in 1827 this small city had nearly a hundred establishments licensed to sell liquor. The temperance forces had been quite successful in alerting businessmen and wage-labor masters to the violence, lost time, and bad workmanship engendered by liquor consumed both on the job and off. But one resource had not been utilized by the Rochester Society for the Promotion of Temperance—a galvanizing speaker who could sway large audiences.

Theodore Weld had received numerous appeals from Charles Finney and others to come and assist them, since his Utica conversion in the spring of 1826. In most instances he had steadfastly refused, heeding the admonition of Charles Stuart to put first his training for the ministry, and not be deterred by urgent pleas.[28] But Weld could not resist the revival in Rochester. He had already spent a few vacations laboring throughout the West for the American Temperance Society, and by 1830 he was said to be the most powerful advocate for the cause in those regions.[29]

For almost a month he worked in small meetings with local advocates, speaking to various gatherings. In conjunction with Finney, it was decided that the regular evangelistic meetings should be suspended for a short while at the end of December, and the entire emphasis be placed on temperance. From the pulpit of the Third Presbyterian Church, Theodore Weld spoke to packed attendances in several meetings, and on New Year's Eve he delivered a lecture that throbbed with crackling vitality and dynamic emotional impact, and lasted for several hours. The audience sat riveted. He demanded that those touched by the revival have nothing further to do with the liquor trade. Indeed, they must not even do business with merchants who trafficked in ardent spirits, for, he explained, this threat of an economic boycott would show that Christians meant what they said.

At the end of this impassioned speech, the Rev. Joseph Penney rose from among the clergy present and demanded that vendors in the congregation cease from the sale of alcohol at once. Eight or ten liquor dealers and manufacturers rose to pledge themselves to abandon the business, and the wholesale grocers went to another room to conduct a meeting on the matter. On the morrow Albert and Elijah Smith, owners of the largest grocery and provisions emporium in Rochester, had their clerks trundle all the liquor casks from the warehouse to the street. Before a great crowd of approving, noisy church members and silent, astonished sinners, the Smith brothers stove in the kegs and allowed thousands of gallons of Demon Rum to flow harmlessly down the gutters of Exchange Street.[30] With that precedent, other merchants followed suit. The *Western Recorder* stated, a week after the meeting at the Third Church:

> Indeed, we have been informed that a large number of wholesale grocers and others, have had a meeting with reference to abandoning the sale of ardent spirits, and we have no doubt they will generally do so. . . . We wish Mr. Weld could visit every town in this region with reference to the promotion of temperance. Should we say what we might anticipate from such a visit, we should be charged with enthusiasm.[31]

Occasionally a well-to-do convert of the revival went into a store, purchased its entire stock of spirituous goods, and had it destroyed before the awestruck employees. In several cases retailers who had been

moved by the temperance argument threw their liquor into the Erie
Canal, the symbolism of which carried afar. Others could not be so
cavalier; Rossiter and Knox, a large establishment, advertised that it
would no longer sell spirits, but "not thinking it a duty to 'feed the
Erie Canal' with their property, offer to sell at cost their whole stock
of liquors."[32] And so it went, until only one or two merchants dared
to defy the mood of the day and continued to handle alcohol.

Finney and Weld were elated at the success of their first determined attempt at reform. Praises crowded upon them from near and
far. Because both of them possessed innately the reforming instinct,
one success would lead to greater determination, and the wedding of
individual conversion to societal renewal and reform was thus established as an ongoing principle of the new measures.

These months also afforded Charles Finney the opportunity to
become acquainted with a number of men who would be his associates
or supporters in the future. The first of these to arrive at Rochester
was the son of the Troy lawyer, Zebulon R. Shipherd, the Rev. John
Jay Shipherd, who would in time be the founder of Oberlin College.
He had heard Finney preach four years previously, and he declared that
he did not like his "impudence and asperity of manner." But Finney
must have liked Shipherd, for in November 1827 the evangelist had
urged Shipherd to come to Stephentown and "preach as candidate for
settlement" at the church that had been built up by Finney's preaching.[33] On September 28, 1830, Shipherd, his wife, two sons, and a
schoolteacher friend boarded the canal boat near Schenectady, intending to go west to do missionary work. They arrived in Rochester on
Saturday afternoon, October 2, the day after the panic at the First
Church. They intended to stay a day or two in the city, not only to
avoid breaking the Sabbath but also to hear Charles Finney preach.
Finney arranged to have Shipherd preach at the Second Church that
Sunday afternoon, and tried to persuade Shipherd to stay and assist
him in the revival. Shipherd declined, but in turn urged Finney to ac-
company him to the West. Neither one of course suspected what the
future would hold in regard to Oberlin College.[34]

With the unblemished reputation of the revival spreading afar,
invitations to Finney for meetings elsewhere crowded in as never before. On November 29, 1830, Anson G. Phelps wrote from New York,
beseeching Finney to return there as soon as the Rochester campaign
was concluded:

> I have often thought that your faith was strong enough to com-
> prehend the whole city, and indeed I do believe if ministers and

Christians had last winter come out on the Lord's side that Satan's kingdom would have trembled. But there is still a great degree
of stupidity among the churches and dissentions among the ministers. Doct. [Samuel] Cox and his party declared that he could
not even sit again in Presbytery with Doct. [Gardiner] Spring, and
the consequence is that the N York Presbytery is divided. I believe we shall form the 3d Presbytery. . . . Remember Bro. Finney
that there is one pulpit in N York always at your command.[35]

Milton Brayton in Utica had fruitlessly besought Finney to return there so many times that he gave up the attempt, and instead
asked Theodore Weld to use his influence with the evangelist. "We
want Brother Finney here," he wrote to Weld, "and must have him and
can't live without him—so set yourself to work and try your best to
get him to come with you."[36] The Presbytery of Ontario sent Finney
a resolution from all of their churches inviting him to preach there:

On motion resolved unanimously that the Rev. Charles G. Finney be invited to come and labour in the bounds of this Presbytery; and that the Rev. Norris Bull be a committee to communicate the resolution to Mr. Finney with such a statement of facts
as he may deem expedient. January 20, 1831.[37]

Several other presbyteries issued similar invitations to him, and
the Rev. J. W. Adams of Syracuse implored Finney to come there in
three different letters, the last of which stated with desperate urgency,
"the wickedest among us, some notorious infidels who have never been
seen within the walls of a church, have solemnly declared that 'if Finney did come here they would certainly go and hear him preach!'"[38]
Several writers begged Finney to travel west to the Mississippi Valley,
and Edward N. Kirk continued to ask him to come to Albany and assist
there. Still another pastor, Rev. Russell Whiting, declared that his
church would be filled on three hours' notice if Finney sent word that
he would preach, "such is the state of feeling in anxious expectation
of the event."[39] And so it went, through dozens of such pleadings.

Rarely was a preacher so sought after. And the most anxious inquiries were from New York City. Joel Parker, Lewis Tappan, Joshua
Leavitt, and Herman Norton all made insistent requests that he return
there without delay, pleading the opportunities of the hour.[40] Leavitt
was hopeful that a reconciliation could be brought about between

Asahel Nettleton and Finney, and he felt strongly that if such happened every pulpit in New York would be open to him.

Some reasons why the reputation of this awakening spread so
rapidly and so far were first, that most of the towns surrounding
Rochester for some distance were touched to a degree by the revival
spirit, and large numbers from these towns were faithful attenders
of the meetings in the city. The *New York Evangelist* said that "We
have an impression, from all that can be learned by private letters,
and by oral testimony, that almost every town within forty or fifty
miles of Rochester is favored more or less with the special presence
of the Lord."[41] Secondly, Finney's own demeanor in the conduct of the
meetings was as impressive, if not more so, as it had been in any previous campaign. Perhaps it was because, unlike the atmosphere of the
major eastern cities, a congeniality and a warmth were here that were
absent in the frenetic pace of New York and Philadelphia, and the
citizens had fewer distractions from the spiritual. Beyond question,
Finney was delighted with the openhearted reception he received on
all hands, and with the fact that the professional men of the city were
responding in such numbers. One sympathetic writer declared that
the services were orderly, solemn, and still, and "never interrupted by
loud and boisterous expressions, either of grief or joy; never rendered
offensive to the ear of refinement by low allusions, or coarse and vul-
gar expressions, nor painful to the ear of piety by an irreverent and
affected familiarity with sacred things."[42]

Charles P. Bush, a student who was converted under Finney's
ministry, gave the following graphic description of one sermon by the
evangelist:

> "You will get your 'wages'; just what you have earned, your due;
> nothing more, nothing less; and as the smoke of your torment
> like a thick cloud, ascends forever and ever, you will see written
> upon its curling folds, in great staring letters of light, this awful
> word, *wages*, WAGES!"
>
> As the preacher uttered this sentence, he stood at his full
> height, tall and majestic — stood as if transfixed, gazing and point-
> ing toward the emblazoned cloud, as it seemed to roll up before
> him; his clear, shrill voice rising to its highest pitch, and pene-
> trating every nook and corner of the vast assembly. People held
> their breath. Every heart stood still. It was almost enough to raise
> the dead — there were no sleepers within the sound of that clarion
> voice.[43]

Charles Finney, exhilarated at his success in Rochester, kept up his furious pace through February and tried to ignore the great strains to which he was subjecting his mind and body. Fortunately, he was still young enough to be resilient, whereas an older person would have crumbled under the demands. He drove himself so because he was mindful that the spring thaw would arrive soon, and while the canal was frozen and some of the other manufactures and activities were in abeyance, he wanted to capitalize to the utmost upon the time people had available for attention to religious matters. When the thaw came the roads would be almost impassable from the mud, and while they were still frozen a greater number came from the surrounding towns in February than in any previous month.[44] With the calendar in mind, Finney planned to conclude the campaign with a series of union meetings from Thursday, February 24, to Sunday, February 27. Finney was not to be the only speaker; singlehandedly he could not possibly cover all the meetings. Rather, simultaneous meetings were to be held to accommodate the crowds, and all the churches of the entire area were invited to participate.

The pastors included Penney of First Church, Sedgwick of Ogden, Barnard of Lima, Wisner of Ithaca, Campbell of Palmyra, Myers of Brockport, Buck of Penfield, Farnsworth of Ovid in Seneca County, Eddy of Canandaigua, Asa Mahan of Pittsford, and Finney. During this final great effort these clergymen preached several times each, and the meetings were begun at six in the morning and ran through the evening, allowing participants to come and go at their convenience. In the mornings there were inquiry meetings, without specific preaching, and they overflowed with "anxious sinners." In the evenings the preaching was conducted in earnest.

Attendances were phenomenal, considering the rural nature of Monroe County and its neighboring counties. Delegations came from Buffalo and Lockport, and some traveled seventy miles, from Ithaca, supporting their pastor, William Wisner. When February 27 came it was felt that the union meetings should not stop, and so all agreed that they might run through to the next Sunday. Crowds continued to come "with unabated zeal." It seemed as if many who had not previously made some decision were anxious to do so before the meetings terminated, for fear that "the day of grace" might pass them by. In one of these last meetings Finney preached on the topic, "What Must I do to be Saved?" It was reported by one in attendance:

> After the discourse was ended, in which the conditions of salvation were laid with perfect conspicuousness before every mind,

and all was said that could be said to urge their immediate acceptance, all who had come to a fixed determination to accept at once,
were requested to tarry after the congregation were dismissed, that
special prayer might be offered in their behalf. The number which
left was small, that the crowd seemed hardly diminished, and the
throng being still so great that it was impossible to separate the
congregation without great inconvenience. Those who were determined to accept at once the conditions laid before them were requested to signify that determination by rising. Simultaneously
hundreds arose from all parts of the house.[45]

With the campaign concluded, converts poured into the churches.
At one point, in January 1831, about one hundred affiliated with First
Church, and about the same number were added to Second Church.
William Wisner accepted a call from this congregation to be its pastor, and during the next several years, 372 new converts were taken
in. Third Church added 158 converts in 1831.[46] Presbyterian churches
in surrounding areas received a considerable accession of new members as well, but this denomination was not the only one to benefit.
The First Baptist Church of Rochester added 203 members during the
awakening. The Methodists in the city were so encouraged by additions to their ranks that they proceeded to build a church seating two
thousand people, or one-fifth of the entire citizenry! The Episcopalians also benefited, and in Rochester Finney carried on the free church
movement as he had in New York City by helping to found two more
open-seated, reform-oriented churches, the Bethel Free Church and
the Rochester Free Presbyterian Church. The latter lasted only from
1832 to 1838, but the former developed into the Central Presbyterian
Church and in time was chiefly responsible for bringing Charles Finney back to the city for the revivals of 1842 and 1855.[47]

The revival was undeniably remarkable for the widespread effects it produced; instead of being confined to a relatively small
geographical area, it touched people at distances as great as one hundred miles and more, leading to conversions and revivals. This is shown
by these additions in 1831 to the following congregations: Troy, Second Presbyterian, 156; Watertown, 100; Ithaca, 220; Geneva, 270; Penn
Yan, 123; Clyde, 100; Seneca Falls, 127; Salem, 212; Auburn, 235; and
Clinton, 134. Robert H. Nichols has said, "The churches of the synod
probably added four or five thousand new members in all. Genesee
Synod reported gains of the same dimensions. . . . Such phenomenal
gains marked an epoch in the church life of the state, and indeed the
revival was felt over much of the nation."[48]

Beyond the salutary effects of the revival on Rochester, it was almost singularly responsible for bringing about the national revival of 1831, in which what had been building up for years throughout the country seemed almost to explode in that one year.[49] Under the ministrations of men influenced by what Finney, Beecher, and a host of lesser evangelists were doing, revivals seemed to be everywhere in 1831. Between 1800 and 1835 the proportion of Protestant church members to the national population almost doubled, from 7 to 12½ percent, but most of that growth came after 1830. The membership of New England churches grew by one-third in 1831.[50] Everywhere, ordinary citizens desired to have duplicated in their town what had happened so sanely and so respectably in Rochester.

Charles Finney's decision to go there (or the mystical promptings that made him go) had proven to be wise, for the Rochester revival was to be the most successful of his entire career. Where churchgoers had been feuding and bickering before he came, and the number of new members in its divided churches had dropped dramatically from 1828 through the fall of 1830,[51] Finney brought about a reversal in what seemed to be an almost hopeless situation. For the extent of interchurch cooperation, and the magnitude of support, it was the first citywide evangelistic effort that may be properly compared with the urban campaigns of the last third of the nineteenth century. After some years of experimentation, Finney had arrived at a mastery of his techniques and theories of mass evangelism, many of which would be further developed by later evangelists and utilized to this day. Part of his methodology was a broad, undenominational approach to presenting the gospel, which might be accepted as much by Methodists, Baptists, and Episcopalians as by Presbyterians.

Over the years, evaluations of the Rochester revival were almost entirely favorable. There was little to criticize. Robert L. Stanton, near the end of a long life of Old School Presbyterianism, wrote to Finney in 1872, "All Rochester was *moved* that winter. . . . The atmosphere . . . seemed to be affected. You could not go upon the streets, and hear any conversations, except on religion."[52] It was often said that the entire character of the city was modified because so many of the converts were leaders of the community, who "would remake society and politics in Rochester."[53] Finney, in his *Memoirs,* wrote of what he was told by the man who became district attorney of Rochester soon after the revival, concerning the drop in the crime rate not only in 1831 but for years afterward.[54]

From the perspective of history, it is apparent that the Rochester campaign served as the watershed in attitudes among clergy and laity toward Charles Finney. Previous to Rochester, he was still suspect to multitudes. After this, he was widely accepted, and his work in this city deserves to be seen as the high point of his career as an evangelist.

II

BOSTON AND BEECHER

From the middle of the eighteenth century an increasing array of liberal ideas were enunciated by leading clergymen of Boston such as Jonathan Mayhew (1720–1766), pastor of the West Church, and Charles Chauncy (1704–1787), pastor of the First Church. These ideas coalesced under the influence of English Unitarianism, and in 1785 the King's Chapel in Boston became the first church in America to declare itself Unitarian. Then, in 1805, the well-known liberal minister of Hingham, Henry Ware (1764–1845), became Hollis Professor of Divinity at Harvard, and the orthodox everywhere became seriously alarmed. Calvinists reacted vigorously, and in a few years Congregationalism was brought to the verge of schism. Jedidiah Morse (1761–1826), minister at Charlestown, a leading scholar, and overseer of Harvard, was furious at Ware's appointment and led the orthodox forces on a number of fronts, including the founding of a new and rigidly Calvinistic seminary at Andover, Massachusetts.

The inevitable split occurred when the quiet and dignified pastor of the Federal Street Church in Boston, William Ellery Channing (1780–1842), took the occasion of Jared Spark's ordination in 1819 at an explicitly Unitarian church in Baltimore to speak on "Unitarian Christianity," a sermon immediately taken as the definitive statement of the new liberal faith. Many congregations in New England separated over the issue, and churches were forced to choose whether they would remain orthodox or go with the liberals. One hundred twenty-five churches had formed themselves into the American Unitarian Association by 1825. According to Lyman Beecher:

> All the literary men of Massachusetts were Unitarian. All the trustees and professors of Harvard College were Unitarians. All the elite of wealth and fashion crowded Unitarian churches. The judges on the bench were Unitarian, giving decisions by which the peculiar features of church organization, so carefully ordained by the Pilgrim fathers, had been nullified.[1]

Lyman Beecher himself led the aggressive campaign against this threat to orthodoxy, and by 1821 strong and trusted pastors had been placed in strategic churches, and a number of other measures to stem the tide were under way. Nathaniel William Taylor, Beecher's close friend and professor of theology at Yale, selected for attack the newly appointed Dexter Professor of Sacred Literature at Harvard, Andrews Norton, a Unitarian, and began a literary battle with him. Amid all the furor, Norton brought the clash down to one point—what Calvinism taught regarding total depravity. "Though I have not before used these precise words," he said, "I now affirm it to be a doctrine of Calvinism, *that God creates men with a sinful nature.*"[2] Insisting that there were several varieties of Calvinist opinion on the issue, Taylor was willing to do battle with Norton on this point, but he immediately demanded that a distinction be made between the nature that is created by God, and that which is "natural, which is not from God, or which is not created by God." When Calvinists use the phrase "depraved by nature," Sidney Mead comments, they "do not mean that man's nature is such that he sins from physical necessity but only that his created nature is the occasion of his sinning without precluding the possibility of the opposite result. His nature is such that it is certain that he will sin, but it does not impinge upon his power to the contrary." Taylor's famous phrase, "certainty with power to the contrary," was meant to say that there are antecedents to all that we do as humans that make happenings certain, but looking back at a later time upon what we did, we are confident that we possessed full power to do otherwise than what we actually did.[3]

While this literary controversy continued through 1822 and 1823, Beecher preached his famous sermon, "The Faith Once Delivered to the Saints," in October 1823. His rationale was the same as Nathaniel Taylor's: to make orthodox doctrine palatable, and more reasonable than the teachings of Unitarianism. He took similar ground to Taylor, arguing for the freedom of the will in order to separate orthodoxy from the idea of predestinated happenings over which humans have no control. This time it was the Unitarians' turn to pounce, and in their paper, the *Christian Examiner*, the reviewer gleefully pointed out that Beecher's desire to modify the harsh aspects of Calvinism was so great that it was *he* who had actually departed from orthodoxy:

> What makes this statement of Christian doctrine remarkable, considered as coming from a reputed Calvinist, is its decidedly *anti*-Calvinistic bearing; expressly denying some of the peculiarities of Calvinism, distinctly asserting none of them, nor even implying any one of them in such a manner, as to make it obvious to a common reader. . . . It begins with asserting, in as strong and unqualified language as was ever used by an Arminian or Unitarian, the doctrine of man's actual *ability* and *free agency*. . . . On the subject of *original sin,* and *native depravity,* our author is hardly less unsound in his orthodoxy, for his statement of the Atonement might also be adopted by all Unitarians of whom we have any knowledge. . . . Enough has been said to show, that, according to Dr. Beecher, "the truth once delivered to the saints" is decidedly *anti-Calvinistic.* This concession, considering the quarter from which it comes, is certainly an important one, and we thank him for it.[4]

If Lyman Beecher and Nathaniel Taylor believed they were the outstanding champions of orthodoxy against the Unitarian threat, others were not so sure, feeling that the New Haven Theology capitulated at major points. Actually, the defenders of Federalist Calvinism had been suspicious of Beecher and the Yale faculty of divinity for several years. Perhaps the first rumble of discontent had been in 1819 when Beecher preached "The Design, Rights, and Duties of Local Churches." A reviewer in an orthodox paper angrily noted that Beecher made statements concerning the constitution of the church "known to him to be in opposition to what a great majority of his Presbyterian brethren hold as most dear."[5] Then, in 1821 Yale professor C. A. Goodrich alarmed conservatives everywhere by stating that "previous to the *first* act of moral agency, there is nothing in the mind which can *strictly* and *properly* be called sin—nothing for which the being is accountable to God."[6] Beecher too became upset over that, fearing that it would precipitate an immediate rupture with the orthodox.

Although he largely agreed with Goodrich's ideas, he knew that such bald statements of the New Divinity could overturn everything for which he was working. Matters simmered for several years, and then in 1826 Ashbel Green, Presbyterian editor of the *Christian Advocate,* attacked in print some sentiments of another Yale divine, Eleazer Fitch.[7]

By 1828 the matter could be sidestepped no longer. Nathaniel Taylor contended that the wisest strategy was to present the New Haven views boldly, and therefore he took the opportunity before the Connecticut Congregational clergy, gathered at Yale chapel on September 10, 1828, to preach his famous sermon, *Concio ad Clerum* (advice to the clergy). His text was Ephesians 2:3, "And were by nature the children of wrath." It was a very direct statement, going to the heart of the issue but in actuality presenting nothing that had not been argued for years by Fitch, Goodrich, and Taylor. We may picture in our imagination the anger of those who were orthodox in the congregation as the handsome and dignified Taylor stood in the pulpit and preached what to them was virtual heresy:

> By the moral depravity of mankind I intend generally, the entire sinfulness of their moral character—that state of the mind or heart to which guilt and the desert of wrath pertain. I may say then negatively,
>
> This depravity does not consist in any essential attribute or property of the soul—not in *any thing created* in man by his Maker. On this point, I need only ask—does God create in men a sinful nature, and damn them for the very nature He creates? Believe this, who can.
>
> Nor does the moral depravity of men consist in a sinful nature, which they have corrupted by being *one* with Adam, and by *acting in his act.* . . .
>
> When therefore I say that mankind are entirely depraved *by nature,* I do not mean that their nature is *itself* sinful, nor that their nature is the *physical* or *efficient* cause of their sinning; but I mean that their nature is the occasion, or reason of their sinning—that *such is their nature, that in all the appropriate circumstances of their being, they will sin and only sin.*

Whatever Taylor may have done to the old orthodox doctrine, he wanted it distinctly known that the new understanding of depravity mitigated not a whit the guilt of the unregenerate. At the conclusion of the discourse (which would have taken perhaps ninety minutes to deliver), Taylor tried to show that he was as evangelical as anyone there by ending with an application which was worthy of Jonathan Edwards:

> Finally, I cannot conclude without remarking, how fearful are the condition and prospects of the sinner. His sin is his own. He yields himself by his own free act, by his own choice, to those propensities of his nature, which under the weight of God's authority he *ought to govern.* . . . God beseeching with tenderness and terror—Jesus telling him He died once and could die again to save him—mercy weeping over him day and night—heaven lifting up its everlasting gates—hell burning, and sending up its smoke of torment, and the weeping and the wailing and the gnashing of teeth, within his hearing—and onward still he goes. See the infatuated immortal!—Fellow sinner,—IT IS YOU.
>   Bowels of divine compassion—length, breadth, height, depth of Jesus' love—Spirit of all grace, save him—Oh save him—or he dies forever.[8]

Despite the fact that all of these positions of the New Divinity had been promulgated previously, the shock waves from Taylor's sermon reverberated throughout the nation, and engaged the attention of the theologically astute for some time. Charles Finney was preaching at the German Reformed church in Philadelphia when Taylor delivered *Concio ad Clerum.* Only a week later, on September 17, 1828, David L. Dodge wrote to Finney:

> At the late commencement at Yale Dr. Taylor I understand came out with his particular views . . . so as to be understood and many of the ablest divines were alarmed. Some I hear have come out boldly against him and Taylor is about to publish his sermon. All were well satisfied that his general views, so far as I hear, were to virtually deny innate depravity. . . . I hear that Dr. Taylor said infants were depraved but not sinful.[9]

Here a fascinating historical coincidence came about. Finney was expounding doctrines very similar to the New Haven Theology, but it is doubtful that he or anyone else in Philadelphia understood that at the time, or recognized the implications that all of this would have for both the Presbyterian and the Congregational churches. Finney, a year after the New Lebanon Convention, may have been sufficiently conversant with the religious situation in America by that point to be aware that Nathaniel Taylor was a close friend of Lyman Beecher, but the lingering antagonism from Beecher at New Lebanon was fresh in Finney's memory, and in all likelihood Finney was still irritated enough to consider all of Beecher's friends automatically hostile to him. During the next two years, he would come to several startling realizations.

Charles Finney was not the only one to be unaware of the meaning of all this. When he preached for a full year in Philadelphia, the very heartland of the Presbyterian Church, and within the hearing of many of its most powerful leaders, they remained completely blind to the real implications of Finney's doctrine. Apparently, from the available evidence, these powerful clergymen were more concerned with the new measures than with the content of Finney's message. They could hardly fail to recognize that his demand for instant decisions in conversion boded changes in the existing methodologies of evangelism, but that did not appear to be of great consequence. To those who were determinedly Old School, Finney seemed to be merely another itinerant evangelist, a bit younger and more vibrant than most, but hardly anyone of intellectual depth. As William G. McLoughlin has said, "They thought him to be merely a crude western exponent of Hopkinsianism, and while they did not like Hopkinsians they had learned to put up with them."[10] As far as they were concerned, Finney had been invited to Philadelphia by a respected member of the Presbytery, James Patterson, and there was nothing out of order about that proceeding. Then, when a number of Finney's supporters arranged to have him preach to larger crowds in the city's most commodious church, the German Reformed, the Old School men sighed and resolved to tolerate his presence for a few more months, thinking he would be gone from them in due time and they would hear no more.

When Charles Finney departed from Philadelphia, on January 5, 1829, events affecting the future of the entire denomination began to occur more rapidly. Albert Barnes (1798–1870) had graduated from Princeton Seminary in 1824 and took as his first pastorate the church at Morristown, New Jersey. Early in 1829 he preached and then published a controversial sermon entitled *The Way of Salvation*. Much of its argument was Edwardean, but it was critical of the Westminster Confession and clearly aligned with the New Haven Theology, for in it Barnes held that a sinner is not "personally answerable for the transgressions of Adam." The published sermon received wide notoriety, and when in 1830 James P. Wilson retired from the pastorate of the prestigious First Church of Philadelphia, the church extended a call to Barnes, and Wilson publicly defended his views. James Patterson in Philadelphia immediately wrote to Finney, in New York City, "Dr. Wilson's people have called Rev. Mr. Barnes of Morristown, N.J. Dr. Green, Dr. Ely, and Mr. Potts, it is said, don't like that he should come into this Presbytery because of his New Divinity. He is a revival man, and it is said he is a very devoted man."[11]

While the Old School advocates of the Philadelphia Presbytery had not perceived Finney to be much of a threat during the year 1828, by 1830 they were thoroughly alarmed by tendencies such as the steady penetration of the Yale New Divinity into Presbyterianism in the Plan of Union parishes served by Congregationalists, and its effect even on a Princeton graduate such as Barnes.

James Patterson had been misinformed in the above letter about Dr. Ezra Stiles Ely, pastor of the Third Church and editor of *The Philadelphian,* a respected Presbyterian periodical, for when Barnes was opposed, Ely took his side in the debate. But George C. Potts, pastor of the Fourth Church, Dr. Ashbel Green, formerly president of Princeton, George Junkin, president of Lafayette College, and other Old School members of Presbytery attempted to block Barnes' call to the First Church. In this they were unsuccessful, but in 1831 Barnes was accused of heresy by them, particularly in regard to the doctrine of original sin, and found guilty by the Presbytery. The case was appealed to the General Assembly that year, and New School adherents throughout the denomination immediately tried to pack the assembly with delegates favorable to their cause. In hearing the case, the General Assembly pronounced some of Barnes' teachings objectionable, but found that there was insufficient evidence to hold him guilty of heresy. It therefore advised the Philadelphia Presbytery to drop the matter. Nonetheless, the entire denomination was by this time rocking from the tremors produced by the trial of such an eminent pastor.[12]

This was where matters stood as Charles Finney concluded his extremely successful Rochester revival in the spring of 1831. Two topics dominated the news for Presbyterians throughout the nation: Finney's admirable revival in New York State, which was largely Presbyterian in auspices, and Albert Barnes' trial before the General Assembly. And now the full significance of what had been developing in the denomination, and in Congregationalism, came home to Finney. Instead of Barnes answering charges of heresy for his views of human depravity, it could have been Charles Finney on trial!

Several factors combined to make Barnes a more logical target than Finney for the Old School, however. First, both Finney and Barnes had only begun to publish by 1831, but Finney's sole published work, the *Can Two Walk Together* sermon preached in Beman's church in Troy back in 1827, was (fortunately for the evangelist) not related to the topic of depravity, but dealt with more innocuous issues, whereas Barnes, inadvertently or otherwise, had laid himself wide open to attack on a crucial problem for Calvinists. Secondly, as the pastor of a powerful and central church in the most important presbytery, Barnes was far more vulnerable than the itinerant Finney, and, it seemed to the Old School, it was of greater urgency to silence him, especially because he seemed much more scholarly than Finney, and would thus have greater literary productivity.

If Charles Finney had any lingering doubts about the significance of the Barnes trial, others were now eager to instruct him. Assisting Ezra Stiles Ely on the staff of *The Philadelphian* was S. B. Ludlow, who wrote to Finney on January 20, 1831, about the latest plans of Ashbel Green and the Old School men:

> Dr. G[reen] and his party (Russell, Engles, McCalla, Potts, etc.) . . . doubtless are engaged in devising ways and means to protect the church against the *deadly heresy* of brother Barnes and all others like him, of which it is *feared* not a little has already leavened the great lump. They seem to be specially troubled, about these days, by *The Philadelphian*. . . . The High Church Regency (Dr. G. etc.) . . . have now resolved to publish a paper of their own, to regulate the faith and practice of the denomination in the U. States, and to make them conform to the *Standards* [the Westminster Confession and Catechisms]. So, you and all *heretics* like you, who sit in darkness, may expect soon to see a great light.[13]

The New School adherents and moderates of the Philadelphia Presbytery were heartened by their victory in the Barnes case, but they knew that relations with their Old School opponents in the presbytery would be exceedingly difficult from that time on. Some of the Old School men were, of course, reasonable people who were not witch-hunters and would not deliberately cause contention, but they were led by the irascible Ashbel Green, the aging ex-president of Princeton. Green had thundered for years that whenever aberrations in theology appeared, he would do all in his power (which was considerable) to root them out. Green was backed up in his threats by the younger president of Lafayette College, George Junkin, who, like Green, had been goaded to fury by Albert Barnes remaining in the pulpit of the First Church.

To try to circumvent the continuing troubles, and following the example of New York City, which had three separate presbyteries as of January 4, 1831, James Patterson, Ezra Ely, Eliphalet Gilbert, and eleven other moderates and New School men petitioned the General Assembly to allow the erection of a second presbytery in Philadelphia, based on "elective affinity" as in New York. This would mean that in the future Green, Junkin, and others who wished to challenge the New School men must do it at the level of Synod or General Assembly, where the outcome of such battles was in much more doubt than it would be in the smaller, more easily controlled presbytery. Understandably, the Old Schoolers howled. But their protests did little good. Delighting to see the mighty Philadelphia Presbytery shorn of some of its power through division into two halves, the New School delegates to the 1831 General Assembly, having a majority, elected Nathaniel Beman as their moderator and allowed the division.

Patterson, Gilbert, Ely, and the other moderates were delighted. Styling the new judicatory a "revival presbytery," they immediately pressed ahead to make alterations that could never have been accomplished in the old, badly divided organization. Chief among these was the determination to license and ordain candidates for the clergy who held New Divinity views. Clearly, changes were in the wind everywhere.[14]

From New York City a constant flow of letters arrived in Rochester, from Finney's many friends, beseeching him to return there. Anson Phelps wrote on January 31, 1831, of the changed attitude in that city. "You would now be surprised, even Doct. Spring and Doct. Cox adopt what has been termed Finney measures, to ask all to rise up in the congregation who wished to be prayed for. . . . All the churches are following the Western measures, even the Dutch begin to talk of a four-day meeting."[15]

On February 21, 1831, Finney heard from Lewis Tappan and Joel Parker, both stating solid reasons why (in their opinion) he should return to New York after concluding in Rochester. Tappan promised: "We have secured Masonic Hall until 1st May, and Tammany Hall after that period indefinitely. Either can be arranged to seat as many as any Presbyterian church in the city."[16] And Joel Parker assured him, "I think you have a fair prospect of being taken by the hand by *all* the Presbyterian clergy, unless it may be Doct. Philips."[17]

From New Haven, Connecticut, Timothy Dwight, Jr., earnestly implored Finney's ministry in that town, stating that a revival had already commenced, and "We are very desirous, sir, that the several thousands in our city, who are still stupid, and unwilling to make an effort for their salvation, should be alarmed, and converted to the Lord."[18]

The six months that Finney labored in the arduous Rochester campaign had taken their toll, and it was clear to all that the evangelist was ill and exhausted. Physicians who examined him diagnosed consumption, and gave as their opinion that he would not live long.[19] Dr. William Wisner, pastor at Ithaca, was so concerned that he attempted to induce Finney to come to his home for a long rest, but the evangelist felt that he suffered only from fatigue. He had received an invitation from Dr. Nott, president of Union College in Schenectady, who was a personal friend, and he set off toward the east in company with Wisner and Josiah Bissell after the conclusion of the Rochester meetings. Leaving his family in Rochester because of the deplorable condition of the roads, Finney and his companions took the stage as far as Auburn. Traveling conditions were so hazardous, however, that they were forced to stay overnight in that town, and they intended to take the morning stage to Schenectady.

Early the next morning, as they were preparing to board the stage, a man came to Finney with "an earnest appeal to me to stop and labor for their salvation, signed by a long list of unconverted men, most of them among the most prominent citizens in the city."[20] They were not reticent in admitting that they were the ones who had tried to undermine Finney's meetings there in July and August of 1826, when Dirck Lansing was the minister of the church, and had broken away to form a new congregation. Finney was so moved by this request that he agreed to stay and preach on a very limited schedule, allowing him to get the rest he so badly needed. He had been told previously by a correspondent that another opposer of 1826, Professor James Richards of the Auburn Theological Seminary, "does not lift a finger nor move his eye nor wag his tongue to oppose you,"[21] and this was another factor in his decision to preach at Auburn.

From approximately March 16 to April 23, 1831, Finney evangelized, on a restricted schedule, in Auburn. He was gratified that there were apologies tendered for the previous opposition, and he noted that none appeared on this occasion.[22]

After five weeks of rest and limited preaching, Finney was sufficiently recovered to continue on his way.[23] As ever, requests and invitations flooded in upon him, and his extant correspondence contains any number of desperate pleadings for his help. For some reason he did not continue on his way to Schenectady, but accepted an invitation from Buffalo, probably because the work at Rochester had already caused increased spiritual interest there, and he felt that revival was in the offing. He arrived in Buffalo near the end of April, and labored there until the first of June, reinvigorated, and having proven that the doctors' diagnosis of consumption was incorrect, and their prediction of his early demise a bit premature.[24]

Having rested somewhat from March through May, 1831, Charles Finney was ready for another great challenge. But he was also wiser than in previous years, and aware that triumphs such as Rochester could come only occasionally. He knew that he must be judicious regarding the supplications and well-meaning advice of his overzealous friends who were forever demanding his presence in locations regardless of the situation among the churches and the clergy. Many were pleading for him to return to Philadelphia, but he now understood, as the Barnes controversy dragged on, that in such a charged atmosphere it was far from the somewhat receptive city of 1828. New York City presented somewhat similar difficulties. Finney was receiving conflicting signals from his supporters in Gotham, some, like Joshua Leavitt, saying that he should keep away for a while until the situation improved, and others, such as Phelps and the Tappans, urging him to come immediately. He had already worked for extended periods in these two greatest cities of the land, despite the fact that neither was, in his terminology, a "revival city." Their eminence, and their wealthy residents such as the Tappans, seem to have clouded his judgment. To continue to minister to individuals of importance, Finney's actions and occasional statements indicate that next he wished to work in New England. Perhaps part of his determination stemmed from the wish to work in the home territory of Asahel Nettleton and Lyman Beecher. Indeed, their presence did not deter him; if anything it seemed to make the challenge more enticing.

At the conclusion of the Buffalo meetings, by June 1, Finney journeyed east with his wife and children to his father-in-law's home in Whitesboro to allow himself further rest, and to escape the summer heat of the cities. Remaining there for a time, he then spent some weeks "journeying for recreation, and for the restoration of my health and strength," traveling to the Albany area to confer with Nathaniel Beman by July 10, and to New York City for the period July 25 through August 8, 1831.

Behind these seemingly innocuous travels, Finney was attempting to work out a plan. In May he had received an invitation from
the Union Orthodox (Congregational) Church of Boston, asking if he
would supply the pulpit in August during the absence of their minister, the Rev. Samuel Green. Here was exactly what he had been seeking
—a legitimate invitation from a church there, to preach for a brief
period while he was able to study the entire situation and the attitudes of the Boston trinitarian clergy. However, using admirable caution, he also accepted an invitation from Josiah Chapin and his pastor
to preach in Providence first, from approximately August 10 through
20. A stay in Rhode Island prior to the Boston appointment would
be even more circumspect, and would allow him time to get his bear-
ings in New England. Finney made no secret of these plans, thinking
that it would do no harm for Lyman Beecher and others to be fore-
warned of his coming.

If Charles Finney expected Beecher to have something to say
about this, he was not disappointed. Even before he reached Providence,
he received two letters, both written on the same day, August 2, 1831.
One was from the Committee of Supply of Boston's Union Church,
which told of a meeting of the city's clergy at which their invitation
to Finney was laid before the assembly:

> At this meeting a very free and full discussion and expression of
> opinion took place, in regard to the expediency of your visiting
> Boston, the result of which was, on the part of the clergymen,
> that your manner of presenting truth is such that the minds of
> Unitarians (we mean men of influence and education who would
> be attracted to hear you from curiosity and reports spread abroad
> concerning you) would be still more prejudiced against it; an evil
> which they have been laboring for years to remove.[25]

However, despite the concerns of the clergy, the laymen of the
Union Church discounted their fears and upheld their earlier invitation to Finney, saying they hoped he would still come.

The second letter was, predictably, from Lyman Beecher, with
an enclosure from Catharine Beecher. It was apparent from the tone
of Beecher's letter that he did not wish to antagonize Finney, knowing that it would be difficult to prevent the evangelist's coming if he
were utterly determined, inasmuch as he possessed a legitimate invitation from a church there. So Beecher squirmed a bit, using alter-
nately firmness then flattery and cajolery:

In respect to the desireableness of your being invited to aid us, by your laboring in this city, at this time. We have been looking at the subject for several months, and had come to the conclusion, which we had expressed to several individuals, sometime since, and repeated in the meeting for consultation yesterday, that *Boston* was not the *best* point of entrance for you into New England, nor the *present* the best time for you to visit Boston.

In this long letter, Beecher went on to say that he held no grudges over "past differences of opinions about measures," because "with very little difference and that now on points of discretion unessential, you and I are as much, perhaps even more, *one* than almost any two men whom God has pleased to render conspicuous in his church." Nonetheless, this was an inopportune and dangerous time for Finney to preach in Boston. Referring to his great dream of evangelical assimilation, Beecher declared that he was sorry for "any division . . . in that great body of Evangelical men who seem to be called by heaven to lift the standard of revivals," but if Finney would be patient a bit longer, perhaps the obstacles would be removed that prevented his coming.[26]

In the enclosure Catharine Beecher explained what the obstacles were:

> There is a large community here of literary, fastidious, powerful, and influential men, earnestly enlisted against revivals, and ardently on the lookout for every indiscreet expression, or impolitic movement, that may be trumpeted in their newspaper and blown through their ranks. There is also a set of timid, though good men, who are already trembling for the present bold measures, and whom it is very important to hold in one united body. . . .
>
> This would throw a man of your generous feelings, and Christian principles, under restraint. . . . I believe you would be much more at your ease, & bring out the peculiar excellencies of your preaching better, where you would be in less critical circumstances, than you would find yourself in at Boston; & for your *comfort*, as well as your usefulness, I am decidedly of opinion, that Hartford or N. Haven would be a better location for you than Boston. You know how anxious I have felt that you and father should be brought together, but father says it cannot be done *here*, without involving the main question now under consideration.[27]

There is every likelihood that, when Finney read these two letters from Beecher and his daughter, he chuckled to himself and nod-

ded knowingly as he thought of the wily Boston pastor hiding behind
Catharine's skirts and conniving frantically on the one hand to keep
Finney out, and on the other to placate him. Did the man never stop?
Finney had had enough of Beecher's pious demagoguery at New Lebanon, and it was enormously rankling that Beecher thought his trans-
parent little tricks were so clever that everyone else, including Finney, was stupid enough to be fooled by them! The evangelist did not
doubt that the Unitarians and the Hopkinsians were waiting to trap
Beecher and the prorevival men in Boston by some foolish or gauche
act, but again, Finney had been stung by Beecher's and Nettleton's insults at New Lebanon about his supposed fanaticisms. Did Beecher
suppose that he acted, in New York and Philadelphia, like a rustic
bumpkin? The man was offensive![28] Finney took pen in hand and
wrote to the Union Church committee:

> I have been extensively supposed by New England ministers to
> be a kind of interloper crowding myself in here and there when
> I was not wanted. Dr. Beecher himself has viewed me in this light
> and accused me of floating upon the tide of popularity, and laying
> ministers under a moral necessity of falling in with me, and in
> my hearing he most solemnly pledged himself to use his influ-
> ence to oppose me if I came to New England. Having no evidence
> that Dr. Beecher had changed his purpose I do not see how I could
> consent to visit Boston. . . . I have always supposed and do now
> believe that Dr. Beecher has been but very imperfectly acquainted
> with my real views and practices.[29]

So much for Beecher's fawning statement in his letter, "you and
I are as much, perhaps even more, *one* than almost any two men."
Finney was not deceived by Beecher. But he was somewhat puzzled
over one item. Why did Beecher continue to oppose him, when that
very summer the periodical to which Beecher contributed, *The Spirit
of the Pilgrims*, had started to publish a series of articles that described
the new measures revivals in Rochester and other cities of New York,
and spoke of them in glowing terms? How could Beecher now justify
his opposition? As William McLoughlin comments, this was "an editorial decision which he must have made before he knew of the invitation to Finney by Green's church."[30] Beecher was indeed in an embarrassing spot, and Finney did not care if the committee at the Union
Church passed his letter about for all to see.

Apparently that is what happened, or the committee told the
clergymen that they would still move ahead to have Finney come, for

we next find that Beecher and the other ministers took quick action. Their expedient to remove themselves from the difficulty was to dispatch one of their number, the Rev. Benjamin B. Wisner of the Boston Old South Church, to Providence for the purpose of hearing Finney. Wisner was to attend the meetings inconspicuously and determine whether there were things said and done that would be unacceptable in Boston, or if Finney might indeed pass muster. After auditing three sermons, Wisner was so pleased with Finney's performance that he introduced himself to the evangelist and said, "I came here a heresy hunter but here is my hand and my heart is with you."[31] Immediately he sent a notice to the clergy declaring that "our difficulties and grounds of hesitation about Mr. Finney's coming to Boston at present were now fully removed."[32]

Beecher and the others felt that this was an admirable way of saving face, and they communicated with the committee of Union Church on August 15, 1831, telling of Wisner's visit to Providence and his approval of Finney's deportment, and continuing, "We are now, not only willing, but desirous that Mr. Finney should come, as soon as may be, to this city, and be engaged for a time in preaching the gospel and in other ways promoting a revival. . . . The public good would be most promoted by his preaching in Park Street Church, especially on Sabbath evenings."[33]

This was exactly what Finney had desired—not to come to Boston merely as a summer replacement for Samuel Green, but at the invitation of the Congregational clergy of Boston. He began preaching toward the end of August, and continued in Boston until the end of April 1832, a total of eight months. During that time he was scheduled to preach in most of the trinitarian churches of the city, although he labored principally in Park Street Church, where Beecher's son Edward had been pastor until October 28, 1830, and which was now vacant.[34]

And yet Finney was not particularly pleased by the public response to his sermons. Had he not been so determined to preach in Boston, he might have guessed this would be the case. As he reported:

> I could not learn that there was among them anything like the spirit of prayer that had prevailed in the revivals at the West and in New York City. There seemed to be a peculiar type of religion there, not exhibiting that freedom and strength of faith which I had been in the habit of seeing in New York.
> I therefore began to preach some searching sermons to Chris-

tians. Indeed I gave out on the Sabbath, that I would preach a series of sermons to Christians, in Park Street, on certain evenings of the week. But I soon found that these sermons were not at all palatable to the Christians of Boston. It was something they never had been used to, and the attendance at Park Street became less and less, especially on those evenings when I preached to professed Christians. This was new to me. I had never before seen professed Christians shrink back, as they did at that time in Boston, from searching sermons. . . . It was evident that they somewhat resented my plain dealing, and that my searching sermons astonished, and even offended, very many of them. However, as the work went forward, this state of things changed greatly; and after a few weeks they would listen to searching preaching, and came to appreciate it.[35]

However, to the intense relief of the clergy, there was no strong opposition, from Hopkinsians or Unitarians, at first. Many of the orthodox Bostonians accepted his circumspect preaching, even though they were a bit shocked at his directness. Lyman Beecher, in his *Autobiography*, hardly mentioned Finney's long campaign in the city, other than to comment that he "did very well."[36] But when Finney preached in Beecher's Bowdoin Street Church there was a predictable clash between them, for if Finney expected his host to sit and listen to him, as all other pastors did, he was to be disappointed.

On this particular evening a large group had gathered for an inquiry meeting in the basement of the Bowdoin Street Church, and Finney prepared to address them. "My object," he told, "was to bring them to renounce themselves and their all, and give themselves and all they possessed to Christ." As he pressed the point for some time, there seemed to be a gratifying response among the audience, and Finney proceeded to invite them to kneel for prayer. At this moment Beecher stood up, unable to contain himself any longer, and interjected, "You need not be afraid to give up all to Christ, your property and all, for he will give it right back to you." Finney was startled and distressed, for Beecher did not go on to be more specific, or make any "just discriminations" as to the sense in which God would return their goods. Finney "felt in an agony. I saw that his language was . . . the direct opposite of the truth." Yet he dared not appear to contradict Beecher, especially in his own church.

So Finney carefully began again, when Beecher had concluded, and attempted to correct the impression Beecher had made. He said that God did require his people to renounce the ownership of material goods, and realize that all things were not theirs, but the Lord's, and that Christians must understand that they are merely stewards of God's gifts. This time Beecher did not interrupt, but let Finney complete his comments, to his great relief.[37]

The more that Finney worked in the Boston area, the more he saw to criticize of Beecher and his tactics. Naturally, Finney still harbored some resentment for the harsh criticisms he had received at New Lebanon, and was alert to respond in kind to any lapses by Beecher. Apparently he was not alone in criticizing "the big gun" of Boston, for Finney recorded in the manuscript of his *Memoirs*, "I was soon informed by Dr. Wisner that my manner of dealing with professors of religion was directly opposite to that of Dr. Beecher; that the standard which he set up was a very low one." But the local clergy stood in fear of his power, and so they suffered in silence. Nonetheless, according to Wisner, there was a general feeling that Beecher "was letting down the standard of orthodox piety and preaching, in such a way that left the doors open too wide altogether to the orthodox Christian church. He said that he felt, and they had felt in Boston for some time, that getting the people into the church under so low a standard of preaching was calculated to do them great mischief."[38] In any other situation, Finney might have lashed out, attempting to restore high standards of Christian belief and conduct. But Boston was unique, and Beecher had proceeded along this path to attempt the nearly impossible task of gaining converts and at the same time doing nothing that might ruffle Unitarian feathers.

The Unitarians were not the only ones who watched Beecher and his allies closely. The Old Calvinists and the Hopkinsians of eastern Massachusetts, following Asahel Nettleton's persistent warnings, were also alert to the momentous changes that were in the offing. At this precise time the controversy was raging between Bennet Tyler, representing the Hopkinsians, and Nathaniel Taylor of the New Haven Theology, and Lyman Beecher was very much caught in the middle of the struggle. The orthodox clergy of Boston were divided between Hopkinsians and Old Calvinists, with only a few, including Beecher, supporting the emphasis on free will and the virtual rejection of innate depravity that was flowing from New Haven. Considering that Charles Finney was increasingly regarded as the most prominent exponent of the New Haven Theology, it may be a matter of some surprise that the orthodox clergymen of Boston had put up as little resistance as they did to his coming.

There was one Boston Hopkinsian, however, who was not so eas-

ily placated. Asa Rand was editor of the *Volunteer*, a religious periodical printed in the city, and he determined to expose to his readers and
the world exactly what Finney was teaching. Accordingly, he attended
Finney's meetings surreptitiously, taking notes and waiting for the best
opportunity to strike. On one occasion at Park Street Church in the
autumn of 1831, Finney preached a new sermon, "Sinners Bound to
Change Their Own Hearts," with his text taken from Ezekiel 18:31,
"Make yourselves a new heart and a new spirit, for why will ye die?"
With unerring instinct, Rand sensed that Finney would use this text
in the service of free will, and he scribbled furiously during Finney's
delivery, taking down as much of the sermon as he could. The crucial
parts of the printed text ran:

> *The spiritual heart, is the fountain of spiritual life, is that deep-
> seated but voluntary preference of the mind, which lies back of
> all its other voluntary affections and emotions, and from which
> they take their character.* . . . It is evident that the requirement
> here, is to change our *moral* character; our moral disposition; in
> other words, to change that abiding preference of our minds, which
> prefers sin to holiness; self-gratification to the glory of God. . . .
>
> It is a change in the choice of a *Supreme Ruler.* The con-
> duct of impenitent sinners demonstrates that they prefer Satan
> as the ruler of the world. . . .
>
> Thus the world is divided into two great political parties;
> the difference between them is, that one party choose Satan as
> the god of this world. . . . The other party choose Jehovah for
> their governor, and consecrate themselves, with all their interests,
> to his service. Nor does this change imply a constitutional al-
> teration of the powers of body or mind, any more than a change
> of mind in regard to the form or administration of a human gov-
> ernment.[39]

If Asa Rand wished to attack the New Divinity doctrine of an
utterly free will unrestricted by any predilections or fetters, he could
hardly have chosen a better example than this statement by Finney.
Here, as in few other places before the appearance of his *Lectures on
Systematic Theology* in 1846, where he covered the same ground at
great length, Finney expounded the idea that all virtue resides in the
proper exercise of the human will. From his earliest days as a Christian, he had been irritated with the Calvinist doctrines of "physical
depravity, consequent inability, and constitutional regeneration." The
first taught that humanity has a weakened and unbalanced physical

condition that contributes to the development of moral depravity, and the second stated that as a result of both physical and moral depravity, humankind is born with a sinful nature, makes only sinful choices, and therefore lacks free will, and is spiritually dead. Man is born not neutral, virtuous, or innocent, but with a constant tendency toward evil that is innate, inherited from Adam. And constitutional regeneration spoke of the absolute need for a new, divine life to be implanted by the Holy Spirit, as it is stated in 1 Corinthians 2:10, 12; Ephesians 1:17–18; 2 Corinthians 4:6; and so on. So, when Finney found people of weak faith who doubted that the Holy Spirit was working in them, he was annoyed that some of them felt they were not of the elect, or if they were eventually to be saved, that they could do nothing but wait prayerfully until the Holy Spirit began to work in them. The popular jingle that summarized this passive attitude went, "You can, but you can't; you will, but you won't; you're damned if you do, and damned if you don't." Finney called this attitude "cannot-ism." It was specifically against this attitude of hopelessness that his "New Heart" sermon was directed.

To Finney, free will was the possession of every person. "The necessary adaptation of the outward motive to the mind, and of the mind to the motive, lies in the powers of moral agency, which every human being possesses. He has understanding to perceive and weigh; he has conscience to decide upon the nature of moral opposites; he has the power and liberty of choice."[40] Finney then attempted to bring a scientific approach into this by using human psychology. In 1831 he, like everyone else, had a mechanistic attitude to psychology, or what he called "the laws of mind," and he assumed as a matter of course that God worked in human nature on the basis of fixed principles of psychology, and that the revival preacher must learn to do the same. "He who deals with souls should study well the laws of mind," applying what he has learned to the "views and feelings in which he may find the sinner at the time," for in so doing conversion may be brought about much more rapidly and easily.[41]

Finney then introduced his well-known illustration of the daydreamer at Niagara Falls, to demonstrate his thinking that there were four separate "agencies" that had to combine in the conversion of a sinner. "As you stand upon the verge of the [Niagara] precipice, you behold a man lost in deep reverie, approaching its verge unconscious of his danger. He approaches nearer and nearer," and at the last moment you cry out, "Stop!" The spell that holds the man is broken, and he sees his danger, retreating just in time. Making applications, Finney said that the daydreamer was the indolent, hell-bound sinner, and "you" who shout to him are the preacher, or evangelistic Christian. The word "stop" was the gospel message that pierced his heart and shattered his complacency. Thus, there were four agencies at work in this conversion: "the actual turning, or change, is the sinner's own act. The agent who induces him, is the Spirit of God. A secondary agent, is the preacher." And the fourth agency is the Word: "Not only does the preacher cry *Stop*, but, through the living voice of the preacher, the Spirit cries *Stop*":

> Thus you see the sense in which it is the work of God, and also the sense in which it is the sinner's own work. The Spirit of God, by the truth, influences the sinner to change, and in this sense is the efficient cause of the change. But the sinner actually changes, and is therefore himself, in the most proper sense, the author of the change.[42]

In a very short time Asa Rand published in his paper, the *Volunteer*, a lead article entitled "The New Divinity Tried," and a bit later the article was reprinted in a sixteen-page booklet. The title amply demonstrates that Rand lumped Finney with Taylor and Beecher, and wished to demonstrate by means of this sermon the inevitable results of weak and illogical reasoning. Rand began by giving a précis of the sermon, to give as precisely as he could what Finney had said. Then he declared that "we perfectly accord with many things in this sermon, which are forcibly exhibited. . . . We can therefore fully accord with most of the 'Remarks' made in the concluding part of the above sermon."[43]

Rand's strictures of the "New Heart" sermon were especially devastating because he approached it in a dignified and respectful fashion, never mentioning Finney by name or speaking offensively of him, and because he exposed the deficiencies of the sermon in a relentless manner. Having given all the credit he could to the things with which Christians were in agreement, and mentioning the favorable items of the message, he then examined the problems. Basically Rand's treatment came under two heads, biblical and doctrinal. Because he wrote in an age when a certain amount of scriptural knowledge was assumed even among the laity, he did not cite or quote the many verses that he took to be common coinage among his readers, but rather he made frequent allusions to them.

His first attack was that Finney ignored or was ignorant of scripture. The basic problem was the moral depravity of fallen human nature, and Rand pointed out that both the Old and New Testaments were in agreement on this: Jeremiah (17:9) said, "The heart is deceitful above all things, and desperately wicked," and Paul said, in Romans 3:23, "For all have sinned, and come short of the glory of God." Rand found that Finney overlooked, or was unaware of, so many sections of scripture that contradicted his assumptions, and could adduce few if any to support them, that he appeared to be little more than a novice in biblical or doctrinal knowledge. Among the biblical passages that Finney overlooked, and which were undoubtedly central sections bearing on the subject, were Genesis 6:5; 8:21; Proverbs 20:9; Ecclesiastes 7:20; Matthew 15:19; Romans 3:9–12; 5:6, 12–19; 7:14–23; 8:6–8; 1 Corinthians 15:21–22, 45–49; Galatians 3:10; 5:17; Ephesians 2:1–3; 4:17–19; James 1:14–15, and others. These passages presented humankind, Rand found, as dead in sin, defiled in the faculties of soul and body, and possessed of a nature that was opposite to good and inclined to do evil out of its profound corruption. In addition, this guilt was indeed imputed to posterity, so that the human being could do no other than sin. As Rand said:

> It will be agreed that all the depravity of a sinner lies in his heart, or heart and will. By the principles of this sermon, the "governing purpose" includes both, and of course contains all the depravity of man. What then becomes of all those "vile affections," whose name is legion, which are entirely separate from that purpose? . . . What becomes of that "body of death," under which every Christian "groans being burdened," and which subjects him to a dreadful conflict from his conversion to his removal to glory? Are these to be *included* in the "governing purpose" or heart? . . .
>
> We have seen already, that he has made off strangely with the doctrine of entire depravity; reducing it to a trifling matter, seated only in the "governing purpose," and put off as easily as persons change their plans of business. The preacher totally discards the doctrine of "original sin," or transmitted pollution, and yet totally fails to account in any other way for the admitted fact, that in every age children take the course of rebellion.[44]

Rand found that a second glaring problem in Finney's sermon was the way in which he had taken the careful progression of logic in the Westminster Confession—Satan's seduction of humankind, death in sin, imputed guilt to posterity, the covenant of works, the covenant of grace, Christ the Mediator, made under the law, effectual calling, adoption, and so on—and attempted to gloss over the theology that made Christianity distinctive, compressing it into the simplicity of an either/or decision. This was no step forward in theology, Rand declared; if anything it was to allow it to be taken over by silliness. It prostrated reason, and gutted terminology of meaning. "On the principles of this sermon," Rand lamented, "there can be no true conversion. Conversion is simply an act of his own will . . . to which the sinner is induced by motives alone. He renounces the world and chooses the service of God."[45]

There was another charge that Finney would have taken very seriously, regarding his cherished idea of "disinterested benevolence." In his "New Heart" sermon, Finney had said, "Look at the utility of benevolence. It is a matter of human consciousness that the mind is so constituted that benevolent affections are the source of happiness; and malevolent ones the source of misery."[46] To this Rand replied, "The essence of true religion is wofully obscured by the sentiments here advanced. The Bible makes it consist in disinterested love to God and man. This doctrine gives it the character of self-interest."[47] Thus Finney's vaunted idea that the sinner opts for God out of love and a desire to further universal happiness are empty boasts, Rand found; the sinner operates only out of selfishness.

Another bone of contention that Rand found was Finney's oversimplification of the Holy Spirit's role in conversion. Rather than the full-orbed doctrine of pneumatology in the Westminster Standards, Finney's reductionism had made of all the scriptural instruction on what the Spirit did a small and weak thing. Whereas in the Confession of Faith the saints are called to Christ by the "Spirit working in due season; are justified, adopted, sanctified, and kept by his power through faith unto salvation" . . . and given the "Holy Spirit, to make them willing and able to believe,"[48] Rand found that Finney had trivialized these crucial operations, or ignored them altogether. In the "New Heart" sermon, "The sole office of the Spirit is to convince and persuade," Rand noted. "His influence is precisely of the same kind with the preacher's. . . . The Spirit *persuades* only; the sinner is convinced and yields to the persuasion. He resolves to serve God, and is a Christian."[49] This, Rand felt, was as notable a lack as Finney's minimizing of human depravity.

When Rand's "New Divinity Tried" appeared in the *Volunteer*, and then in pamphlet form, it caused a furor. By its very title, it was clear that Asa Rand intended to indict not only Finney but all those who held to the New Divinity. Here in this sermon, conveniently for Rand and the other Hopkinsians, all of the heresies that had been suspected in the New Haven Theology were paraded so overtly that it was impossible to miss them. There must have been some hurried consultations between Lyman Beecher, Benjamin Wisner, and other Boston clergymen, for Wisner either volunteered or was appointed to answer Rand in a pamphlet.

Wisner, who was in a sense responsible for Charles Finney's being in Boston, protested vigorously against the blanket indictment of "The New Divinity Tried." It was clear, he said, that Rand was implicating "other orthodox Congregational ministers in the city," and these men were Calvinists of unblemished reputation. Then he proceeded to examine what Finney had preached, and in some very dextrous interpreting he attempted to demonstrate that the doctrines of the "New Heart" sermon could be reconciled, more or less, with some of the Edwardean schools of the last seventy years. Charles Finney, Wisner stated, "agrees with Augustine, Calvin, President Edwards, Dr. Hopkins, Dr. Woods, and the great majority of orthodox divines in New England". . . on the contested issue that "moral character is to be ascribed to voluntary exercises alone."[50] In his attempt to be adroit, however, Wisner neglected to mention that Asa Rand was in agreement with Finney on this point, for to have done otherwise would have been to assert that the human being was a mere automaton. But when it came to the agency of the Holy Spirit, Wisner had to admit that Finney was deficient, and he himself agreed with Rand that the Spirit had a far broader and more active part to play in regeneration than Finney had allowed. However, said Wisner, he could not allow Finney to be condemned; he was orthodox "in doctrine even if not in the philosophical manner of explaining doctrine."

The excitement created by all of this soon reached the Presbyterians of the Middle Atlantic states. There, with the controversy over Albert Barnes at fever pitch, and the distant smoke from the squabble between Nathaniel Taylor and Bennet Tyler drifting down from Connecticut, the moderates of Princeton Seminary read the pamphlets and reviews of Rand and Wisner. Up to this point they had been largely silent on the issues. They had watched as Finney preached in Philadelphia throughout the year 1828, and although they had felt that his coarse, "denunciatory" revivals were backcountry fanaticisms unworthy of dignified Presbyterians, they had kept silent. Over the years the Princetonian Calvinists had been unhappy with the innovations

Lyman Beecher (1775–1863), "father of more brains than any man in America," in his later years. Inheriting the mantle of Timothy Dwight as the evangelical leader of the Second Great Awakening, Beecher exerted enormous labors for years to promote innumerable causes. Beecher's fluctuating relationships with Charles Finney and his converts provide a fascinating study. From *Harper's Weekly Journal of Civilization*, January 31, 1863.

brought about in Edwards' theology by his followers and students, and the Hopkinsians especially had irritated them. Again, they kept silent. Then, when Nathaniel Taylor's *Concio ad Clerum* had been published in 1828, their worst fears over the influence of the Plan of Union Congregationalists who had graduated from Yale were realized. But

Charles Hodge (1797–1878) taught over three thousand students during his fifty years at Princeton Theological Seminary. While Hodge was a moderate in spirit, he emerged as a champion of Old School Presbyterians against the New School theology of Albert Barnes, Nathaniel Beman, and Charles Finney. Courtesy of the Presbyterian Historical Society.

still they remained silent, broaching their anger only to one another. With the coming of the Barnes controversy, they again remained aloof, waiting for the determinations of the General Assembly.

And now this; Charles Finney again, in complete agreement with the New Divinity! The young professor of oriental and biblical literature at Princeton Seminary, Charles Hodge, who had founded the *Biblical Repertory and Theological Review* in 1825, as editor assigned to himself the task of writing on Wisner's *Review of "The New Divinity Tried."* Perhaps it was the silence of years that boiled up in the article. Whatever caused Hodge's anger, his review of Benjamin Wisner's pamphlet ran for twenty-six pages and upheld Asa Rand at each point. Hodge was delighted that the salient ideas of the New Divinity were exposed to public view. "It starts with the assumption that morality can only be predicated on voluntary exercises; that all holiness and sin consist in acts of choice or preference." But, Hodge noted, there is nothing new about this notion; "It is, on all hands, acknowledged to be centuries old. The novelty consists in its being held by men professing to be Calvinists."[51] And it brings "very nearly the same results" when there is an attempt to weld it to Calvinism as it does when used in all other schemes.

Charles Hodge agreed with Rand's other criticisms, but at one point he held that Rand had not gone far enough. This was in the tendency of Finney's mode of evangelism not only to rest largely in the sinner's own determination, which Rand had noted, but that it gave insufficient attention to Christ's work of salvation. Here was an extremely serious criticism, if it be correct. It was of grave consequence that Finney did not include the fulness of the Holy Spirit's work, but if he neglected what Christ did on the cross, that was unforgiveable:

> We believe that the characteristic tendency of this mode of preaching, is to keep the Holy Spirit and his influences out of view; and we fear a still more serious objection is, that Christ and his cross are practically made of none effect. The constant exhortation is, to make choice of God as the portion of the soul; to change the governing purpose of the life; to submit to the moral Governor of the universe. The specific act to which the sinner is urged as immediately connected with salvation, is an act which has no reference to Christ. The soul is brought immediately in contact with God; the Mediator is left out of view. We maintain that this is another Gospel. It is practically another system, and a legal system of religion. We do not intend that the doctrine of the mediation of Christ is rejected, but that it is neglected; that the sinner is led to God directly; that he is not urged, under the pressure of the sense of guilt, to go to Christ for pardon, and then to God; but the general idea of submission (not the specific idea of submission to the plan of salvation through Jesus Christ,) is urged,

or the making a right choice. Men are told they have hitherto chosen the world, all they have to do is choose God; that they have had it as their purpose to gain the things of this life, they must now change their purpose, and serve God. . . . Conviction of sin is made of little account; Christ and his atonement are kept out of view, so that the method of salvation is not distinctly presented to the minds of the people. The tendency of this defect, as far as it extends, is fatal to religion and the souls of men.[52]

For the most part, Charles Finney's plan to modify the theology and practice of the Presbyterian denomination to conform to the new measures, now several years old, had been surprisingly successful. Although Asahel Nettleton and Lyman Beecher had challenged him on behalf of the Congregationalists, until this time the Presbyterians, astonishingly, had taken only sporadic notice of what he was attempting. But now Princeton Seminary had turned its gaze on Finney, with disapproval. Statements from the young and brilliant professor and editor, Charles Hodge, carried enormous weight throughout the church. With the Barnes controversy raging, Finney knew that further progress would be much more difficult.

12

FINNEY ON BROADWAY

By the late 1820s the silk-importing firm of Arthur Tappan was very successful, and his income was enormous for that day. For some years the company grossed over one million dollars annually. Taking the most conservative estimate, if his profits are figured at a modest six percent and the shares of his minor partners are subtracted, Arthur's personal income may have been between twenty-five and thirty thousand dollars, or in today's currency, about four hundred thousand dollars.[1]

The reasons for the success of Arthur Tappan and Company were obvious. First, both he and Lewis rigidly followed Christian ethical practices based on the Bible, such as "Owe no man any thing" (Romans 13:8), and the "golden rule" of Matthew 7:12. Because these principles were adhered to so steadfastly, this built a trust for the brothers among the general public, and even their competitors in business or adversaries were forced to give them a grudging admiration on the score of rectitude. Although there were many who disliked the Tappans, for anyone to question their integrity and honesty was almost unheard of. Secondly, they operated on the undeviating and advertised rule of one price to all customers. As one historian has remarked, "In 1830, New York merchants were notorious for their shifty ethics and higgling habits, and Tappan's single price for all, backed by his rigid and unyielding probity, made money."[2] Dealers in from the country, uncomfortable with the pressures of the city and suspicious of getting cheated, found Arthur's emporium felicitous and trustworthy.

Both brothers took their success with utmost seriousness. Arthur, the older, was distant, taciturn, and stern, but as Gilbert Barnes has pointedly said, "his rigidity of conduct and his deep jealousy and hatred of natural man were somehow joined with an impulsive and winning generosity, an unwearying pity for the unfortunate of whatever rank, and an humble devotion to the welfare of the poor."[3] In all fairness, much of Arthur's abrupt manner and outlook on life were conditioned by the chronic headaches he had suffered since childhood, which rarely abated.

Lewis, free from such physical torment, was a happier sort. Both of them had the glint of mental acuteness in their eyes, but Lewis's countenance was always the more eager and open of the two. In addition, there was a compatibility between them that furthered their mutual aims. Throughout his lifetime Lewis tried to keep out of the limelight and allow Arthur to get most of the credit for their philanthropy, and he did this especially in the biography he wrote of his brother's life. Arthur's great generosity to benevolent causes, colleges, seminaries, and innumerable societies, was already well established by 1830. Their real determination to do more than merely contribute handsomely to benevolent causes came, as we have seen, as early as 1827, when Lewis proposed a chain of "Pilgrim" churches throughout New York City, each of which would continue to spawn churches led by laymen, without the regulation of a presbytery.[4] When this plan was torpedoed by Gardiner Spring and other Presbyterian divines, it resulted only in the Tappans' renewed determination to provide Christian ministry to newcomers to the city, and soon this broadened to include the poor and disadvantaged, in the "free church" movement.

From that point, other interests came rapidly to the Tappans. Next there was the campaign in 1828, in concert with Josiah Bissell, Jr., of Rochester, to stop the delivery of mails on the Sabbath. This was a dismal failure.[5] Next Arthur Tappan turned to temperance, and the allied problem, in his eyes, of allowing wine to be used in the sacrament. But what could conscientious Christians use in the place of wine? Arthur was angry that "the mixture of waste liquids, logwood dyes and cheap French brandy" sold as wine should be used for this purpose. He investigated and then imported from France his discovery, a "non-alcoholic burgundy." As his solution to the country's alcoholism problem, Tappan recommended that this be used by those tempted to vice. It was quickly nicknamed by his enemies "A. T. Burgundy." Undeterred, he went before the temperance society and proposed this "simple juice of the grape, such as was used in primitive times before 'alcohol' was discovered or manufactured," for use in communion and for every occasion. Unimpressed, the society refused to go along with the idea.[6]

Next, the Tappans turned to a most unpopular cause that was to divide even churchgoers. As part of their work among the poor at the First Free Church and other activities at Five Points, the Tappans had been sensitized to the number of bordellos in the area. On the model of the London Magdalen Society, Arthur organized the Magdalen Society of New York, established an "Asylum for Females who have Deviated from the Paths of Virtue," and appointed the Rev. John R. McDowall, a recent graduate of Princeton Seminary, as its superintendent. When in London some years earlier, Arthur had been assured by the managers of the Magdalen Society there that many prostitutes wished to reform, and responded to their efforts. McDowall went into a number of the brothels, spoke with the women, and wrote a pamphlet entitled *The Magdalen Report.* Then he persuaded two prominent physicians, named Brown and Reese, to sign it along with his name and Tappan's. In it McDowall estimated that "every tenth female in our cities is a prostitute." As for these unfortunates, a prostitute's "feet go down to death . . . for in about five years they are carried to the grave and their places are filled by a new class of unfortunate, guilty females." As for New York City, "the number of females in this city who abandon themselves to prostitution is not less than ten thousand!! . . . ten thousand harlots in this city!"[7] The report then went on to be entirely too specific on many details for that delicate age.

When the pamphlet appeared in the summer of 1831, it caused a sensation. Most of the newspapers of the city howled with rage, Tammany Hall politicians roundly denounced it as an attack by ministerial do-gooders, and even many church people were horrified that such things would be made public. Dr. Reese publicly disavowed the pamphlet, but Dr. Brown and the Tappans upheld it. Among the outraged lower classes there was talk of mobbing Arthur Tappan's home, and among the upper classes there were protest meetings to finance a libel suit against the society.

It was not only city editors and ward heelers whose civic pride was wounded. A large number of respected citizens vented their rage as well, and as Bertram Wyatt-Brown has said, "what unified all these civic leaders was a common resentment of the rising 'social influence of New Englanders in the City.'"[8] The pamphlet was pirated, many copies were sold to the inquisitive, and Tappan was forced to publish a statement concerning it in which he apologized that "the language is in some instances indelicate, and the details too minute." As a conclusion to the whole affair, the asylum was closed for lack of funds.

Totally undeterred, the Tappans then turned (their resolution must be admired, if not all their goals!) to the possibilities of providing college education for blacks. In 1828 Arthur Tappan had met Simeon S. Jocelyn, a young Congregational clergyman and home missionary whose dedication to the welfare of blacks, some slave and some free, touched Tappan. Jocelyn had a plan to found a college at New Haven, Connecticut, and to invite blacks there from across the nation. Tappan immediately fell in with the plan, bought several acres of land in the city for a campus, pledged a generous contribution for buildings, and got members of the Yale faculty to promise they would teach in the college when it was established. Then, a public hearing was held before a committee of the Connecticut legislature. The pioneer abolitionist, Benjamin Lundy, was the chief speaker. His address in support of education for blacks was well received, and the legislators gave some hope for support from the state.[9]

Lundy was highly respected by British abolitionists, who had already abolished the slave trade in 1807, and were at that moment trying to garner enough votes in Parliament to outlaw the practice throughout the entire British empire, which victory would come to them in 1833. From England the antislavery leaders sent Lundy their pamphlets and newspapers. His paper, the *Genius of Universal Emancipation,* was published in Baltimore, and he had as his assistant William Lloyd Garrison, a man of meager education and explosive temperament.

In the summer of 1830 Garrison, then only twenty-four, had accused a shipmaster of "domestic piracy" for transporting slaves to a new plantation in Louisiana for their owner. Showing his violent proclivities, he raged in Lundy's paper, "Francis Todd . . . should be sentenced to solitary confinement for life!" He and all who transport slaves "are the enemies of their own species—highway robbers and murders; and their final doom will be, unless they speedily repent, to occupy the lowest depths of perdition." For this he was jailed in Baltimore on a charge of libel.

For seven weeks Garrison languished in jail, until word of his imprisonment reached the ears of Arthur Tappan in New York. Tappan sent money to release Garrison on bail, although the two were strangers. Garrison immediately visited the Tappans, and with gifts from them and other philanthropists he issued the first number of his own paper, the *Liberator*, in Boston on January 1, 1831. This first issue was militant throughout, and demanded the immediate freedom without compensation "of our slave population." Unfortunately, Garrison had no practical plan or interest in the many political, economic, and social difficulties involved in emancipating the millions of slaves in the United States. As Gilbert Barnes says, "His ardent, suggestible imagination seized upon the abstract absolutes of the radical pamphleteers of immediate abolition, and he made them his own."[10]

Garrison's vitriolic attacks were symptomatic of the internal discord that was convulsing the abolitionist movement in America at this very time. Several different struggles agitated the antislavery forces. The first was the argument over African colonization, a plan with a long history. Several years before the Revolutionary War, Dr. Samuel Hopkins, founder of the stricter branch of Edwardean theology, stated that some blacks should be educated and sent back to their native lands as teachers and pastors, to make some slight compensation for the evil and misery of the slave trade. In 1800 the Virginia legislature asked Governor James Monroe to correspond with President Thomas Jefferson regarding the purchase of land to colonize free blacks. Then, on December 21, 1816, The American Society for Colonizing the Free People of Color in the United States was organized in Washington, and in April 1818, Samuel J. Mills, Jr., selected Liberia as an ideal site where free blacks might colonize. But by 1831 opposition to this plan was mounting, as many whites realized that, if all the blacks of the United States were freed, it was utterly improbable that they would all desire to be expatriated. The proponents of colonization, however, did not give up easily.[11]

The second issue that vexed the antislavery forces was that of "immediate emancipation." Until approximately 1830, both British and American abolitionists had been committed to a "gradualist" position regarding emancipation. The earlier abolitionists believed that some sort of transitional arrangements would be needed to prepare the black population for life in a free society. By education and apprenticeship techniques, it was hoped, blacks could be inducted into the responsibilities of a new situation. During the early 1830s there was an astounding change in sentiment toward this, however. Large numbers of abolitionists, fearing that such "gradualism" was merely an excuse for indefinite postponements, switched over to "immediatism." Garrison voiced it for many in his *Liberator* as "the universal, immediate, and unqualified emancipation of all American slaves." But "immediatism," many sympathizers objected, was a most unfortunate choice of term, for its inevitable meaning to those who might otherwise want emancipation properly planned and conducted, was that vast hordes of illiterate, unskilled, and destitute blacks were about to be turned loose on the land. To counter such ideas, others who quailed at Garrison's virulence explained that "immediatism" meant "gradual emancipation immediately undertaken."[12]

The third and probably most explosive issue was the frenzied debate over "amalgamation," the nineteenth-century euphemism for the social interaction and mingling of blacks and whites. Multitudes who were eager for abolition still opposed amalgamation. Charles Finney, strong exponent of freedom for blacks, on the other hand thought that if a white person had a "constitutional taste" that excluded blacks, that was quite legitimate and should be respected. Here he disagreed with the Tappans and Theodore Weld.[13]

In spite of the mounting opposition to the idea of black colonization in Africa, the American Colonization Society was in 1831 the only truly national organization that even professed to deal with the issue of slavery.[14] The Tappans realized this, and with their extensive experience in administration, they resolved to do something about the problem. In June 1831, Arthur Tappan attended the First Annual Convention of People of Color with Garrison and Jocelyn, held in Philadelphia. Conferring there with Lundy and others disturbed over the problem, Tappan and Garrison decided to form a national society without further delay. But public prejudice and other difficulties soon presented themselves, and it was not until the autumn of 1833 that they could begin. Soon Arthur Tappan began the *Emancipator*, an abolitionist journal dedicated to a less inflammatory type of antislavery influence than Garrison's *Liberator*, for the brothers saw the difficulties inherent in trying to attract supporters to Garrison's radical ideas, and wished to find a middle way that might attract much wider support.[15]

The Tappans' next benevolent activity was to provide for theological education in the West. They had for some years been ardent supporters of orthodox colleges in the East. Arthur Tappan was a director of the American Education Society, and he was especially interested in assisting needy young men who wished to prepare for the ministry. Then in 1831 it came time for Lewis Tappan to send his own two sons to a school. In conversation with Charles Finney, Tappan heard glowing praise for George Gale's Oneida Institute at Whitesboro, New York. Its distinguishing feature was the manual labor system, whereby a student paid a very small tuition and board, and combined work on the farm with a portion of the day set aside for lectures. But above and beyond this, its students were quickly imbued with reform principles, and this, perhaps as much as its country location, far from the haunts of sin, immediately impressed Tappan. The boys were enrolled.

Theodore Weld had entered Oneida Institute in the autumn of 1827 to complete his preparation for theological training. The trustees, however, had pressed him into collecting funds for the school, because of his impressive demeanor and number of contacts with important people. At the task of seeking contributions Weld had conspicuous success, and during the next three years at the school he spent more than half of his time traveling and performing this function on its behalf.[16] In addition he was the "monitor-general" of the students, and when Lewis Tappan visited the Institute in August 1831, his sons introduced him to Weld.[17]

Tappan had of course heard a great deal of the amazing Weld before this, and in short order they had compared many notes and become good friends. Perhaps the farsighted Tappan had already formulated his plan involving Weld before he went to Whitesboro. At any rate, it concerned the Society for Promoting Manual Labor in Literary Institutions, which had already been organized with Joshua Leavitt as secretary. In light of the excellent reputation Oneida Institute was enjoying throughout the nation, the society had been set up to propagate the idea of manual labor schools in other parts. And, in light of Weld's abilities as a fund-raiser, Lewis Tappan knew that he was just the man to serve as its traveling agent.

If that position alone had been offered to Weld, he would probably have refused it. But in addition, Lewis Tappan offered him a commission to choose a location for "a great national Theological Seminary on the Manual Labor Plan." A spark was struck. Weld was quite aware that such a seminary was needed, for dozens of Finney's converts in his revivals had expressed their intention to enter the ministry, and many of these had completed their literary training and were ready to advance into theological study. With this combination of possibilities set before him, Weld could not refuse.

With his usual intensity, Weld set to work in the fall of 1831 to determine the best location for the new school. He was approached by some who wished to have it in New York State, but he felt that enough educational institutions were already there. It was the West, others urged him, that desperately needed such a place to train pro-revival clergymen. J. L. Tracy wrote to Weld on November 24, 1831:

[George Whipple] has written to you I know on the subject of the Manual Labor Institution which you are about to establish and which you wish to locate where it will do the world most good. . . . I feel sanguine in the belief that if you would come over and view the land in its length and breadth, bearing upon its surface as it does the germ of a mighty, an all controlling influence, both political and religious, you would be at once in favor of locating the great institution in the Valley of the Miss[issippi]. . . . Tis yet a babe. Why not then come and take it in the feebleness of its infancy and give a right direction to its powers that when it grows up to its full stature we may bless God that it has such an influence? What could be better calculated to do this than an Institution of the character we contemplate? I doubt not Rochester may have some facilities which are not possessed by Cincinnati but it seems to me these facilities should be very great to weigh down the other reasons which present themselves for bringing the institution on this side the mountains. . . . I hope and pray you will not take any decisive step until you come to Cincinnati and see for yourself.[18]

In actuality, such a school already existed at Cincinnati. In 1828 two merchants, Ebenezer Lane and his brother William, met with a board of trustees in Cincinnati and agreed to give an endowment of $4,000 to establish a theological seminary there, and the manual labor system was to be "a fundamental rule or principle" of the school.[19] A tract of land and buildings were secured in the beautiful wooded Walnut Hills, two miles from Cincinnati, and the Ohio legislature granted a charter to "Lane Theological Seminary." But further progress was very slow and funds were not forthcoming.

In desperation an agent of the school traveled to Boston in October 1830 to invite the most famous pastor in the nation, Lyman Beecher, to be the new president. Beecher seemed to fill every criterion admirably; he was an abolitionist, a revivalist, something of a scholar and administrator, had more contacts in churchly circles than anyone else in America, and could attract prospective students to the seminary if anyone could. Beecher was delighted with the offer, saying that "it was the greatest thought that ever entered my soul."[20] The agent, having obtained Beecher's virtual acceptance of Lane's presidency, hurried on to New York to ask for a meeting with the Tappan brothers. Always open to educational enterprises, Arthur Tappan pledged $20,000 to endow a chair of theology, on condition that Beecher would be the first seminary president.

The delight inspired by this turn of events among Lane's supporters soon chilled when Beecher, in Boston, vacillated and delayed for a year and a half over his decision. On the one hand he was indeed eager to be free from the endless skirmishing with the Boston Unitarians, yet on the other he was loath to leave until the debt had been paid to rebuild his burned-out church, and his congregation was refusing to give its consent for him to leave. Despite Beecher's indecision, it soon became evident which city Weld should choose, and he submitted to the Tappans a strong recommendation of Cincinnati and the embryonic manual labor school that already existed there.[21] It would be, Weld believed, an ideal place for the many Finney converts who planned to be clergymen to continue their education.

Finally, in April 1832, Lyman Beecher arrived in Cincinnati, looked over the seminary, consulted with its supporters, debated whether to accept the call of the Second Presbyterian Church as its pastor, and visited relatives. All of this was enough to convince him (if in truth his mind was not already made up) to accept the offers. Back in Boston he resigned his church and, at age fifty-seven, with his usual gleeful confidence, took his family west. Had he known what awaited him, Beecher might not have been so jaunty. As Gilbert Barnes has well said:

> Rejoicing that his fraternity of young converts now had an opportunity for theological training, Weld sent them word that the appointed day was here. By some strange fate, this host of Finney's converts was to confront Beecher as Finney had done in 1827. Once more Finney's new measures, now in antislavery guise, were fated to rouse Beecher's ire; once again there was to be a dispute, a defeat, and a separation.[22]

Most of the students destined for Lane Seminary were from western New York. Twenty came from Oneida Institute, having absorbed all the learning they could there. Several who hailed from Rochester, including H. B. Stanton, floated down the Ohio River from Pittsburgh on a raft. But a smattering came from the South—from Missouri, Virginia, Kentucky, Tennessee, and two from Alabama. This was to be the largest class of theological students ever assembled in an American seminary, and they were, as quite mature men (most of them were well into their twenties), quite aware of the significance of the school, Beecher's leadership, and their own circumstances. As they gathered for the first term, in August 1833, Beecher pronounced them "the most talented, spirited, heroic phalanx I ever met!"[23]

On October 25, 1831, when Charles Finney had been laboring in Boston but two months, Lewis Tappan wrote to Theodore Weld from New York City, "The Free Ch[urc]h have prayerfully determined to take measures preparatory to the formation of a 2d Free Chh. 30 to 40 members of our Chh are to be set apart as Colonists. They will take Masonic Hall; elect a Pastor; and by preaching, praying, and laboring expect the blessing of God upon this Xian [Christian] enterprise."[24] Tappan went on to say that Edward N. Kirk had been offered the pastorate, but that he was uncertain if he could accept, and "whether Mr. Kirk comes or not . . . we want you." The intention was to link the efforts of Weld and Joel Parker in the free church movement. On November 9 Parker also wrote to Weld to bolster Tappan's request, saying "Will you come? Dont send back a crazy fanatical letter about 'city polish' and 'refinement,' etc., etc. We dont want you here to flatter the vanity of the gay nor to make entertainments for the refined. We want you to talk to the consciences of those who are perishing in sin."[25]

Weld, with his characteristic independence, decided against New York. In his dual capacity as agent and recruiter for Lane Seminary, and traveling agent for the Society for the Promotion of Manual Labor in Literary Institutions, he was crisscrossing New England and the West in their interests. In February 1832, near Columbus, Ohio, the drivers of the stage coach in which he was a passenger attempted to ford a rain-swollen river, and Weld, in an incident publicized across the nation, nearly drowned when the coach and horses were swept downstream in the pitch-dark night. Nonetheless, he pressed on after recuperating from the harrowing experience (although he bore some of its effects the remainder of his life), and reached Cincinnati by late February. Having disdained New York, Weld was overwhelmed with the potential of the West for revivals. He wrote to Charles Finney from Cincinnati on February 28:

> You never can move this vast valley by working the lever in Boston, New York or Philadelphia. But I suppose you will still reiterate the old assertion that in *New York* especially you can sway the West thro the hundreds of business men who resort thither from here. Answer: the western merchants and others are but the drop of the bucket in this great population. . . . I tell you my dear brother, the cure, the only cure for prejudice against you is con-

tact. I say *contact,* not a brushing contact of a single sermon or two, but for weeks. . . . The mere *fact of your* coming into the valley would win this population greatly. They would begin *to identify you with themselves.* The obstacles here are very few. You could command audiences of thousands. Their camp meetings all over this region would afford you immeasurably greater fields for effort than you have ever occupied. Think of fifteen thousand souls, and these mainly *those who rarely hear the gospel.* . . . Cincinnati is *the spot* for you to begin by all means. . . . One fact more. The great mass of the population are not gospel hardened. . . . One fact more. The churches at the East are comparatively well under weigh. They are moving upon the full tide of revivals. They dont need you at all as they do here. Thro all the West, revivals of any power are almost unknown. This whole region is half a century behind the East. Besides, here is to be the battlefield of the world. Here Satans seat is. A mighty effort must be made to dislodge him *soon,* or the West is undone.[26]

Finney's campaign in Boston had not been especially successful, and it was coming to a close. Perhaps Weld is correct, he thought. Writing to Lewis Tappan, Finney outlined Weld's arguments for going to the beckoning West. When he received Finney's letter, Tappan, whose power base was solid in New York but did not extend far from there, was alarmed. Charles Finney had been a powerful factor in the success of the Benevolent Empire to this point, and his departure would be a severe blow. Tappan immediately wrote a letter, on March 16, which attempted to counteract Weld's influence by informing Finney that the Chatham Street Theater had been leased as planned, and that if he came to New York it was his to use. In a previous note regarding this Finney had asked, "Is not the location too filthy for decent people to go there?" Tappan responded, "No. It is more decent than I had apprehended and can be made quite so. . . . The *sensation* that will be produced by converting the place, with slight alterations, into a church will be very great, and curiosity will be excited, in the city and out of it, to visit a place thus appropriated." Finney had agreed that a large theater converted into a place of worship would pique the curiosity of many, but he said that this location was "contiguous to Dr. Spring, Mr. Rice," and other important Presbyterian clergymen. Tappan replied to this, "Would it be murdering souls to draw away half of Dr. Spring's congregation?"[27]

In the months prior to this the Association of Gentlemen, with Lewis Tappan taking the lead, had hoped that the good work being done by Joel Parker at the First Free Church might be expanded. By the beginning of 1832 the First Free Church was meeting in Broadway Hall, the largest auditorium in the city. With forty-one of its members who were willing to form the nucleus of the Second Church, this was organized on February 14, 1832, in the Third Presbytery of New York. Although Charles Finney was the first choice of the Gentlemen to head up the new enterprise, he had been gone from New York for a year and a half. In their uncertainty as to the date of his return, they had offered the pastorate first to Edward N. Kirk, then to Theodore Weld, and, disappointed on both counts, had come up with the idea of securing a very large auditorium with which to lure Finney back to the city.

The Chatham Street Theater seemed a good location, and Lewis Tappan approached a clergyman named Dr. Jacob Janeway, one of the trustees of the estate that owned it, and asked the price. Tappan reported that Janeway was somewhat ashamed of the property and wanted to be rid of it, but he had leased it to a circus owner named William Blanchard, who in turn had sublet it to Thomas Hamblin. On contacting Blanchard, Tappan found that he was not only willing to give up his lease, but would assist in renovating the building to change it to a church.[28]

Lewis Tappan kept up his pleas to Finney, begging him to come and pastor the Second Free Church, or Chatham Street Chapel. On March 22 he wrote:

> Again, a man like Weld thinks the center of the world is where he acts. . . . The [Mississippi and Ohio] Valley is important, and very soon Rail roads will bring all the business men to this city twice a year. If converted here they will labor at home effectually. . . . That is not the question, but this, is there a post, all things considered, where such a moral influence can be exerted as in that thoroughfare where 30,000 walk daily? (Chatham Street.)
>
> You say, "I don't know as my coming to N.Y. *now* could help me any in forming a judgment as to what is duty." A view of the premises, the localities, etc. would remove your doubts as to the fitness of the place, its capacity, etc. etc. and enable us to decide about hiring the estate.[29]

Charles Finney could hardly deny that there were advantages in Tappan's offer. For one, he knew the situation in New York, and although it was not ideal, due to the Old School opposition, Tappan's arguments regarding the influence radiating from a pulpit there were certainly correct. Indeed, Finney did feel that his business in the city was unfinished. Also, the Chatham Street Theater was very large, and in its renovated state it would hold twenty-five hundred people, a very substantial audience. And yet, perhaps the most persuasive argument was the fact that he and Lydia had three children, with the birth of Frederic Norton (named after Herman Norton) on March 7, 1832. With an increasing family, Lydia could no longer travel with her husband as she had from time to time in the past. Moreover, Finney's health was not good, and in view of this a settled pastorate seemed most inviting.

With these advantages of New York balanced against the uncertainties of a ministry in Cincinnati—based, for all Finney knew, mainly on Theodore Weld's enthusiasms—the choice became an obvious one. After Lewis Tappan agreed that he might have several months each summer to continue his itinerant evangelism in other places, Finney accepted the offer. On April 11 Tappan wrote jubilantly to the evangelist, "Well, we have possession! Hamden gave it without compensation; our contracts are made; a gang of mechanics began this morning; and the place is to be finished by 8 May!!—in season for the anniversaries."[30] So, when the Boston campaign concluded about May 1, Finney left for New York City. He arrived there by May 6 but had to begin his ministry in temporary quarters until the renovation of the theater could be completed. It had been arranged to dedicate what would become known as the Chatham Street Chapel on Monday, April 23, at half-past five in the morning, to allow businessmen and their employees to be present, and it was reported that well over one thousand attended the service even at that early hour.[31]

Finney may have had some reason to be disappointed with the chapel. Although Lewis Tappan continually boasted of it, stating that it was large enough to "accomodate ever so many anxious," nonetheless it could not be denied that it was a big barn of a place, perhaps better suited for circuses than services. It was not in a good neighborhood, and Finney was concerned that the entire building, while only eight years old, might collapse under the weight of a packed house.[32] Because it was leased and not purchased, as the Association of Gentlemen had enough financial obligations at the time, it was not carpeted, and the clatter and movement even of an orderly congregation must have echoed in the cavernous interior. On Sunday, May 6, renovations were sufficiently complete for the first services to be held, and Charles Finney preached twice and conducted a sacramental service. The *New York Evangelist* reflected the mingled delight of the occasion and the moderate disappointment in the accommodations, as it reported on May 12, 1832:

> Chatham Street Chapel was opened for divine service last Sabbath. Rev. Mr. Finney preached morning and evening. In the afternoon the Lord's Supper was administered, Rev. Mr. Parker's church joining in the ordinance. Vast congregations attended during all the exercises, and accordingly no apprehensions of danger from the structure of the building, are longer felt. The three galleries, and even the aisles were crowded, and great numbers were obliged to leave for want of seats. Not less, however, than two thousand persons were accomodated; and the speaker's voice was distinctly heard in all parts of the house.
>
> Measures, we hope, will be taken to prevent, in future, such a degree of noise and disturbance near the doors, and particularly in the galleries, as was made by the coming in of such crowds of persons after the exercises had commenced. In the front galleries, (which, by the way, afford very agreeable seats,) it was quite impossible to fix one's attention upon the devotional services; and so late was the noise continued, that the first part of the sermon was heard with difficulty. We know not how to avoid this evil entirely, but if the floor and stairs were to be spread with carpets, it would be an essential, if not indeed an entirely effectual improvement.[33]

Perhaps it was in hopes of overcoming some of the esthetic shortcomings that the Tappans and Finney invited Thomas Hastings (1784–1872) to be the director of music at the chapel. Already a well-known church musician, Hastings was by this point composing and writing hymns prolifically. In 1830 he had composed the tune for which he is best remembered, "Rock of Ages, Cleft for Me," to Toplady's verses. In his lifetime he was to write over sixteen hundred hymns, and over a thousand hymn tunes, including the music for "Majestic Sweetness Sits Enthroned" (1837) and "From Every Stormy Wind That Blows" (1842), and the verses for "Hail to the Brightness of Zion's Glad Morning" (1832), among the ones that are still sung. Acutely nearsighted, and an albino, Hastings was able to read a page of music when placed upside down. Singers for years remembered this outstanding choral director conducting large choirs with his face close to the music to be able to read it, a great difficulty for a musician, which he was largely able to overcome.[34]

In 1823 Thomas Hastings had gone to Utica to direct the music of several choirs and churches, at the same time editing and publishing *The Western Recorder*, a religious periodical that he used to popularize his advanced ideas. Here Finney became his close friend during the Utica revival, and the evangelist realized the power that good music could have over audiences. With his fine reputation and innovative techniques, Hastings would surely be a great asset at the Chatham Street Chapel, and he had an unusual assignment. He was not only to direct the music at Second Free Church, but also to improve the musical offerings at the entire group of free churches, which would mean that he would divide his time among them, though giving Second Church priority. Thus, although Finney stated inflexibly his opposition to anything innovative in music,[35] Hastings was encouraged at the chapel to provide a fine background to the preaching, and he set a precedent for future soloists, "choristers," and other elements of modern evangelism. In the 1830s and 1840s in America the most prolific of religious composers were Lowell Mason, William Bradbury, and Hastings, the great trio who ushered in a new period of hymnody. Hastings would assist Finney in the same capacity at the Broadway Tabernacle in 1836 and 1837.

However bare and noisy the Chatham Street Chapel may have been, Lewis Tappan was delighted to show off his acquisition to the gathered delegates of the "Great Eight benevolent societies," who came to New York each May for their "anniversary meetings."[36] There they would report on the progress of the preceding year, and make plans for the next assault on the forces of sin and sickness. It was always a time of jubilation, for "the Great Eight" had already expanded "beyond the most sanguine expectations of their founders." Great amounts of money were rolling in, and they had become, in the view of one observer, "immense institutions spreading over the country, combining hosts . . . a gigantic religious power, systematized, compact in its organization, with a polity and a government entirely its own, and independent of all control." The combined income of the fourteen leading societies had been increasing at an impressive rate, but suddenly in the early 1830s it spurted, and in 1834 it would approach nine million dollars (equivalent to approximately one hundred thirty million dollars today). The combined budgets easily rivaled the major expenditures of the federal government.[37]

In addition to "the Great Eight," there were innumerable lesser societies—to promote prison reform, stop the desecration of the Sabbath, help reform prostitutes, and so on. It seemed that, in this age of societies, everyone in the churches was eager to join one or more. Riding the crest of popularity in 1832 was the American Temperance Society. An incredible web of local groups allowed a vast membership. The New York State Temperance Society was approaching two thousand locals, including young men's societies, infant societies, and female auxiliaries. In 1833 it would print eighty-nine million pages of literature.[38]

At the heart of all this were the Tappans, thoroughly enjoying their role and, in truth, maintaining their lucrative silk business largely as a means to bring in money for what was their consuming interest in life, the Benevolent Empire. Interlocking directorates involved the Tappans and a relative few—Gerrit Smith, Anson Phelps, David Low Dodge, William Jay, and others—who sat on board after board, and thus coordinated the activities of the societies. It was not entirely a coincidence that most of these men were either New School Presbyterians or New Divinity Congregationalists, and thus very compatible with Charles Finney.

In 1832 at the "anniversary meetings" Finney was one of the featured speakers. In a famous message he dwelt on the old Edwardean concept of "benevolence." Challenging the delegates who had come from near and far, Finney rose to the occasion in his new amphitheater by sending out a ringing exhortation sketching the basic outlines of Christian benevolence. Primarily, it was etched on the eschatological doctrine of postmillennialism, which holds that the kingdom of God will increase until it has ultimately converted the world, this period of triumph being the thousand-year peaceful reign of Christ illustrated in Revelation chapter 20.

With the conviction that conditions were improving on the earth (in part, through their efforts), Finney delineated for the societies the demands and motivation necessary to bring in the millennium and complete the task, and he offered a far-sighted national program in which all Americans could combine their efforts to bring about the latter-day glory. Basing this on Jonathan Edwards' idea of "universal benevolence," Finney gave the delegates a panoramic view of the entire universe under the moral government of the Creator, and showed how America could fit into this as a crucial part of the divine plan. Humans everywhere, and especially those under the searching light of the gospel, are to behave in accordance with the "laws of benevolence," which Jesus set forth in terms of love of God and neighbor. In Finney's view, this eventuated in each Christian's obligation to "aim at being useful in the highest degree possible," seeking to advance the interests of God's kingdom above all other things. Some of this was of course simply a recasting of Edwards in a nineteenth-century mold, sharing his view that the world was getting better in a postmillennial sense. But Finney added some significant touches by personalizing it far more than Edwards had, and challenging each Christian in a very relevant way to find his or her place in God's plan.[39]

By this point in Finney's life, through his contact with the Tappans and the Association of Gentlemen, these ideas had become central in his thinking, and a necessary adjunct to the preaching of salvation through Christ. Previously, many of the elements of this theology were more or less present in his thought, but the salvation of the lost was paramount, and they were subservient. By the time of his association with the free churches of New York and elsewhere, and his increased contact with the poor and disadvantaged, these stresses on reform and benevolence were being given equal weight with evangelism. It is not difficult to understand why. As he dwelt in the less affluent area of New York City and brushed shoulders with the teeming and needy masses throughout the day, he was burdened to help these desperate people, and impelled by two growing beliefs. First, many "Christians" were lazy, and contributed little or nothing to God's work. They must see, he felt, that being passive for God will never suffice, that God demanded one's best from every true Christian. As he said, "Every member must work or quit. No honorary members." Secondly, to help cure the world's sickness, full and dedicated service from each child of God was the inevitable consequence of true faith. If, therefore, a person did little for the kingdom, his or her salvation was certainly in question. This was bold and uncompromising doctrine, and it was typically Finney.

Increasingly in his thought at this time was the concept of the church as a reform organization, sustained by the cooperative endeavors of revivals and benevolence. He was later to state that the "great business of the church is to reform the world—to put away every kind of sin."[40] Finney never surrendered the idea that revivals were God's primary means of reforming both the church and the world, because he remained convinced that only individuals who were soundly converted could bring about social reform. As Norman Grover has stated, "The reform of church and society were assumed to follow spontaneously from the total internal transformation of the inner man."[41] This in some degree explains Finney's aversion to denominational bureaucracies and organizational bigness, because he saw the church not as form and structure but as dynamic and life—a fellowship of transformed believers, avidly cooperating for the achievement of the same goals.

New converts were urged by Finney immediately to become "useful in the highest degree possible" by throwing their energies and zeal into every cause that needed assistance. In magnificent harmony with American activism and the democracy of the Jacksonian age, the church too was a voluntaristic society, and it was the Christian's high privilege to cooperate with the Lord in the vanquishing of every sin and human plight, and eventually to bring in, as the final triumph, the millennium. Thus, although Charles Finney had learned much of this from, first, Jonathan Edwards, and later from Lyman Beecher, the Tappans, and the benevolent societies that had been founded in the previous twenty years, he was not to follow along, slavishly accepting their visions. His awareness of the possibilities of Christian service was as great as theirs. Therefore, to Lewis and Arthur Tappan, Phelps, the Platts, and many others, Charles Finney must have seemed to be the very embodiment of what they needed—a masterful orator who could sway great audiences, and enunciate the ephemeral stuff of dreams.

With the "anniversary meetings" over, attendances at the chapel remained high for the next month. All the circumstances of Finney's life pointed to a great period of usefulness in New York. On June 1, 1832, Dr. J. W. C. Bliss, William Green, Jr., and other leaders of the Second Free Church contracted with Finney that he receive a salary of $1,500 per annum, to be paid in quarterly sums.[42] The evangelist had purchased a residence near the chapel, and Lewis Tappan aided him in setting up housekeeping, a new experience for the Finneys. Tappan advised Charles and Lydia to purchase only plain and unadorned furniture, so that they would set a good example to others in the ministry.[43]

Coincidentally, it was at this time that Lydia's parents sold the old family farm in Whitesboro, where she had been born and raised, and where Charles had frequently gone to rest between revivals. Until he purchased the small residence at 177 Grand Street, the Finneys had no home of their own, and for the first seven years of their marriage they had come to regard the farm as home. Lydia had longed for a place of their own[44] and loved the farm, and news of its sale came as a great disappointment. Quite distressed, she wrote to her father:

> Although I am glad you have sold out, still when I reflect, that, that retired spot where I have spent so many of my days, days of

childhood and peace, where I have received and enjoyed so much parental, brotherly, and sisterly affection, when I reflect that I can no longer call it *home*, my tears flow and I cannot refrain from weeping bitterly.[45]

Then, there was the problem of moving their belongings, and pieces of furniture that Lydia wished to have from the old family farmhouse, to 177 Grand Street. "Whatever she has there that can be safely boxed up and transported should not be sold," Finney suggested to his in-laws, and Lydia, elated at owning their own home, wrote a postscript to his letter, "Now I write you for the first time from 'our own house'! . . . Had you been here, my dear Mother, and shared those first nights, you would have smiled to see us—we slept on the floor without a blanket or bed quilt to cover us, but as the weather was warm, we got along very well."[46]

The Chatham Street Chapel rapidly became recognized as the "cathedral" of the new empire of expanding benevolence. Although esthetically it may have left something to be desired, at least it did fulfill the criterion of location in what was rapidly becoming the most important city in the United States, at the heart of that city, and it did possess the necessary capacity for the throngs who came there. For the next several years, until the Broadway Tabernacle was built to Finney's specifications in 1835, vast congregations of delegates, meeting here each year during the first two weeks of May, concentrated the efforts of the benevolence organizations upon the needs of society.

Now a settled pastor, Charles Finney contemplated the demands of the different type of ministry that he had undertaken: he had to produce new sermons regularly, without turning to the old stock that he had preached and repreached for some time; in place of the evanescent crowds he met in each campaign from city to city, which were with him for a time and then were seen no more, he had to adjust to a continuing audience, who would get to know him quite well; there would be the dogging church members who could not be avoided, tedious committee meetings, and the minutia and trivia of balance sheets, reports, and teas with societies of ladies. Then too, the nagging problems, often small but cumulative, that could be brushed aside in going from city to city, could not be evaded when one occupied a station, and was permanently responsible. Once again the comments that he was losing his unction, or becoming dignified and formal, began to come. Herman G. Norton, Finney's old and close friend, charged that "you reason more than formerly," and cautioned him not to lose his enthusiasm.[47] And another friend wrote:

> I fear that the peculiar circumstances in which you have been placed have led you rather to a discussion . . . of abstract theological subjects than to those soul-stirring appeals to the heart and conscience by which you once brought so many sinners to the feet of Jesus.[48]

The dreaded cholera epidemic of 1832 struck New York City in the early summer. The Finneys decided to remain in the city,[49] although attendance at the chapel declined. Panic drove multitudes up into Greenwich Village, out on Long Island, and over into New Jersey. Estimates placed the number of those fleeing to escape the disease from seventy thousand to one hundred thousand.[50] Seemingly healthy people suddenly dropped over, and were dead in a short while. The shock of witnessing such a thing drove others away in terror, in a hasty and totally disorganized exodus, leaving all their material goods behind.

Like many other clergymen, Charles Finney believed that his proper place was where he was needed, amid the sick and suffering, and so he and his family stayed in town till early August. The mortality was very high in the neighborhood of his home, and Finney said "I recollect counting, from the door of our house, five hearses drawn up at the same time, at different doors within sight."[51] In July, deaths from cholera were averaging approximately forty each day in the city.[52] By August 10 he and his wife and children, doubtless to their intense relief, were staying with friends in Whitesboro, far from the dread spectre of death from cholera.

After five weeks of rest and visiting with in-laws and his multitudes of friends in Oneida County, Finney resumed his labors at the Chatham Street Chapel about September 24. His installation as pastor of the chapel was set for September 28, 1832, and during the service he was taken ill. "Soon after I got home," Finney said, "it was plain that I was seized with the cholera. The gentleman at the next door, was seized about the same time, and before morning he was dead."[53] As with all the cases, it was not known for some days whether he would survive. His physician used drastic treatments to cure him, and as Finney's health had not been good for some time before the onslaught of cholera, the disease left him debilitated. "The means used for my recovery, gave my system a terrible shock, from which it took me long to recover." By October 27, however, the *New York Evangelist* reported that he was improving, and was able to receive visitors.[54]

With the cholera epidemic receding in New York, people returned to the churches gradually. It was seen by the Tappans and others that Charles Finney could not possibly shoulder the burden of his pastorate for a time, however, and supply preachers were used in his stead. A young man whom Finney had known during his 1828 Philadelphia campaign, Jacob Helffenstein (1803–84), became an even closer friend during this period, and was called temporarily to the First Free Presbyterian Church. Helffenstein was thirty at the time, a clergyman of the German Reformed Church, and the son of Samuel Helffenstein of Philadelphia, in whose large church Finney had preached for several months to union meetings. The elder Helffenstein had been cool to new measures evangelism, but his son had been thoroughly won over by Finney's methods and remained an ardent evangelist throughout his life.[55]

Finney was not able to resume a regular preaching schedule again until the spring of 1833, and it was only then that business throughout the city had recovered from the epidemic. Eager to draw crowds again, Finney scheduled a series of revival messages for twenty successive evenings in late spring. This was in addition to his Sunday services, and it must have been an enormous drain on his weakened energies. However, five hundred converts were counted as the results of this evangelistic effort. Because the Chatham Street Chapel was once again enjoying vital growth, with overflowing congregations, its original mandate to proliferate the free church cause was followed. A new congregation was organized on December 6, 1833, as the Third Free Presbyterian Church, or the Houston Street Church.[56] A new building had already been erected for this congregation at Houston and Thompson Streets, and Finney's old friend, Dirck C. Lansing, currently serving at the Second Presbyterian Church of Utica, was called as pastor.

The work was becoming so demanding that an assistant to Finney was engaged in April 1834. He was the Rev. John Ingersoll (1792–1859), who came from Rupert, Vermont, and had graduated from Middlebury College in 1825. He had been active in Oneida County for the previous three years as a pastor, and, like Helffenstein, was a thorough new measures man who would work well with Charles Finney. With an associate pastor assisting him, a very large auditorium that could handle crowds, and the encouragement and financial support of men like the Tappans, Finney attempted to recover his health and enter fully into all the activities. He wrote, years later, of the congregation and of his work:

> I instructed my church-members to scatter themselves over the whole house, and to keep their eyes open, in regard to any that were seriously affected under the preaching, and if possible, to detain them after preaching, for conversation and prayer. . . . In this way the conversion of a great many souls was secured. . . . A more harmonious, prayerful, and efficient people, I never knew, than were the members of those free churches. They were not among the rich, although there were several men of property belonging to them. In general they were gathered from the middle and lower classes of the people. This was what we aimed to accomplish, to preach the Gospel especially to the poor.[57]

By 1833, the free church movement was thriving. To abandon the old custom of supporting a church through pew rents, and to provide free seats for all, especially inviting the poor not to be relegated to the back but to have equal prominence with those of better economic station, was a major break with the past. As an egalitarian movement the poor of New York City were bound to appreciate it, and its close connections with New School Presbyterianism were also of interest. Old School churches and pastors looked on them with a combination of dismay and envy, and at times there must have been embarrassment to see what the free churches were doing for the poor they had neglected.[58] A friend wrote to Finney, "The old churches, I think feel a little ashamed to see the new measure churches prosper as they are."[59] By 1834, there were four free churches in New York, and their dynamic growth was described by Lewis Tappan:

> The First Free Church has admitted 753 members; 301 males and 452 females; 493 of whom united on profession of faith, and 260 on certificates from other churches. The adult baptisms have been 303, and 27 young men are preparing for the ministry. . . . The Second Free Church has admitted 426 members; 145 males and 281 females; of whom 302 were added on profession, and 104 on certificate. The adult baptisms have been 106. Nine young men belonging to this church . . . are engaged in the foreign missionary service. . . . The Third Free Church has admitted 344 members; 115 males and 229 females; of whom 203 were added on profession

and 141 on certificate. Twelve are studying for the ministry, and two are in foreign missionary service. . . . The Fourth Free Church has admitted 64 members; 22 males and 42 females; of whom 26 were added on profession, and 38 on certificate. Three are studying for the ministry, and one is preparing for the missionary service.[60]

Joel Parker had been pastor of the First Free Church since its founding in June 1830, and on October 18, 1833, he resigned his charge to take a church in New Orleans. The Rev. Elijah Barrows came as pastor on March 9, 1835. At the Second Free Church, or Chatham Street Chapel, Charles Finney was installed as pastor on September 28, 1832. At the Third Free Church, Dirck C. Lansing was installed as pastor in December 1833, and resigned on July 23, 1835. The Fourth Free Church, a colony from the Second, was organized on April 9, 1834, and called the Rev. Isaac N. Sprague on October 12, 1834.[61] There were in all eleven free churches, the Fifth, organized in 1834, being mainly an overflow church from the Second, the Sixth Charles Finney's new organization formed in 1836, and the rest formed from 1836 to 1840.[62]

These free churches vexed the Old School Presbyteries because, in addition to being new measures congregations, they claimed to accept Presbyterian principles but they acted in ways that were more akin to Congregational practices. Nonetheless, in time they became a very strong part of the New School Third Presbytery, which in 1832 listed its congregations and pastors as follows:[63]

CHURCH	PASTOR	NUMBER OF MEMBERS
Allen Street	Henry White	215
Bleecker Street	Erskine Mason	290
Bowery	Dr. J. Woodbridge	178
Central	William Patton	515
First Free	Joel Parker	217
Laight Street	Dr. Samuel H. Cox	746
Montreal	George Perkins	157
North	Ebenezer Mason	(unknown)
Second Avenue	John Murray	59
Second Free	Charles G. Finney	63
Seventh	Elihu Baldwin	518
Spring Street	Henry Ludlow	482
Union	Herman Norton	348
West	David Downer	32

While the free church movement in New York City was prospering, the Tappan brothers were continuing their abolitionist efforts, funding newspapers and antislavery speakers, and in general doing everything they could to help the blacks. It was slow going, and, with public opinion as it was, increasingly dangerous. All the abolitionists, in the North as well as the South, met violent resistance wherever they turned. But with the Tappans, whose name had been linked to so many unpopular causes in the past, it was even easier for their enemies to spread rumors and raise mobs to fever pitch. Newspapers, especially in New York City, were almost unanimous in vilifying the brothers. Abolitionists such as the Tappans were, after all, touching the pocketbook nerve of all those with an economic stake in slavery, and these included many northerners who traded with the South. Others in the border areas feared the social, economic, and political consequences of freedom for the slaves. In the summer of 1833 one newspaper editor, in a vitriolic blast, warned his readers that the only way to end "the phrensy of Garrison and Arthur Tappan" was by "cutting off their heads."[64]

The Tappans insisted increasingly that blacks be invited to attend services at Chatham Street Chapel. Charles Finney did not object to this, but throughout his ministry at the chapel and the Broadway Tabernacle, blacks were segregated in a place reserved for them to the side of the sanctuary. On July 8, 1833, when some blacks had attended a service and were attacked by some hooligans after leaving, the *Courier and Enquirer* announced, "Another of those disgraceful negro outrages, etc., occurred last night at that common focus of pollution, Chatham Street Chapel."[65]

Despite the threats, the Tappans moved ahead to found the New York City Anti-Slavery Society in October 1833. They had originally planned to hold the organizational meeting in Clinton Hall, but the trustees rebuked Arthur Tappan for attempting to use it for an abolitionist gathering, and Lewis Tappan suggested they use the Chatham Street Chapel instead. The news was quickly passed by word of mouth to the delegates, and when a large, furious mob gathered at Clinton Hall that evening, it was found to be deserted. Gathering at Tammany Hall, the rioters were organized by an old enemy of the Tappans, Robert Bogardus, and then a succession of proslavery speakers whipped the mob to a fury.[66]

Meanwhile, inside the Chatham Street Chapel, the abolitionists had conducted their meeting, adopted a constitution, and elected officers, with Arthur Tappan chosen president. As they came to an end, rioters were heard storming up the street and into the chapel. The delegates scattered, fearful for their lives, knowing that the mob might easily put a torch to the building. Shouts of "Garrison—Garrison—Tappan—Tappan! Where are they? Find them! Find them!" filled the chapel. Some of the abolitionists quickly fled to one of the lecture rooms on the upper floors of the theater, where a Sunday school meeting was in progress, and pretended to be part of that. In a few minutes, rioters were banging on the door, threatening to break it down, and policemen arrived just at that moment to arrest them. In the large lobby on the first floor the lights were out, but one drunken rioter, with a dagger and a lantern, staggered about searching for the Tappans. "As the intruder passed, the janitor blew out his light, then slipped into the darkness," Bertram Wyatt-Brown says, "while the brothers fled out the back door unharmed."[67]

Charles Finney must have been appalled at such activities in his church. To have a drunken mob prowling through the chapel, some with weapons or firebrands, threatening to burn it down! Nonetheless, he had fought with sin and its devotees long enough to know that you must engage it to conquer, and perhaps he had the satisfaction of thinking that the chapel certainly stood in the city as a symbol of Christian involvement and rectitude. During 1833, from all evidence, Finney remained a moderate on the antislavery question. His views were definite and well known, so that no one could accuse him of evasion or cowardice. Still, he attempted to maintain a balance, regarding slavery as one evil (however great) among many to which the gospel addressed itself. Slavery, like all other social problems, was but a symptom of the inner malignity of sin, and the priority was to attack the sinful heart with the cure of conversion; once that was done, the symptoms would begin to take care of themselves.[68] Finney advised Joshua Leavitt, editor of the *New York Evangelist*, to go very slowly into the prospect of involving the paper in the abolitionist controversy. Despite this warning, even before Finney had departed on his trip to the Mediterranean, Leavitt was plunging into the struggle in the columns of his paper.[69]

Over a year after he had contracted cholera, Finney was still a sick man. He stated in his *Memoirs*, "in January, 1834, I was obliged to leave on account of my health, and take a sea voyage."[70] Perhaps it was just as well that he was away, in view of his illness, for the year 1834 brought great violence in New York City, and Finney would have been frustrated in his powerlessness to do anything about it. He did not return from the sea voyage until July 1834.

During this period, Lewis Tappan put the Chatham Street Chapel to uses Charles Finney might well have questioned, because of its susceptibility to arson. During antislavery week in May 1834, Tappan scheduled the chapel for meetings particularly aimed at defeating the goals of the American Colonization Society in attempting to send freed blacks to Africa. This split between the antislavery forces was widely publicized, one paper speaking of a "deep laid plan among these conspiring sectarians to bring us back to the settled gloom and superstitions of the dark ages."[71] On July 4, 1834, Tappan invited the city's blacks to a service of commemoration, during which he read William Lloyd Garrison's Declaration of Sentiments to the audience. Hooligans had been filing into the balconies in the meantime, and they began to shout and create diversions in the noisy theater. Then, two choirs of whites and blacks began singing a new hymn written by John Greenleaf Whittier, and as they did so the balconies erupted in bedlam, and hymnbooks and paper were thrown in abundance. Just in time a group of watchmen from the office of the mayor arrived, and restored order.[72] Three evenings later, however, when another congregation of blacks was in the chapel, rioters had become emboldened enough to throw benches from the balconies.[73] What happened next is perhaps best told in Lewis Tappan's own words, in a letter he sent to Theodore Weld on July 10, 1834:

> Monday evening the Monthly concert of our church was held at my house. The Sexton of the Chapel ran over at half past 9 and told me the mob were demolishing the Chapel. We therefore dismissed the meeting, and I recon[n]oitered. On returning home I saw a crowd in front of my house. I passed through them, rang at the door, and shut myself in, amidst a tremendous noise,— mingled groans, hisses, and execrations. The mob dispersed, after a while, without committing any violence, or "throwing any stones." . . .
>   The newspapers of yesterday continued to "fan the embers." . . . I took my family out of town about the time the mob were collecting at the chapel. On coming into town this morning I stopped to look at a newspaper which revealed the fact of my house having been attacked, furniture destroyed, etc., last night. A crowd has been before the house all day. My wife and myself passed two hours in the house surveying the ruins, and collecting some articles of wearing apparel. The iron railing, blinds, window sashes, glass, etc., in front are destroyed. The windows and door are fastened with rough boards, etc. Inside the appearance is, as you may suppose after *such* a company had passed the evening in my house.

It beggared all description. There was the most wanton destruction of property you can imagine, and some articles were *stolen* by these uninvited guests.

At the end was a postscript dated July 11, which read:

The whole city was in commotion last night. The mob assailed Dr. Cox's house and church, and threatened other buildings, but the magistracy did their duty, and no violence of consequence was effected.

Then another postscript was added, which read:

I am told the mob last night broke the windows of Dr. Cox's church, and also the door and windows of his house. The Cavalry dispersed them. They threatened to assail [Rev. Henry] Ludlow's house tonight. What will be the issue the Lord only knows.[74]

In the next day's edition the *Courier and Enquirer* reported that only a window was broken while a group of gentlemen peacefully demonstrated.[75] In order to publicize his troubles, Lewis Tappan left his gutted house unrepaired for the remainder of the summer, while he and his family lived in Brookline.

The situation rapidly got worse during the rest of 1834, with mobs looting and pillaging almost at will throughout the city, and finally the mayor, a Tammany Democrat named Cornelius Lawrence, was forced to call out the militia. Their orders, however, were to deal leniently with rioters. On one day a band of marauders determined to ransack and burn down the Tappan dry-goods store, and the brothers heard of the mob's coming in time to barricade themselves inside. They passed out an estimated thirty-six stands of rifles and guns to their clerks and friends. As the front door was being smashed in, Arthur Tappan coolly gave the order to shoot the rioters only in the legs; just then a company of militia arrived, and dispersed the mob.[76]

As the center of much antislavery activity, the Chatham Street Chapel was singled out for particular hatred by the city's proslavery forces during 1834. The wonder is that it was not burned to the ground. Blacks suffered especially during the summer, having seven of their churches destroyed or badly injured, and many free blacks had their homes wrecked.[77]

13

AN EXPLOSIVE PERIOD

During the long, hot summer of 1834, as newspaper editors goaded frenzied mobs to place the life of every black person and abolitionist in New York City in danger, Charles Finney was far from the violence. His friends, with every good intention, had persuaded him that a sea voyage and new and distant places might go far to restore his health. In all likelihood they also sensed the approaching turmoil that would engulf the Chatham Street Chapel, and wished to remove Finney from its dangers by urging him to go on an extended leave of absence. Simply to send Finney to Oneida County, to stay with friends or relatives, would not do; malaria had been epidemic there for some time,[1] and in his weakened condition he was too susceptible to any malady. But if a longer trip was advisable, what of Lydia? With three small children to care for, it was apparent that she could not take them on any lengthy sojourn. Therefore Charles would be forced to leave Lydia for a period, as painful as the separation would be. It was agreed to.

The voyage was one of the most unhappy periods of Finney's life, for in every way it was ill considered and unwise. For one, to travel to distant lands by oneself, with only the company of strangers, was bound to be lonely. Then, winter was the worst time to cross the Atlantic, for storms were frequent and fierce. Finney had never been to sea before for any time, and apparently no one advised him of the cramped conditions on ships and the dangers of winter crossings. So, leaving Jacob Helffenstein to do the preaching at the chapel (with John Ingersoll to add his assistance in April 1834), Finney booked passage on board the *Padang,* a small brig bound for Smyrna (Izmir), Turkey.[2] The *Padang* sailed from New York City on January 20, 1834, and it is a fair assumption that Finney began to have second thoughts as soon as he went on board and saw the accommodations. "My state room was small," he recalled in his *Memoirs,* "and I was on the whole, very uncomfortable; and the voyage did not much improve my health."[3]

Travel by sea in the early nineteenth century was terrible. Almost no one traveled for pleasure, even in the better weather of summertime. Seasoned travelers recorded that crossing the Atlantic at any other time was the height of foolhardiness. If you did travel by sailing ships, you went at the whim of the winds. Such ships then were small, and totally lacking in creature comforts. Designed to carry only cargo, they were ill suited to provide for passengers. Built of wood, they leaked incessantly. Their captains were almost invariably gruff old sea-dogs. They were not hotel-keepers or jolly hosts, and they made it clear that they had no time for any passengers who might be aboard. The straining ships got the captains' full attention. Nursing a small sailing packet through gales and shattering seas was their game, not comforting seasick and dismally unhappy travelers.

On shipboard, food depended on the state of the weather, always. When it could be prepared and served, it was coarse at best. There was no refrigeration, and food was served warm *only* if the cook could keep a fire going in his wet galley. If the cook was a poor one (and most of them were), the food was hardly worth swallowing.

In fair weather, a stroll about a deck eight feet wide by ten feet long was one of the few recreations available in the 1830s. If the weather were foul, however, the captain's order was all passengers below, for he would take no chances with some landlubber being washed overboard. Cards, singing, stories, and shared fears were the only distractions below. In bad weather, particularly in wintertime, the terrifying sounds of seas, shrieking winds, and the groaning of ocean-strained timbers were constant, making sleep elusive. Dank cabins, wet bedding, and frequent numbing cold were the rule, not the exception. And on many voyages these miserable conditions had to be endured for months on end.

Predictably, the little brig bearing Charles Finney was badly knocked about by storms during the voyage of sixty-eight days to Malta. He spent some weeks there and then sailed for Sicily, giving up his original idea of continuing to Turkey. Finney had also contemplated sailing on to the Holy Land, but the Mediterranean is hardly at its best in March and inasmuch as he recorded nothing of his feelings at this time, we must assume that he had had enough of sea travel and decided against sailing farther to the east.

With the uncertainties of sailing ships on the wintry Atlantic, Lydia Finney was naturally concerned over her husband's whereabouts and welfare, especially because he was not well to begin with. She remained in Whitesboro during the time he was abroad, enjoying the double benefits of being with her parents and escape from embattled New York City. In those days of dubious communications from overseas, Lydia was greatly helped by Lewis Tappan, who kept her informed of the whereabouts of Finney's ship (when letters from him did not arrive) by means of the London shipping lists.[4] After months of storms at sea and miserable loneliness for his beloved wife and children, Finney decided that he had enough of Europe, and took ship at Messina, Italy.

He arrived in Boston on July 18, went to New York, and found waiting for him the rioting and destruction that has been described.[5] Naturally, he was overwhelmed and disgusted at what the mobs had done and inept politicians allowed, and, in the midst of the summer heat, he left for Whitesboro to join his family. He needed no urging.

During Charles Finney's journey to foreign shores, an event had occurred at Lane Seminary in Cincinnati that was to affect his life — and that of many others — radically. There, soon after the beginning of classes in late 1833, Theodore Weld had kept his promise to Arthur Tappan to spread abolitionist ideology among the students. It was not, at first, an easy task, for most of the students assumed that all antislavery adherents were like the incendiary William Lloyd Garrison. Weld, with his enormous persuasion, worked quietly among his fellow students, and they looked to him with complete trust. Finally, in February 1834, Weld and others felt the time had come to discuss publicly the entire controversy, and they applied to President Beecher for permission, which he reluctantly gave.[6]

What followed were called "debates," but in actuality they were protracted meetings, and for nine evenings, with mounting interest, the students listened raptly. James Bradley, one of their number and a former slave, described from his own background what slavery was like in Kentucky.[7] Then William Allan, son of a slaveholding clergyman in Alabama, gave the arguments for immediate emancipation. Others spoke, or read some of the literature that had been gathered. They told the blood-curdling facts of how blacks were treated in the

South, of the beatings and killings, and the northerners were aghast. Then Weld spoke. "He . . . uttered no malice; sharpened no phrase so that its venomed point might rankle in another's breast. . . . His great soul was full of compassion for the oppressor and the oppressed. . . . Nobly simple in manner, free from thought of self, he touched the springs of the human heart," said the *Emancipator.*[8]

When Theodore Weld completed his talk, a vote was taken, and it was unanimous for immediate emancipation. Then they moved to the debate over colonization, and after hearing arguments on both sides, proceeded to vote against colonization. That completed, they organized an antislavery society at Lane Theological Seminary. And theory must be translated into practice, they declared, and founded for the blacks of Cincinnati three Sunday schools, a lending library, a class to teach reading, a Bible class, and courses of lectures. The students, thoroughly aroused to what they now saw as their Christian duty, went out to elevate the city's blacks, but they received a bitter response from its white citizenry. Several years previously, a series of bloody race riots had torn the city apart, and these were all too fresh in public memory.[9] Many anticipated clashes between the races again as ugly rumors spread of Lane students and blacks socializing in intimate ways.[10] At that point, fortunately, the summer vacation came and students and faculty scattered.

Early May each year was also the occasion for Lyman Beecher's appearance at the New York anniversary meetings, but when he arrived there he found, to his shock, that the Lane debates had become renowned in all American colleges. Everywhere; students were planning discussions, studying propaganda on various issues, and deciding whether to set up antislavery societies themselves. Among the college administrators and officers there present, a meeting was called on this urgent matter, and it was there decided that the violent nature of the matter "imperiously demanded that all anti-slavery agitation should be suppressed."[11] A copy of this resolution was sent to every institution of higher learning in the country.

With Beecher remaining in the East throughout the summer, attending to many interests, the board of trustees of Lane Seminary received this resolution and were appalled at what their students had wrought. Disregarding the fact that the seminary president was absent, they immediately took actions that were extremely high-handed, knowing as they did the sentiments of both Beecher and their benefactors, the Tappans, on the matter. For the most part, the trustees were Cincinnati merchants who did much business across the Ohio

River in Kentucky, and did not want their names tied to a school so publicly connected with antislavery.[12] Then, they were pressured by an editorial in the May issue of the *Western Monthly Magazine*, published in Cincinnati, in which the debates were subjected to excoriation. In addition, a most unpopular member of the faculty, the Rev. Thomas J. Biggs, took advantage of Beecher's absence and led the trustees to take action, proclaiming, "We are a reproach and a loathing in the land."[13] Biggs had already clashed with Theodore Weld over several items, and he wrote to Lyman Beecher on August 18:

> I am favoured today with the letters jointly from yourself and Dr. Vail, its contents I have read and reperused with deep interest . . . and my only regret is that I cannot, in view of facts, *present* and *past*, persuade my mind into sympathy with yours. . . . The public here is calling for some manifesto on the subject from the Trustees. . . . The Trustees feel themselves called upon to furnish something to correct and allay this (not unreasonably) excited state of feeling. We have among us, as all know, the Master Spirit of Abolitionism, we have it here in its sublimated state—it has already inflated and intoxicated nearly all our students—the exhilarations make them soar above all our heads, and the principle is now pretty well settled that the one whose head has most capacity for this empyrical gas, why, he's the Model, and the *best theologian*, and best anything else you please. It is now believed to be time to settle the question, "Who shall govern? Students? or faculty in concurrence with Trustees?"[14]

Biggs acted as prosecutor in the trustees' action. On August 9 he came before the executive committee of the trustees, and argued vehemently against what Weld and the others had done. The report of a special subcommittee was adopted by the executive committee on August 20; it resolved to ban all student societies except those dealing directly with education, to make students obtain permission for any discussions that were "matters of public interest and popular excitement," and to invest themselves with the summary power to expel offenders. The trustees stated that continued abolition activity in the seminary would "pour into the controversies of the community a heated torrent of unextinguishable rancor." Final action by the trustees was postponed because of Beecher's absence, but to make sure that their determination was not misunderstood, they summarily dismissed Professor John Morgan, the only faculty member who had supported the students.[15]

One member of the trustees, the Rev. Asa Mahan of the Sixth Presbyterian Church of Cincinnati, had cooperated with Charles Finney during the Rochester revival of 1830–1831. Of the twenty-five trustees, he was almost the only one familiar with the students, and he knew well that these mature men would not tolerate being treated like children. He forcefully argued against the resolutions, and wrote to Lyman Beecher, imploring him to return immediately and "save the school from dismantlement."[16]

Still Beecher dallied in the East. He wrote to the students, beseeching them to be patient and humble. Without the president, the board of trustees decided to move ahead anyway, and on October 10, 1834, it ratified the action of the executive committee taken on August 20. When he finally returned to Cincinnati, sometime between October 10 and 14, Beecher tried to vacillate and explain away the trustees' action, saying that he found "nothing in the regulations which is not common law in all well regulated institutions."

Predictably, the students were infuriated. Henry Stanton had written to James Thome on September 11, "If the law requiring us to disband the Anti-Slavery Society, is passed, we shall take a dismission from the Seminary. . . . If the laws pass, the theological class will probably all go in a body *somewhere* & pursue our studies. We can have money enough to hire good teachers—perhaps Stowe will go with us—Morgan certainly will if we need him."[17] True to their intention, and disgusted with Beecher, the students withdrew almost to a man; of the over one hundred students at Lane, but eight remained in December.[18]

Much of the blame for the debacle must rest on Lyman Beecher's shoulders. His movements from May through October 1834 were erratic, and indicate strongly that he wished to remain away. In addition, his *Autobiography* cannot be trusted for this period. As Gilbert Barnes has commented, "All the direct evidence, as well as Beecher's own unhappy inconsistencies of action and statement, indicate that he permitted the trustees to do a distasteful job that he wanted done and had promised Tappan not to do, and then attempted to dodge the responsibility for it."[19]

By November 3, Finney was again at the Chatham Street Chapel, attempting to pick up his work after the absence of many months and the horrors of the summer. Letters from him to his wife at this time show him somewhat uncertain as to his future, and seriously giving thought to abandoning the ministry altogether. Certainly his poor health was a major factor in his discouragement, but another, as he

Charles Grandison Finney, about 1834. During his tenure at the
Chatham Street Chapel, this oil portrait was painted by Samuel
Lovett Waldo and William Jewett. Courtesy of the Allen Memorial
Art Museum, Oberlin College. Gift of Lewis Tappan, 16.6.

surveyed the destruction of the mobs in New York, was very likely what was happening to the cause of revivals.

Lewis Tappan, frantically busy in the promotion of a myriad of good causes and currently embroiled in the violence over slavery, had, in a rare moment of reflection, quietly admitted to Lydia Finney that the antislavery cause was replacing revivals in the church.[20] It is possible that Charles Finney saw this letter. If he did (it was retained among his papers), it would have caused him untold grief. He looked on the Tappan brothers kindly, as marvelously generous benefactors, and he regarded Theodore Weld as a brother. But these, and many others, seemed to Finney to be losing sight of priorities in the mad swirl of benevolent enterprises and the evils of slavery. The conversion of sinners was not just another in a long list of good causes that must be attended to, Finney fervently believed. Evangelism was the mainspring from which all else must be energized! And these, his friends, were rapidly losing sight of this bedrock truth. As if to gently rebuke them, in his discussions of evangelistic methods begun in December 1834, which after transcription became the *Lectures on Revivals of Religion*, he said regarding slavery:

> Writings, containing temperate and judicious discussions on this subject . . . should be quietly and extensively circulated, and should be carefully and prayerfully examined by the whole Church. I do not mean by this, that the attention of the Church should be so absorbed by this as to neglect the main question of saving souls in the midst of them.[21]

Certainly it was not that Charles Finney tolerated slavery. He went on to say:

> The subject of Slavery is a subject upon which Christians, praying men, *need not* and *must not* differ. . . . Christians can no more take neutral ground on this subject, since it has come up for discussion, than they can take neutral ground on the subject of the sanctification of the Sabbath. It is a great national sin. It is a sin of the Church. The Churches, by their silence, and by permitting slaveholders to belong to their communion, have been consenting to it. . . . It is the Church that mainly supports this sin. Her united testimony upon the subject would settle the question. Let Christians of all denominations meekly, but firmly, come forth, and pronounce their verdict; let them wash their hands of this

thing; let them give forth and write on the head and front of this great abomination, "SIN," and in three years, a public sentiment would be formed that would carry all before it, and there would not be a shackled slave, nor a bristling, cruel slavedriver, in this land.[22]

Finney not only condemned slavery in the abstract, but he brought his convictions into practice in forbidding slaveholders to take communion in the Chatham Street Chapel. After his return from overseas, he presided at a sacramental service in the church on November 3, 1834. At that time he forbade slaveholders from taking communion, saying that those who held others in slavery, and who claimed a right of property in the bodies of their fellow men, could hardly be in accord with God's will, and therefore were not worthy of taking the sacrament. One slaveholder who was present said, "The preacher was rather hard upon me, but he was right."[23]

And yet, Finney insisted upon taking a moderate stand on the burning issue, knowing full well that it might alienate him from many friends. He opposed the concept of "amalgamation," the term then used for the mingling of whites and blacks. He was not alone in this, as many abolitionists wanted emancipation, but not throwing the races together. During his tenure at the Chatham Street Chapel and the Broadway Tabernacle, Finney was against the two races sitting in the same areas. Blacks were always segregated and put off to the sides or in the balconies.[24] Blacks were welcome as members in the church, but along with women they were prohibited from holding office or voting. When the Tappans wished to have a distinguished black man serve on the board of trustees of the Chatham Street Chapel, Finney and others declared their resistance. The matter was finally dropped, to the Tappans' irate protests.[25] Finney had strong support in his view among a large majority of his congregation, who felt that social mixing of the races had no particular purpose.

Five years later, when his anger had cooled somewhat, Lewis Tappan explained to a friend:

> At an early period in the history of the Free Churches in this city an attempt was made to introduce the peculiar principles of Abolitionism into them. They had been instituted to produce a *reform*, and it was thought that every branch of Christian benevolence . . . ought to be engrafted on the Free Church system. Some of us thought that the "negro pew" should be done away, for . . .

it was understood by whites and blacks, that the colored people should sit by themselves in a certain place in one of the galleries. In the Chatham St. Chapel we succeeded in bringing the colored part of the congregation down stairs to occupy a range of slips on one side of the church, but were never able, though Mr. Finney was the pastor, to abolish the distinction altogether, in seats, and allow people to sit, in fact, as they were invited to do so, wherever they chose. . . . Finding nothing could be done in a matter so dear to my heart, I left the church.[26]

Shortly before departing for the Mediterranean in January 1834, Finney had given some of his more exceptional sermons to a printer. Now that he was a famous pastor in a very well known church, the clamor for copies of his messages had grown until Finney could no longer defer publishing, as he had for years. Previously, his only published work had been the "Can Two Walk Together Except They Be Agreed?" sermon of early 1827. Even the sermon that first stirred the theologians of Princeton, "Sinners Bound to Change Their Own Hearts," delivered in the autumn of 1831, had been transcribed and excerpted in print by Asa Rand, but Finney at that time had done nothing toward seeing it into print.

The volume was ready for the public later in 1834. Entitled *Sermons on Various Subjects*,[27] the collection began with "Sinners Bound to Change," and then included several other sermons very similar in content. "How To Change Your Heart" expounded more of Finney's theories pressing for instantaneous submission to the gospel. Another was entitled "Total Depravity," based on John 5:42, and here Finney boldly presented what had so rankled Asa Rand and Charles Hodge. It was not that humans were not universally depraved and sinful, of course; Finney believed that, but he deviated from orthodoxy in insisting that human sinfulness "does not consist in any want of faculties to obey God. We have all the powers of moral agency, that are needed to render perfect obedience to God."[28]

Humans have only themselves to blame for their depravity, and cannot point to the fall of the first parents. Depravity is not "in any *physical pollution transmitted from Adam*." Finney lamented that there had been so much repetition of this idea for centuries. Nor, he said, does depravity "consist in any *principle* of sin, that is incorporated with our being."[29] It is simply voluntary choice. This is repeated in each mortal, and as there is the ability to fall into sin, there is a commensurate amount of ability to reject sin and opt for God. Otherwise, Finney declared, "if there were any want of faculties, in our nature, our responsibility would cease; and we could not be fully blamed, for not doing that, for the performance of which we do not possess the appropriate moral powers."[30] Here, in a widely sold volume that went through three editions from three different publishers in as many years, Finney's views were available to the entire public, and not just in the scholarly periodicals for a relative few to read.

Not only did Finney send *Sermons on Various Subjects* to the printer before leaving for the Mediterranean, but he also warned Joshua Leavitt not to involve the *New York Evangelist* in the abolition controversy. In the furor that followed, however, Leavitt forgot this excellent advice and devoted many columns to topics regarding slavery. As a result, to Leavitt's horror, cancellations came from multitudes who were not convinced on the slavery question and resented the paper's forthright stand.

As soon as Finney had returned from his voyage, Leavitt appealed to him, "Brother Finney, I have ruined the *Evangelist*. . . . We shall not be able to continue its publication beyond the first of January, unless you can do something to bring the paper back to public favor again."[31] He then asked Finney to write a series of articles on the subject of revivals. The evangelist considered it, and then offered to give a series of lectures in the Chatham Street Chapel on the topic. Leavitt said, "That is the very thing," and in the paper began to advertise that the lectures would be published.

On Friday evening, December 5, 1834, Finney faced an expectant audience in the chapel and delivered the first of a long series of talks. The intention was to give one per week, right into the winter and spring. Characteristically, Finney prepared little, relying on his vast experience for thoughts and illustrations as he progressed. To compound the problem, Leavitt, rather than a professional stenographer, was going to attempt to take down what Finney said in longhand — he did not know shorthand! It seemed like a formula for failure, but despite the potential for difficulties, out of this arrangement came an enormously successful book. Finney explained:

> Mr. Leavitt could not write short-hand, but would sit and take notes, abridging what he wrote, in such a way that he could understand it himself; and then the next day he would sit down and fill out his notes, and send them to the press. . . . I did not myself write the lectures, of course; they were wholly extemporaneous. I did not make up my mind, from time to time, what the next

lecture should be, until I saw his report of my last. Then I could see what was the next question that would naturally need discussion. Brother Leavitt's reports were meagre, as it respects the matter contained in the lectures. The lectures averaged, if I remember right, not less than an hour and three quarters, in their delivery. But all that he could catch and report, could be read, probably in thirty minutes.[32]

Another paper seized upon the difficulties inherent in such a system, and made charges about the accuracy of the transcription. To explain how the talks were being recorded, Leavitt replied:

Our brother editor is in error in regard to the revision of the notes. They are seen by no person but the editor and the printers, until they come out in the paper. It is but justice to the preacher to state this, for it is to be presumed that some statements and positions are often presented either in a less guarded or less impressive position in our brief sketches, which in the sermon itself would be entirely unobjectionable. We have Mr. Finney's consent to our publication of these notes.[33]

There are twenty-two lectures, and some of them run to thirty or thirty-five pages in print. In saying that Leavitt's reports were "meagre," and could be read "probably in thirty minutes," Finney may have been unjust to the editor, for if they were indeed delivered verbally as given in print (and there is no reason to think otherwise), each of the thirty or more printed pages would take at least two minutes, and possibly three, to be spoken. The point is, Leavitt may have captured a good deal more than Finney gave him credit for.

With the series concluded in the spring, it was immediately rushed into book form. Twelve thousand copies were sold soon after, under the title *Lectures on Revivals of Religion*, and it was translated into French and Welsh. One publisher in London printed eighty thousand copies. When they had been translated and published in Welsh, a great revival resulted in that land, and the Congregational clergy of Wales informed Finney by letter of what had happened.[34] The news was equally good for the beleaguered *New York Evangelist;* Leavitt had astutely printed several thousand extra copies of the lectures, which he offered at no cost to new subscribers, and through the fame of the lectures, and promotional means, by the conclusion of the series he had gained twenty-six hundred subscriptions. This was many more than the loss he had earlier suffered, and he said to Charles Finney then, "I have as many new subscribers every day, as would fill my arms with papers, to supply them each a single number."

Lectures on Revivals of Religion was Charles Finney's second major publication. However, the idea behind *Lectures on Revivals* was not new. In 1832, William B. Sprague, pastor of the Second Presbyterian Church in Albany, New York, a theological moderate tending toward Old School positions, had issued a book with the same title that Finney later used.[35] From the vantage point of Albany he had watched the revivals for years, and he tried to distinguish between false excitements and true awakenings. From an Edwardean viewpoint, Sprague grappled with the problem of revivals, showing that (with reservations regarding fanaticism) moderates, Hopkinsians, and Old School adherents could accept awakenings within a certain framework. The work was clearly designed to demonstrate that it was not only new measures adherents who were vitally absorbed in revivals, but that all evangelical groups had become greatly interested since the literal explosion of the latter phase of the Second Great Awakening. No evangelical wished to be shut out.

In addition, Sprague's book was a covert admission that the Old School and the moderates had capitulated on major issues, and now admitted that the Edwardean concept of the unpredictable, "prayed-down" awakening had generally passed on, to be replaced by tacit agreement that "means" were, within bounds, acceptable. All-night prayer meetings, females praying in mixed meetings, the anxious bench, and some other measures were frowned on, but surprisingly, other practices were accepted.[36]

Finney had an entirely different motivation in delivering his lectures; in essence it was to mount a devastating attack on "the traditions of the elders," as he scornfully called the doctrines of hyper-Calvinism. It was his intention to set forth his methods in evangelism, but it was equally his purpose to expose the shortcomings, as he saw it, of all that was adverse to the conversion of great numbers of people.

Charles Finney must have seen a copy of Sprague's book; perhaps he read it. It is intriguing to conjecture what he thought of Sprague. Possibly it was not too positive. When he came to deliver his own view of revivals, there was no temporizing. Evangelism was too vital a matter merely to acquiesce, as he must have felt that Sprague and the others did. William McLoughlin has stated the matter succinctly in his introduction to Finney's *Lectures:*

The first thing that strikes the reader of the *Lectures on Revivals* is the virulence of Finney's hostility toward traditional Calvinism and all it stood for. He denounced its doctrinal dogmas (which, as embodied in the Westminster Confession of Faith, he referred to elsewhere as "this wonderful theological fiction"); he rejected its concept of nature and the structure of the universe (especially its exaltation of the sovereign and miraculous power of God in regard to conversions and the promotion of revivals); he scorned its pessimistic attitude toward human nature and progress (particularly in regard to the freedom of the will); and he thoroughly deplored its hierarchical and legalistic polity (as embodied in the ecclesiastical system of the Presbyterian Church). Or to put it more succinctly, John Calvin's philosophy was theocentric and organic; Charles Finney's was anthropocentric and individualistic. . . . As one prominent Calvinist editor wrote in 1838 of Finney's revivals, "Who is not aware that the Church has been almost revolutionized within four or five years by means of such excitements?"[37]

But Finney was not just mounting a reaction to Calvinism. The *Lectures* were also intended to be a declaration of principles of the revival program he had employed for the past few years, and which he confidently assumed (correctly so) would be the standard of action for much of American Protestantism for years to come. Conveniently, in the first lecture Finney stated the viewpoint and agenda of the entire series, and indeed of the whole new program of evangelical advance. There he declared, a revival "is not a miracle, or dependent on a miracle, in any sense. It is a purely philosophical[38] result of the right use of the constituted means—as much so as any other effect produced by the application of means. . . . The means which God has enjoined for the production of a revival, doubtless have a natural tendency to produce a revival."[39] This was to contradict directly the older view of awakenings held by Edwards, Whitefield, and everyone else until then, that revivals came only in God's good time. "I wish this idea to be impressed on all your minds," Finney declared, "for there has long been an idea prevalent" that revivals are entirely supernatural and beyond explanation, "not to be judged of by the ordinary rules of cause and effect. . . . No doctrine is more dangerous than this to the prosperity of the church, and nothing more absurd."[40] Because this new command of the power of revival in the church was in perfect accord with the advancing scientific knowledge of the day, Christians have had a marvelous tool placed in their hands by God, and they are obliged to use it to the utmost.

Then Finney proceeded to lay the foundation for the bringing of awakening to the churches. Excitements — heightened feelings and enthusiasm — are given by God and not to be despised, Finney said; this has been the manner in which the faith has long been advanced. "The state of the world is still such, and probably will be till the millennium is fully come, that religion must be mainly promoted by these excitements."[41] The new mastery of "the laws of the mind" (or psychology, in our contemporary terminology), which was unknown in Whitefield's and Edwards' day, demands that the church utilize this newfound power to control "excitements," thereby stirring people up to recognize their obligations to God.

Despite the fact that the church could command the new powers of science to its benefit, there were still the age-old reasons why Christians should seek revivals. Nodding in the direction of Jonathan Edwards, and sounding very much like him, Finney listed some of the reasons: "when the wickedness of the wicked grieves and humbles and distresses Christians"; "when the providence of God indicates that a revival is at hand"; "when Christians have a spirit of prayer for a revival," and so on.[42] And how can God's people expedite the coming of an awakening? First, by breaking up the fallow ground of their hearts — "to prepare your minds to bring forth fruit unto God."[43] Then, having begun, they must continue to subdue all sins,[44] to be constant in prayer,[45] to be filled with the Holy Spirit,[46] to deal wisely and conscientiously with sinners,[47] and to preach the gospel intelligently and to the point.

It would be good to pause momentarily and note the impact all this had on nineteenth-century Protestantism. Until this time in America, the great prestige of the clergy had made it its responsibility, and not that of the laity, to be evangelists and win the lost. Lyman Beecher's frantic struggles to shore up a collapsing theocracy in New England were the last gasps of this tradition. With the great influence that his *Lectures on Revivals* were to have for the next century, Charles Finney was bringing about a dramatic reversal of the old understanding, and insisting that *every* Christian was directly and inescapably charged with the responsibility of evangelism.[48] As Finney declared:

> You will be wise in using means for the conversion of sinners. ... But a man who is led by the Spirit of God, will know how to *time* his measures right, and how to apportion Divine truth, so as to make it tell to the best advantage. ...
> Every Christian makes an impression by his conduct, and

witnesses either for one side or the other. His looks, dress, whole demeanor, make a constant impression on one side or the other. . . . He is either gathering for Christ, or scattering abroad. . . . Every moment of your lives, you are exerting a tremendous influence, that will tell on the immortal interests of souls all around you.[49]

This shift away from the primacy of the clergy—utterly foreign to Mather, Edwards, Timothy Dwight, or Beecher—was of course very much in harmony with the Jacksonian democracy of his day.[50] Like almost everyone at that time, Finney believed in the potential and the dignity of the common man, in the benevolence of the Almighty, and in progress. He pointed to the obvious, that in a rapidly growing nation it is necessary for every Christian to "aim at being useful in the highest degree possible" if the millennium were to come soon, and that it is absurd to expect the clergy to do everything.

With this insistence, Finney then turned to attack the restrictive aspects of the Presbyterian Church. It was a denomination, in his opinion, dominated by the Old School element, of frigid, dead formality; "A spirit very different from the spirit of prayer appears to prevail in the Presbyterian church."[51] But especially the heavy hand of Calvinist election produced everywhere the feeling of futility and inability that had frustrated countless people from feeling free to accept God's grace with openness and joy:

> For instance, when you tell sinners that without the Holy Spirit they never will repent, they are very liable to pervert the truth, and understand by it that they *cannot* repent, and therefore are under no obligation to do it until they feel the Spirit. It is often difficult to make them see that all the "cannot" consists in their unwillingness, and not in their inability.[52]

This was only to be expected, Finney proclaimed. What could be produced by clergymen who had been wrongly educated for their profession to begin with? He had found that most pastors were hardly capable of furthering revivals, because their training and understanding were deficient. For over a hundred pages he belabored this point, venting all his pent-up anger against Samuel Cox, Beecher, and a host of other ministers who had opposed him at one point or another:

> A minister may be *very learned and not wise*. . . . A minister may be *very wise*, though he is *not learned*. . . . Those are the best

educated ministers, who win the most souls. . . . There is evidently a great defect in the present mode of educating ministers. This is a SOLEMN FACT, to which the attention of the whole church should be distinctly called; that the great mass of young ministers who are educated accomplish very little. When young men come out from the seminaries, are they fit to go into a revival? . . . Seldom. Like David with Saul's armor, he comes in with such a load of theological trumpery, that he knows nothing what to do. Leave him there for two weeks, and the revival is at an end. . . . [Seminaries] direct the mind *too much to irrelevant matters,* which are not necessary to be attended to. In their courses of study, they carry the mind over too wide a field, which diverts the attention from the main thing, and so they get cold in religion, and when they get through, instead of being fitted for their work, they are *unfitted* for it.[53]

Especially are the theological seminaries deficient in training young men to preach. Here again, Finney found that the misunderstood doctrine of election was at fault, for it stifled seminary graduates in urging their congregations toward immediate response. Once instill that horrid dogma in human minds, and everything thereafter goes awry! "It has been customary, in many places," Finney declared, "for a long time, to bring the doctrine of election into every sermon. Sinners have been commanded to repent, and told that they could not repent, in the same sermon."[54] Is it any wonder that congregations are confused, and revivals are impossible to bring about, in such a state?

Then there is the overwhelming problem of pastors being trained to stay tied to notes in their preaching. Here the examples of Peter Starr and George Gale, in Finney's preconversion days, came before his mind, as he recalled the old, staid, and starched regulation style of homiletics. "Nothing is more calculated to make a sinner feel that religion is some mysterious thing that he cannot understand, than this mouthing, formal, lofty style of speaking, so generally employed in the pulpit."[55] But this was to characterize the Presbyterian and Congregational churches; in contrast the Methodist and Baptist preachers were generally firebrands, and their denominations and churches were adding members rapidly. And then came the section that must have rankled every Calvinist pastor who read it:

Look at the Methodists. Many of their ministers are unlearned, in the common sense of the term, many of them taken right from the shop or the farm, and yet they have gathered congregations, and pushed their way, and won souls every where. Wherever the Methodists have gone, their plain, pointed and simple, but warm and animated mode of preaching has always gathered congregations. Few Presbyterian ministers have gathered so large assemblies, or won so many souls. Now are we to be told that we must pursue the same old, formal mode of doing things, amidst all these changes? . . . It is impossible that the public mind should be held by such preaching. We must have exciting, powerful preaching, or the devil will have the people, except what the Methodists can save. It is impossible that our ministers should continue to do good, unless we have innovations in regard to the style of preaching. Many ministers are finding it out already, that a Methodist preacher, without the advantages of a liberal education will draw a congregation around him which a Presbyterian minister, with perhaps ten times as much learning, cannot equal, because he has not the earnest manner of the other, and does not pour out fire upon his hearers when he preaches.[56]

The new style of preaching that Finney advocated must be extemporaneous, conversational, colloquial, repetitious, practical, lively, and never monotonous. "We can never have the *full meaning* of the gospel, till we throw away our notes," he proclaimed. But he was aware that objections are often brought against extemporaneous preaching, that it was letting down the dignity of the pulpit. This is an argument without merit, he said. "It is only an account of its novelty, and not for any impropriety there is in the thing itself."[57]

Then Finney plunged into the entire issue of innovations in worship. Correctly, he showed that religious people tend to be conservative regarding customs, accepting new ideas slowly. Indeed, all the current customs met opposition when first introduced. So, the new measures are naturally opposed. In time, he was confident, everyone will assume they have been used for ages. Choirs, instrumental music, organs, extemporary prayers and preaching, kneeling in prayer— all these have only recently been accepted. As to his new measures, the blessing of God has certainly been upon them, if success in conversions be any criterion.[58] And Finney expressed astonishment at the well-educated divines of the Old School who opposed anything new, "when the truth is, that every step of the church's advance from the gross darkness of Popery, has been through the introduction of one new measure after another,"[59] as their education should have informed them.

Charles Finney was not through with the ecclesiastical bureaucracy of his church, however. He deeply resented all those pastors who had opposed him — or whose opposition he had imagined. The annual General Assembly was especially infuriating. In one of the more well-known passages he ever spoke or wrote, Finney rasped out, "These things in the Presbyterian church, their contentions and janglings are so ridiculous, so wicked, so outrageous, that no doubt there is a jubilee in hell every year, about the time of the meeting of the General Assembly."[60] In all fairness, chapter 15 of his book is an intemperate diatribe, and although it is extremely quotable because of its quaint expostulations, only a few excerpts can be given here, and the reader urged to examine it directly. Finney fumed that, although real and blessed revivals were in progress, the General Assembly had done nothing but complain, sending forth a "pastoral letter" to the churches "calculated to excite suspicions, quench the zeal of God's people,"[61] and stop the awakening.

Charles Finney bristled with indignation when he considered backslidden, recalcitrant church members, who were the chief source of darkness in the nation, in his view. He may have been thinking of Asahel Nettleton when he cried to his congregation, "If Christians in the United States expect revivals to spread, and prevail, till the world is converted, they must give up writing letters and publishing pieces *calculated to excite suspicion and jealousy in regard to revivals....* The millennium would have fully come in the United States before this day."[62]

There were other hindrances to the spread of the kingdom of God and revivals as well, Finney said, which were cherished by some church people. For one, there was the awful treatment of new converts in most churches. Epitomizing the social reform spirit of the times, Finney demanded that those recently converted "should set out with a determination to *aim at being useful in the highest degree possible....* But if they see an opportunity where they can do more good, they must embrace it, whatever may be the sacrifice to themselves."[63] New converts should be taught (as Finney felt they were not) to cultivate a tender conscience, to pray without ceasing, to look for places where they might sacrifice for God, to be strictly honest in all their dealings, and to be happy and agreeable. In some manner, multitudes of new Christians have come to the conclusion that "they were born to enjoy themselves." Most Christians have a low standard of duty, "and that is the reason why there are so many useless members in our churches." These people may have to go "through fiery trials. Satan may sift them like wheat." Sacrifices and trials are to be expected, Finney stated; do not expect joy now. "They will be happy enough in heaven." Here, there is work to do![64]

Then there were the negative factors in the average Christian life. Most urgent to Charles Finney was the misuse of food and drink. It would be very difficult to change the habits of church members who had been on the wrong course for years, but Finney was adamant that it was with the new, pliable converts that progress could me made:

> Young converts, by proper instructions, are easily brought to be "temperate in all things." Yet this is a subject greatly neglected in regard to young converts, and almost lost sight of in the churches. There is a vast deal of intemperance in the churches. I do not mean intemperate *drinking*, in particular, but intemperance in eating, and in living generally. . . . Ten years ago, most ministers used ardent spirit, and kept it in their houses to treat their friends and their ministering brethren with. And the great body of the members in the churches did the same. Now there are but few of either. . . . It is well known, or ought to be, that TEA AND COFFEE have no nutriment in them. They are mere stimulants. They go through the system without being digested. The milk and sugar you put in them are nourishing. And so they would be just as much so, if you mixed them with rum, and made milk punch. But the tea and the coffee afford no nourishment. And yet I dare say, that a majority of the families in this city give more in a year for their tea and coffee, than they do to save the world from hell.[65]

Here Finney was exposing a concern of his that would expand greatly in years to come, with the more controlled environment that the closed college community of Oberlin would offer, and with young, pliable students who would be more likely to follow whatever regimens were dictated.

And so it went for the remainder of *Lectures on Revivals*. Whatever one's reaction to the sentiments expressed here by Finney, it must in fairness be admitted that he was grappling with innumerable problems that confronted the church of his day, and that he was seeking new answers. Interestingly, in so doing he was not taking the familiar road of capitulation, but instead demanding that Christians have extremely high standards in being the "salt of the earth" and the "light of the world." The Calvinists also had high standards, he felt, but their principles were desiccated and worthless for the emerging demands of the new day. So he would replace the old standards with ones equally demanding if not much more so, and no one would be able to charge him with lowering the criteria of biblical ethics; if anything, he was raising them. Charles Finney was a rigid taskmaster for a sluggish and sinful church, and for impressionable and easily molded new converts. And much of his wrath was turned on the Old School, which in his view was smug, complacent, and obfuscating.

It might be expected that the Old School counterattack would be as savage. The chief article came, as it had in April 1832, in *The Biblical Repertory and Theological Review*, which was edited by Charles Hodge of Princeton Seminary. This time it was not the young editor who blasted Finney, but his close friend, the Rev. Albert Baldwin Dod (1805–1850), a graduate of Princeton College and Seminary who was also an excellent mathematician. Because of his abilities in this field, he had given up the ministry to become professor of mathematics in the college at the age of twenty-five. This did not in any way diminish Dod's intense interest in Calvinism, however, and he remained an Old School adherent until his early death, writing incisive articles for Hodge whenever called upon. As William G. McLoughlin has said, "his review of the *Lectures on Revivals* can and should be properly considered the official and definitive counterattack upon the theological revolution that Finney led. It was so considered by contemporaries, and it merits careful consideration here."[66]

Dod's full review was so lengthy (ninety-seven pages) that the editor was forced to spread it across two issues. McLoughlin calls it, accurately, "biting sarcasm."[67] It becomes obvious that Dod looked upon Finney as an amateur in theology, if not a crude, bungling interloper in ecclesiastical affairs that were simply beyond his ken. He assailed Finney's literary style ("For, surely, it has not often fallen to our lot to read a book, in which the proprieties of grammar as well as the decencies of taste were so often and so needlessly violated; and in which so much that may not inappropriately be termed *slang* was introduced"),[68] knowledge of history and all other academic disciplines ("We were not surprised by Mr. Finney's ignorance in confounding Mary, Queen of Scots, with 'bloody Queen Mary' of England. . . . We do not look indeed for any thing like a thorough knowledge of any one subject, for should he obtain it, it would surely pine away and die for want of company"),[69] and what he saw as Finney's arrogance and pride ("there is a very peculiar self-isolation about him . . . so arrogantly does he assume all knowledge to himself,—so loftily does he arraign and rebuke all other ministers of the gospel. He stands alone in the midst of abounding degeneracy, the only one who has not bowed the knee to Baal. The whole world is wrong, and he proposes to set them right").[70]

Dod combined his review of the *Lectures on Revivals* with a critique of *Sermons on Various Subjects*, which was published a bit earlier. The first half of the review, published in the July issue, was basically on the *Sermons*, and Dod found much there to impugn. Charles Finney was so anxious to propagate the doctrines of the New Divinity, Dod believed, that in the sermons he became tedious: "If we may judge from the tiresome degree of repetition in these productions, the perpetual recurrence of the same ideas, phrases, and illustrations, we should suppose that he can have nothing new to say."[71] Dod then proceeded to attack the sermons on three heads: the government of God; the nature of depravity and sin; and the nature of regeneration.

Regarding the nature of God's government, Dod found that Finney was adhering to the New Divinity of Nathaniel W. Taylor of Yale: "He teaches, without any qualification, the doctrine which the New Haven school was at first understood to teach."[72] But Finney took Taylor's notions to shocking ends, in Dod's view:

> Accordingly, we find Mr. Finney using such language as this: "God has found it *necessary to take advantage* of the excitability there is in mankind, to produce powerful excitements among them, before he *can* lead them to obey." We know of nothing which ought more deeply to pain and shock the pious mind. If the perverseness of man has been able in one instance to prevent God from accomplishing what he preferred, then may it not in any instance obstruct the working of his preferences. . . . We cannot contemplate this doctrine, thus carrying out its lawful consequences, without unspeakable horror and dismay. The blessedness of the Deity! What pious mind has not been accustomed to find in it the chief source of its own joy? . . . If God therefore be, as this doctrine represents him, unable to produce states of things which he prefers, . . . the voice of wailing and despair should break forth from all his moral subjects. . . . If he could not prevent the introduction of sin into our world, we see not upon what principles we are entitled to affirm that he can prevent its reintroduction into heaven.[73]

In Dod's view, Finney had reduced the power of God, and made it much less than infinite. Whether Finney knew the consequences of his ideas or not (and it was quite clear that Dod doubted Finney understood them), he had introduced the old philosophical question of theodicy, with a finite God who did the best he could. "We can see, indeed, but little to decide our choice between such a God as this and no God," thundered the outraged Dod.[74]

When Dod came to his second point, the nature of depravity and sin, he found Finney merely confused and pathetic in his arguments, and hardly worthy of consideration. As we have previously seen in examining "Sinners Bound to Change Their Own Hearts," Finney went to great lengths in denying that there can be a fallen nature that causes all sinful acts and is prior to them. The orthodox view (held by Dod), deriving from St. Paul, Augustine, Luther, and Calvin, held that before the fall of its first parents, humankind did indeed possess free choice, but that when the first parents *of their free will* chose to disobey God, they fell into *voluntarily chosen* sin and lost the freedom to choose good over evil, and that this current predilection toward sin has tainted human nature in its entirety and explains perfectly why humankind universally commits sin.

Against this orthodox view, Finney held to the idea that this makes God "an infinite tyrant." Dod patiently tried to explain that it did no such thing. Indeed, the Creator *might* have been something of a tyrant had he *prevented* that first free choice (out of love and concern for humankind, knowing, as humans did not, the consequences of their tragic choice), but even with the consequences in view, God *allowed* it, Dod said. Further, if there *was* a fall in Adam (which Finney did not deny) it would be astounding to imagine that there would have been no great change in the nature and will of the human being, or what Finney called "physical depravity."

In careless moments, Dod pointed out, Finney slipped into assuming that humankind had something very much like "physical depravity." To show Finney's blunder, Dod needed to demonstrate:

> The doctrine that the mind has tastes and dispositions distinct from its faculties and acts. It is easy to show in contradiction to Mr. Finney, that it may possess such attributes, which nevertheless will not form any part of the substance of the mind. Nay we can make Mr. Finney himself prove it. In one of his sermons, where he has lost sight for a brief space of physical depravity, he speaks on this wise: "Love, when existing in the form of *volition,* is a simple preference of the mind for God, and the things of religion to everything else. This preference may and often does exist in

the mind, so entirely separate from what is termed emotion or feeling, that we may be *entirely insensible to its existence.* But although its existence may not be a matter of *consciousness,* by being felt, yet its influence over our conduct will be such, as that the fact of its existence will in this way be made manifest." Here is a state of mind recognised which Mr. Finney, with an utter confusion of the properties of language, chooses to call love existing in the form of volition, but which we call a disposition. But by whatever name or phrase it may be designated, it is not a faculty of the mind; it is not the object of consciousness, has no sensible existence, and cannot therefore in any proper sense be called an act of the mind—nor yet does it form any part of the substance of the mind.[75]

Dod's third area of attack, the nature of regeneration, found, as Asa Rand did, that Finney espoused Pelagian views, pure and simple. Dod quoted a sentence from one of Finney's sermons: "The *only* sense in which sin is *natural* to man is, that it is natural for the mind to be influenced in its individual exercises by a supreme preference or choice of any object." His words dripping with scorn, Dod retorted, "On reading this last extraordinary declaration the text of an inspired apostle came to mind, in which he assures us, that we are 'by *nature* children of wrath' [Ephesians 2:3]."[76] As McLoughlin has well said, "Dod's strong point, however, was that he could quote a large number of Biblical passages that do indicate men are born sinful by nature. . . ."[77] Knowing perfectly well the thin ice on which Finney here stood, Dod charged, "But texts of Scripture are as nothing in Mr. Finney's way. He makes them mean more or less, stretches or curtails them, just as occasion requires."[78] Dod was in complete agreement with Asa Rand that Finney had so truncated God's sovereignty that it obviously made man and not God the measure of all things. When Finney insisted throughout the sermons that human beings had great power to choose salvation if they so desired, this made the operations of the Holy Spirit so limited that they were almost "superfluous." This, said Dod, means that "Finney's teachings are neither more nor less than the old Pelagian notions."[79]

In the second segment of Dod's review, he turned to the two problems, as he saw it, presented by the *Lectures on Revivals.* The first of these was the extremism and fanaticism promoted by Finney's approach, and the second was the potential of these practices to work their way insidiously into all the operations of the church, thus upsetting its sound doctrine and preventing things from being done "decently and in order." Of these, to Dod the second was the more serious. Belatedly, however, he drew the attention of his readers to the conjunction between the new measures of Finney and the New Divinity of Yale. It is remarkable, as William McLoughlin has pointed out,[80] that the theologians of Princeton were so tardy in realizing that Finney's new measures "were not simply a matter of revival procedure but a matter of doctrine which put him in the camp of the liberalizers." But finally Hodge, Dod, and the moderates of Princeton had caught on. Perhaps piqued as much by their previous blindness as by anything that Finney said, in an important paragraph Dod spoke for all Princeton Seminary when he declared:

> These measures might have had their origin in the "New Divinity," for they are in entire keeping with the theology as well as the religion of the system. Historical facts however have guided us in assigning their origin to erroneous views of religion. The New Measures, we believe, were in full action before the theology of New Haven shed its light upon the world. We recollect that it was a matter of surprise to many when the conjunction took place between the coarse, bustling fanaticism of the New Measures and the refined, intellectual abstractions of the New Divinity.—It was a union between Mars and Minerva—unnatural, and boding no good to the church. But our readers will have observed that there is a close and logical connexion between Mr. Finney's theology and his measures. . . . It is well known that [James] Davenport, against whose extravagant fanaticism Edwards wrote at length, is *redivivus* in Mr. Finney, and that the same scenes over which he grieved and wept have been re-acted in our day under Mr. Finney's auspices.[81]

Of this second section of Dod's review, the first thirty pages are taken up with a treatment of Jonathan Edwards' views as compared to Finney's. Edwards had been cited quite often by Finney as justification for principles and practices,[82] and Dod took up the challenge as to whether Edwards did in fact say the things that Finney attributed to him. In particular, Finney claimed that Edwards defended the practice of lay preaching: "So much opposition was made to this practice nearly a hundred years ago, that President Edwards actually had to take up the subject, and write a labored defence of the rights and duties of laymen."[83]

Not so, said Albert Dod. In truth, it was the very opposite. James Davenport and others had so stirred up laymen during the height of the Great Awakening, 1741–1743, that opprobrium still rested upon lay preaching.[84] Jonathan Edwards, as well as all Presbyterians and Congregationalists, detested lay exhorters, as Edwards made perfectly clear in his *Thoughts Concerning the Present Revival of Religion*, Dod pointed out.[85] Now, it is not that Finney could simply have been mistaken on this, Dod stated, for "in the same work from which Mr. Finney has taken long extracts, and to which he often refers, as if familiar with its contents, Edwards makes known, with all plainness his opposition to lay exhortation."[86] Dod found this to be nothing less than a deliberate misrepresentation of Edwards, and he believed that Finney was guilty of this "unscrupulousness in the use of means for the attainment of his ends" altogether too often.

Dod criticized the *Lectures on Revivals* under five counts that he considered reprehensible. There was its coarseness and vulgarity, particularly referring to the language Finney used. Then there was its extravagance: "It is a peculiar mark of the fanatic that every dogma, every little peculiarity to which he is attached, is made to be infallibly certain, and infinitely important."[87] Here Dod took as one example Finney's statements on preaching. Only *his* methods would do; there must in sermons be the constant telling of stories and parables, just as Finney did. There must be only extemporaneous preaching, just as Finney did, for a speaker can never give the *"full meaning* of the gospel"* until he throws away his notes.[88] And so it went.

Thirdly, Dod found the work full of Finney's "spiritual pride and arrogance." He professed to be shocked. "But there is arrogance and assumption," Dod found, "beyond any thing which it has ever been our fortune previously to encounter."[89] Then, there was the book's censoriousness. Every custom, Dod found, that was alien to the new measures was in danger of condemnation. Particularly was Dod infuriated with Finney's broad assaults on the institutions of the Presbyterian Church, which had nurtured and sustained him through his conversion and until that time. Dod wished to know, What had the church done to harm Finney? Why was he always fulminating violently against the denomination that had for years tolerated so patiently his aberrations and onslaughts? Did nothing ever please the man? Again and again, Dod found, Finney brought down the wrath of the Almighty upon every act of the Presbyterian Church that displeased him, "in the singular prerogative which he enjoys of a back-door entrance into the Court of Heaven, and of unquestioned access to its magazines of wrath."[90] And finally there was the book's irreverence and profaneness, its frantic language, its willingness to adopt any means or reject any principle, for the winning of the immediate argument. All this, as before, Dod found to be simple fanaticism.

> It is too evident to need elucidation, that on all the subjects which we have gone over, his opinions are diametrically opposed to the standards of the Presbyterian church, which he has solemnly adopted. Many of the very expressions and forms of stating those doctrines upon which he pours out his profane ridicule, are found in the Confession of Faith. Why then does he remain in the church? . . . And can he see no moral dishonesty in remaining in a church whose standards of faith he has adopted, only to deny and ridicule them? . . . We tender him our thanks for the substantial service he has done the church by exposing the naked deformities of the New Divinity. He can render her still another, and in rendering it perform only his plain duty, by leaving her communion, and finding one within which he can preach and publish his opinions without making war upon the standards in which he has solemnly professed his faith.[91]

And at the end of the review, regarding what Dod considered Finney's aberrant behavior, he concluded:

> All the known means of kindness and expostulation have been tried to induce him to abandon his peculiarities, but without success. It is the clear duty of the Church now to meet him and his co-reformers with open and firm opposition. . . . The elements of fanaticism exist in the breast of every community, and may be easily called into action by causes which we might be disposed to overlook as contemptible. We conclude this article, as we did our former, by pointing out to Mr. Finney his duty to leave our church. It is an instructive illustration of the fact that fanaticism debilitates the conscience, that this man can doubt the piety of anyone who uses coffee, and call him a *cheat*, who sends a letter to another on his own business, without paying the postage,[92] while he remains, apparently without remorse, with the sin of broken vows upon him. In this position we leave him before the public. Nor will we withdraw our charges against him, until he goes out from among us, for he is not of us.[93]

14

THE BEGINNINGS OF OBERLIN

John Jay Shipherd held Charles Finney in the highest esteem, and had attempted to persuade Finney to come with him to the West when he stopped at Rochester in October 1830 to behold the beginnings of the revival there. But Finney had his eyes fixed on the eastern cities still, with plans to subdue more of them. So Shipherd went on, to Elyria, Ohio, and there worked for a time as a missionary pastor. Among other endeavors, he took on three students, but in a short while only one remained, Philo P. Stewart. Profoundly challenged by the enormous difficulties the frontier presented, Shipherd began to discuss with Stewart plans for a colony and school in northeastern Ohio.

For the colony, Shipherd imagined collecting a number of "right spirits" from New England and New York, people who would each "consider himself a steward of the Lord, and hold only so much property as he can advantageously manage for the Lord." He wished to attract only solid Christians, people who would live in the wilderness with "Gospel simplicity," working hard and hoarding nothing, and doing as much as possible to maintain the educational institution that would enhance the colony. "From the four winds," from "the vain amusements and strong temptations of the world," multitudes might be gathered to the colony and the school. "Connected with the Academy will be a farm & workshop, where, with four hours labor per day, students shall defray their entire expense. . . . We propose a manual labor establishment for *females* also, which in our estimation is immensely important for reasons which I have not room to name, but which will occur to you."[1]

Other schools founded in that day had prospectuses that were similarly idealistic, but as fortune would have it, Shipherd's school from its founding was, as Timothy L. Smith has said, "the seedbed of American Christian radicalism, not only on the question of slavery, but of racial brotherhood, women's rights, peace, prohibition, and a whole range of concerns for the creation of a righteous social order, in the nation and in the world."[2] Hard work and plain, wholesome living was emphasized for the colony, and for the school as well. With mounting enthusiasm, the plans were advanced and the entire enterprise named Oberlin after the French pastor Jean Frederic Oberlin, who had recently died. By August 1832 the plans were complete, and a site of five hundred acres of unscarred wilderness in Russia Township, Lorain County, was chosen as a possible location. The excitement of the founders was not to be dimmed by the fact that this entire area was of such hardscrabble soil that prospective settlers had refused to purchase farms in the vicinity. So nearly waste was the tract regarded that when Shipherd located the owners in Connecticut, they donated the desired land.[3]

Fired with enthusiasm for the enterprise, Shipherd combed New England and New York, attempting to gather subscribers, students, colonists, and a faculty. Philo Stewart was left at Oberlin to oversee the operation there. In Andover, Massachusetts, Shipherd found the man he considered best qualified to be head of the new school, Samuel Read Hall, principal of the Teachers Seminary at Andover, and author of *Lectures on School-Keeping*, a popular manual of pedagogical methodology. In addition Shipherd found Dr. James Dascomb, a young physician recently graduated from Dartmouth, and Shipherd recommended him to teach scientific subjects and to be the colony's doctor. Others whom Shipherd found declined their appointments, and Hall stated that he could not come to Oberlin until late in 1834.[4]

As Shipherd talked with others about his plans, he was persuaded that the new school should add a collegiate course and eventually a theological department. But misfortunes began to come. For one, Samuel Hall's poor health made it doubtful that this distinguished educator would ever be able to endure the rigors of life on the frontier, and by October 1834 he had so informed the trustees.[5] Financial troubles beset the school from its formal opening on December 3, 1833. The amounts raised by Shipherd in the East were far smaller than anticipated. Over one hundred students were enrolled, and the manual labor plan for the students in the collegiate course worked well, but the tuition raised was not sufficient to pay faculty salaries. Increasingly desperate expedients were attempted to keep the school viable. The trustees offered "perpetual scholarships" for $150 each, promising the student who purchased one that the money thus invested in Oberlin would cover his expenses during his time there, "and when he graduates [he can] sell the same scholarship, not diminished but increased in value."[6] The scheme, which it was hoped would provide the chief source of support, caused nothing but confusion and hard feelings.[7]

By the fall of 1834 the entire project was in a desperate condition. As a last recourse, Shipherd determined once again to go east, to appeal to the philanthropists in the major cities. He went to Columbus to catch the stage, and chanced to meet Theodore Keep, son of the newly appointed president of the Oberlin board of trustees. Young Keep amplified the information that Shipherd already possessed from the pages of the *New York Evangelist* concerning the Lane rebels, and Shipherd realized that near Cincinnati there was a large company of young men—with wealthy eastern friends—whose academic future was uncertain. With all dispatch he made for Cumminsville, a suburb of Cincinnati, where the rebels had set up an informal seminary and were trying to keep themselves together, studying their favorite subjects and doing benevolent work among the blacks of Cincinnati.[8]

There, in the home of Asa Mahan, Shipherd met the rebels, and described the Oberlin enterprise. He was persuasive, and found the men favorable to enrolling at Oberlin, providing certain conditions might be met. Because these men had been treated so peremptorily by the Lane trustees, Shipherd could understand that they would make demands. He, for his part, was so eager to save Oberlin in this way that he was willing to concede much. First, Theodore Weld and John Morgan, the Lane professor who had been discharged for siding with the students against the trustees, must be given professorships. Then, blacks must be admitted to the student body. Finally, Asa Mahan, the Lane trustee who had defended the students through the entire debacle, must become the president of Oberlin, and entire freedom of speech on all reform issues must be guaranteed.[9]

Mahan, on being proposed for this office, turned to his friends and supporters, John and James Melendy and William Holyoke; after discussion with them, he accepted.[10] Shipherd, claiming that he had power "in fact and form plenipotentiary" from the trustees, agreed to all the proposals, and wrote to the trustee president, John Keep, that

Mahan was "a revival minister of the millennial stamp . . . a man of inflexible christian principles. . . . His interest in our Institution is intense & he would be willing to toil & sacrifice in its behalf to any extent so would his estimable wife."[11]

When the trustees received these conditions and appointments, there was a willingness to accept all but the one regarding black enrollment. Throughout the small colony, a furor arose. One of the colonists later described the commotion: "A General panic & dispair seized the Officers, Students & Colonists—P.P. Stewart the Organ of Opposition at once proclaimed Bro. Shipherd Mad!! crazy &c &c & that the School was changed into a Negro School. Its founders would be disappointed and hundreds of negroes would be flooding the School."[12]

When Theodore Weld was offered the appointment he declined it, and instead suggested Charles Finney. He wrote to Shipherd that Finney was "in too great a prostration of health for evangelism or pastoral work. Teaching theology would be a needful rest to him."[13] Finney, to Mahan and Shipherd, was an admirable replacement for Weld, and they knew that his appointment would delight the Lane rebels. Without waiting any longer for an answer from the Oberlin trustees, Shipherd started east with Asa Mahan to secure assurance of continued financial aid from the Tappans (who were more or less definitely committed to underwrite the Lane rebels wherever they went), and to induce Charles Finney to accept the theological professorship.

Shortly after the beginning of 1835, the Lane rebels had heard the news that Finney was being invited to accept the post, and they were delighted. William T. Allan wrote to Weld: "This Oberlin plan, however, has opened up a new train. If you and Finney should go there I would try if possible to go with the rest."[14] And Henry B. Stanton wrote to Weld: "We have had no formal expression of opinion since your letter arrived, but we like the plan well. Brother Finney *must* go to O. It is the very kind of contact we need."[15] Then, sensing that Finney would need some persuasion and that their urgings might bestir him, some of them wrote directly to him in New York City:

> Our eyes have for a long time been turned toward you, as possessing peculiar qualifications to fill a professorship in such an institution. Holding and teaching sentiments which we believe are in accordance with the Bible, and having been called by God to participate more largely in the revivals of the last 9 years than any other man in the church, we could not but fix our attention

on you as one whom God had designated for such a work. . . .
Recognizing these truths, and having full confidence in your qualifications, we strongly desire to become your pupils. . . . We need
more practical preaching power—more knowledge of revival measures than we can obtain at any Seminary in the West, or perhaps,
in the country. . . . We cannot but think that the Providence of
God calls upon you to become the professor of theology in that
institution. If you should go there, nearly or quite all the theological students who left Lane, would place themselves at once
under your instruction.[16]

Needless to say, Finney's reaction to all of this was mixed. It
would certainly not be an easy decision to make. Because his health
was still poor, the prospect of leaving an enormously demanding pastorate at the "cathedral of the Benevolent Empire," in America's leading city, the very center of wealth and privilege, would mean that life
elsewhere might be less frenetic. However, this struggling college was
on the frontier, and diseases such as malaria often made such places
dangerous. There were obvious advantages to be seen: many of the
Lane rebels were converts from his Western revivals, and it would be
a pleasure to meet them again and teach them. Then, there was no
question that teaching in an academic environment, with long vacations, would be less taxing than the intense demands of an urban
pulpit such as the Chatham Street Chapel. With the welfare of their
beloved Lane rebels in mind, the Tappans in November 1834 had asked
Finney to consider going to Cumminsville, to teach and lead them.
But, without benefit of an institution behind him, and with the question of how long such a situation could last, Finney had decided against
it.[17]

However, on the other hand, there were pressing reasons to remain in New York City. For one, there were plans to build a fine new
church, to Finney's specifications, to replace the noisy, barnlike Chatham Street Chapel. With ready money available to finance it, the prospect of a superb sanctuary of his own design, and the delight of
preaching in it for years to come, to a man whose whole life was speaking to audiences, there was much here to counterbalance the doubtful allure of the rude buildings and cabins of the frontier. In addition,
he had just begun, on December 5, 1834, the first of the long series
of lectures on revivals, and it was his hope and intention to continue
this right through the winter and spring. With Joshua Leavitt tran-
scribing the lectures for immediate publication in the *Evangelist*, and

every likelihood that at the conclusion of the series they would be combined into a book, Finney could hardly give much attention to other matters, and he surely did not wish to stop the series in the middle and resume it at some later time. What to do?

As is so often the case, money was the deciding factor. And the Association of Gentlemen had the money. When Shipherd and Mahan reached New York City it is likely that they visited the Tappans prior to seeing Finney, although the sequence of events is now unknown. Gilbert Barnes has assumed this order, and with his usual succinctness has said, referring to Arthur Tappan:

> His response was prompt, for Oberlin offered at one stroke a refuge for his homeless protegés, a school for Negroes, and a nursery for abolitionism. . . . He canvassed his wealthy friends for contributions, he pledged tens of thousands on his own account, and lent Oberlin thousands more. He went again to Finney and with an insistence that would not be denied, persuaded him to go."[18]

To Tappan, the combined futures of the Lane rebels, an abolitionist, manual-labor seminary, and blacks who desired to be educated, outweighed the future of Charles Finney at the Chatham Street Chapel. If so much hinged on Finney's move to this new sphere of operations, then the Tappans knew that they must do everything possible to influence the outcome, and Finney's personal preference as to his future was in actuality only a small part of the entire equation.

Rounds of consultations were held with William Green, an antislavery merchant who had helped establish the Chatham Street Chapel, Isaac M. Dimond, a Connecticut manufacturer of jewelry, Joshua Leavitt, Shipherd, Mahan, and the Tappans. Two matters perplexed Finney, and he made it clear that his final acceptance of the offer would largely be determined by the resolutions of these problems. First was the matter of the admission of blacks at Oberlin, and the interrelated problem of the guarantee of freedom of speech on all reform issues. This decision was entirely in the hands of the Oberlin trustees. They had failed to act at their meeting on January 1, 1835, and so it could not be resolved until their next meeting, scheduled for February 9. Meanwhile their new trustee president, the Rev. John Keep, was using his influence to persuade board members to vote favorably on the two items that had been tabled.[19] Understandably, Finney did not want a recurrence of what had happened at Lane Seminary, with a feuding, too-powerful board of trustees. The second matter, however, could be settled in New York—the financial stability of the institution.

Here, Arthur Tappan was as good as his word, as always. He organized those in the consultations into "The Oberlin Professorship Association."[20] What happened next must have overwhelmed Shipherd, for it was beyond his wildest dreams. Arthur Tappan subscribed $10,000, and his brother Lewis, Isaac Dimond, William Green, and some other businessmen promised to pay the sum of $600 annually for each of eight professors. To guarantee Oberlin's stability, Arthur Tappan pledged much of his income, $100,000 per year, until the financial base of the college was secure.[21] Finney was pleased with this arrangement (as were, obviously, Shipherd and Mahan), and made the further stipulation that he be allowed to return to New York City for several months each winter for preaching. This arrangement had been agreed to earlier with the Tappans, and was certainly a clever accommodation as far as they were concerned, for it meant that Finney would continue to influence New York and the Benevolent Empire, would not be permanently relegated to the West, and could remain as pastor there, as the new sanctuary was built. In addition, Finney stipulated, the trustees must "commit the internal management of the institute entirely to the Faculty, inclusive of the reception of students."[22] Everything now hinged on the trustees giving in on these points.

The news of the New Yorkers' generosity flew. Two of the Lane rebels, H. B. Stanton and Huntingdon Lyman, wrote immediately to Theodore Weld:

> Dear Br. Weld
>   We received a letter from Mahan last night and waited for the mail in the hope of receiving one from you. Lest you should not be acquainted with what Br. Mahan has effected, I give a summary of his letter. It is dated 12th Jany. "Five professorships at $10,000 have been secured. A. Tappan has given $10,000 besides. The professorships will be increased to eight, and from 5. to $10,000 obtained for a library all in N.Y. which will make the aggregate in that city from 95 to $100,000.[23]

With Shipherd and Mahan back in Oberlin, the trustees met as scheduled on February 9. The meeting was "riotous, turbulent & filled with detraction [and] slander."[24] John Jay Shipherd, who was not present, had written to them, "I did not desire you to hang out an aboli-tion flag, or fill up with filthy stupid negroes; but I did desire that you should say you would not reject promising youth who desire to prepare for usefulness because God had given them a darker hue than others." He then threatened to resign as their agent if they did not guarantee "that the Faculty shall control the internal affairs of the in-stitute & decide upon the reception of students,"[25] as Finney's condi-tion had specified. After a time the meeting was adjourned, to meet again the next morning. When the vote on the matter was taken, four of the trustees, led by Philo P. Stewart, opposed the admission of blacks. Four voted in favor of it. It was then up to the chairman, John Keep, to cast the decisive ballot, and he voted in favor of their admission. With the matter resolved, the Tappans and others could build up the college. It is altogether likely that, if John Keep had not voted as he did, Oberlin would soon have passed into oblivion.

It was widely recognized what Oberlin's acquisition of Charles Finney, a competent faculty, and the Lane rebels would mean in terms of equipping an enduring educational institution, and a large number of zealous young men, for the propagation of new measures princi-ples. Charles B. Storrs, president of Western Reserve College at Hud-son, Ohio, and "the ablest educator in the West, with a national repu-tation for scholarship and eloquence,"[26] a Finneyite himself, was irate, knowing what this competition would do to his school, and in the next few months he and his faculty did all in their power to upset the arrangement. "At least a week before the trustees' meeting of Feb-ruary 10," Robert Fletcher states, various religious papers were prema-turely reporting that all had been settled at Oberlin, that Finney was expected to come as professor of theology, that Asa Mahan had ac-cepted the presidency, and that professorships had been endowed and $10,000 received for buildings.[27]

The *New York Evangelist* under Leavitt was naturally eager to report the latest tidings to its readership, and on March 21 it announced that Finney and Morgan had accepted the positions offered them. On April 11 Leavitt stated in the paper, "The Rev. Asa Mahan, President of this Institution, Rev. Charles G. Finney, Prof. of Theology, and the Rev. John Morgan, Prof. Rhetoric, are expected to enter upon their of-ficial duties at Oberlin, about the first of May next."[28] And on March 23 John Keep wrote to Finney, "I give you my full and firm belief, that your proposal to be absent from the Seminary 3 or 4 months . . . will be most readily acceeded to by the Board of Trustees."[29]

Despite these hopeful statements, there were also many discordant notes sounded at this time. Multitudes throughout the North wanted no agitation on the abolition question, and violently opposed those who threatened to raise it. John Jay Shipherd and Charles Finney traveled to Philadelphia in March to raise funds for the school, and could not collect enough to pay their railroad fares for the return trip to New York. Oberlin's own financial agent in New England, Benjamin Woodbury, was adamantly against Finney's coming.[30]

While these intrigues were continuing, Finney, trying to recover from his exhaustion and poor health, was busy with a number of important and fatiguing projects. From week to week during the winter and spring of 1835 he continued delivering the lectures on revivals on Friday evenings, and preaching on the standard schedule on Sundays. But another absorbing interest was also beginning to take shape: the design and construction of the Broadway Tabernacle. A study of the extant materials suggests that there were two chief reasons why a new church was sought. First, the Chatham Street Chapel was in a poor neighborhood, and the odium of its having been a theater had never completely worn off;[31] architecturally, it was a theater, not a church. Secondly, Finney wanted a new building constructed distinctly as a sanctuary, whose acoustics and other properties would be superior to those at the chapel. In addition to these considerations, it may also be that, as the site for the annual meetings of the "Great Eight" benevolent societies where thousands of delegates from around the nation gathered, there were matters of self-esteem involved. To have all these strangers to New York City meet in a bad neighborhood, in a building that did not look like a church, doubtless brought on a problem of image. Although the not too opulent surroundings surely suggested Christian self-sacrifice, the delegates were, after all, dispensing millions of dollars each year!

The search for a suitable location was completed in the spring of 1835, when four lots were secured, "one of which was purchased, the others hired from the estate of Peter Lorillard,"[32] in a better area uptown. This site was on the east side of Broadway from Anthony Street[33] north to Catherine Lane. Susan Hayes Ward described the layout: "Its entrance on Broadway, about twenty-five feet wide, in the middle of the block, was secured by a lease of two lots in front of the edifice. . . . This entrance, extending east one hundred feet to the small yard in front of the building, when not in use, was closed with iron gates swinging in from the street."[34]

As pastor of the church, Finney was extremely fortunate in having a number of wealthy supporters to whom he could turn at times such as this. With the Tappans' funds so largely diverted to Oberlin, the main financing of the Broadway Tabernacle came from William Green, Jr., the antislavery merchant, who gave $5,000 and loaned $25,000, and Isaac M. Dimond, the jewelry manufacturer, who contributed the same sum and loaned $20,000, which was never repaid. Other subscriptions came to $6,000; and $5,500 was secured by bonds and mortgage. This totaled $66,500, the cost of the land purchased, and the edifice itself.[35]

Joseph Ditto was chosen to be the architect and builder, but it was understood from the beginning that Charles Finney had certain very specific concepts that he wanted incorporated in the design.[36] Basically, it was the idea of a circular gallery with (as much as possible) an uninterrupted view of the platform given to every person in the house, no matter where seated. Over the years, Finney had preached in many auditoriums where pillars and other obstacles had blocked the view of his hearers; he wished no such hindrance in this sanctuary. Due to the span of the ceiling, Ditto could not comply with this demand entirely, and he was forced to place six pillars in a circle to support the roof.

Another concept embodied in the design, to facilitate communication between the pulpit and each auditor, was to have the eight ranks of pews in the gallery banked at the proper angle so that each person could easily see over the heads of those in front. In actuality — and this accorded perfectly with his theology of preaching — it was not so much that Finney was concerned that each person have a good view; he was determined that *he* would see each one of *them!*[37] This idea that a speaker can be much closer to his audience when they surround him, on at least three sides, and that with a congregation of, say, one thousand, no one with such an arrangement need be seated more than seventy feet from the pulpit, became very influential for churches built during the next hundred years, and resulted in the "Akron plan" of sanctuary design.

Trained in the old school of architecture, Joseph Ditto rebelled at such demands, saying "it would injure his reputation to build a church with such an interior."[38] Faced by the imperious Finney, he of course capitulated and designed as he was told. And Finney was correct. When completed, the sanctuary was all that Finney had hoped for.

The land was cleared and construction begun in the spring of 1835. Work went well for a time, with Finney supplying ideas for the Sunday school rooms, chapels, and halls as well as the sanctuary. He remained in New York City until perhaps the first of May, and then left for Oberlin. Naturally, New York buzzed with rumors about the latest Tappan and Finney venture, because the previous summer had been a time of riots and conflagrations. Hatreds had cooled but little, and in July a rumor circulated that the church being erected was to be an "amalgamation church," in which whites and blacks would be seated together throughout the house, and that it would be used as a center for abolitionist "hot heads." As Finney said, "Such was the state of the public mind in New York at that time that this report created a great excitement and somebody set the building on fire."[39] Several volunteer fire companies answered the alarm, but, typical of the motley crews who were better at parades in the cities than at extinguishing fires, they had heard the rumors also and stood by as the fire raged, refusing to put it out. The roof and the interior were consumed, and had to be rebuilt. Nothing daunted, Dimond and Green were soon pushing construction again, in spite of threats.[40]

With the construction of the Broadway Tabernacle underway, Finney headed west, to view for the first time the land and college to which he had been called. Meanwhile, the president and trustees of Western Reserve College had been doing everything in their power to draw off some of Oberlin's sudden popularity and financial benefactions. The trustees aimed at the heart of the matter, electing Finney professor of pastoral theology[41] and appointing a committee with instructions to visit the Oberlin trustees and convince them that they were conscience-bound to transfer their gifts to Western Reserve. What happened next is best told in Finney's own words:

> In Cleveland I found a letter awaiting me, from Arthur Tappan, of New York. He had in some way become acquainted with the fact, that strong efforts were making to induce me to go to Hudson, rather than to Oberlin.
>
> The college at Hudson, at that time, had its buildings and apparatus, reputation and influence, and was already an established college. Oberlin had nothing. . . . It had, to be sure, its charter, and perhaps a hundred students on the ground; but everything was still to be done. . . .
>
> I left my family at Cleveland, hired a horse and buggy, and came out to Oberlin, without going to Hudson. I thought at least that I would see Oberlin first. When I arrived at Elyria, I found some old acquaintances there, whom I had known in central New York. They informed me that the trustees of Western Reserve College thought that, if they could secure my presence at Hudson,

> it would, at least in a great measure, defeat Oberlin; and that at
> Hudson there was an Old School influence, of sufficient power
> to compel me to fall in with their views and course of action. This
> was in precise accordance with the information which I had re-
> ceived from Mr. Tappan. . . . I therefore wrote to the trustees of
> Hudson, declining to accept their invitation, and took up my abode
> at Oberlin.[42]

By the middle of May Finney had made this decision, and was
settling in Oberlin. On June 30 he officially notified the trustees of
his acceptance of the position offered him.[43] Eager to plunge into the
work, he made do with the few dwellings as yet constructed, living
where he could until better accommodations were available for his
family and himself. Arthur Tappan's money was being used for the
erection of several buildings, among them two substantial brick
houses, each two stories high, which would serve as homes for Asa
Mahan and Finney.[44]

The thoughtfulness of the New York philanthropists was manifested in another gift to the infant school, a large tent intended for
use not only by the school but also for evangelistic work in the West.
An item mentioning it appeared in the *New York Evangelist* on May 23,
1835: "Tent for Mr. Finney.—This tent has been completed, and was
yesterday forwarded from this city to Mr. Finney at Oberlin. It covers
300 feet of ground, will hold 3000 people, and cost $700. The expense
is defrayed by a number of gentlemen in this city."[45] Other accounts
were more specific as to size; James H. Fairchild said that "it was a
circular tent, a hundred feet in diameter—sufficient when closely
seated to shelter three thousand persons."[46] Made of white canvas, the
tent made a majestic appearance with the long blue banner streaming from its center pole, bearing the inscription, "Holiness to the Lord,"
and it was used for some years at commencements and other large
gatherings. Remarking on the possibility of holding protracted meetings in it, John Keep wrote to Finney, "Most of the impenitent in the
vicinity, will wish to come, at least once and see the Tent."[47]

The inaugural ceremonies for the Oberlin Collegiate Institute
were held on the first Wednesday of July, 1835, in this large tent. John
Keep, as president of the trustees, delivered the charge to the president and faculty. Asa Mahan, former member of the trustees at Lane
Seminary, was inaugurated as the first president, occupying that chair
for fifteen years. In addition he was made professor of mental and moral
philosophy. Charles Finney became professor of theology. John Mor-

gan became professor of literature of the Bible and church history. All three gave addresses, which, typical of the time, were not brief. According to the *Evangelist,* however, "the audience hung upon their lips for hours, without indicating a desire through weariness to drop off."[48]

Construction of buildings was being pushed as rapidly as possible, for students were arriving continuously. Thirty-two of the Lane rebels eventually came to study at Oberlin,[49] and especially for them the first of the dormitories, the "Barracks," was rushed to completion by June 1835.

As classes began, although there was a spartan rigor everywhere in Oberlin, it seemed that all was well, and the future was splendidly bright. In August 1835 Mr. and Mrs. William Green, Jr., of New York City arrived with the latest news of Chatham Street Chapel and the continuing work on the Broadway Tabernacle, and Finney may have mused that everywhere in his life there was construction going on, and that was a hopeful sign. Green returned to New York in September to give a favorable report of Oberlin to the Professorship Association.[50]

The next visitor was George W. Gale, on his way west from New York State to Illinois, where he would found Knox College. From his years with the Oneida Institute he was well aware of the difficulties in maintaining a school, and he was greatly impressed by the advances made in such a short time, and by the devoutly Christian atmosphere.[51] He appreciated especially the manual labor system, Oberlin's "peculiarity."[52]

As to Oberlin's other "peculiarity," the admission of black students, although it remained an admirable testimony to the high ideals of Shipherd, Keep, Mahan, Finney, and the Lane rebels, those who had panicked when it was originally proposed might have saved themselves the commotion. For several years there were almost no blacks in the colony; one black student followed the Lane rebels to Oberlin.[53] By 1840 the proportion of black students was somewhere around four or five percent, but it did not reach any significant number for years.[54] As the major benefactor, Arthur Tappan was most proud of this feature of his project, and he took more interest in the college than in any other project of his antislavery career.[55]

If Arthur Tappan and other abolitionists saw a bright spot at Oberlin, it may have been the only cheer they found, for the year 1835 was frenzied in the struggle to free the slave. On July 29, when the U.S. mail boat from New York reached Charleston, S.C., the local newspapers announced that the mail contained a great deal of incendiary abolitionist literature for distribution throughout the South. Copies of *The Emancipator, The Slave's Friend,* and other papers included did not call for a slave insurrection throughout the South, as was charged, but mobs gathered and took the papers to an open area and burned them before an immense crowd. Whoever had sent them, the mobs knew exactly whom to blame, and the next day the *Charleston Courier* reported, "The effigies of Arthur Tappan, Dr. Cox, and W. L. Garrison were at the same time suspended. At nine o'clock the balloon was let off, and the effigies were consumed by the neck, with the offensive documents at their feet."[56]

The matter of sending northern papers to the South was immediately taken to the Congress and the Postmaster General. The latter official, seeking to avoid complicity or further violence, stated that although he had no legal power to stop such mails, "as a measure of public necessity, therefore, you and the other postmasters who have assumed the responsibility of stopping these inflammatory papers will, I have no doubt, stand justified in that step before your country and all mankind."[57] Throughout the South, the name of Tappan was vilified as never before, and a reward of $30,000 was offered for his delivery upon the levee of New Orleans.[58]

Slaveholders could not harm him, and so they took out their rage upon anyone who had anything to do with abolition. In Nashville during July, Amos Dresser, an Oberlin College student and seller of Bibles, a gentle and inoffensive man, was arrested for selling a copy of *Letters on Slavery,* and for having some abolitionist papers in his possession. After a trial before a committee, two of whom were clergymen and seven of whom were Presbyterian elders, he was publicly beaten before a riotous crowd and thrown out of the city, suffering the loss of $300 worth of Bibles.[59]

While these episodes were vexing the nation, the Tappans, as the principal backers of Oberlin Collegiate Institute, were continuing to have their troubles. Where much of it took the form of insults and abuse, attacks upon them in the papers and snubs from former friends, no one doubted that far more sinister danger was indeed close at hand. Many southern merchants—someone estimated seven thousand, and almost all slaveholders—were in New York City at any given time. Rumors circulated that hooligans from Georgia, eager to cash in on the rewards, had a pilot boat ready to carry off Arthur Tappan. That was well within the realm of possibility, for Arthur had moved his residence from the city to Brooklyn Heights, and he commuted regularly by ferry across the East River. With Arthur so exposed in his movements, any clever assassin could have succeeded in his attempt. The mayor of Brooklyn thought the danger sufficiently real to post himself outside Arthur's home at night, and also to station a patrol of men at the Brooklyn Navy Yard in case armed assistance against mobs was needed.[60]

The Oberlin trustees certainly hoped that Arthur Tappan's largesse to their school would continue. But during the summer, after he had given $1,750, they got a warning that his giving might be greatly restricted. John Jay Shipherd, who had been drawing heavily on the merchant's account as instructed, was distraught at the news, and wrote to Tappan for details. He was doubtless relieved when Tappan replied, "The drafts you speak of as *to be* drawn will be duly honored if my life is spared. If I had foreseen the storm that has gathered around my head I should not have dared to assume the responsibilities I did for your Institution."[61] But such assurances from Tappan rang false to those, especially in New York, who knew his circumstances well, and rumors of trouble had certainly gotten back to Oberlin and Shipherd. Tappan's erstwhile southern trade had long been a mainstay of his business, but with the South united in its hatred of his very name, that trade had shriveled to nothing. Because of this, he had been forced to trade on long-term credit while keeping his prices at their former levels. In addition, Tappan's creditors were reacting to an increasingly tight money market throughout the nation, and could advance needed cash to him only at twenty-five to thirty percent interest.[62]

Charles Finney returned from Oberlin to the Chatham Street Chapel in early December 1835, to deliver another series of Friday evening lectures and take up the burdens of his pastorate there.[63] He had not been in New York for many days before another crippling blow to the Tappan fortunes occurred, which would augur the end of their financial support of Oberlin.

If Arthur Tappan had contemplated the possibility of loss from fire, he may have comforted himself on that score (it being only a possibility among many real problems) by noting that his store was near the firehouse of Oceanus Company No. 11, an old volunteer squad with a fine reputation, and that the single water hydrant on Hanover Square was almost directly before his store's entrance. In addition, his building was constructed of solid Maine granite, which was among the most impervious materials to fire.

On the evening of Wednesday, December 16, Arthur Tappan was with the executive committee of the American Antislavery Society at its rooms on Nassau Street, half a mile from his store. The night was bitterly cold, with the mercury standing at zero, and a brisk wind blew across Manhattan from the rivers. As the committee discussed its business, shortly before nine o'clock shouts were heard from the street and the ringing of fire bells warned that there was an alarm somewhere in the business district. This was the oldest section of the city, containing a heterogeneous mix of warehouses, shops, tenements, public buildings, bordellos, tumbledown shanties, and well-built homes.

Most of the abolitionists on the committee accompanied Arthur and Lewis Tappan from the building, and, hurrying in the direction of the clamor, they saw that the fire had engulfed Comstock and Andrews Company, a dry-goods firm off Hanover Square on Beaver Street. Fire companies and residents of the area were making valiant efforts to stop the flames, but the fire hydrants and hoses were freezing up, water was impossible to obtain, and the task appeared impossible. Amid the clutter of tinder-dry old buildings, the wind was whipping the flames to such intensity that they were sending fiery embers into the sky, threatening to spread the conflagration to distant rooftops.[64] As the abolitionists stood horrified, the building next to Tappan's caught fire. One of the partners of that firm, and some employees, were already inside the store removing the goods and tossing them into the center of the small square, but it was soon realized that the blaze would probably engulf the entire area, and valuable merchandise would have to be removed to a much greater distance.[65]

Conditioned to coolness by the attacks that had been made on them, the Tappans surveyed the situation. Fortunately, Arthur had recently installed iron shutters on all his windows as a defense against rioters, and the solid structure promised protection for a period of time. The brothers quickly set about recruiting volunteers, mostly blacks, to remove the merchandise. The blacks responded eagerly to their pleas, for they regarded the Tappans as advocates and friends, and throughout the night they drove themselves without respite to save as much as possible. "Doubtless," Lewis Tappan declared, "they felt that they had worked for a benefactor."[66] Without their efforts, the brothers would have faced ruin. As it was, two-thirds of the stock was removed to safety.

While these frantic exertions were continuing, Arthur Tappan removed from his iron safe $500,000 worth of promissory notes, and they were taken to another place; other papers were left in the safe, in the hope that they would not be burned. It was found afterwards that those left were charred beyond recognition. A vacant store at some distance was quickly hired, and the merchandise taken there, where it remained safe.

The inferno raged through the night, leaping from block to block, and it was noon before demolition crews were eventually successful in checking the fire's advance. Surveying the ruins, the authorities determined that more than fifty acres of the business district were leveled, and the streets obliterated. A total of some six hundred fifty buildings had been destroyed, including the Stock Exchange on Wall Street and the Dutch Reformed church on Garden Street. Damage was estimated at $18 million, or more.[67]

After the night of exhausting labor, and half frozen, the Tappan brothers gathered their chief clerks together for breakfast. Someone asked what was to be done next. "Rebuild immediately," Arthur Tappan responded. A clerk was sent off to a builder, and in a short time a contract had been signed to begin construction as soon as possible, on the same site. In addition, the day's papers carried the notice that "Arthur Tappan & Co. acknowledge with gratitude the efficient exertions of their friends and fellow-citizens in saving (by the blessing of God) the largest portion of their goods, all their books of account, and most of their papers." The address of their new location was given, and the announcement that they intended to rebuild at the old location.[68] On the whole, Arthur Tappan was emerging from the situation in better condition than many of the other merchants, who not only lost everything, but whose insurance firms went bankrupt under the flood of claims. Previously, Tappan had insured his goods with underwriters in Boston and other New England cities[69] as well as in New York, inasmuch as local insurance companies refused to take the full coverage because of the proslavery riots of 1834. Thus, although Tappan was paid in full by the New England companies, he lost $40,000 through the failures of New York firms.

The many reformers and church people who depended on the generosity of Arthur Tappan, including those at Oberlin, were naturally chagrined at his losses. At the Chatham Street Chapel Charles Finney could do little more than give moral support to his benefactor and lend his sympathy, and hope to himself that Tappan's gifts were not ended. Finney was having his own troubles. The chapel and the incomplete Broadway Tabernacle had both been outside the area of the conflagration, so it was not losses from fire that directly affected Finney. The difficulty lay elsewhere—with the Third Presbytery of New York.

Finney had numerous matters of contention with the Presbyterian denomination, but it was the area of discipline that provided
the final, explosive issue that led to his departure from that church.
Since his conversion and early inclination to the ministry under
George Gale's influence, Finney had had differences not only with the
Old School theology but also with the Presbyterian system of graded
judicatories and the appellate procedure for ecclesiastical trials, from
the local session to the presbytery to the synod and, finally, to the
general assembly. His *Lectures on Revivals* teem with his irritation
at meetings of groups of clergymen and elders: they were tedious and
interminable, and (in his opinion) they accomplished little. Even the
much more loosely organized Congregational Church—to which Finney was steadily drifting—had its share of litigation and bureaucracy:
"President Edwards was obliged to be taken up for a long time in disputes before ecclesiastical councils; and in our days, and in the midst
of these great revivals of religion, these difficulties have been alarmingly and shamefully multiplied."[70] To Finney, Presbyterians were far
worse.

Research into the relevant minutes of the presbyteries and synods
to which Finney belonged from 1824 to 1836 shows that he rarely attended meetings, although it was always mandatory that all clergymen attend unless they could present a valid excuse. After he had been
ordained a year or two, Finney (according to these minutes) did not
ask to be excused but simply did not bother to attend, and the presbyteries allowed his cavalier disdain only in deference to his prominence and heavy work load, whereas a lesser man might have been
stringently disciplined. Even when his friends were on trial or urgent
issues were coming up that needed his influence and vote, correspondence from these men shows that they usually pleaded in vain for
him to attend, or that he promised them his presence and then often
disappointed them. Having made himself an outsider to the power
structure of the church, he squawked mightily when it did not defer
to his wishes, and continued his high-flying, independent ways.[71]

For Finney, the crowning touch that provoked his departure was
the Third Presbytery's inconsistency in handling two similar cases
of discipline. A man transferred his membership from another church
to the Second Free Church, and later Finney found that the man had
committed an offense that demanded discipline in his former church.
Finney reasoned that, inasmuch as the offense had been committed
at the other church, and the session there knew the details, they should
be the ones to administer the discipline. This matter was brought

before the Third Presbytery, to which Finney belonged, and its members decided that the Second Free Church, where he was now a member, should discipline the errant one. Finney disagreed, but to keep peace he did as the presbytery wished.

In a short while a similar case arose in which a woman joined the Second Free Church, and then it was found that she had been guilty of an offense that called for discipline. In accordance with the previous ruling of the presbytery, the session excommunicated her. She appealed to the presbytery, and its members ruled the reverse of their previous decision. Finney was astonished. He rose to speak, and told them that he did not know what to do; the two cases were precisely similar, yet their decisions were entirely opposite.

According to Finney, at that point Dr. Samuel H. Cox, pastor of the Laight Street Church,[72] defended their inconsistent decisions. "Dr. Cox replied that they would not be governed by their own precedent, or by any other precedent; and talked so warmly, and pressed the case so hard, that the presbytery went with him."[73] From his *Memoirs*, it would appear that this greatly rankled and disturbed Finney, as naturally it would, and led to his decision to transfer his ordination to the Congregationalists. This left the possibility wide open for the still uncompleted Broadway Tabernacle, not yet affiliated with any denomination, to belong to any group the pastor and members wished. For Finney this was a large opportunity. From his viewpoint, he resented the intrusions of any higher ecclesiastical body. Why, then, should this fine new church, soon to be finished, come under the jurisdiction of the Presbyterians?

On Sunday, March 13, 1836, in a large meeting room in Broadway Hall at 440 Broadway, Charles Finney resigned as pastor of the Second Free Presbyterian Church (Chatham Street Chapel). At the same time he announced his intention to demit the ministry of the Presbyterian Church, and to transfer his ordination to the Congregationalists. Thereupon he stated that he had been offered the pastorate of the new church to be formed, the Sixth Free Church, and that he intended to accept if it proved to be the wish of the congregation. An organizational meeting was then formed, a covenant or constitution of eleven principles passed,[74] which was Congregational, not Presbyterian, in intent, and a board of deacons, which also acted as trustees of the property, was elected. Finney was nominated and elected as the new pastor, and he and the assembled group then adjourned until the service of that evening.

Later, in the Chatham Street Chapel, the sermon was delivered

Interior of the Broadway Tabernacle, New York City. With the deep galleries in a circular design, Charles Finney's radical plan allowed the speaker to have eye contact with almost everyone in the congregation, and no person was seated more than seventy feet from the platform. From an old sketch.

by the Rev. Charles Fitch, pastor of the Free Church of Hartford, Connecticut. When he concluded that, he then read the names of the 118 members who formed the new congregation, the covenant, and confession of faith, and he pronounced them a church, the Broadway Tabernacle Church. A prayer was then offered, and an anthem sung, and the service was concluded.[75] With these actions, Charles Finney had severed his ties with the Presbyterian denomination.

Unfortunately, the new building was not quite complete, and the services were held for a few more weeks in the Chatham Street Chapel. Then on Sunday, April 10, all was in readiness, and the first service was held in the sanctuary that Finney had largely designed. The builder turned over the Broadway Tabernacle at the morning worship, and the excited congregation heard the opening address from the Rev. Nathaniel E. Johnson, pastor of the Third Free Church, who had replaced Dirck Lansing there on August 23.[76] In the evening service that day Finney was installed as pastor by a newly formed Congregational body calling itself "The Association of New York City." The installation sermon was delivered by the Rev. Joel Mann, pastor of the Second Congregational Church of Greenwich, Connecticut. Joshua Leavitt gave the charge to the congregation and also the installation prayer. The man who had taken the pastorate of the Second Free Church, Charles Martyn, then gave the charge to the pastor.[77] The Second Church's superb director of music, Thomas Hastings, was brought by Finney to the Broadway Tabernacle, and he led choirs in stirring anthems during the gala morning and evening services.

In the next issue of the *New York Evangelist*, Joshua Leavitt described the immense crowds that day, who came to view the fine new structure and add their good wishes. He reported with delight on the church's interior: "The internal arrangement is admirably contrived; the galleries and ceiling are low; the sound good. The gallery extends round the house, descending on the backside to the level of the pulpit, thus forming a fine orchestra."[78] As he wrote this, Leavitt was certainly comparing the comfortable, well-lit, and clean new surroundings with the barnlike Chatham Street Chapel with its abominable acoustics and dangerous neighborhood. Now here was a "cathedral" for the Benevolent Empire that it might be proud of! The neighborhood was excellent; it was the active center of New York City in the 1830s, with new business houses and recent construction round about. Immediately across Broadway, on the west side and extending for two blocks, was the New York Hospital, one of the most active and largest hospitals in the United States. Nearby was the beautiful new Masonic Hall. At a short distance was Peale's Museum, and the Washington Hotel. And on Church Street, not far off, was Columbia College. Charles Finney was pleased as well, and as he became accustomed to preaching from its pulpit, he found that the design was all that he had hoped it would be for ease in communication with his audience. As Nelson Nichols said, "he never changed his mind about this first building of his being anything but ideal for his purposes. He summarized his opinion by writing that 'it was a most commodious and comfortable place to speak in.'"[79] Finney also wrote that the Broadway Tabernacle was an "admirable place for preaching the Gospel, where such crowds were gathered within the sound of my voice."[80]

Indeed, the design of the Tabernacle was quite advanced for that day. A few weeks after its completion it was proudly presented by the Tappans and others to the delegates who came from around the nation to the May Anniversary Week of the benevolent societies, and it measured up to all expectations. Approximately one hundred feet square and seating twenty-five hundred persons, the acoustic properties of the sanctuary were excellent, largely because of the bowllike, circular design of the gallery. Below this large gallery the main floor had rank after rank of pews seating hundreds, and the choir loft and organ were at the back of the large platform, with the pulpit in the front center. Susan Hayes Ward described "a stairway running up from the floor to the gallery in which the choir was seated, and, under the stairway, to the left, a mysterious passageway led to the pastor's study, Bible and infant classrooms, and other departments."[81] In the great central domed ceiling there was a skylight. A large gas-lit chandelier hung down over the congregation to provide light for evening worship, and projecting out from the gallery there were a number of gas lamps that added to the illumination. The entire credit for this innovative, extremely functional auditorium goes to Finney, for his instincts that resulted in this design had proven to be abundantly correct.

He was able to enjoy preaching in this new hall for about ten weeks. However enticing it may have been to remain there for a time longer, Finney was well aware that stirring events were happening at Oberlin, and he must return. By late June of 1836 he was again at the Collegiate Institute, ready to take up the new classes that were forming. The antislavery atmosphere there was superheated, and much of the reason for the intensity of interest revolved around the activities of Theodore Weld. With many of the Lane rebels now at Oberlin, and having espoused the West as the scene of his activities, Weld—as well as the others of the institute—viewed the school as a natural center of abolitionist operations.

In the fall of 1835 Weld had given a series of gripping lectures in the unfinished assembly room of Ladies' Hall at Oberlin. He wrote to Lewis Tappan:

> Our meetings are held in one of the new buildings. It is neither plastered nor lathed and the only seats are rough boards—thrown upon blocks; and you may judge something of the interest felt at Oberlin on the subject of abolition when I tell you that from five to six hundred males and females attend every night, and sit *shivering* on the rough boards without fire these cold nights, without any thing to lean back against, and this too until nine o'clock. . . . The weather has been so cold and the place where we meet here is so open that brother Finney has not attended my lectures. His state of health would make it exceedingly presumptuous to do so.[82]

Such rapt loyalty may be rare in this day, but the spartan rigor of Oberlin was able to cultivate it. Regarding the antislavery activities throughout the North, Oberlin's historian has declared, "Everywhere Oberlinites were in the van."[83]

Much of this fervid activity revolved around Weld, who was capable of generating amazing loyalty and the desire to duplicate his own astounding energies. In upstate New York and throughout Ohio, he enjoyed success after success in recruiting supporters of abolitionism. In February 1836, almost seven hundred new members had been taken into the Utica Antislavery Society because of his efforts, and twelve hundred people, mostly men of voting age, signed antislavery petitions there. In March he was in Rochester, and eight hundred new members came into the local society.[84]

But Weld's fortunes changed when he came to Troy in May and June. There he expected to find the usual opposition, which in all previous places he had gradually overcome even to the extent of bringing some of the former antagonists around to his point of view. But in Troy he found a much more determined resistance. As Weld and Nathaniel Beman waited at the front of the First Presbyterian Church for the meeting to begin, mobs outside petrified the trustees into canceling the scheduled lecture series. For weeks the proslavery forces prevented Weld from even speaking, and attack after attack upon him made it doubtful that he would escape the city with his life. At another church he managed to get up to speak, and twice rioters stormed down the aisle and tried to pull him from the pulpit, while his supporters fought them back.

At the head of the opposition was the mayor of Troy himself. With the city in turmoil for weeks, finally the mayor ordered Weld out of Troy, and Weld accepted the inevitable.[85] Although this defeat may have infuriated Weld, it only enhanced his reputation among the antislavery forces of the nation. William Lloyd Garrison praised his bravery, and the numbers of young men who held him in the highest esteem were emboldened by his unconcern for self as he came near to martyrdom.[86]

Charles Finney looked upon these frenzied activities with interest and support. After all, he had been a leader in the interests of reform, and the Benevolent Empire, for years, and it could hardly be denied that slavery was the evil that cried loudest for reform in the country. For Finney, however, it was one reform among many. There can be little doubt that he was somewhat disturbed at the prospect of so many of his youthful, energetic, and highly idealistic converts turning aside from initial intentions to become clergymen, and taking up, however temporarily, the cause of antislavery. To Finney, this was laudatory, but it was also, perhaps, succumbing to the enthusiasms of the day, preferring to be pelted with eggs by mobs rather than to enter the more plodding, unexciting work of preaching the gospel. He held tightly to his conviction that all reforms were good and necessary, but that working with souls was the ultimate reform, and therefore the most necessary.

For Finney the most pressing insight (and also the most elusive) was to comprehend that all evils that afflict human society—wrongs done to women, slavery, drunkenness, war, and all the rest—were but natural consequences of *sin*, and that if faithful pastors attacked this central evil by the cure of conversion, in time all subordinate evils would begin to diminish. To him, mounting campaigns against various problems was a noble thing, but if it was done at the expense of the central Christian mission, evangelism, then it was like spanking the giant dragon but not slaying it. And he simply could not understand why of all the intelligent Christians he knew, including Weld and the Tappans, so few could grasp this insight.

The opposing view, that urgent problems demanded separate remedies, was surely driving a wedge between Finney and these friends. The Tappan brothers had been somewhat miffed with Finney since he had taken a temporizing attitude toward several matters involving blacks at the Chatham Street Chapel. However self-serving, their feelings toward Finney are understandable: they had supported him in every endeavor he had undertaken, including the latest costly gamble at Oberlin; yet he failed to reciprocate and support them in all their policies. By late 1835 and continuing through 1836, Lewis Tappan was accusing Finney of cowardice and "sinning against conviction" in letters to Theodore Weld. To such charges Weld gave an animated rebuttal. On October 14 Tappan wrote voicing several acrimonious sentiments, and Weld's reply is so full of insights and distinctions that it deserves to be quoted at length:

Oberlin, 17 Nov. 1835

My dear brother Tappan,
I received yours of Oct. 14 some days since at Elyria. I am quite at a loss what to say in reply to that part of your last letter which treats of Brother Finney. That Finney is a coward I cannot believe and for this simple reason: I have seen in him more frequent and more striking exhibitions of courage physical and moral than in any other man living. That brother Finney has been (as you say you fear) "sinning against conviction" I cannot believe. An acquaintance with him of the most *intimate* character for *nine years* forbids me to harbour the suspicion for a moment. Everything in his character and history — all that I have seen of him — (and nobody has seen more of him) goes utterly against it.
Nobody on earth could convince me that *you* were deliberately "sinning against conviction." And if you were to do *just the things* which you allege against brother F. I could account for it on a supposition far more charitable than to suppose you were sinning against conviction. I have looked over all the facts and details in your letter on this subject and have talked the whole over and over with brother Finney, and I find my mind exactly in this state. 1- I do not believe he has been "*afraid*" of anything except of *doing wrong*. 2- I believe he is an abolitionist in full. 3- That he has given the subject as much prominence in his preaching, and at Communions, etc., *as he conscientiously believed was his duty*. 4- I have no doubt but he has thought, felt, said and done less on the subject than he should have done. . . .
The truth is Finney has always been in revivals of religion. It is his great business, aim and *absorbing passion* to promote them. He has never had hardly anything to do with Bible, Tract, missionary, Education, Temperance, moral Reform and anti slavery societies. . . .
I fear it is one of your bessettings my brother to put upon actions *bad* constructions, and to infer hastily wrong motives upon *too slight* grounds. You recollect we talked this all over one night at your fireside. Now for *me* to lecture *you* on this po[i]nt is I con-

fess a good deal like Satan rebuking sin. The truth is my dear
brother we both need a great deal of *faithful dealing.* God grant
we may always get it.[87]

As might be assumed, even such strong sentiments from Weld
did little to assuage Lewis Tappan's peevishness toward Finney. It is
not so much that Weld's intercession did not placate Tappan. Rather,
it is quite likely that there was some correspondence between Tappan and Finney, no longer extant, which fanned the sparks to a hotter
flame in Tappan's mind.

His diary records his increasing anger[88] in the spring of 1836, when
Finney returned to New York City and there were several agitated meetings between them over what Tappan had tried to do at the Chatham
Street Chapel in Finney's absence. It had irritated Tappan greatly that
black members were seated in the upper balconies, dubbed "nigger
heaven," and he had launched a determined effort to abolish this practice and bring the blacks down to the main floor. When Finney returned to the city in mid-February he immediately counteracted this
attempt, to Tappan's outrage. Completely unsatisfied with Finney's
response to his charges of weakness on the slavery issue, Tappan combined this with the rebuff to his attempt to desegregate the blacks
and vented his ire to his diary. Finney, he wrote, was doing much "injury to the anti-slavery cause," and he was "unsound on the slavery
question." He sourly commented that "God's blessing in this ch[urc]h
is withheld because the minister & the ch[urc]h have not done their
duty in reference to people of color."[89]

Apparently, during their meetings over these vexing differences
between them, Finney had attempted to maintain an attitude of equanimity as Tappan raged on. He had done so in the hope that he might
cool the merchant's temper by his own example. Tappan, already in
bad financial straits and fast losing power in the benevolent societies
because he and his brother were no longer able to contribute the large
sums of former years, was in no mood to be mollified, and Finney's
calm only agitated him the more. Their meeting ended on a bad note,
with Lewis Tappan refusing to speak to Finney. The evangelist had
not wanted this, and he wrote to Arthur Tappan, pleading for understanding, on April 30, 1836:

I admit that the distinction on account of color and some
peculiarities of physical organization, is a silly and often a wicked

prejudice. I say often, because I do not believe that it always is a wicked prejudice. A man may certainly from *constitutional taste* feel unwilling to mar[r]y a colored woman or have a daughter mar[r]y a colored man and yet be a devoted friend of the colored people. . . .

You err in supposing that the principles of Abolition and Amalgamation are identical. . . . Abolition is a question of flagrant and unblushing wrong. A direct and outrageous violation of fundamental right. The other is a question of prejudice that does not necessarily deprive any man of any positive right. . . . Now it appears to me that to make these two questions identical is to give the opposers of Abolition a great advantage over us in point of agreement, and that to bring forward and insist upon Amalgamation just now would do infinite mischief to our cause.[90]

If Arthur Tappan attempted to reconcile his brother with Finney, his efforts were as fruitless as Theodore Weld's. A petulant letter from Lewis Tappan to Weld on March 1, 1836, demanded to know why Weld had "excluded 3 or 4 colored men from your Convention in Ohio," and Weld was forced to spend half a dozen pages in straightening out this misunderstanding.[91] The letters continued to fly back and forth. On April 5 Weld wrote to Lewis Tappan, obviously pained to the end of his endurance and toleration, "I was grieved and sick at heart [over] that part of your letter in which you speak of our dear brother Finney very like *vindictiveness.* . . . I know Finney is not a perfect man . . . but yet take him for all in all, when shall we look on his like again?"[92]

As Charles Finney returned to take up his work at Oberlin in May of 1836, this increasingly acrimonious give-and-take with Lewis Tappan, and Tappan's threats to cease financial support of Oberlin, combined with the common knowledge that the silk importing firm was in dire straits, may have influenced Finney to decide that he should not be overly concerned with the Tappans, but that he must follow his own lights. Certainly Weld had kept Finney informed of Tappan's charges and countercharges; the evangelist knew too that Weld had defended him courageously in all the salvos of letters. Believing increasingly that he had been correct all along in urging the Lane rebels and others to go into the ministry and treat abolition as a sideline, Finney now attempted to swing Weld to his point of view decisively in July 1836. Perhaps Finney sensed that Weld was coming to a crucial point in his life after the defeat at Troy, New York, in May and June,[93] and that he would welcome support and reorientation. Without question, Finney sensed that the slavery issue would continue to divide

revivalist Christians, and he was very apprehensive that unless abolitionists took a less strident and harsh tone, the nation would be led
into civil war in short order.

Utilizing his conviction that sin was at the core of all human
disorders, and that conversion was the only remedy for sin, Finney
believed that he had arrived at a stunning conclusion: a nationwide
revival would best prepare the land for the alleviation of all its ills,
including slavery! Using his most persuasive rhetoric he wrote to Weld
on July 21:

> Br. Weld is it not true, at least do you not fear it is, that we are
> in our present course going fast into a civil war? . . . How can we
> save our country and affect the speedy abolition of slavery? This
> is my answer. What say you to it? The subject is now before the
> publick mind. It is upon the conscience of every man, so that now
> every new convert will be an abolitionist of course. Now if aboli-
> tion can be made an append[a]ge of a general revival of religion
> all is well. I fear no other form of carrying this question will save
> our country or the liberty or soul of the slave. One most alarming
> fact is that the absorbing abolitionism has drunk up the spirit
> of some of the most efficient revival men and is fast doing so to
> the rest, and many of our abolition brethren seem satisfied with
> nothing less than this. . . .
>
> The causes now operating are in my view as certain to lead
> to this result as a cause is to produce its effect, unless the publick
> mind can be engrossed with the subject of salvation and make
> abolition an appendage, just as we made temperance an append-
> age of the revival in Rochester. Nor w'd this in my judgment re-
> tard the work at all. I was then almost alone in the field as an
> Evangelist. Then 100000 were converted in one year, every one of
> which was a temperance man. The same w'd now be the case in
> abolition.[94]

Underscoring the fact that antislavery was making its agents into
frenzied and defiant men was the recent behavior of Henry B. Stanton, Finney wrote, who deserved a severe castigation for exhibiting
"the spirit and the language of a slave driver."[95] Finney immediately
turned to impress the same message on those under his instruction
at Oberlin, hoping that if he influenced enough of them he might win
his case for the new approach.

About the same time that Finney wrote the above letter, Sereno
W. Streeter wrote to Weld, "Mr. Finney is making a strong effort to

have us Evangelize instead of abolitionizing. . . . It is possible that Mr. Finney will be dismissed from his charge in New York and devote his whole time *here*. He wants to take us out and train us in the field. He will make an effort to have us go with him this winter."[96]

Within a few weeks the matter came to a head. Four of the Lane rebels wrote to Weld at once, on August 9, 1836. The last letter to Weld was from the staunch abolitionist James A. Thome, who stated that "I feel almost like weeping my eyes out" when he read what Streeter and Alvord had written, for "it looks so much like desertion in the hour of darkest trial." He wished to be more exact in informing Weld why the divisions in the group were coming about:

> It may be well to state more explicitly than Bro. Allan has the occasion of this division amongst us. Bro. Finney has had two meetings of our class within the last month to consider this matter. He poured out his soul before us in agony in view of our continuing in the abolition field—said that his great inducement to come to Oberlin was to educate the young men from Lane Seminary (our class)—that the revival part of the church were looking anxiously for us to enter upon the work of Evangelists, and would be exceedingly grieved if we did not—that we would accomplish the abolition work much sooner by promoting revivals—that the present unholy excitement in church and state, which the *present system of measures* had raised, and was directly calculated to *increase*, would soon end in civil war—that the only hope of the country, the church, the oppressor and the slave was in *wide spread revivals*.
>
> Such considerations as these, coming from Bro. F. and accompanied by his fervent earnestness, were designed to make a powerful impression upon hearts so much attached to him. We all felt their influence. But we discussed the various points with him for several hours, stating the reasons which induced us to continue in the ab[olitionist] field.[97]

Despite the sincere defense of Charles Finney that Theodore Weld had made to Lewis Tappan, it is apparent that from this time forward Finney and Weld drew apart, and the cordial relationship they had enjoyed for ten years was never again the same. Surely this was not wanted by Finney, who wished for Weld to continue regarding him as a spiritual father whether or not he was able to swing Weld around to his point of view. But Weld was certainly distressed at the insistence with which Finney presented his view to the Lane rebels. Reacting to Finney's attempts to influence them, Weld became more determined himself to put upon the field a dynamic cadre of antislavery agents, and at the May meeting of the national society he was commissioned to expand the number of agents to seventy.

Weld left New York in July 1836 to go on an arduous four-month search, "winnowing the nation" for "men of the most unquenchable enthusiasm and the most obstinate constancy."[98] By November over fifty of "the Seventy" had been selected, and they gathered in New York for a period of rigorous training under Weld's management. Characteristically, from November 15 through December 2 Weld drove himself unstintingly. William Lloyd Garrison and other antislavery leaders were in attendance. Robert H. Abzug has described those weeks:

> A number of people addressed the meeting, but according to Garrison all revolved around Weld. . . . It was an intense time for all. Day after day delegates met from nine to one, from three to five, and finally from seven to nine in the evening. Theodore tested himself to the limit. Despite a severe cold and failing voice, he spoke often and at length, and kept long hours—sometimes until two or three in the morning—preparing material for presentation. By the final day of the convention, Weld, the master orator training those who would follow, could not speak above a whisper.
>
> Ironically for Weld, the very acceptance and adoption of a strategy for which he had so long fought marked an end to his own participation. The agents' convention was his swan song as an orator. After his final whispered phrases at New York, he rarely ascended the speaker's platform for the fifty-seven remaining years of his life.[99]

This was the beginning of a period of major changes not only for Weld, but for Finney, the Tappans, and others as well. In the period 1836–1837, Weld not only lost his voice but went into periods of depression and debilitating exhaustion. The Tappans, along with multitudes of other businessmen, went into bankruptcy in the Panic of 1837. In the Presbyterian Church, the Old School majority in the General Assembly exscinded the New School, causing a schism that lasted from 1837 to 1869. And Charles Finney, now gone from the Presbyterians but unquestionably partly responsible for the split in the denomination, underwent major changes in his own life as he entered further into the life of an academician, and watched as the Second Great

Awakening rapidly declined and the men whom he had converted—
the Lane rebels and others—spurned his advice for the most part and
became fervid abolitionists.

As the years went on, Asa Mahan became increasingly disen-
chanted with the Lane rebels whom he had supported during their
rebellion at the seminary in Cincinnati. Perhaps from the wisdom
of his own years, he later said that, while still at Lane, "several of the
most talented among them" refused to attend church services, because
they could "receive no benefit from the discourses of Dr. Beecher or
any other pastor in the city." Mahan went on, sadly, "Of these young
men, every one, as far as I could learn, afterwards made shipwreck
of the faith. Only two or three of them entered the ministry at all,
and they soon after left it, under the influence of some of the absurdities that then obtained."[100]

This is, of course, an exaggeration, certainly born out of Mahan's
own dismay. Lawrence Lesick, after giving a very extensive coverage
of the Lane rebels, offers this more balanced judgment:

> It is apparent that the conflict in the relationship between evan-
> gelicalism and antislavery had several ramifications. Some of the
> rebels gave up the antislavery of the Lane debate and rebellion
> for evangelicalism. Others discarded much of evangelicalism in
> favor of antislavery and reform. Weld, and perhaps others, gave
> up both.[101]

OBERLIN PERFECTIONISM

The abolitionist dream obsessed a goodly number of the Oberlin theological students, but the faculty itself—Asa Mahan, Charles Finney, John Morgan, and Henry Cowles—in the fall of 1836 began to stress another product of the religious ultraism of western New York State, perfectionism. This doctrine of the life of perfect holiness and freedom from sin, as Whitney R. Cross has reminded us,[1] had a history in that state going back to its early settling. Much of Burned-over District perfectionism differed little from traditional Methodist teaching stemming from John Wesley, and this can be seen as one contributing source, but unquestionably there were other sources, now lost to history.

It is known that a James Latourette of New York City left the Methodists about 1828 and drew around himself a group seeking holiness, and it was from this group, as far as can be known, that some adherents went to Albany by 1830 and associated with students in Nathaniel Beman's Troy and Albany School of Theology. As this faction proliferated, some of the prominent names were Chauncey Dutton, John B. Foot, Simon and Charles Lovett, and the two Annesley sisters. There is a possibility that Theodore Weld's brother Charles may also have been connected with the group.[2] Eager to spread their ideas, they were found in New Haven, Long Island, western New York, and Ohio within a few years. Cross has found that a second group of perfectionists existed in central New York by 1832, and among the leaders of its various branches were Hiram Sheldon, Jarvis Rider, Erasmus Stone, David Warren, Sophia Cook, Lucina Umphreville, and Jonathan Burt. Charles Weld, ever drifting about among ultraists, was well known to these people by 1834.[3]

These names were eclipsed in time by the well-known John Humphrey Noyes, who was born in Brattleboro, Vermont, in 1811. He graduated from Dartmouth College in 1830 and was converted soon after. Deciding for the ministry, he attended Andover Seminary and Yale Divinity School. He announced that he was sinless in 1834, and for perfectionist and adventist views he was ousted from Yale. It was about this time that he went to New York City and, at the suggestion of Charles Weld, called at the Finney home. Finding that Finney was away on his Mediterranean voyage, Noyes reported:

> By Weld's suggestion I next called on Mrs. Finney, wife of Rev. Charles G. Finney, who was then absent on a voyage for his health. When I made known to Mrs. Finney my profession and my object in calling, she entered into conversation with me on spiritual subjects with considerable interest. I gathered from what she said, that she and her husband were thinking much on the subject of holiness, but were fearful of the errors and fanaticism connected with it.[4]

During his time at Yale, Noyes had formed a close friendship with James Boyle, the former disciple of Father Nash who pastored a free church in New Haven. On August 20, 1834, Boyle, with some assistance from Noyes, founded *The Perfectionist* magazine.[5] During its two-year span this paper circulated among all the New York cults and served as their chief exponent, although Noyes left Boyle after a few months over some differences. For several years after this Noyes drifted about, attempting to mature his theology and meeting with William Lloyd Garrison, the New York philanthropists, and others. He gradually came to dominate the entire eastern group of perfectionists.

Knowing of Finney's growing interest in perfectionism and hoping to claim the evangelist as one of his coterie, Noyes was delighted to report to his mother on March 30, 1837, "Finney, who has been corresponding with some of the brethren here, sent for and received the whole of *The Perfectionist*."[6] Noyes was encouraged by this, and immediately wrote to Finney. He received this answer:

I have often heard of you, and of your extravagances of course. But, precious brother, I have learned not to be frightened if it is rumored that anyone has received any light which I have not myself. . . . I have inquired after you this winter, but have not been able to learn where you were. You are well acquainted with my beloved brother Boyle. I had hoped to see him, and have a full explanation of his views, but believe he has gone west. . . . Now brother, I should like in the warmth of Christian love to converse this matter over with you, and learn whether you have discovered any hidden rocks on the coast, and dangerous quicksands upon which an inexperienced navigator is in danger of falling. I have no fear of the doctrine of holiness — perfect, instantaneous, perpetual holiness; and know full well that like justification, sanctification is to be received by faith.[7]

Noyes was obviously delighted by the attention paid him by the famous evangelist, and reported that "immediately after the receipt of this letter, I went to New York, and had an interview of several hours with Mr. Finney. . . . I rejoice that I have an opportunity by publicly testifying, that the candor and kindness of his behavior toward me was surpassingly beautiful and refreshing. In the course of our conversation, he bore witness repeatedly and with warmth, that he perceived in me no indications of insanity."[8]

Finney would later reconsider his evaluation of Noyes and perfectionism. By 1837 he had learned that several of the itinerants were unstable and inclined toward bizarre fanaticisms, and there were already enough clues to Noyes' being of the same stamp to have alerted Finney. The mention of "insanity" by Noyes himself bears testimony to this. At any rate, in a few years it became apparent that Noyes was developing strange notions of complex marriage and sexual "transactions," and Finney was forced to accept the truth. In 1840 at Putney, Vermont, Noyes established a commune, and by 1846 he was propagating ideas of biblical communism, complex marriage, male continence, population control, mutual criticism and education. This commune lasted until 1848. In that year he founded the second commune, at Oneida, New York, and this lasted until 1881. Under intense public pressure he left the United States in 1876, and lived in Ontario until his death, in 1886.[9]

In the mid-1830s, Oberlin was not so isolated for its people to be unaware of much, if not all, of the perfectionism of New York. The fever of perfectionism was abroad, and it was easily caught by those constitutionally inclined toward ultraisms. Oberlin's settlers were recruited from the class in which New York perfectionism was prevalent, and they had not forgotten their past or broken off their lines of communication when they came to Ohio. Especially among the theology students of Oberlin the literature from Noyes and Boyle had an avid reading audience, and it served, as James H. Fairchild has said, "to raise the question of obligation as to the degree of holiness which Christians might attain."[10]

Fairchild has pointed out that, even without the perfectionist influences flowing out of New York, the Oberlin faculty of theology might have developed an indigenous version simply because of the type of men they were. The gathering of a group of men such as Finney, Asa Mahan, John Morgan, Henry Cowles, and the founders, John Jay Shipherd, John Keep, and others, in a remote place like Oberlin, served to concentrate their personal power specifically on the cultivation of the spiritual life. Previous to their coming to the Ohio wilderness each had been adherents of the Yale New Divinity or of Finney's new measures, and their endeavors had concentrated on the evangelism of the lost. But at Oberlin the situation radically changed: there, in a sparsely populated area, where "there was only here and there a sinner to be converted,"[11] it was natural that they would turn their attention to the perfecting of the saints.

The theologians turned upon the students and settlers with all the intensity of the revivals out of which they had come. "It was not a rare thing," Fairchild declared, "for a large portion of the congregation, after a searching sermon by Prof. Finney or Pres. Mahan, to rise up in acknowledgment that they had reason to apprehend that they were deceived as to their Christian character, and to express their determination not to rest until their feet were established upon the Rock."[12] And yet both Finney and Mahan claimed that they did not realize that they were in effect preaching perfectionism from the first gathering of the college community. Benjamin B. Warfield has clearly stated the problem:

> One of the odd circumstances connected with the situation was that Finney and Mahan knew perfectly well what perfectionism was. They had lived with it in Central and Western New York: their companions in their evangelistic work there had preached it in their presence: their followers had often rushed headlong into it. They themselves had kept their skirts free from it; partly, no doubt, because of their engrossment with the prior matter of conversion; more, no doubt, because of the mystical and anti-

nomian form taken by "the New York Perfectionism," which was abhorrent to them as preachers of righteousness. But they could not help knowing that perfectionism lay at their door; and yet they drove on, preaching an essential perfectionism without, they say, being aware of it.[13]

Warfield's point must be underscored; the New York forms of perfectionism were shot through with socialistic, mystical, and communitarian ideas and antinomian theology, all of which made them completely unacceptable to Finney and Mahan. Boyle, Noyes, and the others in New York, in largely casting aside the restraints or sanctions of the corporate approval of the whole churchly community and of the Bible, had already gone deeply into the antinomian notion that they were responsible to no authority other than God, not even to those appointed by God to regulate human behavior. Holding that under the gospel dispensation the moral law is of no use or obligation, inasmuch as faith alone is necessary to salvation, the New York perfectionists thus took ground that would outrage and offend Charles Finney, whose perfectionism was based upon precisely the opposite approach to behavior. Finney would declare later that "a self-indulgent Christian is a contradiction,"[14] and he had taught since his conversion that self-denial, not license, was the key to Christian morality. To him, Noyes' ideas were shocking and scandalous, and Oberlin perfectionism rejected them outright.

The first real manifestations of Oberlin's version came in the summer of 1836, curiously at the same time as the question arose, whether the Lane rebels would become abolitionists or clergymen. A group of young men at Oberlin had formed a missionary society, and to prepare for their anticipated careers they determined to put away sin and advance in holiness. At a devout consecration meeting they committed their lives to a godly walk, pledging to indulge in known sins no longer. "They left the meeting," D. L. Leonard records, "feeling that they were pledged to a life of entire obedience, chiefly from the side of duty—the obligation and the possibility of it."[15] Immediately the rumor flew that the members of the missionary society had all become perfectionists, although, of course, not of the New York variety.

Meanwhile, Asa Mahan was undergoing changes in his own understanding of theology. For several reasons he felt depressed over the state of the church and the low tone of Christian living, and he and a colleague prayed about this and sought answers from scripture.

"While thus employed," he recalled, "my heart leaped up in ecstasy indescribable, with the explanation, 'I have found it.' . . . The highway of holiness was now, for the first time rendered perfectly distinct to my mind."[16] Mahan always thereafter regarded this discovery as pivotal in his life, a "second conversion." Whether Finney was having similar qualms or not, we do not know, but naturally Mahan related the experience to him. "When my associate, then Professor Finney," he says, "became aware of the great truth that by being 'baptized with the Holy Ghost' we can 'be filled with all the fulness of God,' he of course sought that baptism with all his heart and with all his soul, and very soon obtained what he sought."[17] According to Mahan, it was at this time that Finney received "the second blessing," and the effects on the two of them were dramatic, giving a greater urgency and power to their preaching.

With this new dynamic, President Mahan began a series of revival meetings at Oberlin in the fall of 1836. He did most of the preaching, and there must have been many discussions between Finney and Mahan at this period, as they attempted to understand the full import of their new life of holiness. Still, in their discussions and throughout the revival, neither Finney nor Mahan saw clearly that they had adopted perfectionist principles, pure and simple. Mahan said that it was only "by subsequent reflection . . . that I became aware that the principles which I had practically adopted necessarily involved the doctrine of Christian perfection."[18]

The revival meetings continued to the end of the academic semester, at which the students and faculty would depart for the long winter vacation. At one of the last meetings, after Mahan had again eloquently propounded the ideas of holiness, which now thoroughly absorbed him, a young man who had recently graduated with the first theological class on October 10, 1836, rose to ask a question. This was Sereno Wright Streeter,[19] and he directed his question to Mahan and Finney, asking to what extent he could hope to be delivered from sinning. Could he actually receive entire sanctification in this life? He asked, "When we look to Christ for sanctification, what degree of sanctification may we expect from Him? May we look to Him to be sanctified wholly, or not?"[20]

Suddenly it dawned on Asa Mahan that he was not aware of the full implications of his own preaching. "I do not recollect that I was ever so shocked and confounded at any question before or since," he recalled. "I felt, for the moment, that the work of Christ among us would be marred, and the mass of minds around us rush into Perfectionism."[21] Whether or not they now saw the path before them clearly, Finney and Mahan realized that answers given precipitously could lead to great damage in impressionable student minds, and that wisdom dictated caution here, because they themselves were just beginning to comprehend the matter. They responded that much study would be given to their answers, and that the students would have them in due time, after the winter vacation.

With the conclusion of the fall term, Finney was scheduled to return to the Broadway Tabernacle, which had been struggling on without him under the care of assistant pastors. It was expected, of course, that Finney's coming would be the highlight of the year for the church, and he planned a widely publicized series of lectures for weekday evenings similar to the lectures on revivals that he had given two years previously, and which had done so much to aid the ailing *New York Evangelist* and galvanize attention to the subject of revivalism. He said of this and of the new perfectionist stance:

> I had known somewhat of the view of sanctification entertained by our Methodist brethren. But as their idea of sanctification seemed to me to relate almost entirely to states of the sensibility, I could not receive their teaching. However, I gave myself earnestly to search the Scriptures, and to read whatever came to hand upon the subject. . . . This led me to preach in the Broadway Tabernacle, two sermons on Christian perfection. Those sermons are now included in the volume of lectures preached to Christians.[22]

Asa Mahan accompanied Finney to New York, and the two spent as much time as possible in studying and reading not only the Bible but also books such as John Wesley's *Plain Account of Christian Perfection* and the *Memoir of James Brainerd Taylor*, which they found very much to their liking. When it came time for Finney to begin the weeknight lectures, he did not devote the entire series to perfectionism, as might be expected, but limited his treatment to two sermons. Why he did so is somewhat puzzling. Although there is supposedly a continuity to his topics in that they were all addressed to "professing Christians," thus having to do with various aspects of the believer's life, the effect of the two lectures on perfectionism is certainly muted because of their being placed between sermons on other aspects in the book *Lectures to Professing Christians*. Did Finney feel that he and Mahan were such neophytes on the topic that he could teach no further at that point? Perhaps; but by 1840 he was able to write an entire series of articles on the doctrine for the *Oberlin Evangelist*, and these were immediately published in a full-length book. But it was hardly Finney's style to be modest in the proclamation of any teaching, and so reticence, or the admission that he was yet a learner on this, seems unlikely to be his reason for giving but two lectures on the new and urgent doctrine.

As with the *Lectures on Revivals of Religion*, Joshua Leavitt asked if he might transcribe the spoken lectures for immediate publication in the *New York Evangelist*, and then publish them in book form. As Leavitt accomplished this difficult task, editing was kept to an absolute minimum, and phrases such as "all of you who are here tonight" are frequent in the printed versions. In the first of the two sermons on perfectionism, Finney immediately disavowed the other forms that were causing such antipathy:

> Here let me observe, that so much has been said within a few years about Christian Perfection, and individuals who have entertained the doctrine of Perfection have run into so many wild notions, that it seems as if the devil had anticipated the movements of the church, and created such a state of feeling, that the moment the doctrine of the Bible respecting sanctification is crowded on the church, one and another cries out, "Why, this is Perfectionism." But I will say, notwithstanding the errors into which some of those called Perfectionists have fallen, there is such a thing held forth in the Bible as Christian Perfection, and that the Bible doctrine on the subject is what nobody need to fear, but what everybody needs to know. I disclaim, entirely, the charge of maintaining the peculiarities, whatever they be, of modern Perfectionists. I have read their publications, and have had much knowledge of them as individuals, and I cannot assent to many of their views.[23]

Finney was well aware that he was entering into troubled waters, and this attempt to dissociate his new thinking from that of Noyes, Boyle, and others would not serve to quell criticism for long. But he was completely justified in insisting that there were numerous and major differences between Oberlin perfectionism and Noyes' version. The propagation of complex marriage and communitarian ideas that Noyes undertook were not the only areas of disagreement with Finney and Mahan. In addition Noyes claimed that once persons had achieved full sanctification or freedom from sin, they could never lose such a state. Finney, on the other hand, taught that a life of holiness depended on continuing obedience to the moral law of God. If persons strayed from the path of complete rectitude and disobeyed God, Finney said, they would lose their sanctification until they had thoroughly repented. On this point, James Fairchild wrote:

> There was little said about *sinlessness* in connection with this experience. Perhaps Pres. Mahan was less cautious than others in this respect, and sometimes gave the impression that it was his privilege and duty to testify that under this new experience he was free from the consciousness of sin. Others occupying public positions carefully refrained from such expressions; and confession of sin was, as before, an element in public prayer.[24]

In these two lectures, the first real exposition of Oberlin perfectionism, Finney did not approach the topic without prior theological commitments; all the characteristic traits of his earlier thinking are included. All virtue consists in disinterested benevolence. There is no such thing as a fallen nature, or an inherited depravity; sin consists only in individual acts, which are uniformly indulged in by all human beings. To avoid the charge that God might condemn something for which humans would not be responsible, we have no obligation beyond our ability; we can do all that we ought to do, for we can freely respond in choice to God's demands. All depends, ultimately, upon whether our own will responds to or rejects the influences of the Holy Spirit. These are the familiar concepts that form the skeleton of his thinking.

Almost immediately, Finney mounted an attack upon the Wesleyan doctrine of "evangelical perfection" given to believers by God's grace completely apart from the demands of the Old Testament law, although Finney did not identify the target of his attack:

> I am to show what Christian perfection is; or what is the duty actually required in the text.
> It is perfect obedience to the law of God. The law of God requires perfect, disinterested, impartial benevolence, love to God and love to our neighbour. It requires that we should be actuated by the same feeling, and to act on the same principles that God acts upon; to leave self out of the question as uniformly as he does, to be as much separated from selfishness as he is; in a word, to be in our measure as perfect as God is. Christianity requires that

we should do neither more nor less than the law of God prescribes. Nothing short of this is Christian perfection. This is being, morally, just as perfect as God. . . .

The command in the text, "Be ye perfect, even as your Father which is in heaven is perfect," is given under the gospel. Christ here commands the very same thing that the law requires. Some suppose that much less is required of us under the gospel, than was required under the law. It is true that the gospel does not require perfection, as the condition of salvation. But no part of the obligation of the law is discharged. The gospel holds those who are under it to the same holiness as those under the law.[25]

Having delivered what was intended to be a polemic against the Wesleyan conception, Finney then moved ahead to attempt to demonstrate that it is the plain duty of the Christian to achieve perfection in this life. Should there be doubts or objections, Finney claimed that "God wills it."[26] The scriptures are full of injunctions to the point, and the Savior explicitly commanded all Christians in the Sermon on the Mount (Matthew 5:48) to be as perfect as God. If we examine the Bible, he declared, throughout "you will find that it is everywhere just as plainly taught that God wills the sanctification of Christians in this world, as it is that he wills sinners should repent in this world."[27]

But not only that; all the promises and prophecies of God concerning sanctification of believers "are to be understood of course, of their perfect sanctification."[28] If we make them to mean anything less than full and complete perfection, Finney declares, and therefore speak of a partial obedience, we speak of that which is absurd. And further still; throughout the Bible there is a "great blessing" promised, whether it be under the Abrahamic covenant, or later: "All the purifications and other ceremonies of the Mosaic ritual signified the same thing. . . . Those ordinances of purifying the body were set forth, every one of them, with references to the purifying of the mind, or holiness."[29] And not only that, but the perfect sanctification of believers is the express object for which the Holy Spirit is promised to them.

Benjamin Warfield has responded to these precise claims:

Every one of these propositions is true; and none of them is to the point. The whole point at issue concerns the process by which the believer is made perfect; or perhaps we would better say, whether it is by a process that he is made perfect. Avoiding the hinge of the argument, Finney endeavors to impale his readers on dilemmas. "If it is not a practicable duty to be perfectly holy in this world, then it will follow that the devil has so completely accomplished his design of corrupting mankind, that Jesus Christ is at fault, and has no way to sanctify His people but by taking them out of the world." "If perfect sanctification is not attainable in this world, it must be either from a want of motives in the Gospel, or a want of sufficient power in the Spirit of God." It would be a poor reader indeed who did not perceive at once that such dilemmas could be applied equally to every evil with which man is afflicted—disease, death, the uncompleted salvation of the world. . . . If freedom from death is not attainable in this world, then it must be due to want of sufficient power in the Spirit of God. If the world does not become at once the pure Kingdom of God in which only righteousness dwells, then we must infer either a want of sufficient motives in the Gospel, or a want of sufficient power in the Son of God. There have been people who reasoned thus: the point of interest now is, that it was not otherwise that Finney reasoned—and that accounts for many things besides his perfectionism. It is a simple matter of fact that the effects of redemption, in the individual and in the world at large, are realized, not all at once, but through a long process: and that their complete enjoyment lies only "at the end."[30]

In these two sermons Finney was obviously limited in the amount of time he had to explicate his new ideas, but the surprising thing is that, in the series of lectures he wrote for the *Oberlin Evangelist* on the same topic in 1840, which were immediately brought together in book form under the title *Views of Sanctification*,[31] he added little of importance to what he had already said. Finney was throughout the two sermons, as in 1840, consistently taking Pelagian ground, in line with his previous utterances. Even the natural, unregenerate person has much natural ability, and the power of choice. Christ and the Holy Spirit can work on human beings only by bringing motives for action to bear on them, or by persuading them to act for their own benefit.

This Pelagianism got Finney into real difficulty in the sermons. He said, "The greatest difficulty, surely, is when selfishness has the entire control of the mind, and when the habits of sin are wholly unbroken."[32] Well and good; but the Augustinian and Pauline answer is, of course, that God's all-powerful grace intervenes, and can in numerous ways alter the sinner's path and mind-set. But Finney will not have this. He continued, "This obstacle is so great, in all cases, that no power but that of the Holy Ghost can overcome it; and so great, in many instances, that God himself cannot, consistently with his wisdom, use the means necessary to convert the soul."[33] His phrase "no power" can mislead; Finney has already made clear that the Holy Spirit uses no power except the power of persuasion, which is entirely external to the natural person. Now, he has just stated that, "in many instances," God himself is powerless to effect the conversion of the unregenerate person. Such people, then, are beyond hope of salvation. They are too far gone in depravity for even the grace of God to redeem them.

Warfield has replied to this:

> We have thus reached the astonishing conclusion that men may be too sinful to be saved. They are saved, or they are not saved, according to their determination in sin. Moderately sinful souls can be saved, very sinful souls are beyond the possibilities of salvation. This no doubt is good Pelagian doctrine: it is not Paul's doctrine or Christ's. We are surprised to find it here where Finney had started out to prove that evil habits cannot inhibit the attainment of perfection, because they do not inhibit the attainment of conversion. We have ended by proving that "in many instances" they can and do inhibit the attainment of conversion; and that, whether we are converted or not does not depend therefore on God who in many cases is helpless in the face of our sinfulness, but on the degree of our sinfulness.[34]

As Charles Finney revealed the first accounts of the new Oberlin perfectionism to his listening and reading public, the year 1837 dawned, gloomy and foreboding. It was to be an evil year in many senses. For the Tappan brothers, financial difficulties had been piling up since the disastrous fire of December 1835, and there were hopes for a while that they could come back to a stable condition. Theirs was not the only company to proceed headlong into the multiplied troubles of finding credit hard to obtain at any rate of interest, tradesmen canceling orders or begging extensions on their arrears, and dismal prospects on every hand. Bankruptcies in New York City were increasing, and consternation was being expressed everywhere. Adding to the general confusion was the fact that America had had no previous experience with financial panics as in Europe, and the citizenry did not know what to expect.

As money became more and more scarce, the banks themselves were hard pressed. Arthur Tappan, as one of the best known businessmen in the nation, sent his brother Lewis to Philadelphia for a conference with Nicholas Biddle, president of the Bank of the United States. As Lewis said, he "urged on Mr. Biddle the importance of sustaining the firm, and suggested that any disastrous occurrence to it might involve the stoppage of several others."[35] Biddle agreed, offering Tappan the sum of $150,000, and for a while it appeared that this relief might be sufficient to keep Tappan's credit good.

But the debtors of the firm failed to fulfill their responsibilities, and Tappan appealed again to Biddle for more funds. Biddle replied that it was with the greatest reluctance he was obliged to deny the second application of such a respectable house, but the bank simply could not comply. When Lewis returned from his second trip to Philadelphia, Arthur immediately asked what had happened. As Lewis told him Biddle's answer, Arthur sadly decided to suspend payment of his debts. "He bore the disappointment like a man who had done all he could to avert a calamity," Lewis wrote, "and when it came, resigned himself to the will of God. He felt deeply the necessity of adding to the general distrust, of delaying the payment of his debts to those who needed the money, of disappointing the hopes of parties that leaned upon him, of not continuing the stated sums he had engaged to pay for the support of benevolent objects, and the other contributions he was wont to make."[36] On May 1, 1837, Arthur Tappan publicly announced his suspension of payments to a stunned citizenry. When the total amount of his indebtedness was revealed — $1.1 million — the public could hardly countenance the fact. Throughout the nation, few merchants even grossed such an amount in the best of years.

Lewis Tappan wrote of the Panic of 1837 and of the desperate means that he and his brother used to keep the firm from making all their creditors insolvent as well:

> After taking a full survey of his position and means, he, with the full concurrence of his partners, made a proposition to the creditors of the firm, to give new notes for existing ones, payable in six, twelve, and eighteen months, with interest. . . . The creditors generally complied with the terms proposed, with full reliance that they were the best that could prudently be offered. Within the time the whole amount of indebtedness, with the accruing interest, was paid, together with a million and a half dollars for the purchase of new goods. The scarcity of money during the

time bore heavily upon debtors, and Mr. Tappan had to pay tens of thousands of dollars for extra interest, to enable him to meet the notes given on retiring the previous notes. The result was deemed very creditable to his financial skill and laborious exertions. It raised him still higher in public estimation as an honorable merchant.[37]

While the Tappans manfully attempted to weather the financial storm, Charles Finney in 1837 underwent continued changes in his own life. For one, his family was further enlarged on March 16 with the birth of his fourth child, Julia. Expecting this child, his wife Lydia had remained in Oberlin when Finney had gone to New York City at the end of 1836. Clearly, the fact that he could hardly bring his wife and children with him to New York each year was one among several factors that weighed heavily in his decision to resign from his ministry at the Broadway Tabernacle. In addition, there was the question of his health, and the fact that Finney's importance to the cause at Oberlin meant that he was attempting to serve effectively there as well as be the pastor of a large and vitally important pulpit-centered church. Which had the greater claim upon his loyalties and energies? Even if his health were good, to have tried to perform two such tasks would have taxed the energies of any man. When the question of loyalty had to be faced, the potential of the situation at Oberlin proved to be the stronger attraction.

It must have been extremely difficult for Finney to resign from his fine new Broadway Tabernacle, but if he were to consider his own health and future, there seemed to be little choice. Therefore, on April 6, 1837, Finney sadly tendered his resignation. Lewis Tappan told what happened next:

> The Rev. Messrs. George Duffield, and Jacob Helffenstein, had been elected co-pastors. . . . The church of the Tabernacle was a Congregational one; and after the resignation of Rev. C. G. Finney, Mr Duffield, then residing in Philadelphia, was invited to fill the pastoral office. He preached very acceptably several months. Early in the year 1838, a conference took place between leading individuals of the Dey Street Presbyterian Church (formerly the First Free Church, Rev. Joel Parker, pastor,) and the Congregational church at the Tabernacle, (Rev. George Duffield, pastor elect,) with a view to sell the Dey Street church, and unite both churches at the Tabernacle. . . . The result was, the two churches were united

at the Tabernacle in the spring of 1838, under the ministry of
Messrs. Duffield and Helffenstein; and it was agreed that they
should be connected with the Third Presbytery of New York, with
such principles of the Congregational order to be engrafted as
should be approved by the united churches.

In the course of the following summer, Mr. Helffenstein having contemplated taking charge of a congregation in Pennsylvania,
[a] self-constituted committee . . . conceiving that it might promote the interests of the united churches to have Mr. Duffield
retire also, took measures to induce both of the pastors elect to
resign. . . . Two meetings of the church were held, at which Lewis
Tappan was called to officiate as chairman. Letters from both of
the pastors elect were laid before the last meeting, in which Mr.
Helffenstein absolutely, and Mr. Duffield qualifiedly, resigned; and
it was voted by the church to accept their resignations.[38]

Lewis Tappan still retained his membership, but the Broadway
Tabernacle, along with every other church in the land, faced bleak
times. In addition there was dissension among the members, as indicated in the quotation above. The faction that engineered the resignations of Duffield and Helffenstein wanted to call Joel Parker to the
pulpit, and in this it eventually succeeded, to the anger of Lewis Tappan. Isaac M. Dimond had gone into bankruptcy and had departed.
The *New York Evangelist* had ceased publication for a time, and Joshua
Leavitt had gone to become editor of the *Emancipator*, thus throwing
his energies more fully into the abolitionist struggle. Every bank in
New York City had closed, as well as many across the nation. Multitudes were thrown out of work, and there was rioting in the streets.
Churches were closing, or considering the prospect of consolidat-
ing with other congregations so as to keep their doors open. In May
1837 an Oberlin agent in New York State waxed eloquent as he cried,
"A dreadful panic has seized the nation. Order has become confusion. . . . Paper is almost worthless. I found myself unable to get a
seat in the stage from Syracuse to Madison altho' I had as current
paper money as the nation affords. The stage agent said it would not
buy oats for their horses." Then the agent described the public reaction: "Banks have refused to redeem their Bills. Mobs have been re-
sorted to, to compel them to do it. . . . The pressure is immense.
Famine stares thousands & thousands in the face."[39]

When Charles Finney returned to Oberlin in April 1837, the situation there was equally bleak. By that month the banks of Ohio were
refusing to perform any functions except to receive deposits or pay-

ments. Oberlin until this time had depended for financial support almost entirely on Arthur and Lewis Tappan and the Professorship Association in New York City. With the Tappans in dire straits, the other members of the association wrote on May 12 to Levi Burnell, Oberlin's secretary and treasurer, that they resolved that the school "was worthy of being sustained," but they regretted that they were unable to keep up their pledges, and they suggested that subscribers pay twenty percent on their commitments.[40]

Throughout the summer and the early fall of 1837 the financial situation worsened across the country. Finney reported that the situation for Oberlin was if anything worse than at other schools, because of the general hatred for its antislavery stand. "The great mass of the people of Ohio were utterly opposed to our enterprise," he declared, "because of its abolitionist character." Threats were frequently made that those who sympathized with slavery from the surrounding area would come and tear down the college buildings and scatter the students. "A democratic legislature was, in the meantime, endeavoring to get some hold of us," Finney feared, "that would enable them to abrogate our charter."[41] Faculty salaries at the Oberlin Collegiate Institute could not be paid, and the teachers "did not know, from day to day, how we were to be provided for."[42]

As the winter of 1837 approached, Finney reported that he was very worried about providing for his family throughout the winter:

> Thanksgiving day came, and found us so poor that I had been obliged to sell my travelling trunk, which I had used in my evangelistic labors, to supply the place of a cow which I had lost. I rose on the morning of Thanksgiving, and spread our necessities before the Lord. I finally concluded by saying that, if help did not come, I should assume that it was best that it should not; and would be entirely satisfied with any course that the Lord would see it wise to take. I went and preached, and enjoyed my own preaching as well, I think, as ever I did. . . . After the meeting, I was detained a little while in conversation with some brethren, and my wife returned home. When I reached the gate, she was standing in the open door, with a letter in her hand. As I approached she smilingly said, "The answer has come, my dear;" and handed me the letter containing a check from Mr. Josiah Chapin of Providence, for two hundred dollars.[43]

However, the end was not yet in sight for the travails of church people during the malevolent year of 1837. Charles Finney had recently departed from the Presbyterian Church for the Congregational fold, but this did not prevent the Presbyterians from suffering a major schism during 1837. As we have seen, for some years conditions for making this almost inevitable had been ripening, and only by the merest chance Finney had escaped being the target for those in the Old School who saw in him, and others, all that they considered wrong with the New School ideas. We have seen that it was probably Finney's omitting to publish any of his more substantial collections of sermons before 1831 that led the Old School purists to turn instead to the young pastor of the prestigious Philadelphia First Church, Albert Barnes, and to try him for heresy on the basis of his published New Divinity sermon, *The Way of Salvation*. At the General Assembly of 1831 Barnes was cleared of the charges, but not before the entire denomination was reeling from the effects of the rift between the two factions.

Having been rebuffed in the Barnes case, those of the Old School who were distraught over the inroads made in the denomination by what they considered heresies, next turned their attention westward. There the students of Nathaniel Taylor had infiltrated the denomination in larger numbers through the provisions of the Plan of Union, and there a showdown had to be made. In the year 1833 Edward Beecher, Theron Baldwin, and Julian Sturtevant, all former Congregationalists and former members of Yale College's "Illinois Band" who had been active in founding Illinois College, were charged with heresy, and were eventually exonerated by the synod. Then in 1835, it was Lyman Beecher's turn. Dr. Joshua L. Wilson, pastor of the Cincinnati First Presbyterian Church, was interested in Lane Seminary, and when Beecher was considering the presidency in 1832 Wilson repeatedly wrote to him urging his acceptance. But when Beecher came to Cincinnati, Wilson, an ardent advocate of the Old School, suddenly discovered that Beecher was full of abominable New Divinity notions.

Six weeks after the Lane rebels left Cincinnati for Oberlin, Wilson charged Beecher before the presbytery of having denied original sin, imputed guilt, and humanity's inability to save itself. For years Beecher's prestige in New England, and his adroit nimbleness in ecclesiopolitics and playing all sides, had largely kept him out of trouble in the looser Congregational polity. But suddenly, in the Presbyterian judicatories, he was in the toils. He thrashed and wrestled, trying to dodge the plain meaning of his own words, as Wilson pursued him relentlessly. Acquitted by the presbytery, Beecher appealed to the Synod of Cincinnati, and when asked there of his relationship with Charles Finney, Beecher replied that he had heard more truth from him than from any other man in the same length of time. "I have felt the beatings of his great, warm heart before God," he said.[44]

When Beecher was also acquitted by the Synod, Wilson appealed to the General Assembly of 1836. There Beecher was again exonerated when he delivered a statement of strict (and insincere?) orthodoxy, having learned that he could get away with no less. The *Biblical Repertory and Theological Review* of Princeton Seminary was satisfied with his statement but dubious of his integrity, and in its 1837 review of his *Views in Theology* it highlighted discrepancies between his earlier published works and Calvinism. Frantic after the long legal battle, Beecher lashed back by excoriating the *Review*, his former friends Asahel Nettleton and Joseph Harvey, the editor of the *Southern Christian Herald*, and Joshua Wilson. The *Review* answered by suggesting that Beecher was verging on insanity.[45]

It was everywhere apparent that a showdown was inevitable. Led by George Junkin, president of Lafayette College, the conservatives charged Albert Barnes before the Philadelphia Presbytery with heresy, and the trial was taken on appeal to the Synod and then to the 1835 General Assembly. Here the Old School had a sufficient majority to condemn his writings and to depose him from his ministerial standing. However, at the 1836 Assembly, the New School managed to secure a majority of commissioners, and they immediately proceeded to reverse the direction of the previous year. Because the Barnes case was emblematic of the entire position of the New School, it was imperative for them that he be reinstated, and "Mr. Barnes, by a strong vote, was restored to his ministerial standing, with no condemnation passed upon any of his sentiments."[46]

Then the majority swiftly turned to another vexing issue, the Old School's impending threat to dissociate the church from the American Board of Commissioners for Foreign Missions (ABCFM) and the American Home Missionary Society (AHMS). This assembly was held in Pittsburgh, where an agency of the Pittsburgh Synod, the Western Foreign Missionary Society, was being proposed as the replacement for the ABCFM. The New School majority rejected the proposal, and almost succeeded in merging the denomination's home mission board with the AHMS. Then, because the principle of "elective affinity" had been so helpful in allowing New School presbyteries to flourish without Old School interference in New York City and Philadelphia, the 1836 assembly broadened the policy, hoping to create still more presbyteries. And as a final stroke, the liberals united with the Congregationalists in founding Union Theological Seminary in New York City, which was expressly done without the auspices of the General Assembly in order to have a school that was beyond the control of the denomination.

Such imperious actions by the New School invited not only shock at the inroads but also retaliation. Until this time the Old School, for various reasons, had not been able to gain majorities consistently at the annual assemblies. Finally, and perhaps with some chagrin at their tardy realization of the threat to their common interests, the Old School divines joined ranks with moderates from the southern states, who had become persuaded that the New School advocates were not only heretics but also abolitionists.[47]

When the General Assembly came together on June 5, 1837, it was firmly in the control of the Old School coalition. Wasting no time whatsoever, the conservatives moved to abrogate the Plan of Union. Next, the following act was moved:

> Be it resolved . . . that in consequence of the abrogation by this Assembly of the Plan of Union of 1801, between it and the General Association of Connecticut, as utterly unconstitutional, and therefore null and void from the beginning, the Synods of Utica, Geneva, and Genesee, which were formed and attached to this body under and in execution of said "Plan of Union," be, and are hereby declared to be out of the ecclesiastical connexion of the Presbyterian Church of the United States of America; and that they are not in form, or in fact, an integral portion of said church.[48]

In addition the Synod of the Western Reserve was also exscinded from the church. Thus, in one decisive act in New York State alone nineteen presbyteries, 378 ministers, 444 churches, and probably 40,000–50,000 members were ejected from the denomination, and in the Western Reserve another 131 clergymen, 109 churches, and perhaps 10,000–20,000 members were taken from the rolls.[49] Then, in other actions, the conservatives made the Western Foreign Missionary Society the sole missionary board of the denomination, and warned the ABCFM and the AHMS not to consider themselves in future affiliated with Presbyterian work at home or abroad.

Undeterred by all of the tumult within the Presbyterian fold, and unmindful that at least in some measure he had been a contributing factor toward the schism, Charles Finney busied himself during 1837 and 1838 with his academic work, the financial rigors of the time, and the development of Oberlin perfectionism. Part of this development entailed the dissemination of information about the Oberlin ideas. The *Oberlin Evangelist* was established in November 1838 for this purpose. It was edited by Henry Cowles, was issued twice a month, and soon attained a circulation of five thousand copies. Various members of the Oberlin faculty contributed articles, with those of Finney, Asa Mahan, and Henry Cowles the most frequent. During 1839 Cowles authored a series of articles that were reprinted under the title *Holiness of Christians in the Present Life*. Asa Mahan's book entitled *Scripture Doctrine of Christian Perfection*, published in 1839, also was first run as a series in the paper.

In 1839 also Finney wrote the series that appeared in 1840 under the title *Views of Sanctification*. In it Finney demonstrated that he had drifted somewhat from his original close approximation to John Wesley's ideas, who had said "Christian perfection . . . is not absolute. Absolute perfection belongs not to man, nor to angels; but to God alone. It does not make a man infallible; none is infallible while he remains in the body."[50] But in his book, *Views of Sanctification*, Finney declared:

> *Entire and permanent sanctification is attainable in this life. . . .*
> It is self-evident that entire obedience to God's law is possible on the ground of natural ability. To deny this, is to deny that a man is able to do as well as he can. The very language of the law is such as to level its claims to the capacity of the subject, however great or small that capacity may be. "Thou shalt love the Lord thy God with all thy heart, with all thy soul, with all thy mind, and with all thy strength." Here then it is plain, that all the law demands, is the exercise of whatever strength we have, in the service of God. Now, as entire sanctification consists in perfect obedience to the law of God, and as the law requires nothing more than the right use of whatever strength we have, it is of course forever settled that a state of entire and permanent sanctification is attainable in this life on the ground of natural ability.[51]

Here Finney was doing far more than attempting to counter Noyes' brand of perfectionism with a biblically based exposition of holiness. He was ultimately concerned with the problem of the anemic responses he saw even the most earnest Christians making to the scriptural standard of righteousness. *Must* Christians fall away from the pursuit of holiness, Finney was asking, after being soundly converted and making a good start in the Christian life? If it were a common thing that Christians lapsed, what was the power that they lacked? Finney found the answer in John Wesley: the role of the Holy Spirit in actually bringing into human lives the sanctity provided by Christ's atonement. Here Finney began to use a vocabulary that Wesley feared, of Pentecostal terminology. The "baptism of the Holy Spirit" was to be normative for all Christians, Finney declared. Although he did not profess to have this second work of grace until 1843,[52] Finney was determined to work toward it, saying:

> The provisions of grace are such as to render its actual attainment in this life, the object of reasonable pursuit. It is admitted that the entire and permanent sanctification of the Church is to be accomplished. It is also admitted that this work is to be accomplished "through the sanctification of the Spirit and the belief of the truth." It is also universally agreed that this work must be begun here; and also that it must be completed before the soul can enter heaven.[53]

Identification with the aberrations of John Humphrey Noyes brought increasing censure upon Oberlin in the popular mind. The obvious route, then, for Finney, Mahan, and the others would have been to drop the use of the term "perfectionism," and adopt some other term instead. But other than the occasional use of "sanctification," the damaging term continued to be widely used by the Oberlinites. And that was not the only reason for the rising tide of dislike for the Oberlin theology. Not only did it take a stance akin to John Wesley in the matter of sanctification, but Finney took an increasingly Arminian[54] position (again similar to Wesley's) regarding the eternal security of the believer.

To understand the furor this would cause, it must be borne in mind that all the natural clientele of Oberlin were either Congregationalists or Presbyterians — both Calvinists in greater or lesser degree — and that by his going against the Calvinist tenet of the "perseverance of the saints," Finney would only antagonize them still further, in addition to their previous anger over perfectionism. This is to say that full-blown Arminians, such as the Methodists, were not one of the groups to which Oberlin might easily appeal, and Finney's choosing to do this can only appear to be a reckless act that would

further alienate erstwhile supporters. After all, enough of the old doctrines were being haggled over or denied by Taylor, Finney, and other
liberals, and perseverance was not among them. For Finney to begin
warfare on a new front was only to bring down greater enmity on his
own head, and make it impossible henceforth to claim to be in the
line of Jonathan Edwards. One may say that to deny the security of
the believer is the inevitable tendency of the doctrine of natural ability run rampant, but it is also to say that here Finney had abandoned
a crucial article of faith for most New Englanders and New Yorkers.

Finney's new idea, that believers can lose their salvation, was
revealed in the *Oberlin Evangelist* of December 16, 1840, in a lecture
on 1 Corinthians 10:12, "Let him that thinks he stands, take heed lest
he fall." Most in the line of Edwards would have stressed that this does
not relate to security of salvation, but to the power of temptation, and
would have agreed with Charles Hodge's statement, "This probably
is the kind of false security against which the apostle warns the Corinthians, as he exhorts them immediately after to avoid temptation. . . .
The same apostle . . . at other times breaks out in the most joyful
assurance of salvation, and says that he was persuaded that nothing
in heaven, earth or hell could ever separate him from the love of God.
Romans 8:38,39."[55]

But Finney took Paul to mean salvation itself:

*This confidence, whatever may be its foundation, cannot of it-
self secure the soul against falling into sin and hell.*
1. Because, if it is founded in any thing naturally good in us, it
is ill-founded of course.
2. If it is founded in what grace has already done for us, it is ill-
founded; for however much grace may have done, it has not
changed our nature. Our constitutional susceptibilities remain
the same. It has not so changed our relations and circumstances
as to exempt us from temptation; and consequently, nothing that
grace has done, or ever will do for us, can render our perseverance
in holiness *unconditionally* certain.
3. If this confidence is based upon our purposed watchfulness,
prayerfulness, experience, or faith; these, independent of the sovereign grace of God, afford no such foundation for our confidence,
as to render it at all certain, or even probable, that we shall not
sin again.
4. If this confidence is based upon the promises of God, it will
not render our perseverance *unconditionally* certain; because the
promises of God are all conditioned upon our faith, and the right
exercise of our own agency. . . .

5. Any confidence in the promises of God, either for sanctification or final salvation, that does not recognize this universal principle in the government of God, is ill-founded and vain; because
God has revealed this as a universal principle of his government;
and whether expressed or not, in connection with each promise,
it is always implied.[56]

To anyone but a novice in theology, this central section of Finney's lecture contains a number of problems. For one, Finney offered
no other ground of spiritual confidence but these five, and he said
repeatedly that these depend upon the believer's continued faith and
watchfulness, which if suspended render the promises of God of no
effect. Incredibly, Finney mentioned nothing of the atonement of
Christ as the basis of reconciliation of humanity to God and the foundation of the believer's confidence for salvation—almost as if it did
not exist! Equally incredibly, he mentioned nothing of the Holy Spirit's
office of sealing and building up believers, thus giving them confidence, as in the sense of Ephesians 1:13–14.

But perhaps most astonishing is Finney's point 2, which cannot
be explained on the basis that Finney was quibbling with others over
some obscure theological detail. Here Finney either inexplicably lost
his grasp of Christian doctrine, or he deliberately denied a basic
teaching of the faith, upon which nearly all Christians have been
united—that believers receive a new nature when they become regenerate (2 Corinthians 5:17; Romans 7:6–8:17). Even the New School
and New Divinity rebellion against the doctrine of original sin never
began to suggest that the believer did not receive a new nature at regeneration![57]

With all this in view, it becomes easy to understand why criticisms of Oberlin theology mounted. William Wisner was not the first
when he told Finney in 1839 that a term such as "assurance of faith"
would be far more acceptable than "perfectionism." "I confess for myself," he said, "that there is something revolting to my feelings in having a mere man profess to keep the love of God perfectly."[58] In the
next year Josiah Chapin warned Finney that the *Oberlin Evangelist*
was given over far too much to the teachings of perfectionism.[59] Many
New School adherents, especially after the Presbyterian schism, were
embarrassed at the mounting cry that the Oberlin ideas were the logical tendency of their positions. Most of them severed any connections
with Finney.

Even Finney's closest friends, Herman and Amelia Norton, were quite unhappy with the new stance. Amelia wrote to Lydia Finney in 1839, "When *Oberlin Perfectionism* is spoken of, [we have] often exclaimed 'it is not so. Mr. Finney is not a perfectionist!'" But then Amelia unburdened herself to her friend since childhood, saying, "you must *excuse* us, if in every point we do not agree with you."[60] We have no record as to Herman Norton's feelings on the subject, but in all likelihood they matched his wife's, and it is not difficult to imagine that this issue placed a real strain and anxiety on the close relationship these two couples shared.

In synods and presbyteries throughout the church, committees were frequently appointed to examine the ideas of Oberlin and any of its graduates who came before judicatories for ordination. Two American missionaries to Siam were dismissed by the ABCFM for adherence to perfectionist ideas of the Oberlin variety.[61] In 1841 the Presbytery of Cleveland (the closest to Oberlin) published an 84-page booklet that denounced the tendencies of perfectionism as dangerous to the church, stating:

1. That if it is through the truth God sanctified his people, Oberlin Perfectionism can only hinder the work of grace in their hearts. 2. That any who suppose they have been benefitted by reading the *Oberlin Evangelist,* and other works devoted to the propagation of this system of error, are probably deceived in one of two ways; either they are mistaken in thinking they are growing in grace, or they have been benefitted by what constitutes no part of the *peculiarities* of that system.[62]

Also in 1841 the Synod of Ohio issued a statement declaring, "We regard the errors of that body called the Oberlin Association, as very great. . . . Their preachers ought, by no means, to be received by our Churches as orthodox ministers of the Word."[63] At the same time the Fairchild brothers graduated from the Oberlin Theological Department and applied to the Huron Presbytery for licensure; that body, however, refused even to examine them, because they professed adherence to the Oberlin doctrines.[64]

What was especially distressing to Charles Finney was the awareness that several of his long-time friends joined in condemning the Oberlin position. Samuel C. Aikin, a member of the Presbytery of Cleveland, was among those signing its denunciation of Finney. Perhaps even more painful to him was the realization that Nathaniel S. S.

Beman was one of the signatories of the following condemnation from the Presbytery of Troy in 1841:

> Resolved: That in the judgment of this Presbytery, the doctrine of "Christian Perfection" in this life, is not only false, but calculated in its tendencies, to engender self-righteousness, disorder, deception, censoriousness and fanaticism. . . .
> Resolved, That it is the duty of all orthodox ministers to acquaint themselves with this error. . . .
> Resolved, That we view with regret and sorrow, the ground taken on this subject by the Theological Professors at Oberlin.[65]

Normally Finney did not respond in print to criticisms. In this case, however, he did respond, and this in itself is indicative of how deeply he was hurt by Beman's action, as the language of Finney's reply, in the *Oberlin Evangelist,* conveys: "I cannot, however, refrain from saying, that when I saw the name of one whom I greatly loved, and with whom I had often taken sweet counsel, attached to that report, my heart felt a kind of spontaneous gushing, and I almost involuntarily exclaimed, 'Et tu, Brute.'"[66]

The Presbyterians were often joined by Congregationalists in condemning Oberlin perfectionism. In official actions the General Association of Connecticut did so in 1841, the Genesee Association and the General Association of New York followed suit in 1844, and the Fox River Congregational Union of Illinois did the same in 1845. Lyman Beecher did not publicly denounce Finney, but in a letter he did berate the doctrine in 1844, and this was answered in the *Oberlin Quarterly Review* by Professor John Morgan.[67] Coming later but with no less stinging effect was an attack by the man who followed Finney at the Broadway Tabernacle, George Duffield. In 1847 Duffield wrote a booklet, *Warning Against Error,* excoriating perfectionism. It was issued with the sanction of the Presbytery of Detroit and the Synod of Michigan.[68]

Historians of Oberlin College have often declared that most of the religious press of the United States was arraigned against the school and its perfectionist stance, which is undoubtedly true. Of course neither Finney nor Mahan were of the type to accept this meekly. Not only through the pages of the *Oberlin Evangelist* but also in perfectionist conventions they struck back as best they could, holding such meetings from July 1841 through 1843 in New York and Ohio. And, increasingly, Finney abandoned his previous principle of ignoring attacks, and began to answer some of the most vicious ones. But as Finney and the theological faculty continued to further perfectionism, their best efforts could not arrest the indifference and eventual decay into which the doctrine fell at Oberlin. Finney taught it to the end of his long life, and, after Mahan's departure from Oberlin in 1850, he was even more active than Finney in attempting to promote it, publishing the books that have been noted, toward the end of his life. However, the vogue of the doctrine at Oberlin was rather short-lived. James H. Fairchild said of it:

> The visible impulse of the movement to a great extent expended itself within the first few years. . . . It became more and more a matter of doubt whether the seeking of sanctification as a special experience was on the whole to be encouraged. . . . Indeed, if I have rightly observed, it came at length to be the fact, more than at first, that persons of less balanced character were more likely to share in the special experience.[69]

FINNEY THE EDUCATOR

Gradually the effects of the Panic of 1837 receded across the nation, and the economy regained some vitality. At Oberlin the financial situation was precarious for some years. Because of the school's adamant stand on intensely debated issues, especially abolition, it was difficult to find contributors to replace those who had gone into ruin during the panic. But in Great Britain, where slavery had been abolished some years previously, there were many who sympathized deeply with the American slave, and who recognized that Oberlin was *the* center of antislavery agitation in the Northwest. Among them were numerous Quakers who were persons of property.

Recognizing the potential of England to alleviate their financial plight, in March 1839 the trustees of the college sent John Keep and William Dawes to "Oberlinize" the sister nation, armed with personal letters of introduction to prominent English reformers. They also carried a circular, drawn up by Theodore Weld and signed by outstanding American abolitionists, which described Oberlin as "the great nursery of teachers for the coloured people in the United States and Canada," "an admirable school for the training of anti-slavery lecturers and preachers," and the only college "in the United States in which the black and coloured student finds a home, where he is fully and joyfully regarded as a man and a brother."[1] Throughout Scotland and England the two men lectured and made friends whenever opportunity afforded, and in June 1840 their presence at the World Anti-Slavery

Convention in London gained them an additional number of supporters for Oberlin, especially among Quakers. When they returned to America late in 1840 they had collected the sum of $30,000 and had cultivated much good will toward Oberlin.

With these funds, and gifts from the immensely wealthy abolitionist Gerrit Smith,[2] Oberlin managed to survive somehow. Despite the dismal financial picture, students flocked to the school in increasing numbers, due largely to Charles Finney's influence and reputation. Where in 1835 there were approximately two hundred students, by 1840 there were about five hundred, and in 1852 the number had climbed to a thousand.[3] If sketches and wood engravings of the mid-1840s, and early photographs from the 1850s, can be trusted, the college campus by then had become rather handsome, with the impressive Chapel and the four-storied Tappan Hall dominating the quadrangle, and three smaller buildings, Oberlin Hall, Ladies' Hall, and Colonial Hall, off to its right. Still smaller buildings, and the homes of the faculty, were farther in the distance.

From the very beginning, the settlers at Oberlin had cherished the desire for a religious society that might be powerful in their community. In August 1834 John Jay Shipherd presided at a meeting that resolved that a church be formed, to be named "The First Congregational Church of Christ at Oberlin." When the congregation grew in size, its services for worship were moved from one location to another, from Oberlin Hall to Colonial Hall, and then still larger quarters were sought. Charles Finney had accepted the pastorate after his arrival, and he had immediately announced his intention to conduct a revival ministry, with the desire to convert as many students and citizens of the surrounding areas as was possible. In this he was quite successful, as might be expected. Indeed, the terribly difficult economic crisis may well have stimulated the turning to things of the spirit, and kept everyone mindful of even slight material blessings.[4]

It was natural that those who were so continually involved in matters of the spirit would long for an edifice specifically devoted to the worship of God, which would not have to be shared with the purposes of education in a college community. The minutes of the congregation record that on February 10, 1841, a meeting was held at which it was resolved to "proceed forthwith to take measures for building a meeting house."[5] On May 5, 1842, Elizabeth Maxwell, a student, wrote home to her mother about the effects of Finney's preaching: "The congregations are still growing larger. The Laboratory and Chapel are crowded every Sabbath. A site for the new church has been chosen, and we are told that work on it will begin soon."[6]

As pastor, Charles Finney was naturally at the center of activity. His good friend, Willard Sears of Boston, supplied the plans, which were probably designed by a prominent New England architect, Richard Bond, whom Finney had met while in Boston. The church was fortunate to have Deacon Thomas P. Turner, a Vermont-born house carpenter, on the building committee, and he was given full authority over construction. It is likely Finney had some say in drafting the plans, perhaps telling Bond what he wanted in the way of design. Possibly Finney wished to duplicate as much as possible the superb layout of the Broadway Tabernacle with its circular seating in the gallery and the possibility of eye contact from the pulpit with every person in the audience, to which the extant plans testify.[7]

With the entire community donating to the endeavor and assisting in whatever ways it could, on June 17, 1842, the cornerstone was laid. Appeals for funds were frequently published in the *Evangelist*, and recognition of gifts was also printed. But, due to lack of funds, work on the church went rather slowly. Finally, late in 1844, the building was sufficiently completed for the first services to be held there. In 1845 the unecclesiastical appearance of the structure—due to the flat front and lack of a portico or steeple—was rectified somewhat by the addition of a short tower, its design taken from an Asher Benjamin pattern book. Immediately, as Finney began to preach powerful sermons in the imposing new structure to packed congregations (it would seat perhaps one thousand,[8] and another two or three hundred might be crammed in the aisles and stairways), it became the locale for community revivals. One person stated early in 1846: "Our last communion season—March 15—was a day of precious interest, enhanced by the addition of fifty-two members to our church, of whom thirty-seven were by profession, and most if not all of them the fruits of the recent revival."[9] Charles Finney would remain as pastor of this congregation for thirty-seven years.

In the pulpit, his power over Oberlin students was immense. Years after their graduation, the most vivid memories most former students retained were of the First Church packed with people, and especially of Finney's withering sermons. "To go to Oberlin was to hear Finney, the great actor of the American pulpit,"[10] the college historian has well said, and "his glittering eyes, shaggy brows, beak-like nose and expressive mouth" symbolized perfectly all that Oberlin stood for. But to stress the hard and demanding mien of Finney was to overlook another side, although surely it was the harsher aspects that were re-membered most.

However, Finney also had his gentle side, and this was displayed best during his pastoral prayers, which were apparently the deliberate reverse of his behavior during the sermons. When praying, he became mild, full of love for God and for his hearers, and as intimate as if he were sharing confidences with the Lord in his own private devotions. "Supplications took the place of warning, tears the place of sweeping, stabbing gestures," Fletcher has said.[11] As the consummate actor of the national pulpit, Finney was always mindful of the effect of modification of tone and mood. Becoming as simple and artless as a child, the renowned orator on his knees poured out before God and his audience extemporaneous pleas for the sick and distressed of the congregation, for the welfare of the college, for the farmers, for the nation, and for any that needed divine assistance. Such a prayer could continue for five to seven minutes, and its effect would be melting, persuasive. Then, the prayer completed, Finney would rise to his feet, announce a hymn for all to sing, which would allow time for the transition in mood, and then launch into a penetrating discourse that riveted his hearers to their seats.

On Sundays Finney would normally preach at two services, one in the morning and another in the afternoon, and often the message of the morning would be abruptly cut at a convenient place, and Finney would announce that he would continue from that point later in the day. In addition it was the custom at Oberlin to have a service on Thursday afternoon at which Finney would preach.[12] Wright has said of this, "It was in his sermons upon the Sabbath, and upon Thursday afternoons, that one would hear his most complete and effective presentation of the great themes of the gospel. . . . It was through these means, in fact, that his influence became most extended among the vast body of pupils gathered at Oberlin."[13]

Finney mellowed a great deal after he came to Oberlin; every source bears this out, and we have noted already a gradual softening all along from his early stern, "denunciatory" ways. That was largely attributable to the polishing effect of the larger cities and his well-to-do supporters, who would of course tolerate no fanaticisms. But at Oberlin other forces acted to soften him still further. There, among friends and with admiring students coming distances to sit at his feet, harshness was inappropriate, except perhaps when dealing with certain subjects in the pulpit. His attitudes, reactions, motivations, hopes, and anxieties are illustrated in the fund of anecdotes involving Finney, though many of them are apocryphal and must be rejected. The newspaper writers of his time, both friendly and antagonistic, were eager to seize upon any extravagant story or humorous incident said to involve Finney and to give it currency. However, the well-authenticated incidents, especially of his life at Oberlin, are sufficiently numerous to give us many glimpses into the inner dynamics of the man.

On one occasion he preached to a large audience on the theme, "the signs of a seared conscience." At one point he stated:

> Just consider the condition in which I found myself yesterday. I engaged a number of men to make the garden and put in my crops; but when I went to look for my farming tools, I could not find them. Brother Mahan borrowed my plough some time ago, and has forgotten to bring it back. Brother Morgan has borrowed my harrow, and I presume has it still. Brother Beecher has my spade and my hoe, and so my tools were all scattered. Where many of them are, no man knows. I appeal to you, how can society exist when such a simple duty as that of returning borrowed tools ceases to rest as a burden upon the conscience?

The effects of this sermon on Oberlin were amazing. Very early the next morning, Frederic Norton was asked by his father to go out into the yard and calm down the watch dog, which was making a great din. Norton, who related this account, discovered that a neighbor living across the street, having borrowed a sawhorse, had attempted to return the item under cover of darkness, but as he climbed over Finney's fence he was seized by the watch dog. The sawhorse was lying nearby as mute witness. Throughout the day, farming tools came in from all quarters, and many of them Finney had never owned and never heard of previously. Presumably, the consciences of the guilty were relieved in all the environs of Oberlin!

All the professors and citizens of Oberlin had the best of personal relations with Finney, and with them he was most genial and lively. He recognized their personal weaknesses, and they his, and he could joke about them without giving offense. One of his colleagues was quite sluggish in his movements, and took a very long time to answer his door bell. When Finney rang it one day, the response by one of the children was quite rapid, but Finney had already walked off the porch to the front gate. Hearing the door opening, Finney turned round and exclaimed, "Why, is that you, George? You need not have been in so much of a hurry. I was on my way to the post office, and

I thought I would ring the bell as I went along, and stop as I came back."

Across northern Ohio, the summer of 1853 was hot and dry, the pastures were scorched, and a complete failure of the crops seemed likely. On a sweltering Sunday morning, Finney faced his congregation and prayed:

> We do not presume, O Lord, to dictate to thee what is best for us; yet thou dost invite us to come to thee as children to a father, and tell thee all our wants. *We want rain*. . . . Unless thou givest us rain, our cattle must die, and our harvests will come to nought. O Lord, send us rain, and send it now! Although to us there is no sign of it, it is an easy thing for thee to do. *Send it now*, Lord, for Christ's sake! Amen.

The service then proceeded, but Finney had hardly begun his sermon when the rain descended in such torrents that he could not be heard. He called out, "I think we had better thank God for the rain," and asked that they sing the hymn, "When all thy mercies, O my God, My rising soul surveys, Transported with the view, I'm lost In wonder, love, and praise."

Several years later another dry season came, and Professor Morgan prayed for rain. A slight downpour followed. Afterward, one student remarked that that was a remarkable evidence of answered prayer, but another said, "You ought to hear President Finney pray for rain. When Professor Morgan prays for rain, it just drizzles, but when President Finney prays, it pours!"

Charles Finney made little distinction between the church and the academic activities of the college; to him they were a unit, and he and the rest of the faculty were attempting to minister to the whole person. He saw his role as an educator simply as an extension of his mission, and threw himself into classroom instruction with the same zeal he manifested in the pulpit. This brings into the foreground the question of Finney's competence as an academician, obviously a debatable question. Even his enemies readily granted that he possessed a first-rate mind; it was his training, not his intellect, that was in question.

After Finney's appointment to the post of professor of theology, John Keep confided to Gerrit Smith that quite a few had questioned his educational background, feeling that he would fail at Oberlin from "lack of science."[14] He had, after all, no academic degrees and had gotten very little instruction that might be considered of college level. He had received from Benjamin Wright enough instruction and practical experience to equip him as a lawyer, and later from George W. Gale hardly enough training in theology to satisfy a not-very-scrupulous Plan of Union presbytery! As a lawyer or a clergyman he was adequately equipped, if barely; but as a college professor?

If there were doubts at first about Finney's ability in the classroom, his agile mind and autocratic manner compensated for his educational deficiencies. Many of the students had come from great distances to attend Oberlin largely on the strength of Finney's reputation —and as new students they had no other college experience with which to compare Oberlin. Then, too, he had been instrumental in the conversion of some of those from New York State (the Lane rebels and others), and those students regarded him with unfailing awe. It may be concluded, therefore, that although Finney would have been blocked from most other college faculties, at Oberlin much of the curriculum as it developed was molded around his ideas, and for that place and time he was ideal.[15] It might even be argued that Oberlin, with its abolitionism, perfectionism, and other aspects hated by most of the outside world, needed just such a magnetic, compelling person as Charles G. Finney if it were to survive.

The students were convinced that Finney had much to offer them. Back in the East in 1836 Joshua Leavitt was eager to help the Oberlin cause, and he printed in the *New York Evangelist* a letter from a student there:

> Neither have any of us had occasion to regret our coming here to place ourselves under Mr. Finney's instruction. He has commenced a course with us, which when completed will furnish us with a good practical knowledge of the whole field of theology. He has thus far given ample satisfaction in his department and evinced that he possesses every requisite for a skillful instructor. He does not pursue the old system, of teaching the opinions of great divines and scholars, as oracular authority.[16]

Another student, Elisha Sherwood, was a member of the first graduating class from Oberlin, in 1836, and he was so pleased with his education that he returned the next year to take more work under Finney's instruction, saying:

On the 6th of July, Prof. Finney gave us his introductory lecture to his course on pastoral theology, followed with thirty lectures embodying his rich experience, his sanctified common sense, enforced by the teachings of God's word, and pressed down upon our hearts by his fervent prayers.[17]

Sherwood was an ardent disciple of the great evangelist, believing that his work under Finney "was the most valuable of any course in my whole study." He told of one period in which, as was customary, Finney opened the class with prayer and then became so burdened that he kept praying the entire hour. Sherwood declared, "It was the richest hour of all my theological course. It was an hour that brought with it the enduring power of the Holy Spirit fitting us to be witnesses to the power of the Gospel. Oh, that every candidate for the ministry might enjoy such an hour."[18]

The courses in practical theology that Finney offered were obviously not run on the lecture method; one can hardly picture Charles Finney standing before a class and lecturing on Athanasius or Augustine! As in all he did, he demanded that the topics considered pertain directly to life. Attempting to involve the student completely in the process of learning, he used methods closely akin to today's seminar technique.

George Clarke described what he underwent, and the maturing effect it had on him: "A theme was assigned to each one, on which, after due preparation, he must discourse, and then 'be picked.' It set us all to thinking. The theme that at one time was given to me was Imputation, a doctrine which was then much discussed; and I well remember how I stood for three days and was questioned."[19] This was of course excellent practical experience, to assign to the students extensive reading and then demand of them that they be able to sort out all that they had read and organize it, and then coherently express it orally.

Finney himself said of his methods:

It is our custom in this Institution to settle every question, especially in theology, by discussion. I have now for twelve years been going annually over my course of instruction in this manner, and own not a little to my classes, for I have availed myself to the uttermost of the learning and sagacity and talent of every member of my classes in pushing my investigations. I call on them to discuss the questions which I present for discussion, and take my seat among them and help and guide them according to my ability; and not infrequently, I am happy to say, do I get some useful instruction from them. Thus I sustain the double relation of pupil and teacher.[20]

Oberlin was to be a demanding place, according to Finney and the rest of the faculty; as the manual labor system was to stimulate the physical side of the students, so the intellectual exercises were to be equally demanding. In his *Lectures on Revivals of Religion,* Finney had been devastating on the theological education of his day. He saw little good in it, even as he had refused to attend a seminary when the St. Lawrence Presbytery requested him to do so before his ordination. Now that he was in the full-time business of preparing ministers himself, it was time for him to put into practice all the methods he had upheld for years. What made effective pastors? (Finney was as pragmatic here as any Yankee could be.) *Results,* and nothing else! And that meant *souls converted!* "Those are the *best educated ministers* who win the most souls. . . . God forbid that I should say a word against an educated ministry! But what do we mean by an education for the ministry? . . . Let them be educated *for the work.*"[21]

Finney was very mindful that many students had read these criticisms in his *Lectures on Revivals* before coming to Oberlin, and that the theologs among them wished to be molded in his stamp, for they looked on him as the preacher par excellence. To effect a new method of clergy education, he therefore began with homiletics itself. Thrust the student out into the world—and *make him preach!* But no; students were too reticent (even at Oberlin). The snares of professionalism too quickly clutched at them, and they would give themselves over to laborious preparation, which killed the vital spark that might have set themselves, and others, on fire.[22] Even at his school he found this:

> In our school at Oberlin our students have been led—not by myself, I am bound to say—to think that they must write their sermons; and very few of them, notwithstanding all I could say to them, have the courage to launch out, and commit themselves to extemporaneous preaching.[23]

From the very first, the theological department occupied the front rank in the Oberlin Institute, certainly getting more attention than was given to the preparatory department or the collegiate department. This stems not only from Finney's driving force, but also from the fact that the teachers in that department were the leaders of the entire faculty. President Mahan, Finney, John Morgan, Henry Cowles, and later Henry E. Peck and James H. Fairchild, were all fine teachers whom the students could emulate. For forty years the course of study in this department remained almost unchanged. In the first or "junior" year the curriculum included "Introduction to the Study of the Old and New Testaments; Biblical Archeology; Greek and Hebrew Exegesis; Principles of Interpretation; Evidences of Divine Revelation; Sacred Canon; Mental and Moral Philosophy; and Compositions and Extemporaneous Discussion." In the second or "middler" year the theologs took "Greek and Hebrew Exegesis; Didactic and Polemic Theology; History of Theological Opinions; and Composition and Exposition Discussion." And in the third or "senior" year the curriculum included "Sacred and Ecclesiastical History; Church Government; Pastoral Theology; Sacred Rhetoric; Composition of Sermons; Exegesis (advanced); and Extemporaneous Discussion."

At the heart of the entire theological department was Charles Finney. Robert Fletcher did not exaggerate when he wrote, "Though there were other effective teachers in the old Theological Department, it was for forty years after its founding essentially a one-man institution."[24] Certainly this may be as much a weakness as a strength, especially in later years when Finney was far beyond his prime; and yet the students did not seem to take it as a weakness. When he was off preaching, as occurred so frequently, student attendance fell, and when he returned, it climbed again. With Finney giving so many central courses, and absenting himself so often, it was imperative that the small faculty of theology be flexible and able to take over his courses.

One of Finney's most important courses was didactic and polemic theology. Originally he designed the course to deal with the standard areas of theology, and the difference between it and what would be taught here in most seminaries was that student discussion played a much larger part. But after a few years he shifted the emphasis away from general Protestant teachings to stress his own views on human ability and freedom of the will, moral government, and sanctification.[25]

Another highlight of the theological course was reserved for the senior year: Finney's inimitable treatment of the whole area of the function of the clergy, expressed in practical theology. In the light of

Finney's great interest in a pragmatic approach to the training of pastors, and in view of his personal eccentricities, it was to be expected that he would make the course exceptional. He did. Four different students left notebooks on the course contents, one set taken in 1836, one in 1837, one in 1843, and one in 1857. In addition, there are in the Oberlin library three of Finney's own manuscript lecture outlines for practical theology. As the course was given, it was rapidly expanded. In 1837, Fletcher believed, it consisted of only half a dozen lectures, basically on etiquette and relations with the female sex. But by 1843 it had expanded to over twenty lectures, bringing in many more areas of concern.[26]

The expansion of the course suggests that Finney felt compelled to add more and more areas as he noted the deficiencies of his students. Probably he would have preferred to omit some of these, as being basic; yet he knew full well that some of the men, even at this late stage, needed to be brought up short in regard to their personal care and deportment. Some of them were from cultured homes in the cities, but many others were from farms and small towns and had unpolished manners.[27] From his contacts with the wealthy and the powerful, Finney had himself derived some refinement and polish since 1827. How often, one wonders, did he reflect on his own rather crude ways of yore?

Holding a high view of the clerical office, Finney instructed his students that they must possess "dignity of Character," not in some superficial or hypocritical way such as an "anti-social carriage," "affected sanctity," "studied reserve," or in officious "airs and manners," but rather in "such serious purity of conversation as to forbid all trifling in [their] presence." A clergyman, he instructed them, should have "such a compassionate earnestness of piety as shall force the impression that [he is] a serious and a holy man."[28] Then there were lectures on such diverse topics as overseeing church officers; the pastor's study habits; the care and feeding of the flock; relations with the opposite sex; how the minister should dress, care for his home, his horse, and his family; the preparation of sermons; pastoral visitation; business transactions; the conduct of church services; sincerity in a pastor; and — above all as of supreme importance — the choosing of a proper helpmeet, the minister's wife.

Oberlin graduates (and anyone else) must not use a dirty handkerchief; they must not pull off their stockings when they are out visiting; they must not put their feet and muddy boots on any of the furniture, especially on the sofa; they must not spit on the carpet;

and they must not blow their noses with their fingers! However incredible this advice may seem today, certainly it would not have been repeated year after year, if it were not needed by the unpolished country fellows who made up much of the student body. One of his illustrations (told as if *surely* no one here present would be guilty of such conduct) was of a young *clergyman* who "called on some ladies after walking some distance, took off his boots & hung his socks on the andirons the first thing"! And then there was another parson who "put his feet up in a window in a lady's parlor to enjoy the cool air!" His students were instructed strictly to clean their teeth and keep their nails cut short and cleaned. When they are invited to have dinner with a family, they must be especially mindful of their manners, he said. It was not proper etiquette for them to cut their meat with pocket knives, or to wipe their mouths on the tablecloth. Out of his own painful experiences, repeated many times over, Finney declared, he had been disgusted "in anxious meetings to smell the breath of a filthy mouth."[29] Surely there was much shaking of heads as those guilty of such antisocial conduct realized how many bad habits they would have to break, if they were to please the demanding Mr. Finney.

New ideas about health were another characteristic of the times. Phrenology and total abstinence from alcohol were symptoms of the quest for health that have been noted previously. Nor was Oberlin unique here; it simply pursued the ideal of health more assiduously than most other devotees. One might say that for Oberlin, what perfectionism was to the spirit, health was to the body. Inasmuch as other communities did not have the guiding doctrine of sanctification, perhaps this gives us a clue as to why Oberlin was obsessed with health as much as it was with perfection; they were, in a sense, kindred or parallel ideologies.

So we cannot begin a study of Oberlin's idiosyncracies relating to the perfection of the body with the colony itself. The roots go back to what has been seen of the manual labor scheme at the Oneida Academy in 1827, and to the stress on temperance during the Rochester revival of 1831. Finney's conviction of the holiness of caring for the temple of God (1 Corinthians 6:19), as exemplified in what he repeatedly declared about health and the seared conscience, came into a confluence with dietary and other fads of the time, and eventuated in the health movement at Oberlin. The stress on temperance during the Rochester revival needs no rehearsal, but it may be apropos to review the Oneida Academy regimen of manual labor. On George Gale's farm near Whitesboro, the day began very early for the boys enrolled in the academy, usually about four in the morning. To pay for their tuition, the students worked on an average of four hours a day, and their diet consisted of rice and molasses, codfish and potatoes, griddle cakes and molasses, with bread and milk being served the remainder of the time.[30] The system of manual labor was one of the first stated goals when the Oberlin Collegiate Institute was formed.

The health movement in America and England had a century-old history when Gale and others became convinced of its benefits. Several semipopular medical journals touted the cause in the America of the 1820s and 1830s. One, the *Journal of Health,* was published in Philadelphia from 1829 to 1833, and contained many of the ideas later espoused by Sylvester Graham. In it there were recipes for bran bread and other staples. Readers were urged to have only one type of food per meal, and corsets and feather beds were condemned. Little progress was made, however, until Dr. Sylvester Graham and Dr. William A. Alcott turned the movement into an actual reform. Graham became general agent for the Pennsylvania Temperance Society in 1830, and in time was convinced that intemperance in eating was as wicked and dangerous to the health as the drinking of alcohol. In 1832, during the cholera epidemic, he saw his opportunity and began to deliver lectures on the concept of proper diet and ways to escape disease. The public mind was ready for this, and numbers of people joined the cause. When Graham lectured in Boston, sufficient converts were made to dietary reform that the American Physiological Society was founded there in 1837, and Willard Sears, trustee of Oberlin and close friend of Charles Finney, was placed on the executive committee. Dr. Alcott, trained as a physician at Yale and cousin of Bronson Alcott, was also prominent in the movement.[31]

Briefly, Graham's principles were as follows: tea, coffee, tobacco, all alcoholic beverages, and other stimulants were prohibited; gravies and fats were prohibited; pastries and sweets other than maple syrup and honey were prohibited; pepper, oil, mustard, vinegar, and all other condiments were prohibited. Meat and fish were discouraged from the diet; instead, Graham recommended vegetables and fruit, and bread made of unbolted wheat; rice, sago, Indian corn, rye, and tapioca were also allowed "if plainly cooked." No one should overeat, and all must eat slowly and chew their food thoroughly. Taking medicine was discouraged; in its place abstinence from food was recommended as a curative. Regular exercise in the outdoors was demanded as essential to health. Too warm, tight clothing was discouraged. Bathing in warm or cold water was strongly encouraged, even in the wintertime. Seven hours of sleep were recommended for all, preferably from 10 P.M. to 5 A.M., but never after meals. Feather beds were thought to be highly detrimental, and ventilation for the bedroom was advised.[32]

Sylvester Graham had hardly formulated his opinions than Oberlin, along with other institutions, indicated its eagerness to adopt the latest panacea for all human ills, the use or disuse of this or that particular item of solid or liquid food. Both of Oberlin's founders, John Jay Shipherd and Philo P. Stewart, were early advocates of the view that tea and coffee were deleterious to the health. In 1832 Shipherd began requiring prospective colonists to sign a covenant, article five of which read as follows:

> That we may have time and health for the Lord's service, we will eat only plain and healthy food, renouncing all bad habits, and especially the smoking and chewing of tobacco, unless it is necessary as a medicine, and deny ourselves all strong and unnecessary drinks, even tea and coffee, as far as practicable, and everything expensive that is simply calculated to gratify appetite.

Charles Finney was also said to have adopted the Graham diet early in the 1830s when his health had declined, and he became convinced that it had helped him regain a measure of physical vigor.[33]

It may be asking too much of the imagination to believe that while these varied projects and emphases were being promoted, there was still another thrust receiving almost as much attention at Oberlin as revivalism. But it is so, and this great program was abolitionism. This, however, was not a short-lived fad like some of the others. It had been at the bone and marrow of Oberlin from the very beginning, and was surely a chief reason why the Tappans had been willing to give the school their backing.

Even before Theodore Weld came to Oberlin in the fall of 1835 to deliver his gripping series of lectures on abolition, in June of that year there had been a prayer meeting of most of the colonists there in behalf of the "downtrodden people of color." After the time of prayer, specific action was sought, and appropriate response was found in the formation of the Oberlin Anti-Slavery Society with 230 members. John Jay Shipherd became the first president, and he wrote, "Indeed, when the motion to resolve ourselves into an Anti-slavery Society was decided by rising, the congregation came up en masse, arm and soul to this good work of God."[34] Along with Shipherd, Finney and Mahan were the first to put their signatures to the constitution of the society. By winter the society had grown to 300 members. Soon other societies were added, the Young Ladies' Anti-Slavery Society with 86 members, and the Female Anti-Slavery Society with 48 charter members,[35] and in 1842 the Young Men's Anti-Slavery Society was organized.

Then, in August 1835, there occurred an episode that became a legend: Amos Dresser, a former student of Oneida Institute and Lane Seminary who had enrolled at Oberlin, went to Tennessee, sold a copy of Rankin's *Letters on Slavery*, and was seized by an infuriated crowd and horsewhipped. When he returned to Oberlin it was as a hero, and for the next dozen years Dresser told the story over and over on every possible occasion, and published it repeatedly.[36]

Charles Finney's position in the entire abolition movement at Oberlin was, as has already been seen in his struggle for the allegiance of the Lane rebels, a somewhat ambivalent one. He considered himself adamant in his opposition to slavery; but for many, his resistance to slavery was too moderate. In the frenzied heat of those years, when enthusiasts lost all sense of perspective as they threw themselves without reserve onto one side of the struggle or the other, Finney's attempt to hold a sensible, biblical, moderate stance may have been a greater contribution to the abolition of slavery than has been generally realized. Robert Fletcher has stated, "If the antislavery sentiment in Oberlin was so strong and so general, why then did the College contribute so few abolitionist lecturers after 1837? The answer is—the answer to so many queries about Oberlin—*Finney*."[37]

Finney's struggle with the Lane rebels over their choice of vocations has already been traced. The effect of his efforts may be noted, after the withdrawal of Theodore Weld's influence at Oberlin, in a letter from J. A. Thome to Weld written on February 7, 1839:

Since that time my views have undergone a change, favorable for the most part to the present mode of operations. It is likely however, that I still differ, in some respects, from yourself, and other prominent abolitionists. For example, I am of the opinion that if ministers & professing christians generally were as holy in heart & strong in faith, as they should be, they would further the interests of the oppressed more effectually by preaching the cross— the *Whole Cross* I mean—than by forming Anti Slavery Societies —composed indiscriminately of Christians, worldlings & infidels. The church *ought* to be an anti slavery Society (for certainly its charter is both an Anti Slavery Constitution and Declaration of Sentiments), and if it were there would be no need of other organizations for the same object. . . . But while the estate of church, the ministry, & the religious press remains as it now is, I am satisfied that direct Anti-Slavery efforts, such in the main as are now being made, are proper & necessary.[38]

If some were of the opinion that Oberlin should have been doing more for the abolitionist cause, others continued their opposition to the school over the years because, in their view, it was doing entirely too much for the slave. Finney noted that "the great mass of the people of Ohio were utterly opposed to our enterprise, because of its abolition character."[39]

Whatever calumnies were directed against Oberlin, the truth was in almost all cases something quite different. Undeniably, Oberlin was sold out to the abolitionist cause, but the charges of wild radicalism leveled against the school by Delazon Smith and hosts of others simply do not match the facts. What Oberlin *could* have been was epitomized in the position of William Lloyd Garrison. There were several instances of zealotry in behalf of runaway slaves, as the renowned "Rescue Case" of 1858–1859, and there is no denying that Oberlin was one of the most notorious refuges of fugitive slaves in the north.[40] The point is, however, that the school was prevented from veering into several extremes by Finney's moderate position on slavery, and it is no exaggeration to say that his view eventually prevailed among most of the faculty and students of the institution.

Garrison had founded the New England Anti-Slavery Society and his weekly, the *Liberator*, in 1831. Shortly before that, Arthur Tappan had paid a sum of money to secure Garrison's release from the Baltimore jail where he had languished. Quite naturally, therefore, the Tappans hoped that this firebrand, whom they genuinely liked and admired, would prove to be a man of sentiments similar to their own orthodox Calvinism. Increasingly, they found their hopes disappointed.[41] He was a master of quotable invective in the pages of the *Liberator*, and his unbridled vehemence lashed out increasingly at the things they held dear. At first they were puzzled that Garrison had never claimed conversion to Christ and joined a church. In July of 1836 they were upset to read an editorial in the *Liberator* in which he blasted "pharisaical" Sabbath-keeping.

Then, in the spring of 1837, Garrison came under the influence of John Humphrey Noyes. Garrison eschewed Noyes' ideas of Christian perfectionism and spiritual wifery, but he added to his own inclinations in those directions Noyes' pugnacious pacifism, antiinstitutionalism, and high-sounding logical absolutes. On March 22, 1837, Noyes warned Garrison that the United States, "a country which, by its boasting hypocrisy, has become the laughing-stock of the world, and by its lawlessness has fully proved the incapacity of man for self-government," was "ripe for a convulsion like that of France." But whereas infidels had rushed France into its revolution, Noyes went on, the United States was certain to be upset by the scriptures, by the reform movements, and especially by its own slave system and the abolitionists. Garrison and his fellow reformers must obey the scriptural command, "'Come out of her, my people, that ye be not partakers of her sins and of her plagues.'" If they disobeyed this, Noyes stated, a "UNIVERSAL EMANCIPATION FROM SIN" would never occur in America.[42] Although Garrison was hardly a devotee of the Bible, then or later, this mutilated quote from Revelation 18:4, and the similar sentiments of Paul in 2 Corinthians 6:17, resonated with his own delusions of superiority and grandeur, and immediately became his watchword in all things. In the June 30, 1837, issue of the *Liberator* he adopted Noyes' statement, "*My hope of the Millennium begins where Dr. Beecher's expires — viz.*, AT THE OVERTHROW OF THIS NATION."[43]

Before such sentiments the Tappans stood appalled. The situation, over which they liked to think they retained some control, had gotten entirely out of hand. The Tappans held little liking for Lyman Beecher for his part in driving the rebels from Lane Seminary, and especially for his spiteful act in the summer of 1836 when he went before the Congregational associations of both Connecticut and Massachusetts and persuaded them to pass — without a dissenting vote in either state — resolutions excluding both evangelists *and* abolitionists from the Congregational pulpits of these two states. In Gilbert Barnes' words, these were the actions of "an angry, vengeful old man" who was "impotent to harm abolitionism in the West."[44]

In retaliation for the exclusion of his agents from every pulpit in those states, Garrison dredged the language for epithets to excoriate the Congregational clergymen in his *Liberator*. These pastors stood "at the head of the most implacable foes of God and man," toward whom "the most intense abhorrence should fill the breast of every disciple of Christ." The Methodists were as bad: "a cage of unclean birds and a synagogue of Satan." The Presbyterians equally foul: "anathema." As he flailed away at the "blackhearted clergy" in issue after issue, Garrison eventually concluded that the churches themselves restricted the soaring aspirations of humanity.[45] In a final burst of denunciation, Garrison "renounced all allegiance to his country and had nominated Jesus Christ to the Presidency of the United States and the World."[46]

Naturally, the clergy did not take this passively. Every church in Boston closed its doors to meetings of Garrison's New England Anti-Slavery Society. In the summer of 1837 five Congregational clergymen published *The Appeal of Clerical Abolitionists on Antislavery Measures,* and this was followed by several other "pastoral letters" and "appeals," all of which denounced Garrison and challenged his leadership. He responded with his strongest epithets in print. Then he wrote to Lewis Tappan, his supporter in past controversies with the New York committee, asking, "Does it indeed not concern the Parent Society, that five clergymen, professed abolitionists, have publicly impeached . . . its 'leading' advocates? . . . I maintain, with all seriousness and earnestness, that you are both bound to meet these aspersions promptly, and in an official capacity; and should you refuse to do so, I for one shall feel that you will have greatly misapprehended your duty, and need to be admonished by abolitionists universally."[47]

To these threats from Garrison, the national officers responded in various ways. Elizur Wright, Jr., wrote a bitter letter to Garrison regarding his views, saying, "It is not in the human mind (except in a peculiar and, as I think, diseased state) to believe them."[48] But the Tappans replied in a concerned but evasive fashion, not wishing to be drawn into the Boston broil. They, with most of the officers, were plotting in every way possible to free abolitionism from Garrison's obsessions about the clergy, women, war, and social institutions. However, it was no use. During 1838 and 1839, divisions and splits continued in both camps, and the intrigues and bickering smoldered incessantly. Finally, in mid-May 1840, pro-Garrison forces packed the annual meeting of the American Anti-Slavery Society in New York City, and Arthur Tappan, anticipating "a recurrence of the scenes witnessed last year," resigned as president. His worst fears were realized, and the Tappan element withdrew to reorganize as the American and Foreign Anti-Slavery Society, which had only the most pallid existence for a short time.

For our purposes the point of the Garrison tale is that all of this public vindictiveness, internal wrangling among abolitionists, and anti-ecclesiasticism could easily have been duplicated at Oberlin, had it not been for the more moderate approach demanded by Charles Finney and other members of the faculty there. Robert Fletcher has said,

"Oberlin and Garrison had nothing in common but their consecration to the freeing of the slave. . . . His 'come-outerism' was antipathetic to all that Oberlin held dear. He denounced the organized Christian Church and cast it aside as wholly and hopelessly polluted. Oberlin, as we have seen, sought to make the Church into a great anti-slavery society."[49]

Over the long and painful years leading up to the Civil War, Oberlin mounted many endeavors and programs to help the blacks, both free and slave. Some of its graduates went to Canada to aid fugitive slaves who had gotten to that safe haven, and schools for blacks were opened there and elsewhere. President James H. Fairchild assessed the work of those earlier days:

> There are those among us who could tell some startling tales of anti-slavery campaigns. The ruffianism and malignity of the Missouri border at a later day, scarce exceeded the bitterness and mean hatred which anti-slavery men encountered in many portions of Ohio, and of which Oberlin and its students received a double portion. The terrible mobs which sometimes occurred, were, perhaps, less annoying than the low and contemptible abuse, which was matter of almost daily experience. The schools which our students taught were characterized as "nigger" schools—the churches where they preached were "nigger" churches. . . .
>
> Oberlin was, in those days, a sort of general depot for various branches of the "underground railroad." The charter of the road allowed, at that time, only *night trains*. . . . The fugitives were sent off by night to Cleveland, or Charleston, or Huron, or Sandusky, wherever a steamboat or vessel might be found whose captain would receive the contraband goods.[50]

During all these activities, as the nation lurched its way toward the inexpressible agonies of civil war, Finney gave his support and encouragement in a moderate and steady way to the forces of abolitionism. There was nothing spectacular in the part he took; probably feeling that there was a superabundance of wild-eyed zealots on both sides, Finney maintained the same emphases he had initiated in the early 1830s at the Chatham Street Chapel. Perhaps because of this, historians have largely overlooked Finney's contributions to the anti-slavery movement, preferring instead to highlight the roles of the militants and egotists. This is an oversight on their part. His greatest contribution, first recognized by Gilbert Barnes, was to stab awake the consciences of a large number, after his 1826 debut at Western and Rome, N.Y. Revivalism and reform began to go hand in hand, especially after the beginning of his Rochester revival on September 10, 1830. William G. McLoughlin summarized Barnes' discovery of "a different and incomparably more significant tale":

> [It was] a tale which began with the Great Revival in the "burned-over" region of New York inspired by Charles Grandison Finney (a man as neglected as Weld by historians) and which led through the conversion of Weld and his conversion of other westerners to the formation of a mighty wave of evangelical antislavery sentiment west of the Appalachians; this sentiment brought about the formation of countless abolition societies and the arousing of a religious crusade against slavery which was more significant and important in the election of Lincoln and the outbreak of the Civil War than the work of Garrison in the East.[51]

Another major contribution of Finney to antislavery was his provision of an ideological or theological framework upon which abolitionist ideas could be made to interface with Christian doctrine. A similar framework had been constructed earlier by British evangelicals such as John Newton, Thomas Clarkson, and William Wilberforce as their powerful rationale in undermining all the main grounds of the defense of slavery, combined with a brilliant use of all the weapons available to them in the long struggle in Parliament that resulted in the abolition of the British slave trade in 1807. However, by 1830 the majority of Americans knew little of these British arguments, and American slavery differed on so many points from that of the British Empire that the arguments could hardly be imported wholesale at any rate. Therefore, Charles Finney was not merely parroting the ideas of others when he became incensed over slavery in the early 1830s.[52] And he continued to provide ideology for abolitionism in America in the succeeding decades.

Before William H. Seward stated in the U. S. Senate, on March 11, 1850, that there was a "higher law" than the Constitution (thus giving a catch phrase to the antislavery forces), or Theodore Parker or Henry Ward Beecher picked up the notion and began to speak of it, Charles Finney was using higher law doctrine. In 1847 he stated:

> Nations are bound by the same law as individuals. . . . No human legislature can nullify the moral law. No human legislation can

make it right or lawful to violate any command of God. All human enactments requiring or sanctioning the violation of any command of God, are not only null and void, but they are a blasphemous usurpation and invasion of the prerogative of God.

The same principles apply to slavery. No human constitution or enactment can, by any possibility, be law, that recognizes the right of one human being to enslave another, in a sense that implies selfishness on the part of the slaveholder. Selfishness is wrong *per se*. It is, therefore, always and unalterably wrong. . . . That slaveholding, as it exists in this country, implies selfishness, at least in almost all instances, is too plain to need proof. . . . Deprive a human being of liberty who has been guilty of no crime; rob him of himself—his body—his soul—his time, and his earnings, to promote the interests of his master, and attempt to justify this on the principles of moral law! It is the greatest absurdity, and the most revolting wickedness.[53]

From Finney's prohibiting slaveholders to take communion at the Chatham Street Chapel in 1834, through the Civil War years, he consistently equated slaveholding with sin. In 1846 he wrote:

No generation before us ever had the light on the evils and wrongs of Slavery that we have: hence our guilt exceeds that of any former generation of slave holders; and, moreover, knowing all the cruel wrongs and miseries of the system from the history of the past, every persisting slave-holder endorses all the crimes and assumes all the guilt involved in the system and evolved out of it since the world began.[54]

As Finney grew older, he retained his confidence in human institutions to some degree, but was always mindful that sin blighted every attempt to make a better world. Recognizing that, he freely criticized politicians, as he said in 1856: "The Bible represents Satan as ruling the hearts of men at his will, just as the men who wield the slave power of the South rule the dough faces of the North at their will, dictating the choice of our Presidents and the entire legislation of the Federal Government."[55]

Although he did not favor secular politicians meddling in areas where the church might bring about spiritual reform, Finney came more and more to the conviction that, as Britain had eliminated slavery by legislation, so in America this basic evil could be swept away only in the same fashion. And when war arrived in April 1861, he declared his opposition to Abraham Lincoln because of the President's conservative approach to the slavery issue. In 1864 Finney wrote to Gerrit Smith, who favored Lincoln's reelection, that the Republican Party should nominate someone else:

> We need a more radical man to finish up this war. I hope the radicals in & out of congress, will make their influence so felt in respect to the coming nomination that Mr. L. will see that there is no hope of his renomination & election unless he takes & keeps more radical ground. The people are prepared to elect the most radical abolitionist that is if he can get a nomination.[56]

17

THE CHANGING FACE OF REVIVALS

Τhe financial panic of 1837 spread its pernicious effects over the nation for several years, but by the early 1840s the thoughts of Americans turned once again to more pleasant topics than the chaotic state of the economy. The churches began to prosper once more, and for the most part regained the vitality they had had before the panic. Evangelism again became a priority.

Even with the strictures placed upon Charles Finney because of his perfectionist theology, there were still some who wished his services in conducting revivals. Willard Sears, the wealthy Boston businessman, had been very generous to Finney during the panic, sending him $600 each year to support his family after Josiah Chapin was no longer able to aid.[1] Sears was thoroughly dedicated to reform measures, and felt that the churches of Boston were not sufficiently eager to hear free discussion on all the great questions of reform, especially since Lyman Beecher had persuaded them to close their pulpits to both evangelists and abolitionists in 1836. For this reason Sears had purchased the Marlborough Hotel, on Washington Street, and a large chapel adjacent to it. The entire complex was to be dedicated to the needs of Christian reformers. As Finney said:

> In 1842, I was strongly urged to go and occupy the Marlborough chapel, and preach for a few months. I went and began my labors, and preached with all my might for two months. The Spirit of

the Lord was immediately poured out, and there was a general agitation among the dry bones. I was visited at my room almost constantly, during every day of the week, by inquirers from all parts of the city, and many were obtaining hopes from day to day. . . .

A Unitarian woman had been converted in Boston, who was an acquaintance of the Rev. Dr. Channing. Hearing of her conversion, Dr. Channing, as she informed me, sent for her to visit him, as he was in feeble health, and could not well call on her. She complied with his request, and he wished her to tell him the exercises of her mind, and her Christian experience, and the circumstances of her conversion. She did so, and the doctor manifested a great interest in her change of mind; and inquired of her if she had anything that I had written and published, that he could read. She told him that she had a little work of mine, which had been published, on the subject of sanctification. He borrowed it, and told her that he would read it; and if she would call again in a week, he should be happy to have farther conversation with her. At the close of the week, she returned for her book, and the doctor said, ". . . I should like to see Mr. Finney. Cannot you persuade him to call on me? for I cannot go and see him." She called at my lodgings; but I had left Boston for Providence. After an absence of two months, I was again in Boston, and this lady called immediately to see me, and gave me the information which I have related. But he had then gone into the country, on account of his health. I greatly regretted not having an opportunity to see him. But he died shortly after, and of his subsequent religious history I know nothing. . . . The next time I met Dr. Beecher, Dr. Channing's name was mentioned, and I related to him this fact. The tears started in his eyes, in a moment, and he said with much emotion, "I guess he has gone to heaven!"[2]

The Unitarian leader William Ellery Channing, to whom this refers, despite his sweet temper and warmth of affection, had nonetheless clashed with Lyman Beecher during the latter's tenure in Boston. Channing had founded the Berry Street Conference of liberal Boston ministers in 1820, out of which the American Unitarian Association developed in 1825, and so Beecher naturally regarded him as totally heterodox and apostate, despite his engaging personality. But perhaps, if Beecher's tears and emotion were genuine, he retained real liking for the man who had set forth the tenets of Unitarianism in 1819 at the ordination of Jared Sparks, and who was known thereafter as "the apostle of Unitarianism."[3]

Although Finney had many inquirers, it was a time of religious confusion in the city, engendered by the premillennial prophecies spread by William Miller. For years Miller had been predicting that the Second Advent of Christ would take place "about 1843." Although he held off being more specific about the exact month or time frame until the beginning of 1843,[4] when 1842 arrived the fated year was close enough for multitudes to grow very restive. Finney, like most clergymen at that time, was a postmillennialist, believing that the dedicated work of Christians was bringing in the thousand-year reign of peace, *after which* the Second Coming would transpire, with its Last Judgment. When Miller reversed the order of eschatological events, making the Second Coming imminent, this challenged the assumptions of Finney and the others, and he reported that he attended Miller's Bible class in Boston "once or twice; after which I invited him to my room, and tried to convince him that he was in error. . . . But it was vain to reason with him, and his followers, at that time."[5] That would have been a confrontation to witness, as the fiery-eyed Finney, confident that progress was inevitable and that the reforms he and his friends had undertaken were surely bringing in the millennium, crossed verbal swords with the chief exponent of the view that the efforts of Christians were insufficient, and only the Lord's impending return could vanquish the forces of evil and decay!

During Finney's time in Boston, a revival began there, especially among the Baptists.[6] Naturally Finney hoped to become fully involved in it, but just then "Josiah Chapin and many others, were insisting very strongly upon my coming and holding meetings in Providence."[7] Finney felt greatly indebted to Chapin for all the financial aid he had given to Oberlin, and so he prepared to leave Boston, though regretfully. The Baptist evangelist Jacob Knapp had been conducting meetings in Providence, and he then came to assist in the Boston awakening.[8] Finney and Knapp compared notes on their work in the two cities, and then Finney went to Providence to take up where Knapp had left off. He reported that the great revival in Boston "prevailed wonderfully, especially among the Baptists, and more or less throughout the city. The Baptist ministers took hold with brother Knapp, and many Congregational brethren were greatly blessed, and the work was very extensive."[9] Perhaps as many as four thousand members were added to the Boston churches in the year 1842.[10]

Meanwhile, Finney did his best in Rhode Island. "The work increased, and spread in every part of the city", he reported, "until the number of inquirers became so great, together with the young converts, who were always ready to go below with them, as nearly or quite to fill that large room. . . . This state of things continued for two months."[11] At the end of that time, it was opportune to leave Providence; it was a small city, and Finney felt he had expended enough energy upon it, considering the many demands upon his limited strength.

Leaving the East, Finney took an Erie Canal packet boat on his way home to Oberlin. With his innumerable friends along the route of the canal, it was always difficult not to stop and visit with them, but there were pressing reasons for moving on. As Finney wrote, "I was then, as I thought, completely tired out; having labored incessantly for four months, two in Boston, and two in Providence. Beside, the time of year had come, or nearly come, for the opening of our spring term in Oberlin."[12] Finney had already presumed upon the tolerance of the administration at Oberlin in allowing him to absent himself from teaching duties during the previous term, and his practice of remaining away, involved in revivals, was to become almost habitual in the years to come. In addition to his stated reasons for hurrying home, there was of course also the fact that Lydia was there with the children, and her health was deteriorating. A fifth child, Sarah, had been born to them in 1841, and her birth may have contributed to Lydia's declining health.

Possibly because the packet boats often stopped overnight at the major terminal of Rochester, and because sleeping accommodations aboard the boats were cramped, poor, and lacked privacy, Finney decided to stop off, visit one of his friends there, and take a later boat to continue his journey. For some reason, he did not realize what was bound to happen—that his presence in the city was sure to be detected, and as the one who had led the unforgettable revival eleven years earlier, news of his coming would stir all of Rochester.

Exactly that occurred. Members of the clergy came to him and asked that he preach, and a leading judge of the state court of appeals came and was especially urgent in his appeals to Finney to remain for a time. He gave in, and spoke for them. "But this brought upon me a more importunate invitation," he stated, "to remain and hold a series of meetings. I decided to remain, and, though wearied, went on with the work."[13] The students at Oberlin would have to wait a bit for their favorite professor.

Inasmuch as the Rochester revival of 1830–1831 had brought together in a profoundly ecumenical way not only the Presbyterians (who were numerically predominant there), but also the Baptists, the Methodists, and the Episcopalians to some degree, Finney was naturally hopeful that, if he were to throw his energies into the work, a number of churches might cooperate in it. But, in the nature of things, it was not to be. Finney described what happened:

> Mr. George S. Boardman was pastor of what was then called, the Bethel, or Washington street church; and Mr. Shaw, of the Second or Brick church. Mr. Shaw was very anxious to unite with Mr. Boardman, and have the meetings at their churches alternately. Mr. Boardman was indisposed to take this course, saying that his congregation was weak, and needed the concentration of my labors at that point. I regretted this; but still I could not overrule it.[14]

Frustrated in his attempts at a union effort, Shaw then invited Jedediah Burchard to preach in the Brick Church. For many years warnings about Burchard's eccentric behavior had circulated among the clergy, and Shaw must have been either unaware of the ways in which other pastors and churches had been treated by him, or he was so irritated over his inability to have Charles Finney at the Brick Church that he threw caution to the winds and invited another well-known evangelist, so that he too might have protracted meetings. Finney's earlier warm feelings toward Burchard had cooled for a decade, and although Finney had not publicly censured Burchard for his bizarre conduct, he had let a few close associates know what he thought of the other man.[15]

In his *Memoirs*, Finney was eager to give the impression that the Rochester revival of 1842 was mainly directed at the legal profession. The chapter dedicated to this gives instance after instance of the conversion of lawyers. But others also attended the Finney meetings, as this contemporary description shows:

> Elisabeth has finally finished her letter & sent it off this evening, while I was hearing Mr. Finney preach from the words "He that covereth his sins shall not prosper"—the remainder of the verse tomorrow evening.—I have a very strong, clear & abiding impression that we are indeed to have a *great* revival here. Sabbath evening at a union *tract* meeting of all the churches, (the house was crowded) Mr. Church (I had observed for some time while Mr. Edwards was speaking that he wept)—as they all sat in the pulpit—(the Baptist minister) arose & with great feeling and solemnity, addressed the meeting & soon said "I confess before this whole congregation that a *fragment* of a sermon (Mr. Finneys, 'Put ye

on the Lord Jesus Christ'] that I heard the last evening has lodged an impression in my heart not soon to be forgotten.". . . *Friday*— Mr. Finney continues here still—the result of his preaching none can yet tell—I am confident he preaches the truth as no other minister that I have ever yet heard, has preached it. Mr. Boardman sustains him, so far, I hope he will be here when you come. I have been to hear all his sermons until last evening.[16]

The *Oberlin Evangelist* stated that a gentleman in Rochester had ordered one hundred copies of Finney's *Views of Sanctification,* and had written that "the Lord is doing a great work here, through Brother Finney."[17] Despite the fact that the Brick Church had invited Jedediah Burchard to conduct meetings, apparently from the evidence many of the Rochester churches supported the Finney meetings. Dr. Henry J. Whitehouse, rector of St. Luke's Episcopal Church, had supported Finney's preaching during the 1830–1831 revival, and he did the same in 1842. It was beneficial for his congregation; over seventy persons were converted, and Finney claimed that they were "almost all among the principal people of his congregation."

After two months' work in the city of Rochester, Finney closed his campaign and returned to Oberlin. It was to be like this for years to come. He enjoyed teaching and influencing young people who might spread his ideas far afield, and Oberlin was his home, where Lydia and his beloved family were. But when Charles Finney received a challenging invitation to some field of work, off he went. This was a bit callous, it must be admitted, toward the school and the students. In the years before the Civil War, as Oberlin expanded, multitudes of students were attracted to the college and especially its theological department, chiefly by the prospect of studying under its most renowned teacher, as John Morgan reminded Finney.[18] During his frequent absences, Professors Henry E. Peck and James H. Fairchild carried on as best they could, substituting for Finney in his courses and supplementing his work. Robert Fletcher has said, "When Finney was away, as so often happened, the attendance fell off; when he returned, it climbed again."[19]

Finney's correspondence has frequent complaints about his poor health, and at the same time Lydia's physical condition did not improve. In the midst of his concerns here, Sarah, two years old, fell ill early in 1843. That such a young child—hardly more than an infant— should fall dangerously sick was all the more vexing to Finney, for he was greatly concerned over the salvation of each of his children.

At Sarah's tender age, she was yet unable to understand the Christian doctrine of salvation and rather than trying to explain it to her, Finney had simply to be confident that the Savior accepted all such children who had not reached the age of responsibility. Evangelical faith, as believed by most Protestants in that day, was couched in the harsh absolutes of heaven and hell, but it provided a family like Charles Finney's with an explanation and an appreciation for all the realities of life and death, and made bearable what all must endure ultimately. Sarah died on March 9, 1843.[20]

In December 1843 Finney was back in Boston, preaching again at the Marlborough Chapel at Willard Sears' invitation. Since his previous visit, a congregation had been formed, but Finney was very candid in describing it as "composed greatly of radicals; and most of the members had extreme views, on various subjects . . . not composed of materials that could, to any considerable extent, work healthfully and efficiently together."[21] As he labored there, from late December 1843 until the middle of March 1844, Finney was again distressed with the pall the Unitarians seemed to spread over the city:

> I have labored in Boston in five powerful revivals of religion, and I must express it as my sincere conviction, that the greatest difficulty in the way of overcoming Unitarianism, and all the forms of error there, is the timidity of Christians and churches. . . . The influence of Unitarian teaching has been, to lead them to call in question all the principal doctrines of the Bible. Their system is one of denials. Their theology is negative.[22]

Predictably, not a great deal was accomplished in evangelism at this period, for in addition to the timidity of the orthodox, the hysteria over the supposed Second Coming of Christ induced by William Miller's teaching was at its height,[23] and this served to deflect attention from other religious activities. But Finney reported that, for him personally, a crucial spiritual milestone was reached then, the second work of grace or the "baptism of the Holy Spirit." He had sought this since he had preached and written on the topic in 1837.[24] In a little-noticed section of his *Memoirs*, Finney spoke of the experience of "filling," which, to him, should be normative for every Christian. It brought him spiritual peace and moral triumph, and was the culmination of his long search for "heart purity" and "perfect love," of which John Wesley had written. Finney wrote:

During this winter, the Lord gave my soul a very thorough over-
hauling, and a fresh baptism of his Spirit. . . . But this winter, in
particular, my mind was exceedingly exercised on the question
of personal holiness. . . . I gave myself to a great deal of prayer. . . .

After praying in this way for weeks and months, one morning while I was engaged in prayer, the thought occurred to me,
what if, after all this divine teaching, my will is not carried, and
this teaching takes effect only in my sensibility? . . . Just before
this occurrence, I had a great struggle to consecrate myself to God,
in a higher sense than I had ever before seen to be my duty, or
conceived as possible. . . . I then had a deeper view of what was
implied in consecration to God, than ever before. . . . This was
early in the morning; and through the whole of that day, I seemed
to be in a state of perfect rest, body and soul. . . . Nothing troubled me. I was neither elated nor depressed; I was neither, as I
could see, joyful or sorrowful. My confidence in God was perfect,
my acceptance of his will was perfect, and my mind was as calm
as heaven.[25]

In 1844 another child was added to the Finney family, a girl, Delia.
This pregnancy may have complicated Lydia's physical condition, and
hastened her death in 1847. Finney's correspondence through these
years makes frequent mention of Lydia's frail health, and in addition
Delia herself may not have been a strong child, for she lived to be only
eight years old, dying on September 1, 1852.

It was in 1844 as well that Finney's influence became truly inter-
national, helping to inspire the creation of an organization dedicated
to improving the spiritual and social well-being of young men, the
Young Men's Christian Association. George Williams was born in 1821
in Somerset, England. As a youth he was apprenticed to a draper in
the town of Bridgwater, when he began to read some of Finney's works
published in England. Through them he was converted, and he then
joined the local Congregational church. In 1841 he went to London
and took up work at a draper's there, later rising to be a partner in
the firm. His faithfulness to business did not deter him from becoming increasingly active in religious work, and he was continually
challenged by Finney's writings, especially *Lectures on Revivals*. He
began a prayer meeting at his place of work, and sought to win his
fellow clerks to the Christian life.[26] In June 1844 twelve young men,
all but one of them employees in the firm, met in his room and formed
a society to win other young men to the Christian faith. This group
called itself the Young Men's Christian Association, and the idea

became contagious, for it came on the rising tide of the Evangelical movement in Britain. Similar groups sprang up throughout the British Isles, and within less than a decade they were also to be found in the United States and Canada. In Europe similar societies, some of them older, were also flourishing. In 1854 a confederation of the associations was formed for North America, and in 1855, in Paris at the time of the Industrial Exhibition, the World's Alliance of the Young Men's Christian Associations was constituted by delegates from both sides of the Atlantic.[27]

When Charles Finney approached his half-century mark, he recognized increasingly that with his limited strength, he could accomplish more through publication than by any other means, for his previous writings, as with George Williams, obviously had wide influence. His theology classes at Oberlin enabled him to develop a coherent theology, and his first serious work on systematic theology, intended for more than the lay audience to which he had previously addressed his writings, saw the light of day in 1840: *Skeletons of a Course of Theological Lectures by the Rev. Charles G. Finney*. This will be dealt with shortly.

In 1845 he and others of the Oberlin staff decided that Finney's voice should be heard again on the subject of revivals. It was not so much to further awakenings, as he had attempted to do with his *Lectures on Revivals*. Rather, it was to try to correct glaring abuses that were appearing wherever revivals took place. Certainly this was hardly the first notice of these abuses, or of the poor quality of converts coming from revivalism in later times; notices of these problems had been appearing in print for years. The *New York Evangelist* itself had noted, as early as 1833, the gradual decline of awakenings since the monumental 1830–1831 period: "Revivals of religion have not been as numerous or as powerful, particularly in the Northern and Middle States, as they were the preceding year." And in 1834 the editor stated that the impetus toward awakenings had dropped alarmingly, and he asked, "Have the American churches abandoned revivals?"[28] That was a friend of revivals speaking. The enemies of Finney's new measures were far more eager to point to declensions. Albert Dod, in reviewing Finney's *Lectures on Revivals* in 1835, was quick to charge, "It is now generally understood that the numerous converts of the new measures have been, in most cases, like the morning cloud and the early dew. In some places, not a half, a fifth, or even a tenth part of them remain."[29]

Charles Finney had, of course, erected extremely high standards

of performance for converts in *Lectures on Revivals,* and had dispar-
aged the laxity of most Christians in those pages. After that he became increasingly critical, stating in 1836 in a lecture published in
the *New York Evangelist* that of all the converts of the previous decade of revivals, "the great body of them are a disgrace to religion. Of
what use would it be to have a thousand members added to the Church
to be just such as are now in it."

His critics immediately seized upon this, declaring that Finney
was admitting the failure of his work. No, he retaliated, for this was
not a reflection on the circumstances of their conversion, but rather
on the inabilities of the churches to engender a dynamic piety in them.
However, he accepted the blame, and now recognized that some of
his evangelistic techniques had to be changed: "My stay at every place
was too short to accomplish much in the work of leading converts
to manhood in religion. The same has been true of my brethren who
have been evangelists."[30] The key was greater and more intensive training; evangelism was only the first step, and sound converts would not
necessarily be produced just because their conversions were properly
brought about, any more than a well-adjusted adult would be produced
by a healthy birth years before without much training in the interim.

The 1845 articles in the *Oberlin Evangelist* were based on Finney's mature thinking and years of observation. They were addressed
"To all the friends and especially all the ministers of our Lord Jesus
Christ." Referring to his 1835 work and hoping that his readers had
thoroughly read it, Finney began, "Since the publication of those Lectures, my observation and experience on the subject have been continually developing and ripening until I am very desirous of saying
many additional things to my brethren on this subject." Setting the
tone for what was to come, he admitted to early mistakes in his career: "I can see that in some things I erred in manner and in spirit."[31]
The first of the letters was humble and reflective.

The second letter got down to business immediately:

> *Dear Brethren:*
>   I have observed, and multitudes of others also I find have
> observed, that for the last ten years, revivals of religion have been
> gradually becoming more and more superficial. All the phenomena
> which they exhibit testify to this as a general fact. There is very
> much less deep conviction of sin and deep breaking up of the heart;
> much less depth of humility and much less strength in all the
> graces exhibited by converts in late revivals, than in the converts

from the revivals which occurred about 1830 and '31 and for some time previous.[32]

Now, what was the cause of this? Finney declared that there are often egregious faults in the methodology of the recent evangelists:

> There is much less probing of the heart by a deep and thorough exhibition of human depravity, than was formerly the case. It has been of late a common remark . . . that for the last few years there has been little or no opposition made by impenitent sinners to revivals. Now it is not because the carnal mind is not still enmity against God, but I greatly fear it is for want of thoroughly turning up to the light the deep foundations of this enmity in their hearts.[33]

Finney had spent quite a few pages in his *Lectures on Revivals* in stressing that the evangelist and the pastor should be wise and skillful in dealing with souls, and that their success will be proportionate to their skill. Finney is saying, therefore, that this principle was being overlooked, and that many evangelists were apparently interested chiefly in immediate results, or numbers, rather than in the permanence and stability of their converts.

A second fault of recent evangelists was similar to the first:

> I fear that stress enough is not laid upon the horrible guilt of this depravity. . . . When sinners and backsliders are really convicted by the Holy Ghost, they are greatly ashamed of themselves. Until they manifest deep shame, it should be known that the probe is not used sufficiently, and they do not see themselves as they ought.[34]

A third fault was that recent evangelists relied on their own persuasive power over an audience to get them to express a desire for change, rather than relying upon the power of God. This would be a fundamental fault, Finney believed, in that at the outset an evangelist would not impress upon an audience that only God can bring about any true and complete conversion. Here Finney verged upon a criticism of his own earlier doctrine, as framed in his famous "New Heart" sermon, that the sinner is like the dazed man on the brink of the Niagara River and that when someone cries "Stop!" the man has the power to awaken and turn himself away from the imminent danger.

Finney did not mention his earlier doctrine, but he declared, "I have often thought that at least in a great many instances, stress enough has not been laid upon the necessity of divine influence upon the hearts of Christians and of sinners."[35]

Finney continued in this fashion for numerous issues of the *Oberlin Evangelist*. His overall conclusion that revivals were in decline is certainly correct, and in attempting to pinpoint some of the reasons for this he was also accurate, without question. But he told only part of the story. There are major factors he did not mention. For one, he always assumed that revivals could be a continual experience for the church, whereas history shows them to be relatively rare. The Second Great Awakening was exceptional for its length, over some thirty years, and Finney was fortunate to have lived through its second phase and, indeed, to have prolonged it by his own vastly influential ministry. That revivals must decline eventually, in the nature of things, he could hardly contemplate.

Another aspect of the decline of the Second Great Awakening that Finney did not mention was that evangelism had, in a sense, suffered from its own success. Because the growth of the churches had been so spectacular in some years,[36] in a measure due to Finney's converts, other men desired to emulate him and they also joined the ranks of full-time evangelists. In 1820, throughout New England and the Middle Atlantic states, there was one well-known evangelist: Asahel Nettleton. By the 1840s there were scores of imitators of Finney, Burchard, Knapp, Jabez Swan, and Luther Myrick. Inspired by the success of Finney, these imitators "got on the bandwagon." Generally they itinerated in small towns and villages rather than the cities, and the common people flocked to them because they were commoners themselves, without airs and often without much education.[37] A major difference between them and Charles Finney, however, was that in his later years he became increasingly prone to introspection and the very type of critique of his "letters" in the *Oberlin Evangelist*, being sensitive to difficulties and the need of adjustments, whereas for the most part they brooked no opposition or criticism, and when they met problems they simply flew to another area and began their practices over again.

Whatever differences there were among them, however, Finney was partially responsible for the rise of these itinerants, and that brings us to the point that with them came an inevitable stereotyping of evangelism, an institutionalizing and a woodenness and mechanization that no free and uninhibited movement of the human spirit to meet God could possibly withstand for long. Evangelism of a routine type could indeed plod along endlessly under their aegis, but were these men capable of bringing about a spontaneous outpouring of God's Spirit that would sweep thousands of souls into the kingdom, as happened from 1826 to 1831? More to the point, where now was Finney's concept that a "prayed-down revival" (as opposed to the older idea that they were sent at God's good time) was possible at any time? His earlier confidence that he could always bring about an awakening by "means and measures" seemed to be failing him!

Still a third contributing cause for the decline of revivals was the pressing claims of other emerging causes or crises, combined with the fact that the human mind can bear such excitement for a limited period, and its tolerance for the Second Great Awakening was already vastly extended in time. The slavery issue, at white heat by the mid-1840s, diverted many from attention to salvation. The innumerable reform movements diverted others. Then, after January 13, 1846, when General Zachary Taylor was ordered to march his four thousand troops from the Nueces River to the Rio Grande, the threatened war with Mexico posed a serious issue for the alarmed nation. Taken all in all, the multitude of events that demanded the attention of the rapidly expanding country in the 1840s and 1850s meant that even religious people could no longer concentrate entirely on revivals. In his "Letters on Revivals," Finney nowhere specifically admitted that ominous changes had blighted the freshness and spontaneity of earlier revivals, but it was everywhere apparent.

Other topics demanded attention. His quieter years engaged in pedagogy at Oberlin enabled Finney to develop a mature theology that systematically treated the entire field instead of specific topics. This was first presented in *Skeletons of a Course of Theological Lectures by the Rev. Charles G. Finney,* published in 1840. Originally designed as lectures given to his theological classes, they constitute a rather comprehensive treatment of the whole field of theology. Among the thirty-five lectures are "The Laws of Evidence," "Divine Authority of the Bible," "The Trinity," "The Divinity and Humanity of Christ," "The Personality of the Holy Spirit," "Providence," "Atheism and Deism," "Man, the Moral Law and the Commandments," and "The Atonement." For the most part, these treatises adhere generally to normative Protestant orthodoxy; Christ is God the Son, in two natures yet one Person, and this Person is the second in the Godhead, the Father and the Holy Spirit being the First and Third Persons; the Bible is divinely inspired and infallible, as was generally taught in the period before the rise of higher criticism; as to humankind, forensic laws of evidence demonstrate that it is a rebel against God's holy and just laws, and the stubborn human revolt against the Creator's lordship is shown in continual sin, and the erection of deism and atheism as defenses against the intrusion of truth. Throughout there is no mention of sanctification or perfectionism.

Strict Calvinists might have accepted much of Finney's *Skeletons*, with the exception of two positions it held: general atonement (as opposed to a limited atonement for the elect only), and the objection to substitutionary theories of the atonement. This must be set in context. Over the centuries, theologians have found the atonement so multifaceted that no one doctrine could adequately express it, and three main types of theories have arisen. The first is the Classical, Dramatic, or "Ransom to Satan" theory, based on passages such as Matthew 20:28, 1 Timothy 2:6, and Romans 5:18–19. This theory regards sinners as the possession of Satan since the Fall. Christ on the cross paid the ransom for their redemption, and Satan accepted Christ in their place. In his resurrection Christ rose triumphant, for Satan and death could not hold him, and thus Satan lost both his original captives and their ransom. The second is the Satisfaction or Juridical theory, which originated with Anselm (1033–1109). Here human sin is regarded as an affront to the majesty of God. Such an affront requires an infinite satisfaction. But no human can adequately offer this; only the God-Man can render satisfaction and bear the penalty of sin. The Protestant Reformers tended to adopt penal substitutionist forms of this view, in that (1 Peter 3:18) Christ took upon himself the punishment properly due humankind. The third is the Subjectivist or Moral Influence theory, developed by Abelard (1079–1142). It holds that the chief human problem is how to be freed from the fear of God, that we might respond personally to God's love. This is made possible by the embodiment of God's love in Christ's sacrifice, which is meant to evoke a moral response in human beings, leading them to repentance and amendment of life. But strong objections have been made against this view by many; it may present Christ as doing little more than setting an example of love and sacrifice, to which we respond, for it evades stating specifically what Christ *did*.

Charles Finney espoused the Moral Influence theory, stating, "In the atonement God has given us the influence of his own example, has exhibited his own love, his own compassion, his own self-denial, his own patience, his own long-suffering, under abuse from enemies. . . . This is the highest possible moral influence. . . . The influence of the Atonement, when apprehended by the mind, will accomplish whatever is an object of moral power."[38] In line with Finney's stress on God's moral government of the universe, he called this the governmental theory, but it is merely a variation on Abelard.

Finney spoke repeatedly in his theology of "public justice," and he claimed that he had taught all this from shortly after his conversion. He never defined carefully what he meant by public justice, but he did indicate that it was not in the nature of a transaction, but rather something in the manner of a demonstration to all that in some way God had accepted what Christ did at Calvary.[39] He rejected both the Classical and Satisfaction theories in the *Skeletons:*

> [Christ] could not have endured the literal penalty of the Law of God, for this, we have seen in a former skeleton, was eternal death. . . . He did not suffer all that was due to sinners on the ground of retributive justice. This was naturally impossible, as each sinner deserved eternal death. Inflicting upon him this amount of suffering would have been unjust, as his sufferings were infinitely more valuable than the sufferings of sinners. . . . Neither wisdom nor enlightened benevolence could consent that an innocent being should suffer, as a substitute for a guilty one, the same amount that was justly due to the guilty. We are no where informed, nor is it possible for us to know, or perhaps to conceive, the exact amount of Christ's sufferings as a substitute for sinners. It is enough for us to know that his sufferings, both in kind and degree, were so ample a satisfaction to public justice as to render the universal offer of forgiveness to all the penitent consistent with the due administration of justice.
>
> The Atonement was not a commercial transaction. Some have regarded the Atonement simply in the light of the payment of a debt; and have represented Christ as purchasing the elect of the Father, and paying down the same amount of suffering in his own person that justice would have exacted of them. To this I answer:
> 1. It is naturally impossible, as it would require that satisfaction should be made to retributive justice.
> 2. But as we have seen in a former lecture, retributive justice must have inflicted on them eternal death. To suppose, therefore, that Christ suffered in amount all that was due to the elect, is to suppose that he suffered an eternal punishment multiplied by the whole number of the elect.[40]

Theologically, this presents some problems. For one, Finney did not appear to good advantage in making statements such as this. Here he was the prosecutor of the human race, and he knew no mercy—whereas the New Testament is full of God's mercy. Finney was here the wrathful prosecutor arguing for the death penalty before a jury. Unfortunately, he did not embody the kinder aspects of the law in so acting. That a judge could commute or forgive a sentence was almost beyond Finney's imagination. And yet this is exactly what the New Testament presents.

Secondly, Finney appears to have had a very narrow view of the doctrine of Christ's righteousness. His overwhelming insistence was that sinners deserved *eternal* punishment. All is colored by that. Although he taught in a fashion that the demands of the law were met by Christ *in his death*, he did not come to grips with Romans 3:21–26 and the terms "gift" or "freely" (v. 24). Thus he left himself open to misunderstanding and attack from the orthodox. They would be on firmer ground, with much scripture that they could cite, in showing that Finney was deficient in understanding that Christ was already the righteousness of God *before* his death on Calvary. This would mean, the orthodox would explain, that Christ had already met, in the place and behalf of humankind, every demand of the Old Testament law, thus going to his death as the sinless, perfect substitute for humanity. Therefore, they would explain, as God's perfect righteousness, Christ's death alone was sufficient, according to the writings of Paul, and atonement did not depend on the *amount* of suffering he endured.

Thirdly, Finney was being dishonest in claiming that theologians over the centuries were the first to regard the atonement as a transaction. If he had been candid, he would have admitted that theologians merely tried to work out what the Bible so often presents, in Romans and Galatians, in most of Paul, in Mark 10:45, in the epistle to the Hebrews, and so on. The words, "ransom," "propitiation," "expiation," "righteousness," "justified," "reconciled," and so on are in the New Testament; theologians did not put them there, and it was not they but Finney who was devious in trying to sweep away all that did not agree with his notions.

In essence, Finney was really arguing against scripture itself (and not against interpretations of it), although in that day of strict literalism he dared not reveal this. Finney's crucial point, that inasmuch as punishment for sinners is said to be forever (Matt. 25:46; Rev. 20:10,

15), therefore if Christ was to suffer literally in their behalf it must also be forever, is not supported by the Bible. Finney's legalistic bent prevented him from fully appreciating divine grace or the meaning of the resurrection. To apply these seriously at this point would be to take the New Testament teachings that Christ's righteousness and obedience made his suffering and death *immediately* efficacious (Romans 5:18–19); that he died under our sins (I Peter 2:24; 2 Cor. 5:21); and that he was raised from death and exalted to the Father's right hand (Heb. 9:24) as the token that our sins are gone, that his work for us has the divine approbation and that we, for whom he suffered, are completely justified (Heb. 9:25–28).

Finney revised and expanded all this for his *Lectures on Systematic Theology,* which appeared in two volumes in 1846 and 1847. In the 1846 volume are the subjects of moral government, moral obligation, attributes of love, attributes of selfishness, atonement (which repeated much of the above), human government, moral depravity, and regeneration. In the 1847 volume are the subjects of ability (moral, natural, and gracious), repentance, faith and unbelief, justification, sanctification, election, reprobation, divine sovereignty, and perseverance. In 1851 the work was reissued in one massive volume.

In the 1846 volume Finney made several important statements in the Preface. He admitted that "this volume is much more difficult to understand than any of the remaining volumes will be. I have begun with the second volume, as this was to be on subjects so distinct from what will appear in the first volume that this volume might well appear first."[41] Although he did not specify what subjects would be in a forthcoming first volume, apparently they were some of the items dealt with in the *Skeletons,* such as more on the attributes of God, which naturally belong first in a systematic theology. From his statement he appears to have contemplated several other volumes, but only the third (1847) was to appear, and the promised first volume was never written.

Then in the Preface Finney went on to say, "What I have said on the 'Foundation of Moral Obligation' is the key to the whole subject. Whoever masters and understands that can readily understand all the rest."[42] Obedient to his desire, we begin by noting his adherence to the prevailing theory of pure and applied psychology, the old "faculty psychology" with its totally inadequate categories and explanations for human behavior, and in which he was constrained to work out his theories:

*The ultimate or absolute good can not consist in any thing ex-
ternal to Mind itself. . . .* The Constitution of Moral Agents has
three primary Departments or Faculties as we have formerly seen,
namely, the *Intellect,* the *Sensibility,* and the *Will.* All the demands of our being may be and must be made by one of these
Faculties. The Intellect has its demands or wants. The Sensibility has its objects of desire, or its demands and wants. Our whole
being is comprised in these three departments, and they sustain
such correlations to each other and to the universe that the objects demanded by these powers or susceptibilities are indispens-
ible conditions of our well-being or being *satisfied.* For instance,
the Intellect demands knowledge of Truth; the Conscience demands obedience to Moral Law; the Sensibility demands those
objects that excite its desires. These are only specimens of the
demands or wants of our being.[43]

The insufficiencies of the quagmire of nineteenth-century "mental science" need not be further lamented, but it is important to fix
this approach in the mind to follow Finney's thinking. Each person,
he taught, has complete free will and is a moral agent, and "the *foundation of Moral Obligation is the Reason or Consideration* that im-
poses obligation on a moral agent to obey moral law."[44] Finney then
laid down this proposition: "*The highest Well Being of God and of
the Universe of sentient existences is the end on which ultimate
preference, choice, intention, ought to terminate.*"[45] This is because
the well-being of God and sentient beings must be "*intrinsically and
infinitely valuable in itself.*"

That brought Finney to his concept of "the simplicity of moral
action."[46] He began with the point that all moral character resides in
the ultimate choice. And because this ultimate choice dominates all
subordinate choices, volitions, and acts, it dominates one's entire life.
The moral character of the ultimate choice thus gives its moral character to the whole life. Because the ultimate choice is simple and its
moral character is simple, one must be morally exactly what one's
ultimate choice is morally. This ultimate choice must be completely
moral or completely immoral, completely holy or completely sinful
and evil. Therefore a person must be completely holy or totally sinful. There can be no gradations or degrees. Every person is therefore
at any given instant perfectly sinful or perfectly holy. As Finney
declared, "Moral agents are at all times either as holy or as sinful as
with their knowledge they can be. Consequently, total moral deprav-

ity is an attribute of selfishness in the sense that every sinner is as wicked as with his present light he can be."[47] It cannot be overemphasized that Finney makes these states mutually exclusive: "*Moral Character is always wholly right or wholly wrong, and never partly right and partly wrong at the same time.*"[48] There is no third position, no mixed state between the two. "Sin and holiness, then, both consist in supreme, ultimate, and opposite choices, or intentions, and can not, by any possibility, co-exist."[49]

Here is Oberlin perfectionism applied in a new way: not as a teaching exclusive to itself, but now as the very heart of Finney's entire theology. All subordinate ends, Finney taught, and the choices of will that bring them about, will be determined by this ultimate end. If a person truly wills the good of being as his ultimate end, he cannot make other volitional choices that would bring about other ends. Once having chosen this ultimate end, a person's entire life is determined by it. This inevitably follows from the mechanism of moral action. In addition, it would seem in Finney's system that a Christian cannot sin. "The new or regenerate heart can not sin. It is benevolence, love to God and man. This can not sin." On the other hand, "The carnal heart or mind can not but sin; it is not subject to the law of God, neither can be, because it is 'enmity against God.' . . . These are both ultimate choices or intentions. They are from their own nature efficient in each excluding the other, and each securing for the time being, the exclusive use of means to promote its end."[50] And in another place Finney presses this dichotomy even further; the saints are dead to sin and alive to God, and the reverse is true of sinners. "The Bible . . . often speaks in so strong language as almost compels us to understand it as denying that the saints sin at all, or to conclude that sinning at all proves that one is not a saint."[51]

Throughout much of his *Systematic Theology*, Finney returned again and again to the topics that had been identified with him—and with many of the New Divinity theologians—for nearly two decades. There is no such thing as original sin in the Augustinian sense; "all sin is actual, and . . . no other than actual transgression can justly be called sin":[52]

We deny that the human constitution is morally depraved,
1. Because there is no proof of it.
2. Because it is impossible that sin should be an attribute of the substance of soul or body. It is and must be an attribute of choice or intention and not of substance.

3. To make sin an attribute or quality of substance is contrary to God's definition of sin. "Sin," says the apostle, "is anomia," a "transgression of, or a want of conformity to the moral law." That is, it consists in a refusal to love God or our neighbor, or, which is the same thing, in loving ourselves supremely.[53]

Writing a systematic work on theology gave Finney an opportunity to express in fuller detail many of the positions for which he, Taylor's New Divinity, and the New School had been attacked. One of the most persistent questions urged against the New School was, If there is no particular flaw in the human character, or bent toward sin in the constitution, whence all the sinning? Finney attempted to answer "why sin is so natural to mankind. Not because their nature is itself sinful, but because the appetites and passions tend so strongly to self-indulgence. Besides, selfishness being the ruling passion of the soul, its manifestations are spontaneous." Of course, this answer would hardly satisfy an Augustinian, who would immediately point to the operative verb "tend," and laugh gleefully. But Finney went on, "The constitution of a moral being as a whole when all the powers are developed, does not tend to sin, but strongly in an opposite direction, as is manifest from the fact that when reason is thoroughly developed by the Holy Spirit, it is more than a match for the sensibility and turns the heart to God."[54]

And what is regeneration? The Old School held that regeneration was the actual infusion of a new nature in the person by the Holy Spirit. No, said Finney:

It is not a change in the substance of soul or body. If it were, sinners could not be required to effect it. Such a change would not constitute a change of moral character. No such change is needed, as the sinner has all the faculties and natural abilities requisite to render perfect obedience to God. All he needs is to be induced to use these powers and attributes as he ought. The words conversion and regeneration do not imply any change of substance but only a change of moral state or of moral character. The terms are not used to express a physical, but a moral change. Regeneration does not express or imply the creation of any new faculties or attributes of nature, nor any change whatever in the constitution of body or mind.[55]

It was not long after the publication of the second volume of *Systematic Theology* in 1846 that the Old School responded. The

Princeton faculty took it upon itself to subject Finney's book to close scrutiny in *The Biblical Repertory and Princeton Review,* and its editor, Charles Hodge, entrusted the task to no one but himself. He began his review in a rather complimentary fashion:

> This is in more senses than one a remarkable book. It is to a degree very unusual an original work; it is the product of the author's own mind. . . . The work is therefore in a high degree logical. It is as hard to read as Euclid. Nothing can be omitted; nothing passed over slightly. . . . There is not one resting place; not one lapse into amplification, or declamation, from beginning to the close. . . . The author begins with certain postulates, or what he calls first truths of reason, and these he traces out with singular clearness and strength to their legitimate conclusions. We do not see that there is a break or a defective link in the whole chain. If you grant his principles, you have already granted his conclusions. Such a work must of course be reckless. Having committed himself to the guidance of the discursive understanding, which he sometimes calls the intelligence, and sometimes the reason, and to which he alone acknowledges any real allegiance, he pursues his remorseless course, regardless of any protest from other sources. The scriptures are throughout recognized as a mere subordinate authority. They are allowed to come in and bear confirmatory testimony, but their place is altogether secondary. Even God himself is subordinate to "the intelligence." His will can impose no obligation; it only discloses what is obligatory in its own nature and by the law of reason.[56]

This was the third time that *The Biblical Repertory* had turned its attention to Charles Finney, it will be recalled, and the second time that its editor had taken matters in hand himself (Albert Dod had reviewed the *Lectures on Revivals* in 1835). Although Hodge was not as acerbic toward Finney as Dod had been, he still felt of Finney as he had in 1832, "that Christ and his cross are practically made of none effect." Hodge placed the fault squarely upon Finney's theory of the foundation of moral obligation, declaring that "it changes the whole nature of religion." A massive shift has taken place, Hodge said, and the creation has displaced the Creator; in Finney's system "God is subordinate to the universe," and love to being in general is substituted for love to God.[57] Furthermore, Hodge declared, Finney has so decimated theology that he cannot "attach any other meaning to love than 'good will,' i.e. willing good or happiness to any one. Love of

God therefore can, according to his doctrine, be nothing more than willing his happiness; and this obligation is entirely independent of his moral excellence."[58] But this has staggering consequences, said Hodge; inasmuch as good will has no respect to the moral character of its object, "there is no more virtue in loving God (willing God's good) than in loving Satan."

Charles Hodge believed that Finney had created major problems in making "the Well Being of God and of the Universe," in Finney's phrase, the core of his theology, and in reducing "all virtue and religion to a simple act of the will," as Hodge explained it. "If virtue has no place in the affections," Hodge stated, "neither can sin have." Nonetheless, the Princetonian gave Finney credit: "Mr. Finney is beautifully consistent in all this, and in the consequences, which of necessity flow from his doctrine. He admits that . . . if a man preaches the gospel from a desire to glorify God and benefit his fellow men, he is just as wicked for so doing as a pirate. We may safely challenge Hurtado de Mendoza, Sanchez, or Molina to beat that."[59] Hodge admitted bafflement here: "It passes our comprehension to discover why the will being determined by the desire to honour God is selfishness and sin," whereas when it is determined by the desire of the highest good, it is virtuous.

For forty pages Charles Hodge made the definitive Old School review of Finney's theology in a surprisingly mild tone; there is hardly any vitriol spilled anywhere, and not one approximation to Finney's favorite phrase for his opponents, "it is absurd." Hodge was confident that the weaknesses of *Systematic Theology* were patent. "The doctrine of course rests on a false apprehension of the nature of sin and holiness, and of the grounds and extent of our obligations." No one is perfect, declared Hodge, who is not perfectly like Christ, and he found nothing of such teaching in Finney. To Hodge, "It shocks the moral sense of men to say that a pirate, with all his darkness of mind as to God, and divine things, with all his callousness, with all the moral habits of a life of crime, becomes perfectly holy, by a change of will, by forming a new intention, by mere honesty of purpose."[60]

Hodge's strong point was that he could quote a vast number of biblical passages where the saints and writers of scripture, in spite of their greatest attempts to live consistently holy lives, were forced to bewail their slips and sinful tendencies. "Need any reader of the Bible," he asked, "be reminded that the consciousness of sin, of present corruption and unworthiness, is one of the most uniform features of the experience of God's people as there recorded?" Yet Finney expected people "to believe that 'honest intention' is the whole of duty and religion," and if they have that, they are perfect. Religion, as represented by Finney, "is something exceedingly different from what good people in all ages have commonly regarded it," Hodge concluded.[61]

Some seventy-five years later, Hodge's successor at Princeton Seminary, Benjamin Warfield, was less affable with Finney. "It is quite clear that what Finney gives us is less a theology than a system of morals," Warfield stated. "God might be eliminated from it entirely without essentially changing its character."[62] Warfield found that Finney expressly taught that the ground of human justification was not the obedience of Christ for us, or the atonement, but solely the divine benevolence:[63]

> When Finney strenuously argues that God can accept as righteous no one who is not intrinsically righteous, it cannot be denied that he teaches a work-salvation, and has put man's own righteousness in the place occupied in the Reformation doctrine of justification by the righteousness of Christ.
>
> Finney, it must be confessed, exhibits no desire to conceal from himself the seriousness of his departure from the Reformation teaching in his doctrine of justification. . . . He fairly rages against this forensic doctrine. "Now," he exclaims of it, "this is certainly another gospel from the one I am inculcating. It is not a difference merely upon some speculative or theoretic point. It is a point fundamental to the gospel and to salvation, if any one can be." It is with full consciousness, therefore, that he ranges himself over against this doctrine of the Reformation, as teaching "another gospel."[64]

18

NEW MEASURES IN ENGLAND

During all these years in the Finney household, with the death of little Sarah in 1843 and the birth of Delia in 1844, Lydia's health continued to decline. Given Finney's frequent and extended absences from Oberlin, the work of managing the home and raising the children devolved almost entirely upon Lydia. She employed servants to do as much of the housework as possible, but there was a great deal they could not do. And when her husband was at home, there was if anything more work. As the most popular professor on campus and also the pastor of the town church, Finney constantly had to meet both students and members of the congregation. In the large brick home at the center of the campus there was always activity during the decade of the 1840s, with Helen, Charles, Frederic, and Julia growing rapidly, and their father delighting to romp and play with them, and encourage them in musical activities.

Because so few letters from Charles and Lydia have survived, we are forced to rely upon correspondence written to them to form an adequate idea of the family circle, and thus some of our picture must be inferential. Enough comes through, however, to portray clearly a warm family group and a proud father. The asperity of former years has largely gone from Finney; he now dealt with friends, parishioners, and admiring students. It is clear from all the sources that he came to rely on Lydia's insights and judgments increasingly, and his family was ever dearer to him.

With the Finneys' move to Oberlin, Lydia's opportunity to fill what Leonard I. Sweet has termed the "Assistant model" of the minister's wife broadened still more. As the spouse of the premier evangelist of the time, naturally she shared the limelight, and received the admiration of thousands of women across the nation. In addition, as long as her health permitted, she participated very actively in the Female Department of the college, where young women who wished to achieve careers of greater significance came to prepare themselves. For years she was a member of Oberlin's Female Board of Managers, and served as the "mother-confessor" to hundreds of young ladies for a decade.

As she had done when her husband was itinerating, at Oberlin Lydia found several functions which she could uniquely fulfill. It was most important, although an unofficial role, that the campus have a prominent woman to whom female students could come for advice and help, and Lydia was naturally fitted for that. The archives have many letters from young people seeking admission to Oberlin, recent youthful converts, young pastors and ladies seeking mates—all writing to the Finneys for advice. Because they were so widely trusted and their judgments so revered, Professor Finney and his wife often served as matchmakers, especially for pastors and missionaries, and marriage negotiations were frequently hammered out in their home. In addition, Lydia contributed greatly to the Maternal Association at Oberlin, and was the national society's highest executive officer, its first director, one of its earliest managers, and later a vice president.

While the quest for martyrdom to the cause which manifested itself occasionally in that period does not seem to have come to Lydia, nonetheless all of these demands on her limited strength hastened her decline. Finney sensed as early as 1843 that she might not live much longer, and he wrote in the *Memoirs*, "I had had a great struggle about giving up my wife to the will of God. She was in very feeble health. . . ."[1] He had frequently placed his family upon the altar of God, but suddenly, with the circumstances of Lydia's condition before him, he felt a touch of rebellion. For hours he struggled upon his knees seeking to follow God's will, but found himself unable to do it. "I was so shocked and surprised at this," he wrote, "that I perspired profusely with agony."[2] Nothing availed; though he struggled and prayed until he was exhausted, he found that if she were to be taken from him, he could not be content. While Finney was deeply distressed with himself over his reaction, it does him credit. He loved Lydia so deeply that he put aside all the demands of the moment, and concerned himself with her health unreservedly. Always emotional, Finney was deeply moved throughout her long illness by her calm resignation, religious faith, and her determination to do what she could for her family while any strength remained.

When the year 1847 arrived, four of their children were teenagers: Helen was nineteen and already married to an Oberlin professor, William Cochran; Charles was seventeen, Frederic was fifteen, Julia was thirteen, and the baby, Delia, was three. Thus most of the children could understand that their mother was failing, and the family, during this period, would be knit together very closely. It was probably the darkest time of Finney's life. He and Lydia had been married for twenty-three years, she at age twenty, he at age thirty-two, and during all that time she had been a stalwart support to him, contributing much to his ministry, providing a new role model for Evangelical women, never losing faith in his mission, and rarely complaining even in moments of severe adversity. It had not been easy for Lydia, with her modest and retiring ways, humility, and occasional depressions, being the wife of Charles Finney.

The greatest concern for Christians then was the conversion of their children, and Lydia was absolutely faithful to this. She was uncertain of the spiritual state of several of her offspring, especially Helen, and she admonished her son-in-law, "see to it *dear William* that Helen meets me in Heaven." Then, a few weeks before her death on December 17, 1847, Lydia summoned her children to her bedside and prayed for each of them. She then stated to her husband that "her work was done with and for them. . . . [She] had said all she had to say. She had given them her last advice."[3] The years of her failing health conditioned him to accept what was coming, and when she passed away he was calm.

With five children to raise, Finney was faced with the question of whether he should remarry.[4] His own needs and those of his children seemed to demand that he do so, and on November 13, 1848 President Asa Mahan of Oberlin conducted the wedding of Finney to Mrs. Elizabeth Ford Atkinson, a widow of Rochester, New York. Born in 1799, Elizabeth had married William Atkinson, an early settler of Rochester who had built the first mill there in 1817, an event of great importance to the surrounding country. As the Atkinsons became well-to-do they also became extremely active Episcopalians, and when Charles Finney began his revival in the city in 1830, they threw their support fully behind him. In a few years Elizabeth opened the Atkinson Female Seminary in the city, but an 1843 typhoid epidemic took the lives of her fifty-three-year-old husband as well as two daughters. She was to prove a good mother for Finney's children as well as a bulwark in his work for the next fifteen years. Although Finney had known Elizabeth for eighteen years, the circumstances which brought them together in marriage are not known. While many second marriages then were matters of convenience more than love, in time Elizabeth — so stalwart, self-assured, and utterly different from Lydia — captured all of Finney's affection, and his admiration as well.[5]

For the previous five years, Finney had been faithful to his professional duties at Oberlin. During Lydia's extended illness he had remained at her side. This was unusual for him, with his love for travel and novelty. But now, there were compelling reasons for him to leave for a time. For one, there was the distasteful situation surrounding President Asa Mahan, who was increasingly disliked by the faculty and many of the trustees, and in 1844 had been requested to resign.[6] Mahan had weathered that storm, but his cruel personal attacks and his haughty ways continued to alienate his associates, and in 1848 and 1849 he had become entangled in a church trial that nearly tore the Oberlin community apart. In 1846 Lucy Gillett had abandoned her children and her husband, Robert E. Gillett, who had been the college's general agent and publisher of the *Oberlin Evangelist.* The details are complex, but briefly, several in the community brought charges of improper conduct against Robert Gillett in 1848. Asa Mahan believed the rumors of scandal and charges against Gillett totally false, and he was willing to act as Gillett's counsel. Despite this he was excommunicated in December 1848, and feelings between Mahan and the faculty again reached fever pitch. Finney and Mahan had been close friends for years, but the friendship had faded over the frequent disagreements, and when Mahan left for England and France to attend the World Peace Congress and to conduct a preaching mission, during most of 1849 and part of 1850, few were sorry to see him go.

Another, even more compelling reason for Finney to leave Oberlin, was the attraction of evangelizing in the British Isles. For more than fifteen years he had been urged to go there and conduct a ministry, from the time in 1833 when Anson Phelps had written from Liverpool, telling him that in England there was a very large interest in American revivals and especially in what Finney had been doing.[7] Doubtless, Phelps planted a seed in Finney's mind that took root, describing Britain as a great and waiting field for his labors. But Finney's writings had been converting Britons even before his arrival. After 1837, when his *Lectures on Revivals* were first printed in Britain, awakenings were reported in Scotland and England because of the volume's influence. It was in Wales, however, that the book had its greatest impact from 1839 through 1843, and the resultant awakening was popularly known as "Finney's revival." The Welch Congregational minister Thomas Rees wrote to Finney that the revival had been "chiefly promoted" by his *Lectures*, which had "been instrumental in the conversion of hundreds if not thousands of our countrymen."[8] As Finney contemplated going to Britain in 1849, he may have regretted that he had not seized the opportunity to do so at an earlier time.

In the previous pages the transatlantic character of the First Great Awakening, and the formation of a closely related British and American evangelical Protestant community after the Revolution, have been noted on occasion. Taking these factors into account helps in an understanding of the web of relationships that was to support Finney in England, as well as a grasp of those circles of critics who were to assail the American and his "measures." As George Whitefield had spread the 1740s Awakening throughout the colonies, so Americans had gone to England to return the favor and to evangelize there, and Finney would be merely another in a series. Of his predecessors, perhaps Edward N. Kirk, Lorenzo Dow, and James Caughey had drawn the greatest attention. British Methodists had since their beginnings been deeply involved in itinerancy and revivalist preaching, and they allowed Dow and Caughey to have extensive ministries. Among the Congregationalists, George Redford had been conducting protracted meetings since the 1830s.

Thus, Finney must have been aware of at least some of the factors involved in British Nonconformists' interest in revivalism, although of course he was informed chiefly by those holding positive and enthusiastic views, and he would by the nature of the case be told less of any negative aspects possibly in effect. It would have been hard for him to judge, from his side of the Atlantic, the extent to which English Dissenters were committed to aggressive evangelism, the welcome he might receive among them, and the amount of cooperative support he might expect. He would have been aware of the extensive subculture of Dissent in the Industrial Age taking shape, but he could hardly have known of its sentiments in detail. Had he known how little he would be supported, perhaps he would have taken a different course.

As Finney contemplated the British ecclesiastical scene, he was well aware that to some clergymen there his name stood for all that they considered bad in American Christianity. But he also knew that

Finney in 1850: A daguerreotype taken in England during his first British campaign. In all the likenesses of Finney, his riveting eyes and stern countenance are immediately apparent. Combining these with his intense, direct manner of preaching, one understands why he had such power in the pulpit over multitudes of hearers. Courtesy of Oberlin College Archives.

his *Lectures on Revivals* had gained him many friends, and that his connection with Oberlin would open other doors, inasmuch as the college was well known there for its reforming zeal, especially in the antislavery cause. The efforts in this regard of John Keep and William Dawes have already been described. Their attendance at the World Anti-Slavery Convention in London during June 1840 won many to Oberlin's support, and their lecturing in Scotland and England over a year and a half enabled them to raise a large sum for the college. Then, in 1843, Lewis Tappan attended the Anti-Slavery Convention in England, and further enhanced the reputation of the school.

With these incentives to cross the Atlantic and work with the British Nonconformists, Finney and his fifty-year-old second wife set sail for Southampton in the autumn of 1849, and arrived there on November 6. They were met at the dock by James Harcourt, pastor of a chapel in Houghton, "a village situated midway between the market towns of Huntingdon and St. Ives," as Finney wrote, northwest of Cambridge. He had been sent to meet Finney by Potto Brown, an influential and wealthy flour miller who had become very concerned over the spiritual laxity of Huntingdonshire, and who had advanced money from his own pocket to provide a pastor for the town. Brown was well known for his irenic, broad-based evangelicalism, his generosity toward the temperance cause and the Anti-State Church Association, and for his support of schools. He had brought Harcourt to Houghton, recognizing in him a pastor fully supportive of awakenings.[9] Of all the invitations Finney had received begging him to come to Britain, those from Potto Brown and his friends, offering financial support and promising pulpits available to him, had made the greatest impression on him.[10]

On Sunday, November 11, Finney began preaching in the Union Chapel at Houghton. Opposition began to manifest itself from the Established Church as wealthy landholders forbade their workers to attend, but it did little good. Crowds came, some walking many miles to hear the American evangelist. The small chapel was packed, with hundreds unable to crowd in. Nothing daunted, Potto Brown found a huge tent and had it set up in a field, and this proved adequate to hold more than a thousand auditors. Finney realized that, if Brown's letters had been impressive, the man himself was even more remarkable. "Although brought up a Quaker," Finney wrote, "he was entirely catholic in his views, and was laboring, in an independent way, directly for the salvation of the people around him."[11] One technique Brown utilized was to invite great numbers of people to his home for every meal, each day, that they might meet and converse with Finney.

In a short while the *Oberlin Evangelist* reported, "We learn that Prof. Finney's first labors in England have been chiefly in Houghton for a period of about three weeks, and signally successful."[12] Given Brown's generous support and encouragement of his work, Finney could hardly have given him any less time. Nonetheless he was naturally eager to get on to bigger things, in the cities. This opportunity came through another of the men who had implored Finney to come to England, Charles Hill Roe, pastor of the Heneage Street Baptist Chapel of Birmingham and a close friend of Potto Brown. Roe, formerly the traveling secretary of the Baptist Home Missionary Society, had taken this pastorate in 1842, and he claimed that his congregation had awaited Finney's arrival since that time.[13]

Birmingham was a large and heavily industrialized city in the midlands. Although Finney was happy to be preaching to Roe's congregation, he knew that a ministry in one church could hardly be expected to reach its teeming populace. For him to be generally accepted, it was imperative that he gain the approval of John Angell James, one of Nonconformity's luminaries in the mid-nineteenth century and pastor for forty-five years of the two-thousand-member Carr's Lane Chapel. Finney was later to write that James "wielded a very extensive influence in that city, and indeed throughout England." This was in part because of the vast popularity of his booklet, *The Anxious Inquirer After Salvation Directed and Encouraged*, of which over two hundred thousand copies had been distributed, and which was widely read in America. James, however, was not ready to give his endorsement to Finney's work too readily. He had important friends in many places, was a regular reader of the American religious press, was well aware of the *Biblical Repertory and Princeton Review* attacks on Finney, and had been receiving letters from London and the United States telling of Finney's departure from the Presbyterian denomination, of Oberlin perfectionism, and of other matters in his past.

Having been through some unsettling episodes with itinerants in the past, James was determined to proceed cautiously; yet at the same time he recognized Finney's popularity, and the good that might be done if the American would be found to be cooperative and his theology acceptable — at least within limits. Skillfully maintaining his reserve, James did not invite Finney to preach at his church, but first invited the American and the Nonconformist pastors of Birmingham to breakfast at his home. James was of course eager to avoid importing any problems from across the Atlantic but, wisely, he had a larger purpose in calling the clergy together than merely to discuss Finney's acceptability. He began the meeting by commenting that things were not going well in the churches; that standards were low, and there was altogether too much willingness just to achieve mediocre results, "while the conversions, in most of the churches, were very few, and, after all, the people were going to destruction."[14] James concluded that something must be done, and left the floor open to discussion upon the obvious. Cleverly he had shifted the emphasis from rumors concerning Finney to the spiritual needs of the city.

After some discussion the pastors agreed to invite Finney to hold meetings in their churches in succession. He preached half a dozen times in Carr's Lane Chapel and then made the rounds of several other Birmingham churches, returning to Charles Roe's Heneage Street Chapel and the large Ebenezer Chapel in Steelhouse Lane, which at that time was without a minister. In all these churches he found crowded congregations, but among Birmingham evangelicals generally, Richard Carwardine has concluded, "Finney's three-month stay was little more than an absorbing interlude, regarded with great interest but attracting little organized support."[15] As to the failure of the pastors to organize behind Finney, much of this may be due to the letters that were being circulated warning against his influence. This attempt to mute him was to be continued throughout the English tour. In an effort to counteract this, Finney gave James and his close friend, George Redford, copies of *Lectures on Systematic Theology.* Redford, a theologian in his own right, had been trying to bring revival to his congregation for some years, and he greatly admired Finney. When Redford had an opportunity to interview Finney, he proclaimed to James (according to Finney), "he has his own way of stating theological propositions; but I cannot see that he differs, on any essential point, from us."[16]

In the meantime, the feelings at Oberlin against President Mahan had reached a critical turn. Mahan, away from it all in London, tried to pretend disinterest, writing to Finney on January 5 of his activities and asking for further news.[17] Just two days later John Morgan wrote Finney from Oberlin to inform him that the faculty had decided to ask Mahan to resign, although, given his intransigence, they knew it would be useless.[18] If Mahan was disturbed by this, he did not show it, and took ship shortly thereafter to return to the States and confront his antagonists at Oberlin.

In the interim they had laid their own plans. Joab Seeley, an Oberlin agent, had persuaded the congregation of a church in Newark, New Jersey, to extend a call to Mahan to be their pastor. This would be, they believed, an ideal way for Mahan to save face, allowing him to resign from the presidency under the pretense that he wished to accept this desirable pastoral call. But Mahan would have none of it. When he arrived at Oberlin he mentioned nothing of the Newark call, and proceeded to rally his supporters for another defense of his tenure. Petitions were signed, and little else occupied the students and settlers for more than a month, as they split over the issue. On one petition 285 signatures had been gathered, the signers declaring that they had "heard with pain & regret of the contemplated resignation of President Mahan."

An event of significance for Charles Finney's future was the statement presented to Mahan by the faculty on March 18, in which a recent letter from Finney was quoted. The formal statement read in part:

> Dear Bro. Mahan
>
> We deem it our duty to communicate to you our views of the character of the letter dated March 8th which you have addressed to Bro. Dawes, respecting the document of the same date addressed to you by your associates. . . .
>
> Every assertion respecting the nature of our communication in your letter is entirely erroneous, and every one of its erroneous assertions is fitted to excite odium against us & conciliate sympathy towards yourself. . . .
>
> From the statement that the communication is from your "associates who are on the ground" some may receive the impression . . . that Prof. Finney differs in opinion from us. We have the most ample evidence that it is not so. . . . We think ourselves at liberty to give you the following extract from a recent letter of his.
>
> "I think the *Faculty and nearly all his* [your] *most familiar friends* have substantially one opinion respecting him [you], and that this opinion may be expressed thus; — He is a Christian man, & in many respects a useful & lovely man — upon the whole, honest & well-meaning, but possessing *certain characteristics* which are highly calculated to undermine & finally to annihilate confidence in his discretion & even in his piety where there is a want of intimate acquaintance. . . . The loss of confidence in Bro. M's discretion & fitness for his position in several respects has become so universal in the Faculty & so extensive in the Community that to go on so is useless & *even impossible.* This I have seen clearly for the last year. I have been long dreading to come to the conclusion that it was best for him to leave. But every thing con-

sidered, I am compelled to the above conclusion. May the Lord direct. . . ."[19]

This formal statement to Mahan was signed by the entire faculty, with the exception of Henry E. Peck and, of course, Finney. This was the only recorded instance of Finney's opposing Mahan, but it was enough for the president, as might be supposed. Mahan never forgave Finney for it.

Finally, on April 18, a special meeting of the trustees was called to make some determination of the explosive matter. For three days they wrangled. At last a settlement was reached. Because Mahan would not offer his resignation, the trustees were loath to demand it. It was finally decided that the faculty would withdraw its request for his resignation if Mahan would henceforth change his ways. Accordingly, a paper was drawn up by the faculty and trustees jointly, outlining their major objections to his conduct. The first two points give an idea of the whole: "1. He should see that his self-esteem has amounted to self conceit . . . & that under the same influence he underrates the ability & character of his brethren. 2. He should see his tendency to attribute unworthy motives to his brethren & promise to do so no more."[20] When the paper was read to Mahan, he agreed to mend his behavior; hands were shaken all around, and there was a general hope that this nasty affair was behind them, and concord would now reign.

Of course no such thing happened. Mahan made no changes in his deportment, and other issues only added fuel to the fire. Because of the controversy and Finney's extended absence, student enrollment was down, and John Morgan wrote to Finney on May 7, 1850, expressing the hope that he would soon return, for that would surely provide some relief for the situation.[21] A month later Lewis Tappan wrote an urgent letter to Finney in London, saying that for the sake of the school he should return immediately.[22] On June 18 Willard Sears wrote to Finney from Boston telling of the latest development: fearing that Oberlin was about to collapse, Mahan's followers decided to pull out of the debacle before it was too late, taking with them as many students and supporters as possible, and founding a new school where all would be of one mind under their leader. It was, Sears wrote, to be called a "National University," and it was to be established south of nearby Cleveland![23]

In the latter part of August 1850, there was the annual meeting of the trustees, and Asa Mahan took that opportunity to resign from the presidency of the college. John Keep, president of the trustees, was much relieved that the long struggle was over, and he wrote to Finney, "The President sent in his resignation, and verbally added that he had pledged himself to accept of the Presidency of the contemplated Seminary at Cleveland."[24] John Morgan was appointed president pro tempore, and it was noted with relief during the next weeks that rather than the collapse of Oberlin, which had been forecast by Mahan's supporters, peace once again reigned on the campus.

As for the "National University," the grand pretensions were scaled down to reality and it was called Cleveland University. On the three hundred acres of land that had been purchased about a mile south of Cleveland a campus was laid out, and the erection of a building was begun in the summer of 1851.[25] In the spring of that year the Ohio legislature had granted the school a charter, and instruction began shortly thereafter. As can be guessed, trouble plagued the "university" from the start. Understandably there were hard feelings between Oberlin and anyone connected with the enterprise, especially because many of the two to three dozen students had transferred from the older school. When Mahan and William Dawes approached some of the Oberlin supporters for financial contributions, naturally it was greatly resented, and in retaliation the list of Mahan's faults to which he had admitted in April 1850 was disclosed to the backers of Cleveland University. When they learned of Mahan's weaknesses, there was consternation among those promoting the enterprise. Some withdrew, notably the university's secretary and treasurer, ex-Governor William Slade of Vermont. This was the final blow to the venture. In New England some who had promised substantial subscriptions stated that they were canceled, and with that the school closed forever. Asa Mahan, needless to say, was out of a job—but that was hardly of concern to those at Oberlin. Robert Fletcher has well said of Mahan, "When he was eliminated Oberlin changed. The opposition to the 'heathen classics' died down because the leader of the movement was gone. 'Sanctification' was soon a matter for apology. From 1850 Oberlin moved away steadily from radicalism toward moderation and from heresy toward orthodoxy."[26]

All this while in England, Charles Finney awaited anxiously for the mails to bring him news of the noisy controversy that was disturbing the peaceful serenity of the Ohio forests. He had departed from Birmingham in the middle of March 1850 to preach in George Redford's church in Worcester, the old cathedral city of some thirty thousand residents. Finney was quite eager to claim, in his *Memoirs*, that both Redford and John Angell James had given full approval of his theological views,[27] but the extant correspondence does not quite jibe with the claim. On January 29 James had sent Finney a letter he had received from a pastor who heard him preach in London shortly after his arrival in mid-November. This pastor complained to James that Finney had said that "faith was *not* the gift of God." James chided Finney, "Your sermons in London did not certainly remove the unfavorable impression as you learn from the letter I send you."[28]

Then, as George Redford perused the volumes of *Systematic Theology* Finney had given him to read, on two occasions he wrote to Finney, asking that, if the volumes were to be republished in England, Finney remove some "objectionable phraseology."[29] Because Finney was so eager for acceptance in Britain, especially by a man so influential as George Redford, he went right at the task. John Campbell reported a year later, "Mr. Tegg has purchased the copyright of Mr. Finney's great work on Theology, which, during his residence in London, he has carried through the press, severely revising, and, to considerable extent, re-writing it. In a few days, that goodly volume of nearly a thousand pages will be before the public."[30]

When Finney preached at Worcester he was approached by some "wealthy gentlemen" who, apparently, saw an inherent defect in the way all evangelists had to work in that day. In any city, Finney was forced to depend upon the invitations of pastors to house his meetings in their churches, and, if these were not forthcoming, he was at a loss for hospitality. This dependence plagued Finney throughout his ministry, as we have seen. With the exception of his adequate auditoriums in the Chatham Street Chapel, the Broadway Tabernacle, and the Oberlin First Church, he was always at the mercy of too small buildings. The problem was not merely inadequate churches and the uncertainties of invitations. Compounding this was the difficulty that whenever Finney was invited to a particular church, naturally he was expected to devote his ministry mainly to that congregation, and he was usually prevented from making it a "citywide campaign."

More broadly, Finney at times wished a true ecumenicity—an outreach to entire communities rather than just to one or two churches—and with the exceptions of Philadelphia in 1828 and Rochester in 1831, the innate sectarianism of many clergymen prevented this broader ministry through much of his life. Despite the size of Philadelphia, in 1828 the New School Presbyterians had shared Finney's desire to reach the whole city, and thereby solve the problem, by using the largest auditorium available, which happened to be a German Reformed church. To them, what did that matter?

A century before, George Whitefield (and to a lesser extent John Wesley) had solved the problem simply by preaching outdoors to crowds of ten to thirty thousand. But then, Whitefield had a stentorian voice, which, according to Ben Franklin, "might be heard and understood at a great distance." Franklin was so intrigued with Whitefield's vocal power that he performed some mathematical calculations on the vast audiences; "I computed," he stated, "that he might well be heard by more than thirty thousand."[31] Charles Finney's voice was not that powerful, so he was confined to indoor auditoriums as were his contemporaries Jacob Knapp, Jabez Swan, Jedediah Burchard, A. C. Kingsley, James Caughey, Daniel Baker, Orson G. Parker, and the other itinerant evangelists of the 1840s and 1850s. The well-to-do gentlemen in Worcester, however, offered Finney a solution to the vexing problem: they would have built for his use a portable "tabernacle" that could be taken down and moved in sections by railway car, and then set up again at the next series of meetings. Finney explained:

> They proposed to build it, one hundred and fifty feet square, with seats so constructed as to provide for five or six thousand people. They said if I would consent to use it, and preach in it from place to place, as circumstances might demand, for six months, they would be at the expense of building it. But on consulting the ministers at that place, they advised me not to do it. They thought it would be more useful for me to occupy the pulpits, in the already established congregations, in different parts of England, than to go through England preaching in an independent way, such as was proposed by these gentlemen.
>
> As I had reason to believe the ministers generally would disapprove of a course then so novel, I declined to pledge myself to occupy it. I have since thought that I probably made a mistake; for when I came to be acquainted with the congregations, and places of public worship, of the Independent churches, I found them generally so small, so badly ventilated, so situated, so hedged in and circumscribed by the Church—I mean, of course, the Establishment—that it has since appeared to me doubtful whether I was right; as I have been of opinion that I could, upon the whole, have accomplished much greater good in England, by carrying as it were, my own place of worship with me, going where I pleased, and providing for the gathering of the masses, irrespective of denominations. If my strength were now as it was then, I should be strongly inclined to visit England again, and try an experiment of that kind.[32]

It is not difficult to sympathize with Finney's dilemma. As a foreigner in a new land, with many clergymen and laypeople plying him for favors but with no proven old friends on whom to rely, Finney was literally at the mercy of the whims and demands of strangers. The idea of a portable meeting place for evangelistic services would have to wait until the next generation. Dwight L. Moody utilized the concept of a temporary hall first in February 1875, when none of the Liverpool buildings was deemed adequate for the anticipated crowds, and a huge sheet iron tabernacle, called Victoria Hall, was erected.

In early March 1875, as Moody moved to his spectacular London campaign, the city was so vast that the committee directing the preparations divided the city into four huge sections, with the idea of holding simultaneous meetings in four halls and dividing Moody's time as judiciously as possible among them and using associate evangelists in the interims. Agricultural Hall, the largest auditorium ever occupied by Moody, was rented in the northern part of London; the Royal Opera House in the fashionable West End; and two temporary structures were erected on Bow Road and in Camberwell Green, the working-class areas of the city, each of them seating between eight thousand and nine thousand.[33] In all, during the four months of Moody's London campaign, 285 meetings were held throughout the city, and although the attendance figures certainly included many repeaters, over two and one-half million people heard the heavy-set Yankee speak without benefit of public address systems or other modern aids — a truly astonishing feat. By skirting dependence on clergymen and their churches, and by renting or erecting his own much larger halls, D. L. Moody was able to avoid the problems that beset Charles Finney.

Enough of Finney's labors in England have been examined to begin to answer some questions. Who were the ones who heard him gladly? What was the social context of Finney's preaching in Britain? It does not seem that the upper classes supported his meetings to any extent. Except for well-to-do Quakers and some wealthy individuals who were Dissenters, for the most part the British upper classes belonged to the Church of England. This was still the most powerful religious body in the nation, and Anglican parishes had never cultivated an American-style tradition of occasional revivals. Years later, D. L. Moody's committees, in skirting denominational preferences, were careful to include as many evangelical, low-church Anglican clergymen as possible in their workings and on platforms as Moody spoke, but Finney had no such extensive committees, and no Anglican contacts or backing.

As for the urban lower class, it was already turning away in increasing numbers from organized Christianity by 1850, although in some cities Finney did find moderate support from this segment of society. Finney, like Moody at a later date, was to draw his audiences largely from more direct descendants of the Evangelical Revival, the drapers' assistants of the YMCA clientele, the middle-class shopkeepers, school teachers, and upwardly mobile elements, and from other social groups uncertain about their identity. The middle-class evangelicals who supported Finney took little notice, for the most part, of what was happening among agricultural laborers, miners, and potters. The problem, however, was more complex than that, involving the fact that Finney held the majority of his meetings in cities, with the exception of his work in Huntingdonshire. In 1850, the differences between urban and rural areas were becoming more pronounced. Village depopulation proceeded rapidly as the Industrial Age arrived and called for ever greater numbers of laborers in the factories. As the rural areas declined, towns grew in size and wealth, containing large numbers of newly arrived lower-class laborers. The religious census of 1851 showed that workingmen in the larger, industrial towns and cities were not attending the churches, and were rapidly discarding any religious profession. Neither Finney's work nor the churches were able to reach them.

From the middle of March to May 5, 1850, Finney labored at George Redford's church in Worcester. Requests for his preaching were at this point coming from many quarters, some from prominent pastors such as Benjamin Parsons in Gloucestershire. However, the majority of the extant invitations were from lesser laypeople or pastors. Thus when Finney heard from one of the outstanding Nonconformist leaders, we may imagine his reaction. John Campbell, a large, energetic Scotsman, had left Kilmarnock in 1839 to become pastor of two London churches that had been built for George Whitefield, the Tabernacle in Moorfields and the Tottenham Court Road Chapel. These were situated about three miles apart, and as pastor, Campbell occupied the post in an unusual way. "His voice was such that he did not preach," Finney stated.[34] "He supplied his pulpit by employing, for a few weeks at a time, the most popular ministers that could be employed, to preach to his people." Campbell was nonetheless busy, for he was the editor as well of several religious periodicals in Britain, including the *Christian Witness* and the *British Banner*. At the end of March he wrote to Finney, asking "whether it may not be possible for you to visit London, and give it two, three, or four weeks of your energetic labours? You are aware that it pleased God, now a century ago, through the instrumentality of an Englishman to bless America; and who can tell but it may please him, by means of an American, to bless England? We have much need of a Revival throughout our borders."[35] Knowing well of John Campbell's crucial position among the Nonconformists, and the importance of his London pulpit, Finney was happy to accept the invitation.

Meanwhile, things were going well at Finney's meetings in Worcester, and in a printed circular George Redford praised the American:

> He is making a great impression here; *full* congregations every night, and some hopeful conversions. I am quite satisfied that, if brethren will give him the opportunity, he may be made a great blessing at this juncture. I have now heard many sermons, and all my fears concerning his orthodoxy are dissipated. He sometimes uses a novel, perhaps a strange phraseology; but rarely anything to offend even critical ears. His energy is surprising, and the effect is delightful. HE WILL TEACH many of us to preach in a new way.[36]

This broadside had the apparent purpose of quelling fears among the British that Finney was merely an American humbug or ranter, for after Redford's endorsement of Finney was concluded, the sheet then went on to quote Finney himself. "I find that vast misapprehensions prevail on this side of the Atlantic, in regard to the great revivals on the other side," Finney stated. Had the British forgotten the work of Whitefield, or the great Wesleyan revival?

Finney went on to attempt to draw complete parallels between the historic awakenings and his own work: "I fear and dread," he wrote, "an unintelligent bluster and excitement."[37] Intelligence across the Atlantic had brought disturbing tales of harrowing camp meetings of the Cane Ridge variety in the past fifty years—and were not Oberlin and Rochester, after all, on the *frontier* of America? Finney had his work cut out for him in dispelling notions that he might be another Barton Stone or James McGready.

By the middle of May, Finney was preaching from Whitefield's pulpit. The *Oberlin Evangelist* was delighted that he was now in the "Queen of cities," and was certain that "the London Ministry and churches will be glad to welcome him and to bid him godspeed in his benevolent endeavor to diffuse the religion of the age."[38]

After Finney preached for several weeks to large attendances (the sanctuary seated three thousand), he knew from past experience that there was a large number of concerned people in the congregation who were ready to make some commitment. The coming Sunday evening there was to be a communion service, and Finney believed that would be an ideal time to hold an inquiry meeting, while the sacrament was being served in the sanctuary. Asking John Campbell about the availability of another meeting hall, the pastor "hesitated, and expressed doubts whether there were any that would attend such a meeting as that."[39] Finney was convinced that Campbell, with all his experience and desire for a revival, had no concept of the psychology at work among his people. So the evangelist pressed the pastor about such a room, and Campbell replied that there was the infant school room, which would hold perhaps thirty or forty at most. "O," Finney responded, "that is not half large enough. Have you not a larger room?" Campbell was amazed at Finney's request, and asked if there really was any discernible interest among the congregation in making a commitment at that point. Then he stated that there was the British school room, but that held some fifteen hundred people, and "of course you don't want that." Confidently, Finney replied that that was the very room. Campbell regarded Finney as impetuous, and said with some exasperation, "Do you suppose that in the midst of London, under an invitation to those that are seeking the salvation of their souls . . . that they will single themselves out, right in the daytime, and under such a call as that, publicly given, to attend such a meeting as that?" Elsewhere, Finney wrote of Campbell that he was "an earnest, but a very belligerent, man,"[40] and it was somewhat daring of Finney to reply that he knew the state of the people better than did Campbell, and that the gospel is as well adapted to the English as to the Americans.

Finney preached a short sermon that evening, and then explained to the congregation what he intended. He was precise in delineating the type of person he wished to come to the after-meeting; those confident of their salvation were not invited, nor "careless sinners," but only those truly concerned. Meanwhile, Campbell listened. Then Finney dismissed the congregation. Campbell "nervously and anxiously looked out of the window, to see which way the congregation went," for the way to the British school room was down Cowper Street a few yards and then through a narrow passage. "To [Campbell's] great astonishment, Cowper Street was perfectly crowded with people," Finney related; "When I entered, I found the room packed. . . . I soon discovered that the congregation were pressed with conviction, in such a manner that great care needed to be taken, to prevent an explosion of irrepressible feeling."[41] In the meanwhile, Campbell was consumed with curiosity and went through the communion service as fast as dignity would permit, and then rushed to the British school room to see what was afoot. Entering the room, he was "amazed at the crowd present, and especially at the amount of feeling manifested." Finney then proceeded to deal with the people just as he would have dealt with a group of Americans, with no change in technique whatever.

From mid-May through mid-September 1850, Finney continued at Whitefield's Tabernacle in Moorfields. From the evidence, he had none of the committees and a fraction of the multitudinous publicity that aided in D. L. Moody's great success a quarter-century later in London. To Finney's delight, he found that he was not speaking continually to the same hearers, but constantly new audiences. "Whence they all came," he wrote, "Dr. Campbell did not know, and no one could tell; but that hundreds and thousands of them were converted, there is no reason to doubt."[42] However, if the following account by John Campbell is the case, there was little reason to wonder where the crowds were coming from:

> It is but proper to say, that the extraordinary audiences of Mr. Finney, through so long a period, have not been the sole fruit of mere pulpit attraction. He has been sustained as never was a preacher before in the Metropolis nor in these lands. In addition to the aids he derived from the journals under our conduct, other means have been adopted on an unusual scale to awaken public attention. In addition to the issue of two large Addresses, written by the Pastor, of eight thousand copies each, distributed from house to house throughout the surrounding neighborhood, the young men of the Tabernacle have labored most laudably, and even heroically, to excite the attention of the careless, and to bring them to hear the Word of Life. They actually subscribed among themselves between thirty and forty pounds to work the Press! Fifty thousand copies of another Address, prepared by the Pastor, were circulated by them and the young females throughout the city, and large numbers of other addresses. Besides all this, large bills were extensively posted, and not only so, but carried on the shoulders of men throughout the numerous thoroughfares. . . . These boards, which were borne through the streets, created considerable scandal to

Elizabeth Atkinson Finney and her husband. A daguerreotype taken in England during their first British campaign, about 1850. The silver plate has deteriorated considerably, creating the spots. Elizabeth's determination and strength of character seem apparent here. Note that Finney is no longer smooth-shaven, but has grown sideburns. Courtesy of Oberlin College Archives.

not a few worthy people, who are not quite as wise as the children of this generation. And there were not wanting those to blame both the Pastor of the Tabernacle and Mr. Finney. . . . Neither of them so much as even knew of the thing till it had been some time in operation.[43]

At the same time, antagonists in America attempted to halt the work as well. The *Presbyterian*, published in Philadelphia, carried an article on July 20, 1850, which first quoted from John Campbell's *British Banner*, and then declared:

It is obvious from this, that Finney preaching is to have its run in London, as it had here. Similar accounts, even far more favourable, were given in the early years of his labours in this country; but the churches that *enjoyed* his ministrations have wept bloody tears of regret that he ever saw them. We presume that no man, now living or dead, has inflicted more injury upon the cause of religion, and especially upon revivals of religion, than Charles G. Finney. Thousands, who were once his admirers and friends, are now witness to the truth of this solemn and awful declaration. We make it in view of our accountability to God, as well as to those who read this paper; and if our friends in Great Britain should be tempted to try the experiment of Mr. Finney's gospel in their churches, they will find it eminently successful at first, and disastrous in the end.[44]

The *Presbyterian* was an Old School paper edited by a man named Prime, and this article was reprinted in the *Puritan Recorder* and several other papers, reaching Britain and causing Finney much consternation, for it hinted at far more than it said.[45]

John Campbell, possibly among other reasons because he was Finney's sole host in London, supported the American to the hilt. In all fairness it is remarkable that these two exceedingly strong-willed individuals kept on such good terms, without a single clash recorded, for almost a full year of association.[46] With the power of two prominent journals at his command, Campbell used their columns to praise Finney's ministry: "His voice is clear and remarkably strong. . . . Rarely, on Sabbath or week days, does he preach less than an hour and a half. . . . Yet never a man had less of the meretricious or claptrap than Mr. Finney." Campbell was also struck by Finney's directness and accusation of the unconverted; "In speaking to the multitude, he always addresses them, not as unfortunate, but as criminal, ever pressing upon them the doctrine that nothing prevents them from repenting and believing but their pride and love of sin."[47]

Another aspect of Finney's ministry in London was the part that Elizabeth Atkinson Finney took in the proceedings. Obviously a woman of determination and strength, she was willing to do anything that might assist in bringing people into the church. At Whitefield's Tabernacle a meeting for poor and unchurched women was held, and Elizabeth was invited to attend and address these women. It was the British custom, as in New England, that ladies should not speak in gatherings with gentlemen present, and Elizabeth naturally assumed that none would be there. She was wrong; a number of men were present, and she waited for them to leave. Again she was dismayed, for these gentlemen were vitally interested in the welfare of the poor women, and wished to listen as she spoke, apparently being willing to violate custom. Uncertain of herself, Elizabeth arose and began to give a talk that lasted for forty-five minutes. At the conclusion some of the men stated that they were delighted with her message, and asked her to do the same in other meetings for women. When Elizabeth told her husband what she had done, he too was concerned, fearing that it might bring condemnation down upon them. But this did not happen, and she accepted the challenge to work with women during the remainder of the London meetings.[48]

Still, carping criticisms of Finney came from America, and as from nowhere a defender appeared. He was the 37-year-old Henry Ward Beecher, son of Lyman, who had taken the pastorate of the Plymouth Congregational Church of Brooklyn only three years previously. On a trip to England in the summer of 1850 he stopped by the Tabernacle in Moorfields to hear again the man of whom his father had spoken so often — usually with bitterness — over the past quarter-century, who had doubtless done more than anyone else to frustrate his father's bid for preeminence among the American clergy. Finney and Henry Ward Beecher had met recently, when Finney had been invited to preach in the Plymouth Church pulpit on October 7, 1849, as he came to New York to take ship for England. On that first occasion, and again in London, Beecher was pleased at what he heard from Finney. Inasmuch as he was already in rebellion against much that his father believed, but had not yet adopted his later progressively liberal views, Beecher was able to accept the anti-institutional individualism of Finney at this point in his life, whereas later he would repudiate it utterly.[49] It was only three years since he had come from the Midwest to be a pastor in the increasingly fashionable residential area of Brooklyn Heights, and he was then theologically much like Finney. Lyman Abbott said, "Mr. Beecher's preaching at this period of his life was preeminently revival preaching."[50]

Graciously, John Campbell invited Beecher, along with Finney, to be his guest. In their conversations in Campbell's home, Beecher had all his fears dispelled that his father's old adversary was an ogre. Doubtless Finney was eager to befriend Beecher, recognizing that he was rising fast in the religious world. They discussed the attacks in the American papers on Finney, and of the letters being sent to British pastors. Beecher was appalled, and very sympathetic. In a few days he wrote from Liverpool that he had decided to return to the States. Two days later he wrote again, perhaps thinking that Finney badly needed his encouragement. He urged Finney to remain in London, saying, "if I can do anything for you after my arrival, I shall be glad to do it."[51] And when he arrived home he wrote an open letter in the *New York Independent*, publicly rebuking Finney's American attackers:

> On two occasions we were present, when, at the close of the Sabbath evening's service more than a thousand persons presented themselves in an adjoining hall as inquirers. Nor have we ever witnessed in any place, more solemnity, order, and unexceptionable propriety in the conduct of meetings, than has prevailed under Mr. Finney at the Tabernacle. And now, if we were an English clergyman, and if we were inclined to doubt the reality of Revivals, and, seeing the results of Mr. Finney's labors, should hear it testified from the land of revivals that they were spurious, that good as they might now seem, they would end in mischief, we should conclude, *not* against Mr. Finney, but against revivals. We should say, "If these are spurious, all revivals are spurious." This is the tendency of the efforts put forth by religious newspapers in America to undermine Mr. Finney in England.[52]

Finney had originally anticipated that the meetings at the Tabernacle would terminate in mid-August, but the attendances were so great, and the conversions so numerous, that he was prevailed upon to extend his work. So, through the hot London summer he toiled away on an enormously demanding schedule that would have floored many younger men. But the work took its toll; he reported, "After I had preached for Dr. Campbell about four months and a half, I became very hoarse; and my wife's health also became much affected by the climate, and by our intense labors."[53] Campbell, meanwhile, was ecstatic at the results; he reported in the *British Banner* at the end of August that the number of inquirers was more than one thousand and climbing rapidly.[54] Soon Finney had another visitor:

> In September my friend [Potto] Brown, of Houghton, called on us, and seeing the state of health that we were both in, he said, "This will never do. You must go to France, or somewhere on the continent where they cannot understand your language; for there is no rest for you in England as long as you are able to speak at all."[55]

With that he handed Finney fifty pounds sterling.

Paris was chosen as the place where the American evangelist and his wife would rest, and a letter of introduction for Finney was sent to Mr. Charles Cooke of that City, that they might stay for a time in his home. With the change of climate, and the diversions available, they made rapid strides in recovering their health. But the Finneys had not come to the Old World to see the sights. By October 6 they were back in England. Potto Brown was concerned lest the persuasive John Campbell convince Finney to return to the Tabernacle immediately, and so Brown brought them to his home at Houghton, probably with the intention of allowing Finney to do local preaching only. But sequestering the Finneys in somewhat remote Huntingdonshire did not prevent letters from finding their way to them.

With an insistence that would not be muted, friends at Oberlin continued to request the date of Finney's return. Finney's 22-year-old daughter Helen, now married to Jacob Dolson Cox, was concerned about student attrition due to his absence and wrote on July 31, "the Faculty and students are very anxious to know what you will do about returning, as it will influence the classes greatly in regard to staying."[56] Professor John Morgan wrote frequently, and trustee president John Keep maintained a steady barrage of missives designed to lure Finney back without delay. In late August Keep wrote to hint broadly that the trustees wished to have Finney accept the presidency of the college, and if he were there he would have been offered the post at the last meeting. "I regard it as essential that you return to this Institution as soon as is practicable," Keep stated. "Oh what a relief were you now on the ground."[57]

Charles Finney's response to these demands and allurements

to return is rather puzzling. They swayed him, apparently, not at all. From all available evidence he does not seem to have had any obligations to remain in England, and yet there he stayed until the next spring, turning a deaf ear to all entreaty—even the lure of the college presidency!

Finney wrote to John Campbell at Whitefield's Tabernacle that he needed rest to allow his voice to return to its strength, and that he had decided to confine himself to some preaching at Houghton and to follow that with a few weeks spent in Dr. George Redford's church in Worcester. Campbell had been pursuing Finney with almost as many letters as came from Oberlin, and hearing of the American's plans, he responded, on October 22, 1850:

> You seem to forget that he who labours in London, and in such a sphere as you recently filled, labours not so much for a Congregation as for a City. Your week-day Congregations were generally, at least two thirds, and, I believe, three fourths, entire strangers; so that while the speaker was stationary, the assembly was rotatory; you were in effect preaching to portions of a hundred churches, and to that extent diffusing new life and interest. . . .
>
> I have no conception that any of the principal places will invite you, since ministers will not lay themselves aside, giving you the scope which is essential to the effect of your ministrations. . . .
>
> Once more, and very seriously, should you go to some obscure and new place, you will be toiling in darkness, and the country will hear little more of your labours, and desire no fresh impulse from the publication of facts connected with them, whereas by laboring with us, you will stand connected with "The Banner" and the "Witness."[58]

Laying aside John Campbell's insistence, it was of course true when he declared that nowhere else in Britain could Finney hope to procure such an audience as he had in the heart of London at the Tabernacle. Finney did not try to pretend otherwise, and so when his voice was strong again he returned to Whitefield's pulpit. The *British Banner* of November 20, 1850, trumpeted, "we are now in a condition to make a communication which will cheer the hearts of thousands in this great metropolis. The Rev. C. G. Finney will resume his labours at the Tabernacle next Lord's-day week, first of December."[59]

At the same time Campbell took on the *Puritan Recorder*, which was published in Boston and had taken up the attack on Finney after *The Presbyterian* had begun it on July 20. The *Puritan Recorder,* in its continuing assaults through the autumn of 1850, stated that when Finney began his ministry he had been looked on as the great power of God. But he had not then broached his "heresies" of perfectionism, and now opinions were greatly changed, and most of the pulpits where he had previously preached would not accept him. The reason many pastors opposed him, the paper stated, was to "be found more in the practical results of his preaching than in the doctrines which he avows."[60]

On the basis of the months he had worked with Charles Finney and observed his methods closely, John Campbell sneered at such logic. Those who wrote that, he charged, were listening to hearsay, and knew nothing of the man at firsthand. "Now this is remarkably curious to us, men of the Old World, since we had thought that doctrines determined results—that where the results were good, the doctrines could scarcely be bad," Campbell said. This pragmatic approach served him. Yes, he admitted that Finney entertained some "inaccurate views," but they were somewhat inconsequential, "whereas the doctrines of the great salvation, as by him proclaimed, have proved both the power of God and the wisdom of God to many souls."[61]

Understandably, Charles Finney was incensed as the attacks continued. It was his usual practice over the years to ignore his enemies, but that was on home soil, where facts could rather easily be checked and the truth ascertained. But this was different. With allegations coming from America, from supposedly reputable journals, how could the English determine what was indeed the case? Taking pen in hand on December 12, 1850, Finney wrote a long letter that appeared in the *New York Evangelist* for April 17, 1851. It read in part:

> And now, will you allow me to ask, Where have I done so much to disparage revivals? What churches have I labored in where so much evil has resulted? When have they *"wept tears of blood"* or any other tears, *because of evils* that have resulted from my labors? . . . Where, I ask, have I rent churches, introduced divisions, led the church astray, or unsettled pastors? I appeal to those who *know.* Let those churches and ministers who have been so injured by any fault of mine, speak.
>
> Give us facts, names, dates, places, not hearsay. I have heard much talk; give us truth. . . . But I beseech my brethren, slander not those glorious revivals. If there ever were genuine revivals, I believe those were such. If there is any true religion *in the world,*

I believe it is found in the mass of those precious converts, who have ever since made up no small portion of the membership of those churches.[62]

Finney could do little more than respond in such a manner as this, and hope that the British would listen to him rather than to his detractors. He continued in the Tabernacle to the end of March 1851, and the crowds coming to hear did not diminish. This was surely some gratification in itself, to be able to preach in the most eminent Dissenter pulpit of the world's greatest city for the amazing length of eight months in all, and still to have packed congregations clamoring to hear him until his departure.

On March 31, 1851, a farewell reception was held for Charles and Elizabeth Finney in the Royal British Institution, on Cowper Street, City Road. Over six hundred guests attended the affair, which lasted from five to seven P.M. Then the assembly adjourned to the Tabernacle; here several thousand people had gathered. Finney was presented with the *English Hexapla*, comprising the Greek text of the New Testament with six English translations, and the volume was inscribed, "Presented to the Rev. C. G. Finney, as a token of respect and affection, by his friends in the Tabernacle, London. March 31, 1851, on his departure for his native land." Elizabeth Finney was given the condensed *Commentary of Ingram Cobbin*, and it was inscribed to her.

In a service alternating between laughter and some tears, Campbell, Finney, and others spoke on several matters. Finney commented on the new English edition of his *Systematic Theology*, saying that it was both written and bound better than the Oberlin edition, which "was not very nicely got up," because the author had written it under great pressure, and the publisher "had but just commenced business, and this was the first book they ever produced." Then he turned to John Campbell's invitation to him to come labor at the Tabernacle. Dr. George Redford had said to Finney that Campbell would stand by the American, for he was "not afraid." This comment caused great laughter throughout the congregation. Finney then added (doubtless without intending to be funny), "Now, I wanted to find a man who could stand fire." According to the reporter, at this remark the audience was convulsed in gales of laughter.[63]

When John Campbell arose he surveyed the many months during which Finney had been his co-laborer. Among many other comments, he was perhaps more direct than anyone else had been concerning Finney's abilities in the pulpit:

Well, we cannot say that we are much gratified at the thought
of Mr. Finney's returning to college duties, and the general ministry of a rural charge. We do not consider that such is the place
for the man; and we must be allowed to think that, fifteen years
ago, a mistake was committed when he became located in the
midst of academic bowers. In our view, there are few living men
to whom such an element is less suited. He is made for the millions—his place is the pulpit, rather than the professor's chair.
He is a heaven-born sovereign of the people. The people he loves,
and the mass of the people all but idolize him. He seems specially
created for oral labour. . . .

It is certainly a pity that a man so singularly endowed for
evangelic labour should be chained down by the dull routine of
College duties. If we mistake not, there are a thousand men to
be found in the United States, that would perform Mr. Finney's
professorial duties as well, perhaps in many respects better, than
he; but we doubt if, amongst the three-and-twenty millions American citizens, and the forty thousand ministers, more or less, that
labour among them, there are many, if one, that possess all the
qualifications above enumerated. Thus much for the attributes
of Mr. Finney as a public instructor; and the opinion is given after
hearing him incessantly for about nine months.[64]

Undoubtedly, Finney gave much thought to an evaluation of his
English campaign as he prepared to sail for America. The sentiments
he inscribed in his *Memoirs* are for the most part positive, but his
opinions (written some years later) do not always jibe with the evidence. Sensibly, he used the term "revival" sparingly to refer to his
work in Britain, basically limiting it to what had happened in Birmingham, and even then he complained that there "the ministers were
not then prepared to commit themselves heartily to the use of necessary means, to spread the revival universally over the city."[65] As to
London, although he had won large numbers of converts at the Tabernacle and had gained the endorsement of a number of leading Nonconformists, Finney was aware that he had but scratched the surface
of metropolitan, unchurched London with its vast, sprawling population, challenging extremes of poverty and wealth, and peripheral evangelism. Looking for culprits, he pointed his finger at an old enemy:
"London is, and long has been, cursed with hyper-calvinistic preaching,"[66] but here again his disappointments clouded his judgment and
rendered him inaccurate, for strict Calvinism had long been a minor-
ity evangelical expression.[67]

He does not say it, but perhaps Finney was mindful that his timing was wrong, that he had come to Britain ten to fifteen years too late, and that, had he more of his youthful vigor, he would have accomplished much more. The English publication of his *Lectures on Revivals* in 1837 had coincided beautifully with the peaks of revival interest in many parts of the British Isles, and Edward N. Kirk and James Caughey had conducted quite successful campaigns at that time chiefly because of strong groundswells toward awakening that had largely dissipated by the period of Finney's work. But it was not just timing; as Richard Carwardine has demonstrated, it was also Finney's constituency that was askew.[68] British Baptists and Congregationalists, although they possessed some leaders who were eager for cooperative mass evangelism, were largely unskilled in this and certainly were not totally committed as denominations to evangelism. Perhaps he should have thrown in his lot with the Methodists of England: for years they had wholeheartedly practiced the very type of revivalism —under the leadership of Lorenzo Dow and Caughey—that Finney wished, with excellent results and large membership gains.

As to Finney's British pulpit performances, he had done well, and the burden of his almost sixty years was not overapparent. Nonetheless, he did not possess the vigor of his earlier years, and frequently he described himself as "exhausted." The English tour was then, at best, a qualified success.

19

THE LATER YEARS

While in the midst of his activities at Whitefield's Tabernacle, in December 1850, Charles Finney received a reply to his letter to the Oberlin faculty assuring them that he intended to return to his teaching responsibilities, but pleading for their indulgence for a few more months in light of the success of his work in London. The reply read in part:

> The Faculty agree fully with you that we would better have no President at all than to have a man who is not the right one. When you are here, all that needs to be done on the subject, can be, we trust, with a disposition all round to consult the general good alone. All will be oftener disposed to defer to your feelings, *because you are our natural head & leader*, & we know that your fraternal spirit will sufficiently incline you to wish to act in entire harmony with your sons & brothers. . . .

[Signed] John Morgan	Absent: James Dascomb
Nelson Hodge	Timothy Hudson
James Fairchild	Charles Penfield
George Allen	Henry Whipple[1]
Hamilton Hill	

In subtle hints or overt statements, for months John Keep and others had been saying how much Finney was needed in the Oberlin presidency, and attempting to soften the resistance they knew he would make to their entreaties. This was but the latest in the series, and it would not be the last. But Finney had no particular desire to be the executive head: he had never shown an interest in administrative matters in any position he had ever held. Preaching, teaching, writing, and counseling alone interested him; these were intriguing and produced results. With the tedium of administrative concerns he had, of course, no patience whatsoever. So he gave Keep and the others no assurances.

On the other hand, Finney could hardly deny that he was far and away the most renowned person connected with the college, and that if he were president it would redound to the credit of Oberlin among those who agreed with his theological position. But surely Keep and the faculty and trustees were not thinking narrowly of the benefits to be accrued with Finney as head; they sincerely recognized that in a multitude of ways his moral force had sustained the school all through its rough beginnings, and that he was the main reason why great numbers of students had enrolled there. As Robert Fletcher has said, "The spiritual and moral heat generated by Finney's revivals had produced Oberlin. . . . Finney and Oberlin were inseparable; Oberlin without Finney certainly seemed unthinkable."[2] It is quite likely, therefore, that he recognized the inevitability of his becoming the president.

Early in April 1851, Elizabeth and Charles Finney sailed from England on a large packet ship, the *Southampton*.[3] By May they were again in Ohio. When they arrived it was at a school now officially named Oberlin College, for the change from the old name of Oberlin Collegiate Institute had been approved by the Ohio legislature on March 21, 1850.[4] Frequently friends of the school expressed their belief that the departure of the tumultuous Asa Mahan and the change of name signified a maturing there, a clarification to the outside world that this was not merely a preparatory school but a full-fledged academic institution, that the early days of constant fads and peculiarities were being quietly put behind, and that there was, in Fletcher's phrase, "a conscious desire to conform."[5]

At the annual commencement gathering of the trustees on August 26, 1851, Finney was elected president, and he immediately accepted the post and began his duties. He did this with the stipulation that he was to give general oversight to the direction of the College, and that alone. As James Fairchild described it, "he was elected . . . with the arrangement that he was not to give attention to the details of the position, but only to the more public duties. His work as an instructor was not changed except that he took the Senior college class for some years in moral philosophy."[6] This course had been taught by Asa Mahan until his resignation, as it was traditionally taught by college presidents across America. But when Finney took over, because of the college's willingness to have him conduct revivals elsewhere and be frequently absent, it was determined to remove some of that burden from him. To that end, Henry E. Peck became professor of sacred rhetoric and philosophy in 1851, and James H. Fairchild also began to assist in 1859.[7]

The agreement as to Finney's performance of presidential duties was, therefore, one of convenience among him, the trustees, and the faculty. The college would benefit from his great reputation and general oversight, and at the same time he would still be allowed to travel afield on evangelistic missions, which would also serve to keep the school's name before the general public.

From the outset of his tenure, Finney's attitude to the position was very different from that of Mahan. While his predecessor had no calls to distant places and was able to hover nearby and control the faculty closely, Finney wished to do nothing of the sort. It will be recalled that in 1835, when he was called to the school, he had insisted that the trustees must "commit the internal management of the institute entirely to the Faculty, inclusive of the reception of students."[8] This was still his intention. His style in presiding over faculty or trustee meetings was not to dictate or dominate, but merely to serve as the chairman. Whenever he asserted his own views on any matter, although certainly they carried great influence, they did not necessarily prevail and were often voted down, which bothered him not at all. Fortunately for the school, the faculty was very capable of conducting its affairs and doubtless enjoyed doing so after enduring the heavy-handed tactics of Asa Mahan.[9]

As president, Finney continued to accept engagements elsewhere, as the agreement allowed. In the fall he traveled to New York City to conduct meetings in the Broadway Tabernacle, now under the pastorate of Dr. Thompson. The intention was to stay the winter, but Finney reported that after preaching there a short while he "found so many hindrances in the way of our work, especially the liability to the interruption of our evening services, by the practice of letting the Tabernacle for public lectures," that he concluded his work in the city and accepted an invitation to preach in Hartford.[10]

Horace Bushnell (1802–1876), pastor of its North Church, had recently published several volumes that were broaching innovative concepts and disturbing the orthodox; his *Christian Nurture* (1847) argued, against the revivalism that Finney had done so much to further, that conversion should be educative rather than overwhelming or sudden, and thus it laid the foundation for new approaches to religious education. In 1849 he had published *God in Christ,* and when Charles Finney came to Hartford, Bushnell's *Christ in Theology* (1851) had just come before the reading public. All of these proved quite disturbing to conservatives such as Dr. Joel Hawes, pastor of another Congregational church in Hartford, who, incidentally, had been invited to the July 1827 New Lebanon Conference by Lyman Beecher and had voted against Finney's new measures at that debate. For some time Hawes had been pummeling Bushnell's views, but both of them attended Finney's meetings, and he preached in all three of the Congregational churches of the town. According to Finney, "Dr. Hawes and Dr. Bushnell came to an understanding to lay aside their differences, and go on and promote the work."[11]

We can hardly probe the dynamics of the situation at this remove, but it is tempting to conjecture why Bushnell, who had just written so strongly in deprecating the way revivalism ignored a child's nurture and spiritual roots and made one's entire spiritual state depend on the evangelistic decision, would be willing to support the meetings of the very man who most perfectly epitomized the opposite viewpoint! In all fairness to Bushnell, it must be stressed that he was attempting, in *Christian Nurture,* to restore a balance to the Christian life that he felt revivalism had upset, because he viewed Christian life and conversion not as something beginning instantaneously but as the normal operation of God's grace through the regular channels of home and church life and instruction. He was not opposed to revivals, for he believed that they helped greatly to reach those who were deep in sin. But his attempt to restore balance to the concept of Christian growth faulted revivalism for its lop-sided insistence that the *only* way to salvation was through its "jump and stir," in which the gradually maturing influences of God's grace are often "swallowed up and lost in the extraordinary."[12] Apparently he had been wrangling with Joel Hawes to the point of weariness, and he momentarily tolerated Finney's "jump and stir" for the sake of long-term peace and quiet.

Charles and Elizabeth Finney left Hartford about April 1, 1852, and returned to New York, preaching in the Brooklyn Plymouth Congregational Church several times for Henry Ward Beecher. By this point rumors were flying again at Oberlin, not that Finney would not re-

Tappan Square, Oberlin College, about 1860. This is a rare, early photograph of the school. On the left is the chapel, recently constructed, and on the right Tappan Hall, the men's dormitory which was built in 1835–36. In the background are the homes of professors and villagers. Note the plank sidewalks, the paths which students have cut through the lawn, the small evergreens, and the bandstand. Courtesy of Oberlin College Archives.

turn, but that he was considering giving up the presidency. The rumors were founded in some fact. The trustee president, John Keep, wrote in March beseeching Finney not to resign. After all, he had been president for only six months! If Finney were to resign, and worse yet to cease teaching theology at Oberlin, the theological department would soon close, Keep stated.[13]

Apparently Keep reasoned that a double attack was better than a single, and may have influenced John Morgan to write to Finney three days later. In that letter Morgan took a somewhat different tack from Keep, attempting to woo Finney back to the campus rather than scolding him:

> There is here now the greatest congregation I have ever seen in Oberlin, the galleries of the noble church crowded with masses of young people twice as numerous as usual and on Thursday the Chapel is crowded to a jam, orchestra included. If you have anywhere else a more important assembly to address, it must be an exceedingly interesting one. As I have aimed my feeble pocket-pistol at the vast assembly from Sabbath to Sabbath, I have earnestly wished you were here to pour in your heaviest shot in the name of the Lord.[14]

John Morgan's rationale must have gone home, for Finney wished nothing more than an appreciative audience, and within two months he was back in his Oberlin pulpit, pouring in his "heaviest shot." But there were other problems as well. Finney's health had never been excellent from his first coming to Ohio, and when he reached his sixtieth year his friends increasingly feared a general decline, for he overtaxed himself so often. In addition, Finney became the target of much of Asa Mahan's spite after his departure.

For the next few years after his resignation in August 1850, Mahan continued to demand back salary from the trustees, and even tried to charge them for services rendered during vacations since 1835. For some reason Mahan waited until 1855 to begin a vicious attack on Charles Finney, stating to Lewis Tappan that there had been "a sad declension in purity at Oberlin & especially on the part of Mr. Finney." To one and all he declared that Finney should be asked to resign, and he began to relate fanciful stories of improprieties on his successor's part to anyone who would listen. Tappan, still very protective of Oberlin, knew well that if Finney heard these tales he would be sure to resign immediately. Thereupon Tappan took the responsibility of dressing Mahan down properly: "Your mind has dwelt upon the subject so long, and you are so self-conceited—so sensitive to your reputation—so idolatrous of your influence that you have, I fain believe, done immense injustice to Mr. F. and to yourself."[15] Tappan and others then arranged a meeting between the two men at which they "mutually agreed to 'bridle the tongue.'"[16] After this, Mahan kept his promise and opposition from that quarter ceased.

In the autumn of 1855 Finney returned to the scene of his great revival, Rochester, for his third time there. Again he addressed his sermons particularly to the attorneys of the city, and achieved extraordinary success. Dr. J. H. McIlvaine was then pastor of the First Presbyterian Church and an Old School theologian, and consequently would not invite Finney into his pulpit. In 1891 he wrote of Finney:

> He preached in several of the churches twice or three times every day and Sunday for about eight months. During all this time a prayer meeting was held every day at 10 o'clock a.m., averaging from 800 to 1,000 attendance. The whole population of Rochester rocked as if the city had been shaken by an earthquake. Almost all the churches were opened to Mr. Finney, but I, being a true-blue old Scotch sectarian, would not let him into the First Church, for which I have repented ever since. . . . The number of converts was incredible. . . . Upon the whole, the blessing of that revival to Rochester, in my opinion, can never be over-estimated.[17]

In the fall of 1856, and again the following year, Charles Finney returned to preach in Boston at the Park Street Church. The second visit coincided with the beginning of the Awakening of 1858, which swept through the northern states just before the outbreak of the Civil War.[18] This massive awakening, much briefer than the Second Great Awakening, began inconspicuously in Hamilton, Ontario, in October 1857. Soon religious journals picked up the news and reported that three to four hundred conversions had occurred in a few days. Expectations of a great moving of God became general. On December 1, 1857, two hundred pastors gathered at Pittsburgh for the purpose of discussing the opportunities for and hindrances to an awakening. The meetings continued for three days in an anxious and solemn manner. In a short time a similar convention was brought together at Cincinnati, and hundreds of clergymen studied questions such as the need of the churches and the possibilities of a general awakening. It is no exaggeration to say that it was Charles Finney who had done most to sensitize the consciences of American pastors to wish for periodic revivals, and to recognize that with the cessation of the Second Awakening some twenty years previously, they desperately wished for another such turning to God by a nation that was writhing in agitation over the slavery question.

Although weekly lay prayer meetings had dotted New York City during 1857, the first one to become prominent was organized by Jeremiah C. Lanphier. This tall and quiet 48-year-old businessman began work as an urban missionary for the North Dutch Reformed Church in July 1857. On September 23, 1857, he instituted a noonday prayer gathering for laymen that began attracting large numbers. It was meeting on a daily basis by October 7, just a few days before the stock market crashed and prostrated business everywhere. This financial panic shattered complacency and forced multitudes into bankruptcy. Finney said that before this New York "seemed to be on such a wave of prosperity as to be the death of revival effort."[19] The panic was the catalyst that triggered the awakening, and within six months ten thousand men were gathering daily for prayer in numerous places throughout New York.

In February 1858 James Gordon Bennett, an early exponent of sensational newspaper reporting in America, began to give extensive space to the awakening in his *New York Herald*. Not to be outdone, Horace Greeley, editor of the *New York Tribune*, gave still greater coverage, and in April 1858 he devoted the entire edition of the *Tribune* to a special revival issue. Finney appreciated this, and told an audience in Glasgow, "It ought to be said that the editor and proprietor of the *New York Tribune* has done much that has extended this work. He employed a special and an able Christian editor to collect and arrange the revival intelligence. . . . All honour to Mr Greely for the honourable course he pursued."[20] Other papers quickly followed suit in reporting the great numbers attending prayer meetings and professing conversion everywhere.

When the churches of the large cities were filled to capacity, the meetings were moved to theaters. Prominent pastors such as Theodore Cuyler and Henry Ward Beecher attended and lent their support, but for the most part laymen provided the leadership. On March 17, Burton's Theater in New York City was thrown open for noonday prayer meetings, and half an hour before the service the theater was packed to every corner. Three days later the *New York Times* reported that Beecher led three thousand people in prayer at Burton's Theater, and during his reading from scripture he was interrupted by the singing of hymns from an overflow meeting in the barroom![21] At this Beecher led the packed house in thanksgiving that such a thing could happen.

What amazed secular reporters and other observers was that there was no fanaticism or objectionable behavior to be found, but a moving and orderly impulse to pray among these crowds. Very little preaching was done anywhere. In New York, as the financial panic began to recede, the *New York Herald* of March 6, 1858, commented with amusement, "Satan is busy all the morning in Wall Street among the brokers, and all the afternoon and evening the churches are crowded with saints who gambled in the morning." With the interest of the nation at first centered on New York City, gradually other cities began to duplicate the events there, and soon awakenings were common throughout the nation. Timothy Smith has described this proliferation:

> The Metropolitan Theater in Chicago was crowded with two thousand daily attendants. In Philadelphia mammoth prayer services in Jaynes Hall, Handel and Haydn Hall, and the American Mechanics Auditorium finally gave way in the summer to those held for four months under a great tent. The most spectacular of many revivals in public high schools was in Cleveland, where all but two boys professed conversion. . . .
>
> If the awakening dramatized the nearly complete acceptance of revivalism among Baptists, it evoked surprising support from Old School Presbyterians, Episcopalians, and even Unitarians and Universalists. . . . Low-Church Episcopalians, whose best-known leaders were Charles Pettit McIlvaine, bishop of Ohio, and Stephen Higginson Tyng and his sons, pastors of immense congregations in Philadelphia and New York, welcomed the awakening with more abandon. . . . Even more remarkable is the fact that Unitarian churches in New York and Boston united that spring in "densely crowded" weekly meetings for testimony and prayer.[22]

The influence of the Awakening was felt everywhere in the nation. Most of the colleges had sessions of prayer for their students, and—demonstrating the extremely conciliatory mood of this awakening—even Harvard was led in such services by the Unitarian Frederic Dan Huntingdon, Plummer Professor of Christian Morals and preacher at the Appleton Chapel.[23] A reporter in a leading secular journal summed it up when he wrote, "The Revivals, or Great Awakening, continue to be the leading topic of the day . . . from Texas, in the South, to the extreme of our Western boundaries and our Eastern limits; their influence is felt by every denomination."[24]

Coming on the very eve of the Civil War, with the land being torn apart by the controversy and the hatreds, the Awakening of 1858 was an astounding phenomenon. Calm and impressively orderly, with a massive emphasis on prayer, a truly ecumenical spirit and no sectarian rivalry, and led by dedicated laymen such as Jeremiah Lanphier, the movement continued to exert powerful influences after the outbreak of hostilities at Fort Sumter. During the agonies of the war, both the northern and the southern armies received much attention from the YMCA and its offspring, the United States Christian Commission. Ministering equally to soldiers of the North and the South, 1,375 clergymen, and hundreds of laymen, visited the camps and prisons and sought to bring spiritual comfort wherever possible. Their labors were not without fruit. Early in the war a revival broke out in the Army of Northern Virginia, and in a short time there were reports of other revivals through all the Confederate forces. "Army churches" were organized in the southern army, open to soldiers of all evangelical beliefs, and eventually it was claimed that one hundred fifty thousand converts had been made.[25]

Estimates of the total number of converts in the Awakening of 1858 have varied somewhat. Finney declared, "It was estimated that during this revival not less than five hundred thousand souls were converted in this country,"[26] and this may be one of the lower approximations. At times the reports from various places seemed to indicate that, for the climactic five months from February to June 1858, some fifty thousand persons were making commitments each week, which would raise the estimate considerably above Finney's.[27] The total will never be known, but the fact that the Awakening of 1858 was utterly lacking in fanaticism, solemn, devoted to prayer, and led by laymen, makes it unique in American history.

Charles Finney seems to have been greatly inspired by these months in 1857 and 1858, and he commented:

> The church and ministry in this country had become so very extensively engaged in promoting the revival, and such was the blessing of God attending the exertions of laymen as well as of ministers, that I made up my mind to return and spend another season in England, and see if the same influence would not pervade that country.[28]

Finney had discontinued the Oberlin course in systematic theology in 1858, and so he had more time at his disposal. He recognized that the awakening in the States centered on lay leadership, but longed to see a great renewal of spiritual interest sweep Britain as it had America, and he volunteered himself as one who might be used to bring it about. Undoubtedly he thought back to his first English trip of 1849–1851, which had been moderately successful at the best estimate. Were the revival currents now more powerfully charged, and the times more auspicious? From one aspect, no, for many of his former supporters were no longer available: Charles Roe had emigrated to America; John Angell James was quite elderly (and was to die within a year) and his congregation divided over mass evangelism; George Redford was now retired, and told Finney that his former congregation was split over asking for his assistance. Only a few remained. Nonetheless, Finney determined that he would go to England.

Elizabeth and Charles Finney sailed for Liverpool in late December 1858 on the steamer *Persia*. On landing they were met by their faithful supporter Potto Brown, who requested that Finney labor for a time in his home village of Houghton and neighboring St. Ives in Huntingdonshire. The previous pastor at Houghton, James Harcourt, had in the meantime moved to the Borough Road Chapel in London, and after Finney completed his work at St. Ives he went to London at Harcourt's urgent request to preach for him, arriving there early in March.

He had not been long in London when difficulty appeared. Samuel Tregelles (1813–1875), an English New Testament textual critic who had already become famous for his *The Man of Sin* (1840), *The Prophetic Visions of Daniel* (1845), and *Account of the Printed Text of the Greek New Testament* (1854), wrote to John Campbell, who was still pastor at Whitefield's Tabernacle. Tregelles disagreed strongly with Finney's presentation of the conditions of salvation in his *Theology*, and explained this, hoping of course to have the matter aired in the papers Campbell edited.[29] Finney was well aware that John Campbell was a "very belligerent" individual,[30] but it might be thought that the working relationship and the friendship that had developed between them on the 1849–1851 visit would have prevented what occurred next.

To Finney's dismay, he found that "instead of going to my theology, and seeing just what I did say, Dr. Campbell took it up in his paper and agreed with Dr. Tregelles, and wrote several articles in opposition to what he supposed to be my views."[31] An English friend wrote to Finney at this point, "I have read with intense pain the criticisms which have appeared in the *British Standard*, on your views of Theology, and I regard them as very unnecessary and unfair."[32]

Campbell's article in the *Standard* was sent to Oberlin and appeared in the *Evangelist,* and when Finney heard of this he was incensed, writing to his daughter Julia:

> If you are at Oberlin when this reaches you will you call on one
> of the editors of the O. Evangelist and ask who committed the
> blunder of representing the piece they published from the British
> Standard as Editorial & Dr. Campbell as so great a theologian.
> . . . Dr. C. is anything but a great theologian. When I was with
> him he professed agreement with my views. He now claims to
> differ from me & is out upon me in his paper & claims to be real
> old school.[33]

It may well have been Finney's failure to arrange with Campbell
to preach first in the Tabernacle when he came to London that was
behind the entire quarrel, but obviously after this there was no chance
that he would be invited there. In addition he was in poor health, so
he decided to accept Potto Brown's invitation to rest for some weeks
at his home in Houghton. Once there, however, another problem presented itself: Brown's habit of throwing open his home to all visitors,
which prevented Finney from a proper recuperation. Elizabeth Finney wrote to his daughter Julia from Brown's, "He is always sick and
as he has nothing in particular to deeply interest his mind he feels
the turpitude and I may say ennui of one who has always lived intensely exciting scenes."[34] Although he surely did not want to offend
his dear friend Potto Brown, Finney moved from there to Huntingdon
for a while and recovered a measure of his health. Besieged by invitations to preach throughout the land, Finney chose to return to London, to "several chapels occupied by a branch of the Methodist church,"
in the northeastern part of the city. Not long before he went there,
toward the end of May 1859, one of the pastors described the situation:

> The three chapels are situated in healthy districts, each of them
> a mile from the Thames. . . . They are nearly of a size, the largest
> will hold about 13 or 14 hundred persons. . . . In connection with
> the three chapels . . . we have 30 Leaders, and between Six & Seven
> hundred church members.[35]

Upon arrival, however, Finney came to realize that this was not
so fine an area as that of the Whitefield Tabernacle. Chapel members

labored valiantly to assist, but there was much poverty and crime in the neighborhood, beggars and thieves seemed to abound, many of the homes were delapidated and ancient, and the smoke from little factories and a seemingly infinite number of chimneypots eddied into the sky. It was, perhaps, the poorest area he had ever labored in, and although he stated that "we had a glorious work of grace there," some of his correspondence revealed how moved he was by the destitution of the inhabitants.[36]

For three months Finney labored in this smoky, grimy section, and probably he was pleased to receive an invitation in August to come to Scotland. Here was a new vista! John Kirk of the Evangelical Union in Edinburgh asked him to preach in his church, one of the largest of that city. The Evangelical Union was an offshoot from the Presbyterians, and had stemmed from the deposition of James Morison in 1841 from the United Secession Church. A fine preacher, he held to a general atonement, and drew huge crowds to his Dundas Street church in Glasgow. Holding to a limited atonement, most of the Scottish Presbyterians resisted Morison and the Evangelical Union he founded in 1843. In 1840 Morison had published his phenomenally popular tract, *The Way of Salvation*, which pressed unbelievers to recognize their ability and obligation to repent immediately. Throughout the tract, the influence of Charles Finney was undeniable, and he openly advocated the reading of the American's works by his fellow pastors. By 1843 Morison had swung even further toward Finney's ideas, declaring that the Holy Spirit's influence was resistible and election conditional. A person had simply to believe to be elected and regenerated before God. Following Finney's and Morison's thinking, John Kirk became a well-known radical, agitating for years as he denounced church establishments, the Corn Laws, and much else.

If Charles Finney were to preach in Scotland for the Evangelical Union, it would mean that he would cut himself off from acceptance by the Presbyterians. But they had not invited him to Scotland, whereas John Kirk had. In addition, the Presbyterians still held to the Westminster Confession of Faith, and many of them might be considered (by Finney at least!) high Calvinists. With the Evangelical Union, Finney found a denomination—small though it might have been—that was entirely dedicated to revivalism and his own type of liberalized thinking [37]

During the summer of 1859 the effects of the Ulster revival on Scotland were at their greatest. It was at this time Finney was occupying Kirk's pulpit, for the months of August, September, and October, and it was then that he received an invitation from Fergus Ferguson, Sr., to preach in his Evangelical Union church in the northern city of Aberdeen. Finney accepted the invitation, but in Ferguson's church he came upon more difficulties. The Presbyterians and the Congregationalists had been giving the church much opposition, and Ferguson was discouraged. Finney plunged into the work nonetheless, and surprisingly he received several invitations from Congregational and Presbyterian churches to preach there. After a bit he reported that "numbers had been converted, and a very interesting change was manifestly coming over his congregation and over that city."[38] At the same time from Edinburgh Finney heard from John Kirk that the revival was still in progress at his church,[39] and the *Glasgow Christian News* stated:

> Mr. Finney cannot be expected to go over many of our churches even if his stay in Scotland is greatly protracted; but it will be a greater matter indeed that he gives his precious aid at our great centres, and a still greater matter that we learn the true elements of revival success as a standing experience throughout the length and breadth of our field of influence.[40]

From Aberdeen Elizabeth and Charles Finney journeyed to Bolton, a few miles to the northwest of Manchester, arriving there on December 14, 1859. Apparently Finney was not distressed to leave Scotland, for although he had been well received in Kirk's and Ferguson's churches, the opposition there toward the Evangelical Union had irritated him. On December 23, 1859, George Redford, his old friend in Birmingham, wrote, "I can fully understand what you say of Scotland. It is cold formal unloving. Yet I have no doubt there is good seed that will spring up."[41]

Perhaps lamenting that no record had been kept of the first English visit, Elizabeth Finney began a journal shortly after landing for this second tour. For sixty handwritten pages she recorded the good and bad happenings of the year 1859, but when the Finneys arrived at Bolton, her spirits revived and her reports took on a more sprightly air. She was especially encouraged by the excellent reception given to her work with the women of the town, and she devoted herself to this ministry much more than she had in 1850. Missing no opportunity, Elizabeth Finney began this work on the first Sunday in Bolton: "I met 200 ladies this afternoon—deep solemnity." On January 7, 1860: "Tea meeting from Mr Barlow to his workpeople—1000 present. Mr

Barlow made a good address—Many wept." On January 13: "Meeting at the [Temperance] Hall filled with a very attentive audience. Mr Davidson said 200 had this week been savingly affected by the truth. At the prayer meeting afterward 40 professed to have covenanted that night to be the Lord's." On Sunday, January 15: "Mr Finney preached in the Hall afternoon & evening—a perfect jam—every place filled— ante room, stairs, lobby." On the next Sunday: "Mr Finney preached in the Hall this afternoon to a dense mass of human beings. . . . At six the house was well filled—though the services did not commence till ¼ to 8. . . . It was ½ past eleven before they could have the [in- quiry] meeting—My Husband seems to bear it well—& we both are in better health than we have been in England. I have not heard my Husband complain so little of his Health in a twelve month." On February 2: "At the Hall—the largest meeting of Ladies yet—as many as 400."[42] As Leonard Sweet has shown, Elizabeth and Charles Finney were truly engaged in a team ministry which was extremely effective.

The large increase in attendances and conversions Elizabeth Fin- ney was so pleased to record was due in large measure to the coopera- tive spirit of the Methodists and Congregationalists of Bolton. Between these two groups much of this cotton-manufacturing town was spoken for. Finney noted that the Methodists were very strong in Bolton, and had been since John Wesley found it one of his "favorite fields of labor,"[43] but an irenic mood prevailed among the sects. The Finneys stayed in the home of a wealthy and "very unsectarian" Methodist mill owner, James Barlow. The evangelist preached at the different churches, but it was soon decided that the best effect would be gained by using the huge Temperance Hall for union revival meetings.

Buoyed up by the true ecumenicity manifested in Bolton, Fin- ney regained some of his past energy, as his wife noted. Observers were surprised that this man in his sixty-eighth year could preach with such vigor twice on Sundays and at least four times during the week, but in large measure he was doing this in response to the support given to his revival by the churches. Laypeople canvassed the entire city, inviting the inhabitants of each home to the meetings, and vast quan- tities of handbills, tracts, and posters were utilized to promote what was being done. James Barlow and other influential figures did all they could to promote the work generally. At one point Barlow invited the aged and infirm of Bolton to a dinner, and Elizabeth Finney reported that "about 300 sat down to a bountifully supplied table." "Our meet- ings the largest we have had," she noted on another occasion. Finney's recollections in his *Memoirs* are full of his delight in the great congregations that were drawn from miles around, and the large numbers who would respond to his invitations, making the campaign in Bolton the high point of this second English visit. One clergyman told Finney that every household in the town had been visited.[44]

For approximately three and one-half months the Finneys worked in Bolton, until the beginning of April 1860. At the end of that time, over two thousand inquirers and twelve hundred converts had been counted—a very enviable record.[45] The clergymen and their congregations were delighted with what Finney had accomplished, and on his departure he was given a purse and this testimonial:

> Rev and Dear Sir: It is with deep regret . . . that we assemble to bid you "Farewell" at the close of your arduous labours in our midst. . . . All of us, without exception, have derived unspeakable benefits from your labours. And we gratefully record the fact that these blessings have been shared by vast numbers of our fellow townsmen; that some thousands have been awakened to a sense of the claims of religion—that many hundreds have found a peace and new life in Christ Jesus—that family religion has been greatly promoted—and that there have been large accessions to our various churches.[46]

From Bolton the Finneys went the short distance to Manchester, and hoped to find there the same kind of nonpartisan interdenominationalism they had enjoyed for the previous several months. They were to be sorely disappointed. Rather than the cordiality and sympathy that the clergy practiced in Bolton, in Manchester it was the same as it had been in Scotland. The Congregationalists were in the preponderance here, but Finney discovered "a great lack of confidence and sympathy among the Congregationalists themselves." To his further shock he noted a halfhearted attitude of the clergy toward the work: "they did not generally attend our meetings. They did not follow them from place to place, and were seldom seen in the meetings of inquiry."[47] These problems "grieved the Spirit and crippled the work," and Finney struggled on as best he could until the beginning of August.

During his work in Manchester a weekly periodical entitled *The Revival*, which was a "summary of events connected with the present revivals of religion," spoke of Finney's ministry in these terms:

> Mr. Finney is well known in America and England. His preaching is marked by strong peculiarities. It is highly argumentative—

keenly logical—yet, being composed of good strong Saxon, is intelligible to the common people. Boldness, verging to severity, is one of its chief characteristics. Unpalatable truths are urged with a fearless courage. Human responsibility and the obligation of every one to repent and believe the gospel are handled with a master's grasp. . . . Mr. F. is sixty-eight years of age, and has been a laborious worker in the cause of God forty years; yet he preaches with wonderful energy six times every week, and after every meeting holds meetings for anxious inquirers.[48]

Whatever strength remained to Finney, he devoted tirelessly to the work as he always had done, but the months in the city of Manchester were a discouraging business. Meanwhile, rumors were circulating at Oberlin that he would not return and would resign soon as president, and he received continual pleas from the faculty and others urging his immediate return. So, Finney prepared to leave Manchester for America, and as he did, a message arrived from Dr. John Campbell. Was Campbell regretting his earlier abrupt action in siding with Tregelles against Finney, which meant that Whitefield's Tabernacle in London was deprived of the compelling preaching of the man who had so mesmerized the crowds in 1851? In all likelihood, yes. Campbell wrote, "You will leave behind you in both nations, multitudes to whom your name will be long dear."[49] It was an olive branch extended, as close as the pompous Campbell could bring himself to saying he had made a great mistake.

On August 2 Elizabeth and Charles Finney put Manchester behind them and traveled to Liverpool. They had booked passage on the ship that had brought them to England, the *Persia*. The next day it was to sail, and they "found that large numbers of our friends had assembled from different parts of England, to bid us good-bye." In a touching farewell, the two Americans accepted the gratitude of numbers of Englishmen, boarded the ship, and left on the tide.

Upon reaching the harbor of New York, Charles Finney and his wife went home to Oberlin by the most direct route. He was exhausted and in ill-health, and the sea voyage had been as uncomfortable as usual. In Oberlin, however, he found little time for rest. Much had occurred during his absence. For one, his congregation at the First Church had grown so large that it had spawned a daughter congregation, the Second Church, and they wished Finney to preach to them as well. Also, there was a pressing need for evangelistic services, for many new students were on the campus, and Finney believed that "there was a large number of impenitent persons residing here at that time."[50] The latter item betrays something of his concern for the overall condition of the college as well. Perhaps it was mainly the effects of advancing age with Finney, with its debilities that make one wish he could do as he had in days of yore. But he was unhappy with some aspects of the college; he found the piety declining as the school became more successful, and he objected to the increasing number of activities that were "worldly." While he was on the second British tour he had written about this to the principal of the preparatory department, E. Henry Fairchild, and the latter had replied:

> But from many dissipating things we are free. We have no balls, no cotillion parties, no kissing parties, no late parties, no midnight parades of Sons of Malta, no secret societies of any kind, no horse racing, no circuses, no gambling establishments, no drinking saloons, no brothels, no Sabbath excursions, no street fights, or street drunkards, no military parades, no county fairs, very little swearing, very little smoking, almost no cases of discipline, very little mischief among the students. . . . Indeed, with all our faults, I know of no place that compares with this for the general prevalence of good order and religious principles.[51]

Such assurances assuaged Finney's mind for a time, but on returning to the campus the old irritations cropped up again. During the war years, from 1861 to 1865, with all their uncertainties and upheavals, again it was impossible to attend to religious activities as if nothing was happening, and it is likely the spiritual tone of the campus was severely tested.

A year after Charles Finney turned seventy, on November 27, 1863, his second wife, who had been such a help to him on the campaigns of the fifteen years of their marriage, passed away. He bore up well under the loss, for although he loved Elizabeth well, it was not as when Lydia died and left five children between the ages of three and nineteen. Now his four remaining children were grown, the youngest twenty-six, and they were choosing mates of their own and raising children. A year after Elizabeth's death Finney was married for the third time, to Rebecca Rayl, the assistant principal of the ladies' department at Oberlin.[52]

As if his own advancing age were not troubling enough, Finney suffered from continued ill health, and during the war years as the conflict ground on with all its horrors and depression, he felt burdened beyond endurance. He had resolved years before to vacate the presidency, and in August 1865 he decided that no one would deter him this time. Accordingly, he wrote to the trustees, "Our college needs a President who can give more attention to the details of its duties that I can give. My duties as Pastor & as Professor of Theology demand the use of all my remaining strength."[53]

Accepting the inevitable, the board of trustees recognized what a pivotal point this was in Oberlin's history. Here was the titan who had been with the school almost since its beginning, whose reputation had contributed incalculably to its success, and who had been for thirty years (in 1865) its chief driving force, and for the past fourteen years its president. The college had no right to ask any more of him in his declining years, other than to hope that his fondness and dedication to the work might persuade him to continue teaching at a reduced rate for a bit longer. The board therefore responded:

Beloved Brother in the Lord;
      The accompanying resolutions of the Board of Trust, of Oberlin College, will inform you of the acceptance of your resignation of its Presidency. They will also inform you of the pleasant duty imposed upon us, of expressing to you their deep sense of the value of your influence and labors in the Institution.
      Permit us to say then that we esteem your connection with the Institution as the main earthly source of its popular power and spiritual influence. You came to it in the day of small things. You have stood by it in the days of trial and adversity. You have lived to see it prospered, honored, and useful. You have always been, and always will be while you live, its recognized head. To you the nominal Presidency is of little significance. It was only by great urgency that you were induced to accept it. It, and not you, was honored by that acceptance: and now that you resign it, you only lay aside a name, and not your real power either in the College or in the Estimation of the public. . . .
      Prepared in the great Revivals of your early ministry, you were manifestly fitted for, and called to the work of training young men to preach the Gospel. . . .
      Your clear views in Theology have disentangled the steps of the multitude, and have laid the foundation for sounder thinking among men, on essential doctrines. Oberlin, the Church, and the world have been made wiser and better for your life and labors here as well as elsewhere.[54]

The trustees thus recognized that Charles Finney was utterly unique as the college president, and that whoever was chosen as the next head would have his own style and could not possibly be like Finney. Their first choice was the Rev. Michael E. Strieby, a graduate who was secretary of the American Missionary Association, but when he declined they approached Finney's own son-in-law, James Monroe, who had married Julia Finney. Monroe had graduated from the college in 1846 and from the theological department in 1849, and was professor of rhetoric and belles-lettres from 1849 to 1862, and a state senator. When Monroe also declined, the trustees then offered the position to the man who had been doing much of the real administrative work in Finney's term of office, James H. Fairchild.[55] He had been at Oberlin since 1834 as student, then teacher, and then as administrator, and he was thus thoroughly acquainted with the demands of the office. At almost every point he was a contrast to Charles Finney: "modesty, diffidence, and temperance" are terms the historian of Oberlin has used to describe Fairchild.[56] This is shown even in the way he later edited Finney's *Memoirs* for publication, for he was careful to omit sections that were questionable, potentially embarrassing to someone, or that he considered too involved or lengthy.[57] Fairchild was formally inducted into the office of president by John Keep on August 22, 1866, during commencement week.

Released from these burdens, Finney could concentrate on teaching the classes in practical theology and writing, and preaching at First Church. Because the *Lectures on Revivals of Religion* had had such a large impact on the religious world, it was suggested by several friends that Finney might again have a similar effect by bringing out the story of his work. Finney claimed in his *Memoirs* that "of late the trustees of Oberlin College have laid the matter before me, and urged me to undertake it. They, together with numerous other friends in this country and in England, have urged that it was due to the cause of Christ." At first he had been reluctant to write such a history, for he had kept no diary, and had to rely on memory. But he claimed that "my memory is naturally very tenacious," and those events, especially of years ago, "have made a very deep impression on my mind."[58] However, he wanted it clearly understood that it would not be an autobiography, and he would "enter no farther into a relation of the events of my own private life than shall seem necessary to give an intelligible account of the manner in which I was led."[59] Rather, it would be a history of the revivals he had engaged in, for that, after all, was of far greater consequence than a mere recitation of dates and facts, Finney said.

The fall and winter of 1867–1868 was spent by him in compiling the hundreds of manuscript pages that related to the long sweep of his life. Throughout its pages he steadfastly maintained that, even without a diary to consult and verify dates and details, he was able to "remember, with great distinctness," those distant events. It must have been a great chore to piece together, even with a good memory, occurrences that had transpired forty years before, and to keep the details of work in one city or town separate from those of another location. We have noted that Finney was inaccurate in some of his early dates and specific events until about 1826, by which point he was able to sort things out and become more accurate, but in fairness to Finney his later editor, James H. Fairchild, was at times responsible for some of the errors. In all, however, the *Memoirs* is a remarkable tour de force, for although there is some confusion here and there, Finney's recitation of account after account of long-ago incidents comes across with an impressive clarity.

In the Preface Fairchild wrote that Finney "left the manuscript at the disposal of his family, having never decided, in his own mind, that it was desirable to publish it. Many of his friends, becoming aware of its existence, have urged its publication; and his children, yielding to the general demand, have presented the manuscript to Oberlin College for this purpose."[60] Finney died on August 16, 1875, and Fairchild's preface is dated January 1876, so it is apparent that the decision for him to go ahead with the editing and preparation for publishing was made soon after the evangelist's death.

With his *Memoirs* completed to the beginning of 1868, Finney turned to another cause that might occupy his still vital energies. Some may have regretted it, but the cause which seemed most urgent to him was the fight against Freemasonry. This struggle had been going on for years, since the kidnaping and murder of William Morgan in 1826 at Batavia, New York, and the formation of the Antimasonic Party in 1828, which has been previous related.[61] Finney immediately went to work on an exposé of the Masons based on the recollections of his own rather short membership in the lodge,[62] and on accounts he had heard and read. He wrote to Theodore Tilton, editor of the *New York Independent*, regarding the articles he planned to write, and found that Tilton was very receptive to a full series of pieces on the subject of Freemasonry.

With time at his command for the project, Finney plunged in, and produced a rather verbose article that the paper duly published. The reaction was predictable. Letters poured in to the *Independent*, many howling with rage, and others congratulating Finney for his stand. Some readers canceled their subscriptions. Delighted with the response, Finney increased the pressure in still more articles, and Oliver Johnson, Tilton's assistant editor, wrote asking that he shorten future instalments, for the journal did not have space to print them in full.[63]

Hinting broadly that many other papers would be happy to accept the rest of the series, Finney asked if the furious response from Masons was causing the paper's staff to have second thoughts about continuing.[64] After several angry exchanges between Finney and Johnson, Theodore Tilton returned from his lecture tour, saw Finney's letters, and quickly intervened, fearing that the evangelist might go to another paper to continue the series. On May 2 he wrote to Finney:

> First of all, write your full mind on the subject. Pour the hottest shot you can forge. Spare not. . . . In the second place, don't write so many articles that the people will get tired of reading them. When I told you I would print whatever you wished to say on Masonry, I meant, of course, that I would not shrink from any responsibility which your attacks on the system might bring down on my head. . . . Now it is evident that you are making a book on the subject. I have no room to print a book in the *Independent*. I have now printed four articles: I will print six more: making ten in all. After that the ax must fall.[65]

Other periodicals looked askance at the furor. Nathan Brown, editor of the *American Baptist*, wrote to Finney to declare that his journal stood ready to provide all the space necessary if the *Independent* failed to stand by its promise, or if the evangelist wished to continue the series beyond his original plans.[66] In addition the Western Tract and Book Society offered to gather together the serialized articles and publish them in book form, and to issue any other pieces on Freemasonry that Finney might wish to send forth. He replied that he must be cautious with the society, for he was alarmed over their willingness to allow Masons to be admitted to church membership. To him, this[67] was as serious as admitting slaveowners to the communion thirty years earlier. But with the society having the facilities to promote the proposed book and an enthusiasm to fight the Masons,

Finney could hardly turn down the offer, and the volume, *The Character, Claims and Practical Workings of Freemasonry*, came from the press in 1869.[68]

Finney's chief purpose in the articles and the book was to demonstrate that Freemasonry and Christianity were antithetic, and that no one who claimed to be a Christian could tolerate any longer being a Mason. He cited his own resignation from the lodge in Adams, New York: "The evening passed away, and at the close of the lodge I was requested to pray again. . . . [I] was much depressed in spirit. I soon found that I was completely converted *from* Freemasonry *to* Christ, and that I could have no fellowship with any of the proceedings of the lodge. Its oaths appeared to me to be monstrously profane and barbarous."[69] But Finney gave no dates in writing this, and if he intended to convey that dramatic conversion experiences such as he underwent made the secret lodges immediately repulsive to Christians, he was hardly being above board here. It took him two and a half years from his conversion to summon the determination to leave the Masons! In fact, he did not request dismission until shortly before his ordination to the ministry.

While Finney was conducting his personal attack on the Masons, on a broader front others were preparing their own onslaughts. Amasa Walker wrote to Finney on May 3, 1868, "There is to be a National Convention as you doubtless know at Pittsburg," in regard to all secret societies, and he wanted the evangelist to be there by all means.[70] Jonathan Blanchard was involved with that, and also was planning to launch a paper, as he informed Finney on May 11, 1868: "I shall try and get our Executive Committee together next week and start a paper. . . . If we start a paper we shall want to print all your articles from the first. I have thought of beginning with a small dollar paper once in two weeks."[71] By the next spring the paper, *The Christian Cynosure*, was appearing regularly, with Blanchard as its editor.

With the inexpressible horrors of the Civil War so fresh in the minds of every citizen, other hatreds and rivalries grew dim by comparison. In 1869 the Old and New School Presbyterians reconciled their differences and approved reunion. A similar conciliatory spirit was manifested at the meeting of the National Triennial Congregational Council, which was organized at Oberlin in November 1871. Leaders of Congregationalism from across America gathered there, and Finney was asked to address the council on the topic, "The Gift of the Holy Spirit." Although he was in his eightieth year, Finney spoke for an hour on this, one of his favorite themes. Previously the delegates had been embroiled in discussions over procedure, and Wright says:

He treated the subject so tenderly and delicately as completely to disarm the prejudice of those who had been his lifelong opponents with respect to doctrinal questions. The triumph was complete; the whole audience was suffused with tears as their thoughts were turned from their trifling topics of ecclesiastical machinery toward Christ himself and his salvation.[72]

The next day the council moderator, Dr. Budington, closed the meeting by remarking that, the previous day, they had listened with swelling hearts to President Finney, and he stated, "I rejoice to stand this day upon the grave of buried prejudice. It is true that Oberlin has been a battle-cry in our ranks for a generation. It is so no longer, but a name of peace, of inspiration, and hope."[73]

In May 1872 Finney retired as pastor of the First Congregational Church of Oberlin. On his retirement he received a testimony of thanks from the grateful congregation, which recognized his many years of faithful service "without any adequate pecuniary reward or even support from us."[74] In 1874 the National Congregational Council again met at Oberlin, and again Finney was asked to speak. One eyewitness reported that the council, "filling the large church, rose in a body upon his entrance, and remained standing, while the veteran evangelist, pastor, and president, with unweakened step and fire of early manhood in his eye, moved along the aisle to the pulpit."[75]

Still Finney lectured, as long as strength allowed, to his beloved theological students in the renowned pastoral theology course, completing his last course of lectures in July 1875.[76] According to James H. Fairchild, who knew him so intimately, "the burden of years seemed to rest lightly upon him. He still stood erect, as a young man,"[77] and he retained not only his mental faculties but also that mesmerizing glance from his fiery eyes.

The long journey was nearly over. But the traveler, who had come so far from the crudities of backwoods New York State, and through such powerful experiences, moved on with the old unfaltering step. The young law student, the resolute revivalist, the aged professor, were the same: vitality, utter self-confidence, and a fierce determination of will were his to the last hour. Endowed by nature with a robust constitution, Finney, although for years having complained of periods of poor health, was in remarkable physical condition for his age. Naturally, some of the crippling effects of aging came to him. No specific disease could be singled out, but by the summer of 1875 there were signs of a general physical decay. Yet even in these last months, the strain of iron held firm. The daily work continued: a certain amount of correspondence with old friends, limited teaching until July, interest in his beloved children and grandchildren, and in his fruit trees and garden.

Not long after the college commencement in August 1875, Finney enjoyed a quiet Sunday. At sunset he walked with his wife Rebecca to hear the music from nearby First Church. The worshipers were singing "Jesus, Lover of my soul," and Finney took up the words and sang them from memory to the end. Coming home, he spent the evening with Rebecca and his son Frederic and his wife, and his daughter Julia and her husband. After Finney retired he began to complain of pains around his heart. About two o'clock in the morning he asked for some water. It would not quench his thirst, and he said quietly, "Perhaps this is the thirst of death." A few moments later he added, softly, "I am dying." After a short period of suffering, during which the physicians did all they could to alleviate the pain, he died as the morning dawned on August 16, 1875. He was two weeks short of completing his eighty-third year.[78]

Oberlin mourned for the man who had been its spiritual father for forty years, and buried Charles Grandison Finney in nearby Westwood Cemetery. And across America, and in the British Isles as well, those who had been influenced or converted by him, who numbered in the hundreds of thousands, thanked God for his life.

NOTES

PREFACE

1. Timothy L. Smith, *Revivalism and Social Reform: American Protestantism on the Eve of the Civil War* (New York: Abingdon, 1957), pp. 78–79.

2. Perry Miller, *The Life of the Mind in America: From the Revolution to the Civil War* (New York: Harcourt, Brace, and World, 1965), p. 9.

CHAPTER I — INTRODUCTION

1. William G. McLoughlin, *Revivals, Awakenings, and Reform* (Chicago: University of Chicago Press, 1978), pp. 2, 10.

2. Kenneth S. Latourette, *The Unquenchable Light* (London: Eyre and Spottiswoode, 1945), pp. 9–23.

3. Daniel Dorchester, *Christianity in the United States* (New York: Hunt and Eaton, 1895), p. 316.

4. Timothy Dwight, *Travels in New England and New York* (Cambridge, Mass.: Harvard University Press, 1969), 4:266–67.

5. William W. Sweet, *Methodism in American History* (Nashville: Abingdon, 1954), pp. 158–59.

6. W. M. Gewehr, *The Great Awakening in Virginia, 1740–1790* (reprint, Gloucester, Mass.: Peter Smith, 1965), p. 230.

7. William B. Sprague, *Lectures on Revivals of Religion* (Edinburgh: Banner of Truth, 1958), Appendix, pp. 151–52.

8. William M. Engles, ed., *Minutes of the General Assembly of the Presbyterian Church, 1789–1820* (Philadelphia: Presbyterian Board of Publication, 1847), p. 209.

9. E. H. Gillett, *History of the Presbyterian Church in the United States of America* (Philadelphia: Presbyterian Board of Publication, 1864), 1:299.

10. Based on a letter by McGready quoted in Franceway R. Cossitt, *The Life and Times of the Rev. Finis Ewing* (Louisville: Dart and Ransom, 1853), Appendix F, pp. 494–99.

11. James McGready, "A Short Narrative of the Revival of Religion in Logan County, in the State of Kentucky, and the Adjacent Settlements in the State of Tennessee, from May 1797, until September 1800," *New York Missionary Magazine*, 4 (New York, 1803) 193.

12. Charles A. Johnson, *The Frontier Camp Meeting: Religion's Harvest Time* (Dallas: Southern Methodist University Press, 1955), and John B. Boles, *The Great Revival: 1787–1805* (Lexington: University of Kentucky Press, 1972) provide the finest studies available on the western revivals and the origin and development of the camp meeting.

13. James R. Rogers, *The Cane Ridge Meeting-House* (Cincinnati: Tuthill, 1910), p. 165.

14. Cited in William W. Woodward, *Surprising Accounts of the Revival of Religion in the United States of America* (Philadelphia: Hastings, 1802), pp. 225–26.

15. Jonathan Edwards, *A Treatise Concerning Religious Affections* (Boston: Kneeland and Green, 1746), p. 35.

16. Francis Asbury, *The Journals and Letters of Francis Asbury* (Nashville: Abingdon, 1958), 2:576.

17. William W. Sweet, *The American Churches, An Interpretation* (New York: Scribner's, 1947), p. 54.

18. [Lyman Beecher], *The Autobiography of Lyman Beecher*, B. Cross, ed. (Harvard University, Belknap Press, 1961), 1:27.

19. Cited in Charles E. Cuningham, *Timothy Dwight, 1752–1817* (New York: Macmillan, 1942), pp. 178–79.

20. Ibid., p. 181.

21. Beecher, *Autobiography*, 1:27.

22. Chauncey A. Goodrich, "Narrative of Revivals of Religion in Yale College," *American Quarterly Register*, 10 (1838) 295–96.

23. *American Quarterly Register*, 12 (1839) 57.

24. Charles R. Keller, *The Second Great Awakening in Connecticut* (New Haven: Yale University Press, 1942), p. 42.

25. Charles C. Cole, *The Social Ideas of the Northern Evangelists, 1826–1860* (New York: Columbia University Press, 1954), p. 75.

26. Conrad Wright, *The Beginnings of Unitarianism in America* (Boston: Beacon, 1955), pp. 3–8.

27. Ibid., pp. 252ff.

28. Sidney E. Mead, *Nathaniel William Taylor, 1786–1858: A Connecticut Liberal* (University of Chicago Press, 1942), p. ix.

29. Sydney E. Ahlstrom, *A Religious History of the American People* (New Haven: Yale University Press, 1972), pp. 308ff, 405–14.

30. Joseph Haroutunian, *Piety versus Moralism: The Passing of the New England Theology* (New York: Holt, 1932), pp. 96, 71.

31. Ahlstrom, p. 409.

32. Ibid., p. 414.

33. For studies of Solomon Stoddard, see Perry Miller, "Solomon Stoddard," *Harvard Theological Review*, 34 (1941) 277–320; Thomas A. Schafer, "Solomon Stoddard and the Theology of the Revival," in *A Miscellany of American Christianity*, Stuart C. Henry, ed. (Durham: University of North Carolina Press 1963), pp. 328–61.

34. Mead, p. 119.

35. Ibid., p. 101.

36. Charles G. Finney, *Lectures on Revivals of Religion*, W. G. McLoughlin, ed. (Cambridge, Mass.: Harvard University, Belknap Press, 1960), p. 12.

37. Ibid.

38. The text of the Plan of Union is reprinted in H. S. Smith, R. T. Handy, and L. Loetscher, *American Christianity: An Historical Interpretation with Representative Documents* (New York: Scribner's, 1960–1963), 1:136. See also George M. Marsden, *The Evangelical Mind and the New School Presbyterian Experience* (New Haven: Yale University Press, 1970), pp. 10ff.

CHAPTER 2 — GROWTH AND SEARCHING

1. Dixon Ryan Fox, *Yankees and Yorkers* (New York University, 1940), pp. 175–80.

2. Timothy Dwight, *Travels in New England and New York* (Cambridge, Mass.: Harvard University Press, 1969), 3:101, 185–86, 372–73.

3. Carl Carmer, *Listen For A Lonesome Drum: A York State Chronicle* (New York: McKay, 1950), p. 115.

4. See D. R. Goodwin, "On Religious Ultraism," in *The Literary and Theological Review*, 3 (1836) 56–66; "Radical Opinions," ibid., pp. 253–65.

5. Whitney R. Cross, *The Burned-over District: The Social and Intellectual History of Enthusiastic Religion in Western New York, 1800–1850* (New York: Harper and Row, 1965), p. 173. See also W. W. Sweet, *Religion in the Development of American Culture, 1765–1840* (New York: Scribner's, 1952), pp. 280ff.

6. Critical studies of Mormonism include L. J. Arrington, *The Mormon Experience* (New York: Knopf, 1979); T. F. O'Dea, *The Mormons* (University of Chicago Press, 1957); Fawn Brodie, *No Man Knows My Name: The Life of Joseph Smith* (New York: Wiley, 1946).

7. Cross, p. 38.

8. Frederick M. Davenport, *Primitive Traits in Religious Revivals: A Study in Mental and Social Evolution* (New York: Macmillan, 1905), pp. 183–86.

9. Winthrop S. Hudson, *Religion in America* (New York: Scribner's, 1981), p. 197; David L. Rowe, *Thunder and Trumpets: Millerites and Dissenting Religion in Upstate New York, 1800–1850* (Decatur, Georgia: Scholars Press, 1985).

10. Arthur Conan Doyle, *The History of Spiritualism* (New York: Doran, 1926), 2:61.

11. George W. Noyes, *Religious Experience of John Humphrey Noyes, Founder of the Oneida Community* (New York: Macmillan, 1923), p. 339.

12. G. Frederick Wright, *Charles Grandison Finney* (Boston: Houghton, Mifflin, 1891), pp. 1–2. It has been claimed that Mother Finney was widowed before she left England. See James A. Finney, *The Name and Family of Finney* (Colorado Springs, Col.: n.p., 1952), pp. 5, 13–14.

13. Franklin G. Clark, "The Bristol Branch of the Finney Family," *The New England Historical and Genealogical Register*, 60 (1906) 67.

14. Ibid., p. 71.

15. Ibid., p. 156.

16. Wright, pp. 1–2, completing his biography of Finney in 1891, did not have the benefit of the more complete work of Clark, who published in 1906, and Wright failed to distinguish between the two Josiahs. Regarding Sarah Curtis, Wright got his infor-

mation from Noble B. Strong; see Strong to Wright, March 11, 1890, in Wright Papers, Oberlin College Archives (OCA). In that letter Strong says, "The grandfather of Charles Grandison was Josiah, his wife was a Miss Curtiss, a sister of Major Eleazazor [*sic*] Curtiss of Revolutionary fame. . . . I have copied the following from our town record." There are lists of Finney genealogy in the Connecticut Historical Society, Envelope no. 32101, labeled "Finney," in which the name "Curtis" could be read as "Carter," and this is the source of the confusion. Howard Finney, *Finney-Phinney Families in America* (Richmond: William Byrd, 1957), p. 22 has "Carter." Richard Dupuis has researched this in the Military Archives Division, has located no "Major Carter" who would be appropriate, but has located Major Eleazer Curtis, who served with Enos' Regiment, Connecticut State Troops, in the Revolution. In all probability this is the man, and his sister was Sarah Curtis.

17. Wright, p. 2.

18. See especially Sylvester Finney to Charles Finney, May 21, 1829, Finney Papers, OCA.

19. John A. Haddock, *The Growth of a Century: As Illustrated in the History of Jefferson County, New York, From 1783 to 1894* (Philadelphia: Serman, 1894), p. 573.

20. See H. H. Allen, *A Historical Discussion: The Presbyterian Church of the Holland Patent* (Boonville, N.Y.: n.p., 1900). A newspaper article of 1850 in OCA tells of the Rev. G. W. Finney of Havenhill, Massachusetts, who was a financial agent of the New York State Temperance Society.

21. Sylvester Finney to Charles Finney, May 21, 1829, Finney Papers, OCA.

22. Wright, pp. 2–3; Frank G. Beardsley, *A Mighty Winner of Souls, Charles G. Finney; A Study in Evangelism* (New York: American Tract Society, 1937), pp. 10–12.

23. Julia Finney-Monroe, "Some Statistics Concerning the Finney Family, prepared by Julia Finney-Monroe, Daughter of Charles G. Finney" (n. d., handwritten sheets in the Finney Papers, OCA); William C. Cochran, *Charles G. Finney: Memorial Address* (Philadelphia: Lippincott, 1908), pp. 19–26. But David McMillan has found that at Hamilton College (offspring of Hamilton Oneida Academy) there is no record of Finney; see David K. McMillan, "To Witness We Are Living: A Study of Charles Finney and the Revival of Religion in and about Utica, New York, During the Winter and Spring of 1826" (B.D. thesis, Union Theological Seminary, 1961), p. 39.

24. *The Documentary History of Hamilton College, Clinton, New York* (Clinton, N.Y.: Hamilton College, 1922), p. 106.

25. L. Nelson Nichols, *History of the Broadway Tabernacle of New York City* (New Haven: Tuttle, Morehouse, and Taylor, 1940), p. 43. Regarding the bass viol, which Finney mentions from time to time in his *Memoirs*, this would be called a violincello, or cello, today. Finney purchased a bass viol with the first money he earned from teaching, and he became a skilled performer upon it, as well as a good singer. See Beardsley, pp. 12–13.

26. Charles G. Finney, *Memoirs of Rev. Charles G. Finney* (New York: A. S. Barnes, 1876), p. 4.

27. Wright, p. 19; Cochran, pp. 13–15.

28. Cochran, pp. 17–18.

29. Ibid., pp. 21–24.

30. Wright, p. 1.

31. Finney, p. 6.

32. Beardsley, pp. 15–16.

33. Finney, p. 5; Cochran, pp. 24–26.

34. Fox, p. 192.

35. P. H. Fowler, *Historical Sketch of Presbyterianism Within the Bounds of the Synod of Central New York* (Utica: Curtiss and Childs, 1877), p. 180.

36. Ibid. See also Cross, pp. 9–13.

37. Charles G. Finney, *Lectures on Systematic Theology* (London: William Tegg, 1851), p. 429.

38. Cochran, p. 13.

39. [George W. Gale], *Autobiography of Rev. George W. Gale* (New York: n.p., 1964), p. 183. Gale (1789–1861) is responsible for the idea, frequently distorted by writers, that Finney had "a receding chin and mouth" (Marion L. Bell, *Crusade in the City*, pp. 23–24). Gale adds to the above, "with his upper jaw a little projecting over the under." In several photographs of Charles Finney, the lower jaw appears to recede somewhat, but the chin is prominent. There is the possibility that Finney had an overbite, but this is hardly a "receding chin." Some of the engravings seem to have caught this, and it may have led to the impression of a weak chin, but his photographs show that in actuality the chin was prominent.

40. Cochran, p. 16.

41. Alden Chester, *Courts and Lawyers of New York: A History, 1609–1925*, three volumes (New York: American Historical Society, 1925), 3:1161.

42. Gale, p. 182. There has been some conjecture over whether Finney was actually admitted to the bar. It has been the practice of some writers over the years to refer to his later preaching as reminiscent of his preconversion experiences before judges and juries, and Gale's quote here does support the idea that Finney tried some cases, probably under Wright's supervision, before local justices of the peace or magistrates. Gale's quote, and the rest of the evidence, suggests that Finney was still an apprentice in law, and Wright's law clerk. But it is also clear from contemporary accounts that the entire legal system of the western counties of New York state in the 1820s was rather haphazard. "Western lawyers, as a rule, were the sons of poor or middle-class people and seldom had a college education. They were the products of the law office and courtroom, and in some instances, of self-study (or no study at all). . . . Upon application for a license he was, as a rule, subjected to a purely perfunctory examination as to his knowledge of the law by a disinterested and often ignorant judge or by a 'board' of equally uninterested and ignorant lawyers" (A.-H. Chroust, *The Rise of the Legal Profession in America* [Norman: University of Oklahoma, 1965], 2:106.) All the contemporary evidence supports the idea that, contrary to modern practice, "admission to the bar" was then a rather perfunctory thing in New York state. Basically it was the granting of a license, and apparently Charles Finney had not attained this. See the study of the problem in David L. Weddle, *The Law As Gospel: Revival and Reform in the Theology of C. G. Finney* (Metuchen, N.J.: Scarecrow, 1985), pp. 46–53, and Grace M. Lansing, "Charles G. Finney," mimeographed article, 1942, Documents Room, Watertown Public Library, Watertown, N.Y.

43. Benjamin Wright has been confused by several authors with the well-known man of the same name who became important in connection with the building of the Erie Canal. Even Finney's grandson, William Cochran, was confused on this point, and said that because Finney was studying under Wright, who was a close friend of DeWitt Clinton, this gave him a good opportunity to rise up the political ladder, inasmuch as Clinton's political fortunes were also rising (Cochran, pp. 37–45). Beardsley said that Finney entered "the office of Judge Benjamin Wright, the leading attorney in that part of the state. Active in politics and a warm personal friend of Governor DeWitt Clinton,

Judge Wright was appointed by the latter a Canal Commissioner and at a later time Surrogate of Jefferson County" (Beardsley, p. 15).

44. Finney, *Memoirs*, p. 6.

45. Robert S. Fletcher, *A History of Oberlin College From Its Foundation Through the Civil War* (Oberlin, Ohio: Oberlin College, 1943), 1:9.

46. Finney, *Memoirs*, pp. 7–8.

47. Sir William Blackstone, *Commentaries on the Laws of England* (Chicago: Cooley, 1871), 4:20. See also John Mattson, "Charles Grandison Finney and the Emerging Tradition of 'New Measure' Revivalism" (Ph.D. dissertation, University of North Carolina, 1970), who has argued that the study of law provided Finney with a well-developed set of assumptions and presuppositions.

48. Because of recent revisionist historiography, this point must be made with caution. Previously it was stated frequently that Finney and Andrew Jackson, each in his own way, were striving for much the same kind of free, individualistic, and egalitarian society. Scholars have corrected this view at two points: first, Finney was not carried away by optimism; at many points his theology perceives clearly the dark, pessimistic aspects of mankind. See Leonard I. Sweet, "The View of Man Inherent in New Measures Revivalism," *Church History*, 45 (June 1976) 206–21. Secondly, the supposed egalitarianism and stress on the "common man" of the Jacksonian era have been severely questioned by numerous scholars. The previous idea—that the age was dominated by the "common man"—rested on political assumptions that, as Edward Pessen has declared, "have been pretty well demolished" (*Jacksonian America: Society, Personality, and Politics* [Homewood, Ill.: Dorsey, 1969], p. 58). See also Edward Pessen, ed., *The Many-faceted Jacksonian Era: New Interpretations* (Westport, Conn.: Greenwood, 1977), pp. 7–46 and passim.

49. Wright, p. 37; Gale, p. 254. See also Charles Finney, "Last Sickness and Death of Mrs. Finney," a letter to the editor of the *Oberlin Evangelist*, January 5, 1848. For the two families' close friendship, see Charles Finney to Nathaniel Andrews, July 15, 1832, Finney Papers, OCA.

50. Finney, *Memoirs*, p. 8.

51. Fowler, pp. 278ff.

52. Benjamin B. Warfield, *Perfectionism* (New York: Oxford University Press, 1931), 2:15.

53. Fowler, pp. 277ff.; Gale, pp. 163–70. Shortly after Finney's entrance into evangelistic activity it was reported by his enemies that Burchard had been instrumental in his conversion. The reason for this is not hard to find, for Burchard was never able to cast off the stigma of a mentally unstable, wild fanatic, and if it could be shown that Finney was greatly influenced by him, it would have been a blow struck against the new measures. But there is no conclusive evidence for Burchard's involvement, and indeed George Gale specifically denied it, saying, "It was either late in the month of October or the first of November. I mention the time as it was reported that Mr. Burchard was directly the means of [Finney's] conversion. Mr. Burchard was not in town, nor had he been for some five or six weeks. He had left town, at my suggestion, and was laboring in neighborhood towns" (*Autobiography*, p. 176).

Benjamin Warfield repeated the story (*Perfectionism*, 2:15), based on J. I. Foot, *The Literary and Theological Review* (March 5, 1838), 70. Whitney Cross also gave it, with no references (*Burned-over District*, pp. 188–89). William Weeks gave Burchard credit for Finney's conversion and the new measures (*The Pilgrim's Progress in the Nineteenth Century* [New York: M.W. Dodd, 1848], p. 268). Three histories of Jefferson County carried this story, beginning with Franklin B. Hough, *A History of Jefferson County in the State of New York* (Albany: Munsell, 1854), followed by Haddock, *Growth of a Century* (1894), and Durant and Pierce (1898). Although they do not state that Finney was converted by Burchard, they claim he was influenced by him. The two other histories followed Hough in stating this.

Of all these sources, none of the ones claiming Burchard's influence over Finney was close to the situation, or could adduce proof of the allegation. Burchard himself left no letters or diary from this period, and so he provided no evidence. Finney hardly mentioned Burchard in his *Memoirs*. Therefore, of all the sources treating this matter, Gale was the closest to the situation. As he was a friend and guide to both men, presumably he was impartial, and put the above disclaimer in his *Autobiography* to correct a rumor he knew to be false and malicious. Unless we discover evidence of equal weight that contradicts Gale, or unless we wish to charge him with a flagrant falsification, historical methodology suggests his version must rule. My own conclusion is that Finney knew Burchard and heard him speak in the months before October 1821, but that his conversion was the result of several forces converging, and was not Burchard's doing.

54. Wright, p. 7.

55. *Oberlin Evangelist*, October 13, 1852.

56. Gale, pp. 176–77.

57. Finney, *Memoirs*, p. 12.

58. See C. G. Finney, *Lectures on Revivals of Religion*, W. G. McLoughlin, ed., (Cambridge, Mass.: Harvard University, Belknap Press, 1960), p. 7, and Leonard I. Sweet, "The View of Man Inherent in New Measures Revivalism," *Church History*, 45 (June 1976) 206.

59. Finney, *Memoirs*, p. 24.

CHAPTER 3 — A RETAINER FROM THE LORD

1. William Cochran, *Charles G. Finney: Memorial Address* (Philadelphia: Lippincott, 1908), p. 35.

2. Charles G. Finney, *Memoirs of Rev. Charles G. Finney* (New York: A.S. Barnes, 1876), p. 26.

3. G. Frederick Wright, *Charles Grandison Finney* (Boston: Houghton, Mifflin, 1891) p. 15.

4. Finney, pp. 29–30.

5. Gilbert H. Barnes, *The Antislavery Impulse, 1830–1844* (New York: Harcourt, Brace, and World, 1964), pp. 10ff.

6. Whitney R. Cross, *The Burned-over District: The Social and Intellectual History of Enthusiastic Religion in Western New York, 1800–1850* (New York: Harper and Row, 1965), p. 158.

7. Finney, p. 14.

8. The Christian moralist Pelagius was active in Rome ca. 382–410. He viewed the church as the community of the (adult) baptized committed to perfectionist ideals, and magnified human, incorruptible, created capacity for freedom from sin. Grace comprised this God-given ability, the illumination of instruction and example, and forgiveness of sin. Specifically those teachings of Pelagius and his followers that were con-

troverted by Augustine and condemned as heretical are: (1) there is no such thing as original sin or a hereditary taint or tendency toward sin inherited from Adam; (2) humankind has perfect freedom of will and has no absolute need of divine grace to instigate salvation; (3) humankind, although aided in various ways by God's grace, is virtually the author of its own salvation. See James E. Johnson, "Charles G. Finney and a Theology of Revivalism," *Church History* 38 (1969), 340ff.

9. Finney, p. 44.

10. Ibid., p. 36.

11. Ibid., p. 43.

12. [George W. Gale], *Autobiography of Rev. George W. Gale* (New York: n.p., 1964), pp. 184–85.

13. Ibid., p. 177.

14. Finney, p. 34.

15. Theological seminaries were being founded by the denominations with increasing frequency at this time: New Brunswick in 1784, Pittsburgh in 1794, Andover in 1808, Union at Hampden-Sydney College, Virginia, in 1812, Princeton in 1812, and Auburn in 1821, in addition to General and Colgate in 1817, Hartwick in 1816, Bexley Hall in 1824, Newton and Mercersburg in 1825, and the divinity schools at Harvard (1816) and Yale (1822). See Winthrop Hudson, *Religion in America* (New York: Charles Scribner's Sons, 1981), p. 155.

16. Finney, p. 45.

17. Gale, p. 185.

18. Finney, pp. 45–46. It is important to note that Finney must not be charged with miscalculation on this date; 1822 was inserted by James H. Fairchild, the editor of the *Memoirs* after Finney's death. It is not in the original manuscript.

19. Ibid., p. 42.

20. Ibid., p. 54.

21. Gale, pp. 186, 274 (italics added).

22. Charles Finney, handwritten manuscript of his *Memoirs*, Oberlin College Archives (OCA), p. 9, reverse.

23. Gale, p. 185.

24. Ibid., p. 203.

25. Finney, pp. 50–51.

26. Again James Fairchild has inserted the wrong date, March 1824, into the manuscript, p. 51. See P. H. Fowler, *Historical Sketch of Presbyterianism Within the Bounds of the Synod of Central New York* (Utica: Curtiss and Childs, 1877), p. 258.

27. Gale, pp. 186, 214.

28. Finney, p. 51.

29. Ibid., p. 53.

30. E. H. Gillett, *History of the Presbyterian Church in the U.S.A.* (Philadelphia: Presbyterian Board of Publications, 1864), 2:467, 482.

31. Finney, p. 52.

32. Gale, p. 214.

33. The letter of appointment from the society is among the Finney Papers, OCA.

34. Gale, pp. 278–79.

35. Cross, p. 160.

36. Ibid., p. 161.

37. Ellis H. Roberts, *The History of New York* (Boston: Houghton, Mifflin, 1887), 2:560.

38. Finney, p. 78.

39. Ibid., p. 77.

40. John B. Boles, *The Great Revival: 1787–1805* (Lexington: University of Kentucky Press, 1972), p. 68.

41. Bernard A. Weisberger, *They Gathered at the River* (Boston: Little, Brown, 1958), p. 35.

CHAPTER 4 — THE HALCYON DAYS

1. Material on the anti-Masonic movement is very extensive. For a good overview, see Lee Benson, *The Concept of Jacksonian Democracy: New York As A Test Case* (Princeton University Press, 1961), pp. 14–46. See also W. R. Cross, *The Burned-over District* (New York: Harper and Row, 1965), pp. 113ff., and R. D. Burns, "The Abduction of William Morgan," *Rochester Historical Society Publications*, 6 (1927) 219–30.

2. George Andrews to Finney, May 7, 1824, Finney Papers, Oberlin College Archives (OCA).

3. Adams W. Platt to Finney, June 22, 1824, Finney Papers, OCA.

4. Charles G. Finney, *Memoirs of Rev. Charles G. Finney* (New York: A.S. Barnes, 1876) p. 82.

5. Ibid., pp. 82–84.

6. P. H. Fowler, *Historical Sketch of Presbyterianism Within the Bounds of the Synod of Central New York* (Utica: Curtiss and Childs, 1877), p. 258.

7. Finney, p. 107. See also Bernard A. Weisberger, *They Gathered at the River* (Boston: Little, Brown, 1958), p. 98.

8. Fowler, pp. 198–200.

9. *Eighth Annual Report of the Female Oneida Missionary Society* (Utica: n.p., 1824), pp. 17–18.

10. In the hierarchical order of the Presbyterian denomination in the United States, a presbytery is a collection of churches, represented by their pastors and elders who meet periodically; a synod is a collection of presbyteries that send delegates to periodic meetings, usually annually; the general assembly is the national representative body that meets annually, composed of delegates from the presbyteries.

11. MS minutes, Synod of Albany, p. 230, in the Presbyterian Historical Society.

12. John Frost (1783–1842), Middlebury College, B.A. 1806, Andover Seminary, 1810.

13. [George W. Gale], *Autobiography of Rev. George W. Gale* (New York: n.p., 1964), p. 254; see also Charles Finney, "Last Sickness and Death of Mrs. Finney," a letter to the editor of the *Oberlin Evangelist*, January 5, 1848.

14. G. Frederick Wright, *Charles Grandison Finney* (Boston: Houghton, Mifflin, 1891), p. 37.

15. Ibid., pp. 38–39.

16. Finney, p. 114.

17. Sarah H. A. Parker, *A Brief Historical Sketch of the First Presbyterian Church at Gouverneur* (New York: The Cox Press, 1918), p. 8.

18. C. C. Sears to Finney, May 13, 1825, Finney Papers, OCA.

19. Finney, p. 80.

20. In his writings Finney calls this town both "Western" and "Westernville." The modern name is Westernville. Also, Finney claims (*Memoirs*, pp. 140, 144) that he

met Gale after attending the Synod of Albany meeting in Utica, in October 1825. But the Synod of Albany met at Troy, not Utica, beginning October 4, 1825. Finney has confused two meetings.

21. Gale, pp. 254–55. Gale has made a slip concerning Finney's having a child at this time; his first child was not born until June 1828.

22. Finney, p. 147.

23. *The Western Recorder,* Utica, N. Y., January 9, 1826.

24. Gale, pp. 255ff.

25. Ibid., p. 252.

26. Presbytery of Oneida, *A Narrative of the Revival of Religion in the County of Oneida, Particularly in the Bounds of the Presbytery of Oneida in the Year* 1826 (Utica: Hastings and Tracy, 1826), p. 7.

27. Frank G. Beardsley, *A Mighty Winner of Souls, Charles G. Finney; A Study in Evangelism* (New York: American Tract Society, 1937), pp. 56–57; also *Narrative of the Revival of Religion in the County of Oneida,* p. 7.

28. Moses Gillet (1776–1848), Yale College, B.A., 1804. Private theological training. Both "Gillet" and "Gillett" are to be found in historical records. Finney's *Memoirs* uses "Gillett," as do the minutes of the Oneida Presbytery, but in his letters he spelled his name "Gillet." He was ordained in 1807.

29. Gale, pp. 262–63.

30. F. Daniel Larkin, "Three Centuries of Transportation," *The History of Oneida County* (Oneida County, N.Y.: n.p., 1977), pp. 31–35.

31. Presbytery of Oneida, *Narrative,* p. 10.

32. Finney, pp. 160–61.

33. Presbytery of Oneida, *Narrative,* p. 10.

34. Ibid. Finney (*Memoirs,* p. 167) said that he was in Rome, N.Y., for twenty days, but surely Gillet's account written in late 1826 is to be preferred to Finney's, written in 1868.

35. Presbytery of Oneida, *Narrative,* pp. 10–11.

36. Finney, p. 164.

37. Ibid., pp. 169–70.

38. Ibid., pp. 160, 169.

39. Ibid., pp. 164–65.

40. Beardsley, p. 68; Finney, p. 116.

41. *The Western Recorder,* April 18 and June 27, 1826.

42. Presbytery of Oneida, *Narrative,* pp. 15–16.

43. Pomroy Jones, *Annals and Recollections of Oneida County* (Rome, N.Y.: published by the author, 1851), p. 390.

44. Finney, p. 165.

45. Ibid., p. 173.

46. Presbytery of Oneida, *Narrative,* p. 12.

47. Almira Selden to Mrs. Lydia Finney, June 5, 1826, Finney Papers, OCA.

CHAPTER 5 — GATHERING STORMCLOUDS

1. Samuel C. Aikin (1790–1879), Middlebury College, B.A., 1814; Andover Theological Seminary, 1817.

2. [George W. Gale], *Autobiography of Rev. George W. Gale* (New York: n.p.,

1964), pp. 269–72. Regarding the pastor's name, he consistently signed it "Aikin," and that is the way it is spelled throughout the original manuscript of the *Memoirs*.

3. Presbytery of Oneida, *A Narrative of the Revival of Religion in the County of Oneida, Particularly in the Bounds of the Presbytery of Oneida in the Year 1826* (Utica: Hastings and Tracy, 1826), pp. 24–25.

4. *The Western Recorder*, April 4, 1826.

5. Presbytery of Oneida, *Narrative*, pp. 14, 16, 20–21, 25.

6. Ibid., pp. 24–26.

7. There are several sources that report on the number of converts, and in each case the figures are the same: Pomroy Jones, *Annals and Recollections of Oneida County* (Rome, N.Y.: published for the author, 1851), pp. 568–70; Moses M. Bagg, *The Pioneers of Utica* (Utica: Harper and Brothers, 1856), pp. 459–62; and Presbytery of Oneida, *Narrative*, pp. 24–25. Bagg also renders a fine account of the influence of the revival on Utica.

8. Charles G. Finney, *Memoirs of Rev. Charles G. Finney* (New York: A.S. Barnes, 1876), p. 180.

9. See David K. McMillan, "To Witness We Are Living" (B.D. thesis, Union Theological Seminary, 1961), p. 47. Generally, Finney's statements are incorrect concerning this episode.

10. Noah Coe (1786–1871), Yale College, B.A., 1808; Andover Seminary, 1811.

11. Presbytery of Oneida, *Narrative*, pp. 20–21.

12. Ibid., p. 18.

13. Ibid., p. 19.

14. Bennet Tyler, *Memoir of the Life and Character of Rev. Asahel Nettleton, D.D.* (Hartford: Robbins and Smith, 1844), pp. 12–26, 97–102.

15. *New York Observer*, December 8, 1827, p. 193.

16. Moses M. Bagg, *Memorial History of Utica, N.Y. From Its Settlement to the Present Time* (Syracuse: Mason and Co., 1892), p. 399.

17. [Lyman Beecher], *The Autobiography of Lyman Beecher*, B. Cross, ed. (Harvard University, Belknap Press, 1961), 2:67–68.

18. Finney, p. 186.

19. See, for the derivation of many of these techniques from the Methodists, Richard Carwardine, "The Second Great Awakening in the Urban Centers: An Examination of Methodism and the 'New Measures,'" *Journal of American History*, 59 (Sept. 1972) 327–40. See also Garth M. Rosell, "Charles Grandison Finney and the Rise of the Benevolence Empire" (Ph.D. dissertation, University of Minnesota, 1971), pp. 48ff.

20. *Letters of the Rev. Dr. Beecher and Rev. Mr. Nettleton, on the "New Measures" in Conducting Revivals of Religion* (New York: G. and C. Carvill, 1828), pp. 1–18 and passim.

21. John Frost to Finney, March 22, 1827, Finney Papers, Oberlin College Archives (OCA).

22. Presbytery of Oneida, *Narrative*, p. 26.

23. Ibid., pp. 59–60.

24. L. Nelson Nichols, *History of the Broadway Tabernacle of New York City* (New Haven: Tuttle, Morehouse, and Taylor, 1940), p. 46.

25. Charles G. Finney, *Lectures on Revivals of Religion*, W. G. McLoughlin, ed. (Harvard University, Belknap Press, 1960), pp. 133–34, 254–57.

26. Beecher, 2:232. See also Robert H. Abzug, *Passionate Liberator: Theodore Dwight Weld and the Dilemma of Reform* (New York: Oxford University Press, 1980), pp. 47ff.

27. Finney, *Memoirs*, p. 185.

28. Beecher, 2:233–34.

29. Benjamin P. Thomas, *Theodore Weld, Crusader For Freedom* (New Brunswick: Rutgers University Press, 1950)p. 16; Finney, *Memoirs*, p. 178; Gilbert H. Barnes and Dwight L. Dumond, eds., *Letters of Theodore Dwight Weld, Angelina Grimké Weld and Sarah Grimké, 1822–1844* (New York: D. Appleton-Century, 1934), 1:432ff.; Gilbert Barnes, *The Antislavery Principle* (New York: Harcourt, 1964), pp. 12ff.

30. Hiram Huntington Kellogg (1803–81), later president of Knox College, was an evangelist working in half a dozen struggling churches of the Oneida Presbytery. See H. R. Muelder, *Fighters For Freedom* (New York: Columbia University Press, 1959), pp. 14, 58ff., and E. E. Calkins, *They Broke the Prairie* (New York: Doubleday, 1937).

31. Hiram H. Kellogg to Finney, May 20, 1826, Finney Papers, OCA.

32. Orin Gridley to Finney, June 24, 1826, Finney Papers, OCA. The matter is discussed in Tyler O. Hendricks, "Charles Finney and the Utica Revival of 1826; The Social Effect of a New Religious Paradigm" (Ph.D. dissertation, Vanderbilt University, 1983), pp. 67ff.

33. Finney, *Memoirs*, p. 194.

34. Dirck C. Lansing (1785–1857), Yale College, B.A., 1804; Williams College, D.D., 1826.

35. Henry Fowler, *History of the Church of Christ in Auburn. A Discourse Preached at the First Presbyterian Church, Thanksgiving Day, November 28, 1867, Containing A Review of the Planting and Growth of All the Denominations in the City, And Of the Theological Seminary, With Statistics of Present Membership, Finances, Sabbath Schools, and Sketches of Eminent Pastors and Professors of the Past* (New York: Chas. Scribner, n.d.), p. 30.

36. Ibid., p. 32.

37. Charles Hawley, *The History of the First Presbyterian Church, Auburn, New York* (Auburn: Daily Advertiser, 1876), p. 12.

38. Zephaniah Platt to Finney, June 19, 1826, Finney Papers, OCA.

39. Minutes of the Oneida Presbytery for the years 1824–1827, p. 55, in the Presbyterian Historical Society.

40. In recent years the term "Holy Band" has been plucked from nineteenth-century writings and applied to those who were either converts of Finney or who worked closely with him, removing the phrase from its original context and distorting its meaning. Gilbert Barnes popularized the phrase in *The Antislavery Impulse, 1830–1844,* but he even included Lyman Beecher, saying, "He [Beecher] even labored with a specious willingness in Finney's Holy Band" (p. 16). This has created an inaccurate portrayal of the actual relationship of these men to Finney. In actuality the bands were not tightly organized at all, and any loyalty their members had was directed at least as much toward "Father" Nash as toward Finney, as George Gale has made clear:

> Perhaps I ought to say something about the religious character of the young men. It partook of the peculiar notions and habits of Mr. Finney, *but more especially of the Rev. Mr. Nash,* who had been much with Mr. Finney. . . . They were in the habit of praying very loud, so that at certain times of the day they could be heard all over the premises. . . . They would sometimes have what was called spiritual travail, or travail for souls, and pray so loud in the school room that people going along the street would stop, and sometimes inquire if anything was the matter. . . . Mr. Finney

and Mr. Nash erred in their treatment of young men, and young converts generally. In avoiding the error of keeping them back . . . they urged them forward, and ran to the other extreme. Many of these youths thought themselves far in advance of ordinary Christians [Gale, pp. 278–81; italics added].

Many of Finney's early co-workers are obscure and lacking in consequence. Itinerant preachers who may be included in the "Holy Band" are Daniel Nash; Luther Myrick, who became Nash's assistant; Nathaniel Smith (1790–1881); Theodore Dwight Weld; Henry Hotchkiss; James Eells; Charles Stuart (1783–1864); and Horatio Foote (1796–1886), who has been miserably slandered by one writer on the basis of a muckraking letter (Cross, *Burned-over District*, p. 195). Records of Foote exist to the end of his life in 1886; there is no evidence that he "seduced a girl" and was "renounced" by the presbytery. Foote was a close friend of Abraham Lincoln, and was given an honorary doctorate by Chadwick College in 1846. See W. H. Collins and C. F. Perry, *Past and Present of the City of Quincy, and Adams County, Illinois* (Chicago: Clarke, 1905), pp. 600, 205–6. Charles Finney had numerous contacts with both Jedediah Burchard (1790–1864) and James Boyle, but neither qualifies as a co-worker with Finney. Some writers have tried to associate Finney with the "mad enthusiast" Augustus Littlejohn, but the only point of contact between them was the financial aid they both received on occasion from the Oneida Evangelical Association.

41. Ephraim Perkins, *A "Bunker Hill" Contest, A.D. 1826. Between the "Holy Alliance" For the Establishment of Hierarchy and Ecclesiastical Domination Over the Human Mind, On the One Side, And the Asserters of Free Inquiry, Bible Religion, Christian Freedom and Civil Liberty on the Other. The Rev. Charles Finney, "Home Missionary" and High Priest of the Expeditions of the Alliance in the Interior of New York; Headquarters, County of Oneida* (Utica: printed for the Author, 1826), p. 100.

42. John Ware, *Memoir of the Life of Henry Ware, Jr.* (Boston: James Munroe and Co., 1846), p. 179.

43. The evidence for Perkins' existence is as follows: Trenton church baptism records show the baptism in 1815 of "a colored child of Rose, slave to Bro. Ephraim Perkins." Records of the Oneida Agricultural Association, of which he was a prominent member, disclose that he was a horse breeder and farmer. And, most conclusively for his authoring the *"Bunker Hill"* booklet, is a letter unearthed by David McMillan, Ephraim Perkins to A. Bancroft, June 10, 1826, in the correspondence files of the American Unitarian Association at Andover-Harvard Theological Library. This letter is one of the most important Finney sources to come to light in recent years. See David K. McMillan, unpublished manuscript on the confrontation between Finney and James Richards, pp. 80–81 and 95, and Tyler O. Hendricks, "Charles Finney and the Utica Revival of 1826," pp. 235ff. Perkins' letter to Bancroft is a blistering attack on Finney, and shows Perkins to have been capable of writing the booklet.

44. Perkins, *"Bunker Hill" Contest*, pp. 58–59.

45. Presbytery of Oneida, *Narrative*, p. 34.

46. Ibid., p. 65.

47. Ibid. "Oldenbarnevelt" was the local Dutch name for the town of Trenton.

48. Ibid., pp. 74–75.

49. Ibid. p. 79.

50. George W. Gale to Finney, March 14, 1827, Finney Papers, OCA.

51. P. H. Fowler, *Historical Sketch of Presbyterianism Within the Bounds of the Synod of Central New York* (Utica: Curtiss and Childs, 1877), p. 673.

52. Frank G. Beardsley, *A Mighty Winner of Souls, Charles G. Finney; A Study in Evangelism* (New York: American Tract Society, 1937), p. 69.

53. Fowler, pp. 673–74; Minutes of the Oneida Presbytery, in the Presbyterian Historical Society.

54. Finney, *Memoirs*, p. 179.

55. Fowler, p. 261.

56. William G. McLoughlin, Jr., *Modern Revivalism: Charles Grandison Finney to Billy Graham* (New York: Ronald Press, 1959), p. 33.

57. See Robert H. Nichols, *Presbyterianism in New York State* (Philadelphia: Westminster Press, 1963), p. 100.

58. William R. Weeks, *A Pastoral Letter of the Ministers of the Oneida Association To The Churches Under Their Care on the Subject of Revivals of Religion* (Utica: Ariel Works, 1827), passim.

59. Ibid., p. 17.

60. Ibid., p. 11.

61. Ibid., p. 8.

62. Herman Norton to Finney, May 15, 1827, Finney Papers, OCA.

63. P. H. Fowler, *Historical Sketch of Presbyterianism*, p. 274.

64. Stanley N. Gundry, *Love Them In: The Proclamation Theology of D. L. Moody* (Chicago: Moody, 1976), p. 46; James F. Findlay, Jr., *Dwight L. Moody, American Evangelist 1837–1899* (Chicago: University of Chicago Press, 1969), p. 126.

65. Leonard I. Sweet, *The Minister's Wife: Her Role in Nineteenth-Century American Evangelicalism* (Temple University Press, 1983), pp. 76–172. For any study of Finney, this excellent work should be consulted. I am indebted to Leonard Sweet for many insights in this section.

66. Ibid., p. 76.

67. Ibid., p. 103.

68. Ibid., p. 109.

69. Whitney R. Cross, *The Burned-over District* (New York: Harper and Row, 1965), p. 177.

70. Sweet, p. 126.

71. Julia Frances Tracy to Lydia Finney, August 27, 1827, Finney Papers (OCA).

CHAPTER 6 — CIVIL WAR IN ZION

1. Nathaniel Beman to Finney, June 9, 1826, Finney Papers, Oberlin College Archives (OCA). Nathaniel Sydney Smith Beman's life (1785–1871; Middlebury College, B.A., 1807) was crowded with events; see *Dictionary of American Biography*, 2:171. He was an evangelist in Georgia after 1812, marrying a woman who held slaves. Thus he became a slaveholder, which became a sore point later. In 1818 he became president of Franklin College in Georgia. He was pastor in Troy, N.Y., 1823–1863, and a highly respected and powerful figure there. In 1845 he was elected president of the Rensselaer Polytechnic Institute. He became a close friend of Finney, and the recognized leader of the New School faction of the Presbyterian Church. Unable to prevail at the 1837 Presbyterian General Assembly, the New School under Beman's direction was exscinded, and became a new denomination.

2. G. Frederick Wright, *Charles Grandison Finney* (Boston: Houghton, Mifflin, 1891), p. 53.

3. Ibid., p. 55.

4. Charles G. Finney, *Memoirs of Rev. Charles G. Finney* (New York: Barnes, 1876), p. 204.

5. Arthur J. Weise, *The History of the City of Albany, New York* (Albany: Bender, 1884), pp. 156–57.

6. William H. Hollister, *The Second Presbyterian Church of Troy, New York* (Troy: n.p., 1915), pp. 6–7, and William Irvin, *Centennial Sermon of the Second Presbyterian Church, 1876* (Troy: Whig, 1876), p. 45.

7. Joseph Brockway, *A Delineation of the Characteristic Features of A Revival of Religion in Troy, in 1826 & 1827* (Troy: Adancourt, 1827), Preface.

8. Ibid., p. 59.

9. *A Brief Account of the Origin and Progress of the Divisions in the First Presbyterian Church in the City of Troy,* "By a number of the late Church and Congregation" (Troy: Tuttle and Richards, 1827), pp. 19–20. Weisberger, in *They Gathered At the River* (p. 298, n. 74), discusses Wright's belief that Brockway also authored that pamphlet.

10. *Brief Account,* p. 22.

11. John P. Cushman to Finney, November 6, 1826, Finney Papers, OCA.

12. It was at this time that Finney was offered financial support by the Oneida Evangelical Association. On December 5, 1826, its president, A. B. Johnson, wrote to Finney: "At a recent meeting of the managers, a resolution was passed that the appointment of Evangelist should be offered to you for the first year; as soon as $600. should be subscribed." Finney accepted the offer, but apparently returned more money to the association than he took. Information on its history is scanty; Daniel Nash, Jedediah Burchard, Herman Norton, Horatio Foote, Luther Myrick, Nathaniel Smith, Daniel Nash, Jr., and Augustus Littlejohn also received aid for perhaps ten years.

13. Several biographies of Asahel Nettleton have been written: John F. Thornbury, *God Sent Revival: The Story of Asahel Nettleton and the Second Great Awakening* (Grand Rapids: Evangelical, 1977); Sherry P. May, "Asahel Nettleton," Ph.D. dissertation, Drew University, 1969; George H. Birney, "The Life and Letters of Asahel Nettleton, 1783–1844," Ph.D. dissertation, Hartford Seminary, 1943; and Andrew A. Bonar, *Nettleton and His Labours,* which follows with few changes Tyler, *Memoir of the Life and Character of Rev. A. Nettleton;* in addition to having the faults of Tyler's work, is also flawed by a lack of historical perspective and objectivity.

14. Dumas Malone, ed., *Dictionary of American Biography* (New York: Charles Scribner's Sons, 1934), 13:432–33.

15. [Lyman Beecher], *The Autobiography of Lyman Beecher,* B. Cross, ed. (Harvard University, Belknap Press, 1961), 2:364–65.

16. Lyman Beecher, "To The Congregational Ministers and Churches of Connecticut" (copy of a letter to the editor of the *Christian Spectator,* Boston, December 18, 1827). For an overview of Lyman Beecher's role see George M. Marsden, *The Evangelical Mind and the New School Presbyterian Experience* (New Haven: Yale University Press, 1970), pp. 20–30.

17. Beecher, *Autobiography,* 2:69–70.

18. An extended account of Nettleton is found in Charles C. Cole, Jr., *The Social Ideas of the Northern Evangelists, 1826–1860* (New York: Columbia University Press, 1954), pp. 20–24, but he too falls into Charles Beecher's trap of portraying Nettleton as aged.

19. Finney, p. 202.

20. Ibid., p. 203.

21. Bennet Tyler, *Memoir of the Life and Character of Rev. Asahel Nettleton, D.D.* (Hartford: Robbins and Smith, 1844), p. 247.

22. Finney, p. 203.

23. Tyler, p. 247.

24. *New York Observer*, February 16, 1828, p. 25.

25. Beecher, *Autobiography*, 2:69.

26. Ibid., 2:71.

27. Tyler, pp. 248–49.

28. Ibid.

29. Ibid., pp. 249–50.

30. Ibid., pp. 252–53.

31. Ibid., p. 250.

32. Charles G. Finney, *Sermons on Important Subjects* (New York: John S. Taylor, 1836), pp. 186–88.

33. Ibid., pp. 189–90.

34. Ibid., pp. 190–94.

35. Ibid., p. 199.

36. Ibid.

37. Jonathan Dickinson, *The Witness of the Spirit. A Sermon Preached at Newark in New-Jersey, May 7, 1740. Wherein is Distinctly Shewn, In What Way and Manner the Spirit Himself beareth Witness to the Adoption of the Children of God. On Occasion of a Wonderful Progress of Converting Grace in these Parts* (Boston: S. Kneeland and T. Green, 1740), pp. 17–20.

38. Jonathan Edwards, *A Treatise Concerning Religious Affections* (Boston: S. Kneeland and T. Green, 1746), p. 8.

39. Ibid., pp. 24–27.

40. Ibid., pp. 103, 268, 279.

41. Perry Miller, *Jonathan Edwards* (New York: William Sloane, 1949), p. 51.

42. Tyler, p. 287.

43. Ibid., pp. 301–2.

44. Ibid., p. 263.

45. Ephraim Perkins, *A Serious Address to the Presbytery of Oneida on the Manner of Conducting Revivals Within their Bounds* (Trenton, N.Y.: Bennett and Bright, 1831), p. 34.

46. Sydney E. Ahlstrom, *A Religious History of the American People* (New Haven: Yale University Press, 1972), p. 422.

47. Beecher, *Autobiography*, 1:410. The full development of the New Haven Theology is given in Sidney E. Mead, *Nathaniel W. Taylor, 1786–1858: A Connecticut Liberal* (University of Chicago Press, 1942), pp. 211ff.

48. The evangelical assimilation is discussed in J. Earl Thompson, Jr., "Lyman Beecher's Long Road to Conservative Abolitionism," *Church History*, 42 (March 1973) 98ff. Because Beecher was so visible, much of what he said and wrote has been taken as representative of the sentiments of clergymen generally at that time, and has been misrepresented. An excellent corrective to this is Lois W. Banner, "Religious Benevolence as Social Control: A Critique of an Interpretation," *Journal of American History*, 60 (June 1973) 23–41, reprinted in Edward Pessen, ed., *The Many-Faceted Jacksonian Era: New Interpretations* (Westport, Conn.: Greenwood, 1977), pp. 302–21. See also Marsden, pp. 20–30.

49. Mead, pp. 76ff. and passim.

50. *Letters of the Rev. Dr. Beecher and Rev. Mr. Nettleton on the "New Measures" in Conducting Revivals of Religion, With a Review of a Sermon by Novanglus* (New York: G. and C. Carvill, 1828), p. 99.

51. Ibid.

52. Ibid.

53. Ibid., p. 91.

54. Ibid.

55. Ibid., p. 80.

56. Beecher, *Autobiography*, 2:71–72.

57. *Beecher-Nettleton Letters*, p. 90.

58. Beecher, *Autobiography*, 2:72.

59. Ibid.

60. Ibid.

61. Ibid.

62. *The Christian Examiner and Theological Review* (Boston), 4 (May–June, 1827) 265.

63. Beecher, *Autobiography*, 2:73.

64. Ibid.

65. George W. Gale to Finney, June 6, 1827, Finney Papers, OCA.

66. Nathaniel S. S. Beman to Finney, May 26, 1827, Finney Papers, OCA.

67. Milton Brayton and J. H. Whipple to Finney, May 18, 1827, Finney Papers, OCA.

68. Joel F. Benedict to Finney, July 5, 1827, Finney Papers, OCA.

69. After Finney left New Lebanon, he conducted a revival in Little Falls from June 18 to July 14.

70. Nathaniel S. S. Beman to Finney, July 7, 1827, Finney Papers, OCA.

CHAPTER 7 — NEW LEBANON AND ITS AFTERMATH

1. The complete minutes of the convention were printed in the Unitarian *Christian Examiner and Theological Review*, 4 (July–August 1827), with these introductory comments: "We republish the following document without hope that it will afford *gratification* to any of our readers. We should be sorry to believe it would. But though a most melancholy, it is a most instructive display of the state of religious character in a portion of our community. On this account it deserves to be read attentively" (p. 357). The minutes were first published in the *New York Observer*, August 4, 1827, and in an abbreviated form in the *Christian Spectator*, 1, new series (September 1827) 499–501. Beecher's account of it is in his *Autobiography*, 2:74–80. Finney's is in his *Memoirs of Rev. Charles G. Finney* (New York: A.S. Barnes, 1876), pp. 201–25. See Charles C. Cole, Jr., "The New Lebanon Convention," *New York History*, 31 (1950) 385–97.

2. G. Frederick Wright, *Charles Grandison Finney* (Boston: Houghton, Mifflin, 1891), pp. 84–85.

3. *Christian Examiner*, p. 359.

4. Ibid.

5. Ibid., p. 360.

6. Ibid., p. 361.

7. Finney, p. 214.

8. Ibid., p. 213.

9. Ibid.

10. *Christian Examiner*, p. 363.

11. Finney, p. 213.

12. *Christian Examiner*, pp. 365–66.

13. Ibid., pp. 366–67.

14. [Lyman Beecher], *The Autobiography of Lyman Beecher*, B. Cross, ed. (Harvard University, Belknap Press, 1961), 2:75.

15. *Christian Examiner*, p. 368.

16. Ibid., p. 215.

17. Ibid.

18. Ibid., p. 216.

19. Ibid., p. 217.

20. Beecher, 2:75.

21. Finney, p. 220.

22. Bernard A. Weisberger, *They Gathered at the River* (Boston: Little, Brown, 1958), p. 120.

23. Wright, p. 94.

24. Don C. Seitz, *Uncommon Americans. Pencil Portraits of Men and Women Who Have Broken the Rules* (Indianapolis: Bobbs-Merrill, 1925), p. 98.

25. Cole, p. 396. Robert H. Nichols has agreed with this estimate, saying: "The apparent outcome of the New Lebanon Convention was a stalemate." See his *Presbyterianism in New York State* (Philadelphia: Westminster, 1963), p. 101.

26. George W. Gale to Finney, July 28, 1827, Finney Papers, Oberlin College Archives (OCA).

27. "Dr. Beecher and Mr. Beman's Convention on Revivals," *Christian Examiner*, 4 (1827) 370.

28. *The Western Recorder*, August 21, 1827, p. 134.

29. Beecher, 2:75.

30. Ibid., 2:76.

31. David L. Dodge to Finney, December 18, 1827, Finney Papers, OCA.

32. Samuel C. Aikin to Finney, December 18, 1827, Finney Papers, OCA.

33. William G. McLoughlin, Jr., *Modern Revivalism: Charles Grandison Finney to Billy Graham* (New York: Ronald, 1959), p. 39.

34. Beecher, 2:77 and Wright, 94–95.

35. Finney, p. 223.

36. Wright, p. 95.

37. Lyman Beecher and Catharine Beecher to Finney, August 2, 1831, Finney Papers, OCA.

CHAPTER 8 — INTO THE LIONS' DEN

1. Perry Miller, *The Life of the Mind in America* (New York: Harcourt, Brace & World, 1965), pp. 23–24.

2. Charles G. Finney, *Lectures on Revivals of Religion*, W. G. McLoughlin, ed. (Harvard University, Belknap Press, 1960), p. 306.

3. The millennial thrust of the times has been emphasized in Ernest L. Tuve-

son, *Redeemer Nation: The Idea of America's Millennial Role* (University of Chicago Press, 1968), and in works by Donald Cherry and James H. Moorhead.

4. Perry Miller stressed the search for national unity in *The Life of the Mind in America*, whereas Alice Felt Tyler, *Freedom's Ferment: Phases of American Social History to 1860* (University of Minnesota Press, 1944), Whitney Cross, *The Burned-over District*, and works by Charles Cole and Gilbert Seldes stressed the trends toward individualism and diversity.

5. Charles G. Finney, *Memoirs of Rev. Charles G. Finney* (New York: A.S. Barnes, 1876), p. 234.

6. James Patterson to Finney, April 20, 1827, Finney Papers, Oberlin College Archives (OCA).

7. George W. Gale to Finney, September 8, 1827, Finney Papers, OCA.

8. For a listing of the petitions circulated by Joseph Brockway, and an account of Beman's trials, see J. P. Cushman to Finney, March 12, 1828, Finney Papers, OCA.

9. [Lyman Beecher], *The Autobiography of Lyman Beecher*, B. Cross, ed. (Harvard University, Belknap Press, 1961), 2:122, 134; see also W. G. McLoughlin, *Modern Revivalism: Charles Grandison Finney to Billy Graham* (New York: Ronald, 1959), p. 38.

10. Finney, *Memoirs*, p. 241.

11. McLoughlin, p. 19.

12. Finney, *Memoirs*, pp. 234–38.

13. James Patterson to Finney, January 12, 1828, Finney Papers, OCA.

14. Finney, p. 238.

15. Ellis P. Oberholtzer, *Philadelphia: A History of the City and Its People* (Philadelphia: Clarke, n.d.), 2:79.

16. Ibid., 2:104.

17. Marion L. Bell, *Crusade in the City: Revivalism in Nineteenth-Century Philadelphia* (Lewisburg, Pa.: Bucknell University Press, 1977), p. 44, states that there were twelve Presbyterian churches in 1828 in Philadelphia, but the Presbytery of Philadelphia Records in the Presbyterian Historical Society lists sixteen for that year. Bell's work has inaccuracies throughout, e.g., "Philadelphia, like the entire North, was strongly 'New School'" (p. 45).

18. Leonard J. Trinterud, *The Forming of an American Tradition: A Reexamination of Colonial Presbyterianism* (Philadelphia: Westminster, 1949), p. 250.

19. Dietmar Rothermund, *The Layman's Progress: Religious and Political Experience in Colonial Pennsylvania, 1740–1770* (Philadelphia: University of Pennsylvania Press, 1961), pp. 32–35.

20. Alfred Nevin, *History of the Presbytery of Philadelphia* (Philadelphia: W. S. Fortesque, 1888), pp. 829ff.

21. *Records* of the Presbytery of Philadelphia, Pa., vol. 3, p. 62, in the Presbyterian Historical Society, Philadelphia. See also Beecher, 2:99ff.

22. Finney's *Memoirs* (pp. 238–39) say he was Old School, and Bell (p. 53) says he was New School. Actually he was a moderate, like Wilson and Skinner, generally holding the Princeton view but tempering this with his concern for evangelism.

23. Finney, pp. 252–53.

24. Thomas J. Shepherd, *History of the First Presbyterian Church of Northern Liberties* (Philadelphia: privately printed, 1882), p. 36.

25. Robert Adair, *Memoir of Rev. James Patterson* (Philadelphia: Perkins, 1840), p. 45.

26. Thomas J. Shepherd, *The Days That Are Past* (Philadelphia: Lindsay and Blakisman, 1871), p. 42.

27. Finney, p. 239.

28. Ibid., p. 255.

29. Ibid., p. 240.

30. David L. Dodge to Finney, February 25, 1828, Finney Papers, OCA.

31. Zephaniah Platt to Finney, March 10, 1828, Finney Papers, OCA.

32. Eliphalet Gilbert to Finney, March 14, 1828, Finney Papers, OCA.

33. Finney, p. 242.

34. Gilbert H. Barnes and Dwight L. Dumond, eds., *Letters of Theodore Dwight Weld, Angelina Grimké Weld and Sarah Grimké, 1822–1844* (New York: Appleton-Century-Crofts, 1934), 1:10–11. The "Hopkinsian Triangle" was a term derived from a series of pamphlets called *The Triangle*, by "Investigator" (Rev. Samuel Whelpley). This was later published in book form (*The Triangle*, New York, 1832). Whelpley was a leading exponent of Hopkinsianism in his day, and he attacked the three Calvinist doctrines of original sin, inability, and limited atonement, which formed the triangle and, to him, entrapped humankind. He demanded the right to interpret these doctrines following the moderate method of Jonathan Edwards and Samuel Hopkins. The New School avidly studied the pamphlets, and they became important influences in the approaching Old School–New School controversy. For an excellent discussion of this, see McLoughlin, pp. 43ff.

35. Ibid., 1:15. Some errors in the Weld-Grimké transcription have been corrected.

36. *Minutes of the General Assembly of the Presbyterian Church in the United States*, MS for the years 1826 through 1830, pp. 228, 237, and 239, at the Presbyterian Historical Society.

37. Helen first married Oberlin professor William Cochran (b. 1814) on May 6, 1846, and he died August 15, 1847. Helen's second marriage on November 29, 1849, was to Jacob Dolson Cox (b. 1828), who became governor of Ohio and secretary of the Interior.

38. First Presbyterian Church in the Northern Liberties to Finney, July 14, 1828, Finney Papers, OCA.

39. Oliver Smith to Finney, July 24, 1828, Finney Papers, OCA; Diary of Lewis Tappan, July 20, 1828, Library of Congress.

40. *Minutes of the Corporation of the German Reformed Church in Philadelphia*, MS for the years 1824 through 1830, pp. 160–61, in the archives of the church. See Bell, pp. 62ff., and John B. Frantz, "Revivalism in the German Reformed Church in American to 1850, with Emphasis on the Eastern Synod" (Ph.D. dissertation, University of Pennsylvania, 1961). Frantz is an accurate guide here.

41. David Van Horne, *A History of the Reformed Church in Philadelphia* (Philadelphia: Reformed Church Publication Board, 1876), pp. 71ff.

42. *Minutes of the Corporation of the German Reformed Church*, pp. 170–71.

43. Caspar Schaeffer to Finney, May 7, 1829, Finney Papers, OCA.

44. Finney, p. 245.

45. Lewis A. Drummond, *Charles Grandison Finney and the Birth of Modern Evangelism* (London: Hodder and Stoughton, 1983), p. 237.

CHAPTER 9 — THE FREE CHURCH MOVEMENT

1. Charles Finney in his *Memoirs*, pp. 258ff., spelled the name "Greer," but a check of the *Records* of the Philadelphia Presbytery, of which Grier was a member, shows that the spelling was consistently "Grier."

2. For the arrival date of January 9, 1829, see "A Religious Revival in Reading, 1829," *The Historical Review of Berks County*, 15 (October 1949) 149.

3. Gilbert H. Barnes and Dwight L. Dumond, eds., *Letters of Theodore Dwight Weld, Angelina Grimké Weld and Sarah Grimké, 1822–1844* (New York: Appleton-Century-Crofts, 1934), 1:23–24.

4. Charles G. Finney, *Memoirs of Rev. Charles G. Finney* (New York: A.S. Barnes, 1876), pp. 260–61.

5. *The Western Recorder*, February 24, 1829.

6. Finney, pp. 269, 271. In "A Religious Revival in Reading, 1829," p. 149, one of Finney's letters states that he "left for Lancaster the 7th of May," and "we left Lancaster for Whitestown N. York the 15th of June."

7. Edward N. Kirk to Finney, July 29, 1829, Finney Papers, Oberlin College Archives (OCA).

8. Bertram Wyatt-Brown, *Lewis Tappan and the Evangelical War Against Slavery* (Cleveland: Case Western Reserve University, 1969), pp. 30ff.

9. For information on the "Benevolence Empire," see Clifford Griffin, *Their Brother's Keepers* (New Brunswick: Rutgers University Press, 1960); Charles C. Cole, Jr., *The Social Ideas of the Northern Evangelists, 1826–1860* (New York: Columbia University Press, 1954); Oliver Elsbree, *The Rise of the Missionary Spirit in America* (Williamsport, Pa.: for the author, 1928); Charles Foster, *An Errand of Mercy: The Evangelical United Front, 1790–1830* (Chapel Hill: University of North Carolina Press, 1960).

10. The "Association of Gentlemen" was a term used on the masthead of the *New York Evangelist*, referring to themselves. See Wyatt-Brown, p. 61.

11. Wyatt-Brown, p. 61.

12. Ibid., p. 62.

13. Gardiner Spring, *Personal Reminiscences of the Life and Times of Gardiner Spring* (New York: Tatlow, 1866), 1:217–18, 225–26.

14. D. L. Dodge to Finney, December 18, 1827, Finney Papers, Oberlin College Archives (OCA).

15. Zephaniah Platt to Finney, December 20, 1827, Finney Papers, OCA.

16. Anson G. Phelps to Finney, January 7, 1828, Finney Papers, OCA.

17. Anson G. Phelps' diary, July 27, 1828, New York Public Library.

18. D. Stuart Dodge, ed., *Memorials of William E. Dodge* (New York: Randolph, 1887), pp. 199, 210ff. Fletcher, *A History of Oberlin College*, 1:26–27, places the meetings in Phelps' home when Beman, Aikin, Lansing, and others were in attendance in December 1827, but all the evidence points rather to August 1828. Fletcher also states that Weld and Zebulon Shipherd participated, but the letters he cites do not support this in any way. Dodge said that this meeting was "in the fall of 1828," and to this Fletcher states, "Dodge is wrong in the year as is indicated in various letters in the Finney MSS, for example: Zephaniah Platt to Finney, New York City, Dec. 20, 1827." But Dodge *was* correct, and there is nothing in Platt's letter to support the December 1827 dating. Unfortunately, several authors have followed Fletcher here.

19. Arthur Tappan to Finney, Sept. 25, 1828, Finney Papers, OCA.

20. Robert S. Fletcher, *A History of Oberlin College: From Its Foundation Through the Civil War* (Oberlin, Ohio: Oberlin College, 1943), 1:25–26.

21. N.S.S. Beman to Finney, October 15, 1829, Finney Papers, OCA.

22. S.C. Aikin to Finney, October 12, 1829, Finney Papers, OCA.

23. L. Nelson Nichols, *History of the Broadway Tabernacle of New York City* (New Haven: Tuttle, Morehouse, and Taylor, 1940), pp. 49–50; Susan H. Ward, *The History of the Broadway Tabernacle Church* (New York: Trow Print, 1901), pp. 21–22.

24. N.S.S. Beman to Finney, Oct. 23, 1829, Finney Papers, OCA.

25. Moses Gillet to Finney, Oct. 26, 1829, Finney Papers, OCA.

26. Wyatt-Brown, p. 61.

27. Anonymous [Calvin Colton], *A Voice from America to England* (London: n.p., 1839), p. 64. See Gilbert H. Barnes, *The Antislavery Impulse, 1830–1844* (New York: Harcourt, Brace, and World, 1964), passim. For studies of the women's movement see Carroll Smith Rosenberg, *Religion and the Rise of the American City* (Ithaca, New York: Cornell University Press, 1971); Nancy F. Cott, *The Bonds of Womanhood* (New Haven: Yale University Press, 1978); Barbara J. Berg, *The Remembered Gate: Origins of American Feminism* (New York: Oxford University Press, 1978); Paul Boyer, *Urban Masses and Moral Order in America, 1820–1920* (Cambridge, Mass.: Harvard University Press, 1978); and Leonard I. Sweet, *The Minister's Wife* (Philadelphia: Temple University Press, 1983), pp. 144–83.

28. *New York Evangelist*, May 29, 1830.

29. Wyatt-Brown, pp. 54, 68.

30. D. L. Dodge to Finney, Dec. 18, 1827, Finney Papers, OCA.

31. N.C. Saxton to Finney, Sept. 27, 1830, Finney Papers, OCA.

32. Joshua Leavitt to Finney, Nov. 15, 1830, Finney Papers, OCA.

33. G. W. Gale to Finney, January 21, 1830, Finney Papers, OCA.

34. Dirck Lansing to Finney, May 25, 1830, Finney Papers, OCA.

35. Lewis Tappan, "History of the Free Churches in the City of New York," in Andrew Reed and James Matheson, *A Narrative of the Visit to the American Churches, By the Deputation from the Congregational Union of England and Wales* (New York: Harper & Brothers, 1835), 2:772.

36. *New York Evangelist*, June 26, 1830.

37. Anson G. Phelps to Finney, September 2, 1830, Finney Papers, OCA. Herman Norton (1799–1850), Hamilton College, B.A., 1823; Auburn Theological Seminary, 1826. Norton was a store clerk in 1817 when he was converted under the preaching of Dirck Lansing at the Auburn Presbyterian church. He met Finney at the revival in Utica early in 1826, and the two formed a close friendship that lasted the rest of their lives. Their friendship was further strengthened in 1826 by Norton's marriage to Amelia Flint of Utica, Lydia Finney's closest friend. When the Finneys' second son was born in 1832, he was named Frederic Norton in his honor.

38. James Patterson to Finney, March 26, 1830, Finney Papers, OCA.

39. S. D. Alexander, *The Presbytery of New York, 1738 to 1888* (New York: Randolph, 1888), p. 101.

40. Tappan, "History of Free Churches," p. 773.

41. Charles C. Cole, Jr., "The Free Church Movement in New York City," *New York History*, 34 (July 1953) 284–88.

42. Herman Norton to Finney, November 1830, Finney Papers, OCA.

CHAPTER IO — REVIVAL AT ROCHESTER

1. Robert S. Fletcher, *A History of Oberlin College: From Its Foundation Through the Civil War* (Oberlin, Ohio: Oberlin College, 1943), 1:23. The entire background and socio-economic aspects of the Rochester revival have been superbly studied in Paul E. Johnson, *A Shopkeeper's Millennium: Society and Revivals in Rochester, New York, 1815–1837* (New York: Hill and Wang, 1978).

2. Josiah Bissell to Finney, September 15, 1829, Rochester Public Library.

3. *The Craftsman*, March 9, 1830; Charles G. Finney, *Memoirs of Rev. Charles G. Finney* (New York: A.S. Barnes, 1876), pp. 284–85.

4. Minutes of the Rochester Presbytery for the years 1828–1838, pp. 77–78, manuscript in the Presbyterian Historical Society; Fletcher, 1:18.

5. Finney, p. 285.

6. Ibid., pp. 285–86.

7. *Atlas of New York* (New York: Lipton, 1838), p. 58.

8. Johnson, pp. 17–18.

9. Ibid., p. 37.

10. Harriet A. Weed, comp., *Autobiography of Thurlow Weed* (Boston: Moore, 1884), pp. 270ff, 296ff.; Johnson, pp. 65, 68, 91.

11. Lyman Beecher, *Six Sermons on the Nature, Occasions, Signs, Evils, and Remedy of Intemperance* (Boston: Burrows and Farr, 1828). For the temperance crusade, see George M. Marsden, *The Evangelical Mind and the New School Presbyterian Experience: A Case Study of Thought and Theology in Nineteenth-Century America* (New Haven: Yale University Press, 1970), pp. 23–30.

12. Johnson, p. 55.

13. Whitney R. Cross, *The Burned-over District: The Social and Intellectual History of Enthusiastic Religion in Western New York, 1800–1850* (New York: Harper and Row, 1965), p. 154.

14. Johnson, p. 85.

15. Levi Parsons, ed. *History of Rochester Presbytery From the Earliest Settlement of the County* (Rochester: Democrat-Chronicle Press, 1889), pp. 251–52.

16. *Rochester Observer*, December 24, 1830. This paper had been founded several years before for the distinct purpose of disseminating information about Christian work, and Josiah Bissell had largely financed it himself

17. Cross, p. 155.

18. Finney, pp. 288–89. Finney had first asked converts to come forward in the January 1826 revival at Rome (see above), but on previous occasions at Evans Mills and Rutland he had asked converts to rise, or take the front bench. Finney, pp. 116, 164–65.

19. Finney, pp. 290–91.

20. *Rochester Observer*, October 22, 1830.

21. Barnes and Dumond, 1:40–41.

22. *Publications of the Rochester Historical Society*, Edward R. Foreman, ed. (The Rochester Historical Society, 1925), 4:288–89; Henry B. Stanton, *Random Recollections* (New York: Pollard, 1855), pp. 40–42.

23. *Rochester Observer*, October 15, 1830.

24. *New York Evangelist*, November 20, 1830.

25. *Rochester Observer*, December 24, 1830.

26. Barnes and Dumond, 1:11.

27. Johnson, p. 82.

28. Gilbert H. Barnes, *The Antislavery Impulse, 1830–1844* (New York: Harcourt, Brace, and World, 1964), p. 207.

29. Ibid., p. 15.

30. Johnson, pp. 113–14.

31. *Western Recorder*, January 7, 1831.

32. *Daily Advertiser* (Rochester), March 19, 1831.

33. Fletcher, p. 64.

34. See Ibid., pp. 19, 67–68.

35. A. G. Phelps to Finney, November 29, 1830, Finney Papers, Oberlin College Archives (OCA).

36. M. Brayton to Theodore Weld, January 22, 1831, Finney Papers, OCA.

37. Parsons, p. 23.

38. J.W. Adams to Finney, November 25, 1830, and January 1, 1831, Finney Papers, OCA.

39. R. Whiting to Finney, January 2, 1831, Finney Papers, OCA.

40. Joel Parker and Lewis Tappan to Finney, Feb. 21, 1831; Lewis Tappan to Finney, Feb. 2, March 17, 18, April 3, 1831; Joshua Leavitt to Finney, Feb. 24, 1831; Herman Norton to Finney, Feb. 1, 1831; Finney Papers, OCA.

41. *New York Evangelist*, Feb. 26, 1831.

42. James H. Hotchkin, *A History of the Purchase and Settlement of Western New York, And of the Rise, Progress, and Present State of the Presbyterian Church in That Section* (New York: Dodd, 1848), p. 163.

43. Charles P. Bush, "Mr. Finney in Rochester and Western New York," *Reminiscences of Rev. Charles G. Finney. Speeches and Sketches At the Gathering of His Friends and Pupils in Oberlin, July 28, 1876, Together With President Fairchild's Memorial Sermon, Delivered Before the Graduating Class, July 30, 1876* (Oberlin: E.J. Goodrich, 1876), pp. 12–13.

44. *Rochester Observer*, February 17, 1831.

45. Ibid., March 3, 1831.

46. Parsons, pp. 245ff.; Hotchkin, pp. 490ff. See Fletcher, pp. 21ff.

47. Parsons, pp. 194, 254–59.

48. Robert H. Nichols, *Presbyterianism in New York State* (Philadelphia: Westminster Press, 1963), p. 102.

49. Johnson, pp. 3–5.

50. Estimates of Protestant church membership are from Johnson, p. 4; Charles C. Cole, *The Social Ideas of the Northern Evangelists, 1826–1860* (New York: Columbia University Press, 1954), pp. 13ff; Winthrop S. Hudson, *Religion in America: An Historical Account of the Development of American Religious Life* (New York: Scribners, 1981), pp. 128–30.

51. Ibid., p. 93.

52. R. L. Stanton to Finney, January 12, 1872, Finney Papers, OCA.

53. Johnson, p. 102. The massive statistics Johnson had compiled on the ages, occupations, backgrounds, etc., of converts are most impressive.

54. Finney, p. 298. Regarding the drop in crime in Rochester, the Rev. C. P. Bush stated, "Even the courts had little to do and the jail was nearly empty for years thereafter. The only theater in the city was converted into a livery stable and the circus into a soap factory." Quoted in H. Pomeroy Brewster, "The Magic of a Voice," *Rochester Historical Society Publications*, 4 (1925) 281.

CHAPTER II — BOSTON AND BEECHER

1. [Lyman Beecher], *The Autobiography of Lyman Beecher*, B. Cross, ed. (Harvard University, Belknap Press, 1961), 2:82.

2. Andrews Norton, "Views of Calvinism," *Christian Disciple*, 4 (new series, 1822) 271.

3. Sidney Earl Mead, *Nathaniel William Taylor, 1786–1858, A Connecticut Liberal* (University of Chicago Press, 1942), p. 189.

4. "Beecher's Sermon at Worcester," *Christian Examiner*, 1 (January–February, 1824) 48–81.

5. Quoted in Mead, p. 212.

6. Beecher, 1:348, quoting Goodrich's letter of January 6, 1822.

7. Mead, p. 218. For a review of the New Haven Theology, see George M. Marsden, *The Evangelical Mind and the New School Presbyterian Experience: A Case Study of Thought and Theology in Nineteenth-Century America* (New Haven: Yale University Press, 1970), pp. 45–52.

8. Nathaniel William Taylor, *Concio ad Clerum, A Sermon Delivered in the Chapel of Yale College, September 10, 1828* (New Haven: Hezekiah Howe, 1828), pp. 5–8, 13–14, 38. The full text can be found in Sydney Ahlstrom, *Theology in America* (Indianapolis: Bobbs-Merrill, 1967), pp. 213–49.

9. David L. Dodge to Finney, September 17, 1828, Finney Papers, Oberlin College Archives (OCA).

10. William G. McLoughlin, Jr., *Modern Revivalism: Charles Grandison Finney to Billy Graham* (New York: Ronald Press, 1959), p. 45.

11. James Patterson to Finney, March 26, 1830, Finney Papers, OCA.

12. Sydney E. Ahlstrom, *A Religious History of the American People* (New Haven: Yale University Press, 1972), p. 467.

13. S. B. Ludlow to Finney, January 20, 1831, Finney Papers, OCA.

14. Samuel J. Baird, *A History of the New School, and of the Question Involved in the Disruption of the Presbyterian Church in 1838* (Philadelphia: Claxton, Remsen and Hoffelfinger, 1868), pp. 392ff.; E. H. Gillett, *History of the Presbyterian Church* (Philadelphia: Presbyterian Board of Publication, 1864), 2:467ff.; McLoughlin, pp. 49–50.

15. Anson Phelps to Finney, January 31, 1831, Finney Papers, OCA.

16. Lewis Tappan to Finney, February 21, 1831, Finney Papers, OCA.

17. Joel Parker to Finney, February 21, 1831, Finney Papers, OCA.

18. Timothy Dwight, Jr., to Finney, March, 1831, Finney Papers, OCA.

19. Charles G. Finney, *Memoirs of Rev. Charles G. Finney* (New York: A.S. Barnes, 1876), pp. 302–4. See also J. Hopkins to Finney, December 13, 1830, Finney Papers, OCA.

20. Finney, p. 303.

21. J. Hopkins to Finney, February 15, 1831, Finney Papers, OCA.

22. See M. R. Bodley to Finney, April 20, 1831, Finney Papers, OCA.

23. Charles Hawley, *The History of the First Presbyterian Church, Auburn, New York* (Auburn: Dennis, 1869), pp. 49–51.

24. *Manual of the First Presbyterian Church of Buffalo, New York, with Historical Sketch and Account of the Centennial Celebration, February 2 to 5, 1912* (Buffalo: n.p., 1912), p. 19.

25. Committee of Supply of the Union Church, Boston, to Finney, August 2, 1831, Finney Papers, OCA.

26. Lyman Beecher to Finney, August 2, 1831, Finney Papers, OCA.

27. Catharine Beecher to Finney (enclosure with letter of Lyman Beecher), August 2, 1831, Finney Papers, OCA.

28. Beecher was not always so dignified in his conduct before congregations himself, and it was certainly hypocrisy on his part to pretend to be the orderly urban pastor who was able to look down on the unruly country ranter, Finney. In M. Brayton and J. H. Whipple to Finney, May 8, 1827, Finney Papers, OCA, Brayton described his visit to hear Beecher at his Boston church, during which, to Brayton's astonishment, Beecher stopped his sermon, took a *tree* and began to *whirl it around* over his head (showing his agility and strength), and when he had given it enough momentum, *threw it* entirely over the heads of the congregation and beyond them! Was it a "large branch" rather than a "tree"? No matter; the episode is incredible, but Brayton claimed to have been an eyewitness.

29. Finney to John Starkweather, August 8, 1831, Finney Papers, OCA.

30. McLoughlin, p. 62.

31. Ibid.; Phineas C. Headley, *Evangelists in the Church from Philip, A.D. 35, to Moody and Sankey, A.D. 1875* (Boston: Hoyt, 1875) pp. 164f.

32. Benjamin B. Wisner to the clergy of Boston, August 16, 1831, Finney Papers, OCA.

33. Beecher, B. B. Wisner, J. H. Fairchild, G. W. Blagden et al., to the Committee for Supplying the Pulpit of the Union Church, August 15, 1831, Finney Papers, OCA.

34. H. Crosby Englizian, *Brimstone Corner: Park Street Church, Boston* (Chicago: Moody, 1968), pp. 105–12.

35. Finney, pp. 314–15.

36. Beecher, 2:80.

37. Finney, pp. 315–16.

38. This section is on p. 635 of the original manuscript of Finney's *Memoirs*, and was edited out by J. H. Fairchild. It belongs on p. 315 of the printed edition. The original may be seen in OCA.

39. C. G. Finney, *Sermons on Various Subjects* (New York: S. W. Benedict, 1834), pp. 4–8.

40. Ibid., p. 6.

41. Ibid., p. 39.

42. Ibid., pp. 15–16.

43. Asa Rand, *The New Divinity Tried* (Boston: n.p., 1832), p. 8.

44. Ibid., pp. 9–11.

45. Ibid., p. 11. The extent to which Finney taught "self-conversion" has been debated for years. Leonard I. Sweet ("The View of Man Inherent in New Measures Revivalism" [*Church History*, 45 (June 1976)] 208f.) argues that Finney taught "entire dependence on the Spirit of God."

46. Finney, *Sermons on Various Subjects*, p. 43.

47. Rand, p. 11.

48. *The Westminster Confession of Faith*, ch. 3, section 6, and ch. 7, section 3.

49. Rand, p. 14.

50. This statement from Wisner is quoted from a review of both Wisner's and Rand's booklets in *The Spirit of the Pilgrims*, 5 (March 1832) 167.

51. [Charles Hodge], "The New Divinity Tried," *The Biblical Repertory and Theological Review*, 4 (April 1832) 279.

52. Ibid., 4:301–2.

CHAPTER 12 — FINNEY ON BROADWAY

1. Bertram Wyatt-Brown, *Lewis Tappan and the Evangelical War Against Slavery* (Cleveland: Case Western Reserve University, 1969), pp. 44–45.

2. Gilbert H. Barnes, *The Antislavery Impulse, 1830–1844* (New York: Harcourt, Brace and World, 1964), p. 20.

3. Ibid.

4. Barnes, p. 20, is incorrect in stating that the Tappans' benevolent activities "were confined largely to generous contributions to the existing benevolent societies" before 1830.

5. [Lewis Tappan], *The Life of Arthur Tappan* (New York: Hurd and Houghton, 1870), pp. 96–102; Wyatt-Brown, pp. 53–54.

6. Tappan, pp. 102–8.

7. *The New York Evangelist*, July 2, 1831. See Tappan, pp. 110–25.

8. Wyatt-Brown, p. 68.

9. Wyatt-Brown, pp. 87ff.; Tappan, pp. 147ff.

10. Barnes, p. 42; see also, for a balance to Barnes' discounting of Garrison, Anne C. Loveland, "Evangelicalism and 'Immediate Emancipation' in American Antislavery Thought," *Journal of Southern History*, 32 (1966) 172–88.

11. See, for the entire episode, Barnes, pp. 25–28.

12. David Brion Davis, "The Emergence of Immediatism in British and American Antislavery Thought," in David Brion Davis, ed., *Ante-Bellum Reform* (New York: Harper & Row, 1967), pp. 139–52.

13. Charles Finney to Arthur Tappan, April 30, 1836, Finney Papers, Oberlin College Archives (OCA).

14. Wyatt-Brown, p. 84.

15. See Wyatt-Brown, pp. 78ff. for a vivid account of this, and Tappan, pp. 164ff.

16. See Gilbert H. Barnes and Dwight L. Dumond, eds., *Letters of Theodore Dwight Weld, Angelina Grimké Weld and Sarah Grimké, 1822–1844* (New York: Appleton-Century-Crofts, 1934), 1:13. Weld was so successful in collecting funds for the school that Gale may have been somewhat jealous.

17. Benjamin Thomas, *Theodore Weld, Crusader for Freedom* (New Brunswick: Rutgers University Press, 1950), pp. 24ff.

18. Barnes and Dumond, 1:56–57.

19. Hermann R. Muelder, *Fighters For Freedom* (New York: Columbia University Press, 1959), pp. 49ff. The standard work on the Lane episode is Lawrence T. Lesick's excellent *The Lane Rebels: Evangelicalism and Antislavery in Antebellum America* (Metuchen, N.J.: Scarecrow, 1980), from which this account is largely drawn.

20. [Lyman Beecher], *The Autobiography of Lyman Beecher*, B. Cross, ed. (Harvard University, Belknap Press, 1961), 2:184.

21. Lesick, p. 77.

22. Barnes, p. 41.

23. See Barnes, p. 46.

24. Barnes and Dumond, 1:50.

25. Ibid., 1:55.

26. Ibid., 1:66–68.

27. Lewis Tappan to Finney, March 16, 1832, Finney Papers, OCA.

28. Lewis Tappan to Finney, March 22, 1832 (first letter), Finney Papers, OCA;

George C. D. Odell, *Annals of the New York Stage* (New York: Columbia University Press, 1927–49), vol. 3.

29. Lewis Tappan to Finney, March 22, 1832 (second letter), Finney Papers, OCA.

30. Lewis Tappan to Finney, April 11, 1832, Finney Papers, OCA. Tappan has misspelled Thomas Hamblin's name here.

31. Susan Hayes Ward, *The History of the Broadway Tabernacle Church: From Its Organization in 1840 to the Close of 1900, Including Factors Influencing Its Formation* (New York: Trow, 1901), p. 24.

32. Lewis Tappan to Finney, March 22, April 11, 1832, Finney Papers, OCA. The theater was not old, as some have suggested; it was built in 1824.

33. *New York Evangelist*, May 12, 1832.

34. Fowler, p. 696; *Dictionary of American Biography*, 8:387–88; Armin Haeussler, *The Story of Our Hymns* (St. Louis: Eden, 1952), pp. 704–5.

35. Charles G. Finney, *Lectures on Revivals of Religion*, W. G. McLoughlin, ed. (Harvard University, Belknap Press, 1960), pp. 133–34, 254–57.

36. The "Great Eight" benevolent societies included:

1) The American Board of Commissioners for Foreign Missions, founded in 1810 and located in Boston.

2) The American Education Society, founded in 1815 and located in Boston, published the *Quarterly Register and Journal of the American Education Society*.

3) The American Bible Society, founded in 1816 and located in New York City, published *Annual Reports of the American Bible Society*.

4) The American Colonization society, founded in 1816 and located in New York City.

5) The American Sunday School Union, founded in 1817 and located in Philadelphia.

6) The American Tract Society, founded in 1826 and located in New York City, published yearly *Reports of the American Tract Society*.

7) The American Temperance Society, founded in 1826 and located in New York City, published *Annual Reports of the American Temperance Society*.

8) The American Home Missionary Society, founded in 1826 and located in New York City, published *Annual Reports of the American Home Missionary Society*.

For information on the "Great Eight," see Charles Cole, *The Social Ideas of the Northern Evangelists, 1826–1860* (New York: Columbia University Press, 1954); Oliver Elsbree, *The Rise of the Missionary Spirit in America* (Williamsport, Pa.: n.p., 1928); Charles Foster, *An Errand of Mercy: The Evangelical United Front, 1790–1830* (Chapel Hill: University of North Carolina Press, 1960); Colin Goodykootz, *Home Missions on the American Frontier* (Caldwell, Idaho: Caxton, 1939); Clifford Griffin, *Their Brothers' Keepers* (New Brunswick, N.J.: Rutgers University Press, 1960).

37. George M. Marsden, *The Evangelical Mind and the New School Presbyterian Experience* (New Haven: Yale University Press, 1970), pp. 14ff.

38. Barnes, p. 18.

39. Charles G. Finney, *Sermons on Various Subjects* (New York: Benedict, 1835), pp. 96–103. Optimistic postmillennialism was largely replaced in Protestantism, after the Civil War, by premillennialism, which holds that evil is increasing and good declining.

40. Charles G. Finney, "The Pernicious Attitude of the Church on the Reforms of the Age," Letters on Revivals, no. 23, *The Oberlin Evangelist*, January 21, 1846, p. 11.

41. Norman Grover, "The Church and Social Action in Finney, Bushnell, and Gladden" (Ph.D. dissertation, Vanderbilt University, 1957), p. 199.

42. J. W. C. Bliss, William Green, Jr., Joel Parker et al., to Finney, June 1, 1832, Finney Papers, OCA.

43. Lewis Tappan to Finney, April 11, 1832, and June 28, 1832, Finney Papers, OCA.

44. Mary Ann Andrews and C.S. Andrews to Lydia Andrews Finney, January 1, 1828, Finney Papers, OCA.

45. Lydia Finney to Nathaniel Andrews, July 15, 1832, Finney Papers, OCA.

46. Charles Finney to Mr. and Mrs. Nathaniel Andrews, July 15, 1832, Finney Papers, OCA.

47. Herman G. Norton and Amelia Norton to Charles and Lydia Finney, March 19, 1832, Finney Papers, OCA.

48. E. W. Clarke to Finney, May 23, 1832, Finney Papers, OCA.

49. Charles Finney to Mr. and Mrs. Nathaniel Andrews, July 15, 1832, Finney Papers, OCA.

50. Ward, p. 25.

51. Charles G. Finney, *Memoirs of Rev. Charles G. Finney* (New York: A.S. Barnes, 1876), p. 320.

52. *Western Recorder*, July 17, 1832.

53. Finney, *Memoirs*, p. 320.

54. *New York Evangelist*, October 27, 1832.

55. Jacob Helffenstein, "C. G. Finney and New Measures; View Of A Contemporary Minister," in *New York Evangelist*, July 20, 1876. L. Nelson Nichols, *History of the Broadway Tabernacle of New York City* (New Haven: Tuttle, Morehouse, and Taylor, 1940), p. 53, states that Helffenstein was an associate pastor at the Chatham Street Chapel at the time Finney was there, but all the evidence is against that. He made no mention of serving at the Chapel in the above article, while he did write of being a successor to Finney at the Broadway Tabernacle. In addition, William Green Jr. to Finney, June 25, 1833 (Finney Papers, OCA) states that Green had been trying to get Helffenstein to supply the pulpit in Finney's absence, and if Helffenstein was already an associate pastor there, that would obviously have been unnecessary.

56. Ward, p. 25; Nichols, p. 54.

57. Finney, *Memoirs*, p. 321–24.

58. Nichols, pp. 54–55.

59. William Green, Jr. to Finney, July 9, 1833, Finney Papers, OCA.

60. Andrew Reed and James Matheson, *A Narrative of the Visit to the American Churches, By the Deputation From the Congregational Union of England and Wales* (New York: Harper and Brothers, 1835), 2:347.

61. S. D. Alexander, *The Presbytery of New York* (New York: Randolph, 1888), p. 108; Jonathan Greenleaf, *A History of the Churches of New York* (New York: E. French, 1846), pp. 176–77. Nichols, p. 54, says the Fourth Free Church called the Rev. Arthur Granger as pastor, but Greenleaf corrects him (p. 176), saying Granger was merely a temporary stated supply for several months before Sprague was installed as pastor in October.

62. See Nichols, pp. 68–69.

63. From the *New York Evangelist*, May 26, 1832.

64. *The Emancipator*, September 21, 1833.

65. *The Courier and Enquirer*, July 8, 1833.

66. G. Frederick Wright, *Charles Grandison Finney* (Boston: Houghton, Mifflin, 1891), pp. 118–19; Wyatt-Brown, pp. 104–5.

67. Wyatt-Brown, p. 106.

68. Ibid., pp. 72–73.
69. Finney, *Memoirs*, p. 328.
70. Ibid., p. 325.
71. Wyatt-Brown, p. 116.
72. *Liberator*, July 12, 1834; *New York Evangelist*, July 13, 1834.
73. *Liberator*, July 12, 1834.
74. Barnes and Dumond, 1:153–56.
75. Tappan, p. 208.
76. Ibid., pp. 222, 284.
77. Ward, p. 26.

CHAPTER 13 — AN EXPLOSIVE PERIOD

1. Gilbert H. Barnes, *The Antislavery Impulse, 1830–1844* (New York: Harcourt, Brace and World, 1964), p. 40.

2. The city of Smyrna, or Izmir, is the site of one of the seven churches of Revelation chapters 2 and 3, and a frequent tourist stop.

3. Charles G. Finney, *Memoirs of Rev. Charles G. Finney* (New York: A.S. Barnes, 1876), p. 325. G. Frederick Wright, *Charles Grandison Finney* (Boston: Houghton, Mifflin, 1891), p. 108, refers to an episode on this voyage that Finney does not record. The ship's captain "was given to strong drink," and "at one time, when a storm was raging and the vessel was in great peril, and the captain was disabled by drink, the command of the ship temporarily devolved on Finney." Wright claims that Finney's "knowledge of seamanship, early acquired on Lake Ontario," enabled him to perform this feat of commanding the ship. The source of Wright's story is a letter, Frederic Norton Finney to Wright, February 10, 1890, in the G. F. Wright Papers, Oberlin College Archives (OCA). It says, "Father's experiences on the water and to which he frequently referred, were those that he had on a trip that he took from N.Y. to points in the Mediterranean Sea on a sailing ship in the early part of his ministry." Later in the letter he continues that during the voyage "the captain was disabled in some way and Father was for a time either wholly or partially in command and it was just the thing that he loved."

It is difficult to accept this story at face value, or to believe that Finney was capable of commanding an ocean-going vessel, during such a storm as the Mediterranean often produces, while apparently the other officers and the crew stood by and allowed this passenger to overrule them. Previous to this Finney had been on a few small ships on the Great Lakes, and he had no experience with major storms at sea, or the management of ocean-going vessels during such emergencies. Inasmuch as Norton himself says "either wholly or partially in command," the story may be in the process of embellishment, an example of a fond son's esteem of his father.

4. Lewis Tappan to Lydia Finney, June 7 and July 18, 1834, Finney Papers, OCA.

5. *New York Evangelist*, January 25 and July 26, 1845; Robert S. Fletcher, *A History of Oberlin College: From Its Foundation Through the Civil War* (Oberlin, Ohio: Oberlin College, 1934), 1:32.

6. J. Earl Thompson, Jr., "Lyman Beecher's Long Road to Conservative Abolitionism," *Church History*, 42 (March 1973) 98ff.; Lawrence T. Lesick, *The Lane Rebels: Evangelicalism and Antislavery in Antebellum America* (Metuchen, N.J.; Scarecrow, 1980), pp. 77ff.

7. [Henry B. Stanton], *Debate at the Lane Seminary, Cincinnati; Speech of James A. Thome, of Kentucky, Delivered at the Annual Meeting of the American Anti-Slavery Society, May 6, 1834* (Boston: Morehouse, 1834), p. 4.

8. *The Emancipator*, April 22, 1834.

9. Robert H. Abzug, *Passionate Liberator: Theodore Dwight Weld and the Dilemma of Reform* (New York: Oxford University Press, 1980), pp. 99–100.

10. *The Cincinnati Journal*, December 13, 20, and 27, 1833; April 5, May 16, 1834; Asa Mahan, *Out of Darkness Into Light; or The Hidden Life Made Manifest* (Boston: Willard, 1876), pp. 116ff. Here Mahan tells vividly the story of Lane from his own viewpoint.

11. Barnes, pp. 70–71.

12. See Fletcher, 1:55, where he identifies the members of the board of trustees.

13. Thomas J. Biggs to F. Y. Vail, July 23, 1834, quoted in Fletcher, 1:157.

14. Thomas J. Biggs to Lyman Beecher, August 18, 1834, Lane Seminary MSS, McCormick Theological Seminary Library, Chicago.

15. Executive Committee Minutes, August 20 and 23, 1834, Lane Seminary MSS, McCormick Theological Seminary, Chicago.

16. Asa Mahan, *Autobiography, Intellectual, Moral, and Spiritual* (London: T. Woolmer, 1882), pp. 179ff.

17. H. B. Stanton to James Thome, September 11, 1834, Miscellaneous MSS, OCA.

18. Barnes, p. 230. Mahan, *Out of Darkness Into Light*, pp. 118–20, also places much of the blame for the Lane debacle on Beecher.

19. Barnes, p. 230.

20. Lewis Tappan to Lydia Finney, July 18, 1834, Finney Papers, OCA.

21. Charles G. Finney, *Lectures on Revivals of Religion*, W. G. McLoughlin, ed. (Harvard University, Belknap Press, 1960), p. 299.

22. Ibid., pp. 298, 302.

23. *New York Evangelist*, November 8, 1834.

24. Gilbert H. Barnes and Dwight L. Dumond, eds., *Letters of Theodore Dwight Weld, Angelina Grimké Weld and Sarah Grimké, 1822–1844* (New York: Appleton-Century-Crofts, 1934), 1:276; William G. McLoughlin, Jr., *Modern Revivalism: Charles Grandison Finney to Billy Graham* (New York: Ronald Press, 1959), p. 110.

25. Lewis Tappan, Diary MS, entry for February 25, 1836; pp. 2–5, Lewis Tappan Papers, Library of Congress.

26. Lewis Tappan to S. D. Hastings, April 11, 1841, Lewis Tappan Papers, Library of Congress.

27. Charles G. Finney, *Sermons on Various Subjects* (New York: Benedict, 1834). This was reissued in 1835 with the same title but with a change of content. In 1836 it again appeared, under a new title, *Sermons on Important Subjects* (New York: Taylor, 1836).

28. Ibid., p. 57.

29. Ibid., p. 84.

30. Ibid., p. 57.

31. Finney, *Memoirs*, p. 329.

32. Ibid., p. 330.

33. *New York Evangelist*, January 24, 1835.

34. Finney, *Memoirs*, p. 330.

35. W. B. Sprague, *Lectures on Revivals of Religion* (Albany: Webster and Skinner and Little, 1832).

36. See, for a good overview of Sprague's work, McLoughlin, pp. 124–25.

37. Finney, *Lectures*, pp. ix–x. McLoughlin states in his introduction (p. lix), "It is also a painful duty to point out that Finney evidently had been reading Calvin Colton's book on this subject prior to delivering his lectures (or else Leavitt turned to it to fill out some passages he had missed), for there are parallels between the two volumes that are too similar to be coincidental." A comparison of the pages cited does show some general similarities, particularly on the topics of pastors knowing the human heart, and sudden conversions versus long conversions. I feel, however, that in these sections there are no actual borrowings, only somewhat parallel sections, and that we need not necessarily infer that either Finney or Leavitt plagiarized from Sprague. It is possible that Finney retained some ideas from an earlier reading of Sprague, of course, and unconsciously repeated them in the lectures. I once sat on a college committee on student plagiarism where the comment was made by a professor, "After all, in the strictest sense of the word 'plagiarism,' who of us does not borrow from previous scholars constantly, in our lectures, etc., without giving credit?"

38. In contemporary terminology we would say "scientific."

39. Finney, *Lectures*, p. 13.

40. Ibid., p. 14.

41. Ibid., p. 10.

42. Ibid., pp. 28ff.

43. Ibid., p. 38.

44. Ibid., pp. 41–51.

45. Ibid., pp. 52–106, 124–39.

46. Ibid., pp. 107–23.

47. Ibid., pp. 140–73.

48. This was a distinct departure from the clergy-centered evangelism propagated by Beecher and Nettleton, and furthered in New England and elsewhere since the days of Increase Mather and Solomon Stoddard; see ibid., p. 122, footnote 5.

49. Ibid., pp. 120, 153.

50. This point must be made with some caution. For years it has been common to state that revivalism was the religious manifestation of Jacksonian democracy, as if all those who were against Jackson were also against equality. Lee Benson has shown convincingly that the major political parties in New York State, for example, both "accepted egalitarianism as the ideology of the Good Society," and that it is wrong to assume that only the Jacksonians promoted individual liberty. See his *The Concept of Jacksonian Democracy: New York As a Test Case* (New York: Atheneum, 1964), pp. 336ff., and Leonard Sweet, "The View of Man Inherent in New Measures Revivalism," *Church History*, 45:2 (June 1976).

51. Finney, *Lectures*, p. 105.

52. Ibid., p. 107.

53. Ibid., pp. 185–87.

54. Ibid., p. 205.

55. Ibid., p. 208.

56. Ibid., pp. 273–74.

57. Ibid., 219.

58. Ibid., p. 270.

59. Ibid., p. 271.

60. Ibid., p. 290.

61. Ibid., p. 273.

62. Ibid., p. 305. Although Finney may have had Nettleton in mind here, an-

other, more pressing controversy was raging at that very time, to which he refers immediately after the cited quotation, "Instead of standing still and writing letters from Berkshire. . . ." It began when David Dudley Field made some "Remarks" on "The Evils of Hasty and Extravagant Accounts of the Results of Protracted Meetings" at a meeting of the Berkshire and Columbia ministers in western Massachusetts on November 5, 1834. These remarks were published in the *New York Observer*, November 29, 1834. Field challenged the alleged number of converts of recent revivals. The *Boston Recorder* took up the controversy, and just when Finney was delivering this lecture, on March 13, 1835, the *Recorder* was publishing a very lengthy reply by Field to some of those who had attacked his findings. Later the *Recorder* noted Finney's remark on "letters from Berkshire," and because they were in the middle of the controversy they answered Finney on April 3, 1835: "We will tell Mr. Finney how to stop this 'writing letters.' Let Evangelists and others 'give up' doing things, which cannot be told of without exciting 'suspicion and jealousy in regard to revivals.' Then 'this writing letters' will cease of course. This would be a much better way than to insist that, when 'many wrong things' are done in the name of the Holy Ghost, no one shall say a word about them." The *Recorder*'s reply to Finney went on for nearly a full column in this fashion.

Field had collected statistics for some years on the number of converts made throughout the area. His chief complaint was that the numbers of new members taken into the churches of the region did not seem to match the numbers given by evangelists, and he naturally asked the question, Were the evangelists exaggerating the number of converts? He especially directed some of his complaints against Horatio Foote.

63. Ibid., p. 404.

64. Ibid., pp. 404–5.

65. Ibid., p. 416.

66. Ibid., p. xxii. See McLoughlin's comments on Dod's review, pp. xxi–xl.

67. Ibid.

68. [Albert Dod], "Review of *Lectures on Revivals of Religion* and *Sermons on Various Subjects*," *The Biblical Repertory and Theological Review*, 7 (July and October 1835), 484.

69. Ibid., 7:657.

70. Ibid., 7:484.

71. Ibid., 7:483.

72. Ibid., 7:486.

73. Ibid., 7:491–92.

74. Ibid., 7:492. See McLoughlin's explication of this at greater length in Finney, *Lectures*, pp. xxiii–xxx.

75. Dod, review, 7:495–96.

76. Ibid., 7:505.

77. Finney, *Lectures*, p. xxviii.

78. Dod, review, 7:505.

79. Ibid., 7:504.

80. McLoughlin, pp. 45–46.

81. Dod, review, 7:656–57.

82. Finney, *Sermons*, p. 80.

83. Finney, *Lectures*, p. 258.

84. Edwin S. Gaustad, *The Great Awakening in New England* (New York: Harper, 1957), pp. 37–41, 70–76.

85. Dod, review, 7:657–58.

86. Ibid., 7:658.

87. Ibid., 7:664.

88. Finney, *lectures,* p. 218.

89. Dod, review, 7:666.

90. Ibid., 7:671.

91. Ibid., 7:526–27.

92. If a letter was not prepaid at its posting in the 1830s, the post office would deliver it and charge postage-due to the recipient.

93. Dod, review, 7:674.

CHAPTER 14 — THE BEGINNINGS OF OBERLIN

1. John Jay Shipherd to Fayette Shipherd, August 13, 1832, Shipherd Papers, Oberlin College Archives (OCA).

2. Timothy L. Smith, "The Cross Demands, the Spirit Enables," *Christianity Today,* February 16, 1979, p. 24.

3. Robert S. Fletcher, *A History of Oberlin College: From Its Foundation Through the Civil War* (Oberlin, Ohio: Oberlin College, 1943), 1:94ff.; Gilbert H. Barnes, *The Antislavery Impulse, 1830–1844* (New York: Harcourt, Brace, and World, 1964), 1:75ff.

4. Fletcher, 1:100.

5. Ibid., 1:128.

6. *The Ohio Observer,* July 17, 1834.

7. Fletcher, 1:132–36.

8. Bertram Wyatt-Brown, *Lewis Tappan and the Evangelical War Against Slavery* (Cleveland: Case Western Reserve University, 1969), pp. 127–31; Barnes, pp. 75f.; Fletcher, 1:139–69.

9. Fletcher, 1:165–69; Barnes, pp. 75–76.

10. Asa Mahan, *Autobiography, Intellectual, Moral, and Spiritual* (London: T. Woolmer, 1882), pp. 191–92.

11. J. J. Shipherd to John Keep, December 13, 1834, Miscellaneous MSS, OCA.

12. N. P. Fletcher, quoted in Fletcher, 1:170.

13. Barnes, p. 76; G. Frederick Wright, *Charles Grandison Finney* (Boston: Houghton, Mifflin, 1891), p. 132.

14. Gilbert H. Barnes and Dwight L. Dumond, eds., *Letters of Theodore Dwight Weld, Angelina Grimké Weld and Sarah Grimké, 1822–1844* (New York: Appleton-Century-Crofts, 1934), 1:190.

15. Ibid., 1:188.

16. George Whipple and Henry B. Stanton to Finney, January 10, 1835, Finney Papers, OCA.

17. Charles Finney to Lydia Finney, November 10, 1834, Finney Papers, OCA; Charles G. Finney, *Memoirs of Rev. Charles G. Finney* (New York: A. S. Barnes, 1876), p. 332.

18. Barnes, p. 76.

19. Fletcher, 1:176–78.

20. James H. Fairchild, *Oberlin: The Colony And The College, 1833–1883* (Oberlin: Goodrich, 1883), p. 65.

21. [Lewis Tappan], *The Life of Arthur Tappan* (New York: Hurd and Houghton, 1870), pp. 238ff.

22. Fletcher, 1:175; Finney, p. 333. See Finney to Trustees of Oberlin Collegiate Institute, June 30, 1835, Finney Papers, OCA. Finney specified these conditions for his coming: he must be allowed to return to New York for a part of each year; there must be adequate funds available so that the school will not get into financial straits; the internal regulation of the school must be left to the faculty. Fletcher, 1:177–78, points out that the major concern was that freedom of discussion was possible on all issues.

23. Barnes and Dumond, 1:201.

24. John Keep to N.P. Fletcher, Peter Pease, and P.P. Stewart, February 29, 1835, quoted in Fletcher, 1:177.

25. J. J. Shipherd to Oberlin Trustees, January 19, 1835, Miscellaneous Papers, OCA.

26. Barnes, p. 40.

27. Fletcher, p. 181.

28. *The New York Evangelist*, April 11, 1835.

29. John Keep to Finney, March 23, 1835, Finney Papers, OCA.

30. Benjamin Woodbury to N.P. Fletcher, February 12, 1835, Miscellaneous Papers, OCA. See also D. L. Leonard, *The Story of Oberlin* (Boston: Pilgrim, 1898), pp. 243ff.

31. Generally, theaters at that time in the major cities were looked down upon as the haunts of prostitutes.

32. Susan H. Ward, *The History of the Broadway Tabernacle Church* (New York: Trow Print, 1901), p. 28.

33. L. Nelson Nichols, *History of the Broadway Tabernacle of New York City* (New Haven: Tuttle, Morehouse, and Taylor, 1940), pp. 60–61 says: "The name of Anthony Street was not changed until 1855, when it became Worth Street in honor of our New York City Mexican War General whose statue is now in Union Square."

34. Ward, p. 28.

35. Ibid.

36. Finney, p. 326.

37. The same concept was carried out at Oberlin, 1842–1844, when the First Church was constructed from plans by Richard Bond, a prominent New England architect whom Finney met in Boston. Finney doubtless guided Bond in utilizing this concept, for on the back of the extant plans for First Church, in OCA, is a drawing showing the speaker at the pulpit having eye contact with all members of the audience, both those in the balcony and those on the main floor.

38. Nichols, p. 60.

39. Finney, p. 328.

40. Nichols, p. 61.

41. George E. Pierce to Finney, May 12, 1835, Finney Papers, OCA.

42. Finney, pp. 342–43; see also L. A. M. Bosworth, "A Stormy Epoch, 1825–1850," *Papers of the Ohio Church History Society*, 6 (1895) 19.

43. Finney to Trustees of Oberlin Collegiate Institute, June 30, 1835, Finney Papers, OCA.

44. Fairchild, pp. 69ff.

45. *The New York Evangelist*, May 23, 1835.

46. Fairchild, p. 73; Finney, p. 336.

47. Fletcher, pp. 182–83, 829–30. John Keep to Finney, June 12, 1835, Finney Papers, OCA.

48. *The New York Evangelist*, July 18, 1835.

49. Fletcher, p. 183.

50. William Green to Finney, August 20 and 28, 1835, Finney Papers, OCA; Manuscript Minutes of the Professorship Association, October 9, 1835; Miscellaneous Archives, OCA.

51. George W. Gale to Asa Mahan, October 22, 1835, Finney Papers, OCA.

52. In Fletcher, chapters 39 and 40 contain a detailed account of the manual labor system at Oberlin.

53. Fairchild, p. 74.

54. Ibid., pp. 111–12.

55. Wyatt-Brown, p. 130.

56. *Charleston Courier*, July 30, 1835.

57. Wright, p. 143.

58. Tappan, pp. 264–65; Wyatt-Brown, pp. 151–52.

59. Tappan, p. 249.

60. Ibid., pp. 243–52.

61. Arthur Tappan to J. J. Shipherd, September 16, 1835, Miscellaneous MSS, OCA.

62. Tappan, pp. 279–81; see also Lewis Tappan to Arthur Tappan, October 5, 1838, Lewis Tappan Papers, Library of Congress.

63. Ward, p. 27, says that Finney began the lectures on December 18, but his correspondence is indefinite on the date of his return to New York City.

64. Tappan, pp. 272ff.; *Niles' Weekly Register*, December 26, 1835; *The Emancipator*, January 1836; C. Foster, *An Account of the Conflagration* (New York: n.p., 1836?).

65. Tappan, p. 273.

66. Ibid., pp. 278, 275.

67. *Niles' Weekly Register*, January 9, 1836; Wyatt-Brown, p. 168; Lewis Tappan to Gerrit Smith, December 21, 1835, Gerrit Smith Miller MSS, Syracuse University Library.

68. *The Journal of Commerce*, December 17, 1835.

69. Tappan, p. 277.

70. Charles Finney, *Lectures on Revivals of Religion*, W. G. McLoughlin, ed. (Harvard University, Belknap Press, 1960), p. 291.

71. I have made a thorough search of the extant minutes of the presbyteries to which Finney belonged, in which attendance at stated meetings is always kept, and Finney's name is among the "absent" at least 90% of the time. These records are in the Presbyterian Historical Society.

72. According to S. D. Alexander, *The Presbytery of New York* (New York: Randolph, 1888), p. 103, Cox left the Laight Street Church on February 3, 1835, so this incident could not have been as near to the resignation of Finney from the Second Free Church as he intimates in his *Memoirs*, p. 325.

73. Finney, *Memoirs*, p. 325.

74. Ward contains this, in Appendix B.

75. Ward, pp. 27–28; Nichols, pp. 62–63.

76. Alexander, p. 108.

77. *The New York Evangelist*, April 16, 1836

78. Ibid.

79. Nichols, p. 60; Finney, *Memoirs*, p. 326.

80. Finney, *Memoirs*, p. 334.

81. Ward, p. 29.

82. Barnes and Dumond, 1:244–45.

83. Fletcher, p. 240.

84. Henry B. Stanton to A. A. Phelps, March 5 and April 13, 1836, in Phelps Papers, Boston Public Library.

85. Theodore Weld to A. A. Phelps, June 1836, in Phelps Papers, Boston Public Library; Barnes and Dumond, 1:309–10; Robert H. Abzug, *Passionate Liberator: Theodore Dwight Weld and the Dilemma of Reform* (New York: Oxford University Press 1980), pp. 147–49.

86. See Abzug, pp. 150–55, for a perceptive treatment of this period.

87. Barnes and Dumond, 1:242–44.

88. Lewis Tappan's diary is among the Tappan Papers, Library of Congress.

89. Lewis Tappan's diary, February 25, March 5, March 14, 1836.

90. Charles Finney to Arthur Tappan, April 30, 1836, Finney Papers, OCA.

91. Barnes and Dumond, 1:270–74.

92. Ibid., 1:288–89.

93. See Abzug, pp. 147–55.

94. Barnes and Dumond, 1:318–19.

95. Ibid., 1:319–20.

96. Ibid., 1:317. In chapter 5 of Lawrence T. Lesick, *The Lane Rebels: Evangelicalism and Antislavery in Antebellum America* (Metuchen, N.J.: Scarecrow, 1980) there is an overview of the motivations and eventual careers of the Lane rebels.

97. Barnes and Dumond, 1:327–28.

98. *Zion's Herald*, 8:25.

99. Abzug, p. 152.

100. Mahan, pp. 239ff.

101. Lesick, p. 199.

CHAPTER 15 — OBERLIN PERFECTIONISM

1. Whitney R. Cross, *The Burned-over District: The Social and Intellectual History of Enthusiastic Religion in Western New York, 1800–1850* (New York: Harper and Row, 1965), pp. 238–51. There are several important sources for the understanding of perfectionism in America; a balanced treatment is John L. Thomas, "Romantic Reform in America," in David Brion Davis, ed., *Ante-Bellum Reform* (New York: Harper and Row, 1967), pp. 153–76; defending Finney is James H. Fairchild, "The Doctrine of Sanctification at Oberlin," in *The Congregational Quarterly*, 18 (April 1876) 237–59; by far the most complete coverage is Benjamin B. Warfield, *Perfectionism* (New York: Oxford University Press, 1931), in two volumes, which was reprinted from articles in *The Princeton Theological Review*. Warfield strongly defends Old School Calvinism, and attacks Finney.

2. Cross, p. 240.

3. Ibid., p. 241.

4. George W. Noyes, ed., *Religious Experience of John Humphrey Noyes, Founder of the Oneida Community* (New York: Macmillan, 1923), p. 135.

5. It is frequently stated that *The Perfectionist* was founded by Noyes, but he repeatedly insisted that it was really Boyle's magazine. In *The Witness*, vol. 1, no. 1 (August 20, 1837), Noyes wrote: "I confess I have long anticipated and desired the ministry upon which I am now entering. But especially since the publication of The Perfection-

ist ceased, I have sought the opportunity which is now presented of effectually declaring that that paper *does not* contain my views, as Mr. Finney, and others suppose. It ought to be known, if it is not, that, although I was several months connected with James Boyle in the publication of that paper, I held but a subordinate office in the business, and that there was a material difference of sentiment between him and me, insisted upon by him and acknowledged by me from the beginning. My liberty of testimony was limited always by his judgment, and within a few months after I abandoned the partnership, my writings were rejected or tardily published. Moreover, many things appeared, especially in the second year of The Perfectionist, which I have been constrained to condemn." See Ernest Sandeen, "John Humphrey Noyes as the New Adam," *Church History,* 40/1 (March 1971) 82–90.

6. J. H. Noyes to his mother, March 30, 1837, cited in *Religious Experience of John Humphrey Noyes,* p. 330.

7. Finney to J. H. Noyes, April 3, 1837, cited in ibid., pp. 333–34.

8. *The Witness,* I/1 (August 20, 1837).

9. See Robert A. Parker, *A Yankee Saint, John Humphrey Noyes and the Oneida Community* (New York: G.P. Putnam's Sons, 1935).

10. Fairchild, pp. 238–39; see also idem, *Oberlin: The Colony and the College, 1833–1883* (Oberlin: E. J. Goodrich, 1883), pp. 90ff.

11. Fairchild, "Doctrine of Sanctification," p. 238.

12. Ibid.

13. Warfield, 2:48.

14. Charles G. Finney, *Systematic Theology* (Oberlin: Strong, 1878), p. 312.

15. Delavan L. Leonard, *The Story of Oberlin: The Institution, The Community, The Idea, The Movement* (Boston: Pilgrim, 1898), p. 238.

16. Asa Mahan, *Scripture Doctrine of Christian Perfection* (Boston: Waite, Pierce, 1849), p. 187. The development of Oberlin perfectionism is presented in Edward H. Madden and James E. Hamilton, *Freedom and Grace: The Life of Asa Mahan* (Metuchen, N.J.: Scarecrow, 1982), pp. 59–67, but Finney's role is played down.

17. Asa Mahan, *Out of Darkness into Light; or, The Hidden Life Made Manifest* (Boston: Willard, 1876), p. 180.

18. Ibid., p. 182.

19. Sereno Wright Streeter (1810?–1880) had been converted under Finney in New York state. He studied at the Oneida Institute from 1828 to 1830, had entered Lane Seminary in 1833, and was among the rebels coming to Oberlin in 1834, where he studied for two years. See Fairchild, "Doctrine of Sanctification," pp. 239–40, and Warfield, 2:54.

20. Mahan, *Christian Perfection,* p. 188; Fairchild, "Doctrine of Sanctification," p. 240.

21. Mahan, *Christian Perfection,* p. 188.

22. Charles G. Finney, *Memoirs of Rev. Charles G. Finney* (New York: A.S. Barnes, 1876), pp. 340–41.

23. Charles G. Finney, *Lectures to Professing Christians* (London: Chidley, 1839), pp. 218–19.

24. Fairchild, "Doctrine of Sanctification," p. 241.

25. Finney, *Lectures,* pp. 215–16.

26. Ibid., p. 219.

27. Ibid.

28. Ibid., p. 220.

29. Ibid.

30. Warfield, 2:59–60.

31. Charles G. Finney, *Views of Sanctification* (Oberlin: Steele, 1840).

32. Finney, *Lectures*, p. 223.

33. Ibid.

34. Warfield, 2:61–62.

35. [Lewis Tappan]. *The Life of Arthur Tappan* (New York: Hurd and Houghton, 1870), p. 280.

36. Ibid., p. 281.

37. Ibid., pp. 281–82.

38. [Lewis Tappan], *Proceedings of the Session of Broadway Tabernacle, Against Lewis Tappan, With the Action of the Presbytery . . .* (New York: n.p., 1839), p. 4. L. Nelson Nichols' statements in *History of the Broadway Tabernacle*, pp. 62 and 68, about Duffield having been with Finney at Chatham Street Chapel and the Broadway Tabernacle are incorrect. Duffield came to the Tabernacle after Finney left.

39. O. D. Hibbard to Levi Burnell, May, 1837, as cited in Robert S. Fletcher, *A History of Oberlin College: From Its Foundation Through the Civil War* (Oberlin, Ohio: Oberlin College, 1943), 1:455.

40. Ibid.

41. Finney, *Memoirs*, p. 337.

42. The situation is described vividly in Fletcher, 1:452ff.

43. Finney, *Memoirs*, pp. 338–39.

44. "The Trial of Dr. Beecher for Heresy," in *The Christian Examiner and General Review* (Unitarian, Boston), 19 (September 1835) 116ff.

45. "Beecher's Views in Theology", *Biblical Repertory and Theological Review*, 9:216–37, 364–407. For an overview of these developments, see George M. Marsden, *The Evangelical Mind and the New School Presbyterian Experience: A Case Study of Thought and Theology in Nineteenth-Century America* (New Haven: Yale University Press, 1970), pp. 55ff.

46. James H. Hotchkin, *A History of the Purchase and Settlement of Western New York, and of the Rise, Progress, and Present State of the Presbyterian Church in That Section* (New York: Dodd, 1848), p. 243.

47. See Bruce Staiger, "Abolition and the Presbyterian Schism of 1837–38," *Mississippi Valley Historical Review*, 36 (1949–1950) 391–415; Sydney E. Ahlstrom, *A Religious History of the American People* (New Haven: Yale University Press, 1972), p. 468.

48. Hotchkin, p. 222–23.

49. Ibid., p. 231; Ahlstrom, p. 468.

50. John Wesley, *A Plain Account of Christian Perfection* (New York: Emory and Waugh, 1829), pp. 59–60.

51. Finney, *Views of Sanctification*, p. 59.

52. Timothy L. Smith has stimulating treatments of Oberlin perfectionism in *Revivalism and Social Reform: American Protestantism on the Eve of the Civil War* (New York: Abingdon, 1957) and "The Cross Demands, the Spirit Enables," *Christianity Today*, February 16, 1979, pp. 22–26. For Finney's own "second baptism," see Finney, *Memoirs*, pp. 375–81.

53. Finney, *Views of Sanctification*, p. 61.

54. See the discussion on Arminianism in Chapter One.

55. Charles Hodge, *An Exposition of the First Epistle to the Corinthians* (London: Banner of Truth, 1959), pp. 181, 169.

56. *Oberlin Evangelist*, December 16, 1840.

57. Elsewhere Finney did maintain two natures in regenerate human nature, as in his *Lectures on Systematic Theology*, 1851 ed., p. 261. Point 2 of this article in the *Oberlin Evangelist* may have been an unfortunate slip on Finney's part, but nonetheless it remains an astonishing statement.

58. William Wisner to Charles Finney, December 23, 1839, Finney Papers, Oberlin College Archives (OCA).

59. Josiah Chapin to Charles Finney, November 9, 1840, Finney Papers, OCA.

60. Amelia Norton to Lydia Finney, March 11, 1839, Finney Papers, OCA.

61. Mahan, *Out of Darkness into Light*, p. 191.

62. *An Exposition of the Peculiarities, Difficulties and Tendencies of Oberlin Perfectionism, Prepared by a Committee of the Presbytery of Cleveland* (Cleveland: Smead, 1841), p. 84.

63. Fletcher, 1:226.

64. Ibid., 1:227.

65. *Minutes* of the Presbytery of Troy, New York, for the Years 1840 to 1842, pp. 236, in the Presbyterian Historical Society. Warfield, 2:209, claims that Beman "was the actual author of the uncompromising refutation."

66. *Oberlin Evangelist*, September 15, 1841.

67. In the *Oberlin Quarterly Review*, February, 1846, p. 318. It had originally appeared in the *New York Evangelist* for September 11, ·1845, pp. 145–46.

68. Warfield, 2:210; Finney, *Memoirs*, p. 348.

69. Fairchild, "Doctrine of Sanctification," pp. 244–45; see Fletcher, 1:228.

CHAPTER 16 — FINNEY THE EDUCATOR

1. Cited in Robert S. Fletcher, *A History of Oberlin College: From Its Foundation Through the Civil War* (Oberlin, Ohio: Oberlin College, 1943), 1:458. I am indebted to Fletcher for unearthing much of the primary material used in this chapter.

2. Ibid., 1:469–70.

3. Enrollment figures are given in Fletcher, 1:501, and in G. Frederick Wright, *Charles G. Finney* (Boston: Houghton, Mifflin, 1891), pp. 157–58, but they disagree somewhat.

4. *Oberlin Evangelist*, January 6, 1841.

5. Ibid., February 17, 1841. There are many details of the activities of the Oberlin church from its inception to the 1870s in Delavan L. Leonard, *The Story of Oberlin* (Boston: Pilgrim, 1898), pp. 180–212.

6. Elizabeth Maxwell to Mrs. Rebecca Maxwell, May 5, 1842, in the possession of Mrs. E. N. Fitch. See also James H. Fairchild, *Oberlin* (Oberlin: Butler, 1871), pp. 11ff.

7. See footnote 37, chapter 14, above. Wright, p. 158, says, "In 1845, a commodious church building had been erected, after the plan of the original Broadway Tabernacle, seating fifteen hundred." But this is not so, based either on the dimensions or on the internal arrangements. The Broadway Tabernacle was a square building, about 100 ft. by 100 ft., whereas First Church is rectangular, its sanctuary measuring about 68 ft. by 96 ft., and is thus considerably smaller and able to hold fewer. Also, the Tabernacle balcony, according to the views in Susan Hayes Ward, *The History of the Broadway Tabernacle* (New York: Trow, 1901), was much deeper, having at least seven pews,

whereas the First Church balcony has four and is elliptical rather than circular, following the contour of the building.

8. Fletcher, 2:575, quotes a visitor in 1853 who stated that First Church was "immense" and would seat "twenty-five hundred persons." I have carefully counted the seats and believe this statement and Wright's claim of fifteen hundred to be evangelistic counts, not based on careful calculation. One thousand would be a much closer approximation.

9. *Oberlin Evangelist*, April 1, 1846.

10. Fletcher, 2:576. Fletcher has much on Finney's activities as pastor of First Church; see especially his chapter 36.

11. Fletcher, 2:578.

12. Wright, pp. 156–57.

13. Ibid., p. 157. See, for many authentic Finney stories, Frances J. Hosford, "Finney the Inscrutable," *Oberlin Alumni Magazine* 30 (1934), 233–36.

14. John Keep to Gerrit Smith, January 16, 1836, Gerrit Smith Miller Papers, Syracuse University Library. See also on this, Wright, pp. 139–53.

15. Although Western Reserve College at Hudson, Ohio, had extended an invitation to Finney in 1835 to serve there as professor of practical theology, it was not so much on the strength of his academic qualifications, but rather a desperate move to attempt to frustrate Oberlin's plans. See Fletcher, 1:430ff.

16. *New York Evangelist*, January 16, 1836.

17. Elisha B. Sherwood, *Fifty Years on the Skirmish Line* (New York: Revell, 1893), p. 37.

18. Ibid., pp. 37–38.

19. Quoted in Wright, p. 154.

20. Charles G. Finney, *Lectures on Systematic Theology* (Oberlin: E. J. Goodrich, 1847), III, Preface.

21. Charles G. Finney, *Lectures on Revivals of Religion*, W. G. McLoughlin, ed. (Harvard University, Belknap Press, 1960), pp. 187–89.

22. Ibid., pp. 189–91. See also Charles G. Finney, *Memoirs of Rev. Charles G. Finney* (New York: A.S. Barnes, 1876), pp. 85–97.

23. Finney, *Memoirs*, p. 91.

24. Fletcher, 2:727.

25. Ibid., 2:733.

26. Ibid., 2:728.

27. Robert S. Fletcher, "The Pastoral Theology of Charles G. Finney," *Ohio Presbyterian Historical Society Proceedings*, 3 (1941) 28–33.

28. Fletcher, *History of Oberlin*, 2:729. All of this will be found, at greater length, in Fletcher, 2:726–34.

29. Fletcher, "Pastoral Theology," 3:32.

30. Articles in the *Western Recorder*, May 25, 1830, and the *Rochester Observer*, May 12, 1831.

31. Fletcher, *History of Oberlin*, 1:318–19; see, for a discussion of the health movement, his chapter 22.

32. *The Graham Journal of Health and Longevity* (April 18, 1837), 1:17.

33. Leonard, p. 219.

34. J. J. Shipherd, July 6, 1835, in the *New York Evangelist*, July 18, 1835.

35. Fletcher, *History of Oberlin*, 1:237.

36. See Wright, pp. 144–45, and *The Emancipator*, December 8, 1835; January 19, February 9, April 27, 1837, and Amos Dresser, *Narrative of the Arrest, Lynch Law Trial,*

and Scourging of Amos Dresser, at Nashville, Tennessee, August, 1835 (Oberlin: E. J. Goodrich, 1849).

37. Fletcher, *History of Oberlin*, 1:252.

38. Gilbert H. Barnes and Dwight L. Dumond, eds., *Letters of Theodore Dwight Weld, Angelina Grimké Weld and Sarah Grimké, 1822–1844* (New York: Appleton-Century-Crofts, 1934), 2:751.

39. Finney, *Memoirs*, p. 337.

40. Fletcher has given many instances relating to this in *History of Oberlin*, chapters 18, 19, 25, and passim.

41. This entire episode is related in Gilbert H. Barnes, *The Antislavery Impulse, 1830–1844* (New York: Harcourt, Brace and World, 1964), pp. 88ff.

42. John Humphrey Noyes to William Lloyd Garrison, March 22, 1837, William Lloyd Garrison Papers, Boston Public Library; also given in Wendell P. Garrison and Francis J. Garrison, *William Lloyd Garrison, 1805–1879* (New York: Arno, 1969), 2:145ff.

43. *Liberator*, June 30, 1837.

44. Barnes, p. 95. See, for an alternate view on this, J. Earl Thompson, Jr., "Lyman Beecher's Long Road to Conservative Abolitionism," *Church History*, 42 (March 1973), p. 102.

45. Garrison's characterization of the Methodist Church is quoted from *Zion's Herald*, 8/123 (August 12, 1837); his statement on the Congregationalists in the *Liberator* for July 14, 1837; and on the Presbyterians in the *Liberator* for September 5, 1837.

46. *The National Enquirer*, 3:33.

47. William Lloyd Garrison to Lewis Tappan, September 13, 1837, Lewis Tappan Papers, Library of Congress.

48. Garrison, *Garrison*, 2:168.

49. Fletcher, *History of Oberlin*, 1:265.

50. Fairchild, pp. 28–31.

51. Barnes, p. viii.

52. Finney's contacts in 1829 with the Association of Gentlemen in New York City may have first sensitized him to the problem of abolition, for the Tappans had become interested in the plight of the blacks in 1828. See Barnes, pp. 25ff. If Finney was influenced by any particular theories regarding abolition, it was probably those of Charles Stuart in England, perpetuated in America by Theodore Weld, in the years 1829 to 1834.

53. Finney, *Lectures on Systematic Theology*, 2:446.

54. *Oberlin Evangelist*, February 4, 1846.

55. *Oberlin Evangelist*, August 13, 1856.

56. Charles G. Finney to Gerrit Smith, January 29, 1864, Gerrit Smith Papers, Syracuse University Library.

CHAPTER 17 — THE CHANGING FACE OF REVIVALS

1. Charles G. Finney, *Memoirs of Rev. Charles G. Finney* (New York: A.S. Barnes, 1876), p. 347.

2. Ibid., pp. 353–57. In Finney's original manuscript "Channing" was spelled out.

3. Arthur W. Brown, *William Ellery Channing* (New York: Twayne, 1961); John W. Chadwick, *William Ellery Channing, Minister of Religion* (Boston: Houghton, Mifflin, 1903), passim.

4. Whitney R. Cross, *The Burned-over District: The Social and Intellectual History of Enthusiastic Religion in Western New York, 1800–1850* (New York: Harper and Row, 1965), p. 291.

5. Finney, pp. 370–71. See the discussion of postmillennialism on pp. 152, 254, and 374.

6. Ibid., p. 354. It is difficult to determine the exact dates of Finney's labors in Boston, Providence, and Rochester, for two reasons: his correspondence, voluminous for earlier years, is very sparse for the years 1836 to 1849, when once again most of it was kept; secondly, with the exception of the *Oberlin Evangelist*, the religious periodicals mentioned Finney only rarely after Oberlin perfectionism was advanced, as if fearful of the repercussions of carrying even news items that might be construed as supportive of Finney. Even the *New York Evangelist* for the months September 1841 through July 1842 fails to mention Finney's activities! His name, apparently, was anathema. We know that Finney was in Rochester by February 1, 1842. That being so, his dating of his labors in Boston and Providence must be off by several months (*Memoirs*, p. 353). If he did indeed work for two months each in Boston, Providence, and Rochester, then a likely time frame would be: Boston, October and November, 1841; Providence, December 1841 and January 1842; Rochester, February and March 1842. See *Memoirs*, p. 355.

7. Ibid., p. 354.

8. See, for Jacob Knapp's ministry, William G. McLoughlin, Jr., *Modern Revivalism: Charles Grandison Finney to Billy Graham* (New York: Ronald, 1959), pp. 140ff.

9. Finney, p. 354.

10. R. W. Cushman, *A Calm Review of the Measures Employed in the Religious Awakening in Boston in 1842* (Boston: Stone, 1847), pp. 33ff.

11. Finney, p. 355.

12. Ibid., pp. 355–56.

13. Ibid., p. 358.

14. Ibid.

15. See, for instance, J. Hopkins to Finney, July 29, 1833, Finney Papers, Oberlin College Archives (OCA).

16. Mrs. Elizabeth Selden Spencer Eaton to her husband, February 15, 1842, cited in *Publications of Rochester Historical Society*, 21:76–77.

17. *Oberlin Evangelist*, March 30, 1842.

18. John Morgan to Finney, March 15, 1852, Finney Papers, OCA.

19. Robert S. Fletcher, *A History of Oberlin College: From Its Foundation Through the Civil War* (Oberlin, Ohio: Oberlin College, 1943), 2:727.

20. See Josiah Chapin to Finney, March 31, 1843, Finney Papers, OCA; also in the OCA is a manuscript by Julia Monroe Finney that gives vital statistics on the family, from which dates here are taken.

21. Finney, pp. 372, 379.

22. Ibid., pp. 372, 385.

23. *Signs of the Times*, January 25, 1843; Finney, pp. 370–71.

24. For an insightful treatment of Finney's "second work of grace," see Timothy L. Smith, "The Cross Demands, the Spirit Enables," *Christianity Today*, February 16, 1979, pp. 22–26.

25. Finney, pp. 373–77.

26. See Clyde Binfield, *George Williams and the Y.M.C.A.* (London: Heinemann, 1973), and Lawrence L. Doggett, *History of the Young Men's Christian Association* (New York: Association Press, 1922), passim; Kenneth S. Latourette, *A History of Christianity* (New York: Harper & Brothers, 1953), pp. 1187f.

27. Doggett, pp. 304–10 and passim.

28. *The New York Evangelist*, January 5, 1833, p. 2; and December 6, 1834, p. 194.

29. [Albert Dod], "Review of *Lectures on Revivals of Religion* and *Sermons on Various Subjects,*" *The Biblical Repertory and Theological Review*, 7 (October 1835) 660–61.

30. *Literary and Theological Review*, 5 (March 1838) 66.

31. *Oberlin Evangelist*, January 29, 1845, p. 19.

32. *Oberlin Evangelist*, February 12, 1845, p. 27.

33. Ibid.

34. Ibid.

35. Ibid.

36. Statistics for the various Protestant denominations are not always extant, but for the Presbyterians, from 1826 through 1832, the church membership increase averaged 11,000 per year. In 1832 it increased by 35,000. But from 1833 to 1837 it dropped to only 2,200 per year on average. Of course, for the Presbyterians this great drop may be largely explained by the withdrawal of many Plan of Union churches to Congregationalism, and other factors that led to the schism of 1837.

37. See McLoughlin, pp. 136–65, for a discussion of these men; also see his chapter 6, "Itinerants."

38. Charles G. Finney, *Skeletons of a Course of Theological Lectures by the Rev. Charles G. Finney* (Liverpool, England: Johnson, 1842), p. 259.

39. See Richard Shelly Taylor, "The Doctrine of Sin in the Theology of Charles Grandison Finney," (Ph.D. dissertation, Boston University, 1953), pp. 185ff.

40. Finney, *Skeletons*, pp. 253–55. Finney repeated much of this section in his *Systematic Theology*, but there he was even more explicit about the everlasting duration of the sinner's punishment:

> The justice, holiness and benevolence of God demand that the penal sanctions of his law should be endless; and if they are not, God can not be just, holy or benevolent. Unless the penal sanctions of the law of God are endless, they are virtually and really no punishment at all. . . . Sin deserves endless punishment just as fully as it deserves any punishment at all. If, therefore, it is not forgiven, if it be punished at all with penal suffering, the punishment must be endless [*Systematic Theology*, 1846 ed., p. 381].

41. Charles G. Finney, *Lectures on Systematic Theology* (Oberlin: Fitch, 1846), p. v.

42. Ibid.

43. Ibid., pp. 49–50.

44. Ibid., p. 41.

45. Ibid., p. 43.

46. Numerous scholars have held that the concept of "the simplicity of moral action" was first developed at Oberlin by William and Samuel Cochran about 1840, and that Finney and Mahan adopted it and incorporated it into their writings; see J. H. Fairchild, "The Doctrine of Sanctification at Oberlin," *The Congregational Quarterly*, 18 (April 1876) 247ff. However, I am indebted to Richard Dupuis for pointing out that an English student at Oberlin, William E. Lincoln, on December 30, 1889, wrote a letter to G. F. Wright (now in the Wright Papers, OCA) saying:

I notice you are preparing a life of Finney. You may need the following. I see Fairchild in one of his works, perhaps his history of Oberlin, says that the doctrine of "simplicity of Moral Intention" (if that's the term) was first heard of by him from a Prof. Cochrane. This is correct & only thus far. Finney in March 1853 in the first interview I had with him after I came to this country told me the following fact. I had been giving forth so many new ideas that I tho't it better that this shd come thro' a different man, hence I clearly instructed Prof. Cochrane . . . in the truth & bade him agitate the community with it & I in due time would notice it & thus perhaps secure a better result than if I gave it in person. He made this remark because I had told him of the long controversy that my teacher Prof. De Morgan of London University had had with Hamilton of Edinburg as to wh. was the first to announce the "Quantification of the predicate." . . . Finney told me the fact saying What matters it who announces first a truth, The Truth is the great thing & it is of slight consequence who gets the honor. In my own case, the doctrine of the simplicity etc. is given to Prof. Cochrane, when the truth is that I etc etc.

47. Finney, *Systematic Theology*, p. 344.
48. Ibid., p. 156.
49. Ibid., p. 158.
50. Ibid., p. 310.
51. Ibid., p. 536.
52. Ibid., p. 478.
53. Ibid., p. 473.
54. Ibid., p. 488.
55. Ibid., p. 494.
56. [Charles Hodge], "Review of *Lectures on Systematic Theology*," *The Biblical Repertory and Theological Review*, 19 (April 1847) 237.
57. Ibid., 19:266–67.
58. Ibid., 19:267.
59. Ibid., 19:272.
60. Ibid., 19:275.
61. Ibid., 19:276.
62. Benjamin B. Warfield, *Perfectionism* (New York: Oxford University Press, 1931), 2:193.
63. Ibid., 2:153–54.
64. Ibid., 2:154–55.

CHAPTER 18 — NEW MEASURES IN ENGLAND

1. Charles G. Finney, *Memoirs of Rev. Charles G. Finney* (New York: A.S. Barnes, 1876), p. 375.
2. Ibid.
3. Charles G. Finney, "The Last Sickness and Death of Mrs. Finney," *Oberlin Evangelist*, January 5, 1848; The Oberlin Maternal Association Minutes, vol. 2, Annual Report, 1848, Oberlin College Archives (OCA).

4. Finney, "Last Sickness . . ."

5. The story of Elizabeth Atkinson Finney is told in Leonard I. Sweet, *The Minister's Wife: Her Role in Nineteenth-Century American Evangelicalism* (Philadelphia: Temple University, 1983), pp. 184–211. Sweet presents the thesis that Elizabeth in numerous ways broadened still further the concept of the pastor's wife, toward fuller, more equal partnership in the ministerial vocation. He has termed her activities, accurately, the "partner model." While I fully concur in Sweet's presentation of Lydia Finney's model, life and labors, I feel that Sweet has portrayed Elizabeth as too successful in dominating Finney, and him as far too "weak and vacillating, buffeted about by popular opinion and frightful anxieties," insecure, indecisive, and over-dependent. I also feel that the sources do not support the grand picture of Elizabeth's British work as Sweet has portrayed it, practically on a par with her husband's.

6. The story of Mahan's clashes with the Oberlin faculty and trustees is told in Edward H. Madden and James E. Hamilton, *Freedom and Grace: The Life of Asa Mahan* (Metuchen, N.J.: Scarecrow, 1982), pp. 99–126.

7. Anson Phelps to Finney, August 29, 1833, Finney Papers, OCA. The standard works on American evangelists in Britain are Richard Carwardine's excellent *Transatlantic Revivalism: Popular Evangelicalism in Britain and America, 1790–1865* (Westport, Conn.: Greenwood, 1978), and John Kent, *Holding the Fort: Studies in Victorian Revivalism* (London: Epworth, 1978). Kent is occasionally inaccurate.

8. Thomas Rees to Finney, April 19, 1850, Finney Papers, OCA.

9. *Oberlin Evangelist*, December 3, 1850; Finney, pp. 386ff; Carwardine, pp. 136f.

10. In the absence of any journal kept on this visit to England, it is difficult to determine exact dates of Finney's meetings in any city. I have tried to establish dates from the extant correspondence.

11. Finney, p. 389. Finney preached for a short while in London also, soon after his landing in Britain, at the Borough Road Chapel (*Oberlin Evangelist*, May 21, 1851, p. 84). In his letter of January 29, 1850, to Finney, John Angell James wrote, "Your sermons in London did not certainly remove the unfavorable impression as you learn from the letter I send you." The overall chronology for the period November 1849 through April 1850 has been taken from a letter by Elizabeth Finney to her sister-in-law, written April 22, 1850, from Worcester. Both letters are in the Finney Papers, OCA.

12. *Oberlin Evangelist*, January 16, 1850.

13. Carwardine, p. 137; Finney, p. 390.

14. Finney, p. 391.

15. Carwardine, p. 139.

16. Finney, p. 394.

17. Asa Mahan to Finney, January 5, 1850, Finney Papers, OCA; also January 25, 1850.

18. John Morgan to Finney, January 7, 1850, Finney Papers, OCA.

19. The Oberlin Faculty to Asa Mahan, March 18, 1850, Miscellaneous Archives, OCA.

20. John Morgan to Finney, May 7, 1850, Finney Papers, OCA; also Treasurer's Minutes of Oberlin College, April 20, 1850, and elsewhere.

21. John Morgan to Finney, May 7, 1850, Finney Papers, OCA.

22. Lewis Tappan to Finney, June 7, 1850, Finney Papers, OCA.

23. Willard Sears to Finney, June 18, 1850, Finney Papers, OCA.

24. John Keep to Finney, August 30, 1850, Finney Papers, OCA.

25. Fletcher, 1:483–86.

26. Ibid., 1:488.

27. Finney, pp. 393–99.

28. John Angell James to Finney, January 29, 1850, Finney Papers, OCA.

29. George Redford to Finney, February 5 and March 7, 1850, Finney Papers, OCA.

30. *British Banner*, March 26, 1851, reprinted in the *Oberlin Evangelist*, May 21, 1851.

31. Nathan G. Goodman, ed., *A Benjamin Franklin Reader* (New York: Crowell, 1971), pp. 142–43.

32. Finney, p. 400.

33. James F. Findlay, Jr., *Dwight L. Moody, American Evangelist, 1837–1899* (University of Chicago Press, 1969), pp. 166–73; William R. Moody, *the Life of Dwight L. Moody* (New York: Revell, 1900), pp. 223–37; William G. McLoughlin, Jr., *Modern Revivalism: Charles Grandison Finney to Billy Graham* (New York: Ronald, 1959), pp. 196ff.

34. Finney, p. 401. Campbell's life has been treated in Robert Ferguson and A. Morton Brown, *Life and Labours of John Campbell, D.D.* (London: Bentley, 1867).

35. John Campbell to Finney, March 28, 1850, Finney Papers, OCA.

36. This is a printed circular enclosed in John Campbell to Finney, May 1, 1850, Finney Papers, OCA.

37. Finney's statement is printed on the same circular.

38. *Oberlin Evangelist*, May 22, 1850.

39. Finney, p. 403.

40. Ibid., p. 404.

41. Ibid., pp. 405–6. The *Oberlin Evangelist* of July 17, 1850, cites a statement in the *British Banner* that between seven and eight hundred persons went to the inquiry meeting.

42. Finney, p. 409.

43. *Oberlin Evangelist*, May 21, 1851.

44. *The Presbyterian*, July 20, 1850.

45. The article was reprinted in the *Puritan Recorder* for July 25, 1850. Finney refers to this attack on him in the manuscript of his *Memoirs*, pp. 964–65, a section edited out by James H. Fairchild.

46. Richard Carwardine has treated Campbell's prickly personality, and the entire situation, at some length; see Carwardine, pp. 141f.

47. *Oberlin Evangelist*, August 28, 1850.

48. Finney, pp. 412–13.

49. Beecher's changing views are explored in William G. McLoughlin, *The Meaning of Henry Ward Beecher: An Essay on the Shifting Values of Mid-Victorian America, 1840–1870* (New York: Knopf, 1970), pp. 34ff.

50. Lyman Abbott, *Henry Ward Beecher* (Boston: Houghton, Mifflin, 1903), p. 63.

51. Henry Ward Beecher to Finney, August 30, 1850, Finney Papers, OCA.

52. *The New York Independent*, November 21, 1850, reprinted in the *Oberlin Evangelist*, December 3, 1850.

53. Finney, p. 412.

54. *British Banner*, August 28, 1850.

55. Finney, p. 413.

56. Helen and Dolson Cox to Elizabeth and Charles Finney, July 31, 1850, Finney Papers, OCA.

57. John Keep to Finney, August 30, 1850, Finney Papers, OCA.

58. *British Banner,* November 20, 1850, reprinted in the *Oberlin Evangelist,* January 1, 1851.

59. *Oberlin Evangelist,* January 1, 1851.

60. Ibid.

61. *British Banner,* January 15, 1851.

62. *The New York Evangelist,* April 17, 1851.

63. *Oberlin Evangelist,* May 21, 1851.

64. Ibid.

65. Finney, p. 395.

66. Ibid., p. 406.

67. Carwardine, pp. 148ff.

68. Ibid., pp. 147–48.

CHAPTER 19 — THE LATER YEARS

1. John Morgan and the Faculty to Finney, December 10, 1850, Finney Papers, Oberlin College Archives (OCA); italics added.

2. Robert S. Fletcher, *A History of Oberlin·College: From Its Foundation Through the Civil War* (Oberlin, Ohio: Oberlin College, 1943), 2:889.

3. Charles G. Finney, *Memoirs of Rev. Charles G. Finney* (New York: A.S. Barnes, 1876), p. 414.

4. Fletcher, 2:887.

5. Ibid.

6. James H. Fairchild, *Oberlin: The Colony and the College, 1833–1883* (Oberlin, Ohio: Goodrich, 1883), pp. 279–80.

7. Ibid., and Fletcher, 2:700–703.

8. Charles Finney to Trustees of Oberlin Collegiate Institute, June 30, 1835, Finney Papers, OCA.

9. G. Frederick Wright, *Charles Grandison Finney* (Boston: Houghton, Mifflin, 1891), pp. 160ff.

10. Finney, p. 415.

11. Ibid., p. 416.

12. Horace Bushnell, "The Spiritual Economy of Revivals of Religion," *The Quarterly Christian Spectator,* 10 (1838) 143ff.

13. John Keep to Finney, March 12, 1852, Finney Papers, OCA.

14. John Morgan (unsigned) to Finney, March 15, 1852, Finney Papers, OCA.

15. Lewis Tappan to Asa Mahan, September 2, 1855, Tappan Papers, Library of Congress (LOC).

16. Lewis Tappan to Finney, September 15, 1855, Tappan Papers, LOC.

17. H. Pomeroy Brewster, "The Magic of a Voice," *Rochester Historical Society Publications,* 4 (1925) 284.

18. Historians have almost ignored the Awakening of 1858, just as they have passed lightly over the significance of Finney in American history. Even several of the standard histories of awakenings hardly mention it, or they discount its effects, partially because it was so lacking in fanaticism or sensationalism and was largely led by laymen. The best treatment is in Timothy L. Smith, *Revivalism and Social Reform: American Protestantism on the Eve of the Civil War* (New York: Harper & Row, 1957), pp. 63–79.

19. Charles G. Finney, *The Prevailing Prayer-Meeting* (London: Ward, 1859), p. 25.

20. Ibid., pp. 26–27.

21. *The New York Times*, March 20, 1858.

22. Smith, pp. 64, 69, 70.

23. Ibid., p. 70.

24. The *Washington National Intelligencer*, March 20, 1858.

25. Smith, pp. 76–78.

26. Finney, *Memoirs*, p. 444.

27. J. Edwin Orr, *The Second Evangelical Awakening in America* (London: Marshall, Morgan & Scott, 1952), pp. 31–33.

28. Finney, *Memoirs*, p. 447. This may be Finney's version of the decision to go to England in 1858, but Elizabeth Finney told a different and surely more accurate tale in her manuscript "Journal" in OCA, Special Collections. Here she disclosed that, in her view, "God would have us go this Autumn [1858]" to the British Isles, but her husband was uncertain. "He had commenced his writing, he thought he should remain at home. . . . I was blamed for pleading for England. Some [at Oberlin] again spoke of my influence over my Husband. Some thought I was ambitious—some, self willed." (Journal, pp. 3–6) Leonard Sweet has told the story, properly portraying a "defiant" Elizabeth, but exaggerating Finney's "pitiful dependence on his wife." See Sweet's *The Minister's Wife: Her Role in Nineteenth-Century American Evangelicalism* (Philadelphia: Temple University Press, 1983), p. 196. Finally, of course, Elizabeth persuaded her vacillating husband to leave for England.

29. Finney, *Memoirs*, pp. 450–51.

30. Ibid., p. 402.

31. Ibid., p. 451.

32. Thomas Lawson to Finney, April 20, 1859, Finney Papers, OCA.

33. Finney to his daughter Julia, May 5, 1859, Finney Papers, OCA.

34. Elizabeth Finney to Julia Finney, April 29, 1859, Finney Papers, OCA.

35. The Rev. R. B. Salisbury to Finney, May 23, 1859, Finney Papers, OCA.

36. Finney to his daughter Julia, July 20, 1859, Finney Papers, OCA.

37. William Adamson, *The Life of the Rev. James Morison, D.D.* (London: Hodder Stoughton, 1898), passim; Richard Carwardine, *Transatlantic Revivalism* (Westport, Conn.: Greenwood, 1978), pp. 97ff.

38. Finney, *Memoirs*, p. 457.

39. John Kirk to Finney, December 19, 1859, Finney Papers, OCA.

40. *Glasgow Christian News*, n.d., quoted in the *Oberlin Evangelist*, December 21, 1859.

41. George Redford to Finney, December 23, 1859, Finney Papers, OCA.

42. Excerpts from the Journal of Elizabeth Finney, January–February 1860, OCA.

43. Finney, p. 461.

44. Elizabeth Finney's Journal for January 9, 1860, and December 29, 1859; Finney, p. 466.

45. *Oberlin Evangelist*, April 11 and May 23, 1860.

46. Cited in Frank G. Beardsley, *A Mighty Winner of Souls: Charles G. Finney* (New York: American Tract Society, 1937), pp. 156–57.

47. Finney, pp. 468–69.

48. Quoted in the *Oberlin Evangelist* for August 15, 1860.

49. John Campbell to Finney, July 28, 1860, Finney Papers, OCA.

50. Finney, p. 471.

51. E. Henry Fairchild to Finney, July 10, 1860, Finney Papers, OCA.

52. Fletcher, p. 898. Whereas Elizabeth Ford Atkinson Finney was close to Finney's own age, Rebecca Allen Rayl Finney was much younger, having been born in 1824. She died on September 12, 1907, at the age of 83. Her obituary is in the *Oberlin Alumni Magazine*, 4 (Oct. 1907) 33–34. See Sweet, pp. 212ff.

53. Finney to the Oberlin Trustees, August 19, 1865, Finney Papers, OCA.

54. John Keep and the Trustees to Finney, August 21, 1865, Finney Papers, OCA.

55. Fletcher, pp. 899ff. and passim.

56. Ibid., p. 902.

57. Fairchild cut from Finney's manuscript of the *Memoirs* perhaps twenty percent of the material, and he was quite consistent in attempting to conceal the identity of anyone then living whom Finney had named. Throughout, in the published edition by Fleming H. Revell Co., wherever there is a person's initial followed by a long dash, that is Fairchild's deletion. The new edition of the *Memoirs* edited by Mr. Richard Dupuis and Dr. Garth Rosell restores all of Fairchild's cuts. His most significant omissions are Lydia's severe illness, Finney's Michigan campaign of 1847, the Taylor lynching scandal, many mentions of Asahel Nettleton and Lyman Beecher and the opposition Finney encountered, and the anti-Masonic material at the conclusion.

58. Finney, p. 2. It is quite likely that Finney referred frequently to the vast amount of correspondence he had retained over the years to check facts and dates, and to jog his memory, and it was well that he had saved it.

59. Ibid., p. 4.

60. Finney, p. IV.

61. See chapter 4, and Whitney R. Cross, *The Burned-over District: The Social and Intellectual History of Enthusiastic Religion in Western New York, 1800–1850* (New York: Harper and Row, 1965), pp. 114ff.

62. Finney received his discharge from the Masonic lodge in Adams, New York, on May 7, 1824, shortly before his ordination.

63. Oliver Johnson to Finney, April 23, 1868, Finney Papers, OCA.

64. Finney to Oliver Johnson, April 25, 1868, Finney Papers, OCA. See also Lewis Tappan to Finney, April 30, 1868, and Jonathan Blanchard to Finney, July 4, 1868, Finney Papers, OCA. Blanchard gave his opinion that it probably cost the *Independent* more than $50,000 in the risk it took to print Finney's articles.

65. Theodore Tilton to Finney, May 2, 1868, Finney Papers, OCA.

66. Nathan Brown to Finney, July 1 and 3, 1868, Finney Papers, OCA.

67. A. Ritchie to Finney, November 5, 1868; Finney to A. Ritchie, November 19, 1868; Finney Papers, OCA.

68. Charles C. Cole, Jr., "Finney's Fight Against the Masons," *Ohio State Archeological and Historical Quarterly*, LIX (1950), 275–85.

69. Charles G. Finney, *The Character, Claims, and Practical Workings of Freemasonry* (Cincinnati: Western Tract and Book Society, 1869), p. 6.

70. Amasa Walker to Finney, May 3, 1868, Finney Papers, OCA.

71. Jonathan Blanchard to Finney, May 11, 1868, Finney Papers, OCA.

72. Wright, p. 267.

73. *Oberlin News*, August 20, 1874.

74. First Church of Oberlin to Finney, May 10, 1872, Finney Papers, OCA.

75. Phineas C. Headley, *Evangelists in the Church From Philip, A.D. 33, to Moody and Sankey, A.D. 1875* (Boston: Hoyt, 1875), p. 153.

76. Fairchild, p. 280.

77. Finney, p. 476.

78. Ibid., pp. 476–77; Headley, p. 168.

BIBLIOGRAPHY

The following primary and secondary sources are only a partial list. Throughout the footnotes, many other sources are given.

PRIMARY SOURCES

Alexander, S.D. *The Presbytery of New York, 1738 to 1888.* New York: Randolph, 1888.

Baird, Samuel J. *A History of the New School, and of the Questions Involved in the Disruption of the Presbyterian Church in 1838.* Philadelphia: Claxton, Remsen and Hoffelfinger, 1868.

Barnes, Albert. *Sermons on Revivals.* New York: Taylor, 1841.

Barnes, Gilbert H., and Dumond, Dwight L., eds. *Letters of Theodore Dwight Weld, Angelina Grimké Weld and Sarah Grimké, 1822–1844.* New York: Appleton-Century-Crofts, 1934.

Bartlett, David W. *Modern Agitators, or Pen Portraits of Living American Reformers.* New York: Miller, Orton and Mulligan, 1855.

[Beecher, Lyman.] *The Autobiography of Lyman Beecher.* Barbara Cross, ed. Cambridge, Mass.: Harvard University, Belknap Press, 1961.

[——, and Nettleton, Asahel.] *Letters of the Rev. Dr. Beecher and Rev. Mr. Nettleton, on the "New Measures" in Conducting Revivals of Religion, with a Review of a Sermon by Novanglus.* New York: G. and C. Carvill, 1828.

A Brief Account of the Origin and Progress of the Divisions in the First Presbyterian Church in the City of Troy; Containing, also, Strictures upon

the New Doctrines Preached by the Rev. C.G. Finney and N.S.S. Beman, with a Summary Relation of the Trial of the Latter before the
Troy Presbytery. Troy: Tuttle and Richards, 1827.

Brockway, Joseph. A Delineation of the Characteristic Features of a Revival
of Religion in Troy, in 1826 & 1827. Troy: Adancourt, 1827.

Colton, Calvin. History and Character of American Revivals of Religion. London: Westley and Davis, 1832.

Committee of the Synod of New York and New Jersey. A History of the Division of the Presbyterian Church in the United States of America. New
York: Dodd, 1852.

Conant, William C. Narrative of Remarkable Conversions and Revival Incidents: Including a Review of Revivals, from the Day of Pentecost to
the Great Awakening in the Last Century— Conversions of Eminent
Persons—Instances of Remarkable Conversions and Answers to Prayer
—An Account of the Rise and Progress of the Great Awakening of 1857–
8. New York: Derby and Jackson, 1858.

Crocker, Zebulon. The Catastrophe of the Presbyterian Church in 1837, Including a Full View of the Recent Theological Controversies in New
England. New Haven: Noyes, 1838.

Cushman, R.W. A Calm Review of the Measures Employed in the Religious
Awakening in Boston in 1842. Boston: Stone, 1847.

Dill, James H. "Congregationalism in Western New York." The Congregational
Quarterly, 1 (April 1859) 151–58.

[Dod, Albert.] "Review of Finney's Lectures on Revivals of Religion and Sermons on Various Subjects." The Biblical Repertory and Theological Review, 7 (July and October 1835) 482–527, 626–74.

Dodge, D. Stuart, ed. Memorials of William E. Dodge. New York: Randolph,
1887.

Eastman, C.G., ed. Sermons, Addresses & Exhortations, by Rev. Jedediah Burchard: with an Appendix, Containing Some Account of Proceedings
during Protracted Meetings, Held under his Direction, in Burlington,
Williston, and Hinesburgh, Vermont, December, 1835, and January, 1836.
Burlington: Goodrich, 1836.

[Eaton, Sylvester.] Burchardism vs. Christianity. Poughkeepsie: Platt and
Romney, 1837.

Engles, William M., ed. Minutes of the General Assembly of the Presbyterian Church, 1789–1820. Philadelphia: Presbyterian Board of Publication,
1847.

Finney, Charles G. The Character, Claims, and Practical Working of Freemasonry. Cincinnati: Western Tract and Book Society, 1869.

———. Guide to the Savior, or Conditions of Attaining to and Abiding in
Entire Holiness of Heart and Life. Oberlin: Fitch, 1848.

———. Lectures to Professing Christians. London: Milner, 1837.

———. Lectures on Revivals of Religion. William G. McLoughlin, ed. Harvard University, Belknap Press, 1960.

————. *Lectures on Systematic Theology.* Oberlin: Fitch, vol. 2, 1846; vol. 3, 1847.

————. *Lectures on Systematic Theology.* London: Tegg, 1851.

————. *Letters on Revivals.* New York: Wright, 1845.

————. *Memoirs of Rev. Charles G. Finney, Written by Himself.* New York: Barnes, 1876.

————. *A Reply to Dr. Duffield's "Warning against Error."* Oberlin, Fitch, 1848.

————. *The Prevailing Prayer-Meeting.* London: Ward, 1859.

————. *The Reviewer Reviewed: or Finney's Theology and the Princeton Review.* Oberlin: Fitch, 1847.

————. *A Sermon Preached in the Presbyterian Church at Troy, March 4, 1827, from Acts 3:3 — Can Two Walk Together Except They Be Agreed?* Philadelphia: Geddes, 1827.

————. *Sermons on Gospel Themes.* Oberlin: Goodrich, 1876.

————. *Sermons on Important Subjects.* New York: Taylor, 1836.

————. *Sermons on Various Subjects.* New York: Taylor, 1834.

————. *Skeletons on a Course of Theological Lectures.* Oberlin: Steele, 1840.

————. *Views of Sanctification.* Oberlin: Steele, 1840.

Fowler, Henry. *The American Pulpit; Sketches, Biographical and Descriptive, of Living American Preachers, and of the Religious Movements and Distinctive Ideas Which They Represent.* New York: Fairchild, 1856.

[Gale, George W.] *Autobiography of Rev. George W. Gale.* New York: n.p., 1964.

Greenleaf, Jonathan. *A History of the Churches of New York.* New York: French, 1846.

Haddock, John A. *The Growth of a Century: As Illustrated in the History of Jefferson County, New York, from 1783 to 1894.* Philadelphia, Sherman, 1894.

Hawley, Charles. *The History of the First Presbyterian Church, Auburn, New York.* Auburn: Daily Advertiser, 1876.

Headley, Phineas C. *Evangelists in the Church from Philip, A.D. 35, to Moody and Sankey, A.D. 1875.* Boston: Hoyt, 1875.

[Hodge, Charles.] "Review of *Lectures on Systematic Theology.*" *The Biblical Repertory and Theological Review,* 19 (April 1847) 237–77.

————. "Review of 'The New Divinity Tried'; or, an Examination of the Rev. Mr. Rand's Strictures on a Sermon Delivered by the Rev. C. Finney, on Making a New Heart." *The Biblical Repertory and Theological Review,* 4 (April 1832) 278–304.

Hotchkin, James H. *A History of the Purchase and Settlement of Western New York, and of the Rise, Progress, and Present State of the Presbyterian Church in that Section.* New York: Dodd, 1848.

Hough, Franklin B. *A History of Jefferson County in the State of New York.* Albany: Munsell, 1854.

Humphrey, Heman. *Revival Sketches and Manual.* New York: American Tract Society, 1859.

Irvin, William. *Centennial Sermon of the Second Presbyterian Church, 1876.* Troy: Whig, 1876.

Jones, Pomroy. *Annals and Recollections of Oneida County.* Rome, N.Y.: n.p., 1851.

Mahan, Asa, *Autobiography, Intellectual, Moral and Spiritual.* London: Woolmer, 1882.

————. *Out of Darkness into Light; or the Hidden Life Made Manifest.* Boston: Willard, 1876.

————. *The Doctrine of the Will.* New York: Fairchild, 1845.

————. *Scripture Doctrine of Christian Perfection.* Boston: Waite, Pierce, 1849.

Mears, David O. *Life of Edward Norris Kirk, D.D.* Boston: Lockwood, Brooks, 1877.

Miller, James A. *The History of the Presbytery of Steuben.* Angelica, N.Y.: Potter, 1897.

Miller, Samuel. *Letters to Presbyterians, on the Present Crisis in the Presbyterian Church in the United States.* Philadelphia: Finley, 1833.

Nevin, Alfred. *History of the Presbytery of Philadelphia.* Philadelphia: Fortesque, 1888.

Norton, Herman. *The Life of the Rev. Herman Norton, to Which Are Added Startling Facts, and Signs of Danger and of Promise, from his Pen, while Corresponding Secretary of the American Protestant Society.* New York: American and Foreign Christian Union, 1854.

Olds, Gamaliel S., and Corning, Richard S. *Review of a Narrative by Rev. John Keep.* Syracuse: Smith, 1833.

Parker, Sarah. *A Brief Historical Sketch of the First Presbyterian Church at Gouverneur.* New York: Cox, 1918.

Parsons, Levi, ed. *History of Rochester Presbytery from the Earliest Settlement of the County.* Rochester: Democrat-Sentinel, 1889.

Perkins, Ephraim. *A "Bunker Hill" Contest, A.D. 1826. Between the "Holy Alliance" for the Establishment of Hierarchy and Ecclesiastical Domination over the Human Mind, on the One Side, and the Asserters of Free Inquiry, Bible Religion, Christian Freedom and Civil Liberty on the Other. The Rev. Charles Finney, "Home Missionary" and High Priest of the Expeditions of the Alliance in the Interior of New York; Headquarters, County of Oneida.* Utica: n.p., 1826.

————. *Letter to the Presbytery of Oneida County, New York, and their "Committee, the Rev. John Frost, Rev. Moses Gillet, and Rev. Noah Coe," "Appointed to Receive Communications from Ministers and Others Respecting the Late Revival, in this County," by Ephraim Perkins, a "Plain Farmer" of Trenton.* Utica: Dauby and Maynard, 1827.

————. *A Serious Address to the Presbytery of Oneida on the Matter of Con-*

ducting Revivals within their Bounds. Trenton, N.Y.: Bennett and Bright, 1831.

Presbytery of Oneida. *A Narrative of the Revival of Religion in the County of Oneida, Particularly in the Bounds of the Presbytery of Oneida in the Year 1826.* Utica: Hastings and Tracy, 1826.

Rand, Asa. *The New Divinity Tried, Being an Examination of a Sermon Delivered by the Rev. C.G. Finney, on Making a New Heart.* Boston: Lyceum, 1832.

———. *A Vindication of "The New Divinity Tried," in Reply to a "Review" of the Same.* Boston: Pierce and Parker, 1832.

Robinson, Charles F. *Weld Collections.* Ann Arbor: University of Michigan Press, 1938.

Shepherd, Thomas J. *The Days That Are Past.* Philadelphia: Lindsay and Blakisman, 1871.

———. *History of the First Presbyterian Church of Northern Liberties.* Philadelphia: n.p., 1882.

Spring, Gardiner, *Personal Reminiscences of the Life and Times of Gardiner Spring.* New York: Tatlow, 1866.

Stanton, Henry B. *Debate at the Lane Seminary, Cincinnati; Speech of James A. Thome, of Kentucky, Delivered at the Annual Meeting of the American Anti-Slavery Society, May 6, 1834.* Boston: Morehouse, 1834.

———. *Random Recollections.* New York: Pollard, 1855.

Tappan, Lewis. *The Life of Arthur Tappan.* New York: Hurd and Houghton, 1870.

Taylor, James H. *Historical Discourse.* Rome, N.Y.: n.p., 1888.

Thompson, Joseph P. *The Faithful Preacher. A Discourse Commemorative of the Late Dirck C. Lansing, D.D.* New York: Calkins and Stiles, 1857.

Tyler, Bennet. *Memoir of the Life and Character of Rev. Asahel Nettleton, D.D.* Hartford: Robbins and Smith, 1844.

Ware, John. *Memoir of the Life of Henry Ware, Jr.* Boston: Munroe, 1846.

Weeks, William R. *A Pastoral Letter of the Ministers of the Oneida Association to the Churches under their Care on the Subject of Revivals of Religion.* Utica: Ariel, 1827.

———. *The Pilgrim's Progress in the Nineteenth Century.* New York: Dodd, 1848.

Wesley, John. *A Plain Account of Christian Perfection.* New York: Emory and Waugh, 1829.

Whittemore, Thomas. *The Modern History of Universalism: Extending from the Epoch and the Reformation to the Present Time.* Boston: Tomkins, 1860.

[Wisner, Benjamin.] *Review of "The New Divinity Tried;" or an Examination of Rev. Mr. Rand's Strictures on a Sermon Delivered by the Rev. C.G. Finney, on Making a New Heart.* Boston: Pierce and Parker, 1832.

SECONDARY SOURCES

Abzug, Robert H. *Passionate Liberator: Theodore Dwight Weld and the Dilemma of Reform.* New York: Oxford University Press, 1980.

Ahlstrom, Sydney E. *A Religious History of the American People.* New Haven: Yale University Press, 1972.

————. "The Scottish Philosophy and American Theology." *Church History,* 24 (September 1955) 257–72.

Atkins, Gaius Glenn, and Fagley, Frederick L. *History of American Congregationalism.* Boston: Pilgrim, 1942.

Banner, Louis. "Religious Benevolence as Social Control: A Critique of an Interpretation." *Journal of American History,* 60 (June 1973) 23–41.

Barnes, Gilbert Hobbs. *The Antislavery Impulse, 1830–1844.* New York: Harcourt, Brace, and World, 1933.

Beardsley, Frank G. *A History of American Revivals.* New York: American Tract Society, 1912.

————. *A Mighty Winner of Souls: Charles Grandison Finney.* New York: American Tract Society, 1937.

Bell, Marion L. *Crusade in the City: Revivalism in Nineteenth-Century Philadelphia.* Lewisburg, Pa.: Bucknell University Press, 1977.

Belt, R.A. *Charles Finney, A Great Evangelist.* Des Moines: Boone, 1944.

Berg, Barbara J. *The Remembered Gate: Origins of American Feminism.* New York: Oxford University Press., 1978.

Berthoff, Rowland. "The American Social Order: A Conservative Hypothesis." *American Historical Review,* 65 (April 1960) 496–514.

Bodo, John R. *The Protestant Clergy and Public Issues, 1812–1848.* New York: Random House, 1965.

Boles, John B. *The Great Revival, 1787–1805.* Lexington: University of Kentucky Press, 1972.

Boorstin, Daniel J. *The Americans: The National Experience.* New York: Random House, 1965.

Boyer, Paul. *Urban Masses and Moral Order in America, 1820–1920.* Cambridge, Mass.: Harvard University Press, 1978.

Brackett, William O. "The Rise and Development of the New School in the Presbyterian Church in the U.S.A. to the Reunion in 1869." *Journal of the Presbyterian Historical Society,* 13 (1928) 117–40, 145–74.

Carwardine, Richard. *Transatlantic Revivalism: Popular Evangelicalism in Britain and America, 1790–1865.* Westport, Ct.: Greenwood, 1978.

Cheesebro, Roy Alan. "The Preaching of Charles G. Finney." Ph.D. dissertation, Yale University, 1948.

Clark, Franklin C. "The Bristol Branch of the Finney Family." *The New England Historical and Genealogical Register.* Boston: New England Historical Society, 1906.

Cochran, William C. *Charles Grandison Finney. Memorial Address at the*

Dedication of the Finney Memorial Chapel, Oberlin, June 21, 1908. Philadelphia: Lippincott, 1908.

Cole, Charles C. "The Free Church Movement in New York City." *New York History,* 34 (July 1953) 284–97.

———. "The New Lebanon Convention." *New York History,* 31 (October 1950) 385–97.

———. *The Social Ideas of the Northern Evangelists, 1826–1860.* New York: Columbia University Press, 1954.

Cott, Nancy F. *The Bonds of Womanhood: "Women's Sphere" in New England, 1780–1835.* New Haven: Yale University Press, 1978.

Cross, Whitney R. *The Burned-over District: The Social and Intellectual History of Enthusiastic Religion in Western New York, 1800–1850.* Ithaca: Cornell University Press, 1950.

Davis, David Brion. *Ante-bellum Reform.* New York: Harper and Row, 1967.

Day, Richard Ellsworth. *Man of Like Passions: A Dramatic Biography of Charles Grandison Finney.* Grand Rapids: Zondervan, 1942.

Dix, John Ross. *Pen Pictures of Popular English Preachers: With Linnings of Listeners in Church and Chapel.* London: Partridge and Oakey, 1852.

Drummond, Lewis A. *Charles Grandison Finney and the Birth of Modern Evangelism.* London: Hodder and Stoughton, 1983.

Dumond, Dwight L. *Antislavery: The Crusade for Freedom in America.* Ann Arbor: University of Michigan Press, 1961.

———. *Antislavery Origins of the Civil War of the United States.* Ann Arbor: University of Michigan Press, 1939.

Edman, V. Raymond. *Finney Lives On.* Minneapolis: Bethany, 1971.

Englizian, H. Crosby. *Brimstone Corner: Park Street Church, Boston.* Chicago: Moody, 1968.

Fairchild, James H. "The Doctrine of Sanctification at Oberlin." *The Congregational Quarterly,* 18 (April 1876) 237–59.

———. *Oberlin: The Colony and the College, 1833–1883.* Oberlin: Goodrich, 1883.

———. *Oberlin: Its Origin, Progress and Results. An Address Prepared for the Alumni of Oberlin College.* Oberlin: Strong, 1860.

Filler, Louis. *The Crusade against Slavery, 1830–1860.* New York: Harper and Row, 1960.

Finney, Howard, Sr. *Finney-Phinney Families in America.* Richmond: William Byrd, 1957.

Finney, James A. *The Name and Family of Finney.* Colorado Springs: n.p., 1952.

Fladeland, Betty. *James Gillespie Birney: Slaveholder to Abolitionist.* Ithaca: Cornell University Press, 1955.

Fletcher, Robert S. *A History of Oberlin College from its Foundation through the Civil War.* Oberlin: Oberlin College, 2 vols., 1943.

————. "The Pastoral Theology of Charles Finney." *Ohio Presbyterian Historical Society Proceedings*, 3 (1941) 28–33.

Foster, Charles I. *An Errand of Mercy: The Evangelical United Front, 1790–1837.* Chapel Hill: University of North Carolina Press, 1960.

Foster, Frank Hugh. *A Genetic History of New England Theology.* University of Chicago Press, 1907.

Fowler, Philemon H. *Historical Sketch of Presbyterianism within the Bounds of the Synod of Central New York.* Utica: Curtiss and Childs, 1877.

Fox, Dixon Ryan. *Yankees and Yorkers.* New York University Press, 1940.

Gaddis, Merrill E. "Christian Perfectionism in America." Ph.D. dissertation, University of Chicago, 1929.

Garrison, Winfred E. "Interdenominational Relations in America before 1837." *Papers of the American Society of Church History*, 9 (1934) 62–63.

Gillett, E. H. *History of the Presbyterian Church in the United States of America.* Philadelphia: Presbyterian Board of Publication, 1864.

Goodykoontz, Colin B. *Home Missions on the American Frontier, with Particular Reference to the American Home Missionary Society.* Caldwell, Idaho: Caxton, 1939.

Griffin, Clifford S. *Their Brothers' Keepers: Moral Stewardship in the United States, 1800–1865.* New Brunswick: Rutgers University Press, 1960.

————. "Religious Benevolence as Social Control, 1815–1860." *Mississippi Valley Historical Review*, 44 (December 1957) 423–44.

Grover, Norman L. "The Church and Social Action in Finney, Bushnell, and Gladden." Ph.D. dissertation, Vanderbilt University, 1957.

Handy, Robert T. *A Christian America: Protestant Hopes and Historical Realities.* New York: Oxford University Press, 1971.

Harding, William H. *Finney's Life and Lectures.* London: Oliphant, 1943.

Harlow, Ralph V. *Gerrit Smith, Philanthropist and Reformer.* New York: Holt, 1939.

Hendricks, Tyler O. "Charles Finney and the Utica Revival of 1826: The Social Effect of a New Religious Paradigm." Ph.D. dissertation, Vanderbilt University, 1983.

Hollister, William H. *The Second Presbyterian Church of Troy, New York.* Troy: n.p., 1915.

Johnson, James E. "The Life of Charles Grandison Finney." Ph.D. dissertation, Syracuse University, 1959.

Johnson, Paul E. *A Shopkeeper's Millennium: Society and Revivals in Rochester, New York, 1815–1837.* New York: Hill and Wang, 1978.

Keller, Charles Roy. *The Second Great Awakening in Connecticut.* New Haven: Yale University Press, 1942.

Kent, John. *Holding the Fort: Studies in Victorian Revivalism.* London: Epworth, 1978.

Kuhns, Frederick. "New Light on the Plan of Union." *Journal of the Presbyterian Historical Society*, 26 (March 1948) 19–43.

Lamb, Wallace E. "George Washington Gale, Theologian and Educator." Ph.D. dissertation, Syracuse University, 1949.

Leonard, Delevan L. *The Story of Oberlin. The Institution, the Community, the Idea, the Movement.* Boston: Pilgrim, 1898.

Lesick, Lawrence T. *The Lane Rebels: Evangelicalism and Antislavery in Antebellum America.* Metuchen, N.J.; Scarecrow, 1980.

Loud, Grover C. *Evangelized America.* New York: Dial, 1928.

McClelland, William L. "Church and Ministry in the Life and Thought of Charles Grandison Finney." Ph.D. dissertation, Princeton Theological Seminary, 1967.

McGiffert, Arthur C. "Charles Grandison Finney: Frontier Preacher and Teacher, 1792–1875." *Christendom,* 7 (Autumn 1942) 496–506.

McLoughlin, William G. *Modern Revivalism: Charles Grandison Finney to Billy Graham.* New York: Ronald, 1959.

———. *Revivals, Awakenings, and Reform.* University of Chicago Press, 1978.

Madden, Edward H., and James E. Hamilton. *Freedom and Grace: The Life of Asa Mahan.* Metuchen, N.J.: Scarecrow, 1982.

Marsden, George M. *The Evangelical Mind and the New School Presbyterian Experience: A Case Study of Thought and Theology in Nineteenth-Century America.* New Haven: Yale University Press, 1970.

Marty, Martin E. *Righteous Empire: The Protestant Experience in America.* New York: Dial, 1970.

Matthews, Donald G. "The Second Great Awakening as an Organizing Process, 1780–1830." *American Quarterly,* 21 (Spring 1969) 23–43.

Mattson, John S. "Charles Grandison Finney and the Emerging Tradition of 'New Measure' Revivalism." Ph.D. dissertation, University of North Carolina, 1970.

Mead, Hiram. "Charles Grandison Finney." *The Congregational Quarterly,* 19 (January 1877) 1–28.

Mead, Sidney E. *Nathaniel William Taylor, 1786–1858: A Connecticut Liberal.* University of Chicago Press, 1942.

Melder, Keith E. "Ladies Bountiful: Organized Women's Benevolence in Early Nineteenth Century America," *New York History* 48 (1967), 231–46.

Miller, Basil W. *Charles Grandison Finney: He Prayed Down Revivals,* Grand Rapids: Zondervan, 1942.

Miller, Perry. *The Life of the Mind in America: From the Revolution to the Civil War.* New York: Harcourt, Brace and World, 1965.

Mode, Peter G. *The Frontier Spirit in American Christianity.* New York: Macmillan, 1923.

Moorhead, James H. "Charles Finney and the Modernization of America." *Journal of Presbyterian History,* 62 (Summer 1984) 95–110.

Morrison, Howard A. "The Finney Takeover of the Second Great Awakening During the Oneida Revivals of 1825–1827." *New York History,* (January 1978) 27–53.

Nichols, L. Nelson. *History of the Broadway Tabernacle of New York City.* New York: Tuttle, Morehouse, and Taylor, 1940.

Nichols, Robert H. "The Plan of Union in New York," *Church History,* 5 (March 1936) 29–52.

———. *Presbyterianism in New York State: A History of the Synod and its Predecessors.* Philadelphia: Westminster, 1963.

Oliphant, U. Orin. "The American Missionary Spirit, 1828–1835." *Church History,* 8 (June 1938) 125–37.

Opie, John. "Conversion and Revivalism: An Internal History from Jonathan Edwards through Charles Grandison Finney." Ph.D. dissertation, University of Chicago, 1964.

Richards, Leonard L. *Gentlemen of Property and Standing: Anti-Abolition Mobs in Jacksonian America.* New York: Oxford University Press, 1969.

Rosell, Garth M. "Charles Grandison Finney and the Rise of the Benevolence Empire." Ph.D. dissertation, University of Minnesota, 1971.

Rosenberg, Carroll Smith. *Religion and The Rise of The American City: The New York City Mission Movement, 1812–1870.* Ithaca, N.Y.: Cornell University Press, 1971.

Ryan, Mary P. *Cradle of the Middle Class: The Family in Oneida County, New York, 1790–1865.* Cambridge: Cambridge University Press, 1981.

———. "The Power of Women's Networks: A Case Study of Female Moral Reform in Antebellum America," *Feminist Studies* 5 (1979), 66–86.

Scott, Donald Moore, "Watchmen on the Walls of Zion: Evangelicals and American Society, 1800–1860." Ph.D. dissertation, University of Wisconsin, 1967.

Seitz, Don C. *Uncommon Americans. Pencil Portraits of Men and Women Who Have Broken the Rules.* Indianapolis: Bobbs-Merrill, 1925.

Smith, Delazon. *Oberlin Unmasked, or A History of Oberlin, or New Protestantism on the Eve of the Civil War.* New York: Abingdon, 1957.

Sorin, Gerald. *The New York Abolitionists: A Case Study of Political Radicalism.* Westport, Ct.: Greenwood, 1970.

Staiger, C. Bruce, "Abolitionism and the Presbyterian Schism of 1837–1838." *Mississippi Valley Historical Review,* 36 (December 1949) 391–414.

Strong, Augustus Hopkins. "Reminiscences of Charles G. Finney," in *Christ in Creation and Ethical Monism,* pp. 364–87. Philadelphia: Williams, 1899.

Sweet, Leonard I. *The Minister's Wife: Her Role in Nineteenth-Century American Evangelicalism.* Philadelphia: Temple University Press, 1983.

———. "The View of Man Inherent in New Measures Revivalism." *Church History,* 45 (June 1976) 206–21.

Sweet, William Warren. *Religion on the American Frontier, 1783–1850: The Congregationalists.* University of Chicago Press, 1939.

———. *Religion on the American Frontier, 1783–1850: The Presbyterians.* University of Chicago Press, 1936.

————. *Religion in the Development of American Culture, 1765–1840*. New York: Scribner's, 1952.

————. *Revivalism in America: Its Origin, Growth and Decline*. New York: Scribner's, 1944.

Taylor, Richard S. "The Doctrine of Sin in the Theology of Charles Grandison Finney." Ph.D. dissertation, Boston University, 1953.

Thomas, Benjamin P. *Theodore Weld, Crusader for Freedom*. New Brunswick: Rutgers University Press, 1950.

Thomas, John L. "Romantic Reform in America, 1815–1865." *American Quarterly*, 17 (Winter 1965) 656–81.

Tuveson, Ernest Lee. *Redeemer Nation: The Idea of America's Millennial Role*. University of Chicago Press, 1968.

Twaddle, Elizabeth. "The American Tract Society, 1814–1860." *Church History*, 15 (1946) 116–32.

Tyler, Alice Felt. *Freedom's Ferment: Phases of American Social History to 1860*. Minneapolis: University of Minnesota Press, 1944.

Vulgamore, Melvin. "Social Reform in the Theology of Charles Finney." Ph.D. dissertation, Boston University, 1963.

Walzer, William C. "Charles Grandison Finney and the Presbyterian Revivals of Northern and Western New York." Ph.D. dissertation, University of Chicago, 1944.

Ward, Susan Hayes. *The History of the Broadway Tabernacle Church: From its Organization in 1840 to the Close of 1900, Including Factors Influencing its Formation*. New York: Trow, 1901.

Warfield, Benjamin B. *Perfectionism*. New York: Oxford University Press, 2 vols., 1931.

Weddle, David L. *The Law as Gospel: Revival and Reform in the Theology of Charles G. Finney*. Metuchen, N.J.: Scarecrow, 1985.

Weisberger, Bernard A. *They Gathered at the River: The Story of the Great Revivalists and their Impact upon Religion in America*. Boston: Little, Brown, 1958.

Weise, Arthur James. *History of the City of Troy, from the Expulsion of the Mohegan Indians to the Present Centennial Year of the United States of America, 1876*. Troy: Young, 1876.

Wright, George Frederick. *Charles Grandison Finney*. Boston: Houghton, Mifflin, 1891.

Wyatt-Brown, Bertram. *Lewis Tappan and the Evangelical War against Slavery*. Cleveland: Case Western Reserve University, 1969.

INDEX